The Lingua Franca

Whose name is hidden behind the anonymity of the key publication on Mediterranean Lingua Franca? What linguistic reality does the label "Lingua Franca" conceal? These and related questions are explored in this new book on an enduringly important topic. The book presents a typologically informed analysis of Mediterranean Lingua Franca, as documented in the *Dictionnaire de la langue franque ou petit mauresque*, which provides an important historical snapshot of contact-induced language change. Based on a close study of the *Dictionnaire* in its historical and linguistic contexts, the book proposes hypotheses concerning its models, authorship, and publication history and examines the place of the *Dictionnaire*'s Lingua Franca in the structural typological space between Romance languages, on one hand, and pidgins, on the other. It refines our understanding of the typology of contact outcomes while at the same time opening unexpected new avenues for both linguistic and historical research.

NATALIE OPERSTEIN'S publications include *Consonant Structure and Prevocalization* (2010), *Zaniza Zapotec* (2015), *Valence Changes in Zapotec* (ed. with A. H. Sonnenschein, 2015), and *Language Contact and Change in Mesoamerica and Beyond* (ed. with K. Dakin and C. Parodi, 2017). She is a recipient of the National Endowment for the Humanities Fellowship.

Cambridge Approaches to Language Contact

Cambridge Approaches to Language Contact is an interdisciplinary series bringing together work on language contact from a diverse range of research areas. The series focuses on key topics in the study of contact between languages or dialects, including the development of pidgins and creoles, language evolution and change, world Englishes, code-switching and code-mixing, bilingualism and second language acquisition, borrowing, interference, and convergence phenomena.

Published titles:
Salikoko Mufwene, *The Ecology of Language Evolution*
Michael Clyne, *Dynamics of Language Contact*
Bernd Heine and Tania Kuteva, *Language Contact and Grammatical Change*
Edgar W. Schneider, *Postcolonial English*
Virginia Yip and Stephen Matthews, *The Bilingual Child*
Bernd Heine and Derek Nurse (eds.), *A Linguistic Geography of Africa*
J. Clancy Clements, *The Linguistic Legacy of Spanish and Portuguese*
Umberto Ansaldo, *Contact Languages*
Jan Blommaert, *The Sociolinguistics of Globalization*
Carmen Silva-Corvalán, *Bilingual Language Acquisition*
Lotfi Sayahi, *Diglossia and Language Contact*
Emanuel J. Drechsel, *Language Contact in the Early Colonial Pacific*
Enoch Oladé Aboh, *The Emergence of Hybrid Grammars*
Zhiming Bao, *The Making of Vernacular Singapore English*
Braj B. Kachru, *World Englishes and Culture Wars*
Bridget Drinka, *Language Contact in Europe: The Periphrastic Perfect through History*
Salikoko Mufwene, Chistophe Coupé, and François Pellegrino (eds.), *Linguistic Ecology and Language Contact*
Ralph Ludwig, Peter Mühlhäusler and Steve Pagel (eds.), *Linguistic Ecology and Language Contact*

Sandro Sessarego, *Language Contact and the Making of an Afro-Hispanic Vernacular: Variation and Change in the Columbian Chocó*

Rajend Mesthrie, Ellen Hurst, and Heather Brookes (eds.) *Youth Language Practices and Urban Language Contact in Africa*

Further titles planned for the series:

Rakesh Bhatt, *Language Contact and Diaspora*

Gregory D. S. Anderson *Language Extinction*

Cecile Vigouroux, *Migration, Economy, and Language Practice*

Agnes He, *The Voice of Immigration: Transcultural Communication and Language Shift*

Yaron Matras and Leonie Geiser, *Reading the Linguistic Landscape: An Ecology of Practices in the Multilingual City*

Pui Yiu Szeto, *Language Contact and Areal Convergence*

The Lingua Franca

Contact-Induced Language Change in the Mediterranean

Natalie Operstein
University of California

Shaftesbury Road, Cambridge CB2 8EA, United Kingdom

One Liberty Plaza, 20th Floor, New York, NY 10006, USA

477 Williamstown Road, Port Melbourne, VIC 3207, Australia

314–321, 3rd Floor, Plot 3, Splendor Forum, Jasola District Centre, New Delhi – 110025, India

103 Penang Road, #05–06/07, Visioncrest Commercial, Singapore 238467

Cambridge University Press is part of Cambridge University Press & Assessment, a department of the University of Cambridge.

We share the University's mission to contribute to society through the pursuit of education, learning and research at the highest international levels of excellence.

www.cambridge.org
Information on this title: www.cambridge.org/9781108999854

DOI: 10.1017/9781009000161

First published 2022
First paperback edition 2024

A catalogue record for this publication is available from the British Library

Library of Congress Cataloging-in-Publication data
Names: Operstein, Natalie, author.
Title: The lingua franca : contact-induced language change in the Mediterranean / Natalie Operstein.
Description: First edition. | Cambridge, UK ; New York : Cambridge University Press, 2022. | Series: Cambridge approaches to language contact | Includes bibliographical references and index.
Identifiers: LCCN 2021017361 (print) | LCCN 2021017362 (ebook) | ISBN 9781316518311 (hardback) | ISBN 9781108999854 (paperback) | ISBN 9781009000161 (epub)
Subjects: LCSH: Lingua francas–Mediterranean Region–History. | Languages in contact–Mediterranean Region–History. | French language–Africa, North–History. | Dictionnaire de la langue franque ou petit mauresque. | BISAC: LANGUAGE ARTS & DISCIPLINES / Linguistics / General
Classification: LCC PM7807.M47 O64 2021 (print) | LCC PM7807.M47 (ebook) | DDC 401/.309822–dc23
LC record available at https://lccn.loc.gov/2021017361
LC ebook record available at https://lccn.loc.gov/2021017362

ISBN 978-1-316-51831-1 Hardback
ISBN 978-1-108-99985-4 Paperback

Contents

Tables

Series Editor's Foreword

The series Cambridge Approaches to Language Contact (CALC) was set up to publish outstanding monographs and, occasionally, anthologies on language contact. Our goal is to integrate the ever-growing scholarship on the subject matter from a diachronic or developmental perspective. Topics of interest to us include but are not limited to the following: language diversification (e.g., the emergence of creoles, pidgins, and indigenized varieties of colonial European languages), multilingual language development and practice, code-switching/mixing (translanguaging), and language endangerment. We provide a select forum to scholars who contribute insightfully to understanding (dynamics of) language evolution from an interdisciplinary perspective. We favor approaches that highlight the role of ecology and draw inspiration both from the authors' own fields of specialization and from related research areas in linguistics or other disciplines. Eclecticism is one of our mottoes, as we endeavor to comprehend the complexity of evolutionary processes associated with contact.

We are proud to add to our list Natalie Operstein's *The Lingua Franca: Contact-Induced Language Change in the Mediterranean*. It is a thorough documentation of a language variety that has caught the attention of students of creoles and pidgins since the late nineteenth century, starting with Hugo Schuchardt's (1909) article "Die Lingua franca." For both good and mistaken reasons, its nineteenth-century variety, called Sabir, was invoked as the proto-variety of pidgins lexified by European languages around the world, having putatively morphed into them through what creolists refer to as relexification (see, e.g., Keith Whinnom 1965, 1977a, 1977b). For sure, the role Lingua Franca played in the Mediterranean trade from the Middle Ages to the nineteenth century explains why it has become customary in modern linguistics to characterize as *lingua francas* various languages with similar roles, regardless of whether their standard varieties are used and/or whether the users include native or heritage speakers. Pidgins themselves are usually associated with the lingua franca function (i.e., as bridge language varieties arising in multilingual contexts in which typically the trading parties have had no common language), by opposition to creoles and expanded pidgins, which have a vernacular function.

Let me note that Lingua Franca arose in the trade between Arabs in North Africa and Europeans in Northern Mediterranean, at a time when Venetians dominated in the trade, before being joined by people in Iberia and by the Ottomans. Iberia then included Arab and Moor colonists who must have been able to speak Iberian language varieties. Those of these colonists and Jews who did not want to convert to Christianity during the Inquisition – practiced during the Reconquista – left for North Africa especially from the thirteenth to fifteenth centuries. We can expect them to have spoken some Iberian language varieties too, regardless of the extent to which their nonheritage systems were undoubtedly influenced by Arabic or Hebrew. Judeo-Spanish is evidence of this. There is no reason why some of these people and their descendants would not have participated in the Mediterranean trade. This is to say that some North African Arabs and Jews were familiar with some Romance languages, which some other Arabs identified collectively as the "language of the Franks," the meaning of *Lingua Franca*. The label was not in reference to the Germanic Franks (who had invaded Gaul) but to Europeans north of the Mediterranean. This information is relevant to the discussions that this book is likely to generate, as I point out below.

How uniform was Lingua Franca? Was it not a continuum from native-like to nonnative varieties of the languages of the "Franks," regardless of whether the poles may be characterized as acrolectal and basilectal, respectively? I add this because what is identified as acrolectal in creole continua is a standard variety, and I wonder how much standardization or social stratification of European language varieties was in place in the trade in which Lingua Franca served as a bridge language. In any case, Natalie Operstein shows that Lingua Franca existed as a continuum, with variation in its grammatical system (albeit not of the kind described by Derek Bickerton as macaronic), and she provides many useful philological considerations on the structures that she has documented and analyzed meticulously. We are told that many of the structures and forms are retentions from its lexifiers, which were genetically related, being Romance languages. Although they did not have identical structural templates, congruence among them played an important role in producing the common features of different varieties of Lingua Franca.

According to Operstein, Lingua Franca was only in some respects like a pidgin and in some others like a koiné. This conclusion should not be surprising, since nonnative speakers of the Romance lexifiers were involved in shaping it, contributing their adstrate features to the feature pool. On the other hand, structural congruence between the primary lexifiers is consistent with the traditional conception of koinéization as reduction to a common denominator of structures of genetically related language varieties in contact, especially if in the case of Lingua Franca, in the formation of which the role of foreigner talk is partial but enhanced by congruence between the lexifiers. What is also remarkable is the lack of evidence for a break in the transmission of the lexifier, bearing in mind the historical context I present above.

The book is a gold mine likely to generate much discussion about the emergence of Lingua Franca and comparative studies between it and pidgins, incipient (still to be documented in the creolistics literature) and expanded ones alike. I am happy to recommend it to our readers.

Abbreviations

1	first person
2	second person
3	third person
A	adjective
Adv	adverb
Ar.	Arabic
ART (art.)	article
Cat.	Catalan
ChI	chancery Italian
CS	code-switching
DO	direct object
DOM	differential object marker
DOM	differential object marking
Eng.	English
F (f.)	feminine
FAI	Fremdarbeiteritalienisch
Ferr.	Ferrarese
Fr.	French
FT	foreigner talk
FUT	future
GRD	gerund
Gr.	Greek
IMPF	imperfect, imperfective
IND	indicative
INF	infinitive
intr.	intransitive
IO	indirect object
It.	Italian
J.-Sp.	Judeo-Spanish
L1	first language
L2	second language

Lat.	Latin
LF	Lingua Franca
lit.	literally
M (m.)	masculine
MCA	Moroccan Colloquial Arabic
N (n.)	noun
neut.	neuter
NEG	negative morpheme
Num	numeral
OBJ	object
OBL	oblique
Oc.	Occitan
PF	perfect, perfective
PL (pl.)	plural
POSS	possessive
PPLE (Pple)	participle
PREP (P)	preposition
PRES	present
PRET	preterit
PRO	pronoun
Ptg.	Portuguese
REFL	reflexive
S (sg.)	singular
SBJ	subject
Sard.	Sardinian
Sic.	Sicilian
SIE	Simplified Italian of Ethiopia
SLA	second language acquisition
Sp.	Spanish
SUBJ	subject
TAM	tense-aspect-mood
TMA	tense-mood-aspect
tr.	transitive
TTR	type–token ratio
Tu.	Turkish
V (v.)	verb
Ven.	Venetian
VL	Vulgar Latin

1 Introduction

1.1 Book Goals

In 1830, the printshop Typographie de Feissat ainé et Demonchy, located at Rue Cannebière 19 in Marseilles, published a slim volume called *Dictionnaire de la langue franque ou petit mauresque, suivi de quelques dialogues familièrs et d'un vocabulaire de mots arabes les plus usuels; à l'usage des Français en Afrique* [Dictionary of Lingua Franca or Petit Mauresque, followed by a few familiar dialogues and a vocabulary of the most common Arabic words, for the use of the French in Africa] (Anonymous 1830a; the *Dictionnaire*). This work would effect a permanent change in the bleak documentary landscape that underlies our knowledge of Mediterranean Lingua Franca (LF), a language which has fascinated generations of scholars:

> Forse nessun altro pidgin ha tanto eccitato la fantasia degli studiosi: le lingue di scambio dell'Africa nera, o il pidgin usato in età moderna fra balenieri baschi ed eschimesi di Groenlandia, o il russenorsk, non mi risulta che abbiano mai stimolato a questo punto l'immaginazione di quelli che se ne occupavano. (Cifoletti 2004: 9–10)
>
> [Perhaps no other pidgin has so excited scholarly imagination: the exchange languages of Black Africa, the pidgin used in the modern age between Basque whalers and Greenlandic Eskimos, or Russenorsk do not seem ever to have stimulated the imagination of those who dealt with them to quite such an extent.]

Despite the sustained interest in LF reflected in the above quotation and evidenced by a steady trickle of publications, there remain considerable lacunae both in our knowledge of the *Dictionnaire*, "la nostra fonte principale di lingua franca algerina (e di lingua franca *tout court*)" [our main source of Algerine Lingua Franca (and Lingua Franca period)] (Cifoletti 2004: 32) and in our understanding of LF, in particular, its place in the taxonomy of the outcomes of language contact. This book engages with both these issues, while combining a descriptive with a theoretical goal.

The descriptive goal of the book is a linguistic and philological study of the *Dictionnaire*, with the focus on its authorship, the models that have served as its blueprints and sources of inspiration, and the structural characteristics of the

LF variety that it describes and documents. The book's theoretical goal is to contribute to our understanding of the "typology of contact outcomes" (Winford 1997: 3) by situating the LF variety captured by the *Dictionnaire* in relation to the structural-typological features of LF's Romance lexifiers, on the one hand, and those of pidgins, with which LF has been routinely classified, on the other.

The organization of the book reflects its dual goals. The remainder of this chapter provides general overviews of LF (in Section 1.2) and this volume (in Section 1.3). Chapters 2–4 are devoted, respectively, to the authorship, models, and practical orthography of the *Dictionnaire*; and Chapters 5–8 engage in a detailed study of the various structural components of the *Dictionnaire*'s LF, situating each in relation to those of LF's lexifiers and those of pidgins. The taxonomic status of the *Dictionnaire*'s LF is the focus of the last chapter, Chapter 9, which revisits the key structural features of LF and separates those which may be due to pidginization from those which receive a better explanation within the framework of koineization.

1.2 Lingua Franca

The ethnonym *Frank* and the glottonym *lingua franca* "the Frank language" reflect an outsider, Byzantine Greek and Muslim, perspective on Western European peoples and languages (Castellanos 2006: 13). As observed by Coutelle (1977: 538), "[s]euls des non-Francs ont pu penser que tous les Francs parlaient le même idiome" [only non-Franks could have supposed that all Franks speak the same language]. Depending on the context, period, and area, the label *Frank* could be applied to Westerners in general, Romance language speakers in particular, or simply foreigners. As a common designation of European Christians it gained currency in most Muslim states between the sixteenth and nineteenth centuries (Lapiedra Gutiérrez 1997: 249). This last sense is reflected, e.g., in the eighth edition of the *Encyclopedia Britannica*:

> FRANK, the name by which the Turks, Greeks, Arabs, &c, designate a Christian. It probably originated during the crusades, in which the French (descendants of the German Franks) particularly distinguished themselves. Europe itself, too, was named *Frankistan*, or the country of the Franks. (*The Encyclopaedia Britannica* 1856: 287)

In the *Dictionnaire*, the word *franco* is listed as a translation for French *franc* (*étranger*) 'Frank (foreigner).' The far-flung currency of the term is apparent from contemporary travel accounts; for example, Paul Theroux reports hearing it in Sudan and Ethiopia ("Almost the entire time I spent in Harar, I was followed by children chanting, 'Faranji! Faranji! Faranji'") (Theroux 2003: 104).

The glottonym *lingua franca* is understood as a (Latin) calque on Arabic *lisān al-faranğ* "language of the Franks" (Schuchardt 1909: 448; Tagliavini 1932: 373–383; Kahane and Kahane 1976: 26; Aslanov 2006: 16–20); the corresponding calques in other languages include *hablar franco* (Haedo 1612), *Frank Language* (Shaw 1757), and *langue franque* (Anonymous 1830a). By absorbing the polysemy of the ethnonym *Frank*, the label *lingua franca* was, over time and space, applied to a variety of linguistic realities (Cortelazzo 1965: 108–109; Kahane and Kahane 1976: 26ff.; Castellanos 2006: 13). Thus, in the Levant, it could cover a gamut of Romance speech, from a Romance-derived pidgin to rudimentary L2 Italian and to regional Italian (Vianello 1955; Cortelazzo 1977: 524–528; Cifoletti 1978: 208). Aslanov (2002) suggests that such indiscriminate use may be explained by the appearance of homogeneity of Romance speech for non-Romance speaking outsiders. Since the Middle Ages, this language label could refer to the languages of the Crusaders and, by extension, auxiliary languages that facilitated communication between the Easterners and Westerners (Aslanov 2006: 16–19; 2010: 105). Its application to the Romance-based contact vernacular a version of which is recorded in the *Dictionnaire* became fixed sometime between the sixteenth and nineteenth centuries (Castellanos 2006: 14–15).

The period of existence of *lingua franca* in the last-mentioned sense is bookended by the earliest and the latest textual samples believed to reflect this language. The earliest is a composition with the first line "Oi Zerbitana retica!" (known as *Contrasto della Zerbitana*).[1] This piece, written in what its first editor identifies as a "dialetto franco delle isole Gerbe" [Frank dialect of the Djerba Islands] (Grion 1890–1892: 183), is included in a manuscript written shortly after 1353; based on historical considerations, Grion pushes back its composition to 1284–1304 (see also Minervini 1996a: 249–252; Lang 2000: 28–29; Cifoletti 2004: 17). The latest textual samples in Arends's (1998)

[1] Cifoletti (1978: 209n14) expresses reservations about identifying the language of the *Contrasto* as LF based on its structural and chronological distance from the other known LF samples and suggests that "la lingua qui usata pare semplicemente un italiano del Sud parlato male" [the language used here appears to be simply southern Italian spoken badly]. Whinnom (1965: 523) characterizes the language of the *Contrasto* as "an inconsistently pidginized Italian," and Minervini (1996a: 250) as "una varietà ritenuta affine alla lingua franca" [a variety considered akin to Lingua Franca]; see, most recently, Baglioni (2018: 75–81). There is also a lack of consensus as to whether pre–sixteenth century texts are to be included in the LF corpus at all: while this is done by some researchers (cf. Arends 1998, Couto 2002), Cifoletti (1989: 220), for instance, considers the earliest LF text to be Juan del Encina's jocular *Villançico contrahaziendo a los mocaros que sienpre van ynportunando a los peregrinos con demandas*, dating from about 1520 and written "in imitation of the donkey- and camel-boys who plagued Christian pilgrims with their sales-talk" (Harvey et al. 1967: 572), while Minervini (2010) points to Haedo (1612) as containing the first documentation of LF. Scholarly opinion is also divided with respect to the LF samples generated outside the Maghreb; compare, for example, the differing assessments of Goldoni's LF in Zago (1986) and Camus Bergareche (1993a).

annotated bibliography of LF date from 1887. A letter from the Semiticist Marcel Cohen to Hugo Schuchardt, dated 13 November 1909 and prompted by the publication of the latter's article on LF,[2] establishes definitively that LF was no longer spoken in early twentieth-century Algiers. Cohen, whose research in Algeria was conducted in 1908–1909, writes:

Comme vous l'avez très bien vu, la Langue franque peut être considérée comme morte; il n'existe plus de langue *neutre* parlée au cours de relations entre des gens qui ont respectivement d'autres langues maternelles (arabe et français s'entretenant en sabir à base d'espagnol ou d'italien – tel qu'on le voit dans la relation d'Haedo ou dans des oeuvres écrites aux environs de 1830–1840, comme les mémoires de Léon Roche). (cited in Swiggers 1991–1993: 273, emphasis original)

[As you saw very well, the Lingua Franca may be considered dead; there no longer exists a neutral language spoken in the course of dealings between persons with different native languages (Arab and Frenchman conversing in Spanish- or Italian-based *sabir*, such as we see in Haedo's account or works written around 1830–1840, such as the memoirs of Léon Roche.[3])]

The LF samples that emanate from the Maghreb between the sixteenth and nineteenth centuries stand out in terms of their quantity and the structural consistency of the LF they represent. Guido Cifoletti has argued extensively (c.g., Cifolctti 1978, 1991, 2000, 2004) that this is not fortuitous but is inseparable from the social and demographic conditions that obtained in that area during the period in question. He does not question the presumed existence of LF in other parts of the Mediterranean (cf. Cifoletti 1991, 2000, 2004: 18–19), however, he hypothesizes that it was only in the Maghreb that LF was able to achieve sufficient independence from its Romance lexifiers to acquire structural stability.[4] Cifoletti (2000: 15–16; 2004: 14, 18–19) argues that the stabilization of LF in the Maghreb became possible owing to the fact that, in the linguistic and social ecologies of the Maghrebi societies, the North Africans and Middle Easterners were in the right social position to be able to impose this vehicular language on the subordinate population of Europeans:

Dunque la conoscenza della lingua di prestigio per la maggior parte dei Mediorientali e Magrebini si fermava allo stadio di pidgin: ma nei porti dei pirati barbareschi i Musulmani si trovarono ad avere un enorme prestigio sugli Europei capitati laggiù (che erano per lo più prigionieri o schiavi), per questo motivo poterono imporre anche a questi ultimi la variante pidginizzata che era a loro usuale, e così la lingua franca divenne bilaterale e si stabilizzò. (Cifoletti 2000: 16)

[2] See Schuchardt (1909). Schuchardt's seminal article is available in English (Schuchardt 1979, 1980) and Italian (Venier 2012) translations, the latter supplied with an extensive commentary.
[3] See Roches (1904).
[4] Chaudenson (2001: 127) refers to this process (in relation to creoles) as *autonomization*.

[Thus the knowledge of the language of prestige by most Middle Easterners and Maghrebis stopped at the pidgin stage, but in the ports of the Barbary pirates Muslims came to have an enormous prestige over the Europeans found there (most of them prisoners or slaves), and for that reason were able to impose even on the latter the pidginized variety that was usual for them, and this way Lingua Franca became bilateral and was stabilized.]

A contributing factor in the imposition of LF on the population of European captives, as discussed by Davis (2003: 114), may have been the fact that many of the slave owners were renegades (Christian converts to Islam) with Romance language backgrounds. Between the late sixteenth and the end of the seventeenth centuries, the elite of Algiers was dominated by converts as well as Andalusians[5] (Muslim refugees from Spain) (McDougall 2017: 30). Converts occupied an important place in Algerine society, serving as rulers of Algiers, as bodyguards and administrators to rulers of Algiers, as corsair captains, and as slave owners (Clissold 1977: 87). Additional factors for the popularity of LF may include the fact that some local slave owners had Christian wives or had themselves been once enslaved by Europeans, which suggests their prior familiarity with LF (Clissold 1977: 55), as well as the fact that Christian slaves were often employed as domestic servants by European consuls to the regency (McDougall 2017: 30, 34).

Outside the Maghreb, the position of LF is less clear-cut. The literary sources through which the Venetian variety of LF has been handed down leave it up to the reader to figure out whether the language they portray is LF, L2 Italian, or L2 Venetian, with differences in scholarly opinion: thus, while Camus Bergareche (1993a) views Goldoni's *lengua de levantinos* as an imperfect L2 variety, Cifoletti (2000: 15) suggests that the differences between Goldoni's and Maghrebi LF may be due to the existence of "una variante locale, un 'dialetto veneziano' della lingua franca" [a local variant, a 'Venetian dialect' of LF].[6] The existence of LF in Egypt in the eighteenth and nineteenth centuries appears certain in view of its mention in Frederic Norden's account

[5] Epalza and Slama-Gafsi (2010: 36) use the terms *andalusí* (Andalusian) and *morisco* (Morisco) "para designar a los últimos musulmanes de España y a sus descendientes en el Mágreb" [to designate the last Muslims of Spain and their descendants in the Maghreb].

[6] "Non mi sentirei di affermare d'altra parte che la lingua franca di Venezia fosse soltanto una serie di casi di mancato apprendimento dell'italiano (o del veneziano): alcuni dei parlanti potevano avere imparato nel loro Paese il pidgin a base italiana, ed essersi fermati a quel livello; ma certo a noi che disponiamo solo di documenti letterari appare difficile separare nettamente la loro realtà da quella di stranieri che semplicemente difettavano nella padronanza della lingua locale" [I would not assert, on the other hand, that the Lingua Franca of Venice was only a series of cases of failed acquisition of Italian (or Venetian): some of the speakers could have acquired the Italian-based pidgin in their country and stopped at that level; but certainly for us, who have only literary documents at our disposal, it appears difficult to clearly separate their reality from that of foreigners who simply lacked mastery of the local language] (Cifoletti 2000: 16).

of his voyage there (Norden 1755: 40) and in a letter written from Cairo by Gérard de Nerval (Nerval 1911: 132) (Sammarco 1937: 148; Cifoletti 1983: 1262; Mallette 2014: 338).

Aslanov (2010: 105–108) suggests that LF did not exist outside Western Mediterranean, and views the sources in which LF is placed in the mouths of Levantines as "une projection de la réalité linguistique prévalent en Méditerranée occidentale à un contexte levantin" [a projection of the linguistic reality prevalent in Western Mediterranean onto the Levantine context] (Aslanov 2006: 23). He hypothesizes that the basis of LF was laid with the beginning of commerce, after the twelfth century, between Pisa, Genoa, Venice, and the ports of the Maghreb and Moorish Spain, and finds it significant that the aforementioned *Contrasto della Zerbitana* is recorded in an island off the coast of Tunisia (Aslanov 2006: 23–25).

Castellanos (2006, 2007) expresses similar views with respect to the origin of LF, dividing its evolution into three phases. The initial phase (*Lingua Franca Originària*) would have taken place between the tenth and fifteenth centuries in the context of Western commercial expansion in the Western Mediterranean, which brought Romance-speaking peoples into contact with Berbers and Arabs. The second phase (*Lingua Franca Evolucionada*) took place between the sixteenth and early nineteenth centuries in the context of a large-scale confrontation between the Ottoman Empire and the West and involved stabilization of LF and its evolution into local varieties. During this period, LF emerges as more Italianized east of Algiers and more Hispanized in its central and western domains. The third phase is conventionally counted from 1830, the year of the French military occupation of Algiers. During this period, LF is also known as *petit mauresque* and *sabir*; Castellanos (2007) suggests that these labels refer to ways of speaking the colonial languages by the local populations, though they may have contained remnants of LF.

The division into three periods is also present in the work of Cifoletti (1989: 22–23). It is primarily based on written documentation from the Maghreb, mainly Algiers, whose LF variety is "di gran lunga la più tipica, la meglio conosciuta e più coerente" [by far the most typical, the best known, and the most coherent]" (Cifoletti 2000: 16–17). Cifoletti identifies the three periods as "il periodo delle origini" [the period of origins], "il periodo dei pirati barbareschi" [the period of the Barbary pirates], and "il periodo del sabir" [the *sabir* period].

The earliest period is documented in the handful of texts that predate Haedo (1612) and reflects the use of LF in travel and commerce and in European-controlled Muslim territories such as Djerba. The second period contains the bulk of the extant documentation of LF. It begins and ends with our two most important documentary sources on this language, both of which were composed by outsiders temporarily residing in Algiers: Haedo (1612) and

Anonymous (1830a). Haedo's *Topografia e historia general de Argel*[7] [Topography and general history of Algiers] contains approximately twenty sentences in LF totaling about a hundred lexical types and presents a snapshot of the LF of Algiers in the last quarter of the sixteenth century. Its value for the study of LF is enhanced by the accompanying metalinguistic commentary, which informs us about how this language fit within the polyglot city's linguistic ecology. This work was published in 1612 by the abbot of Frómista Fray Diego de Haedo, who attributed its co-authorship to his uncle of the same name, Archbishop of Palermo and President and Captain-General of the Kingdom of Sicily (Camamis 1977: 63–64). Based on a detailed analysis of the *Topographia*, Camamis (1977) concluded that this work was likely to have been composed between 1578 and 1581, in Algiers rather than Sicily, and by an eyewitness rather than someone writing from second-hand accounts. As the true author of this work he identified the priest Antonio de Sosa, whose captivity in Algiers partly overlapped in time with that of Cervantes (Camamis 1977: 124–150; see also Medina Molera 2005: 37).

The second period reflects structural stabilization of LF and a certain degree of prestige: as emphasized by Cifoletti (1994b: 146), in written sources from the period LF is depicted as being used by individuals of high social standing, such as corsair captains and various Turkish dignitaries. This period incorporates within its span "the 'golden age' of the privateer economy," which ran from the late sixteenth until the end of the seventeenth century (McDougall 2017: 30). It coincides with the Ottoman domination of the Maghreb and with the rise of Italian to the status of the default language of communication between Ottoman authorities and Western Europe (Cremona 1996, 2002; Minervini 2006; Cifoletti 2007; Baglioni 2010, 2011, 2016).

The last, or *sabir*, period is documented in post-1830 sources (Cifoletti 2004: 261–292). Linguistically, it reflects gradual Gallicization of LF; Cifoletti (2004: 19) speaks of the term *sabir* as capturing a "post-pidgin continuum" that resulted from LF's contact with French. This period also reflects a sharp decline in the social status of the typical users of LF, whom Cifoletti describes (1994b: 146) as "indigeni tra i più ignoranti" [some of the most ignorant natives].

Following the Muslim conquest of Spain in the early eighth century, there had been continuous human movement between the Iberian Peninsula and North Africa, leading to the creation of ethnically and linguistically mixed populations in North African cities like Algiers (Clissold 1977: 20). In Haedo's time, the majority of Algiers's population was born nonlocally; as remarked by McDougall (2017: 30), "the defining feature of Ottoman Algiers

[7] Available online at http://purl.pt/14495.

was perhaps the significance of its immigrants, who may have constituted a majority of the total population in the period 1580–1640." The complex and stratified society of upward of 60,000 souls included an estimated 16,000 Arabs and Berbers, 10,000 Levantines, 6,000 Andalusians (Iberian Muslims), 5,000 Jews, and 30,000 converts, the majority of whom hailed from Italy, Spain, Provence, and the Balkans.[8] The distinctive social/occupational groups in the Barbary Regency period included janissaries (infantrymen recruited from outside North Africa), *raïs* (corsair captains), *spahis* (cavalry-men), and *kuluglis* (sons of janissaries and native women). In addition to its other residents, the city housed about 25,000 Christian captives, most of whom were speakers of Romance languages including Spanish, Italian, Catalan, Occitan, French, and Portuguese (Clissold 1977: 27; Hess 1978: 254–255; Cifoletti 1989: 17–18; Medina Molera 2005: 37ff.).

The linguistic situation of Algiers was characterized by widespread bi- and multilingualism, and simultaneous use of Berber, Arabic, Turkish, various European languages, and LF (Couto 2002: 29, citing Morsly 1996; Planas 2004). To this should be added the "international" languages of the port societies of Western Mediterranean (Spanish, Catalan, Occitan, French, Italian) as well as the languages of religion and culture: Latin, Hebrew, and Classical Arabic (Epalza and Slama-Gafsi 2010: 67–108). Each language was characterized by a variety of contact effects and multidimensional internal variation. The former include, for example, reciprocal influence between Arabic and Berber (Sayahi 2014) and koineization in Judeo-Spanish (Minervini 2002); and the latter includes a distinction between the Muslim and Jewish dialects of Arabic (Cohen 1912: 7; Larzul 2010: 91; Khan 2016; Tirosh-Becker 2019). The languages nonautochthonous to the area also differed with respect to their entrenchment in its linguistic ecology: for example, while Spanish was "[t]he third oldest language of continuous presence in the Maghreb after Berber and Arabic," Turkish "did not filter through to the general public and remained a language of the governing elite" (Sayahi 2014: 46, 50; see also Meouak 2004; Benkato 2020).

The domains of use of LF are known from contemporary eyewitness accounts (Planas 2004). From these we learn that LF was known to all the inhabitants of Algiers and was used by them for communication with the numerous European captives and slaves; in the absence of a shared language, it was also used by the latter for communication among themselves. The condition of being a slave in the Maghreb included the ability to understand orders in LF. Newly captured Europeans were allowed a brief breaking-in

[8] See Shuval (1998: 39–55) and Cresti (2005) concerning the difficulty of estimating the population of Algiers during this period and Borg (1996: 131n11) regarding the presence in Algiers of numerous Maltese.

period to facilitate their adjustment to the local ways and slave life. This included communication with more experienced slaves who, among other things, introduced the new captives to LF (Davis 2003: 57).

Davis (2003: 15) estimates that at the peak of the corsair activity, between 1580 and 1680, the average number of European slaves held in the Barbary regencies at any given time was about 35,000, with around 27,000 held in Algiers and its dependencies, 6,000 in Tunis, and 2,000 in Tripoli and the smaller centers. The sources of the slaves included captured European vessels and corsair raids on the coastal villages of Europe, particularly those populated by Romance-speaking peoples (Italy, Sicily, Sardinia, France, Spain, the Balearic Islands), as well as Greece, the British Isles, and occasionally as far north as Iceland. A glimpse at the ethnic composition of the slave population is afforded by the following eyewitness account:

> As to the slaves of both sexes that are in Barbary today, there are a quantity of them from all the Christian nations, such as France, Italy, Spain, England, Germany, Flanders, Holland, Greece, Hungary, Poland, Slovania, Russia, and so forth. The number of these poor captives reaches about thirty-six thousand, according to the enumeration that I have carried out on the spot and to the records that have been furnished and sent to me by the Christian Consuls who live in the Corsair Cities. (Dan 1649: 318; the English translation cited here is from Davis 2003: 15)

Some of the captured Christians were sold to private individuals while others were owned by the state. The living and working conditions of the state-owned slaves were particularly harsh. During the day, the state slaves worked in heavy construction or rowed the galleys, while during the night they were incarcerated in slave prisons known locally as *bagnos* 'baths' (Davis 2003: 12); Clissold (1977: 56) describes these as "a cross between a Nazi concentration camp, an English debtors' prison, and a Soviet labour camp." Successful escapes were rare. The slaves' only hope of returning home was through the agency of one of the ransoming orders, and they also could try to improve their lot by converting to Islam. Hard labor, beatings, malnutrition, and plague outbreaks resulted in the annual mortality rate of about 17 percent in the slave population (Davis 2003: 17–19). At least 90 percent of the Maghreb slaves were men, and they were denied access to slave or free women and prevented from raising families (Davis 2003: 15, 25, 113). These conditions help explain why LF, "the pidgin of slaves and masters in the Mediterranean" (Davis 2003: 57), was able to survive for centuries without becoming anyone's native language (Operstein 1998, 2007).

Outside slave/slave and master/slave interactions, LF was used for communication between European consuls, naval officers, and other Franks arriving in Algiers on business, and Algerine authorities. Unlike in some other linguistic ecologies (see, e.g., Minervini 1996b; Mufwene 2014), the availability of dragomans[9] apparently did not override or interfere with the use of LF in these exchanges. The French diplomat Laugier de Tassy, writing from personal observation, informs his readers on this point:

> Tous les étrangers qui arrivent dans la Ville d'Alger, sont conduits, dès qu'ils ont débarqué, devant le Dey par le Capitaine du Port ou un de ses Officiers. Le Dey leur donne la main à baiser, & leur demande en langue Franque d'où ils viennent, ce qu'ils viennent faire, & des nouvelles du lieu de leur départ & de la route qu'ils doivent suivre; après quoi ils sont renvoyez. Ordinairement le Truchement de leur Nation est avec eux, pour leur servir de Guide & d'Interprête. (Laugier de Tassy and Philippe 1725: 103)

> [All foreigners who arrive to the city of Algiers are taken, as soon as they have landed, before the *dey* by the captain of the port or one of his officers. The *dey* gives them his hand to kiss and asks them in Lingua Franca where they come from, what they are here for, and the news from their place of departure and the route they will follow; after which they are sent back. Usually the dragoman of their nation is with them, to serve them as a guide and interpreter.]

Laugier de Tassy's testimony is echoed nearly a century later by Mrs. Broughton's (1840). The daughter of the British Consul General in Algiers refers to the period between 1806 and 1812:

> Shortly after our going to Algiers, one of our naval friends accompanied my father to an audience of the Minister of Marine, to lay claim to a vessel, which had been taken and condemned by the Algerines, previous to my father's arrival. The vessel was, I believe, a Maltese or a Sicilian, which had some claims to British protection. It had been on its way from Sicily to Valetta, laden with wheat. Captain _____ considered himself a good Italian scholar, and therefore dispensed with the aid of an interpreter, as did my father also, for Sidi Yussuf, the Minister of Marine, spoke *Lingua Franca* perfectly in all its eloquent and terse abruptness. (Broughton 1840: 281, emphasis original)

In the 1820s, the demographic situation in Algiers was changed compared to what it had been in Haedo's time. Anonymous (1830b) estimates the city's population in 1823 at 40,000; of these, this source describes 4,000 as Turks ("l'aristocratie du pays" [the country's aristocracy]), 10,000 as *kuluglis* (descendants of Turkish men and Algerian women),[10] 20,000 as Moors,[11] and 6,000 as Jews (Anonymous 1830b: 32–38, 66). The number of European captives dropped steadily over the period that separated Haedo (1612) from Anonymous (1830b), with an estimated 500 at the end of the 1780s and 122 discovered in the *bagno* upon the French capture of Algiers in 1830

[9] Ross (1991: 34) notes that, in the period 1785–1830, "[t]he Dey . . . provided [Consuls] with a janissary guard and a dragoman who served as an interpreter and fixer."

[10] See Shuval (2000: 331–336) and McDougall (2017: 36) regarding this term and its transliterations.

[11] See Harvey (2005: 2) and Epalza and Slama-Gafsi (2010: 101n182, 104) on the use of the term *Moor* (Sp. *moro*) to refer to North Africans / Maghrebis.

(Venture de Paradis 1898; Davis 2003: 14; McDougall 2017: 36). A source dating from within a few years of the French conquest provides a lively snapshot of the ethno-linguistic mosaic of Algiers in the early 1830s:

Alger est une véritable tour de Babel. Il n'est peut-être pas de ville dans le monde où l'on parle plus de langues. Après le turc, l'arabe, et l'hébreu, dont les rabbins ne font usage qu'entre eux, celles dont on se sert le plus sont le français, l'italien, l'espagnol, l'anglais et l'allemand, et enfin, cette langue franque qu'on retrouve partout sur le littoral de l'Afrique, et dont les règles cependant ne sont tracées nulle part. (Genty de Bussy 1839: 222)[12]

[Algiers is a veritable tower of Babel. There is perhaps no city in the world where more languages are spoken. After Turkish, Arabic and Hebrew, which the rabbis use only among themselves, those that are used the most are French, Italian, Spanish, English and German, and finally this Lingua Franca which is found everywhere along the coast of Africa but whose rules are nevertheless not recorded anywhere.]

1.3 Chapter Summaries

Chapter 2 "The Author" fleshes out the hypothesis that the basis for the *Dictionnaire* was laid by the work of the American consular officer William Brown Hodgson, who made a fieldwork-based study of LF between 1826 and 1829 within the framework of his language-training mission in Algiers. It is shown, on the basis of Hodgson's correspondence with the US Department of State, that drafts of three of the sections that make up the published version of the *Dictionnaire* – the dialogues in LF, the LF vocabulary, and the Arabic vocabulary – were probably composed by Hodgson early in his stay in Algeria, between April 1826 and May 1827. It is hypothesized that Hodgson subsequently shared his LF manuscript with the French, who saw to its publication.

Chapter 3 "The *Dictionnaire*" focuses on the key publications that provided Hodgson and/or the *Dictionnaire*'s subsequent French editor with the conceptual models that underlie this work. It is shown that three of the sections that compose the published version of the *Dictionnaire* – the dialogues in LF, the Arabic vocabulary, and the structural outline of LF – were prepared with the help of two grammars which were widely circulated at the time, Angelo Vergani's *Grammaire italienne* (Vergani 1823) and Giovanni Veneroni's *Maître italien* (Veneroni 1800). An examination of the multiword lexemes and example sentences in the LF vocabulary shows that, in compiling this part of the *Dictionnaire*, Hodgson and/or the French editor are likely to have relied on definitions and usage examples in a monolingual French dictionary.

[12] Pierre Genty de Bussy was posted to Algiers in 1832. The first edition of his book, which is the source of the quotation, was published no later than 1835 (Robert et al. 1891: 154). See also Piesse (1862: lxxxv–cxxiii).

Chapter 4 "The Orthography" takes a close look at the *Dictionnaire*'s practical orthography of LF, focusing primarily on the sources of the various orthographic conventions, including orthographic solutions that may have been inspired by Vergani (1823) and/or Veneroni (1800), and the sound inventory and phonological processes that the orthography reflects. It is shown that the *Dictionnaire*'s orthography provides no orthographic evidence for consonant or vowel sounds that are not found in either Hispano- or Italo-Romance, and that the sound inventory of LF is not impoverished in comparison with the sound inventories of its Romance lexifiers. Both characteristics support the key role of inter-Romance koineization in the genesis and transmission of LF.

Chapter 5 "The Lexicon" examines the lexical composition of the *Dictionnaire*'s LF, placing particular emphasis on its main Romance components – Italian, Spanish, and French – as well as its "exotic" Turco-Arabic component. The issues discussed include the layered nature of the LF lexicon, the diachronic relationship between its Romance lexical components, the adaptation of French words to the Hispano-Italian molds of LF, and the key typological features of the LF lexicon in relation to the lexicons of pidgins. It is shown that the lexicon of the *Dictionnaire*'s LF differs from what has been identified as typical of pidgins, displaying instead detailed, specific, and interlocking continuity with the lexical and idiomatic features of LF's Romance lexifiers.

Chapter 6 "The Word Formation" examines the patterns of word and lexeme formation in the *Dictionnaire*'s LF, situating them in relation to those of LF's Romance lexifiers and those of pidgins. It is shown that the *Dictionnaire*'s patterns continue the former with a substantial degree of detail by exhibiting such features as the prevalence of suffixation, less productive use of prefixation, moderate use of lexical nominal compounds, preference for syntagmatic nominal compounds, an overall preference for analytic lexeme formation techniques, and little use of conversion and reduplication. It is further shown that LF's reliance on the vocabulary enrichment strategies characteristic of pidgins – rampant polysemy, circumlocutions, and multifunctionality – is less in evidence. In combination, these features argue against categorizing the *Dictionnaire*'s LF as a pidgin.

Chapter 7 "The Inflection" situates the inflectional categories of the *Dictionnaire*'s LF and their morphosyntactic expression in relation to those that are typical of pidgins and those that characterize LF's Romance lexifiers. It is shown that, in contrast to most or all pidgins, LF displays such functional categories as inherited definite and indefinite articles, clause connectors, substantial sets of question words and prepositions, verb allomorphy, a morphologically expressed aspect distinction, gender distinction in nouns and personal pronouns, and adjectival gender agreement. Retentions in the area of inflection which specifically reflect the Romance structural background of LF include inflectional classes in nouns, verbs, and adjectives. LF's inflectional innovations include refunctionalization of the lexifier infinitive and past participle into members of an aspectual opposition, copularization of the locative copula *(e)star*, grammaticalization of the periphrastic possessive construction with *di* 'of,' and grammaticalization of the preposition *per* 'for' into a DOM marker. Retention of lexifier inflectional categories, together with innovations that advance or parallel those found in the lexifiers, result in a substantial degree of typological continuity between LF and its Romance lexifiers in the domain of inflection.

Chapter 8 "The Syntax" examines the syntactic structures of the *Dictionnaire*'s LF as reflected in the *Dictionnaire*'s sentences, usage examples, and multiword lexemes in LF. It is shown that the syntactic structures of LF represent a combination of constructions inherited from the lexifiers, innovations resulting from functional expansion of the corresponding lexifier constructions, and innovations which have close parallels in the Romance domain. Among the inherited constructions are periphrastic causatives with the verbs *make* and *let*, predicative possession with *have*, double negation, adverbial use of adjectives, gender agreement in the noun phrase, obligatory fronting of the interrogative phrase in content questions, and word-order features, such as determiner-noun, possessed-possessor, degree word-adjective, negative morpheme-verb, noun-relative clause, and the basic SVO order with nominal objects. LF innovations include fixing of the SVO order, development of DOM, use of overt pronominal subjects, and complete grammaticalization of *(e)star* and the periphrastic possessive with *di* 'of.' Overall, the syntactic constructions of the *Dictionnaire*'s LF show detailed continuity with those of its Romance lexifiers.

Chapter 9 "The Lingua Franca" closes the book by engaging with the longstanding issue of the taxonomic status of LF. The chapter endeavors to separate the structural components of the *Dictionnaire*'s LF which may be attributed to pidginization from those which may be due to koineization. Methodologically, this involves a comparison between the key structural features of LF and the corresponding properties of naturalistically acquired and foreigner talk versions of its Romance lexifiers, on the one hand, and between the structural developments of LF and the corresponding diachronic structural drifts of the lexifiers, on the other. The comparison shows that LF exhibits both features which are consistent with processes underlying koineization and those which are consistent with processes underlying pidginization. This suggests that LF is best viewed as a structural continuum ranging from more pidgin-like to more koine-like lects, with the formative processes at the basilectal end displaying more drastic restructuring of the lexifier grammar than those at the acrolectal end.

1.4 Acknowledgments

I would like to take this opportunity to thank Derek C. Carr, Armin Schwegler, and Edward F. Tuttle for their valuable feedback and their support and encouragement at different stages of the research and writing that have resulted in this book; Daniele Baglioni for sharing with me his publications on Lingua Franca and related subjects; and the anonymous Cambridge University Press reviewers for their comments, suggestions, and bibliographical references.

I am grateful to Salikoko Mufwene and Ana Deumert, the series editors, for selecting this work for the series. I am especially grateful to Salikoko Mufwene for his support for and interest in this project, his thought-provoking comments and suggestions, generous help with every stage of the preparation of the manuscript, and inspiration. My thanks are also due to Helen Barton of Cambridge University Press for her expert guidance of the book through the publication process and to Isabel Collins for her editorial assistance.

Various parts of the book represent revised and/or expanded versions of journal articles (Operstein 2017a et seq.), and I wish to thank the journal editors and the anonymous reviewers of the manuscripts for their valuable comments and suggestions, which have helped to sharpen this work.

This book project was supported by a National Endowment for the Humanities Fellowship.

2 The Author

This chapter substantiates the hypothesis that the key publication on Lingua Franca, the *Dictionnaire de la langue franque ou petit mauresque* published anonymously in 1830, is based on the work of the US consular officer William Brown Hodgson carried out in Algiers in the late 1820s. By removing the anonymity of the *Dictionnaire*, and by linking its compilation to the activities of the American consulate in Algiers shortly before the French invasion of Algeria, the hypothesis presented in this chapter opens new avenues for both linguistic and historical research. The chapter is structured as follows. Section 2.1 introduces the argument. Section 2.2 lays out the structure of the *Dictionnaire* and highlights its importance for Lingua Franca scholarship. Section 2.3 contains the bulk of the chapter, and Section 2.4 provides a succinct summary of the main points.

2.1 Introduction

In the spring of 1824, an ambitious young man applied for a position as clerk-translator with the US Department of State. The application was in the form of a letter to the then secretary of state John Quincy Adams and had the support of Congressman Daniel Pope Cook from Illinois and the attorney Francis Scott Key, author of "The Star-Spangled Banner," who had known the applicant since he was a boy. Two years later the young man would sail for Algiers as the State Department's first language officer, his mission: to engage in an intensive study of local languages over the period of three years. A year after his arrival in Algiers, in what for him would be a routine progress report to Adams's secretary of state Henry Clay, he would relate that he now speaks "with tolerable facility" Lingua Franca, and that he has "compiled a Vocabulary and Dialogues in Lingua Franca, and Arabic" to which he intends to "add the corresponding Turkish" (Hopkins and Hardgreaves 1973: 235; Bryson 1979: 3–32; Hardgreaves and Hopkins 1981: 511).

The young man's name was William Brown Hodgson, and his three-and-a-half-year stint in Algiers would end in 1829. His departure would take place on 9 October of that year, and on 14 June of the following, 1830, year a 37,000 men strong French army would disembark in the bay of Sidi Fredj west of Algiers, ushering in a long history of French rule in Algeria (Ageron 1991: 5; McDougall 2017: 49). Sometime in the course of the same year, the Marseilles printshop Typographie de Feissat ainé et Demonchy would publish anonymously a short practical guide to LF to facilitate "les communications des Français avec les habitans du pays sur lequel ils vont combattre" [the communication of the French with the inhabitants of the country in which they are going to fight]. The contents of this volume, fully disclosed in its descriptive title *Dictionnaire de la langue franque ou petit mauresque, suivi de quelques dialogues familièrs et d'un vocabulaire de mots arabes les plus usuels; à l'usage des Français en Afrique* [Dictionary of Lingua Franca or Petit Mauresque, followed by a few familiar dialogues and a vocabulary of the most common Arabic words, for the use of the French in Africa], would replicate almost exactly those of Hodgson's description of the work he has completed on LF.

2.2 *Dictionnaire*

The *Dictionnaire*[1] is divided into four parts. The first six pages, which are unnumbered, are occupied by the preface (*Préface*). In its fifteen unnumbered double-spaced paragraphs it briefly introduces LF, provides a bareboned sketch of its grammar, and explains the *Dictionnaire*'s purpose. The next section, which dominates the book in terms of length, occupies pages [11] (the last of the unnumbered pages) through 92, and is titled *Dictionnaire de la langue franque, ou petit mauresque*. Printed in two columns, this is a vocabulary of LF which uses French as the entry and LF as the exit language. The lines in this part appear to be about 1.5 spaced, resulting in about 25–27 entries per page, except for the first and last pages which have fewer entries; according to Baglioni (2017: 187), the total number of French entries in the vocabulary is 2,035. The next section occupies pages 93–98 and is titled *Dialogues*. It is single-spaced and contains eight learner's dialogues in French on the left and their translations in LF on the right; each dialogue is preceded by its number and title, given on separate lines. The final section occupies pages 99–107 and contains a vocabulary of Maghrebi Arabic divided into eleven unnumbered but titled sections and printed in two single-spaced columns, with French as the entry and Arabic as the exit language.

The importance of the *Dictionnaire* for our understanding of LF is hard to overestimate. Without it, our knowledge of LF would have been confined to a highly inadequate patchwork of literary imitations and stylized fragments in

[1] Available online at https://gallica.bnf.fr/ark:/12148/bpt6k6290361w.texteImage.

travelers' accounts and narratives of Barbary captivity (see Arends 1998). This latter documentation was generated by Europeans from various nations who spoke different first languages, wrote in different historical periods, visited different parts of the Mediterranean, and, for the most part, had no serious intention to document LF, reporting the words and phrases in LF for their comic and local color effect (Rossi 1928; Whinnom 1965; Cifoletti 1989, 1994a, 1994b, 2004; Couto 2002; Dakhlia 2008; Selbach 2009). Without the *Dictionnaire*, the combined multicentury textual corpus of LF would have amounted to a small and geographically and chronologically scattered collection of words, phrases, sentences, and items of poetry whose linguistic side defeats a coherent interpretation if tackled as a whole. Publication of the *Dictionnaire* wrought a definitive change in this state of affairs, shaping our entire vision of LF, beginning with Hugo Schuchardt's seminal article in which this work is acknowledged as "the only extensive source for our knowledge of Lingua Franca" (Schuchardt 1979: 40).

The *Dictionnaire*'s importance for LF scholarship is reflected in the studies that either examine this source for its own sake or use it as their foundation. In the majority of the studies, the *Dictionnaire* is mined for information about the structural features of LF, both for general outlines of LF grammar and for more specific studies of its lexical or structural features (e.g., Schuchardt 1909; Coates 1971; Cifoletti 1980, 1989, 2002, 2004; Cornelissen 1992; Russo 2001; Velupillai 2015; Baglioni 2017). The *Dictionnaire* has also been examined in relation with the hypothesis about the internal evolution of LF (e.g., Collier 1977; Foltys 1987; Operstein 2007). The most consistent interest in the *Dictionnaire* has been maintained by Guido Cifoletti, whose published work includes inverse versions of the French-LF vocabulary (Cifoletti 1980, 1989) and a reprinting of the entire *Dictionnaire* (Cifoletti 2004). In the accompanying linguistic and philological studies, Cifoletti examines a number of issues pertaining to the *Dictionnaire* as a self-standing publication, including its orthography, the structural and lexical characteristics of the LF variety it records, and indications about its authorship.

Cifoletti's inferences about the *Dictionnaire*'s authorship are based on a variety of clues that range from the *Dictionnaire*'s practical orthography of LF to the phonological features and lexical composition of the LF variety that it captures. For example, from the orthographic vacillation in the use of geminates and affricates in LF words of Italian provenance Cifoletti infers that the *Dictionnaire*'s compilers' knowledge of Italian was nonnative. Their (or their informants') familiarity with Provençal is inferred from the fact that the *Dictionnaire* is practically the only source to record words of Provençal origin in LF. Their limited knowledge of Spanish is inferred from the absence of Spanish orthographic conventions in the transliteration of LF, the modest number of the recorded Hispanisms, as well as the phonological shape of the latter, which betrays their acquisition via Arabic speakers. The inference about the compilers' (or their informants') limited knowledge of Arabic is supported by the small number of the recorded Arabisms, their adapted phonological shape (as seen, e.g., in the loss of pharyngeals), and the absence of any discernible phonological influence of Arabic on LF outside the Spanish portion of its lexicon (Cifoletti 1980: 17; 1989: 88–89; 1991; 2004: 83–86).

The *Dictionnaire* has attracted a fair amount of criticism for its appearance of hasty composition. This perception stems from typographical errors in both the LF and French, from a less than consistent use of the practical orthography of LF, and a certain unevenness of the LF vocabulary: thus, Cifoletti (1989) notes that, while the initial letters of the alphabet contain relatively few entries, the final letters, particularly the <s>, are disproportionately large, with the increase in the number of entries accompanied by "un incremento vertiginoso dei francesismi ... scarsamente credibili" [a staggering increase in barely believable Gallicisms] (p. 88). As discussed below, these issues stem from the circumstances of the *Dictionnaire*'s publication, particularly the fact that it was brought to publication by someone other than its author.

2.3 William Hodgson

William Brown Hodgson (1801–1871) held many honors and distinctions in his life. He was the US State Department's first language officer. His secret mission to Egypt in 1834 would serve "as a model for later American diplomatic missions to the Middle East" (Bryson 1979: 97). During his lifetime, Hodgson "associated with presidents, secretaries of state, congressmen, senators, justices of the Supreme Court, not to mention the wide range of dignitaries whom he met in Algiers, Turkey, Egypt, Tunis, and Tangier" (Bryson 1979: 191). "He was one of the very first Americans to receive the Legion of Honor from France" (Mackall 1931: 328). "[I]n his day ... he enjoyed a really international reputation in the field of his special studies" (Mackall 1931: 324). Hodgson held honorary degrees from Princeton and was a member of several learned societies, including the American Philosophical Society, American Oriental Society, Royal Asiatic Society, Asiatic Society of Paris, Ethnological Societies of Paris, London, and New York, and Geographical Societies of Paris and London (Mackall 1931: 327–328). Yet, in spite of his distinguished trajectory and significant diplomatic and scholarly contributions, little has been written about Hodgson's life, work, and writings. The only full-fledged biography of Hodgson is Bryson (1979), based mainly on archival materials located in the United States and in part on Hodgson's own publications. Brief sketches of Hodgson's life and various facets of his work are presented in Mackall (1931), Ives (1937), Finnie (1967), Field

(1969), Brower (2009), and Kennedy (2015). The substance of Hodgson's correspondence with Henry Clay, John Quincy Adams's secretary of state, during Hodgson's stay in Algiers is summarized, with selected direct quotations, in Hopkins and Hardgreaves (1973), Hardgreaves and Hopkins (1981), and Seager (1982). Some relevant information is also to be found in Adams's diaries (Adams 1875, 1876). The outline below weaves together the strands scattered throughout these publications.

Hodgson's mission in Algiers as the US State Department's language officer was prompted by the increased commercial traffic between the United States and the Mediterranean, which created the need for trained personnel to "converse and correspond with the peoples along the coast of North Africa" (Bryson 1979: 11). The opportunities that Algiers provided for such training were clearly discerned by William Shaler, the consul general in Algiers since 1815, who "recommended that a young man be sent to the Consulate General at Algiers to study the Arabic and Turkish languages" (Ives 1937: 333) shortly after his arrival there. Ten years would elapse before Shaler's recommendation would be acted upon, and several circumstances would converge to make William Hodgson the first young man to be selected for the task. Chief among these were Hodgson's natural gift for the study of languages, his skill in securing political patronage, and John Quincy Adams's ascendance to presidency, which permitted him to realize his plans to professionalize the consular and diplomatic service, among other things, by "the development, within the structure of the federal government, of a fund of competence in exotic tongues" (Field 1969: 193).

William Hodgson was born on 1 September 1801 in Georgetown, Washington, DC, into a middle-class family. Following the death of his father, while Hodgson was still young, his mother moved the family to Richmond, Virginia. In Georgetown, Hodgson attended the classical academy, where he studied classical Greek and Latin and also assisted the Reverend James Carnahan, his mentor and future president of Princeton. In 1824, Princeton conferred on Hodgson the honorary degree of Master of Arts, of which he was informed by a letter from Carnahan dated 15 April 1824, stating in pertinent part "that in consideration of your attainments in sciences and literature the honorary degree of Master of Arts was conferred on you by an unanimous vote of the Trustees of the College of New Jersey at a meeting held at Princeton on the 14th instant" (cited in Ives 1937: 333; see Bryson 1979: 6–8). On 29 April 1824, in a letter to the then secretary of state John Quincy Adams, Hodgson applied for a position as clerk-translator with the Department of State. In May 1824 he was offered, and declined, the Professorship of Languages and Mathematics at Asbury College in Baltimore, Maryland. His letter to the Reverend John Emory, President of Asbury College, indicates that his employment with the State Department had already commenced. Hodgson's letter outlines his aspirations for a future in the government's employ and provides information about the range of languages he commanded at the time:

> [M]y prospects at present are somewhat flattering, as to my obtaining a place under my Govt. If I be not sent abroad, there is every possibility of my securing a place in the Dept. of State. ... An annual appropriation is made for the Translation of Languages, in the Dept. of State. The papers to be translated, are chiefly, the correspondences of Diplomatic Agents, in their respective languages. The intercourse of this Govt. must be extended under succeeding administrations, which will embrace, Modern Greece, Turkey and perhaps some other Eastern Nations. These negotiations will require a Knowledge of the Oriental Living languages, to which I shall immediately devote myself for their acquisition. At present, there are not more than $500 appropriated for the French and Spanish. I incline to believe, that the Govt. will in the event, as suggested above, make an ample provision for a Translator, of the requisite qualifications. I translate at present 4 Modern Languages and have a foundation (in Hebrew) for the Arabic, Persian, etc. At my age, and with my laborious Habits, how vastly important it would be for me, to commence a regular course of Study, for the acquisition of languages. What might not 5 years of steady applications effect? ... At present I am employed in Translating Portuguese & Spanish but do not know how long I may be wanted. (cited in Ives 1937: 333)

Hodgson's desire to advance his career in the government through dedicated study of oriental[2] languages got a chance to be realized after John Quincy Adams became president and determined to develop personnel proficient in these languages "in order to facilitate diplomatic negotiations in the Mediterranean and the Middle East" (Bryson 1979: 8). In a letter of 29 December 1825, Adams's secretary of state Henry Clay advised William Shaler about Adams's intention to send Hodgson to Algiers to serve under Shaler as a language student. Hodgson was advised of his posting to Algiers via a letter from Clay dated 14 January 1826 (Bryson 1979: 12). His language training was to last for three years and he was to receive a salary of $600 a year, a sum Shaler found "quite equal to what the case requires" (cited in Ives 1937: 333). Clay instructed Hodgson "to report, 'from time to time,' on the progress made in his studies and to add 'such observations and remarks' as he supposes 'will be either useful or interesting'" (Hardgreaves and Hopkins 1981: 37).[3] On 19 January 1826 the grateful Hodgson paid a visit to Adams,

[2] "Prior to the twentieth century, at least, 'the Orient' comprised a vast area stretching from Anatolia and Western Thrace to North Africa and Egypt, and from Arabia to the Persian Gulf. [. . .] These lands were linked in the American mind by a common civilization, by similarities of dress, architecture and art, religious beliefs, and modalities of government" (Oren 2007: 12; see also Said 1978).

[3] Hopkins and Hardgreaves (1973), Hardgreaves and Hopkins (1981), and Seager (1982) summarize Hodgson's letters to the State Department with selected direct quotations. Here and below, these editors' summaries are enclosed in double quotation marks; the direct quotations, if included by the editors, are given in single quotation marks.

who recorded the meeting in his diary. This entry is worth quoting in full as it sheds light on Adams's purpose in sending Hodgson to Algiers and specifically identifies LF as one of the languages he was being sent there to study:

> Hodgson came to say he was preparing to embark for Algiers, and to thank me for the opportunity of going there. My purpose is to attach to each of the Consulates in Barbary a young man for three years, to learn the Turkish and Arabic languages, and the lingua Franca, with a view to have persons among our public officers versed in those languages. I have desired that Hodgson might be one of those persons, as he has a fondness and a facility for acquiring languages quite uncommon. The other three students of this class I propose to select among the midshipmen of the squadron in the Mediterranean. (Adams 1875: 106–107)

When Hodgson's departure for Algiers was unexpectedly delayed, he employed the time profitably by studying Italian and German and acquiring "a collection of books on language" (Bryson 1979: 12). He sailed from Baltimore on 11 February 1826, and reported his arrival in Algiers in a letter to Clay dated 12 April 1826 (Bryson 1979: 12–13; Hardgreaves and Hopkins 1981: 235).

Upon reaching his destination, Hodgson was greeted by a magnificent view of the city in which he was to spend the next three and a half years:

> Algiers, as discovered from the sea, resembles in form and colour a ship's topsail, spread out upon a green field; and, with its surrounding hilly and well cultivated territory, thickly studded with white buildings, several of which are magnificent edifices, developes, on approach, one of the most agreeable views on the shores of the Mediterranean. (Shaler 1826: 47–48)

At the time of Hodgson's arrival, the "highly stratified ... diverse and polyglot society" of Algiers consisted of indigenous inhabitants, migrants from the interior, an Ottoman military-administrative elite and their descendants, renegades (European converts to Islam) and their descendants, Andalusians (Muslim refugees from Spain) and their descendants, Sephardic Jews and their descendants, local Jews, European and African slaves, and European diplomats with their families and servants (Shuval 1998, 2000; McDougall 2017: 30–37). Ageron (1991: 4) estimates the population of the Regency of Algiers in 1830 at 3 million. In his book *Sketches of Algiers*, Shaler (1826: 47) estimated the population of the city of Algiers at 50,000, while Anonymous (1830b: 66) gave the figure of 40,000 for the year 1823 (for other contemporary estimates, see Cresti 2005: 466–468).

Shaler's correspondence in the wake of Hodgson's arrival indicates that he was well pleased with the young man; Hodgson's letters, in turn, show that the feeling of appreciation was mutual (Bryson 1979: 14). In his dispatch to Clay dated 1 June 1826, about a month and a half after Hodgson's arrival, Shaler writes:

> I am very much pleased to find that the government have at length determined to avail themselves of the great advantages offered by the Barbary Consulates for the

> instructions of young men, which must result in important benefits to the public service. Mr. Hodgson appears to possess all the qualifications necessary to avail himself of these advantages, and if I have not erred in my judgment of him, he will not disappoint the expectations of the President. The salary which has been assigned to him, is quite equal to what the case requires, and I have denominated him Secretary to the Consulate. I have already sent to my bookseller in Paris for the elementary books necessary to the study of the Arabic and Turkish languages, and in the meantime, I have borrowed from friends, such as are sufficient to begin with. (cited in Ives 1937: 333, 360)

In his subsequent correspondence Shaler would continue to comment on Hodgson's excellent classical education, "uncommon genius for philological pursuits," and rapid progress in the study of Arabic, Turkish, and Persian, predicting that he "may become a very useful man and may probably rank amongst the first philologists of his time"; Shaler would also characterize the young man as "an excellent scholar of industrious habits and reputable talents" (cited in Ives 1937: 360; Bryson 1979: 15–17, 19). Shaler's favorable opinion of Hodgson's scholarly abilities and his overall potential would be echoed by Peter S. Duponceau (see below), who would write: "I have satisfied myself that he is a young man of extraordinary genius, of great industry, and of sound judgement, and that he will be an honor to his country" (cited in Bryson 1979: 24).

Shaler's letter of 1 June 1826, part of which was quoted earlier, also contains the first indication of the difficulty that was to hinder the progress of Hodgson's language studies: the scarcity of proper learning materials. During the first year in Algiers, this subject would recur in Hodgson's reports to Clay with monotonous regularity. In his first report, dated 1 June 1826, he notes that the consul general (William Shaler) "has furnished him with some books until he 'can be better supplied from Paris'" (Hopkins and Hardgreaves 1973: 411). In the report of 1 December 1826, he again comments on "the slow progress of his language studies because of lack of books," adding that "he plans to resort 'to Paris, and the school of Oriental languages in that University'" (Hopkins and Hardgreaves 1973; Bryson 1979: 16).[4] In the report of 20 January 1827, Hodgson expresses "continuing hope that he will receive 'the books necessary to prosecute ... Oriental Studies; and notwithstanding present difficulties, ... accomplish the object of ... [his] mission in the course of this year'" (Hardgreaves and Hopkins 1981: 101). In the report of 2 May 1827, he again observes "that the 'difficulties' mentioned in his 'letter of

[4] To Hodgson's acute disappointment, "the President had disapproved his request for a leave of absence and had expressed a wish that he remain at his post"; Hodgson was informed of the denial by a letter of 12 July 1827 from Daniel Brent of the State Department (Hardgreaves and Hopkins 1981: 101). The denial to visit Paris was related to Shaler's departure, on 20 April 1827, for a lengthy leave of absence to improve his health and Hodgson's appointment as *chargé d'affaires* during Shaler's absence (Bryson 1979: 16).

January 25th [i.e., 20th]' remain, although he expects to receive his 'Oriental books . . . in a few weeks'" (Hardgreaves and Hopkins 1981: 511).

In his initial report of 1 June 1826, Hodgson also informed Clay that he had "applied himself to the Lingua Franca" (Bryson 1979: 16). Adams's inclusion of LF within the contours of Hodgson's mission was significant as the language was not considered worthy of serious study. This dismissive attitude is clearly articulated in Shaler's letter to Clay of 1 June 1826:

As to the Lingua Franca it cannot properly be termed a language; it is a barbarous jargon compounded of Spanish, French and Italian, and is naturally understood by all who are acquainted with its elements. It is not used in any serious business, and is spoken with any fluency only by the lowest vulgar. (cited in Ives 1937: 360)

The same attitude is apparent in Shaler's book *Sketches of Algiers*, which came out the same year. The passage in question is additionally useful in that it enumerates the languages current in Algiers and their respective spheres of use:

The languages spoken in Algiers are the Turkish, the Arabic, the Hebrew, and what Doctor Shaw calls the Showiah, or that which is spoken by the independent mountaineers, which there is strong reason for believing an ancient and original language. The Turkish is the language of the government, though the Arabic is the predominant tongue; French is in general use in the society of the foreign agents residing here, and the *Lingua Franca*, which is a barbarous compound of Spanish, French, Italian, and Arabic, is the ordinary medium of communication between foreigners and natives. (Shaler 1826: 13)

It is worth noting that, despite Shaler's assertion in his letter that LF "is not used in any serious business," the following fragment from his own book suggests that, on occasion, the language came in useful for translating diplomatic correspondence:

In April, 1812, a letter from the Prince Regent of England to the Dey of Algiers was brought by the Drogoman of the latter to the late Colonel Lear, then Consul General of the United States in Barbary, on the pretext of obtaining a correct translation of it into the *lingua Franca*. (Shaler 1826: 118)

The usefulness of LF for "serious business" is also underscored by a 1828 pamphlet expounding "the means to employ to punish Algiers" (*Mémoire sur les moyens a employer pour punir Alger*) whose author, a cavalry officer during Napoleon's Egyptian campaign and a Marseilles delegate to the Chamber of Deputies (Weiss 2011: 162–163), suggested that, in order to counteract the *dey*'s propaganda against the invading French,

Il est donc indispensable de répandre des proclamations aussitôt qu'on sera débarqué. Elles porteraient en substance, "que nous reconnaissons un seul Dieu miséricordieux, et que nous respectons Mahomet son prophète; que nous ne venons pas faire la guerre aux habitans, mais au Dey, pour nous venger d'insultes personnelles; que la vie, les propriétés, les femmes, et la religion seront respectées; que ceux qui prendraient les armes contre les Français seront punis de mort; et que chacun peut vaquer à ses affaires comme de coutume. Ces proclamations devront être écrites en langue franque, qui est connue du peuple et des marchands. (Chatelain 1828: 60–61)

[It is therefore essential to spread proclamations immediately upon landing. They would communicate, in a nutshell, "that we recognize a single merciful God, and that we respect Muhammad, his prophet; that we are not here to wage war against the people but against the *dey*, to avenge personal insults; that lives, property, women, and religion will be respected; that those who will take up arms against the French will be punished by death; and that everyone can go about their business as usual. *These proclamations will have to be written in Lingua Franca, which is known by the people and traders.*]

Fortunately, Hodgson was serious about his assignment, which included the study of LF. Ambitious, energetic, and eager to prove himself, he was able to approach the task with fresh eyes. It is clear from Hodgson's reports to Clay that he focused on LF during his first year in Algiers. This may have been prompted by the usefulness of the language, its novelty, and its comparative easiness, especially in light of Hodgson's knowledge of the Romance languages which formed its basis. An additional factor may have been the absence of learning tools for Arabic and Turkish, the more "serious" languages included in Hodgson's assignment, and the need to spend lengthy periods waiting for the language materials to arrive from Paris. Hodgson's work on LF is circumscribed by his report of 1 June 1826 to Clay informing the latter that he has "applied himself to the Lingua Franca" and his report of 2 May 1827 stating "that he has 'compiled a Vocabulary and Dialogues in Lingua Franca, and Arabic' and that he intends 'to add the corresponding Turkish'" (Hardgreaves and Hopkins 1981: 511). The information that Hodgson's preparation of the Arabic vocabulary preceded his anticipated work on a Turkish one squares with his initial plan, outlined in his letter of 1 June 1826 to Clay, to defer "his study of Turkish until he had attained a grasp of Arabic, because study of the former presupposed a knowledge of the latter" (Bryson 1979: 16). The letter of 2 May 1827 also informs us that Hodgson has acquired active rather than merely structural knowledge of LF, and contains his assessment of the language's usefulness:

I speak the Lingua Franca with tolerable facility, from my knowledge of the Romanic languages of which it is compounded. It is a useful medium of intercourse in these countries, being used from Constantinople to Morocco. (cited in Bryson 1979: 17)

Hodgson's focus on LF early on in his stay may also be seen as related to his study of Italian, initiated in Baltimore while he was waiting for his passage to Algiers. Since Shaler and Hodgson both had to procure language books from Paris, it is likely that Hodgson's study of Italian proceeded with the help of a

French textbook, such as *Maître italien* (Veneroni 1800) and/or *Grammaire italienne* (Vergani 1823). French textbooks may also have been regarded as superior to textbooks in English; Shaler's letter to his friend Senator Johnston of Louisiana appears to indicate as much: "As I provided myself with elementary books in France I had occasion to remark the excellency of their methods for studying the classical languages. They appear to me superior to ours in simplicity of arrangement and perspicuity of demonstration. My Greek grammar was composed in 1813 by an illustrious professor for the use of the celebrated normal school in France . . .; it has gone through the 13th edition and is the best synopsis of any language that I have ever seen" (cited in Nichols 1950: 136).

Relying on a third language was not unusual in Hodgson's practice of language study; thus, in the spring of 1827 he reported on translating a US–Algerian treaty from Turkish into English with the help of an *Arabic-Turkish-Persian Lexicon*. Later he would rely on Arabic to study Berber, and in 1832, in a letter to the Department of State, he would point out that successful study of Turkish depends on the student's knowledge of Greek, Latin, Italian, and French and is best carried out simultaneously with the study of Arabic and Persian (Bryson 1979: 63, 75). In addition, we know from Shaler's testimony that French was the usual language of communication among the resident foreign agents. Hodgson's ambitious project to create, perhaps the first ever, learning tool for LF may thus be seen as a natural extension of his nearly simultaneous study of Italian, and also perhaps as a reaction to the probable lack of learning tools of any kind for this language. Hodgson's reliance on Veneroni (1800) and Vergani (1823) as his models for such a project, to be addressed in the next chapter, naturally flows from these assumptions.

According to the published summaries and excerpts of Hodgson's reports to Clay, his report of 2 May 1827 is the last to contain a reference to LF. Coupled with the fact that the *Dictionnaire* contains no promised addition in Turkish, this appears to indicate that after May 1827 Hodgson's attention and priorities had turned to other matters and other languages. In fact, his stay in Algiers would be increasingly occupied by administrative duties. In the spring of 1828, Shaler would depart for the United States for the reasons of health and to accept another diplomatic assignment, appointing Hodgson as *chargé d'affaires*. Hodgson's work at the consulate and his progress in language studies subsequent to Shaler's departure are summarized in his letter to Clay of 10 April 1828, in which he reports "that he has taken over the direction of the consulate following the departure of William Shaler, and that he has studied the history and character of 'these asiatic Turks, and of their piratical republic,' as well as the Arabic, Turkish, Persian, Modern Greek, and Berber languages" (Seager 1982: 221). On 27 September 1828, in a letter to Shaler, Hodgson would add all the Romance languages and German to the list of languages in which he claimed competence: “I shall return home with a competent knowledge of all the Romance languages, plus German, Greek, Arabic, Turkish, and Persian” (cited in Bryson 1979: 18). Hodgson’s studies during the later part of his stay in Algiers were facilitated by an “extensive Oriental library” which he was able to amass by acquiring books from Paris. We learn from Hodgson’s letter of 25 June 1829 to Adams that these were paid for with his own funds (Bryson 1979: 24, 171).

Hodgson’s above-mentioned interest in the then little-studied Berber language initially grew out of a suggestion from Shaler, who had been engaged in the study of Berber for several years before Hodgson’s arrival (see Shaler 1824). Hodgson’s interest was further nurtured and encouraged by his correspondence with Peter S. Duponceau, an officer of the American Philosophical Society who had been instrumental in getting Shaler interested in the study of Berber and Berbers (Shaler 1824: 6; Nichols 1950: 136). In a letter to Duponceau of 15 February 1823, the “Old Consul” (Bryson 1979: 14) writes:

> I really wish that our government would determine to educate a youth here, through whom, when well instructed, and under able direction, we might take our share in the honourable task of unrolling the records of time. He might, through such recommendations as the government might command, learn the rudiments of the Hebrew and Arabic in the Oriental School of Paris, and then come here and acquire a perfect familiarity with the dialects of this country. With such an instrument, if he should happen to be of the right stuff, there can be no conjecture as to what could be obtained. (Shaler 1824: 14)

Between 18 May 1828 and 18 October 1829, Hodgson sent Duponceau a series of letters on Berbers and the Berber language, several of which were published in Transactions of the American Philosophical Society and the North American Review (e.g., Hodgson 1829; see Bryson 1979: 19, 169). From these we learn that Hodgson’s study of Berber proceeded with the help of a 21-year-old Berber-speaking student of the Koran, with whom Hodgson communicated in Arabic, and that it did not involve acquiring active competence in the language; instead, Hodgson engaged in a fieldwork-type study that comprised recording the language’s vocabulary, writing its grammar, collecting tales and songs in it, and translating into it portions of the Bible. His letter of 28 May 1828 to Duponceau, as summarized by Hodgson’s biographer, shows that he viewed this research as a way to enhance his career:

> [Hodgson] advised [Duponceau] that he had completed a vocabulary of some Berber words and was at work preparing a grammar as well as a translation of one of the Gospels. He said he hoped that publication of his earlier letter would aid his election into the American Philosophical Society, a reality that would abet his career. (Bryson 1979: 20–21)

Hodgson's other linguistic and ethnographic research during his stay in Algiers is reflected in his etymological musings on selected Berber words (his etymological research was severely hampered by lack of access to pertinent literature) and his notes on various northern and central African peoples whose languages, customs, environment, geography, agriculture, trade, political situation, and military capabilities he studied with avid interest. This information was gathered and confirmed through repeated interviews with native travelers, traders, and slaves (Brower 2009: 59–61). In the preface to his *Notes on Northern Africa, the Sahara and Soudan*, published in 1844, Hodgson explicitly notes that the information he is about to present is the result of his "personal intercourse with the natives of Africa," there being "no other mode . . . of obtaining information so important to science" (Hodgson 1844: n.p.). Some of Hodgson's letters related to these investigations would be published by and/or presented to the American Philosophical Society, and his efforts at building a scholarly reputation would be rewarded by his election as a corresponding member of the Royal Asiatic Society of London, as a member of the American Philosophical Society and, subsequently, of other learned societies (Mackall 1931: 327–328, 344; Bryson 1979: 21–24).

Hodgson's departure from Algiers took place on 9 October 1829. He sailed for Barcelona, traveling overland to Paris where he purchased some books and manuscripts and made "the acquaintance of some professors of Oriental literature." In late November he proceeded to Le Havre, departing for New York City on 1 December 1829 (Bryson 1979: 31).

The results of Hodgson's stint in Algiers are summarized by John Quincy Adams in his diary entry of 16 January 1830, the date Hodgson paid Adams a visit upon his return to the United States. The entry shows that Adams is aware of Hodgson's pioneering research on Berber, and names LF as one of the languages Hodgson has acquired:

> Mr. Hodgson called upon me this morning, a young man whom in the summer of the year 1825 I sent to Algiers, there to learn the Oriental languages. He had an extraordinary facility at learning languages, and had already made some progress in the Hebrew, Arabic, and Persian; and we were in this country so destitute of persons versed in the Oriental languages that we could not even procure a translation of any paper which occasionally came to us in Arabic. He has been absent about four years, and has acquired the Arabic, Turkish, the Lingua Franca, and the Berber, a language concerning which he has made very interesting discoveries. (Adams 1876: 170)

Adams's diary entry also briefly mentions another activity that Hodgson was engaged in during his stay in Algiers: collecting books and manuscripts in "Oriental languages."

> He [Hodgson] said he had brought home some valuable books and manuscripts relating to the Oriental languages, which had cost him about fifteen hundred dollars, which he

had hoped would be taken by the Department of State, but he might now find it difficult to dispose of them. (Adams 1876: 171)

The extent of Hodgson's collection, apparently purchased with his own funds, is mentioned in his letter of 4 September 1829 to Duponceau, cited in Bryson (1979: 24, 170): "I have collected 250 manuscripts in Arabic, Turkish, Persian, and Berber."

In summary, Hodgson's activities in Algiers, as relevant to his language training, may be divided into three rough areas. The first is his study of the languages that the State Department needed for the serious business of diplomatic translation and interpreting, primarily Arabic and Turkish, to a lesser extent Persian and Greek. Given that Hodgson's continued employment with the government depended on his proficiency in these languages, acquiring them, and perfecting his active competency in them, were uppermost on his list of priorities. He would reiterate his proficiency in these languages in his correspondence; for example, in a letter to his political patron John McLean, written in 1834, "he could not help but relate that he could now translate letters from the Sultan of Turkey, the Pacha of Egypt, the Shah of Iran, and the King of Greece" (Bryson 1979: 88).

The second area of Hodgson's linguistic activities was his pioneering research on the Berber language, Berbers, and other African peoples and languages. This work was undertaken, at least in part, with a view to furthering Hodgson's career aspirations by establishing his reputation as a serious scholar. It bore fruit in the form of recognition of his scholarly abilities, dissemination of his work, and his election as a member of prestigious scholarly societies, with further such honors and distinctions to follow (Mackall 1931: 327–328).

While the first and the second type of activities represented time-consuming investment into Hodgson's professional future, activities in the third area apparently aimed at supplementing his meager and intermittent income as a State Department employee, as well as at compensating him for the constant uncertainty of his prospects of continued employment with the government. As his biographer remarks, "[Hodgson] was not above making a profit on his work" (Bryson 1979: 40). One of the activities that fall under this category is his acquisition of Maghrebi books and manuscripts with a view to selling them: after an unsuccessful attempt to sell his valuable collection to the US government, he would sell it to the British Museum (Bryson 1979: 39, 171). Another activity from which Hodgson derived some profit was his work on Berber. Under his direction, his Berber-speaking consultant translated into Berber parts of the Bible; in 1831, Hodgson would sell the translation to the British and Foreign Bible Society in London (Hodgson 1844: 12; Bryson 1979: 23, 170). Hodgson's ability to conduct such a transaction while a State Department employee is interestingly reflected in Adams' diary entry of 19 May 1830:

> Mr. Shaler paid me a morning visit. . . . Shaler spoke of W. B. Hodgson, and asked me if I thought there would be any impropriety in his selling to the British Foreign Bible Society the manuscript translation of the Book of Genesis and three of the Gospels, which he had procured to be made in the Berber language. I said, No; but that while he remained in office in the Department of State he should receive nothing from any foreign individual or society but with the knowledge and approbation of the President and Secretary of State. (Adams 1876: 227)

Hodgson's work on LF encompassed all three types of the above activities. It involved acquiring active proficiency in the language, while at the same time including a research aspect since the only way to attain such proficiency was through a fieldwork-type study. In addition, sometime prior to his departure, Hodgson apparently sold or donated his manuscript containing the "Vocabulary and Dialogues in Lingua Franca, and Arabic" to the French.

There may have been a number of reasons for his decision to part with this work. By the end of his three-and-a-half-year stay in Algiers, Hodgson had progressed immeasurably in his study of Arabic and Turkish, the languages that were essential for his future career prospects, as he envisioned them at the time, and had also established himself as a respectable scholar. His work on Berber commanded respect from serious scholars and got him elected to a learned society; by contrast, similar research on LF, a low-prestige language viewed as a "barbarous jargon," would not have added appreciably to his scholarly reputation (and may even have detracted from it). While Hodgson's progress in Arabic, Turkish, and Persian was praised unstintingly in Shaler's letters, his study and command of LF were entirely self-reported and are left without mention in Shaler's correspondence. Under these circumstances, and in light of Hodgson's meager earnings and uncertain job prospects, it is likely that if there was a demand for a manuscript for which he saw no other useful purpose, he may have welcomed an opportunity to part with it.

That such a demand existed is clear from the contemporary political situation and the events to follow on the heels of Hodgson's departure. For the better part of Hodgson's stay there Algiers had been at war with France: the infamous diplomatic incident involving a French consul, an irate *dey*, and a fly-whisk took place on 29 April 1827, leading to a prompt recall of the consul, imposition of a French naval blockade on Algiers that was to last for three years, and invasion of Algeria by the French forces mere months after Hodgson's departure (Ageron 1991: 5). Due to Shaler's leave of absence during the period that coincided with these developments, it became Hodgson's duty to report home on the "State of Hostilities … between this Regency and France," which he did by closely monitoring and recording the events in the journal of the consulate, acting in effect as an intelligence officer (Bryson 1979: 25–26; Hardgreaves and Hopkins 1981: 723; see more generally Morgan and Kennedy 1991: 8). Preparation of the French military move against Algeria was under way during the period that substantially coincided with Hodgson's stay in Algiers, and he was exceedingly well positioned to observe it and, if he was so inclined, to participate in it.

From the beginning of his assignment, Hodgson's instructions from the State Department included the charge to report on more than just his progress in languages; he was also instructed to add to his reports "such observations and remarks" as "will be either useful or interesting" (Hopkins and Hardgreaves 1973: 37). For most of his stay, Hodgson would also function as *chargé d'affaires*; his direct duties in that capacity involved reporting on economic and political developments in the region by gathering "information of a commercial value to the nation's commercial interests" (Bryson 1979: 25). He apparently discharged his intelligence-gathering duties competently for, after his appointment as dragoman to the American legation in Constantinople some years later would fail due to a personality clash with the local *chargé d'affaires*, he would be entrusted with a secret information-gathering mission to Egypt, one that would serve "as a model for later American diplomatic missions to the Middle East" (Bryson 1979: 97).

Hodgson must also have been well acquainted with other foreign agents residing in Algiers. Owing to the temporary and official nature of his stay there, it is likely that his only opportunity to socialize was within the close circle of his colleagues in the consular corps and their families. This is the impression conveyed by Shaler after his over a decade-long residence in the city:

> The foreign agents residing in Algiers have no intercourse except officially, with the Turks or natives, their society is, consequently confined to their own circle; but as the representatives of foreign states here are generally men of respectable talents and character, enjoying the confidence of their respective governments, the union of their families forms one of the most friendly and pleasing societies that I have ever met with; indeed, in this respect, leaving nothing to desire. ... [S]hould I ever be called away from Algiers, I should not cease to regret being deprived of the kind hospitality and friendly fascinations of its interesting society. (Shaler 1826: 82–83)

In the estimate of Anonymous (1830b: 38), this contingent amounted to no more than sixty individuals: "Les familles de Consuls sont les seules familles chrétiennes qui habitent Alger; elles ne s'élèvent pas, maîtres et domestiques, à soixante individus" [The families of the consuls are the only Christian families to reside in Algiers; they do not amount, masters and servants together, to sixty individuals]. Hodgson's initial introductions to this milieu were made by Shaler, and it was from these colleagues that he was to learn about the political situation in the region (Bryson 1979: 14).

The highlights of the foreign agents' social life are summarized by Ives (1936a: 186): "There were the usual dinners, dances and garden parties, as well as festivities during the infrequent visits of foreign naval vessels."[5] Hodgson's linguistic activities often led him to borrow language materials from his colleagues. For example, upon Hodgson's arrival in Algiers Shaler jump-started his studies by borrowing textbooks from friends: "I have already sent to my bookseller in Paris for the elementary books necessary to the study of the Arabic and Turkish languages, and in the meantime, I have borrowed from friends, such as are sufficient to begin with" (Shaler's letter to Clay of 1 June 1826, cited in Ives 1837: 333, 360). In the spring of 1827, we learn that Hodgson has translated the US–Algerian treaty of 1816 from Turkish to English with the help of a dictionary borrowed from the Sardinian consul general (Bryson 1979: 17). The combination of Hodgson's duties at the consulate, his social life, and his language-training activities provided him with ample opportunities for networking in the diplomatic milieu, while his direct duty to report on political and commercial developments in the region, coupled with his sustained research on the local peoples, customs, and languages, would have caused him to amass a wealth of factual information on Algeria that would have been of great value to the French war effort.

During Hodgson's aforementioned troubled stint as a dragoman in Constantinople he would be described as a spy, "leading us to believe," observes his biographer, "that Hodgson was in the pay of some foreign government" (Bryson 1979: 74–75). That this hypothesis is not without a foundation is suggested by the recognition that Hodgson would receive some twenty years later for "services rendered to French colonial officials in Algiers":

On 15 November of that [1855] year the French government conferred on him La Medaille des Recompenses in recognition of his services rendered to French colonial officials in Algiers. (Apparently Hodgson had made available to these agents of French imperialism his wealth of material on the geography and culture of the Algerian people.) The certificate of conferral was signed by Emperor Napoleon III. (Bryson 1979: 144)

[5] The journal of the British consul's wife mentions the following for February 1809:

"1lth.-All the different Consular families spent the evening at our house; a supper and great squeeze."

"12th.-A great rout and supper at the Swedish Consul's. We refused going, because it was Sunday."

"13th.-A masked ball at the American Consul's. I went as a black woman, in the complete dress of a Moorish slave."

"14th.-Mr B. accompanied me to a masked ball at the French Consul's. I performed the part of an old woman. We stayed till past four o'clock." (Broughton 1840: 123)

Hodgson's surviving papers contain a draft of his letter to Arnaud d'Avezac, the general secretary of the Geographical Society of Paris, dated 10 November 1838 and written to accompany some of his materials collected in Algiers. In it, Hodgson references an earlier honor conferred on him by a French monarch and expresses his hope that the materials he is sending would be of use to the French colony at Algiers:

> I should feel happy to know that the information which I now have the honor to communicate, has been deemed of any importance by His Majesty's Govt. Always deeply impressed with a sense of the high distinction conferred upon me, by His Majesty, I should be greatly pleased if the present document or any others of the numerous papers which I possess should be found useful in the interest of the French Colony at Algiers. (cited in Mackall 1931: 333)

In an earlier open letter to d'Avezac, Hodgson offered to the Geographic Society of Paris some of his materials on "la géographie, les langues et la statistique de l'Afrique septentrionale" [the geography, languages, and statistics of North Africa] (Hodgson 1836). Brower (2009: 271n50) suggests that Hodgson's inscribing a copy of his *Notes on Northern Africa, the Sahara and Soudan* (Hodgson 1844) to General Daumas is revealing of his "close ties to the French policymaking elites." In light of these facts and observations, it is likely that Hodgson's LF manuscript was among the materials that he either donated or sold to the French prior to his departure from Algiers in October 1829.

What happened to Hodgson's manuscript after it was handed over to the French? I noted earlier (see Section 2.2) that certain aspects of the *Dictionnaire* suggest that it was brought to publication by someone other than its author. One of these is the inconsistent use of the practical orthography of LF, in particular, the presence of variant spellings for about a hundred words and inconsistent notation of the geminates and affricates, both of which are nonexistent in French, in words of Italian origin (see Cifoletti 1989: 42; 2004: 83–84). Another aspect is the uneven distribution of the entries in the LF vocabulary, with a larger number of entries overall, and a larger number of Gallicisms, in the later rather than earlier letters of the alphabet (Cifoletti 1989: 88). With respect to this last issue, Cifoletti (1980: 18–20) additionally observes that French-origin words are not found in the *Dictionnaire*'s preface and dialogues, and notes that some of the words express unexpectedly abstract concepts while having the appearance of having been mechanically adapted to Italian phonology. These features are consistent with the hypothesis that the *Dictionnaire* was prepared for publication by a French editor who either did not entirely appreciate the logic behind the practical orthography of LF or had no time to implement it consistently. It is also possible that the editor may have incorporated into the *Dictionnaire* other works that may have been in circulation at the time. The possibility that there may have been other written materials in LF is raised, e.g., by the mention of "two dictionaries and a grammar" by Gérard de Nerval in a 1843 letter written from Cairo (see Mallette 2014: 338):

Je possède assez d'italien, d'arabe et de grec déjà pour parler ce qu'on appelle la langue franque qui se compose arbitrairement de mots de ces trois langues. ... j'ai deux dictionnaires et une grammaire, mais j'apprends bien plus par la nécessité de demander les choses. (Nerval 1911: 132)

[I already have enough Italian, Arabic, and Greek to speak what they call Lingua Franca, which is composed arbitrarily of words from these three languages. ... I have two dictionaries and a grammar, but I learn much more by the necessity to ask for things.]

The printshop that published the *Dictionnaire* also issued, in the same year, the pamphlet entitled *Alger. Topographie, population, forces militaires de terre et de mer, acclimatement et resources que le pays peut offrir à l'armée d'expédition, precedé d'un résume historique; suivi d'un précis sur le service des troupes pendant un siège et orné d'un plan très exact de la ville et de ses environs. Par un Français qui a résidé à Alger* (see Cifoletti 2004: 255–257). As is clear from its title, this work "by a Frenchman who has resided in Algiers" provides a wealth of practical information about the regency and the city of Algiers for the use of the French army. The description of the regency's linguistic situation, supplied in the section *Langue, moeurs, arts* [Language, Customs, Arts], makes no mention whatsoever of the complex multilingual mosaic of Algeria and instead zooms in on the practicalities of communication by mentioning only one language: Lingua Franca. The passage in question, reproduced below, refers to LF in the same way as the *Dictionnaire*, namely, as *Langue Franque ou Petit Mauresque*, seemingly to establish a deliberate link between the two publications:

A Alger, comme dans presque tout le Levant, mahométans et étrangers se servent d'un jargon composé d'italien, de français et d'espagnol, qu'on appelle Langue Franque ou Petit Mauresque, à l'aide de laquelle on entend facilement les trois langues, et l'on se fait entendre de toutes les espèces d'habitans. (Anonymous 1830b: 70)

[In Algiers, as in almost the whole of Levant, Mahometans and foreigners make use of a jargon composed of Italian, French, and Spanish, which is called Lingua Franca or Petit Mauresque, by means of which one understands the three languages easily and makes oneself understood by all sorts of inhabitants.]

The preface to the *Dictionnaire*, similarly, assures the reader that with the help of LF the French will be able to communicate with the locals without the need of an interpreter:

Notre recueil facilitera les communications des Français avec les habitans du pays sur lequel ils vont combattre, et à son aide, il n'est aucun de nos compatriotes qui ne puisse se passer d'interprète, et en servir au besoin. (Anonymous 1830a: n.p.)

[Our compendium will facilitate communication of the French with the inhabitants of the land in which they are going to fight and, with its help, there is no one among our fellow countrymen who will not be able to manage without an interpreter and make use of it as needed.]

The above passages from the *Dictionnaire* and *Alger* indicate that the former was envisioned as a companion publication to this more general volume about Algeria. In fact, the exclusion, in *Alger*, of all languages spoken natively in the regency does not make sense except as a way to point to the *Dictionnaire*. The inconsistency of mentioning only LF in *Alger* while including an Arabic vocabulary in the *Dictionnaire* may be explained by the haste with which the volumes were apparently produced; as noted by Nichols (1950), barely five months separated the adoption of a plan for the invasion of Algeria by the French council of state and the actual invasion.

The author of *Alger*, though not identified by name, is nonetheless described on the cover as "un Français qui a résidé à Alger" [a Frenchman who has resided in Algiers]. The fact that the author of the *Dictionnaire* is not given even this modicum of identification suggests that his identity could not have been alluded to in similar terms. The French Romanist Alfred Morel-Fatio, who had furnished Hugo Schuchardt with a copy of the *Dictionnaire*, was emphatic in his opinion that the author of the *Dictionnaire* was not French: "Je vais m'informer auprès de personnes qui connaissent l'histoire de la conquête dans ses détails si on peut retrouver le nom de l'auteur et les circonstances de la publication (l'auteur n'est pas français: il y a de grossières fautes de grammaire dans la préface)" [I will ask persons with detailed knowledge of the conquest if it is possible to discover the name of the author and the circumstances of the publication (the author is not French: there are rough grammatical mistakes in the preface)] (Morel-Fatio 1882a). Given the coordination between the two publications, it is possible that the *Dictionnaire*'s final editing was done by the individual hiding behind the description "un Français qui a résidé à Alger."

In places, the descriptions of Algeria in *Alger* (Anonymous 1830b) bear more than a passing resemblance to comparable passages in Shaler's *Sketches of Algiers* (Shaler 1826). For example, the similarities between the two descriptions of an armed janissary, given below as an illustration, are too specific to be coincidental. It is possible that the parallels in question derive from their authors' reliance on common sources (both mention Shaw 1757, for example), exposure to similar information through their likely concurrent residence in Algiers, or the practice of sharing books among the foreign agents.

A Janissary, when equipped for battle, has one or more pairs of large pistols in his belt, with his scimitar or yatagan, a dagger in his bosom, and a long musket on his shoulder; all which are as highly ornamented as his circumstances will permit. When, costume included, he is not unfairly represented by the knave of diamonds in a pack of cards. (Shaler 1826: 27–28)

Un janissaire sous les armes, dit un voyageur qui a décrit ces contrées, a au moins une paire de pistolets, un cimeterre, un poignard et un fusil, le tout aussi riche que ses facultés peuvent le lui permettre. Avec cet équipement et son costume, il ne ressemble pas mal à un valet de carreau. (Anonymous 1830b: 77)

[A janissary under arms, says a traveler who has described these lands, has at least one pair of pistols, a scimitar, a dagger, and a rifle, all of it as rich as his circumstances will permit. With this equipment and his costume, he looks not unlike a jack of diamonds.]

Prior to the publication of his book, Shaler spent the summer of 1825 in France, endeavoring to convince influential individuals "that French enterprise should encompass Algiers" (Nichols 1950: 139). On his return to the United States, in the spring of 1828, he would again travel through France and renew his urging. The *Sketches of Algiers* would soon be circulated in French translation (Shaler 1830), and France's policy toward Algiers would follow the general direction urged by Shaler; the plan for the invasion of Algeria adopted by the French council of state in January 1830 would be "very similar to that of Shaler, and the French expedition which captured Algeria in July, 1830, followed the general strategy laid down by the American consul" (Nichols 1950: 141). Shaler's probable influence on the actions of France in Algeria was commonly assumed by his contemporaries, as evidenced by the following excerpt from his obituary (see also Frost 1965: 10):

In 1826, Mr. Shaler published his sketches of Algiers. This book was highly complimented by French writers and particularly in the "Revue Encyclopedique" at Paris. . . . From these sketches the French learned the best method of attacking the city of Algiers with success: and they followed the directions most minutely. (Knapp 1833)

Nathaniel Shaler confirms the above account of William Shaler's role in the invasion of Algeria, adding the interesting detail that Shaler refused to be remunerated for his services to the French government. His information derives in part from Shaler's diaries:

At the end of his service as consul-general, William Shaler, disgusted with the state of affairs in the principality, went to France and had much to do in persuading the French to invade and occupy the country, acting as the adviser of that government in its plans for the expedition, particularly in the operations which led to the capture of Algiers. For this service he received and refused the offer of a sum of money said to have been the equivalent of a hundred thousand dollars. (Shaler 1909: 7)

Though their friendship was cut short by Shaler's untimely demise from cholera (Ives 1936b: 633), William Shaler had been a profound influence in Hodgson's life. The younger man gratefully acknowledged Shaler's impact:

There [in Algiers] it was my good fortune first to have acquired his [Shaler's] friendship. The official dependence which I bore to him, secured for me, the invaluable lessons of his large experience with men and things, and what I esteemed more, the

> instruction of his virtuous mind. . . . I shall conclude this brief sketch of my lamented friend, with the heartfelt testimony, that never had my youth a more faithful guardian and counsellor, or my manhood a nobler object of grateful retrospect and worthy example. (Hodgson 1845: 166–168)

It would be safe to suppose that the ongoing and constantly evolving conflict between France and Algeria, along with the overall political situation with the Barbary regencies, were among the topics that Hodgson and Shaler had discussed, and where their views coincided. Hodgson's (1844: 9) description of the then ongoing military conflict in North Africa as one between "undisciplined hordes and the science of European warfare," and one of "civilization with semi-barbarism," leaves us in no doubt as to his sympathies. His sharing of his considerable archive on Algeria with the French, whether or not he was rewarded for doing so, was clearly in line with Hodgson's political views.

2.4 Chapter Summary

This chapter has shown that the basis for the key publication on LF, the *Dictionnaire de la langue franque* published anonymously in 1830, was laid by William Brown Hodgson's work on this language carried out during his language-training mission in Algiers. The dialogues in LF, the French-LF vocabulary, and the French-Arabic vocabulary were compiled by Hodgson during the first year of his stay in Algiers, between April 1826 and May 1827, and were either donated or sold to the French before his departure from Algiers in October 1829. The next chapter will show that, in his work on the LF manuscript, Hodgson made extensive use of two textbooks which may have served him well in his study of Italian: Vergani's *Grammaire italienne* (Vergani 1823) and Veneroni's *Maître italien* (Veneroni 1800).

Neither LF nor the LF manuscript is mentioned again in Hodgson's reports to the Department of State, and there is no indication in the materials assembled by Hodgson's biographer of their being mentioned in his other surviving papers. Hodgson would not wipe LF from his memory, however. In his lecture "The Science of Language: Sanscrit and Hebrew, the Two Written Primitive Languages Compared," published in 1868, he writes:

> An educated African may be taught to speak English grammatically; but never will a whole people, conquered or subject, acquire the syntax of the dominant race. Hence, in this process of adopting a foreign language, an irregular or inchoate form of speech is produced. Here, it is called *patois*; and on the shores of the Mediterranean, *Lingua Franca*. (cited in Bryson 1979: 148)

3 The *Dictionnaire*

The preceding chapter has substantiated the hypothesis that the basis for the *Dictionnaire de la langue franque* was laid by the diplomat scholar William B. Hodgson who conducted research on LF in Algiers. The present chapter develops our knowledge of the *Dictionnaire*'s sources by focusing on the publications which provided Hodgson with conceptual models for this work. Section 3.1 introduces two Italian grammars which were used as models for the *Dictionnaire*'s preface, LF dialogues, and Arabic vocabulary: Veneroni (1800) and Vergani (1823). Section 3.2 examines the use of the learner's dialogues in Vergani (1823) as a model for the *Dictionnaire*'s dialogues in LF. Section 3.3 looks at the list of commonly used nouns in Veneroni (1800) as a model for the *Dictionnaire*'s Arabic vocabulary. Section 3.4 examines the influence of Vergani (1823) and Veneroni (1800) on the structural outline of LF in the *Dictionnaire*'s preface. Section 3.5 highlights selected aspects of the *Dictionnaire*'s LF orthography in relation to Vergani's (1823) and Veneroni's (1800) shared practice of drawing on French orthographic resources to represent the pronunciation of Italian. Section 3.6 examines the LF vocabulary, focusing on the grammatical information provided in the entries, the use of grammatical and semantic markers, the types of LF translations for the French lexical entries, and the possible models for multiword LF lexemes. Section 3.7 contains a brief summary of the main points.

3.1 Model Grammars

In 1800, the thirty-fifth installment of that year's *Journal Typographique et Bibliographique (Ou recueil consacré à tout ce que parait de nouveau en Littérature, Sciences et Arts)* gave notice of an Italian grammar entitled *La grammaire italienne de Veneroni, simplifiée et réduite à vingt leçons, avec de nouveaux thêmes, de nouveaux dialogues, et un nouveau recueil de traits d'histoire, suivis de quelques morceaux choisis de poésie italienne.*

The publisher's description contrasted this abridgment with the ponderous volume from which it was drawn:

Tous ceux que connoissent la Grammaire italienne de *Veneroni*, conviennent qu'elle est trop diffuse et trop compliquée. L'Abrégé que nous publions est écrit avec beaucoup de clarté et de précision. Il contient plusieurs règles essentielles que manquoient dans Vénéroni. Les thêmes joints à chaque leçon sont intérressans, les dialogues agréables, les traits d'histoire piquans, et les morceaux de poésie italienne choisis avec goût. Sous tous ces rapports, nous ne saurions trop en recommander la lecture. Du reste, le citoyen *Vergani* est très-avantageusement connu dans ces sortes d'ouvrages, qui nous offrent l'utile et l'agréable. (Roux 1800: 285)

[All those who are familiar with the Italian grammar of Veneroni recognize that it is too unfocused and complicated. The Abridgment that we are bringing out is written with great clarity and precision. It contains many essential rules that are absent from Veneroni. The passages attached to each lesson are interesting, the dialogues pleasant, the historical anecdotes spicy, and the snippets of Italian poetry chosen with taste. We cannot recommend reading it too highly in all respects. Moreover, citizen Vergani is very favorably known for this kind of works, which combine the useful and the pleasant.]

The *Journal*'s subscribers were well familiar with the earlier grammar, the *Maître italien* by Giovanni Veneroni (1642–1708). Born in Verdun as Jean Vigneron, Veneroni was able to acquire such outstanding knowledge of Italian as to be able to pass himself off as a Florentine. He enjoyed a successful career teaching Italian in Paris and serving as an Italian language interpreter to the king; an encyclopedic dictionary from the late nineteenth century credits him with greatly contributing to spreading the interest in the Italian language and literature in France (Pinheiro Chagas 1884: 311). The *Maître italien* was first published around 1686 and went through multiple reprintings, and revisions by both Veneroni and others (e.g., Veneroni 1700, 1800). The latter include a 1816 revision whose third edition predates the *Dictionnaire* by a mere decade (Quérard 1839: 96–97); and an English translation was published as well (Veneroni 1823). Angelo Vergani's *Grammaire italienne*, advertised by the *Journal*, was thus one in a long line of revisions of this popular text:

La Grammaire italienne de Veneroni parut pour la première fois vers 1686; depuis cette époque, elle a été réimprimée un grand nombre de fois; mais, ayant vieillie, elle a été remaniée, améliorée par des nouveaux éditeurs. . . . La Grammaire italienne, publiée par Vergani . . . est encore une réduction de celle de Veneroni. (Quérard 1839: 97)

[The Italian grammar of Veneroni appeared for the first time around 1686; since then, it has been reprinted many times, but, having become dated, it has been revised, improved by new editors. The Italian grammar published by Vergani is yet another reduction of Veneroni's.]

Angelo Vergani, an Italian by birth, successfully taught Italian and English in France. In an encyclopedic dictionary from the late nineteenth century, his "simplified grammar of Veneroni" is given first in the list of works he left behind:

Gramatico italiano da segunda metade do seculo XVIII e m. em Paris pelos annos de 1813. Ensinou em França a lingua italiana e abriu em Paris un curso facultativo no collegio da Marca. No tempo da Revolução emigrou para a Allemanha e reappareceu em França depois do 18 de brumario e ahí continuou dedicando se ao ensino das linguas italiana e inglesa. Deixou as seguintes obras: *Grammatica de Veneroni simplificada; Grammatica ingleza simplificada*. (Pinheiro Chagas 1884: 327)

[An Italian grammarian from the second half of the eighteenth century; died in Paris around 1813. Taught Italian in France and opened in Paris an optional course at the collège de la Marche. During the revolution he emigrated to Germany and reappeared in France after 18 Brumaire, there to continue to devote himself to the teaching of Italian and English. He left behind the following works: *Simplified Grammar of Veneroni; Simplified English Grammar*.]

Vergani's condensed and streamlined version of Veneroni's grammar enjoyed a lasting success, going through multiple reprintings and revisions; ten of these are listed in Quérard (1839: 108) alone, including several in the years immediately predating the *Dictionnaire*. The success of the Vergani text led to its use as a model for other grammars (cf. Vergani 1820); from the preface to its 1826 adaptation to Spanish (Rementería y Fica 1826) we learn that it had gone through seven editions. The Spanish version is energetic in its praise of the Vergani text (see also Arce 1988: 11–12; Lombardero Caparrós 2015: 204–205). In light of its ready availability and widely acknowledged usefulness as a teaching tool for Italian, coupled with the fact that it is likely to have been familiar to at least some of the intended users of a LF manual, Hodgson's turning to Vergani's *Grammaire italienne* as a model for a learning tool for a language substantially based on Italian appears a natural choice.

The *Grammaire italienne* (Vergani 1823) is sectioned into definitions of grammatical terms (pp. 1–2), twenty lessons (pp. 3–189), a *Recueil des noms les plus usités* [Collection of nouns in most general use] (pp. 190–194), *Phrases familières, en François et en Italien* [Familiar phrases in French and Italian] (pp. 195–217), and *Scelta di varie storie, per uso de' principianti* [Selection of miscellaneous stories for beginners] (pp. 218–226). It will be shown below that *Phrases familières* were likely to have been used as a template for the *Dictionnaire*'s learner's dialogues in LF, that Vergani's arrangement and explanation of key Italian grammar topics were followed in the *Dictionnaire*'s description of LF, and that his transliteration of Italian sounds influenced certain aspects of the *Dictionnaire*'s orthography of LF. It will be further shown that the *Dictionnaire*'s Arabic vocabulary is more likely to have been compiled with the help of Veneroni's *Recueil des noms les plus nécessaires à savoir et à retenir* [Collection of nouns most necessary to know and remember] (Veneroni 1800: 261–298) than the corresponding section in Vergani (1823: 190–194). Since the exact edition of Vergani's *Grammaire italienne* which was used by Hodgson is unknown, the 1823 edition is used here due to its temporal proximity to the *Dictionnaire* and the fact that this particular edition was often reprinted, including more than once in the years immediately predating the *Dictionnaire*'s publication (see Quérard 1839: 108). Veneroni's *Maître italien* will be cited in its 1800 edition due to its comparative proximity to the period of the *Dictionnaire*'s compilation.

3.2 Lingua Franca Dialogues

3.2.1 Model Dialogues

The section entitled *Phrases familières, en François et en Italien*[1] [Familiar phrases in French and Italian] is found on pages 195–217 of Vergani (1823). The phrases that compose this section are arranged in two columns, with the French prompts on the left and their Italian translations on the right, and are divided into fourteen unnumbered thematic blocks. As shown in Table 3.1, nine of these were used as models for the similarly titled LF dialogues in the *Dictionnaire*. Five of the thematic sections – *Du verbe Avoir* [Of the verb *to have*], *Du verbe Etre* [Of the verb *to be*], *Du lever* [On rising], *Du dîné* [Of dinner], and *De la promenade* [Of taking a walk] – were left out altogether, while two more, *De l'heure* [Of the hour] and *Du temps* [Of the weather], were merged, resulting in the total of eight dialogues in LF.

The selection of the sentences in the LF dialogues as well as the dialogues' titles and topics point to Vergani's (1823) *Phrases familières* as their model. The influence of the corresponding section in Veneroni (1800: 306–321) is, nonetheless, detectable in the fact that this section of the *Dictionnaire* bears the title *Dialogues* and the fact that each dialogue in LF is supplied with a number as well as a title. In Veneroni (1800), the relevant section is called *Dialogues familièrs*; and it will be recalled that the dialogue section is referred to as *dialogues familièrs* in the *Dictionnaire*'s title. Also, all of Veneroni's dialogues except the first have both a number and a title (see Table 3.2). Finally, the exchange *Comment vous portez-vous? – Je suis bien, et vous* [How are you? – I am well, and you?] (see Table 3.4) has no model in Vergani (1823) while Veneroni's (1800) first dialogue contains a close equivalent: *Bonsoir,*

[1] This is the title given in the table of contents; in the body of the grammar, this section is called *Phrases familières, a l'usage des commençans* [Familiar phrases for beginners].

Table 3.1. Phrases familières *in Vergani (1823) and* Dialogues *in Anonymous (1830a)*

Vergani (1823)			Anonymous (1830a)	
Section title (French)	Section title (Italian)	Page	Dialogue title (French)	Page
Du verbe Avoir	Del verbo Avere	195	–	–
Du verbe Etre	Del verbo Essere	197	–	–
Pour affirmer et nier	Per affermare e negare	199	Pour Affirmer ou Nier [*To affirm or deny*]	93
Pour remercier et complimenter	Per ringraziare e complimentare	200	Pour Remercier et Complimenter [*To thank and pay compliments*]	93
Pour consulter	Per consultare	201	Pour Consulter [*To consult*]	94
Pour aller et venir	Per andare e venire	202	Pour Aller et Venir [*To go and come*]	95
D'entendre, de comprendre et de connoître	Dell'intendere, capire e conoscere	203	D'Entendre, de Comprendre et de Connaître [*To hear, to understand, and to know*]	95
Du lever	Del levarsi	205	–	–
Du déjeuné	Della colazione	206	Du Déjeûner [*Of breakfast*]	96
De l'heure	Dell' ora	208	De l'Heure et du Temps [*Of the hour and weather*]	97
Du temps	Del tempo	209		
Pour demander ce qu'on dit de nouveau	Per chiedere ciò che si dice di nuovo	210	Pour Demander ce qu'il y a de Nouveau [*To inquire the news*]	98
Du dîné	Del pranzo	212	–	–
De la promenade	Del passeggio	215	–	–

Table 3.2. Dialogues familièrs *in Veneroni (1800)*

Dialogue	Dialogue title (French)	Dialogue title (Italian)	Page
Premier dialogue	–	–	306
Second dialogue	Pour faire une visite le matin [*To make a visit in the morning*]	Per fare una visita la mattina	307
Troisième dialogue	Pour s'habiller [*To dress oneself*]	Per vestirsi	308
Quatrième dialogue	Le Gentilhomme et le Tailleur [*The gentleman and the tailor*]	Il Gentil'uomo e'l Sartore	309
Cinquième dialogue	Pour déjeûner [*To go to breakfast*]	Per far colazione	311
Sixième dialogue	Pour parler Italien [*To speak Italian*]	Per parlare Italiano	312
Septième dialogue	Du Temps [*Of the weather*]	Del Tempo	313
Huitième dialogue	Pour écrire [*To write*]	Per iscrivere	314
Neuvième dialogue	Pour jouer [*To play*]	Per giuocare	316
Dixième dialogue	Pour monter à cheval [*To mount on horseback*]	Per montar a cavallo	317
Onzième dialogue	Du souper et du logement [*For supper and lodging*]	Della cena, et dell' alloggiamento	318
Douzième dialogue	De la Civilité [*On civility*]	Della Civiltà	319

Monsieur: comment vous portez-vous? – Bien [Good evening, sir, how are you? – I am well].

In Tables 3.3–3.10, the French prompts from the *Dictionnaire*'s dialogues are juxtaposed with their models in Vergani (1823); the translations of the prompts into LF and Italian, respectively, are also supplied.

Table 3.3. *No. 1: Pour Affirmer ou Nier*

Vergani (1823)		Anonymous (1830a)	
French	Italian	French	Lingua Franca
Il est vrai.	È vero.	*Cela est vrai.*	qouesto star véro.
Cela n'est pas vrai.	Non è vero.	*Cela n'est pas vrai.*	qouesto non star véro.
Cela n'est que trop vrai.	Quest' è pur troppo vero.	*Cela n'est que trop vrai.*	qouesto star tropo véro.
Qui en doute?	Chi ne dubita?	*J'en doute.*	mi doubitar di questo.
Il n'y a point de doute.	Non v'è dubbio alcuno.	*Il n'y a point de doute.*	non tenir doubio.
Que voulez-vous parier?	Che volete scommettere?	*Que voulez-vous parier?*	cosà volir scométir?
Je gagerois quelque chose.	Scommetterei qualche cosa.	*J[a] gagerais quelque chose.*	mi scométir qualqué cosa.
Je gagerai ce que vous voudrez.	Scommetterò quel che volete.	*Je gagerais ce que vous voudrez.*	mi scométir cosa ti quérir.
Croyez-moi; je puis vous l'assurer.	Credetemi; ve lo posso assicurare.	*Croyez-moi, je puis vous l'assurer.*	ti crédir per mi, mi poudir assicourar per ti.
C'est ainsi.	È così.	*C'est ainsi.*	star acoussi.
Je crois qu'oui.	Credo di sì.	*Je crois que oui.*	mi pensar si.
Je crois que non.	Credo di no.	*Je crois que non.*	mi pensar no.
Je dis que oui.	Dico di sì.	*Je dis que oui.*	mi ablar si.
Je dis que non.	Dico di no.	*Je dis que non.*	mi ablar no.
Sur ma parole.	Sulla mia parola.	*Sur ma parole.*	per la palabra di mi.
Je dis toujours la vérité.	Dico sempre la verità.	*Je dis la vérité.*	mi ablar dgiousto.
Je vous crois.	Vi credo.	*Je vous crois.*	mi crédir per ti.
Je n'en crois pas un mot.	Non ne credo una parola.	*Je n'en crois pas une parole.*	mi non crédir ouna palabra.
Je ne saurois le croire.	Non posso crederlo.	*Je ne saurais croire.*	mi non poudir crédir.
Cela est faux.	Quest' è falso.	*Cela est faux.*	qouesto star falso.

Table 3.4. *No. 2: Pour Remercier et Complimenter*

Vergani (1823)		Anonymous (1830a)	
French	Italian	French	Lingua Franca
Bon jour, Monsieur.	Buon giorno, Signore.	*Bon jour, Monsieur.*	bon dgiorno Signor.
–	–	*Comment vous portez-vous?*	commé ti star?
–	–	*Je suis bien, et vous.*	mi star bonou, é ti.
Je suis bien aise de vous voir en bonne santé.	Godo di vedervi in buona salute.	*Je suis bien aise de vous voir.*	mi star contento mirar per ti.
Je vous remercie de tout mon coeur.	Vi ringrazio di tutto cuore.	*Je vous remercie.*	gratzia.
Puis-je vous servir en vuelque chose?	Posso servirvi in qualche cosa?	*Puis-je vous servir en quelque chose?*	mi poudir servir per ti per qualké cosa?
Je vous suis fort obligé, obligée.	Vi sono molto obbligato, obbligata.	*Je vous suis fort obligé.*	mouchou gratzia.
Donnez une chaise à Monsieur.	Date una sedia al Signore.	*Donnez une chaise à Monsieur.*	ti dar una cadiéra al Signor.
Il n'est pas nécessaire.	Non è necessario.	*Il n'est pas nécessaire.*	non bisogna.
Je suis fort bien comme cela.	Sto benissimo così.	*Je suis bien comme cela.*	mi star béné acoussi.
Comment se porte monsieur votre frère?	Come sta il vostro Signor fratello.	*Comment se porte votre frère?*	commé star il fratello di ti?
Il se porte fort bien, grâces à Dieu.	Sta benissimo, grazie a Dio.	*Il se porte fort bien.*	star mouchou bonou.
Est-il à la maison?	È egli in casa?	*Est-il à la maison?*	star in casa?
Non, Monsieur; il est sorti.	No, Signore; è uscito.	*Non, il est sorti.*	no, star forà.

Table 3.4. *(cont.)*

Vergani (1823)		Anonymous (1830a)	
French	Italian	French	Lingua Franca
Et Madame votre mere, comment se porte-t-elle?	E la vostra Signora madre, come sta ella?	*Et Monsieur votre père comment est il?*	E il padré di ti commé star?
Pas trop bien.	Non troppo bene.	*Il n'est pas bien.*	non star bonou.
Qu'a-t-elle?	Che ha?	*Qu'a-t-il?*	cosa ténir?
Elle a la fièvre.	Ha la febbre.	*Il a la fièvre.*	ténir fébra.
J'en suis bien fâché.	Me ne dispiace moltissimo.	*J'en suis bien fâché.*	dispiacher mouchou per mi.
Y a-t-il long-temps que vous n'avez vu Monsieur N?	È un pezzo che non avete veduto il Signor N?	*Y a-t-il long-tems que vous n'avez vu Monsieur M.?*	molto tempo ti non mirato Signor M.?
Je l'ai vu hier, l'autre jour, la semaine passée.	L'ho veduto jeri, l'altro giorno, la settimana passata.	*Je l'ai vu hier.*	mi mirato iéri.
C'est un honnête homme.	È un uomo di garbo.	*C'est un brave homme.*	star bouona genti.
Quand vous le verrez, faites-lui mes complimens.	Quando lo vedrete, fategli i miei complimenti.	*Quand vous le verrez faites lui mes complimens.*	quando ti mirar per ellou saloutar mouchou per la parté di mi.
Adieu, mon cher ami.	Addio, mio caro amico.	*Adieu mon ami.*	Adios amigo.

The caption of each table reflects the number and title of the corresponding dialogue in the *Dictionnaire*; and the French prompts and their corresponding translations follow the order in which they appear in the *Dictionnaire*. Vergani's French prompts which were omitted from the *Dictionnaire*, as well as those which were modified in the process, are discussed in the next section.

Table 3.5. *No. 3: Pour Consulter*

Vergani (1823)		Anonymous (1830a)	
French	Italian	French	Lingua Franca
Que ferons-nous?	Che faremo?	*Que fesons-nous?*	cosa counchar?
Que faut-il faire?	Che si ha da fare?	*Que faut-il faire?*	cosa bisognio counchar?
Qu'en pensez-vous?	Che ne pensate?	*Qu'en pensez-vous?*	qué pensar?
Que voudriez-vous faire?	Che vorreste fare?	*Que voudriez-vous faire?*	cosa ti quérir counchar?
Faisons comme cela.	Facciamo così.	*Fesons comme cela.*	bisognio counchar acoussi.
Il me semble qu'il vaudroit mieux . . .	Mi pare che sarebbe meglio . . .	*Il me semble qu'il vaudrait mieux.*	mi pensar star meïo.
Si j'étois à votre place, je ferois . . .	S' io fossi in luogo vostro, farei . . .	*Si j'étais à votre place je ferais.*	sé mi star al logo di ti, mi counchar, *ou* fazir.
A quoi servira tout cela?	A che servirà tutto questo?	*A quoi servira tout cela?*	qué servir touto qouesto?
Laissez-moi faire.	Lasciatemi fare.	*Laissez-moi faire.*	ti laschiar counchar per mi.

Table 3.6. *No. 4: Pour Aller et Venir*

Vergani (1823)		Anonymous (1830a)	
French	Italian	French	Lingua Franca
Qui est là?	Chi è là.	*Qui est là?*	qui star aki?
Entrez.	Entrate.	*Entrez.*	intrar.
D'où venez-vous?	Di dove venite?	*D'où venez-vous?*	oundé ti vénir?
Je viens de chez moi.	Vengo di casa mia.	*Je viens de chez moi.*	mi vénir della casa di mi.

Table 3.6. *(cont.)*

Vergani (1823)		Anonymous (1830a)	
French	Italian	French	Lingua Franca
Où allez-vous?	Dove andate?	*Où allez-vous?*	ové ti andar?
Je vais me promener.	Vado a spasso.	*Je vais me promener.*	mi andar spasségiar.
Je vais voir un ami.	Vado a veder un amico.	*Je vais voir un ami.*	mi andar mirar oun amigo.
Je vais chez Monsieur N.	Vado dal Signor N.	*Je vais chez Monsieur M.*	mi andar in casa del Signor.
Voulez-vous que j'aille avec vous?	Volete ch' io venga con voi?	*Voulez-vous que j'aille avec vous?*	ti quérir mi andar con ti?
Allons ensemble.	Andiamo insieme.	*Oui, allons ensemble.*	si, andar siémé siémé.
Venez ici.	Venite qua.	*Venez ici?*	ti vénir aki?
Montez.	Salite.	*Montez, descendez.*	ti mountar, ti baschiar.
Descendez.	Scendete.		
Allez-vous en.	Andatevene.	*Allez-vous en.*	andar fora.
Sortez de la maison.	Uscite di casa.	*Sortez de la maison.*	andar fora di casa.
Dépêchez-vous.	Sbrigatevi.	*Dépêchez-vous.*	fazir ou counchar presto.
Revenez tout de suite.	Tornate subito.	*Revenez de suite.*	tornar soubito.
Allez plus doucement.	Andate più adagio.	*Allez doucement.*	andar poco poco.
Je suis pressé.	Ho fretta.	*Je suis pressé.*	mi tenir prémoura.
Asseyez-vous.	Sedete.	*Asseyez-vous.*	ti sentar, *ou* ti sédir.
Attendez un peu.	Aspettate un poco.	*Attendez un peu.*	spétar oun poco.
Ouvrez la fenêtre.	Aprite la finestra.	*Ouvrez la fenêtre.*	aprir la bentana.
Fermez la porte.	Chiudete la porta.	*Fermez la porte.*	sarar la porta.

Table 3.7. *No. 5: D'Entendre, de Comprendre et de Connaître*

Vergani (1823)		Anonymous (1830a)	
French	Italian	French	Lingua Franca
Ecoutez-moi.	Ascoltatemi.	*Écoutez.*	sentir.
M'entendez-vous?	M' intendete?	*M'entendez-vous?*	sentir per mi?
Me comprenez-vous?	Mi capite?	*Comprenez-vous?*	capir?
Je vous entends bien.	V' intendo bene.	*J'entends bien.*	mi sentir bonou.
Je vous comprends un peu.	Vi capisco un poco.	*Je vous comprends un peu.*	mi capir oun poco per ti.
Que dites-vous?	Che cosa dite?	*Que dites-vous?*	cosa ti ablar?
Répondez-moi.	Rispondetemi.	*Répondez-moi.*	respondir per mi.
Qui est ce Monsieur qui nous parloit tantôt?	Chi è quel Signore, che parlava con voi poco fa?	*Qui est-ce Monsieur qui vous parlait tantôt.*	qui star qouesto signor qué poco poco ablar per ti.
Le connaissez-vous?	Lo conoscete?	*Le connaissez vous?*	ti conoscir per ellou?
Je le connois de réputation.	Lo conosco per fama.	*J'ai entendu parler de lui.*	mi sentito hablar di ellou.
Je l'ai vue plusieurs fois.	L' ho veduta parecchie volte.	*Je l'ai vu chez vous.*	mi mirato in casa di ti.
Où demeure-t-elle?	Dove sta di casa?	*Où demeure-t-il?*	ové sentar?
Dans la rue de . . .	Nella strada di . . .	*Dans la grand'rue.*	in strada grandi.
De quel pays est-elle?	Di che paese è?	*De quel pays est-il?*	di qué païsé star?
Elle est Italienne.	È Italiana.	*Il est français, anglais, espagnol, portuguais, napolitain, toscan, autrichien, russe, américain, danois, suédois, hollandais.*	star francis, inglis, esbagniol, portugués, nabolitan, toscan, nemsa, moskovit, amérikan, danès, suédés, flamin.

Table 3.7. *(cont.)*

Vergani (1823)		Anonymous (1830a)	
French	Italian	French	Lingua Franca
Y a-t-il long-temps que vous la connoissez?	È un pezzo che la conoscete?	*Y a-t-il long-temps que vous le connaissez?*	mouchou tempou di conoschir per ellou?
Il y a environ deux ans.	Sono due anni incirca.	*Il y a peu de temps.*	ténir poco tempo.
Je serois bien aise de faire sa connoissance.	Avrei a caro di far la sua conoscenza.	*Je serais bien aise de faire sa connaissance.*	mi ténir piacher conoschir per ellou.
Nous irons ensemble la saluer.	Andremo insieme a riverirla.	*Nous irons le voir ensemble.*	bisognio andar mirar per ellou siémé siémé.
Quand il vous plaira.	Quando vi piacerà.	*Quand il vous plaira.*	qouando piacher per ti.
Nous irons demain matin.	Vi andremo domattina.	*Nous irons demain.*	bisognio andar domani.

Table 3.8. *No. 6: Du Déjeûner*

Vergani (1823)		Anonymous (1830a)	
French	Italian	French	Lingua Franca
Avez-vous déjeuné, Monsieur?	Avete fatto colazione, Signore?	*Avez-vous déjeuné?*	ti fato colatzioné?
Non, Monsieur.	No, Signore.	*Non, Monsieur.*	non, Signor.
Vous venez à propos; le déjeuné est prêt.	Venite a proposito; la colazione è pronta.	*Vous venez à propos, le déjeuné est prêt.*	ti venir dgiousto, la mangiaria star pronta.
Je suis venu exprès pour déjeuner avec vous.	Son venuto apposta per far colazione con voi.	*Je suis venu exprès pour déjeuner avec vous.*	mi venouto aposto per far mangiaria con ti.

Table 3.8. *(cont.)*

Vergani (1823)		Anonymous (1830a)	
French	Italian	French	Lingua Franca
Fort bien. Que voulez-vous prendre?	Benissimo. Che cosa volete prendere?	*Bien, que voulez-vous prendre?*	bonou? qué ti quérir mangiar.
Ce qu'il vous plaira.	Quel che vi piacerà.	*Ce qu'il vous plaira.*	qouello qué ti quérir.
Voulez-vous le chocolat ou le café.	Volete la cioccolata o il caffè?	*Voulez-vous du café?*	ti quérir café?
Apportez la chocolatière; mettez-la sur le feu.	Portate la cioccolattiera; mettetela sul fuoco.	*Apportez le café.*	portar café.
Allons, faites chauffer de l'eau; je veux faire du thé.	Animo, fate scaldar dell'acqua; voglio far del tè.	*Faites chauffer de l'eau; je veux faire du thé.*	fazir scaldar agoua; mi quérir counchar thé.
N'en faites pas pour moi; une tasse de chocolat me suffit.	Non ne fate per me; una chicchera di cioccolata mi basta.	*N'en faites pas pour moi, le café me suffit.*	non counchar per mi, il café basta.
J'ai du thé délicieux; je veux que vous en goûtiez.	Ho un tè delizioso; voglio che l'assaggiate.	*J'ai du thé délicieux; je veux que vous en goûtiez.*	mi tenir thé mouchou bonou; mi quérir ti goustar per ellou.
Monsieur, je vous suis bien obligé de votre bonté.	Signore, sono molto tenuto alla vostra bontà.	*Je vous suis bien obligé.*	mouchou gratzia.
Mettez-y un peu plus de sucre.	Metteteci un poco più di zucchero.	*Mettez-y un peu plus de sucre.*	ti métir oun poco piou zoukro.
–	–	*J'en ai assez.*	mi ténir bastantza.

Table 3.9. *No. 7: De l'Heure et du Temps*

Vergani (1823)		Anonymous (1830a)	
French	Italian	French	Lingua Franca
Quelle heure est-il?	Che ora è?	*Quelle heure est-il?*	qué ora star?
Quelle heure croyez-vous qu'il soit?	Che ora credete che sia?	*Quelle heure croyez-vous qu'il soit?*	qué ora ti pensar star?
Je crois qu'il n'est pas encore deux heures.	Credo che non siano ancora le due.	*Je pense qu'il n'est pas trois heures.*	mi pensar non star tré ora.
Il sera bientôt dix heures.	Saranno presto le dieci.	*Il est bientôt quatre heures.*	poco poco star quatr'ora.
Il n'est pas tard.	Non è tardi.	*Il n'est pas tard.*	non star tardi.
Voyez quelle heure il est à votre montre.	Vedete che ora è al vostro oriuolo.	*Voyez quelle heure il est à votre montre.*	mirar qué ora star al orlogio di ti.
Elle ne va pas; elle n'est pas montée.	Non va; è scarico.	*Elle ne va pas bien.*	non andar bonou.
Elle avance; elle retarde.	Va avanti; va addietro.	*Elle avance, elle retarde.*	andar avanti, andar indiétro.
Quel temps fait-il aujourd'hui?	Che tempo fa oggi?	*Quels temps fait-il?*	Comé star il tempo?
Il fait beau temps.	Fa bel tempo.	*Il fait beau temps.*	il tempo star bello.
Il fait mauvais temps.	Fa cattivo tempo.	*Il fait mauvais temps.*	il tempo star cativo.
Il fait chaud.	Fa caldo.	*Il fait chaud.*	fazir caldo.
Il fait froid.	Fa freddo.	*Il fait froid.*	fazir frédo.
Il fait du vent.	Tira vento.	*Il fait du vent.*	fazir vento.
Il pleut.	Piove.	*Il pleut.*	cascar agoua.
Il fait une chaleur étouffante.	È un caldo affannoso.	*Il fait une chaleur étouffante.*	fazir caldo mouchou.

Table 3.10. *No. 8: Pour Demander ce qu'il ya de Nouveau*

Vergani (1823)		Anonymous (1830a)	
French	Italian	French	Lingua Franca
Que dit-on de nouveau?	Che si dice di nuovo?	*Que dit-on de nouveau?*	qué nouova?
Je n'ai rien entendu.	Io non ho inteso nulla.	*Je n'ai rien entendu.*	mi non sentito nada.
Que dit on à la cour?	Che si dice in corte?	*Que dit-on dans la ville?*	qué hablar in chità?
Avez-vous entendu dire que nous aurons la guerre.	Avete inteso dire che avremo la guerra?	*On dit que nous avons la guerre.*	genti hablar tenir gouerra.
On parle d'un voyage du roi.	Si parla d'un viaggio del re.		
–	–	*La guerre, avec quelle nation?*	Gouerra, con qué natzion?
–	–	*Avec les Français.*	con Francis.
–	–	*Que peuvent faire les Français contre Alger?*	qué poudir counchar il Françis contra di Algieri?
–	–	*Par mer rien, mais par terre ils sont redoutables.*	per maré nada, ma per terra il Francis star mouchou forti.
–	–	*Si les Français débarquent Alger est perdu.*	sé il Françis sbarkar, Algiéri star perso.
–	–	*Je pense que les Algériens ne se batront pas.*	mi pensar l'Algérino non combatir.
–	–	*Le Pacha sera donc obligé de demander la paix.*	dounqué bisogno il Bacha quérir paché.
–	–	*Oui, s'il ne veut périr.*	si, sé non quérir morir.
–	–	*S'il veux la paix les Turcs feront tapage.*	sé quérir paché l'Yoldach fazir gribouila.
–	–	*Pour quoi ne fait-on pas la paix?*	perqué non counchar paché
–	–	*Parce que le Pacha est entêté.*	perqué il Bacha tenir fantétzia.

3.2.2 *Simplification Strategies*

In the preceding section it was shown that the number of the dialogues in LF is appreciably smaller than the available models in Vergani (1823); specifically, the content of five of the thematic sections of *Phrases familières* was left out of the *Dictionnaire*. The reduction in the number of dialogues may be seen as the first step in their adaptation as a learning tool for LF. As a result of this pruning, the users of the dialogues are not provided with the linguistic tools to construct conversations about getting up in the morning, going for a walk, or dining out. Wholesale elimination of the sections *Du verbe Etre* [Of the verb *to be*] and *Du verbe Avoir* [Of the verb *to have*] has also led to lexical reduction by eliminating the many names of professions and objects of possession they contain.

Reduction of informational content has been described as one of the simplification strategies of teacher talk, a simplified oral register directed by language teachers at students with low proficiency in the target language. Berretta (1988: 369) describes the reduction of informational content as "[l]a semplificazione ... contenutistica" [content simplification], opposing it to simplification which is "specificamente linguistica" [specifically linguistic]. Both simplification strategies – "simplification of language and simplification of content" (Honeyfield 1977: 431) – are also present in written language teaching materials, such as graded readers, in which literary texts in the target language are adapted for second and foreign language learners. It has been suggested that such simplified reading matter may be regarded as a subtype of teacher talk (Moretti 1988: 222).

Further reduction of informational content was achieved by shortening the model dialogues. The French prompts omitted from the *Dictionnaire*'s dialogues are given in Table 3.11; the first column reflects the number of the corresponding dialogue in the *Dictionnaire*.

The phrases and sentences in Table 3.11 fall into several, not mutually exclusive, categories. These include conventional expressions of politeness, sentences with female participants, sentences perceived as redundant or repetitive with respect to adjacent sentences, sentences omitted due to the overall pruning of the dialogue, and sentences on topics which may have been perceived as irrelevant in the context of anticipated conversations in LF in the Algerian setting, such as rumors about a king's trip abroad, a recent duel, an exquisite china tea set, and varied ways of telling time and describing weather. In the last dialogue, which was subjected to the greatest amount of reduction, the excised portion was replaced with a whole new set of exchanges whose content anticipates the landing of the French army and the commotion this would cause. It is possible that some of the prompts were left out for purely linguistic reasons, such as their syntactic complexity (cf. *Je ne crois pas la moitié de ce qu'on dit* [I do not believe half of what is said]) or the unavailability in LF of some key word, such as the words for *rainbow* or *cloud* (see Table 3.12).

Table 3.11. *Vergani's (1823) French prompts not included in Anonymous (1830a)*

No.	French prompt	Italian translation
1	*Sur mon honneur.* [Upon my honor]	*Sull' onor mio.*
	Foi d'honnête homme. [On the faith of an honorable man]	*Da galantuomo.*
	Je ne crois pas la moitié de ce qu'on dit. [I do not believe half of what is said]	*Non credo la metà di quel che si dice.*
	Cela est imposible. [It is impossible]	*È impossibile.*
	C'est un mensonge. [It is a lie]	*È una bugia.*
2	*Votre très-humble serviteur.* [Your most humble servant]	*Servitore umilissimo.*
	Vous me faites trop d'honneur. [You do me too much honor]	*Mi fate troppo onore.*
	Couvrez-vous. [Cover yourself]	*Copritevi.*
	Ne faites point de céremonies. [Be on no ceremony]	*Non fate ceremonie.*
	Depuis quand? [Since when?]	*Da quando in qua?*
	Depuis hier. [Since yesterday]	*Da jeri in qua.*
3	*Que me conseillez-vous de faire?* [What do you advise me to do?]	*Che mi consigliate di fare?*
	Quel parti prendrons-nous? [What course shall we take?]	*Che partito prenderemo?*
	Faisons une chose. [Let us do something]	*Facciamo una cosa.*
	Que vous en semble-t-il? [What do you think of it?]	*Che ve ne pare?*
4	*Je vais chez Madame N.* [I am going to Mrs. N's]	*Vado dalla Signora N.*
	Je vais ici près; au logis; à la comèdie; à l'église.	*Vado qua vicino; a casa; alla commedia; alla chiesa.*

Table 3.11. *(cont.)*

No.	French prompt	Italian translation
	[I am going close by; home; to the play; to church]	
	Retournons sur nos pas. [Let's go back]	*Torniamo indietro.*
	Allez à droite, à gauche. [Go to the right, to the left]	*Andate a destra, a sinistra.*
	Ne marchez pas si vite. [Don't walk so fast]	*Non camínate così presto.*
	Arrêtez-vous. [Stop]	*Fermatevi.*
	Ne bougez pas de là. [Don't move from there]	*Non vi movete di costà.*
	Pourquoi restez-vous debout? [Why are you standing?]	*Perchè restate voi in piedi?*
5	*Parlez haut.* [Speak loudly]	*Parlate forte.*
	Vous parlez trop bas. [You speak too softly]	*Voi parlate troppo piano.*
	Je le connois de vue. [I know him by sight]	*Lo conosco di vista.*
	Je n'ai pas l'honneur de le connoître. [I do not have the honor of knowing him]	*Non ho l' onor di conoscerlo.*
	Connoissez-vous cette Dame? [Do you know this lady?]	*Conóscete voi quella Signora?*
	Ici près. [Close by]	*Qui vicino.*
	Dans quelle rue? [On what street?]	*In che strada?*
	Où l'avez-vous connue? [Where did you meet her?]	*Dove l' avete conosciuta?*
	A Venise, à Milan, à Paris. [In Venice, in Milan, in Paris]	*In Venezia, in Milano, in Parigi.*
	Il y a environ deux ans. [About two years]	*Sono due anni incirca.*
	Quand? [When?]	*Quando?*

Table 3.11. *(cont.)*

No.	French prompt	Italian translation
6	*J'aime beaucoup le chocolat.* [I am very fond of chocolate]	*Mi piace molto la cioccolata.*
	Où sont les tasses? [Where are the cups?]	*Dove sono le chicchere?*
	Les voici. [Here they are]	*Eccole.*
	Ces tasses sont superbes; je n'ai jamais vu de si belle porcelaine. [These cups are magnificent; I have never seen such fine china]	*Queste chicchere sono superbe; non ho mai visto una così bella porcellana.*
	C'est le prèsent d'un de mes amis, qui les a fait venir de Saxe. [They are a present from a friend of mine who has procured them from Saxony]	*È il regalo d'un mio amico che le ha fatte venir di Sassonia.*
	Le cabaret aussi est magnifique. [The tea-tray is also beautiful]	*Anche il vassojo è magnifico.*
	Votre thé est excellent; où l'achetez-vous? [Your tea is excellent; where do you buy it?]	*Il vostro tè è ottimo; dove lo comprate?*
	Si vous souhaitez, je vous en donnerai l'adresse. [If you wish, I will give you the address]	*Se bramate, vi darò l'indirizzo.*
	Vous me ferez plaisir. [That would please me]	*Mi farete piacere.*
7	*Il est deux heures et demie.* [It's half past two]	*Sono due ore e mezzo.*
	Il est deux heures et trois quarts. [It's three quarters past two]	*Sono due ore e tre quarti.*
	Il est quatre heures moins un quart. [It's quarter to four]	*Sono le quattro meno un quarto.*
	Il s'en va cinq heures. [It's going to strike five]	*Son cinque ore le prime.*
	Comment, cinq heures! il est six heures sonnées. [How five! It has struck six]	*Come, le cinque! sono sonate le sei.*

Table 3.11. *(cont.)*

No.	French prompt	Italian translation
	J'entends l'horloge. [I hear the clock]	*Sento l'orologio.*
	L'horloge sonne. [The clock is striking]	*L'orologio suona.*
	Comptez les heures. [Count the hours]	*Contate le ore.*
	Il est midi. [It's noon]	*È mezzodì.*
	Il est une heure, une heure et demie. [It's one o'clock, half past one]	*È un' ora, un' ora e mezzo.*
	Il est encore de bonne heure. [It is still early]	*È ancora a buon' ora.*
	Il faut que je la monte. [I must wind it up]	*Bisogna ch'io lo carichi.*
	Il est presque nuit. [It is almost night]	*È quasi notte.*
	Il se fait tard. [It is late]	*Si fa tardi.*
	A quelle heure vous couchez-vous? [What time do you go do bed?]	*A che ora andate a letto?*
	A minuit. [At midnight]	*A mezza notte.*
	Nous nous verrons demain à dix heures. [We'll meet tomorrow at ten o'clock]	*Ci vedremo domani alle dieci.*
	Je vous attendrai jusqu'à onze heures, à onze heures et un quart. [I'll wait for you till eleven, till a quarter past eleven]	*Vi aspetterò fino alle undici; alle undici e un quarto.*
	Il me semble qu'il fait un grand brouillard. [It seems to me that there is a great fog]	*Mi pare che vi sia una gran nebbia.*
	C'est vrai. [It's true]	*È vero.*
	Il gèle. [It's freezing]	*Gela.*

Table 3.11. *(cont.)*

No.	French prompt	Italian translation
	Il neige. [It's snowing]	*Nevica.*
	Il tonne. [It's thundering]	*Tuona.*
	Il éclaire. [It's lightning]	*Lampeggia* ou *balena.*
	Il grêle. [It's hailing]	*Grandina.*
	Il pleut à verse. [It's pouring]	*Diluvia.*
	Ce n'est qu'une ondée; elle passera bientôt. [It's only a shower; it will soon be over]	*Non è che una scossa; passerà presto.*
	Je n'ai pas pris mon paraplouie. [I haven't taken my umbrella]	*Non ho preso l'ombrella.*
	Mettons-nous à couvert. [Let us take shelter]	*Mettiamoci al coperto.*
	L'orage est passé. [The storm is over]	*La burrasca è passata.*
	Les nuages se dissipent peu à peu. [The clouds disperse little by little]	*Le nuvole spariscono a poco a poco.*
	Le soleil commence à luire. [The sun is beginning to shine]	*Il sole comincia a risplendere.*
	Je vois l'arc-en-ciel. [I see a rainbow]	*Vedo l'arcobaleno.*
	Il fait un temps humide et mal-sain. [It's damp and unhealthy weather]	*È un tempo umido e malsano.*
	Le temps est inconstant et variable. [The weather is uncertain and changeable]	*Il tempo è incostante e variabile.*
8	*De quoi parle-t-on à présent?* [What are the rumors now?]	Di che si parla adesso?
	On ne parle de rien. [Nothing in particular]	Non si parla di niente.

Table 3.11. *(cont.)*

No.	French prompt	Italian translation
	Je n'en ai pas entendu parler. [I have not heard it mentioned]	Io non ne ho inteso parlare.
	Au contraire, on parle de paix. [On the contrary, they talk of peace]	Al contrario, si parla di pace.
	Quand croit-on qu'il partira? [When do they think he will leave?]	Quando si crede che partirà?
	On ne le sait pas. [It is not known]	Non si sa.
	Où dit-on qu'il ira? [Where do they say he will go?]	Dove si dice ch' andrà?
	Les uns disent en Italie, les autres en Allemagne. [Some say to Italy, others to Germany]	Chi dice in Italia, chi in Germania.
	Et la gazette que dit-elle? [And what does the gazette say?]	E la gazzetta che dice?
	Je ne l'ai pas lue. [I haven't read it]	Non l' ho letta.
	Est-il vrai ce qu'on dit de Monsieur N? [Is it true what they say of Mr. N?]	È vero quel che si dice del Signor N?
	Qu'en dit-on? [What do they say about him?]	Che se ne dice?
	On dit qu'il a été blessé à mort. [They say he has been mortally wounded]	Si dice che sia stto ferito a morte.
	J'en serois fâché; car c'est un honnête homme. [I should be sorry for it, for he is an honorable man]	Me ne dispiacerebbe; perchè è un galantuomo.
	Qui l'a blessé? [Who has wounded him?]	Chi l' ha ferito?
	Le capitaine N. [Captain N]	Il capitano N.
	Sait-on pourquoi? [Do we know why?]	Si sa il perchè?

Table 3.11. *(cont.)*

No.	French prompt	Italian translation
	Le bruit court que c'est pour avoir mal parlé de lui. [There's a rumor going round that it's for having spoken badly of him]	La voce corre che sia per avere sparlato di lui.
	Je ne le crois pas. [I don't not believe it]	Non lo credo.
	Ni moi non plus. [Me neither]	Nemmeno io.
	Quoi qu'il en soit, on saura bientôt la vérité. [Be it as it may, the truth will soon be known]	Comunque sia, si saprà presto la verità.
	Connoissiez-vous Monsieur N? [Did you know Mr. N?]	Conoscevate il Signor N?
	Je le connoissois très-bien. [I knew him very well]	Lo conosceva benissimo.
	Il est mort la semaine passée. [He died last week]	È morto la settimana scorsa.
	Je le sais. [I know]	Lo so.
	Il étoit mon grand ami. [He was my great friend]	Era mio grande amico.
	Il est regretté de tout le monde. [He is mourned by everyone]	È compianto da tutti.
	Etoit-il marié? [Was he married?]	Era egli ammogliato?
	Oui, Monsieur. [Yes, sir]	Si, Signore.
	Sa femme doit être fort affligée. [His wife must be devastated]	Sua moglie deve essere molto afflitta.
	Elle est inconsolable. [She is inconsolable]	Ella è inconsolabile.
	On croit qu'elle mourra de chagrin. [It is thought that she will die of grief]	Si crede che morrà di dolore.

Table 3.12. *A selection of the omitted French prompts*

Category	French	Translation
Politeness formulae	*Sur mon honneur.*	[Upon my honor]
	Foi d'honnête homme.	[On the faith of an honorable man]
	Vous me faites trop d'honneur.	[You do me too much honor]
	Je n'ai pas l'honneur de le connoître.	[I do not have the honor of knowing him]
	Ne faites point de céremonies.	[Be on no ceremony]
	Votre très-humble serviteur.	[Your very humble servant]
Female participants	*Je vais chez Madame N.*	[I am going to Mrs. N's]
	Connoissez-vous cette Dame?	[Do you know this lady?]
	Où l'avez-vous connue?	[Where did you meet her?]
Repetitive prompts	*Sur mon honneur* (omitted) *Sur ma parole* (retained)	[Upon my honor] [Upon my word]
	Faisons une chose (omitted) *Faisons comme cela* (retained)	[Let us do something] [Let us do like this]
	Je le connois de vue (omitted) *Je le connois de réputation* (retained)	[I know him by sight] [I know him by reputation]
Dialogue shortening	*Où demeure-t-elle?* (model dialogue) *Ici près.* *Dans quelle rue?* *Dans la rue de …* ================ *Où demeure-t-il?* (simplified dialogue) *Dans la grand' rue.*	[Where does she live?] [Close by] [On what street?] [On the street …] ============== [Where does he live?] [On the main street]
Irrelevant topics	*Ces tasses sont superbes; je n'ai jamais vu de si belle porcelaine.*	[These cups are magnificent; I have never seen such fine china]
	C'est le prèsent d'un de mes amis, qui les a fait venir de Saxe.	[They are a present from a friend of mine who has procured them from Saxony]
	Le cabaret aussi est magnifique.	[The tea-tray is also beautiful]

Table 3.12. *(cont.)*

Category	French	Translation
	Votre thé est excellent; où l'achetez-vous?	[Your tea is excellent; where do you buy it?]
	Si vous souhaitez, je vous en donnerai l'adresse.	[If you wish, I will give you the address]
	Vous me ferez plaisir.	[That would please me]
	Il est deux heures et demie.	[It's half past two]
	Il est deux heures et trois quarts.	[It's three quarters past two]
	Il est quatre heures moins un quart.	[It's quarter to four]
	Il est une heure, une heure et demie.	[It's one o'clock, half past one]
	Il gèle.	[It's freezing]
	Il grêle.	[It's hailing]
	Je vois l'arc-en-ciel.	[I see a rainbow]
	Les nuages se dissipent peu à peu.	[The clouds are dispersing little by little]
	Est-il vrai ce qu'on dit de Monsieur N?	[It is true what they say of Mr. N?]
	On dit qu'il a été blessé à mort.	[They say he has been mortally wounded]

The reduction of the informational content of the dialogues is accompanied by structural and/or lexical reduction of the French prompts. The changes in question are summarized in Table 3.13. The order of the prompts follows the order in which they appear in the *Dictionnaire*'s dialogues; the translations of the prompts are also provided.

The adaptations seen in Table 3.13 result in both content and linguistic simplification of the French prompts in the *Dictionnaire* as compared to their models in Vergani (1823). The reasons for the simplification may have included the need to adjust the prompts to the reduced expressive possibilities of LF, achieved by aligning them more closely with their LF translations; and to accommodate the, possibly imperfect, knowledge of French on the part of the consultant whose services were employed.

Table 3.13. *Adaptation of Vergani's (1823) French prompts in Anonymous (1830a)*

Vergani (1823)		Anonymous (1830a)	
French	Italian	French	Lingua Franca
Il est vrai.	È vero.	*Cela est vrai.*	qouesto star véro.
Qui en doute?	Chi ne dubita?	*J'en doute.*	mi doubitar di questo.
Je dis toujours la vérité.	Dico sempre la verità.	*Je dis la vérité.*	mi hablar dgiousto.
Je n'en crois pas un mot.	Non ne credo una parola.	*Je n'en crois pas une parole.*	mi non crédir ouna palabra.
Je suis bien aise de vous voir en bonne santé.	Godo di vedervi in buona salute.	*Je suis bien aise de vous voir.*	mi star contento mirar per ti.
Je vous remercie de tout mon coeur.	Vi ringrazio di tutto cuore.	*Je vous remercie.*	gratzia.
Je vous suis fort obligé, obligée.	Vi sono molto obbligato, obbligata.	*Je vous suis fort obligé.*	mouchou gratzia.
Je suis fort bien comme cela.	Sto benissimo così.	*Je suis bien comme cela.*	mi star béné acoussi.
Comment se porte monsieur votre frère?	Come sta il vostro Signor fratello.	*Comment se porte votre frère?*	commé star il fratello di ti?
Il se porte fort bien, grâces à Dieu.	Sta benissimo, grazie a Dio.	*Il se porte fort bien.*	star mouchou bonou.
Non, Monsieur; il est sorti.	No, Signore; è uscito.	*Non, il est sorti.*	no, star forà.
Et Madame votre mere, comment se porte-t-elle?	E la vostra Signora madre, come sta ella?	*Et Monsieur votre père comment est il?*	E il padré di ti commé star?
Pas trop bien.	Non troppo bene.	*Il n'est pas bien.*	non star bonou.
Qu'a-t-elle?	Che ha?	*Qu'a-t-il?*	cosa ténir?
Elle a la fièvre.	Ha la febbre.	*Il a la fièvre.*	ténir fébra.

Table 3.13. *(cont.)*

Vergani (1823)		Anonymous (1830a)	
French	Italian	French	Lingua Franca
Je l'ai vu hier, l'autre jour, la semaine passée.	L'ho veduto jeri, l'altro giorno, la settimana passata.	*Je l'ai vu hier.*	mi mirato iéri.
C'est un honnête homme.	È un uomo di garbo.	*C'est un brave homme.*	star bouona genti.
Adieu, mon cher ami.	Addio, mio caro amico.	*Adieu mon ami.*	adios amigo.
Que ferons-nous?	Che faremo?	*Que fesons-nous?*	cosa counchar?
Allons ensemble.	Andiamo insieme.	*Oui, allons ensemble.*	Si, andar siémé siémé.
Revenez tout de suite.	Tornate subito.	*Revenez de suite.*	Tornar soubito.
Allez plus doucement.	Andate più adagio.	*Allez doucement.*	Andar poco poco.
Écoutez-moi.	Ascoltatemi.	*Écoutez.*	sentir.
Me comprenez-vous?	Mi capite?	*Comprenez-vous?*	capir?
Je vous entends bien.	V' intendo bene.	*J'entends bien.*	mi sentir bonou.
Je le connois de réputation.	Lo conosco per fama.	*J'ai entendu parler de lui.*	mi sentito hablar di ellou.
Je l'ai vue plusieurs fois.	L' ho veduta parecchie volte.	*Je l'ai vu chez vous.*	mi mirato in casa di ti.
Où demeure-t-elle?	Dove sta di casa?	*Où demeure-t-il?*	ové sentar?
Dans la rue de . . .	Nella strada di . . .	*Dans la grand'rue.*	in strada grandi.
De quel pays est-elle?	Di che paese è?	*De quel pays est-il?*	di qué païsé star?
Elle est Italienne.	È Italiana.	*Il est français, anglais, espagnol, portuguais,*	star francis, inglis, esbagniol, portugués,

Table 3.13. *(cont.)*

Vergani (1823)		Anonymous (1830a)	
French	Italian	French	Lingua Franca
		napolitain, toscan, autrichien, russe, américain, danois, suédois, hollandais.	nabolitan, toscan, nemsa, moskovit, amérikan, danès, suédés, flamin.
Y a-t-il long-temps que vous la connoissez?	È un pezzo che la conoscete?	*Y a-t-il long-temps que vous le connaissez?*	mouchou tempou di conoschir per ellou?
Il y a environ deux ans.	Sono due anni incirca.	*Il y a peu de temps.*	ténir poco tempo.
Nous irons ensemble la saluer.	Andremo insieme a riverirla.	*Nous irons le voir ensemble.*	bisognio andar mirar per ellou siémé siémé.
Nous irons demain matin.	Vi andremo domattina.	*Nous irons demain.*	bisognio andar domani.
Avez-vous déjeuné, Monsieur?	Avete fatto colazione, Signore?	*Avez-vous déjeuné?*	ti fato colatzioné?
Fort bien. Que voulez-vous prendre?	Benissimo. Che cosa volete prendere?	*Bien, que voulez-vous prendre?*	bonou? qué ti quérir mangiar.
Voulez-vous le chocolat ou le café.	Volete la cioccolata o il caffè?	*Voulez-vous du café?*	ti quérir café?
Apportez la chocolatière; mettez-la sur le feu.	Portate la cioccolattiera; mettetela sul fuoco.	*Apportez le café.*	portar café.
Allons, faites chauffer de l'eau; je veux faire du thé.	Animo, fate scaldar dell'acqua; voglio far del tè.	*Faites chauffer de l'eau; je veux faire du thé.*	fazir scaldar agoua; mi quérir counchar thé.
N'en faites pas pour moi; une tasse de chocolat me suffit.	Non ne fate per me; una chicchera di cioccolata mi basta.	*N'en faites pas pour moi, le café me suffit.*	non counchar per mi, il café basta.

Table 3.13. *(cont.)*

Vergani (1823)		Anonymous (1830a)	
French	Italian	French	Lingua Franca
Monsieur, je vous suis bien obligé de votre bonté.	Signore, sono molto tenuto alla vostra bontà.	*Je vous suis bien obligé.*	mouchou gratzia.
Je crois qu'il n'est pas encore deux heures.	Credo che non siano ancora le due.	*Je pense qu'il n'est pas trois heures.*	mi pensar non star tré ora.
Il sera bientôt dix heures.	Saranno presto le dieci.	*Il est bientôt quatre heures.*	poco poco star qouatr'ora.
Elle ne va pas; elle n'est pas montée.	Non va; è scarico.	*Elle ne va pas bien.*	non andar bonou.
Quel temps fait-il aujourd'hui?	Che tempo fa oggi?	*Quels temps fait-il?*	Comé star il tempo?
Que dit on à la cour?	Che si dice in corte?	*Que dit-on dans la ville?*	qué hablar in chità?

The categories of simplification attested in the prompts coincide with those described for teacher talk, specifically its written variety used in readings adapted for second and foreign language learners: omissions, and replacement of structures judged as complex with equivalents perceived as being simpler (Moretti 1988: 221).

Omissions are by far the larger category. The types of elements that are omitted include clauses, prepositional phrases, object personal pronouns, adverbs, an adjective, an expletive, a term of address, and alternatives, if present in the original prompts (see Table 3.14; the omitted elements are underlined). Some of the prompts show more than one type of omission; for example, *Je vous suis bien obligé* [I am much obliged to you] dispenses with both the prepositional phrase *de votre bonté* [for your kindness] and the term of address *Monsieur* [sir], which form part of the original prompt *Monsieur, je vous suis bien obligé de votre bonté* [Sir, I am much obliged to you for your kindness].

The last example in Table 3.14 forms part of a more general category of adaptations which consist of eliminating references to females. An unfortunate consequence of this simplification strategy is the absence of usage examples of

Table 3.14. *Omission of elements in the French prompts*

Vergani (1823)	Anonymous (1830a)
Je dis toujours la vérité. [I always speak the truth]	*Je dis la vérité.* [I speak the truth]
Je suis fort bien comme cela. [I am very well like this]	*Je suis bien comme cela.* [I am well like this]
Revenez tout de suite. [Come back right away]	*Revenez de suite.* [Come right back]
Allez plus doucement. [Go more slowly]	*Allez doucement.* [Go slowly]
Nous irons demain matin. [We will go tomorrow morning]	*Nous irons demain.* [We will go tomorrow]
Fort bien. Que voulez-vous prendre? [Very good; what will you take?]	*Bien, que voulez-vous prendre?* [Good; what will you take?]
Je crois qu'il n'est pas encore deux heures. [I believe it is not yet two o'clock]	*Je pense qu'il n'est pas trois heures.* [I think it is not three o'clock]
Quel temps fait-il aujourd'hui? [How is the weather today?]	*Quel temps fait-il?* [How is the weather?]
Je vous remercie de tout mon coeur. [I thank you with all my heart]	*Je vous remercie.* [I thank you]
Je suis bien aise de vous voir en bonne santé. [I am glad to see you in good health]	*Je suis bien aise de vous voir.* [I am glad to see you]
Il se porte fort bien, grâces à Dieu. [He is very well, thank God]	*Il se porte fort bien.* [He is very well]
Monsieur, je vous suis bien obligé de votre bonté. [Sir, I am much obliged to you for your kindness]	*Je vous suis bien obligé.* [I am much obliged to you]
Apportez la chocolatière; mettez-la sur le feu. [Bring the chocolate-pot; put it on the fire]	*Apportez le café.* [Bring coffee]
Elle ne va pas; elle n'est pas montée. [It does not go; it is not wound up]	*Elle ne va pas bien.* [It does not go well]
Ecoutez-moi. [Listen to me]	*Écoutez.* [Listen]
Me comprenez-vous? [Do you understand me?]	*Comprenez-vous?* [Do you understand?]
Je vous entends bien. [I understand you well]	*J'entends bien.* [I understand well]

Table 3.14. *(cont.)*

Vergani (1823)	Anonymous (1830a)
Adieu, mon cher ami. [Adieu, my dear friend]	*Adieu, mon ami.* [Adieu, my friend]
Allons, faites chauffer de l'eau; je veux faire du thé. [Come, heat up some water; I'll make some tea]	*Faites chauffer de l'eau; je veux faire du thé.* [Heat up some water; I'll make some tea]
Comment se porte monsieur votre frère? [How does your brother do?]	*Comment se porte votre frère?* [How does your brother do?]
Non, Monsieur; il est sorti. [No, sir, he is out]	*Non, il est sorti.* [No, he is out]
Avez-vous déjeuné, Monsieur? [Have you had breakfast, sir?]	*Avez-vous déjeuné?* [Have you had breakfast?]
Monsieur, je vous suis bien obligé de votre bonté. [I am much obliged to you for your kindness, sir]	*Je vous suis bien obligé.* [I am much obliged to you]
Je l'ai vu hier, l'autre jour, la semaine passée. [I saw him yesterday, the other day, last week]	*Je l'ai vu hier.* [I saw him yesterday]
Voulez-vous le chocolat ou le café. [Will you take chocolate or coffee?]	*Voulez-vous du café?* [Would you like some coffee?]
Je vous suis fort obligé, obligée. [I am very much obliged (m., f.) to you]	*Je vous suis fort obligé.* [I am very much obliged to you]

the feminine form of the LF perfect (see Chapter 8). Table 3.15 presents the French prompts in which the feminine forms have been replaced with suitable masculine equivalents. This type of adaptation clearly straddles the border between linguistic and content simplification.

Table 3.16 presents other lexical and structural replacements attested in the French prompts; as previously, the relevant forms are underlined.

The first three prompts in Table 3.16 are adapted by replacing the underlined words with (near-)synonyms: *mot* with *parole*, *croir* with *penser*, *se porter* with *être*. The replacements simplify the prompts by eliminating nonessential semantic distinctions of the source language while at the same time aligning the vocabulary of the prompts more closely with that of the target language. As seen in Table 3.17, LF can render both Fr. *croir* and *penser* with *pensar* 'to think,' and it renders both *se porter* and *être* with *star* 'to be.'

Table 3.15. *Replacement of feminine with masculine forms*

Vergani (1823)	Anonymous (1830a)
Et Madame votre mere, comment se porte-t-elle? [And your mother, how is she?]	*Et Monsieur votre père comment est il?* [And your father, how is he?]
Qu'a-t-elle? [What is the matter with her?]	*Qu'a-t-il?* [What is the matter with him?]
Elle a la fièvre. [She's got a fever]	*Il a la fièvre.* [He's got a fever]
Je l'ai vue plusieurs fois. [I have seen her many times]	*Je l'ai vu chez vous.* [I saw him at your house]
Où demeure-t-elle? [Where does she live?]	*Où demeure-t-il?* [Where does he live?]
De quel pays est-elle? [What country is she from?]	*De quel pays est-il?* [What country is he from?]
Elle est Italienne. [She is Italian]	*Il est français, anglais, espagnol, portuguais, napolitain, toscan, autrichien, russe, américain, danois, suédois, hollandais.* [He is French, English, Spanish, Portuguese, Neapolitan, Tuscan, Austrian, Russian, American, Danish, Swedish, Dutch]
Y a-t-il long-temps que vous la connoissez? [Have you known her long?]	*Y a-t-il long-temps que vous le connaissez?* [Have you known him long?]
Nous irons ensemble la saluer. [We will go together to pay her our respects]	*Nous irons le voir ensemble.* [We will go to see him together]

The next two lexical replacements in Table 3.16 consist of using a more general and/or more frequent term for a semantically contiguous term that is more specific and/or less frequent: *voir* 'to see' for *saluer* 'to pay one's respects' and *brave* 'good' for *honnête* 'honorable.' The next two replacements avoid the use of future tense verb forms by using present tense forms instead (*fesons* 'we do' for *ferons* 'we shall do,' *est* 'is' for *sera* 'will be'). The replacement of *à la cour* 'at court' with *dans la ville* 'in the city' is prompted by the altered content of the dialogue and involves no changes in complexity; the same is true of the change from *Dans la rue de ...* 'on the street ...' to *Dans la grand' rue* 'on the main street,' and from *plusieurs fois* 'many times' to *chez vous* 'at your house.' The replacement of *la chocolatière* 'chocolate-pot' with *le café* 'coffee' is inseparable from the elimination of the second clause of the original prompt.

Table 3.16. *Other replacements in the French prompts*

Vergani (1823)	Anonymous (1830a)
Je n'en crois pas un mot. [I do not believe a word of it]	*Je n'en crois pas une parole.* [I do not believe a word of it]
Je crois qu'il n'est pas encore deux heures. [I believe it is not yet two o'clock]	*Je pense qu'il n'est pas trois heures.* [I think it is not yet three o'clock]
Et Madame votre mere, comment se porte-t-elle? [And your mother, how is she?]	*Et Monsieur votre père comment est il?* [And your father, how is he?]
Nous irons ensemble la saluer. [We will go together to pay her our respects]	*Nous irons le voir ensemble.* [We will go to see him together]
C'est un honnête homme. [He is an honorable man]	*C'est un brave homme.* [He is a good man]
Que ferons-nous? [What shall we do?]	*Que fesons-nous?* [What do we do?]
Il sera bientôt dix heures. [It will soon be ten o'clock]	*Il est bientôt quatre heures.* [It is almost four o'clock]
Que dit on à la cour? [What are they saying at court?]	*Que dit on dans la ville?* [What are they saying in the city?]
Dans la rue de ... [On the street ...]	*Dans la grand'rue.* [On the main street]
Je l'ai vue plusieurs fois. [I have seen her many times]	Je l'ai vu chez vous. [I saw him at your house]
Apportez la chocolatière; mettez-la sur le feu. [Bring the chocolate-pot; put it on the fire]	Apportez le café. [Bring coffee]
Il y a environ deux ans. [About two years]	*Il y a peu de temps.* [Not long]
Je le connois de réputation. [I know him by reputation]	*J'ai entendu parler de lui.* [I've heard about him]
N'en faites pas pour moi; une tasse de chocolat me suffit. [Don't make any for me; a cup of chocolate will suffice]	*N'en faites pas pour moi, le café me suffit.* [Don't make any for me, coffee will suffice]
Qui en doute? [Who doubts it?]	*J'en doute.* [I doubt it]
Il est vrai. [It is true]	*Cela est vrai.* [This is true]

Table 3.17. *Lexical reduction in the French prompts*

Vergani (1823)	Anonymous (1830a)	
French	French	Lingua Franca
Sur ma parole. [Upon my word]	*Sur ma parole.*	*per la palabra di mi.*
Je n'en crois pas un mot. [I do not believe a word of it]	*Je n'en crois pas un parole.*	*mi non crédir ouna palabra.*
Quelle heure croyez-vous qu'il soit? [What time do you think it is?]	*Quelle heure croyez-vous qu'il soit?*	*qué ora ti pensar star?*
Je crois qu'il n'est pas encore deux heures. [I believe it is not yet two o'clock]	*Je pense qu'il n'est pas trois heures.*	*mi pensar non star tré ora.*
Comment se porte monsieur votre frère? [How is your brother?]	*Comment se porte votre frère?*	*commé star il fratello di ti?*
Il se porte fort bien, grâces à Dieu. [He is very well, thank God]	*Il se porte fort bien.*	*star mouchou bonou.*
Et Madame votre mere, comment se porte-t-elle? [And your mother, how is she?]	*Et Monsieur votre père comment est il?*	*E il padré di ti commé star?*
Je suis fort bien comme cela. [I am very well like this]	*Je suis bien comme cela.*	mi star béné acoussi.

The change from *environ deux ans* 'about two years' to *peu de temps* 'not long' falls under what Moretti (1988: 241) calls "[a]pprossimazioni generiche" [generic approximations]. The change from *Je le connois de réputation* 'I know him by reputation' to *J'ai entendu parler de lui* 'I've heard about him' avoids using the abstract word *réputation* by a complete syntactic overhaul of the prompt. The replacement of *une tasse de chocolat* 'a cup of chocolate' with *le café* 'coffee' achieves structural simplification of the noun phrase. The replacement of the question *Qui en doute?* 'Who doubts it?' with the statement *J'en doute* 'I doubt it' may also be seen in terms of structural simplification.

Several of the adjustments may be examined in the light of the tendency toward greater explicitness, "un aumento del grado di esplicitezza dei messaggi" [an increase in the degree of expliciteness of the messages] (Moretti 1988: 223). This is achieved through both replacements and insertions / "nondeletions" (Mesthrie 2006). Examples include replacement of *il* with *cela* in the change from *Il est vrai* to *Cela est vrai* 'It is true,' perhaps enhanced by the perceived need to match the LF subject *qouesto* 'this' with an equivalent subject in the French prompt. The change from *Pas trop bien* 'Not too well' to *Il n'est pas bien* 'He is not well' involves inserting a subject, a copula, and a preverbal negator. The inserted elements in *Allons ensemble* 'Let's go together' > *Oui, allons ensemble* 'Yes, let's go together' and *Elle ne va pas; [elle n'est pas montée]* 'It does not go; it is not wound up' > *Elle ne va pas bien* 'It does not go well' also appear to make the prompts more explicit. The increase in the explicitness of the prompts is explainable by the didactic intent of the *Dictionnaire*, and is a feature the dialogues share with other didactic speech modes, whether directed at native or nonnative speakers (Berretta 1988a: 374–375).

The strategies of simplification seen in the *Dictionnaire*'s French prompts have clear correspondences in a range of contexts that call for lexical simplification, including teacher talk, language learning, translation, and adaped written materials for second and foreign language learners (Honeyfield 1977; Blum and Levenston 1978; Moretti 1988; Menegaldo, n.d.). Representative examples from Moretti's (1988) study of simplified Italian literary texts include omissions, as in *quelle parole deliziose* 'those delightful words' > *quelle parole* 'those words,' *si alzò di scatto* 'he leapt to his feet' > *si alzò* 'he got up'; and replacements of various kinds, including with (near-)synonyms, as in *la genesi* 'genesis' > *l'origine* 'origin,' *pare* 'appears' > *sembra* 'seems'; with generic or contiguous terms, as in *passeri* 'sparrows' > *uccelli* 'birds,' *contemplava* 'gazed at' > *guardava* 'looked at'; with generic approximations, as in *Ispettore generale* 'inspector general' > *direttore* 'director'; with syntactically simpler forms, as in *pacchetti di sigarette* 'packs of cigarettes' > *sigarette* 'cigarettes'; and of future with present tense forms, as in *mangeremo* 'we will eat' > *mangiamo* 'we eat.'

3.3 Arabic Vocabulary

The Arabic vocabulary occupies the last nine pages of the *Dictionnaire*. As will be shown below, its composition suggests reliance on Veneroni's *Recueil des noms les plus nécessaires à savoir et à retenir* [Collection of nouns most necessary to know and remember] (Veneroni 1800: 261–298), rather than Vergani's *Recueil des noms les plus usités* [Collection of nouns in most general use] (Vergani 1823: 190–194), and familiarity with the French-Arabic dictionary of Jean-Joseph Marcel (Marcel 1799). Both Veneroni's and Vergani's lists are divided into thematic blocks and use French as the entry language. This arrangement is followed in the Arabic vocabulary, with the Arabic words transcribed in Roman letters. Table 3.18 provides the titles of the sections of the Arabic vocabulary in Anonymous (1830a) and the corresponding sections of the wordlists in Veneroni (1800) and Vergani (1823).

Table 3.18. *Wordlists used in the compilation of the* Dictionnaire*'s Arabic vocabulary*

Recueil des noms les plus nécessaires a savoir et a retenir (Veneroni 1800: 82–83, 261ff.)	*Recueil des noms les plus usités* (Vergani 1823: 62–63, 190ff.)	*un vocabulaire des mots arabes les plus usuels* (Anonymous 1830a: 99ff.)
Adjectifs numériques cardinaux [Cardinal numeral adjectives]	*Des noms de nombre* [On names of numbers]	*Manière de Compter en Arabe* [How to count in Arabic]
Du Ciel et des Élemens [Of the sky and elements]	*Du ciel et des élémens* [Of the sky and elements]	*Quelques Mots Arabes* [A few Arabic words]
Du Temps et des Saisons [Of time and seasons]	*Du temps et de ses parties* [Of time and its parts]	*Du Temps* [Of time]
Les jours de la Semaine [Days of the Week]	*Les jours de la semaine* [Days of the week]	
Noms des choses que l'on est le plus accoutumé de manger; Ce que l'on mange à table pour le bouilli; Pour les entrées; Ce que l'on fait rôtir; Pour assaisonner les viandes; Pour la salade; Pour les jours maigres; Pour le dessert [Names of things one is most accustomed to eating; What is eaten at table as boiled meat; For the first course; What is roasted; To season meat with; For salad; For meatless days; For desert]	—	*Objets de Nourriture* [Articles of food]
Le couvert de la Table [The covering of the table]	*Les meubles de la maison* [The furniture of a house]	*Meubles et Ustensilles* [Furniture and utensils]
Des parties de la maison [Of the parts of a house]	*Des parties de la maison* [Of the parts of a house]	*Des Parties de la Maison* [Of the parts of a house]
Des parties du corps [Of the parts of the body]	*Des parties du corps* [Of the parts of the body]	*Des Parties du Corps* [Of the parts of the body]
Professions et Métiers [Professions and trades]	—	*Etats* [Conditions]
Degrés de parenté [Degrees of kinship]	*Degrés de parenté* [Degrees of kinship]	*Parenté* [Kinship]

Table 3.18. *(cont.)*

Recueil des noms les plus nécessaires a savoir et a retenir (Veneroni 1800: 82–83, 261ff.)	*Recueil des noms les plus usités* (Vergani 1823: 62–63, 190ff.)	*un vocabulaire des mots arabes les plus usuels* (Anonymous 1830a: 99ff.)
Les Métaux [The metals]	—	*Métaux* [Metals]
—	—	*Supplément* [Supplement]

The first section of the Arabic vocabulary, *Manière de Compter en Arabe* [How to count in Arabic], contains cardinal numbers and may have been modeled after Marcel (1799),[2] which begins with a section on cardinal numerals and appears to have made use of an earlier edition of Veneroni (1800) for the rest. For its next section, *Quelques Mots Arabes* [A few Arabic words], the *Dictionnaire* is more likely to have relied on Veneroni's list *Du Ciel et des Élemens* [Of the sky and elements] than on the similarly titled list in Vergani (1823). This inference is based on the order of the entries, which is closer to that of Veneroni (1800), and on the absence in Vergani (1823) of the prompts *le ciel* 'the sky,' *les étoiles* 'the stars,' *le paradis* 'heaven,' and *le diable* 'the devil.' In (1) below, the list of the French prompts in the Arabic vocabulary and the model list from Veneroni (1800) are given side by side, with the nonoverlapping entries marked by shading. For reasons of space, the English glosses are provided only for the first list and omit the definite article. The plural *Les cieux* 'the skies' and the singular/plural pair *L'Ile/Les îles* 'the island/the islands' may have been added to illustrate the Arabic plurals.[3] The adjective *chaud* 'hot' may have been added to highlight the contrast with the noun *le chaud* 'the heat.' The added entry *Eau chaude* 'hot water' suggests familiarity with the Vergani list, which contains the entry *l'eau* 'the water.' The omitted entries pertain to weather and Christianity.

(1)

QUELQUES MOTS ARABES (Anonymous 1830a: 100–101)		DU CIEL ET DES ÉLÉMENS (Veneroni 1800: 261–262)	
Dieu 'God'	*Les nues* 'clouds'	*Dieu*	*les Etoiles*
Le ciel 'sky'	*Le brouillard* 'fog, mist'	*Jesus-Christ*	*les rayons*
Les cieux 'heaven'	*Le pluie* 'rain'	*le Saint-Esprit*	*les nues*
	Le tonnerre 'thunder'	*la Trinité*	*le vent*

[2] This edition of Marcel's dictionary is cited after Larzul (2010); the version consulted is posted at https://gallica.bnf.fr/ark:/12148/btv1b11003907g.image.

[3] Marcel's (1830) French-Arabic dictionary also provides the plural forms for these nouns.

Le paradis 'heaven'			
Le diable 'devil'	*L'Éclair* 'lightning'	*la Vierge*	*la pluie*
Le feu 'fire'	*La grêle* 'hail'	*les Anges*	*le tonnerre*
L'air 'air'	*La foudre* 'thunderbolt'	*les Archanges*	*l'éclair*
Le vent 'wind'	*La neige* 'snow'	*les Saints*	*la grêle*
La terre 'earth'	*La glace* 'ice'	*les Bienheureux*	*la foudre*
La mer 'sea'	*Le tremblement de terre* 'earthquake'	*le Ciel*	*la neige*
Les îles 'islands'	*Le chaud* 'heat'	*le Paradis*	*la gelée*
L'Ile 'island'	*Chaud -de* 'hot'	*l'Enfer*	*la glace*
Le soleil 'sun'	*Eau chaude* 'hot water'	*le Purgatoire*	*le verglas*
La lune 'moon'	*Le froid* 'cold'	*les Diables*	*la rosée*
Les étoiles 'stars'		*le feu*	*le brouillard*
		l'air	*le tremblement de terre*
		la terre	*le déluge*
		la mer	*le chaud*
		le Soleil	*le froid*
		la lune	

The order of the entries in the next section of the Arabic vocabulary, *Du Temps* [Of time], likewise points to Veneroni's (1800) as the more likely model wordlist; this conclusion is bolstered by the absence, in the corresponding list in Vergani (1823), of the entries *semaine* 'week' and *trois quarts d'heure* 'three quarters of an hour.' Several of Veneroni's prompts, including *un moment* 'a moment,' *jour ouvrier* 'working day,' *le point du jour* 'daybreak,' and *l'aurore* 'dawn,' were omitted from the Arabic vocabulary. The prompts *ce soir* 'this evening,' *ce matin* 'this morning,' and *un an* 'a year' were replaced, respectively, with *aujourd'hui soir* 'tonight' (lit. 'today evening'), *aujourd'hui matin* 'this morning' (lit. 'today morning'), and *année* 'year.' The prompt *une heure* 'an hour' was split into two, *heure* 'hour' and *une heure* 'one hour.' Finally, the Arabic vocabulary begins its list of the days of the week with *dimanche* 'Sunday' rather than *lundi* 'Monday.'

(2)	*Du Temps*	Du Temps et des Saisons & Les jours de la Semaine
	(Anonymous 1830a: 101–102)	(Veneroni 1800: 262–263)

Le jour 'day'	*Après soupé* 'after supper'	*Le jour*	*un mois*
La nuit 'night'	*Semaine* 'week'	*la nuit*	*un an*
Midi 'noon'	*Mois-lune* 'month'	*le midi*	*un moment*
Minuit 'midnight'	*Année* 'year'	*le minuit*	*le Printemps*
Le matin 'morning'	*Le printems* 'spring'	*le matin*	*l'Eté*
Le soir 'evening'	*L'été* 'summer'	*le soir*	*l'Automne*
Heure 'hour'	*L'automne* 'fall'	*une heure*	*l'Hiver*
Une heure 'one hour'	*L'hiver* 'winter'	*un quart-d'heure*	*jour de fête*
Un quart d'heure 'a quarter of an hour'	*Jour de fête* 'holiday'	*une demi-heure*	*jour ouvrier*
Trois quart d'heure 'three quarters of an hour'	*Dimanche* 'Sunday'	*aujourd' hui*	*le coucher du soleil*
Demi heure 'half an hour'	*Couché du soleil* 'sunset'	*trois quarts d'heure*	*le point du jour*
Aujourd'hui 'today'	*Lundi* 'Monday'	*hier*	*l'aurore*
Hier 'yesterday'	*Mardi* 'Tuesday'	*demain*	*Lundi*
Demain 'tomorrow'	*Mercredi* 'Wednesday'	*avant-hier*	*Mardi*
Après-demain 'the day after tomorrow'	*Jeudi* 'Thursday'	*après-demain*	*Mercredi*
Avant-hier 'the day before yesterday'	*Vendredi* 'Friday'	*ce soir*	*Jeudi*
Aujourd'hui soir 'tonight'	*Samedi* 'Saturday'	*ce matin*	*Vendredi*
		a[p]rès-dîné	*Samedi*
Aujourd'hui matin 'this morning'		*aprés-soupé*	*Dimanche*
		une semaine	

Objets de Nourriture [Articles of food] is the longest section of the vocabulary, occupying over two pages. There is no section devoted to foodstuffs in Vergani's *Recueil des noms les plus usités*, while Veneroni's list comprises several categories of foodstuffs, with each section containing significantly more items than are included in the Arabic vocabulary. Since listing all of Veneroni's prompts would make for a rather long list, (3) below includes only the items that are present in the Arabic vocabulary. To separate the sections of the Veneroni list from each other, the first relevant entry in each section is given in bold font. The French prompts which are listed by Veneroni more than once are included in (3) only once. As seen below, the Arabic vocabulary contains some twenty additional names of foods, including such items as mulberry, jujube, prickly pear, eggplant, and sour milk.

(3)

Objets de Nourriture (Anonymous 1830a: 102–104)		*Noms des choses que l'on est le plus accoutumé de manger; Ce que l'on mange à table pour le bouilli; Pour les entrées; Ce que l'on fait rôtir; Pour assaisonner les viandes; Pour la salade; Pour les jours maigres; Pour le dessert* (Veneroni 1800: 264–268)	
Le pain 'bread'	*Raves* 'turnips'	***Du pain***	*des citrons*
L'eau 'water'	*Laitue* 'lettuce'	*de l'eau*	*du persil*
Le vin 'wine'	*Piment* 'pepper'	*du vin*	***de la laitue***
La viande 'meat'	*Percil [sic]* 'parsley'	*de la viande*	*du céleri*
Le poisson 'fish'	*Poireau* 'leek'	*du poisson*	***Du beurre***
Morceau de pain 'piece of bread'	*Céleri* 'celery'	*un morceau de pain*	*du lait*
Salade 'salad'	*Choux* 'cabbage'	*une salade*	*des oeufs*
Fruit 'fruit'	*Choux fleur* 'cauliflower'	*du fromage*	*des pois*
Le fromage 'cheese'	*Oefs* 'eggs'	***Du boeuf***	*des féves*
Le sel 'salt'	*Beurre* 'butter'	*du mouton*	*des épinards*
Le poivre 'pepper'	*Lait* 'milk'	*une poule*	*des choux*
Le mouton 'mutton'	*Lait aigri* 'sour milk'	***un haricot***	*des choux-fleurs*
Le boeuf 'beef'	*Carottes* 'carrots'	*des raves*	*des betteraves*
La poule 'hen'	*Feves* 'beans'	*un melon*	***Des pommes***
Le petit poulet 'chicken'	*Épinard* 'spinach'	***les poulets***	*des poires*
Le pigeon 'pigeon'	*Beteraves* 'beets'	*les pigeonneaux*	*des péches*
Le canard 'duck'	*Aubergines* 'eggplants'	*les perdrix*	*des abricots*
L'oie 'goose'	*Courge* 'pumpkin'	*les cailles*	*des cerises*
La caille 'quail'	*Concombre* 'cucumber'	*une oie*	*des figues*

Petits oiseaux 'small birds'	*Amande* 'almond'	*un canard*	*des prunes*
Étourneau 'starling'	*Noix* 'nut'	*un lièvre*	*des raisins*
Cochon 'roasting pig'	*Noisette* 'hazelnut'	*un cochon de lait*	*des noix*
Haricot 'bean'	*Pistache* 'pistachio'	***Du sel***	*des noisettes*
Pois chiches 'chickpeas'	*Châtaigne* 'chestnut'	*du poivre*	*des châtaignes*
Pois 'peas'	*Mûre* 'mulberry'	*de l'huile*	*des amandes*
Citrons 'lemons'	*Olive* 'olive'	*du vinaigre*	*des mûres*
Limons doux 'sweet lemons'	*Huile* 'oil'	*du laurier*	*des coins*
Orange 'orange'	*Coing* 'quince'	*des oignons*	*des grenades*
Raisin 'grape'	*Péche* 'peach'	*un ail*	*des olives*
Jujubes 'jujubes'	*Prune* 'plum'	*des oranges*	
Pommes 'apples'	*Cérise* 'cherry'		
Grenade 'pomegranate'	*Abricot* 'apricot'		
Cédrat 'citron'	*Poire* 'pear'		
Perdrix 'partridge'	*Melon* 'melon'		
Perdreaux 'partridges'	*Pastéque* 'watermelon'		
Lièvre 'hare'	*Figue* 'fig'		
Gazelle 'gazelle'	*Figue de Barbarie* 'prickly pear'		
Vinaigre 'vinegar'	*Raisin sec* 'raisin'		
Laurier 'laurel'	*Eau-de-vie* 'brandy'		
Oignon 'onion'	*Anisette* 'anisette'		
Ail 'garlic'			

The content of the next section, *Meubles et Ustensilles* [Furniture and utensils], is derived from Veneroni's (1800: 265) list *Le couvert de la Table* [The covering of the table], though its title suggests familiarity with Vergani's (1823: 194) *Les meubles de la maison* [The furniture of a house]. As seen in (4), this section is both much shorter than the corresponding wordlist in Veneroni (1800) and incorporates items not found there. These include *bougie* 'wax candle,' *ciseau* 'chisel,' *éponge* 'sponge,' and *café* 'coffee.'

(4)

Meubles et Ustensilles (Anonymous 1830a: 99–100)		*Le couvert de la Table* (Veneroni 1800: 265)	
La table 'table'	*Chandelier* 'candlestick'	*La table*	*une aiguiere*
La chaise 'chair'	*Ciseau* 'chisel'	*une chaise*	*un pot à l'eau*

La serviette 'napkin'	*Rechaud* 'chafing dish'	*la nappe*	*un verre*
La fourchette 'fork'	*Tasse* 'cup'	*un couteau*	*une tasse*
Le couteau 'knife'	*Verre* 'glass'	*la serviette*	*une bouteille*
La cuillère 'spoon'	*Éponge* 'sponge'	*une fourchette*	*une soucoupe*
L'assiette 'plate'	*Café* 'coffee'	*une cuiller*	*une écuelle*
Bougie 'wax candle'		*une assiette*	*une saucière*
		un plat	*un essuie-main*
		une salière	*un couvert*
		un chandelier	*un service*
		une chandelle	*la corbeille à porter le couvert*
		les mouchettes	*un demi-setier*
		un réchaud	*une chopine*
		un bassin	*une pinte*
		un vinaigrier	*un pot*

The list *Des Parties de la Maison* [Of the parts of a house] is based on the similarly titled list in Veneroni (1800); the corresponding list in Vergani (1823) lacks several of the words, including *le jardin* 'garden,' *la fontaine* 'fountain,' and *la terrasse* 'terrace.' Since Veneroni's list is much longer than the corresponding section of the Arabic vocabulary, only the items that are included in the latter are listed in (5) below. The Arabic vocabulary also includes an entry not found in either Veneroni (1800) or Vergani (1823): *la citerne* 'cistern.'

(5)

Des parties de la Maison		Des parties de la maison	
(Anonymous 1830a: 105)		(Veneroni 1800: 276–277)	
La maison 'house'	*Le jardin* 'garden'	*La maison*	*le jardin*
La chambre 'room'	*La fontaine* 'fountain'	*la porte*	*la fontaine*
La porte 'door'	*La terrasse* 'terrace'	*la chambre*	*la terrasse*
La salle 'hall'	*La muraille* 'wall'	*la salle*	*la muraille*
La fenêtre 'window'	*Le four* 'oven'	*la fenêtre*	*le four*
La cuisine 'kitchen'	*Les planches* 'planks'	*la cuisine*	*les planches*
Le puit 'well'	*La pierre* 'stone'	*le puits*	*la pierre*
La citerne 'cistern'			

The list *Des Parties du Corps* [Of the parts of the body] is more likely to be based on the similarly titled list in Veneroni (1800) than Vergani (1823) based on the order of the entries (for example, in Vergani *les cheveux* 'hair' immediately follows *la tête* 'head,' and *le coeur* 'heart' precedes rather than follows *le sang* 'blood'), the shape of the prompt for 'neck' (given as *le cou* by Vergani and as *le col ou le cou* by Veneroni), and the absence in Vergani (1823) of the entry *le ventre* 'belly.' Since the Arabic vocabulary contains only a fraction of the terms included in Veneroni's much more detailed list, only the relevant entries from the latter are given below in (6). The Arabic vocabulary additionally differs from the model list by pluralizing the prompts for 'hand' and 'finger' and by including the entries *l'homme* 'man' and *enfant* 'child.' Variants of these entries, *un homme âgé* 'aged man' and *un petit enfant* 'infant,' are found in the otherwise unused list *Des états de l'homme et de la femme* [Of the conditions of man and woman] present in both Vergani (1823: 192) and Veneroni (1800: 270); the latter list also contains the entry *l'homme* 'man.'

(6)	Des Parties du Corps		Des parties du corps	
	(Anonymous 1830a: 105–106)		(Veneroni 1800: 269–270)	
	La tête 'head'	*Les bras* 'arms'	*La tête*	*les bras*
	Le visage 'face'	*Les mains* 'hands'	*le visage*	*la main*
	Les yeux 'eyes'	*Les doigts* 'fingers'	*les yeux*	*le doigt*
	Les oreilles 'ears'	*Le ventre* 'belly'	*les oreilles*	*le ventre*
	Les cheveux 'hair'	*Les genoux* 'knees'	*les cheveux*	*les genoux*
	Les joues 'cheeks'	*La jambe* 'leg'	*les joues*	*la jambe*
	Le nez 'nose'	*Le pied* 'foot'	*le nez*	*le pied*
	La bouche 'mouth'	*Le sang* 'blood'	*la bouche*	*le sang*
	Les dents 'teeth'	*La peau* 'skin'	*les dents*	*la peau*
	La langue 'tongue'	*Le coeur* 'heart'	*la langue*	*le coeur*
	Le menton 'chin'	*L'homme* 'man'	*le menton*	
	Le col 'neck'	*Enfant* 'child'	*le col* ou *le cou*	

The title of the section *États* [Conditions] is modeled after that of the aforementioned section *Des états de l'homme et de la femme* [Of the conditions of man and woman], present in both Veneroni (1800: 270) and Vergani (1823: 192), while its content is related to that of a different section in Veneroni, *Professions et Métiers* [Professions and trades] (Vergani 1823 lacks a comparable section). As in the preceding cases, Veneroni's wordlist is far too long to reproduce in full; only the relevant entries are given in (7) below.

(7)	États		Professions et Métiers
	(Anonymous 1830a: 106)		(Veneroni 1800: 288–289)
	Le maçon 'bricklayer'	*Le cordonnier* 'cobbler'	*un Médecin*
	Le tailleur 'tailor'	*Le barbier* 'barber'	*un Barbier*
	L'horloger 'watchmaker'	*La cafetier*	*un Tailleur*

L'épicier 'grocer'	*Le cordonnier* 'cobbler'[4]	*un Cordonnier*
L'armurier 'gunsmith'	*L'orfèvre* 'goldsmith'	*un Maçon*
Le médecin 'physician'		*un Horloger*
		un Orfèvre

The list titled *Parenté* [Kinship] is based on the list of *Degrés de parenté* [Degrees of kinship] in Veneroni (1800) based on the absence, in Vergani (1823), of the entries *époux* 'spouse (m.),' *épouse* 'spouse (f.),' *ami* 'friend (m.),' and *amie* 'friend (f.).' In the Arabic vocabulary, the entry *le fils* 'son' is replaced with *le garçon* 'boy.' As in the previous sections, Veneroni's list is too long to reproduce in full, and only the relevant entries are included below.

(8)

PARENTÉ (Anonymous 1830a: 106–107)		DEGRÉS DE PARENTÉ (Veneroni 1800: 269–270)	
Le père 'father'	*Le frère* 'brother'	*Le père*	*le frère*
La mère 'mother'	*La soeur* 'sister'	*la mère*	*la soeur*
Le grand-père 'grandfather'	*Époux* 'spouse (m.)'	*le grand-père*	*l'époux*
La grand-mère 'grandmother'	*Épouse* 'spouse (f.)'	*la grand' mère*	*l'épouse*
Le garçon 'boy'	*Ami* 'friend (m.)'	*le fils*	*l'ami*
La fille 'girl, daughter'	*Amie* 'friend (f.)'	*la fille*	*l'amie*

The list of *Métaux* [Metals] is modeled after the section *Les Métaux* [The metals] in Veneroni (1800); Vergani (1823) lacks a comparable section. Veneroni's list comprises fifteen items, including the four shown below which coincide with the entries in the Arabic vocabulary. The latter also adds the entry *acier* 'steel.'

(9)

MÉTAUX (Anonymous 1830a: 107)		LES MÉTAUX (Veneroni 1800: 296)	
Or 'gold'	*Fer* 'iron'	*L'or*	*le fer*
Argent 'silver'	*Acier* 'steel'	*l'argent*	*le plomb*
Plomb 'lead'			

The final wordlist in the Arabic vocabulary, titled *Supplément* [Supplement], contains words relevant to the period's warfare. While most of these words are found in Veneroni (1800), as a self-standing unit the list represents a new addition.

[4] The French prompt *Le cordonnier* appears twice, with different translations.

(10) *Supplément*
(Anonymous 1830a: 107)

Poudre à tirer 'gunpowder'	*La selle* 'saddle'
Fusil 'rifle'	*La bride* 'bridle'
Pistolet 'pistol'	*Chameau* 'camel'
Sabre 'saber'	*Mulle* 'mule'
Le cheval 'horse'	*Ane* 'donkey'

In summary, the *Dictionnaire*'s Arabic vocabulary was clearly modeled after Veneroni's (1800) vocabulary list for learners of Italian. In the context of the *Dictionnaire* as a whole, Veneroni's list may have even farther reaching effects: for example, the ethnonym-rich prompt from the fifth dialogue, which elaborates on Vergani's (1823) simple prompt *Elle est Italienne* [She is Italian], appears to have been inspired by the section *Des Nations* [Of nations] of Veneroni's wordlist (Veneroni 1800: 296) (see Table 3.7 and 11 below).

(11)

Dialogue No. 5 (Anonymous 1830a: 96)	*Des Nations* (Veneroni 1800: 296)		
Il est français, anglais, espagnol, portuguais, napolitain, toscan, autrichien, russe, américain, danois, suédois, hollandais. 'He is French, English, Spanish, Portuguese, Neapolitan, Tuscan, Austrian, Russian, American, Danish, Swedish, Dutch.'	*Italien*	*Ecossois*	*Suédois*
	Allemand	*Hollandois*	*Polonois*
	François	*Flamand*	*Hongrois*
	Espagnol	*Lorrain*	*Danois*
	Portugais	*Bourguignon*	*Turc*
	Anglois	*Suisse*	*Tartare*
	Irlandois	*Piémontois*	

3.4 Preface

The preface is another section of the *Dictionnaire* where the impact of Vergani (1823) and Veneroni (1800) is felt. It consists of fifteen short paragraphs three of which introduce LF, nine provide its structural outline, and two more introduce the LF dialogues and Arabic vocabulary. The last paragraph states that the purpose of this *recueil* is to facilitate "les communications des Français avec les habitans du pays sur lequel ils vont combattre" [communications of the French with the inhabitants of the land in which they are going to fight].

The paragraphs that provide the structural outline of LF consist of terse descriptive statements and examples. The outline follows, in a highly condensed form, the presentation of Italian grammar in Vergani (1823) and/or Veneroni (1800). Evidence of this reliance is present in the topics covered, and the order and certain details of the coverage, such as its wording, conceptual apparatus, and choice of examples. The congruence in the grammar topics covered and their order may be appreciated from Table 3.19, which collates the

Table 3.19. *The order of grammar topics in Vergani (1823) and Anonymous (1830a)*

Vergani (1823)	Anonymous (1830a)
Leçon Ire *De la Prononciation Italienne.* [Lesson 1: On Italian pronunciation]	*§2: C'est surtout le petit mauresque qui se parle dans les villes maritimes de l'état d'Alger, que nous avons dû recueillir dans ce Dictionnaire, et nous nous sommes attachés à donner aux mots l'orthographe que se rapproche le plus de la prononciation en usage dans ce pays.* [It is primarily the Petit Mauresque that is spoken in the seaside towns of the state of Algiers that we had to collect in this Dictionary, and we have endeavored to give the words the spelling that comes closest to the pronunciation used in this country]
Leçon II. *De l'Article.* [Lesson 2: On the article]	*§4: Les noms se déclinent par l'apposition de l'article comme dans le français et l'italien.* [Nouns are declined by attaching the article like in French and Italian]
Leçon IV. *Règles pour former le Pluriel des Noms.* [Lesson 4: Rules for forming the plural of nouns]	*§5: Les noms n'ont pas de pluriel.* [Nouns have no plural]
Leçon VI. *Des Adjectifs.* [Lesson 6: On adjectives]	*§6: Les adjectifs en* o *ont seuls un féminin.* *§7: Mais les adjectifs en* e *n'ont pas de féminin.* [Only adjectives in *o* have a feminine form] [But adjectives in *e* have no feminine]
Lesson XVI. *Des Verbes réguliers.*[a] [Lesson 16: On regular verbs]	*§8: Les verbes ne se conjuguent pas, ils n'ont que deux temps: l'infinitif qui est toujours terminé en* ir *ou en* ar, *et le participe passé en* ito *ou* ato, *fém.* ita, ata. *§9: On supplée aux autres temps par un sorte d'artifice de langage, dont nous allons donner quelques exemples:* [Verbs are not conjugated, they have only two tenses: the infinitive which always ends in *ir* or in *ar*, and the past participle in *ito* or *ato*, feminine *ita*, *ata*] [Other tenses are supplied by a sort of linguistic artifice of which we are going to give a few examples]

Table 3.19. *(cont.)*

Vergani (1823)	Anonymous (1830a)
Leçon XV. *Des Verbes auxiliaires.* [Lesson 15: On auxiliary verbs]	*§10: Il n'y a qu'un seul verbe auxiliaire,* star *être, qui s'emploie également pour nos deux auxiliaires* être *et* avoir. *§11: Le verbe* avir *ou* tenir *(*avoir*), ne s'emploie pas comme auxiliaire, mais seulement comme verbe possessif.* [There is only one auxiliary verb, *star* to be, which is used for our two auxiliaries *to be* and *to have*] [The verb *avir* or *tenir* (*to have*) is not used as an auxiliary but only as a possessive verb]

[a] In the body of the grammar, this lesson is titled *Des verbes et des participes* [Of verbs and participles].

Dictionnaire's descriptive statements with the numbers and titles of the corresponding lessons in Vergani's (1823) table of contents.

The similarity of the coverage of the grammar topics may be appreciated from juxtaposition of the *Dictionnaire*'s descriptive statements with the corresponding statements in Vergani (1823) and/or Veneroni (1800) in Tables 3.20 and 3.21. Table 3.20 shows that the *Dictionnaire* relies on Vergani's (and Veneroni's) conceptual apparatus when it speaks of "declension" of LF nouns by attaching the article and in following the order of the nominative, genitive, dative, and ablative "cases" in its example nouns *amigo* 'friend' and *casa* 'house' (Vergani's accusative is omitted). Furthermore, the *Dictionnaire* directly compares LF with French and Italian with respect to this aspect of the grammar. The corresponding statements in Veneroni (1800) are even closer to the *Dictionnaire*'s in that they make no explicit reference to cases or include the accusative, as seen in the following example:

Déclinaison de l'Article IL, avec un nom masculin commençant par une consonne.
Sing. le livre, *il libro.*
du livre, *del libro.*
au livre, *al libro.*
du livre,
ou par le livre, *dal libro.*

(Veneroni 1800: 69)

[Declension of the article *il* with a masculine noun beginning with a consonant. Singular the book, of the book, to the book, from *or* by the book.]

Table 3.20. *Description of articles in Vergani (1823) and nouns in Anonymous (1830a)*

Vergani (1823: 11–12)		Anonymous (1830a: n.p.)	
Leçon II. De l'Article. *Les Italiens ont trois articles:* lo, il, la. *L'art.* lo *se décline ainsi [. . .] Il se met devant les noms masculins [. . .]* [Italians have three articles: *lo*, *il*, *la*. The article *lo* is declined as follows . . . It is placed before masculine nouns . . .]		§4 *Les noms se déclinent par l'apposition de l'article comme dans le français et l'italien.* [Nouns are declined by attaching the article like in French and Italian]	
Exemple		*Exemple.*	
Singulier.			
Nom. Lo specchio.	Nom. *Le miroir.*	*L'ami.*	*l'amigo.* 'the friend'
Gén. Dello specchio.	Gén. *Du miroir.*	*De l'ami.*	*del'amigo.* 'of the friend'
Dat. Allo specchio.	Dat. *Au miroir.*	*A l'ami.*	*al'amigo.* 'to the friend'
Acc. Lo specchio.	Acc. *Le miroir.*	*Par l'ami.*	*per l'amigo.* 'by the friend'
Abl. Dallo specchio.	Abl. *Du* ou *par le miroir.*	*La maison.*	*la casa.* 'house'
. . .	. . .	*De la maison.*	*della casa.* 'of the house'
		A la maison.	*alla casa.* 'to the house'
		Par la maison.	*per la casa.* 'by the house'

Table 3.21 juxtaposes the *Dictionnaire*'s description of LF adjectives with the corresponding descriptive statements in Vergani (1823). The similarity between the two descriptions extends to the lexical choice to illustrate gender-neutral adjectives.

In summary, in its structural outline of LF the *Dictionnaire*'s preface follows Vergani's (1823) and Veneroni's (1800) order of the presentation of the grammar and relies on the conceptual apparatus of these texts in its description of LF. The model grammatical descriptions are stripped of their complexity to accommodate the comparative structural simplicity of LF.

Table 3.21. *Description of adjectives in Vergani (1823) and Anonymous (1830a)*

<table>
<tr><th>Vergani (1823: 44)</th><th colspan="2">Anonymous (1830a)</th></tr>
<tr><td rowspan="7">Leçon VI. Des Adjectifs.
Les adjectifs terminé en o servent pour le masculin; comme bello, dotto, *beau, savant. On change l'o en* a *pour former le féminin; comme* bella, dotta, *belle, savante, etc.*
[Adjectives ending in *o* serve for the masculine, as in *bello, dotto,* beautiful, learned. The *o* is changed to *a* to form the feminine, as in *bella, dotta,* beautiful, learned, etc.]
Les adjectifs qui finissent en e *ou en* i *servent pour les deux genres; comme* un uomo prudente, *un homme prudent;* una donna prudente, *une femme prudente ....*
[Adjectives that end in *e* or *i* serve for both genders, as in *un uomo prudente,* a prudent man; *una donna prudente,* a prudent woman]</td><td colspan="2">§6
Les adjectifs en o *ont seuls un féminin.*
[Only adjectives in *o* have a feminine form]</td></tr>
<tr><td>*Masculin.*</td><td>*Féminin.*</td></tr>
<tr><td>Bon, bono.</td><td>bonne, bona.</td></tr>
<tr><td colspan="2">§7
Mais les adjectifs en e *n'ont pas de féminin.*
[But adjectives in *e* have no feminine]</td></tr>
<tr><td>*Masculin.*</td><td>*Féminin.*</td></tr>
<tr><td>Prudent.</td><td>prudente.</td></tr>
<tr><td>Prudenté.</td><td>prudenté.</td></tr>
</table>

3.5 Aspects of the Orthography

The orthography with which the *Dictionnaire* represents LF sounds is another area in which the influence of Vergani (1823) and Veneroni (1800) is perceptible. The preface informs the reader that LF has no spelling ("[c]et idiome ... n'a ni orthographe" [this language has no spelling]) and states that the orthography endeavors to reflect the pronunciation current in the coastal cities of Algeria:

C'est surtout le petit mauresque qui se parle dans les villes maritimes de l'état d'Alger, que nous avons dû recueillir dans ce Dictionnaire, et nous nous sommes attachés à donner aux mots l'orthographe que se rapproche le plus de la prononciation en usage dans ce pays. (Anonymous 1830a: n.p.)

[It is primarily the Petit Mauresque that is spoken in the coastal cities of the state of Algiers that we had to collect in this Dictionary, and we have endeavored to give the words the spelling that comes closest to the pronunciation used in this country.]

As will be discussed in the next chapter, the *Dictionnaire*'s orthography of LF draws inspiration from several sources, most notably the French orthography. Since the sound-letter correspondences are not explained, the orthography employed for both LF and Arabic is meant to be self-evident for the French users. While the majority of the *Dictionnaire*'s solutions – such as the use of the letter <z> for a phonetic [z] – are unremarkable, in the sense that they cannot be traced to a specific source, a case can be made that at least some may have been inspired by Vergani's (1823) and Veneroni's (1800) shared practice of drawing on French orthographic conventions to represent the sounds of Italian.

One such solution is the *Dictionnaire*'s spelling of the affricate [dʒ] by means of the multigraphs <dg> (before front vowels) and <dgi> (before back vowels) (exemplified in 12).

(12)	dgitar	'throw'	(It. gettare)
	dgélosia	'shutter'	(It. gelosia)
	dgialo	'yellow'	(It. giallo)
	dgioco	'game'	(It. gioco)
	dgiousto	'just'	(It. giusto)

This spelling convention may be traced to Veneroni's (1800) and Vergani's (1823) representation of Italian <g> by means of <dg>, cf.: "*G*, devant les voyelles *e* ou *i*, se prononce comme s'il y avoit un *d* devant le *g*: *gelo*, gelée; *giro*, tour; lisez *dgelo*, *dgiro*" [*G*, before the vowels *e* or *i*, is pronounced as if there were a *d* before the *g*: *gelo*, frost; *giro*, tour; read *dgelo*, *dgiro*] (Veneroni 1800: 59). Similarly, in Vergani's (1823: 5–6) list of *Consonnes qui s'éloignent de la prononciation française* [Consonants that differ from the French pronunciation] we find: "*G* comme en français *dgé* . . . . *Ge* comme *dgé*: *Gelato*, *gelosia* . . . . *Gi* comme *dgi*: *Girare*, *gire*, *girasole*" [*G* as in French *dgé* . . . *Ge* as *dgé*: *Gelato*, *gelosia* . . . *Gi* as *dgi*: *Girare*, *gire*, *girasole*].

Another type of influence is discernible in the transliteration of [k] by means of <k>, regardless of its spelling in the source languages (see 13).

(13)	aki	'here'	(Sp. aquí)
	perké	'why, because'	(It. perché)
	kiavé	'key'	(It. chiave)
	markar	'mark'	(Sp. marcar, It. marcare)

médiko	'doctor'	(Sp. médico, It. medico)
fondouk	'market'	(Ar. funduq)[5]

This transliteration convention is derivable from Veneroni's (1800):

Les syllabes *che*, *chi* ... se prononcent commes les syllabes *que*, *qui*, en François, ou comme *ke*, *ki*: *Cherubino*, Chérubin; *ciechi*, aveugles; *chiodo*, clou; *giovenchi*, jeunes boeufs: prononcez *querubino*, *tchiequi*, *kiodo*, *giovenki*. (Veneroni 1800: 59)

[The syllables *che*, *chi* are pronounced like the syllables *que*, *qui* in French, or as *ke*, *ki*: *Cherubino*, cherub; *ciechi*, blind people; *chiodo*, nail; *giovenchi*, bullocks: pronounce *querubino*, *tchiequi*, *kiodo*, *giovenki*.]

In Vergani (1823), similarly, we find <k> as a way to transliterate Italian <q> as well as <ch> before <e> and <i>:

Che comme *ké* en français, *cheto*, *cherubino*. *Chi*, *chia*, *chie*, *chio*, *chiu*, comme en français *ki*, *kia*, *kié*, *kio*, *kiou*. Ex. *Chi*, *chiamare*, *chiaro*, *chiave*, *chiedere*, *chiodo*, *chiudere*. ... *Q* comme en français *kou*. *Qua* (koua): *Quale*, *quadro*, *quasi*, *quaranta*. *Que* (koué): *Quercia*, *querela*, *questione*. *Qui* (kui): *Qui*, *quiete*, *quinci*, *quivi*. *Quo* (kouo): *Quotidiano*. ... *Sche* comme ské en français: *Scherma*, *scherzo*, *scherno*. *Schi*, *schia*, *schie* comme ski, skia, skié: *Schifo*, *schiamazzo*, *schiera*. (Vergani 1823: 5–7)

[*Che* as *ké* in French, *cheto*, *cherubino*. *Chi*, *chia*, *chie*, *chio*, *chiu* as in French *ki*, *kia*, *kié*, *kio*, *kiou*. Examples *Chi*, *chiamare*, *chiaro*, *chiave*, *chiedere*, *chiodo*, *chiudere*. ... *Q* as in French *kou*. *Qua* (koua): *Quale*, *quadro*, *quasi*, *quaranta*. *Que* (koué): *Quercia*, *querela*, *questione*. *Qui* (kui): *Qui*, *quiete*, *quinci*, *quivi*. *Quo* (kouo): *Quotidiano*. *Sche* as *ské* in French: *Scherma*, *scherzo*, *scherno*. *Schi*, *schia*, *schie* as *ski*, *skia*, *skié*: *Schifo*, *schiamazzo*, *schiera*.]

A final spelling convention to be noted is the use of <ou> for both [u] and [w]:

(14)	piou	'more'	(It. più)
	sigouro	'sure'	(Sp. Ptg. seguro)
	chinqoué	'five'	(It. cinque)
	agoua	'water'	(Sp. agua, Ptg. água)

The digraph <ou> is used for transliterating both [u] and [w] in Veneroni (1800), cf. "*publicazione*, lisez *poublicazione*" [*publicazione*, read *poublicazione*] (p. 55), "le mot italien *aurora* ... se prononce *aou-ro-ra*" [the Italian word *aurora* is pronounced *aou-ro-ra*], "l'italien *Europa* ... se prononce *Eou-ro-pa*" [Italian *Europa* is pronounced *Eou-ro-pa*] (p. 56). Vergani (1823) writes about Italian <u> that "[o]n le prononce comme les Français

[5] Russo (2001: 241–242); Cifoletti (2004: 61–62).

prononcent la voyelle composée *ou*" [it is pronounced as the French pronounce the compound vowel *ou*] (p. 4) and uses <ou> to represent the labial glide, as in "*Gua*, *gue* (goua) (goué): *Guadagno*, *eguale*, *guerra*, *guercio*" and "*Qua* (koua): *Quale*, *quadro*, *quasi*, *quaranta*. *Que* (koué): *Quercia*, *querela*, *questione*" (pp. 6–7). Though this transliteration convention is not unusual (cf. Baglioni 2010: 54–56), in combination with the others it gives some of the LF words in the *Dictionnaire* the appearance of having sprung directly from the pages of Veneroni's grammar; for example, in a single page of the latter (Veneroni 1800: 64) we find *dgiro*, *dgiardino*, *dgiousto*, *bouono*, and *virtou*.

Finally, even though the *Dictionnaire*'s spelling of LF is not entirely consistent (cf. Cifoletti 2004: 84), there is a clear tendency to use an acute accent over <e> when it occurs in what appear to be open syllables (see Table 3.22). This spelling convention is particularly clear when comparing related words in which the spelling of <e> varies with its syllable position (see 15a), and in words in which this vowel occurs more than once (see 15b). This orthographic convention is clearly aimed at facilitating the French speakers' pronunciation of LF, and it is perhaps not too far-fetched to suppose that Veneroni's (1800: 57) warning "Dans aucun cas, et sur-tout à la fin des syllabes ou des mots, l'*e* en Italien n'a le son muet que nous lui donnons en François" [In no case, especially at the end of syllables or words, does the *e* in Italian have the silent sound we give it in French] may have contributed to the decision to implement it.

(15) a.

<é> in open syllables	<e> in closed syllables
offérir	offertà
libérar, libéro	liberta
tré, trédichi	trenta

b.

Words with two <e>s	Words with three or more <e>s
béné	bénédéto
mélé	dgénéralé
barbiéré	candéliéré
testamento	tésoriéré
estesso	tonéliéré
permettir	présenté
vermé	ténenté
verdé	négligenté
sempré	fédellé
setté	ségoundamenté
terréno	indépendenté
vendéta	serpenté
mercolédi	gouerriéré
déserto	mestiéré
intéresso	

Table 3.22. *Accented <é> and unaccented <e> in Anonymous (1830a)*

Open syllables		Closed syllables	
Word finally	Elsewhere	Before geminates	Elsewhere
ré	albéro	terra	escapar
sé	biéra	gouerra	esbagniol
qué	quérir	verro	testa
thé	amérikan	serrar	peska
arté	téla	stella	vertou
cané	ciélo	sorella	verdoura
carné	méno	fratello	gerba
café	caténa	vitello	germana
padré	baréta	ellou	persona
oumbré	aspétar	piselli	encora
sangré	frédo	letto	vento
roubié	orékia	tetto	ventro
scarpé	botéga	setté	vendir
cortiné	bévir	lounetta	sentza
doué	época	adesso	pensar
chinqoué	ébriacar	altessa	tempo
grandé	allégro	vessiga	nemsa
fachilé	diétro	cabessa	harem

3.6 Lingua Franca Vocabulary

3.6.1 Structural Aspects

The LF vocabulary is the largest section of the *Dictionnaire*, occupying 81 out of the total of 107 pages. Its title, *Dictionnaire de la langue franque, ou petit mauresque*, is followed by the bold capital letter A and two columns of lexical entries, with alphabetically arranged French entries on the left and their translations in LF on the right. The lines appear to be 1.5 spaced, resulting in about 25–27 entries per page, except for the first and last pages which have fewer entries (Baglioni 2017: 187 estimates the total number of French entries in the vocabulary at 2,035). The French entries are capitalized and end with a period; the subentries with example phrases or sentences, if provided, typically appear on an indented line under the entry word. The translations in LF are not capitalized and end with a period; if the LF translation is longer than one line, the subsequent line(s) is/are indented. In a few of the entries, only the subentry is translated into LF, which leaves the entry word without a translation; in some of these cases, the subentry follows the entry word on the same line and may be enclosed in brackets (see 16 below).

(16)

French	Lingua Franca
effrayant (cela est effrayant) 'scary (this is scary)'	*qouesto fasir paoura* 'this is scary'
egal (cette chose est égale à celle-ci) 'equal (this thing is equal to that one)'	*qouella cosa star come qouesta* 'that thing is like this one'
offenser (s') cela m'offense 'offend (take offense) it offends me'	*qouesto offendir per mi*[6] 'this offends me'

3.6.2 Grammatical Information

The structural sketch in the *Dictionnaire*'s preface informs the reader that the inflectional categories that find morphological expression in LF are the imperfective/perfective aspect distinction in the verb and the masculine/feminine gender distinction in the perfective verb form and a subset of the adjectives (see Chapter 7). This grammatical information is supplied, more or less systematically, in the verb and adjective entries of the LF vocabulary.

For the verbs, the French entry form used is the infinitive; in many of the entries, the infinitive is followed by the masculine and feminine forms of the past participle. The verb forms in the French entry are meant to match, in form and etymology, the two aspectual verb forms of the LF verb, imperfective (derived from the Romance infinitive) and perfective (derived from the Italian past participle). The examples in (17a) and (17b) below show selected verb entries with and without such grammatical information. The forms in (17c)

[6] In the cited examples, the capitalization of the French entries and the periods after the entries are omitted. Entries that look in the original like this:

Acheter, acheté -ée.	*crompar, crompato -ta.*
Affaire.	
J'ai affaire avec vous.	*mi tenir oun conto con ti.*

are reproduced as follows:

acheter, acheté -ée	crompar, crompato -ta
affaire	–
j'ai affaire avec vous	mi tenir oun conto con ti

illustrate the situation when a single-word entry in French is, or may be, translated into LF with a multiword lexeme.

(17)

	French	Lingua Franca	
a.	acheter, acheté -ée	crompar, crompato -ta	'buy'
	briser, brisé -ée	rompir, roto, rota	'break'
	coudre, cousu, cousue	cousir, cousito -ta	'sew'
	feindre, feint, feinte	fingir, finto -ta	'pretend'
b.	cuire	cousinar	'cook'
	enlever	forar	'remove'
	luire	louchir	'shine'
	manger	mangiar	'eat'
c.	brider, bridé -ée	méttir l'eskima	'bridle'
	enterrer, enterré -ée	mettir in terra, messo in terra	'bury'
	enfermer, enfermé -ée	sarar dentro, sarato -ta	'lock up'
	emporter, emporté -ée	forar, forato, portar fora	'take away'

In a number of the verb entries, the French verb is followed by the third-person reflexive pronoun (see 18a). In some of these, the presence of the reflexive pronoun apparently serves to indicate the lack of a formal valency (transitivity) distinction in the corresponding LF verb. This inference is likely in light of the entries in which the French verbs varying in transitivity are translated with the same verb in LF (see 18b).

(18)

	French	Lingua Franca	
a.	dépêcher (se)	far presto	'hurry'
	habiller (s')	vestir	'dress'
	hasarder (se)	risikar	'risk'
	hâter (se)	andar ou fazir presto	'hurry'
	imaginer (s')	pensar	'imagine'
	irriter, s'irriter	irritar, rabiar	'annoy, get annoyed'
	promener (se)	spassegiar	'go for a walk'
b.	réjouir	gaudir	'delight'
	réjouir (se)	gaudir	'rejoice'
	relever	rilévar, alsar	'raise'
	relever (se)	rilevar, alsar	'get up'
	rompre	rompir	'break (tr.)'
	rompre (se)	rompir	'break (intr.)'

For adjectives that distinguish gender in French, the entry form used is masculine (see 19a). In selected adjective entries the feminine form is supplied as well, both in the French prompt and, often, in the LF translation (see 19b and 19c).

(19)

	French	Lingua Franca	
a.	blanc	bianco	'white'
	bon	bonou	'good'

	clair	kiaro	'clear'
	curieux	curioso	'curious'
b.	agé -ée	vekio, vekia	'old'
	bas, basse	basso, bassa	'low'
	noir, noire	négro, négra	'black'
	sec, sèche	séco, séca	'dry'
	séditieux -euse	rivoltato -ta	'rebellious'
c.	amer, ère	amaro	'bitter'
	orné -ée	ornato	'ornate'
	sauf -ve	salvo	'safe'

The structural outline of LF in the preface and the phrase- and sentence-long examples in the body of the *Dictionnaire* suggest that LF lacks nominal number (see Chapter 7). The vocabulary entry in (20) appears to be the only one to supply both a singular and a plural form for a LF noun.

(20)	French	Lingua Franca	
	oreille	orékia -é	'ear'

3.6.3 *Disambiguation Markers*

The French entries which are ambiguous with respect to gender or part of speech are disambiguated via grammatical markers. These are placed after the entry word, usually in brackets, and take the form of a full or abbreviated term for the entry word's part of speech (see 21a) or an article reflecting the entry noun's gender (see 21b).

(21)	French	Lingua Franca	
a.	fort (subst.)	forteretza	'fort' (noun)
	fort (adject)	forti	'strong' (adjective)
	général (substantif)	dgénéralé	'general' (noun)
	général (adjectif)	dgénéralé	'general' (adjective)
	mal (adjectif)	malé	'bad' (adjective)
	mal (adverbe)	malé	'badly' (adverb)
	la (article)	la	'the' (article)
	là (adverbe de lieu)	là	'there' (adverb of place)
	neuf (nomb.)	nové	'nine' (number)
	neuf (adj.)	nouové	'new' (adjective)
	pouvoir (substantif)	poder	'power' (noun)
	pouvoir (verbe)	poudir	'be able' (verb)
	calme (substantif)	bonassa	'calm' (noun)
	devoir (subst.)	dovéré	'duty' (noun)

fin (subst.)	finé	'end' (noun)
même (le) pron.	l'estetzo	'the same one' (pronoun)
peine (à), adv.	a péna	'hardly' (adverb)
sous, prépos.	sotto	'under' (preposition)
suivant, préposition	sécoundo	'according to' (preposition)
sur (préposition)	sopra	'on' (preposition)
surtout (adverbe)	sopra toutto	'above all' (adverb)
tant (adverbe)	tanto	'so much' (adverb)
tard (a[d]verbe)	tardi	'late' (adverb)
tendre (adjectif)	ténéro	'tender' (adjective)
ton (pron. poss.)	di ti	'your' (possessive pronoun)

b.

garde (la)	gouardia	'guarding'
garde (un)	gouardian	'guard'
tour (la tour)	toré	'tower'
tour (un tour)	torno, dgiro(r)	'turn'
voile (une voile)	vela	'sail'
voile (un voile)	vélamé	'veil'

The French entries that are ambiguous semantically are disambiguated by means of words or phrases which specify the intended meaning. Such semantic markers are separated from the entry word by a comma or placed after it in brackets. They may consist of a more generic term, as in *métal* 'metal' next to *argent* 'money; silver' or *barque de pêcheurs* 'fishing boat' next to *sandal* 'sandalwood; sandal';[7] or a synonym or phrase specifying the intended meaning of a polysemous word or disambiguating homophones, as in *miroir* 'mirror' next to *glace* 'ice; mirror,' *bruit* 'noise' next to *son* 'sound; his, her, its,' or *à tirer* 'for shooting' after *poudre* 'powder; gunpowder' (see Table 3.23).

When the LF lexeme provides a very approximate rendition of the French prompt, it is supplied with a literal translation (see 22).

(22)

French	Lingua Franca	
admirable	mouchous bello (très-beau)	'admirable' (very beautiful)
faire attention	mirar bonou (voir bien)	'pay attention' (look well)
amusant	piacher (il plait)	'amusing' (it pleases)

3.6.4 *Lingua Franca Lexemes*

There exist several types of correspondences between the French entries and their LF translations. In the default case, a one-word lexeme in French is translated with a one-word equivalent in LF (illustrated in 23).

7 See Urban (2015: 330–332) regarding the etymology of *sandal*.

Table 3.23. *Semantic markers clarifying the meaning of the French entries*

French	Lingua Franca	Gloss
franc (monnaie)	franco	'franc' (money)
franc (étranger)	franco	'Frank' (foreigner)
argent, métal	plata	'silver' (metal)
argent, monnaie	aspra	'silver' (money)
nègre, esclave	ousif	'black' (slave)
scène, dispute	baroufa	'scene' (quarrel)
sac, saccagement	sackedgio	'sack' (pillage)
satisfaction, réparation	scouza	'satisfaction' (amends)
son, bruit	sono	'sound' (noise)
sorte, espèce	généro, sorté, maniera	'sort' (kind)
répéter, redire	ablar encora	'repeat' (tell again)
amande (fruit)	amanda	'almond' (fruit)
grenade (fruit)	granata	'pomegranate' (fruit)
limon (fruit)	limoun	'lemon' (fruit)
mûre (fruit)	tout	'mulberry' (fruit)
pois (légume)	piselli	'pea' (vegetable)
rouget (poisson)	tria	'mullet' (fish)
cousin (insecte)	mousquita	'cranefly' (insect)
pot (marmite)	pignata	'pot' (cooking pot)
fosse (tombeau)	fossa, tomba	'pit' (grave)
solde (paye)	paga	'salary' (pay)
glace (miroir)	maréia	'mirror' (mirror)
bas (à chausser)	calceta	'stocking' (for putting on)
poudre (à tirer)	polvéré	'powder' (for shooting)
poêle (ustensile de cuisine)	sartan	'frying pan' (kitchen utensil)
poèlon id.	casserola	'casserole' (same)
poste (terme de guerre)	logouo	'post' (military term)
siége (terme de guerre)	sédio	'siege' (military term)
retrancher (se) t. de guer.	fortificar	'entrench' (military term)

Table 3.23. *(cont.)*

French	Lingua Franca	Gloss
retranchement (t. de guer.)	fortificatzion	'entrenchment' (military term)
proue (t. de marine)	proua	'prow' (nautical term)
sandal (barque de pêcheurs)	sandal	'sandal' (fishing boat)
marché (où l'on vend)	fondouk	'market' (where they sell)
traite (lettre de change)	cambialé	'bill' (bill of exchange)
pêche, act. de pêcher	peska	'fishing' (act of fishing)
prise (action de prendre)	préza	'taking' (act of taking)

(23)

French	Lingua Franca	
aiguille	agouilla	'needle'
aigre	aïgro	'sour'
agé -ée	vekio, vekia	'old'
aider	ajudar	'help'
acheter, acheté -ée	crompar, crompato -ta	'buy'

In a little over 100 cases, the French word is translated into LF with two or more single-word alternatives. In most cases, the alternative translations derive from Romance sources, though Arabic and Turkish lexemes are also attested (see 24).

(24)

French	Lingua Franca		
jeune	dgiovine, picolo	'young'	(< It.)
dey	dey, bacha	'dey'	(< Tu.)
tète	testa, cabessa	'head'	(< It., Sp.)
esprit	spirito, cabessa	'wit'	(< It., Sp.)
très	molto, mouchou	'very'	(< It., Sp.)
canonier	canoniéré, tobgi	'gunner'	(< It., Tu.)
verre	verro, tassa	'glass'	(< Fr., Sp.)
désirer	désirar, quérir	'wish'	(< Fr., Sp.)
vide	basio, vouoto	'empty'	(< Sp., It.)
femme	mouchéra (épouse), dona (dame)	'woman, wife'	(< Sp., It.)
fou, folle	maboul, locou, maboula -loca	'crazy'	(< Ar., Sp.)

Such (near-)synonyms are also listed as alternatives in some of the multiword lexemes (see 25).

(25)

French	Lingua Franca	
dévaliser, dévalisé -ée	forar roba *ou* mercantzia	'rob'
quereller (se)	far gribouilla[r] ou baroufa	'quarrel'
souffrir	ténir dolor, ou malé	'be in pain'
embellir, embelli -ée	vernir bello, tornar bello	'grow lovelier'

In some cases, a one-word lexeme in French is rendered in LF with both a single-word and a multiword translation equivalent. This type of correspondences is illustrated in (26).

(26)

French	Lingua Franca	
baguette	picolo bastone, bagueta	'stick'
meuble	mobili, roba di casa	'furniture'
brave	bonou, ténir coragio	'brave'
intrépide	intrépido, tenir coragio	'intrepid'
emporter, emporté -ée	forar, forato, portar fora	'carry away'
saler	salar, mettir salé	'salt'
ignorer	ignorar, non sabir	'ignore'
leur	loro, di loro	'their'
ranger	rangiar, componir, mettir in logo	'arrange'
réfléchir	reflétir, pensar, mirar bonou	'think'

In over 100 cases, the multiword translation is the only one provided. This translation strategy is illustrated in (27).

(27)

French	Lingua Franca	
limonade	agoua di limoun	'lemonade'
belle-fille	moukera del filio	'daughter-in-law'
hachoir	cortello grosso	'cleaver'
multitude	molto genti	'crowd'
délicieux	molto bouno	'delicious'
nuisible	fasir malé	'harmful'
mon, ma, mes	di mi	'my'
opposer (s')	non quérir	'oppose'
nuire	far malé	'be harmful'
sabrer	toccar con yatagan	'slash'

In a small number of the cases, both the French entry and the LF translation are multiword (see 28).

(28)

French	Lingua Franca	
aiguiser un couteau	passar oun cortello	'sharpen a knife'
pétrir le pain	pastar pano	'knead bread'
repasser du linge	passar ferro	'iron clothes'
tacher de	provar di	'try to'

In some instances, the French entry word is supplied with a usage example. In some of these, both the entry and the example are translated into LF, while in others, the entry word is left without a translation (see Table 3.24).

Table 3.24. *Usage examples in the Lingua Franca vocabulary*

French	Lingua Franca	Gloss
appartenir *il m'appartient*	*estar di* *estar di mi*	'belong' 'it's mine'
apporter, apporté -ée *apportez-moi*	*porter per, portato -ta* *portar per mi*	'bring' 'bring me'
approuver, approuvé -ée *approuvez-vous cette chose?*	*goustar* *ti goustar qouesta cosa?*	'approve' 'do you approve of this?'
affront *vous m'avez fait un affront*	*vergognia* *ti fato vergognia per mi*	'insult' 'you have offended me'
affaire *j'ai affaire avec vous*	— *mi tenir oun conto con ti*	— 'I have business with you'
agréable *cette chose est agréable*	— *qouesta cosa piacher*	— 'this thing is nice'
arrêt *(par arrêt du Pacha)*	— *d'ordine del Bacha*	— 'by the order of the Pasha'
effrayant *(cela est effrayant)*	— *qouesto fasir paoura*	— 'this is scary'
égal *(cette chose est égale à celle-ci)*	— *qouella cosa star come qouesta*	— 'this thing is equal to that'

3.6.5 *Multiword Lexemes*

While our ability to trace the sources of the *Dictionnaire*'s Arabic vocabulary is facilitated by its limited size and coverage, the sources of the LF vocabulary, which is much more substantial and varied in its coverage, are far more difficult to trace. Certain inferences in this regard are, nonetheless, possible because

> each dictionary relies to a certain extent on its predecessors, so that for each dictionary compiled today it is possible to construct a kind of genealogical tree in which its origins can (with sufficient patience) be traced back through several centuries. It is in fact impossible to compile a completely new dictionary. Even if no other dictionaries are physically consulted, the compilers' efforts are inevitably drawn from their education and experience, both of which depend on a general consensus concerning derivation, history, pronunciation, meaning, etc., of the

individual words and phrases, all of which can be traced to the influence of dictionaries published in the past. (Collison 1982: 19–20)

One inference that may be drawn from the face of the LF vocabulary is that it is likely to have been modeled after a monolingual French dictionary, or a bilingual or polyglot dictionary compiled by using a monolingual dictionary as its blueprint. The impact of a monolingual dictionary is seen in the multiword LF lexemes, some of which have the appearance of having been calqued on, or at least inspired by, definitions of the type found in a monolingual dictionary.

The issue of potential models for the LF vocabulary is further complicated by the consideration that the actual dictionary used for the purpose could have been the product of a much earlier age. This inference is plausible in the light of what is known about Hodgson's other known use of language-learning materials: thus, Veneroni's *Maître italien*, used as one of the *Dictionnaire*'s models, was first published around 1686, while Meninski's *Arabic-Turkish-Persian Lexicon*, used by Hodgson for translating the US–Algerian treaty of 1816, dates from 1680 (Bryson 1979: 17). In the absence of direct evidence about the actual dictionary used, it would be profitable to compare the multiword LF translations of selected French entries with the multiword definitions of the corresponding entries in Richelet's *Dictionnaire françois* (Richelet 1680). This choice of dictionary is justified by its extensive circulation: not only was it "an enormous commercial success," going through sixty editions between its initial publication in 1680 and its final edition in 1811 (Bray 1986: 15; 1990: 1798), but it had also served as a template for a range of other monolingual, bilingual, and polyglot dictionaries (Collison 1982: 85; Bray 1986: 15; Loving 2012: 82). Additionally, Richelet was one of the first French lexicographers to perform the mammoth task of creating initial, largely original, definitions for the about 20,000 words and senses recorded at the time the first monolingual dictionaries made their appearance (Quemada 1967: 391). This makes it likely that the dictionary relied on for the compilation of the *Dictionnaire* contained at least some definitions and examples ultimately traceable to Richelet's.

The comparison is provided in Tables 3.25 and 3.26. The first column in each table contains the French entry word from the LF vocabulary, the second column contains its LF translation, and the third column provides the relevant definition for the same entry word from Richelet (1811) (see Bray 1990: 1802, 1809 regarding this edition). Richelet (1811) often provides more than one definition for a word, each corresponding to its different sense; for example, the definitions for *enterrer* include *Mettre en terre une personne morte* 'to put a dead person in the ground,' *Mettre dans la terre* 'to put in the ground,' and *Tenir caché* 'to keep hidden.' The definitions included in the tables are the

Table 3.25. *Multiword Lingua Franca lexemes compared with Richelet's definitions*

French	Lingua Franca	Definition (Richelet 1811)
brider	*méttir l'eskima* 'to put the bridle'	*Mettre une bride* 'to put a bridle'
sceller	*mettir taba* 'to put seal'	*Mettre un sceau* 'to put a seal'
enterrer	*mettir in terra* 'to put in ground'	*Mettre dans la terre* 'to put in the ground'
poster	*mettir in oun logouo* 'to put in a place'	*Mettre, placer en un poste* 'to put, to place in a place'
remplacer	*rimettir in logo* 'to put back in place'	*Remettre en place* 'to put back in place'
embraser	*metter fugo* 'to set fire'	*mettre en feu* 'to set on fire'
ferrer	*mettir ferro* 'to put iron'	*Garnir de fer* 'to furnish with iron'
sabler	*mettir sabia* 'to put sand'	*Couvrir de sable* 'to cover with sand'
sabrer	*toccar con yatagan* 'to strike with sword'	*Donner un coup de sabre* 'to give a blow with a sword'
seller	*mettir la sérigia* 'to put a saddle'	*Mettre la selle sur le dos d'un cheval, d'une mule* 'to put a saddle on the back of a horse, a mule'
débrider	*forar l'esquima* 'to take off the bridle'	*Oter la bride* 'to take off the bridle'
déshabiller	*forar roba* 'to take off clothes'	*Oter les habits* 'to take off clothes'
défoncer	*forar il foundo* 'to remove the bottom'	*Oter le fond d'un tonneau* 'to remove the bottom of a barrel'
dévaliser	*forar roba ou mercantzia* 'to take away luggage or goods'	*Oter la valise, les hardes et les marchandises à des passants* 'to take away travelers' suitcase, clothes and goods'

Table 3.25. *(cont.)*

French	Lingua Franca	Definition (Richelet 1811)
déplaire	*non piacher* 'to not like'	*Ne plaire pas* 'to not like'
taire	*non hablar* 'to not say'	*Ne dire pas* 'to not say'
traverser	*passar per metzo* 'to pass across'	*Passer au travers* 'to pass across'
escorter	*dar scorta* 'to give escort'	*Faire escorte* 'to give escort'
secourir	*dar agioudo* 'to give help'	*Donner du secours* 'to give help'
nuire	*far malé* 'to do badly'	*faire tort* 'to do wrong'
bâtir (une maison)	*counchiar, una casa* 'to make a house'	*Faire un édifice* 'to make a buiding'
hacher	*cortar minouto* 'to cut finely'	*Couper fort menu* 'to cut very finely'
souffrir	*ténir dolor, ou malé* 'to have sorrow or pain'	*avoir de la peine, de la douleur, etc.* 'to have sorrow, pain etc.'
répéter, redire	*ablar encora* 'to say again'	*Dire de nouveau* 'to say again'
réussir	*sortir bonou* 'to come out well'	*Venir bien* 'to come well'
reculer	*andar in diétro* 'to go back'	*(se reculer) Se retirer en arrière* 'to go back'
embellir	*vernir bello, tornar bello* 'to turn beautiful'	*Devenir plus beau*[a] 'to become more beautiful'
rougir	*tornar rosso* 'to turn red'	*Devenir rouge à cause de quelque chose qui peut causer de la honte, ou par une autre raison* 'to become red because of someting that can cause shame, or for some other reason'

Table 3.25. *(cont.)*

French	Lingua Franca	Definition (Richelet 1811)
sain-doux	*grasso di porco* 'fat of pig'	*Graisse de pourceau fondüe* 'melted fat of pig'
sentier	*picolo camino* 'small road'	*Petit chemin battu* 'small beaten road'
bienfaiteur	*quello che fasir béné* 'he who does good'	*Celui . . . qui fait . . . quelque bien à quelqu'un* 'he who does some good to someone'
suffisant	*qué bastar* 'which suffices'	*Qui suffit* 'which suffices'
opulent	*molto riko* 'very rich'	*Qui est riche* 'who is rich'
vivant	*in vita* 'alive'	*Qui est en vie* 'who is alive'
successivement	*ouno dopo l'altro* 'one after another'	*L'un après l'autre* 'one after another'
secrètement	*con ségréto* 'in secret'	*En secret* 'in secret'
vis-à-vis	*in fachia* 'in front'	*En face* 'in front'

[a] From Richelet (1761); Richelet (1811) offers only *embellir* 'rendre plus beau' [render more beautiful].

ones that match the corresponding LF periphrases; in the case of *enterrer*, for instance, the only one included is *Mettre dans la terre* 'to put in the ground.'

Table 3.25 displays selected French entries whose multiword translations in LF match the corresponding multiword definitions from Richelet (1811). In some of these, the correspondence between the LF lexeme and Richelet's definition is precise, or more or less so: compare, for example, the LF translations of *suffisant* (*qué bastar* 'which suffices') and *sceller* (*mettir taba* 'to put seal') with the corresponding definitions, *qui suffit* 'which suffices' and *mettre un sceau* 'to put a seal.' The verbal lexemes in LF may employ a more generic or semantically contiguous verb; compare the LF translation of *sabler* (*mettir sabia* 'to put sand') with its definition, *couvrir de sable* 'to cover with sand.' Inevitably, some of the definitions are more wordy than the corresponding LF lexemes: compare, for example, the LF translation of *seller* (*mettir la sérigia* 'to put a saddle') with this verb's definition, *mettre la selle sur le dos d'un cheval, d'une mule* 'to put a saddle on the back of a horse, a mule.'

Table 3.26. *Selected single- and multiword synonyms in Lingua Franca*

French	Lingua Franca	Definition (Richelet 1811)
ignorer	*ignorar, non sabir* 'to ignore, to not know'	*Ne savoir pas* 'to not know'
favoriser	*favorisar, counchar favour* 'to favor, to do favor'	*Faire quelque faveur* 'to do some favor'
permettre	*permettir, dar licentzia* 'to permit, to give permission'	*Donner permission* 'to give permission'
remercier	*ringratziar, ablar gratzia* 'to thank, to say thanks'	*Faire des remercîmens* 'to say thanks'
soigner	*servar, tenir coura* 'to take care'	*Avoir soin* 'to take care'
ranger	*rangiar, componir, mettir in logo* 'to arrange, to compose, to put in place'	*Mettre en ordre* 'to put in order'
sucrer	*zoukar, mettir zoukaro* 'to sugar, to put sugar'	*Mettre du sucre sur quelque chose* 'to put sugar on something'
saler	*salar, mettir salé* 'to salt, to put salt'	*Mettre du sel dans quelque chose qu'on assaisonne* 'to put salt into something one seasons'
brave	*bonou, ténir coragio* 'good, to have courage'	*Hardi, courageux, honnête* 'bold, corageous, honorable'
baguette	*picolo bastone, bagueta* 'little stick, rod'	*Bâton long et délié* 'long and thin stick'

Table 3.26 presents selected French entry words whose LF translations include both single- and multiword lexemes. Some of the single-word translations have the appearance of French words adapted to LF's Hispano-Italian phonology (see Chapter 4) while their multiword counterparts that of having been calqued on or inspired by definitions similar to Richelet's (1811).

The repertoire of techniques involved in rendering French words with periphrastic lexemes in LF represents a subset of those employed by lexicographers for creating dictionary definitions (Quemada 1967: 431–435, 441–451). These include reliance on a (morphologically) related word, as when Fr. *suffisant* 'sufficient' is translated into LF as *qué bastar* 'which suffices,' *secrètement* 'secretly' as *con ségréto* 'with secret,' and *sceller* 'to seal' as *mettir taba* 'to put seal' (compare with the corresponding definitions *qui suffit* 'which suffices,' *en secret* 'in secret,' and *mettre un sceau* 'to put a seal'); translation by means of antonyms, as when Fr. *taire* 'to be silent' is translated as *non hablar* 'to not say' (compare with the definition *ne pas dire* 'to not say'); and translation by modifying a word with a more generic meaning, as when Fr. *baguette* 'rod' is rendered as *picolo bastone* 'small stick,' *opulent* 'opulent' as *molto riko* 'very rich,' and *hacher* 'to chop' as *cortar minuto* 'to cut finely' (compare with the definition *bâton long et délié* 'long and thin stick' for *baguette* and *couper fort menu* 'to cut very finely' for *hacher*). The above examples also illustrate such definition techniques as rendering of adjectives by means of relative clauses (*qué bastar* 'which suffices' for 'sufficient') and adverbs by means of prepositional phrases (*con ségréto* 'with secret' for 'secretly') (see Quemada 1967: 460–461). These and similar definition techniques were routinely used in dictionaries Hodgson would have consulted during his language studies and which could have influenced his work on LF, both directly through the dictionary used for vocabulary elicitation and indirectly through his familiarity with dictionaries in general.

Reliance on a preexistent dictionary may also be inferred from the example sentences that accompany some of the entry words in the LF vocabulary. For the purposes of illustration, Table 3.27 juxtaposes selected usage examples from the *Dictionnaire* with matching examples for the same entry words from the sixth edition of the Dictionary of the French Academy (Institut de France 1835).[8] The word exemplified by each sentence is underlined.

3.7 Chapter Summary

This chapter has shown that the creation of the *Dictionnaire*'s LF dialogues, Arabic vocabulary, and preface involved reliance on two Italian grammars for French learners, Veneroni's *Maître italien* (Veneroni 1800) and Vergani's *Grammaire italienne* (Vergani 1823). Both grammars were widely circulated in the years closely predating the *Dictionnaire*'s publication, and were highly regarded by language teachers. It has further been shown that in compiling the LF vocabulary, Hodgson is likely to have used as his model a dictionary which included word definitions as part of its entries. The Arabic vocabulary was also informed by Hodgson's familiarity with Marcel (1799).

In his seminal article on LF, Hugo Schuchardt described the *Dictionnaire* as "a quite paltry concoction afflicted with every possible fault" (Schuchardt 1979: 40). This assessment is echoed by some of the later researchers, and is justified by a

[8] This edition, which postdates the *Dictionnaire*, is used here for reasons of accessibility.

Table 3.27. *Selected usage examples in the Lingua Franca vocabulary*

French	Lingua Franca	Dictionary of the French Academy
j'ai affaire avec vous 'I have business with you'	*mi tenir oun conto con ti* 'I have business with you'	*Avoir affaire ... avec quelqu'un* 'To have business with someone'
vous m'avez fait un affront 'You have insulted me'	*ti fato vergognia per mi* 'You have insulted me'	*On lui a fait un affront* 'He has been insulted'
cela m'offense 'this offends me'	*qouesto offendir per mi* 'this offends me'	*Cela m'offense* 'This offends me'
solder un compte 'settle an account'	*spachiar oun conto* 'to settle an account'	*Solder un compte* 'to settle an account'

number of the *Dictionnaire*'s properties, such as its inconsistent use of the LF orthography, typographical errors in both French and LF words, and certain unevenness of the LF vocabulary. However, an examination of the *Dictionnaire*'s sources, and a close look at some of the processes that went into its making, alter this perception. They reveal that the *Dictionnaire* relies on solid language teaching tools; that the terse grammatical description and a self-explanatory, from a French speaker's point of view, orthography have been tailored for the practical needs of its users; and that the learner's dialogues in, and the vocabulary of, LF are adapted to its communicative environment in their content, and its expressive possibilities in their complexity. The Arabic vocabulary shows both judicious pruning of the model wordlists and a few strategic additions, such as the names of local foods and the word for *citerne* 'cistern,' a typical feature of an Algerine house ("[i]n houses where good and capacious cisterns are constructed, water enough for the ordinary use of a family is obtained by the terraces during the season of rain") (Shaler 1826: 72). The *Dictionnaire*'s Arabic vocabulary may also have the distinction of being among the first efforts in Algerian Arabic lexicography (Larzul 2010). Given the care that went into the *Dictionnaire*'s compilation, its "untidy" appearance furnishes additional proof that it was brought to publication by someone other than its author.

4 The Orthography

This chapter takes a look at the orthography of Lingua Franca in the *Dictionnaire de la langue franque* and examines the sound inventory and phonological processes that the orthography reflects. Following preliminary observations (Section 4.1), the chapter discusses the orthographic representation and phonological processes of Lingua Franca vowels (in Section 4.2) and consonants (in Section 4.3). Section 4.4 addresses the aspects of Lingua Franca phonology revealed by the phonological adaptation of French words. Section 4.5 zooms in on the various influences on the *Dictionnaire*'s orthography, expanding and supplementing the earlier discussion of this issue in Chapter 3. Section 4.6 summarizes the main issues, situating the sound inventory of Lingua Franca in the context of the hypothesized role of inter-Romance koineization in its genesis.

4.1 Introduction

The *Dictionnaire*'s orthography of LF appears to have been designed specially for this work. This inference is suggested by the statement, in the *Dictionnaire*'s preface, that "[c]et idiome ... n'a ni orthographe, ni règles grammaticales bien établies" [this language has neither an orthography nor well-established grammatical rules] (Anonymous 1830a: n.p.).

A number of interesting observations about the LF orthography are made by Guido Cifoletti in the studies accompanying his editions of the *Dictionnaire*'s LF vocabulary in the inverse order (Cifoletti 1980: 17–21; 1989: 37–48, 85–89) and his republication of the complete *Dictionnaire* (Cifoletti 2004: 33–41, 83–86). Cifoletti notes the lack of an established norm for spelling LF, points out numerous inconsistencies in the LF orthography, and observes that it is based on French with an occasional influence from Italian. These conclusions are apparent in the following observations:

> L'ortografia è estremamente trascurata. ... [L]'autore non poteva rifarsi a nessuna norma stabilita, e cercò soltanto di adattare alla grafia francese la pronuncia che sentiva, ma senza mettere a punto un coerente sistema di scrittura. ... Qualche volta sembra invece comparire un influsso dell'ortografia italiana. ... L'ortografia spagnola al contrario sembra ignorata. (Cifoletti 1980: 17)

Table 4.1. *Lingua Franca vowels*

i		*u*
e		*o*
	a	

[The spelling is very sloppy. The author could not adhere to any established norm and only sought to adapt the pronunciation he heard to the French spelling, without, however, developing a coherent system of writing. Sometimes there seems to appear an influence of the Italian orthography. The Spanish orthography, by contrast, appears to be ignored.]

In addition to remarks of a general nature, Cifoletti makes a number of observations about specific graphemes and multigraphs, the LF sound system and phonological processes, and the probable linguistic background of the *Dictionnaire*'s compilers or their informant (cf. Cifoletti 1980: 25; 1989: 88–89; 2004: 86). These will be pointed out, as appropriate, in the course of the discussion below.

4.2 The Vowels

4.2.1 Spelling

The *Dictionnaire*'s spelling of LF reflects the vowel inventory shown in Table 4.1 (see also Cifoletti 1989: 39; 2004: 34).

The vowel [i] is spelled <i>, except the rare cases when the hiatus between it and a flanking <a> is emphasized by diaeresis (see 2 below). The use of diaeresis is not consistent across the lexical entries: compare, for example, the spelling of *boutïa* (< It. *bottiglia*) with that of *famia* (< It. *famiglia*) and *cavia* (< It. *caviglia*).

(2)

inberno	'winter'	fantazia	'pride'
piselli	'pea'	famia	'family'
rovina	'ruin'	cavia	'peg'
sabir	'know'	boutïa	'bottle'
riou	'stream'	sïa	'namely'
zio	'uncle'	ossïa	'namely'
zia	'aunt'	païsé	'country'

The vowel [e] tends to be spelled <e> in closed syllables and <é> in open ones (see 3 below and Section 3.5 of Chapter 3). A few of the words are variably spelled with and without the diacritic.

(3)

esbinac	'spinach'	qué	'what'
bestia	'animal'	béné	'well'

cabessa	'head'	ézilar	'exile'
terra	'earth'	quérir	'want, ask'
bello	'beautiful'	oumbré	'man'
tempo	'time'	ove ~ ové	'where'

The usual spelling for the vowel [a] is <a>. The spelling <à> is attested word-finally, on both etymologically stressed and unstressed [a]s, and with some words variably spelled with and without the diacritic (see 4).

(4)	agoua	'water'	cativitÃ	'nastiness'
	anima	'soul'	offertà	'offer'
	ablar	'say, speak'	platzà	'square'
	sabato	'Saturday'	cosà ~ cosa	'thing'
	qoualita	'quality'	chità ~ chita	'city'
	fantazia	'pride'	forà ~ fora	'outside'

The vowel [o] is consistently spelled <o> (see 5).

(5)	ockio	'eye'	sporco	'dirty'
	molto	'very'	séco	'dry'
	fatzoletto	'handkerchief'	botoné	'button'

The vowel [u] is spelled <ou>, less commonly <u> or <ù> (word-finally), with variant spellings in some words (see 6). Cifoletti (1989: 40) attributes the use of <u> to the influence of Italian orthography or introduction of Gallicisms, and briefly considers the possibility that <u> may reflect a phonetic [y].

(6)	ouso	'habit, use'	ultimo	'last'
	oumido	'damp'	turco	'Turk'
	paoura	'fear, dread'	trucheman	'interpreter'
	frouto	'fruit'	dgioventù	'youth'
	piou	'more'	ouna ~ una	'one (f.)'
	limoun	'lemon'	oumbré ~ umbré	'man'

The vowel symbols <i> ~ <ï> and <ou> ~ <u> are also used for spelling the corresponding glides (see Section 4.3.1). No orthographic distinction is made between a [u] in hiatus with another vowel and a [w] (see 7a). Some graphic distinction between a [i] in hiatus and a [j] is present due to the use of the diaeresis mark (see 7b), however, this differentiation is not implemented consistently: for example, no graphic differentiation between the vowel-vowel and glide-vowel sequences is present in the word pairs (7c)–(7e).[1]

[1] The judgments about the surface phonetics of these spellings are based on the assumed etyma of the LF words; for example, in *piou* 'more' and *adios* 'goodbye' <i> is assumed to represent a glide rather than a syllabic vowel based on its realization in the assumed source words, It. *più* and Sp. *adiós*, respectively.

(7)

a.	[ua]		[wa]	
	proua	'prow'	agoua	'water'
b.	[ia]		[ja]	
	ossïa	'namely'	bestia	'animal'
c.	[iu]		[ju]	
	riou	'stream'	piou	'more'
d.	[io]		[jo]	
	basio	'empty'	adios	'goodbye'
e.	[ai]		[aj]	
	païsé	'country'	traïdor	'traitor'

4.2.2 *Vocalic Processes*

The most prominent vocalic process reflected in the *Dictionnaire*'s spelling of LF is the raising of unstressed mid vowels (or, more precisely, vowels which are unstressed in the source forms) (Cifoletti 1989: 39; 2004: 35) (see 8).

(8)

a.	[e] > [i]		
	firmar	'detain'	(< It. fermare)[2]
	dgitar	'throw'	(< It. gettare)
	reflétir	'reflect'	(< It. riflettere)
	miscolantza	'mixture'	(< It. mescolanza)
	vindémia	'grape harvest'	(< It. vendemmia)
	rigar	'water'	(< Sp. regar)
	inchito	'full'	(< Sp. henchido)
b.	[o] > [u]		
	bouriqua	'donkey'	(< Sp. borrica)
	locou	'crazy'	(< Sp. loco)
	mouchou	'very'	(< Sp. mucho)
	mouchachou	'child, son'	(< Sp. muchacho)
	riou	'stream'	(< Sp. río)

[2] Due to the closeness of many Romance cognates, assigning LF words to a specific source is not always possible. This difficulty is acknowledged by previous researchers; Cornelissen (1992) estimates that as many as 27% of the LF words listed in the *Dictionnaire* exist in more than one Romance language. The same researcher also finds that only about 60 of the Italianisms do not correspond in form to modern written Italian. This fact, along with some orthographic, phonological, and/or morphological considerations, provides some guidance in assigning LF words to their probable sources. For example, LF *timoun* 'helm' is more likely to derive from Sp. *timón* than It. *timone*, particularly in view of its doublet *timone*. Furthermore, the raising [o] > [u] is more typical of Spanish than Italian words, which argues for the Spanish provenance not only of *timoun* 'helm' but also of *limoun* 'lemon' and *salmoun* 'salmon.' LF *païsé* 'country' is more likely to derive from It. *paese* than Sp. *país* on account of the final *-e* and the *Dictionnaire*'s practice to use <s> for spelling a [z] rather than [s] between vowels; the alternative spelling *païzé* strengthens this conclusion. LF *cédar* 'give up' is more likely to derive from Fr. *ceder* than It. *cedere* because, with few exceptions, LF adapts French verbs in *-er* to its *-ar* conjugation and Italian verbs in *-ere* to its *-ir* conjugation. The issues inherent in attempting to assign LF words to their etymological sources are further addressed in Chapter 5.

bakalaou	'cod'	(< Sp. bacalao)
troumpetta	'trumpet'	(< Fr. trompette)

Some of the words so affected are given alternative spellings (see 9).

(9)	bono ~ bonou	'good'	(< It. buono)
	tempo ~ tempou	'time, season'	(< It. tempo)
	lévante ~ lévanti	'Levant'	(< It. levante)
	grandé ~ grandi	'big, vast'	(< Sp. It. grande)
	fermar ~ firmar	'detain, arrest'	(< It. fermare)
	mescolar ~ miscolar	'mix, falsify'	(< It. mescolare)
	rompir ~ roumpir	'break, split'	(< Sp. romper, It. rompere)
	montar ~ mountar	'go up'	(< Sp. montar, It. montare)

It is unclear whether the words in (10) form part of the same pattern or whether they derive from the lexifier's plural forms instead. The latter possibility is likely in view of the existence of other plurals in the *Dictionnaire* which are glossed with singular nouns, such as *douros* 'piaster' (< Sp. *duro*, pl. *duros*) and *gouanti* 'glove' (< It. *guanto*, pl. *guanti*) (Schuchardt 1909: 444–445) (cf. also plural Italian loanwords like *guwanty* 'glove(s)' in Egyptian Arabic; Spiro 1937).

(10)	denti	'tooth'	(< It. dente, pl. denti)
	genti	'man, people'	(< It. gente, pl. genti)
	pechi	'fish'	(< It. pesce, pl. pesci)
	pernichi	'partridge'	(< It. pernice, pl. pernici)
	turbanti	'turban'	(< It. turbante, pl. turbanti)
	pésanti	'heavy'	(< It. pesante, pl. pesanti)
	forti	'strong'	(< It. forte, pl. forti)

Occasionally, stressed mid vowels are also raised (see 11).

(11)	oumbré ~ umbré	'man'	(< Sp. hombre)
	ratoun	'rat'	(< Sp. ratón)
	païsé	'country'	(< It. paese)
	maloura	'misfortune'	(< It. malora)

The raising of the stressed vowel in nouns ending in *-on* / *-one* in the source languages does not affect all the relevant lexical items (compare 12a with 12b).

(12)	a.	ratoun	'rat'	(< Sp. ratón)
		limoun	'lemon'	(< Sp. limón)
		timoun	'helm, rudder'	(< Sp. timón)
		salmoun	'salmon'	(< Sp. salmón)
		pigioun	'pigeon'	(< Fr. pigeon)
		trahisoun	'betrayal'	(< Fr. trahison)
	b.	ladron	'thief, rascal'	(< Sp. ladrón)
		padron	'owner'	(< It. padrone)
		canton	'corner'	(< It. cantone)

natzion	'nation'	(< It. nazione)
canon ~ canone	'cannon'	(< It. cannone)

A handful of LF words show variable treatment of the stressed mid vowel:[3]

(13)	rosso ~ rousso	'red, scarlet'	(< It. rosso)
	inglés ~ inglis	'English'	(< Sp. inglés)

The following examples show lowering of both stressed and unstressed high vowels of the source forms:

(14)	invédia	'envy'	(< It. invidia, Sp. envidia)
	bekiéré	'glass'	(< It. bicchiere)
	coquiaré	'spoon'	(< Sic. cucchiara)
	dobitar ~ doubitar	'doubt'	(< It. dubitare)

The raising of mid vowels in LF has been attributed to the substrate or adstrate effect of Berber and Arabic (Schuchardt 1909: 449; Cifoletti 1989: 39; Castellanos 2007: 3–4). Cifoletti finds that mid vowel raising is more at home in Spanish- than Italian-origin words, and attributes this effect to the probable acquisition of the Spanish words via Arabic (Cifoletti 1980: 25; 1989: 39, 88). The hypothesis of the Arabic speakers' input into the vowel raising process finds confirmation in similar processes in Romance borrowings in North African colloquial Arabics, including Spanish borrowings in Northern Moroccan Arabic (Sayahi 2005, 2011), French and Spanish borrowings in the Fes/Meknes area of Morocco (Heath 1989), and Italian borrowings in Egyptian Arabic (Spiro 1937; Cifoletti 1975) (see 15). Another source of variable mid vowel realization in LF is similar variability in the lexifiers (cf. Campos-Astorkiza 2012: 90–91 for Spanish).

(15) a.

Spanish	Northern Moroccan Arabic	
premio	[primio]	'prize'
seguro	[siguru]	'sure'
monja	[munxa]	'nun'
cocina	[kuzina]	'kitchen'

(Sayahi 2005: 256; 2011: 93–94)

b.

Spanish	Morroccan Colloquial Arabic	
inglés	[ingliz]	'English (people)'
guerra	[girra]	'war'
gancho	[ganšu]	'pitchfork'
calzón	[garṣun]	'man's underpants'

(Heath 1989: 275–279)

[3] Cf. also the treatment of stressed and unstressed [o]s in the derivationally related pair *moska* 'fly,' *mousquita* 'cranefly' (< Sp. It. *mosca*, Sp. *mosquita*).

c.

French	Moroccan Colloquial Arabic	
gamelle	[gamila]	'cooking pot'
goufrette	[gufrit]	'ice-cream cone'
garçon	[gaṛṣun]	'waiter'
gateau	[gaṭu]	'cake'

(Heath 1989: 275–277)

d.

Italian	Cairene Arabic	
vitello	[bitillu]	'calf'
opera	[ʔubira]	'work'
gonnella	[gunilla]	'skirt'
domino	[duminu]	'dominoes'

(Cifoletti 1975: 138, 146)

A type of vowel raising which stands out by its systematic nature is the raising of the theme vowel *-e-* in LF imperfectives that derive from Spanish infinitives in *-er* and Italian infinitives in *-ere*. As shown in (16), raising of the theme vowel makes these imperfectives indistinguishable from those deriving from Spanish infinitives in *-ir* and Italian in *-ire*.

(16)

a.

quérir	'want'	(< Sp. querer)
sabir	'know'	(< Sp. saber)
rompir	'break'	(< Sp. romper)
escondir	'hide'	(< Sp. esconder)
inchir	'fill'	(< Sp. henchir)

b.

volir	'want'	(< It. volere)
avir	'have'	(< It. avere)
crédir	'believe'	(< It. credere)
conoschir	'know'	(< It. conoscere)
capir	'understand'	(< It. capire)

Given the simplification effect of the above change, Cifoletti hypothesizes that the motivation for it is only partly phonetic:

> Credo perciò che la generalizzazione della desinenza **-ir** sia da attribuire più che altro al bisogno di semplificare e normalizzare, anche se possono avervi giocato un ruolo le difficoltà di pronuncia di alcuni arabofoni. (Cifoletti 1989: 40)

> [That is why I believe that the generalization of the ending *-ir* is attributable mostly to the need to simplify and standardize, even if the pronunciation difficulties of some Arabic speakers may have played a part in it as well.]

Cifoletti's hypothesis is supported by the fact that the raising of [e] in the word-final [er] ~ [ere] sequences is sensitive to morphological environment. For example, while [e] is raised in the verbs *poder*, *piacere*, and *dovere*, it fails to do so in the homophonous nouns (see the verb/noun pairs in 17a–17c).

The forms in (17d) and (18b) provide further examples of [e]'s failure to undergo raising when the word-final [er] ~ [ere] sequences occur in nonverbs.

(17)	a.	poudir	'to be able'	(< Sp. poder (v.))
		poder	'power'	(< Sp. poder (n.))
	b.	piachir	'to please'	(< It. piacere (v.))
		piacher, piachéré	'pleasure'	(< It. piacere (n.))
	c.	dévir	'to owe'	(< It. dovere (v.), Sp. deber)
		dovéré	'duty'	(< It. dovere (n.))
	d.	per	'by, for'	(< It. per)
		bièra	'beer'	(< Fr. bière)
		mouchéra, moukera	'woman'	(< Sp. mujer)

The loss of *-e* in the word-final sequence [ere] is also sensitive to morphological context: while the verbs shed this vowel, the nouns keep it (compare the forms in 18a and 18b).

(18)	a.	volir	'to want'	(< It. volere)
		avir	'to have'	(< It. avere)
		scrivir	'to write'	(< It. scrivere)
		scométir	'to bet'	(< It. scommettere)
	b.	polvéré	'gunpowder'	(< It. polvere)
		dovéré	'duty'	(< It. dovere (n.))
		bekiéré	'cup'	(< It. bicchiere)
		barbiéré	'barber'	(< It. barbiere)

The adaptation of the Romance infinitives in *-er / -ere* to the *-ir* conjugation in LF finds a typological parallel in the borrowing of Italian infinitives in Arbrisht, an Albanian dialect spoken in Calabria in southern Italy. Prior to the onset of borrowing from Italian, Arbrisht had been in prolonged contact with the local Calabrese dialect in which the conjugations in the infinitive have been reduced to two, *-are* and *-ire* (Rohlfs 1968: 359, 362; Breu 1991: 48–49; Trumper 1997: 264). Italian infinitives in *-ere* are borrowed into Arbrisht with the formative *-ir-*, which makes them indistinguishable from borrowed Italian infinitives in *-ire* (the examples in 19 are from Breu 1991: 48).

(19)	Italian	Arbrisht	
	piacere	[pjatʃir-]	'to please'
	invadere	[invaðir-]	'to invade'
	ingrandire	[ingrandir-]	'to enlarge'

The above borrowing behavior exemplifies what Heath (1984, 1989) terms *routines*, "productive processes by which speakers with at least some bilingual competence introduce new borrowings from L2 into L1" (Heath 1984: 372; Gardani 2016: 235). Knowledge of regular processes for converting "L2 items into L1 borrowings" "permits 'instant' borrowing of new L2 items (with Ll affixation) so that it is not necessary for each new L2 item to go through successive stages of assimilation (from CS to fully adapted borrowing)" (Heath 1984: 375). Adaptation of Romance infinitives in *-er / -ere* to the *-ir* conjugation in the *Dictionnaire*'s LF is analyzable in similar terms. Further conversion routines are observable in the adaptation of French words to the phonological and morphological molds of the *Dictionnaire*'s LF, to be examined in Section 4.4.

A few additional vocalic processes may be discerned in the *Dictionnaire*'s spelling of LF. One of them is occasional lowering of mid vowels (see 20a). In (20b), we observe raising of the low vowel.

(20)	a.	sartan	'frying pan'	(< Sp. sartén)
		tartouga	'turtle'	(< Sp. tortuga)
		sackadgio	'plunder'	(< It. saccheggio)
	b.	encora	'again'	(< It. ancora)

Mid vowel lowering is reported in Romance loanwords in North African colloquial Arabics, as seen below in (21a) (from Sayahi 2011: 93) and (21b) (from Cifoletti 1975: 147). Nevertheless, such cognates of the affected LF words as It. *tartaruga*, Fr. *saccage*, and Cat. *encara* also raise the possibility that the forms in question are inter-Romance hybrids. The form *reflétir* 'to reflect' (< It. *riflettere*), given earlier as an example of high vowel lowering, may also betray influence from Fr. *refléchir*.

(21)	a.	Spanish	Northern Moroccan Arabic	
		chocar	[tʃakar]	'collide'
	b.	Italian	Cairene Arabic	
		veranda	[varanda]	'veranda'
		vetrina	[batri:na]	'shop window'

Another vocalic process is loss, addition, or variable realization of the prosthetic vowel in word-initial [s] plus consonant sequences (see 22 below and Cifoletti 2004: 38–39). Related variation is seen in *spétar* ~ *aspétar* 'to wait' (< It. *aspettare*).

(22)	scopéta	'rifle, gun'	(< Sp. escopeta)
	scriban	'secretary'	(< Sp. escribano)
	escambio	'exchange (n.)'	(< It. scambio)
	escambiar	'exchange (v.)'	(< It. scambiare)
	star ~ estar	'to be'	(< It. stare, Sp. estar)
	scaldar ~ escaldar	'heat'	(< It. scaldare, Sp. escaldar)
	scala ~ escala	'stairs, ladder, quay'	(< It. scala, Sp. escala)

The loss of the prosthetic vowel is reported, e.g., by Sayahi (2005: 260; 2011: 95) for Spanish borrowings in Northern Moroccan Arabic (see 23).

(23)

Spanish	Northern Moroccan Arabic	
espía	[spia]	'spy'
estufa	[stufa]	'stove'

Additionally, Sayahi (2005: 260; 2011: 96) reports the loss of initial vowel-consonant sequences in polysyllabic borrowings from Spanish, cf.:

(24)

Spanish	Northern Moroccan Arabic	
enfermero	[frmiro]	'nurse'
ambulancia	[bolansia]	'ambulance'
instalación	[stalasion]	'installation'
entrenador	[trenador]	'trainer'

The process illustrated in (24) resonates with the process seen in (25) (see Cifoletti 2004: 39–41 for a discussion of this pattern).

(25) bassar 'to lower' (< It. abbassare)
bastantza 'enough' (< It. abbastanza)

4.3 The Consonants

4.3.1 Spelling

The *Dictionnaire*'s orthography of LF reveals the consonant inventory shown in Table 4.2. The orthographic representation of each consonant may be seen in Table 4.3.

Table 4.3 requires few comments.

Stops. The digraphs <th> for [t], <ch> for [k], and <gu> for [g] appear to be found in one word each; <qu> spells [k] before a nonfront vowel only in *bouriqua* 'donkey' (< Sp. *borrica*). There appear to be only two examples of <ck>; in both, <ck> corresponds to a geminate in the source language (*ockio* 'eye' < It. *occhio*, *sackadgio* 'plunder' < It. *saccheggio*).

Affricates. The digraph <ti> in *impatientza* 'impatience' is analyzable as an affricate ([ts]) in light of the spelling of what is presumably the same consonant in *patzientza* 'patience': it is more likely that <ti> and <tz> spell the same sound in these related words than that they spell different sounds. The same conclusion regarding the surface value of <ti> is suggested by the variable spelling of the suffix in *fortification* ~ *fortificatzion* 'fortification; entrenchment.' The spelling variant with <ti> is also found in such words as *attention*, *condanation*, *condition*, *dispération*, *protection*, *sitouation*, *sommation*, *sostraction*, *spédition*, and *sujetion*; while the variant with <tz> is used, e.g., in

Table 4.2. *Lingua Franca consonants*

p	*t*		*k*
b	*d*		*g*
	ts	*tʃ*	
		dʒ	
f	*s*	*ʃ*	
v	*z*		
m	*n*	*ɲ*	
	l	*ʎ*	
	r		
w		*j*	

obligatzion, *occoupatzion*, *pounitzion*, *précautzion*, *resolutzion*, *revolutzion*, *sédouctzion*, *significatzion*, *souplicatzion*, *spéculatzion*, *spoliatzion*, and *supositzion*. It appears more likely that the suffix is pronounced the same in all these words than that it is meant to be pronounced with [s] when spelled with a <ti> and [ts] when spelled with a <tz>. The nonuniformity of the transcription may be due to the use of different spelling variants by different compilers.

The use of <sch> and <schi> for what is a [tʃ] in the source words is rare. Cifoletti (1989: 42) considers this use in conjunction with the occasional use of <ch> for [ʃ], as in *pechi* 'fish' (< It. *pesce/i*), attributing both to underdifferentiation between [tʃ] and [ʃ] on the part of the compilers. The more frequent ways of spelling [dʒ] are by means of <dg>, <gi>, or <g> (before front vowels); <dji> appears to be confined to one word.

Fricatives. The more usual way of spelling [s] is by means of <ss> intervocalically and <s> elsewhere; [c] and [ç] are used rarely. The usual way of spelling [ʃ] is by means of <sch> or <schi>; <sc> is used rarely, while <ch> spells [ʃ] almost exclusively in words of non-Romance origin, such as *yoldach* 'janissary,' *bacha* 'pasha,' *bakchich* 'gift,' *chetan* 'Satan, devil,' *cherub* 'drink' (also spelled *scherrub*), and *trucheman* 'interpreter.' Cifoletti (1989: 42) attributes the use of <ch> for [ʃ] in Romance words like *pechi* 'fish' to underdifferentiation between [tʃ] and [ʃ] on the part of the compilers. This analysis suggests that <ch> is employed for [ʃ] only in words of non-Romance ("Oriental") provenance.

<tz> is occasionally found where the source word has an intervocalic [s], and <dz> is always found where the source word has an intervocalic [z].

Table 4.3. *Orthographic representation of Lingua Franca consonants*

p	**<p>**			
	poco 'little'	prouna 'plum'	sempré 'always'	colpo 'blow'
b	**<b>**			
	béné 'well'	bruto 'ugly'	ombra 'shade'	albéro 'tree'
t	**<t>, <th>**			
	tout 'mulberry'	gato 'cat'	montar 'go up'	thé 'tea'
d	**<d>**			
	dolche 'sweet'	nada 'nothing'	andar 'go'	dey 'dey'
k	**<c>, <q>, <k>, <ch>, <qu>, <ck>**			
	cané 'dog'	qouazi 'almost'	aki 'here'	che ~ qué 'that; what'
	ockio 'eye'			
g	**<g>, <gu>**			
	gato 'cat'	gréco 'Greek'	fouogo 'fire'	portuguès 'Portuguese'
ts	**<z>, <tz>, <ti>**			
	zoukaro 'sugar'	*patzientza 'patience'*	impatientza 'impatience'	
tʃ	**<ch>, <chi>, <c>, <ci>, <sch>, <schi>**			
	chita 'town'	lanchia 'boat'	cento 'hundred'	bilancia 'scales'
	caschador 'hunter'	caschia 'hunt'		
dʒ	**<dg>, <gi>, <g>, <ji>, <j>, <dji>, <dgi>**			
	dgélosia 'shutter'	mangiar 'eat'	genti 'man'	jiovédi 'Thursday'
	justo 'just'	sedjiorno 'stay'	dgioco 'game'	
f	**<f>**			
	figa 'fig'	garofan 'clove'		
v	**<v>**			
	vita 'life'	trovar 'find'		
s	**<s>, <ss>, <c>, <ç>, <tz>**			
	séco 'dry'	cabessa 'head'	cédar 'give up'	Françis 'French'
	estetzo 'same'			

Table 4.3. *(cont.)*

z	**<z>, <s>, <dz>**			
	mézé 'month'	rosa 'rose'	nadzo 'nose'	
ʃ	**<sc>, <ch>, <sch>, <schi>**			
	scélérato 'villain'	pechi 'fish'	conoschir 'know'	conoschiuto 'known'
n	**<n>**			
	nada 'nothing'	sentza 'without'	limoun 'lemon'	
m	**<m>**			
	millé 'thousand'	nemsa 'Austrian'	harem 'harem'	
ɲ	**<gn>, <gni>, <ni>**[a]			
	pignata 'pot'	bisognio 'need'	vergonia 'shame'	
r	**<r>**			
	ratoun 'rat'	avaro 'stingy'	ridir 'laugh'	
l	**<l>**			
	limoun 'lemon'	malato 'sick'	maboul 'crazy'	
ʎ	**<ill>, <gli>, <li>**			
	agouilla 'needle'	figlio 'son, boy'	folia 'leaf'	
j[b]	**<i>, <ï>, <y>**			
	iéri 'yesterday'	noïa 'worry'	yoldach 'janissary'	
w	**<ou>, <u>**			
	qouatro ~ quatro 'four'			

[a] The spelling of *mensongua* 'lie' (< It. *menzogna*) may be a typo for the intended *mensogna* or *mensongna*; cf. also *sponga* 'sponge' (< It. *spugna*) (see Baglioni 2010: 48 on the use of <ngn> for <gn>).

[b] The phonological status of the glides is ignored here.

Cifoletti (1989: 43–44; 2004: 36–37, 85n4) assumes that <tz> and <dz> always spell dental affricates, concluding that the former is used "spesso a sproposito" [often erroneously] and the latter "sempre dove non ce l'attenderemmo" [always where we wouldn't expect it] (2004: 37), and ascribing the resulting errors to the compilers' nonnative command of Italian and/or incorrectly assumed inter-Romance sound correspondences. For example, the <tz> in *scométza* 'bet' (< It. *scommessa*) is attributed to hypercorrection due to underdifferentiation between [ts] and [s], and the <tz> in words like *patzion* to the incorrectly assumed sound correspondence between French [s] and Italian ~ LF [ts] (Cifoletti 1989: 44). While this analysis is plausible, the fact that <dz> is used for [z] consistently also makes it possible that this digraph is being used in an innovative way. The same analysis may be applicable to <tz>, particularly in view of the spelling variants *estesso ~ estetzo* (< It. *stesso* 'same') and the use of <tz> for what is likely a [s] in *plàtza* 'square' (< Sp. *plaza*, Fr. *place*) and *platzar* 'place' (< Fr. *placer*) (though the possibility that these are inter-Romance hybrids cannot be excluded, cf. It. *piazza*, *piazzare*). As in the case of the <tz> ~ <ti> variants, this nonuniformity may be due to the use of different spelling conventions by different compilers.

Palatal nasal and liquid. It is unclear whether the spellings <ni> and <li> represent sequences of sounds or the palatal /ɲ/ and /ʎ/, respectively. The variants in (26) lend themselves to different interpretations, as variant spellings for /ɲ/ and /ʎ/ or sequences /ni/ and /li/, or as indicative of actual variation.

(26)	figlio ~ filio	'son, boy'	(< It. figlio)
	vergognia ~ vergonia	'shame, affront'	(< It. vergogna)

Glides. <ï> is used for the palatal glide after a vowel, though this use is more consistent when there is a vowel on either side of the glide. <y> is confined to words of non-Romance ("Oriental") origin: *dey* 'dey,' *yoldach* 'janissary,' *yatagan* 'dagger' (< Tu. *dayı* '(maternal) uncle,' *yoldaş* 'travelling companion; comrade,' *yatağan* 'yataghan'). The more usual way of spelling [w] is by means of a <ou>.

A number of the words display different spellings for what is presumably the same consonant; selected examples are shown in (27). The presence of variant spellings is instrumental for establishing the surface value of some of the nonobvious orthographic solutions, such as the use of <tz> for [s] (in addition to its far more frequent use for [ts]).

(27)	fazir ~ fasir	'to do'	(< Sp. Ptg. fazer)
	mezo ~ metzo	'half, means, medium'	(< It. mezzo)
	estesso ~ estetzo	'same'	(< It. stesso)
	perké ~ perqué	'why, because'	(< It. perché)
	bouco ~ bouko	'opening'	(< It. buco)

dgiousto ~ jiousto ~ justo[4]	'just'	(< It. giusto)
fortification ~ fortificatzion	'fortification' 'entrenchment'	(< It. fortificazione)

In certain cases, the variant spellings may stand for different pronunciations. The <ni> ~ <gni> and <li> ~ <gli> variants have been discussed earlier; additional examples are given in (28). It is possible that the variants in (28a) may reflect etymological doublets deriving from different source languages, while the variants in (28b) – unless <ch> stands for [k] or represents an attempt to spell Spanish [x] or [χ] – may evidence either different input dialects or different periods of entry for the same word (Cifoletti 2004: 71; see Section 4.6).

(28) a. forsa 'effort' ~ fortza 'force' (< Ptg. força, Fr. force, It. forza)
b. moukera ~ mouchéra 'woman' (< Sp. mujer)

Another area of variation is the spelling of geminates in words of Italian origin (see 29). As noted by Cifoletti (e.g., 2004: 83–84), the notation of geminates in the *Dictionnaire* is inconsistent. This spelling variation may be interpreted as reflecting variation in actual speech, especially given the probability of multiple sources for some of the words and/or nonnative knowledge of Italian on the part of the informant and/or compiler(s), as suggested by Cifoletti.

(29)			
a.	capello	'hat'	(< It. cappello)
	obédientza	'obedience'	(< It. obbedientza)
	cativo	'bad'	(< It. cattivo)
	orékia	'ear'	(< It. orecchia)
	frédo	'cold'	(< It. freddo)
	avichinar	'approach, advance'	(< It. avvicinare)
	canoné	'cannon'	(< It. cannone)
	balar	'dance'	(< It. ballare)
	toré	'tower'	(< It. Sp. torre)
b.	apparir	'seem'	(< It. apparire)
	occupar	'occupy'	(< It. occupare)
	offérir	'offer'	(< It. offrire)
	ogietto	'object'	(< It. oggetto)
	colonna	'column'	(< It. colonna)
	bollir	'boil'	(< It. bollire)
	terra	'earth, soil, ground'	(< It. terra)
c.	tropo ~ troppo	'too'	(< It. troppo)
	laté ~ latte	'milk'	(< It. latte)
	noté ~ notte	'night'	(< It. notte)

[4] Cifoletti (1989: 42–43) hypothesizes that there may have existed variation between [dʒ] and [ʒ], with the affricate realization being the default one.

touto ~ toutto	'all'	(< It. tutto)
tocar ~ toccar	'hit, touch'	(< Sp. tocar, It. toccare)
metir ~ mettir	'put'	(< Sp. meter, It. mettere)

Some of the geminate spellings appear to be a carryover from the French orthography:

(30)	commé	'as, how'	(< Fr. comme, It. come)
	comminchiar	'to begin'	(< Fr. commencer, It. cominciare)
	raccommodar	'to repair'	(< Fr. raccommoder, It. raccomodare)
	tassa	'cup'	(< Fr. tasse, Sp. taza)
	terrassa	'roof'	(< Fr. terrasse, Sp. terraza)

Finally, some of the spelling variants, such as *yoldah* for *yoldach*, clearly represent typographical errors (see pertinent remarks in Cifoletti 2004: 83).

4.3.2 Consonantal Processes

One consonantal phonological process reflected in the *Dictionnaire* is replacement of [p] with [b], e.g.:

(31)	nabolitan	'Napolitano'	(< It. napolitano)
	esbagniol	'Spaniard'	(< Sp. español)
	esbinac	'spinach'	(< Cat. espinac)
	osbidal	'hospital'	(< Sp. hospital, It. ospedale)
	balla di canone	'cannonball'	(< It. palla di canone)[5]

This replacement has been attributed to the Arabic substrate or adstrate influence in LF, especially in light of SLA data (cf. Vedovelli 1989) and similar processes in loanwords from Romance languages in North African Arabic (Spiro 1937; Cifoletti 1975: 147; Heath 1989: 260–263; Ahmed 2009: 102):

(32)	[biljatʃu] (Cairene Arabic)	(< It. pagliaccio 'clown')
	[blaṣa] (Algerian Arabic)	(< Fr. place 'square')
	[birsi] (Moroccan Arabic)	(< Fr. épicerie 'grocery store')
	[bṣṣita] (Moroccan Arabic)	(< Sp. peseta 'peseta')

Cifoletti (2004: 36) notes that relatively few instances of this phenomenon are recorded in the *Dictionnaire*, which may be attributed to the long-term contact of North African Arabic with various European languages, making this sound available via loanwords. Sayahi (2011: 94) reports cases of hypercorrection in Northern Moroccan Arabic in which the [b] in the Spanish

[5] LF *balla* may also reflect Sp. *bala* and/or Fr. *balle* (Sp. *bala de cañón*, Fr. *balle de canon* 'cannonball').

loan is replaced with [p], as in [patido] for Sp. *batido* 'milk shake.' The *Dictionnaire* displays an instance of this kind in *piskéri* 'porter' (< Ar. *biskri*, from the city name Biskra).[6]

The existence of some phonological processes may be inferred from variant spellings. The <ni> and <li> spellings for what is a palatal nasal (resp. lateral) in the source word may indicate actual unpacking of these segments in LF, at least in some of its lects. Thus, Sayahi (2011: 94) reports decomposition of Spanish [ɲ] into the [nʲɟ] sequence in Spanish loanwords in Northern Moroccan Arabic, while the transcriptions in Cifoletti (1975: 141, 144, 146–147) point to unpacking of Italian [ɲ] and [ʎ] in Cairene Arabic (see 33).

(33) a. Northern Moroccan Arabic

[banʲɟador]	(< Sp. bañador 'bather')
[punʲɟos]	(< Sp. puños 'fists')

b. Cairene Arabic

[banjo]	(< It. bagno 'bath')
[bunja]	(< It. pugno 'fist')
[biljatʃu]	(< It. pagliaccio 'clown')
[midilja]	(< It. medaglia 'medal')

In some words, the palatal lateral is apparently lost or replaced with [j] (cf. Cifoletti 2004: 37 and the examples in 34).

(34)

meïo ~ mélio	'better'	(< It. meglio)
païa	'straw'	(< It. paglia)
boutïa	'bottle'	(< It. bottiglia)[7]
tria	'mullet'	(< It. triglia)
cavia	'ankle'	(< It. caviglia)
famia	'family'	(< It. famiglia)

The glided realization of [ʎ] in *paglia* 'straw' has produced the minimal pair in (35).

(35)

païo	'pair'	(< It. paio)
païa	'straw'	(< It. paglia)

[6] In Algiers "[s]ome immigrant groups . . . specialised in niche occupations which they dominated (without having a legally recognised monopoly): Jijelis were bakers, Mzabis bath-house managers, Biskris porters and couriers" (McDougall 2017: 36); see also Piesse (1862: cxiv), Venture de Paradis (1898: 14).

[7] Other possible sources of *boutïa* and *famia* are Sp. *botella* and *familia*, given the loss of [ʎ] (including one resulting from earlier [lj]) in certain environments in dialectal and Judeo-Spanish, as in *bolsillo* > *bolsío* 'pocket,' *familia* > *famía* 'family' (Penny 2000: 180, 188).

4.4 The Gallicisms

The *Dictionnaire*'s LF vocabulary contains a substantial number of French words; Cornelissen (1992: 221) estimates that about 4 percent of the total number of LF words reported in it derive from that source. The French words are not inserted into LF as unassimilated items but, rather, are adapted to its Hispano-Italian phonological and morphological patterns (see Chapter 5). The relevant adaptation strategies ("conversion routines"; Heath 1989: 4) provide additional information about LF's phonological and morphological patterns.

The basis for some of the conversion routines is clearly phonological. For example, adaptation of French [y] as [u] or [i] is attributable to the probable absence in LF of the front rounded vowel:

(36)	amousar	'to amuse'	(< Fr. amuser)
	rifousar	'to refuse'	(< Fr. refuser)
	soupliar	'to beg'	(< Fr. supplier)
	riban	'ribbon'	(< Fr. ruban)

There is no orthographic evidence for the presence in LF of nasal vowels; the examples in (37) show French [õ] being unpacked to [un], spelled <oun>. Heath (1989: 82) notes a similar adaptation strategy in Moroccan Arabic, as seen in the loanwords [bun] 'coupon' and [br̥misjun] 'military leave' (< Fr. *bon*, *permission*); see Cohen (1912: 448) regarding Fr. *bidon* 'can' in Algerian Arabic.

(37)	pigioun	'pigeon'	(< Fr. pigeon)
	trahisoun	'betrayal'	(< Fr. trahison)

Other adaptation patterns can simultaneously have a phonological and a morphological basis. One consists in furnishing consonant-final nouns and adjectives with a final *-o* or *-a* (see 38). At the morphological level, this adaptation strategy points to preference for overt gender marking in LF nominals. At the phonological level, it points to preference for ending words from these parts of speech in vowels.

(38)	verro	'glass'	(< Fr. verre)
	savento	'learned'	(< Fr. savant)
	caserna	'barracks'	(< Fr. caserne)
	biéra	'beer'	(< Fr. bière)

The above "LF-ization" of French words is parallel to, and may have been facilitated by, adaptation of French loans in North African Arabic to match the shape of Spanish and/or Italian loanwords, which have had a longer history in the respective varieties. Thus, Lévy (1997: 177) notes that Fr. *machine* and *bière* (and/or Eng. *beer*) become *machina* and *birra*, respectively, in Moroccan Arabic; while Nissabouri (1997: 188–189) discusses a similar adaptation strategy for Fr. *place*, *cuisine*, *ferme*, *poste*, and *valise*, which become [ḅḷaṣa], [kuzina], [firma], [boṣṭa], and [bæliza], respectively. Examples from Algerian Arabic include [bu:sta], [blaṣa], [ri:gla], [pi:ppa], [vi:sta], and [valiza] for Fr. *poste*, *place*, *règle*, *pipe*, *veste*, and *valise* (Ahmed 2009: 102–103). Both in LF and in Arabic, subjecting the French loans to such adaptation routines makes it impossible to identify the specific input language for many of the Romance-origin words. For example, Cifoletti (1975: 144) notes that the presence in Cairene Arabic of such borrowings as [budra] and [lamba] (< Fr. *poudre*, *lampe*) makes the provenance of such loans as [bubi:na] (Fr. *bobine*, It. *bobina*) and [binsa] (Fr. *pince*, It. *pinza*) unclear; Heath (1989: 131–133) discusses this issue in connection with Romance loans in Moroccan Arabic.

Some of the other patterns of “LF-ization” of French words, noted by previous researchers, reveal the compilers’ familiarity with some of the more salient phonological and morphological correspondences between French and Italian / LF. These include the patterns seen in (39) (Cifoletti 1980: 17–21; 2004: 47–49; Baglioni 2017: 195–196).

(39)		French	Lingua Franca	
	a.	*re-*	*ri-*	
		refuser	rifousar	‘to refuse’
		rebuter	riboutar	‘to reject’
	b.	*en-, -ê-*	*in-, -es-*	
		entêté	intestato	‘stubborn’
		entendu	intenduto	‘heard’

Unlike Romance words, consonant-final words of Arabic provenance do not acquire a final vowel in LF (this observation does not apply to verbs, as there are no non-Romance verbs in the *Dictionnaire*’s LF; cf. Cifoletti 1980: 26; 2004: 37–38). This fact ties in with the special orthographic treatment of non-Romance words discussed in Section 4.3.1, and serves as another indication that, at some levels, words from Romance and non-Romance (“Oriental”) sources were kept distinct in LF.

The last pattern to be discussed consists of replacing the French infinitive ending *-er* with *-ar* or (more rarely) *-ir*, and the French past participle ending *-e* with *-ato*, *-ito*, or *-uto* (*-outo*) (illustrated in 40). This adaptation pattern has a phonological effect in that it helps to achieve uniformity in the endings of LF imperfective (*-ar*, *-ir*) and perfective (*-ato*, *-ito*, *-uto*) verb forms, making LF verbs distinguishable from other parts of speech.

(40)	avalar, avalato	‘to swallow’	(< Fr. avaler, avalé)
	cédar, cédouto	‘to give up’	(< Fr. céder, cédé)
	composir, composito	‘to arrange’	(< Fr. composer, composé)

Bakker (2003) and Parkvall and Bakker (2013) make the interesting observation that formal marking of word classes is a recurrent feature of pidgins aligning them with some artificial languages and distinguishing them from other natural languages. The marking is achieved by adding a certain morpheme to each member of the respective word class, "even though they are never applied completely consistently" (Bakker 2003: 13). In the illustrative examples assembled by Bakker (2003: 14), the word classes so distinguished include verbs, nouns, and adjectives, with two of the languages treating their nouns and adjectives as a single class. The situation seen in LF appears to confirm this insight, with words from the noun and adjective classes tending to end in *-o*/*-a* and verbs consistently ending in *-ar*/*-ir* in the imperfective and *-ato*/*-ito*/*-uto* in the perfective form. A comparison of the treatment of similarly shaped Spanish nouns and verbs ending in *-er* provides further illustration of the reality of this part-of-speech distinction (see 41).

(41)	a. poder	'power'	(< Sp. poder)
	mouchéra ~ moukera	'woman'	(< Sp. mujer)
	b. poudir	'to be able'	(< Sp. poder)
	quérir	'to ask, want'	(< Sp. querer)

4.5 The Orthography

4.5.1 Orthographic Contributions

The *Dictionnaire*'s orthographic representation of LF sounds is summarized in Table 4.4. As discussed below, these orthographic devices derive inspiration from several existing orthographies while also displaying several original solutions (see also Section 3.5).

The heaviest contributing orthographies are French and Italian. The contributions traceable to the orthographic conventions of these languages, some of which necessarily overlap and/or are shared by other languages, are summarized in Tables 4.5 and 4.6. Some of the spellings are restricted to specific environments, or are only found in one or a few words.

A few of the solutions are traceable to English and/or German orthographies; these are summarized in Table 4.7. The use of <ch> for [tʃ] may derive from the Spanish orthography as well.

Table 4.8 summarizes what appear to be the *Dictionnaire*'s orthographic innovations. Most of these consist of adding <i> to an existing grapheme or multigraph to indicate or reinforce palatalization; these include <ji>, <ni>, <li>, <chi>, <gni>, <dgi>, and <schi>. The use of <dji> for [dʒ] is a novel recombination of <dg>, <g>, and <ji>, all of which are also used for

Table 4.4. *Orthographic representation of Lingua Franca sounds*

a	<a>, <à>	*k*	<c>, <q>, <k>, <ch>, <qu>, <ck>	*ʃ*	<sc>, <ch>, <sch>, <schi>
e	<e>, <é>	*g*	<g>, <gu>	*n*	<n>
i	<i>, <ï>	*ts*	<z>, <tz>, <ti>	*m*	<m>
o	<o>	*tʃ*	<ch>, <chi>, <c>, <ci>, <sch>, <schi>	*ɲ*	<gn>, <gni>, <ni>
u	<ou>, <u>, <ù>	*dʒ*	<dg>, <gi>, <g>, <ji>, <j>, <dji>	*r*	<r>
p	<p>	*f*	<f>	*l*	<l>
b	<b>	*v*	<v>	*ʎ*	<ill>, <gli>, <li>
t	<t>, <th>	*s*	<s>, <ss>, <c>, <ç>, <tz>	*j*	<i>, <ï>, <y>
d	<d>	*z*	<z>, <s>, <dz>	*w*	<ou>, <u>

spelling this affricate. The only truly novel solutions consist of using <tz> and <dz> for intervocalic [s] and [z], respectively.

The above orthographic conventions are also used in the transliteration of Arabic; as stated in the *Dictionnaire*'s preface, the Arabic words were given "l'orthographe de la prononciation" [the orthography of the pronunciation]. Thus, we find <ou> used for both [w] and [u] (*kaoué / boun* 'coffee'), <ï> used for both [j] and [i] (*el ïoum* 'today,' *halïb* 'milk,' *leïl* 'night,' *aïnïn* 'eyes'), both <ch> and <sch> used for [ʃ] (*cheumz* 'sun,' *mechmech* 'apricot,' *schïtan* 'devil'), and <dg>, <g>, <gi> all used for [dʒ] (*dgemél* 'camel,' *radgel* 'man,' *caouagi* 'coffee-house keeper,' *fingian* 'cup'). Some of the words which are present in both the LF and Arabic vocabularies are spelled in similar or identical ways (illustrated in 42).[8]

[8] Larzul (2010: 91) notes, citing Bresnier (1855: 618), that a distinctive characteristic of the Jewish Arabic dialect of Algiers was pronunciation of the feminine final *-a* as *-é*. The relevant passage from Bresnier (1855) reads as follows: "[L]es Juifs d'Alger, plus particulièrement que ceux des autres localités, changent en *èh* toutes les finales *a* du féminin, qu'ils prolongent d'un manière affectée" [the Jews of Algiers, more so than those of other communities, change into *e* all the feminine final *a*'s, which they prolong in an affected manner]. A number of nouns in the *Dictionnaire*'s Arabic vocabulary appear to reflect this feature (e.g., *sené* 'year,' *kaoué* 'coffee,' *loubié* 'bean,' *zouroudié* 'carrots'), which appears to indicate that more than one informant took part in its compilation.

Table 4.5. *French orthographic contributions*

Grapheme or multigraph	Sound	Example
<ou>	[u]	gousto 'taste'
	[w]	agoua 'water'
<ï>	[i]	païsé 'country'
	[j]	meïo 'better'
<é>	[e]	mézé 'month'
<qu>	[k]	qui 'who'
<gu>	[g]	portuguès 'Portuguese'
<th>	[t]	thé 'tea'
<ch>	[ʃ]	bakchich 'gift'
<ss>	[s]	tassa 'cup'
<c>	[s]	cédar 'give up'
	[k]	esbinac 'spinach'
<ç>	[s]	Françis 'French'
<s>	[z]	rosa 'rose'
<z>	[z]	izola 'island'
<ill>	[ʎ]	agouilla 'needle'
<gn>	[ɲ]	pignata 'pot'

(42)

Lingua Franca	Arabic	
pistola	pistola	'pistol'
yatagan	yatagan	'saber'
mantéga	mantéga	'butter'
festouk	festouk	'pistachio'
esbinac	sbinak	'spinach'
salata	el salata	'lettuce'
taoula	el taoula	'table'
roubié	el roubié	'spring'
seubt	el seubt	'Saturday'
eskima ~ esquima	el skima	'bridle'

4.5.2 Orthographic Tendencies

The *Dictionnaire*'s practical orthography is dominated by two partially contradictory tendencies. The first is preference for a phonetic spelling of LF

Table 4.6. *Italian orthographic contributions*

Grapheme or multigraph	Sound	Example
<i>	[j]	iéri 'yesterday'
<u>	[u]	umbré 'man'
	[w]	quatro 'four'
grave accent	(stress)	chità 'town,' dgioventù 'youth'
<ch>	[k]	che 'that, what'
<z>	[ts]	zoukaro 'sugar'
<c>	[tʃ]	cento 'hundred'
<ci>	[tʃ]	bilancia 'scales'
<g>	[dʒ]	genti 'man, people'
<gi>	[dʒ]	mangiar 'eat'
<sc>	[ʃ]	scélérato 'villain'
<s>	[z]	rosa 'rose'
<gli>	[ʎ]	figlio 'son, boy'
<gn>	[ɲ]	pignata 'pot'

Table 4.7. *English and/or German orthographic contributions*

Grapheme or multigraph	Sound	Example
<j>	[dʒ]	justo 'just'
<dg>	[dʒ]	dgiléko 'waistcoat'
<sch>	[ʃ]	conoschir 'know'
<tz>	[ts]	patzientza 'patience'
<ti>	[ts]	impatientza 'impatience'
<k>	[k]	aki 'here'
<ck>	[k] or [kk]	ockio 'eye'

words over their etymological spelling. This aspect of the orthography may be appreciated by comparing the spelling of selected LF words with their spelling in the source languages (see 43a). Etymological spellings appear occasionally as well (see 43b). Interestingly, the variant <hablar> in (43b) is only used

Table 4.8. *Orthographic innovations in Anonymous (1830a)*

Grapheme or multigraph	Sound	Example
<chi>	[tʃ]	lanchia 'boat'
<schi>	[ʃ]	conoschiuto 'known'
<ji>	[dʒ]	jiovédi 'Thursday'
<gni>	[ɲ]	pagnio 'sheet'
<ni>	[ɲ]	vergonia 'shame'
<li>	[ʎ]	folia 'leaf'
<dji>	[dʒ]	sedjiorno 'stay'
<dgi>	[dʒ]	dgiorno 'day'
<tz>	[s]	estetzo 'same'
<dz>	[z]	nadzo 'nose'

twice, both times in the last dialogue, whereas <ablar> appears thirteen times (Cifoletti 1989: 90).

(43) a. dginokio 'knee' (< It. ginocchio)
kiavé 'key' (< It. chiave)
riquiesta 'search' (< It. richiesta)
chità ~ chita 'city' (< It. città)
fachia 'face' (< It. faccia)
mézé 'month' (< It. mese)
nadzo 'nose' (< It. naso)
scometza 'bet' (< It. scommessa)
pagnio 'sheet' (< Sp. paño)
basio 'empty' (< Sp. vacío)
aki 'here' (< Sp. aquí, Ptg. aqui)
agoua 'water' (< Sp. agua, Ptg. água)
cabessa 'head' (< Sp. cabeza, Ptg. cabeça)
agouilla 'needle' (< Cat. agulla, Ptg. agulha)

b. ablar ~ hablar 'to speak' (< Sp. hablar)
habilé 'skillful' (< Fr. habile, It. abile)
qué ~ che 'what; that' (< Sp. que, qué, It. che)

The concern over accurate phonetic representation of LF is explicitly articulated in the *Dictionnaire*'s preface:

C'est surtout le petit mauresque que se parle dans les villes maritimes de l'état d'Alger, que nous avons dû recueillir dans ce Dictionnaire, et nous nous sommes attachés à donner aux mots l'orthographe quì se rapproche le plus de la prononciation en usage dans ce pays. (Anonymous 1830a: n.p.)

[It is primarily the Petit Mauresque spoken in the coastal cities of the state of Algiers that we had to assemble in this Dictionary, and we have endeavored to give the words a spelling that comes closest to the pronunciation used in this region.]

The second tendency of the orthography is for the convenience of French-language users. The spelling of words beginning with a [k], illustrated in (44), is a case in point. The examples in (44a) show that in contexts which would be unambiguous for readers familiar with the French orthography, before back vowels and [r], word-initial [k] is spelled with a <c>. Before [w], the velar stop is spelled with a <q>,[9] whereas the glide itself is spelled with a <ou> rather than <u> (see 44b). The fact that this choice is deliberate is shown by the spelling variants such as *qouello* ~ *quello* 'that' and *qouando* ~ *quando* 'when,' in which the phonetic spelling <qou> alternates with the etymological spelling <qu>. Before front vowels and the palatal glide, [k] is spelled with <qu> or <k>: these spellings avoid the potential ambiguity that keeping the Italian digraph <ch> in such words would have had for the French-language user (shown in 44c). The fact that this spelling choice is deliberate is shown by the variant spelling <che> for <qué> 'what, that.'

(44)

a. [k] spelled with <c>

capello	'hat'	(< It. cappello)
conoschir	'to know'	(< It. conoscere)
coura	'to care'	(< It. cura)
crédir	'to believe'	(< It. credere)

b. [k] spelled with <q>

qouazi	'almost'	(< It. quasi)
qoualita	'quality'	(< It. qualità)
qouindichi	'fifteen'	(< It. quindici)

c. [k] spelled with <qu> or <k>

quiodo	'nail'	(< It. chiodo)
kiavé	'key'	(< It. chiave)
kiamar	'to call'	(< It. chiamare)

Another spelling convention favoring the French-language user is the employment of single <s> and double <ss> to distinguish between intervocalic [z] and [s]. That <ss> can be used for spelling a single rather than geminate [s] is indicated by the fact that the source words in (45) below contain a single [s].

(45)

cabessa	'head'	(< Sp. cabeza, Ptg. cabeça)
terrassa	'roof'	(< Sp. terraza, Fr. terrasse)
tassa	'cup'	(< Sp. taza, Fr. tasse)

[9] Except <couoré> 'heart' (< It. *cuore*).

Finally, <y> is only used for [j], and <ch> (with very few exceptions) for [ʃ], in words of non-Romance, "Oriental" origin. In Romance-origin words, <ch> normally spells [tʃ] while the palatal glide is spelled with a <i> or <ï> (see 46). It is likely that there was no ambiguity in the use of the digraph because of the French readers' familiarity with these "Orientalisms" (cf. the spellings *bakchich*, *truchement*, *yataghan*, *bey*, *dey* in Devic 1876). An additional reason for giving these words an unusual orthographic representation may have been to emphasize their foreignness, to better convey the local color of the North-African setting of LF.

(46) a. Spelling of [j]

Romance words		*Oriental words*	
iéri	'yesterday'	yoldach	'janissary'
païo	'pair'	dey	'dey'

b. Phonetic values of <ch>

Romance words		*Oriental words*	
chita	'city'	chetan	'Satan, devil'
paché	'peace'	bacha	'pasha'

4.6 Chapter Summary

The sound inventory of LF, as revealed through the spelling practices of the *Dictionnaire*, combines an Italian-type consonant system with the five-vowel system found in Spanish and certain contact varieties of Italian (Hull 1985: 247; Cifoletti 1989: 39). This result is in harmony with the view of LF as a Hispano-Italian koine, articulated by Arends (2005) (see Chapter 9) and described by Aslanov (2014: 132) as an "attempt to find a lowest common denominator for Italo-Romance and Ibero-Romance languages." The *Dictionnaire* provides no orthographic evidence for consonant or vowel sounds that are not found in either Italo- or Hispano-Romance; word-final pharyngeals in words of Arabic origin, such as *taba* 'seal' (< Ar. [ṭa:baʕ]), do not survive in LF (Russo 2001: 242; Cifoletti 2004: 38). The absence of non-Romance sounds in LF further supports the key role played in its genesis by inter-Romance koineization (cf. congruent remarks in Castellanos 2007 and Aslanov 2014).

As regards the consonant system, the koineization hypothesis is supported by the absence in LF of the Spanish velar (or uvular) fricative, rendered with a [k] in *moukera* 'woman' (< Sp. *mujer*). The presence of [dʒ], [ts], and [z], which are absent in modern Spanish, may be connected with the existence of one or more of these sibilants in other Romance lexifiers of LF, such as Catalan and Portuguese, and the Spanish of Moriscos (Iberian Muslims) and Sephardic

Jews (cf. Penny 2000: 181–182). The last two groups formed immigrant communities in North Africa, particularly after their expulsion from Spain, between the fifteenth and seventeenth centuries, conserving for generations thereafter their use of Ibero-Romance vernaculars. According to Whinnom's (1977a, 1977b) estimate, based on Haedo (1612) and cited in Cifoletti (1989: 17–18) and Epalza and Slama-Gafsi (2010: 86–87), the population of Algiers around 1580 included about 10 percent Moriscos and 8 percent Jews (see also Cresti 2005: 468ff.). The phonological impact of premodern or conservative varieties of Spanish on the *Dictionnaire*'s LF is evidenced by such items as *mouchéra*, a variant of *moukera* 'woman': while the latter spelling corresponds to the modern, velar or uvular, realization of <j> in Sp. *mujer*, the former appears to reflect its earlier and/or more conservative palatal value. Similar realization of Spanish <j> appears to be captured by Pellow's (1739: 36) spelling *travacho* of Sp. *trabajo* 'work' (cf. also Fronzaroli 1955: 226). Coexistence of two different realizations of Spanish <j> in Algerian LF was remarked upon by Marcel Cohen, who, in his letter to Schuchardt, commented on the incongruity of *travağar* (< Sp. *trabajar*) and *mukẹ̄r* (< Sp. *mujer*) in the same refrain (Swiggers 1991–1993: 274). Pananti's (1817: 133) spelling *cavezza* 'head' of Spanish *cabeza* reflects an earlier or more conservative affricate realization of the sibilant, which contrasts with the *Dictionnaire*'s spelling *cabessa* reflecting its more recent fricative realization.

The phonological shape of some of the LF lexical items may reflect inter-Romance hybridization. The relevant instances include the boldfaced sounds in *t**a**rtouga* 'turtle' (< Sp. *t**o**rtuga*, It. *t**a**rtaruga*), *sack**a**dgio* 'plunder' (< It. *sacch**e**ggio*, Fr. *sacc**a**ge*), ***e**ncora* 'again' (< It. ***a**ncora*, Cat. ***e**ncara*), *dé**v**ir* 'to owe' (< Sp. *de**b**er*; It. *do**v**ere*), and *scrivir* 'to write' (< Sp. *escri**b**ir*, It. *scri**v**ere*).

Prominent vocalic processes in the *Dictionnaire*'s LF include variable realization of mid vowels and the prosthetic vowel in initial sC-sequences. Prominent consonantal processes include replacement of [p] with [b] and possible mergers of [ɲ] with [nj] and [ʎ] with [lj]. Each process may have multiple sources of origin, including variability and in-progress changes carried over from the lexifiers, phonological transfer from substrate and/or adstrate languages, and internal developments. Regular adaptation of Romance infinitives in *-er(e)* to the LF imperfective conjugation in *-ir* appears to be an instance of a regular borrowing routine.

The sound inventory and phonological processes of LF are conveyed through an orthography that is predominantly French-based and meant to be self-explanatory for those who are familiar with the French orthography. Among the features that are particularly designed with the French-language user in mind are an acute accent over <e> in open syllables; context-dependent spelling of [k], [g], [s], and [z]; and variable uses of such graphemes as <c> and <g>, all of which rely on the users' familiarity with the French orthographic conventions. The *Dictionnaire*'s orthography also draws on several other orthographic traditions, while at the same time incorporating selected transliteration conventions from Veneroni (1800) and Vergani (1823).

5 The Lexicon

This chapter takes a look at the Lingua Franca lexicon as reflected in the *Dictionnaire de la langue franque*. Section 5.1 offers a bird's-eye view of the etymological sources of the lexicon. Section 5.2 focuses on the core vocabulary of the Swadesh wordlists. Section 5.3 addresses the layered nature of the Lingua Franca lexicon, focusing on its Romance and "exotic" (Turkish and Arabic) components. Section 5.4 scrutinizes selected typological features of the Lingua Franca lexicon in relation to properties which have been identified as characteristic of pidgin lexicons, such as typical vocabulary sources and sizes; and discusses features that specifically characterize the lexicon of Lingua Franca: doublets, suppletion patterns, and selected aspects of lexical typology and idiomatic structure. It is shown throughout that the lexicon of the *Dictionnaire*'s Lingua Franca displays detailed, specific, and interlocking continuity with the lexical and idiomatic features of its Romance lexifiers. Section 5.5 recapitulates the main points.

5.1 Total Vocabulary

The etymological composition of the vocabulary of the LF of Algiers is predominantly Romance. Cornelissen (1992: 220) estimates that 97 percent of the approximately 100 lexical types found in Haedo (1612) derive from Romance sources, and only 3 percent from Turkish and Arabic. The Romance portion of Haedo's lexicon is composed of Spanish words (41 percent), Italian words (17 percent), and words traceable to more than one Romance source (39 percent). With respect to the approximately 2,000 lexical types documented in the *Dictionnaire*, Cornelissen estimates over 95 percent to be of Romance origin. Of these, 58 percent derive from Italo-Romance, 4 percent from Gallo-Romance, 6 percent from Spanish, and 27 percent may have more than one Romance language as their source; while the remaining 5 percent derive from Arabic (3 percent), Turkish, Catalan, or Portuguese (2 percent) (Cornelissen 1992: 221; see also Baglioni 2017). Table 5.1 summarizes the percentages of Romance and non-Romance words in the LF of Algiers as reflected in these key primary sources (based on the estimates in Cornelissen 1992).

Table 5.1. *Etymological composition of the Lingua Franca of Algiers*

Lexical sources		Haedo (1612)	Anonymous (1830a)
Romance	Spanish	41%	6%
	Italo-Romance	17%	58%
	Other and multiple Romance sources	39%	over 31%
Non-Romance	Turkish and Arabic	3%	under 5%

In terms of absolute figures, Cornelissen (1992: 221) identifies in the *Dictionnaire* well over a thousand Italo-Romance words, the vast majority of which are "largely identical with the written Italian of the 17th and 18th centuries" and only about sixty are "informal," "archaic," or "dialectal."[1] Baglioni (2017: 191) confirms that "[t]he Italian words generally show a form compatible with the Tuscan-based literary language." In the remaining portion of the lexicon, Cornelissen identifies about eighty words as Gallo-Romance (French and Occitan) and about seventy as Turkish or Arabic; of this last number, Turkish contributes only a dozen words. Other Romance lexical contributors to LF include Spanish, Portuguese, Catalan, and Northern and Southern Italian varieties, particularly Venetian, to a lesser extent Ligurian, Sicilian, and others (Schuchardt 1909; Coates 1971; Cifoletti 1989, 2004; Castellanos 2007; Baglioni 2017).

The non-Romance portion of the *Dictionnaire*'s lexicon is conspicuous by the small number of nonnouns and the complete absence of whole categories of words, including verbs, function words, words for abstract concepts, and Berber words (Schuchardt 1909: 447; Cifoletti 1980: 26; Russo 2001: 227; Aslanov 2014: 124; Baglioni 2017: 198). The most substantial non-Romance lexical component is Arabic; there is also a modest contingent of words from other sources, including Turkish, Latin, Greek, and English (Cifoletti 1980: 29–35; 1989: 62–70; 2002; 2004: 56–73; Russo 2001: 228ff.; Baglioni 2017: 197–202).

[1] "Von den ca. 2.000 Wörtern entstammt mehr als die Hälfte dem Italienischen und ist weitgehend identisch mit dem Schriftitalienischen des 17. und 18. Jhs. Unter den weit über tausend Italianismen entsprechen lediglich 60 Wörter nicht der neuitalienischen Schriftnorm, sondern sind als 'familiär,' 'archaisch' oder 'dialektal' zu bezeichnen . . ." [From about 2,000 words more than half come from Italian and are largely identical with the written Italian of the 17th and 18th centuries. From among well over a thousand Italianisms a mere 60 words do not correspond to the modern Italian written norm but are to be qualified as 'informal,' 'archaic' or 'dialectal'].

Aslanov (2014: 124) observes that the size of the Arabic lexical component of LF does not exceed those of Sicilian, Spanish, or Portuguese, the Romance languages that historically have been in direct contact with Arabic. His assessment resonates with Schuchardt's observation that "[t]he Romance vocabulary of Lingua Franca appears to have been enriched by a number of Arabic words, but for comparative purposes the number is probably not greater than that of the Arabic loans in Spanish" (Schuchardt 1909: 446; see also Fronzaroli 1955: 221). (Here and throughout, the English translation of Schuchardt's article is cited after Schuchardt 1979.) For comparative purposes, the following figures for Iberian Romance languages, quoted in Sayahi (2014: 157–158), are of interest: based on the 2001 edition of the Dictionary of the Royal Spanish Academy (Real Academia Española 2001), there are 1,188 direct loans from Arabic in modern Spanish; the figures for Portuguese and modern Galician quoted by Sayahi are around 1,000 and 450, respectively. Rafael Lapesa's (1981) estimate for Spanish Arabisms mentions about 850 direct loans, 780 derivatives, and over 1,500 toponyms (133n5 bis). Of related interest is the Arabic component in the vocabulary of the various Romance-speaking communities settled in North Africa (cf. Hull 1985: 254).

The shape of some of the Turkish and Arabic words indicates that their immediate source in LF was not Turkish or Maghrebi Arabic but rather one of LF's Romance lexifiers. This observation applies to such items as *harem*, *catramé*, and *magazino*, whose phonological shape points to acquisition from Italian (*harem*, *catrame*, *magazzino*); as well as *sultan* and *minaret*, likely acquired from French (*sultan*, *minaret*) (Schuchardt 1979: 30; Russo 2001: 228ff.; Cifoletti 2004: 53; Aslanov 2014: 126–127; Baglioni 2017: 197–198, 200–201). Baglioni (2017: 198) suggests that only about thirty of the Arabisms may have entered LF directly from Maghrebi Arabic. Some of the Arabic words are somewhat marked in the LF phonology. For example, unlike consonant-final nouns of Romance origin, Arabic nouns ending in a consonant tend not to acquire a final vowel in LF; compare the adaptation of Ar. /tu:t/, /ru:z/, /funduq/, and /fustuq/ (LF *tout* 'mulberry,' *rouss* 'rice,' *festouk* 'pistachio,' *fondouk* 'market') with that of Fr. *baguette*, *brosse*, and *attaque* (LF *bagueta* 'little stick,' *brossa* 'brush,' *attaca* 'attaque') (Cifoletti 2004: 37–38, 60–64; Baglioni 2017: 195ff.). As pointed out in Chapter 4, some of the Turkish and Arabic words are also singled out in the *Dictionnaire*'s orthography.

5.2 Core Vocabulary

This section contributes to our understanding of the etymological makeup of the *Dictionnaire*'s LF by focusing on its core vocabulary, as embodied in the Swadesh wordlists (see Appendix A).

Before turning to the data, a few preliminary observations are in order relating to the difficulty of tracing word origins in multilingual contact situations, particularly where, as here, the languages in contact are closely related, making attractive the concept of multiple etymologies (Cassidy 1966; see also Zuckermann 2003: 53–56; Klimenkowa 2017: 25–26; and Section 5.5). Given the closeness of many Spanish and Italian cognates, some guidelines had to be adopted when assigning the individual words to one or the other language. For instance, since the *Dictionnaire*'s LF often degeminates geminate consonants (see Chapter 4), the source of a word like *séco* 'dry' was assumed to be uncertain since it can derive from Sp. *seco*, It. *secco*, or both. If the Italian and Spanish cognates are identical except for the quality of the stressed nucleus, the word with a nondiphthongized nucleus was assumed to derive from Italian; e.g., LF *terra* 'earth' is derived below from It. *terra* rather than Sp. *tierra*. If the Italian and Spanish nouns are identical except for the final *-e*, the LF word with the *-e* was assumed to derive from Italian; e.g., LF *cané* 'dog' is derived from It. *cane* rather than Sp. *can*, and LF *sol* 'sun' from Sp. *sol* rather than It. *sole*. Some of the identifications, which are pointed out individually, were guided by the word's meaning in LF.

It is also worth noting that the etyma of some of the LF words are close or identical in a number of Romance languages (cf. discussions of this issue in Cifoletti 1989: 65; 2004: 56; Cornelissen 1992: 220–221; Russo 2001: 220–226; Baglioni 2017: 189–190). This concerns such items as, for example, *saber* 'to know,' which has an identical form in Spanish, Portuguese, Catalan, and Occitan; and LF *cousir* 'to sew,' for which Catalan *cosir*, Occitan *cóser*, Venetian *cuser*, and Sicilian *cùsiri* all vie as potential sources (Castellanos 2007: 17; Baglioni 2017: 192). In such cases, it is not claimed that the LF word actually derives from, say, Spanish, but is merely assumed that its shape is compatible with the hypothesis of its Spanish origin (cf. related discussion in Castellanos 2007, who adopts a similar procedure). This observation applies with equal force to some of the LF words derivable from Italian, since nondiphthongization of the stressed nucleus is shared by a number of Romance languages, including Catalan and Portuguese, and is also a feature of Judeo-Spanish (possibly resulting from Portuguese/Leonese influence; Derek C. Carr, p.c.; cf. Penny 2000: 188). The difficulty of separating Italianisms from forms deriving from one of the nondiphthongizing Iberian languages is well known to language contact researchers (Minervini 2014: 73).

With the above caveats in mind, an etymological analysis of each of the Swadesh wordlists yields the following categories:

(A) Words derivable from Italian
(B) Words derivable from Spanish
(C) Words derivable from either Italian or Spanish

(D) Hispano-Italian doublets
(E) Words derivable from Gallo-Romance, hybrids, and/or innovations

The term *doublets*, as used here and elsewhere in this book, includes both etymological doublets, or Romance cognates deriving from different languages or dialects, such as *mouchou* ~ *molto* 'very' (< Sp. *mucho*, It. *molto*, both from Lat. *mŭltus* 'much'); and lexical doublets, or referential synonyms, whether derived from the same or different languages, cf. *largo* ~ *spacioso* 'spacious' (< It. *largo*, *spazioso*), *mas* ~ *piou* 'more' (< Sp. *más*, It. *più*) (see Appendix B).

5.2.1 100 Swadesh Wordlist

(A) There are fifty-two words derivable from Italian; this number includes items like *mi* 'I,' *ti* 'you,' and *massar* 'kill' identifiable as Venetian (Cifoletti 1991: 35; Baglioni 2017: 192). LF *foumo* 'smoke' is assumed to derive from Italian rather than Judeo-Spanish (cf. Penny 2000: 183).

mi 'I'	albéro 'tree'	lingoua 'tongue'	nébia 'cloud'
ti 'you'	sementza 'seed'	piedi 'foot'	foumo 'smoke'
noi 'we'	folia 'leaf'	dginokio 'knee'	fouogo 'fire'
cosa 'what'	scorsa 'bark'	ventro 'belly'	bruchar 'to burn'
qouesto 'this'	pellé 'skin'	collo 'neck'	rosso 'red'
qouello 'that'	osso 'bone'	couoré 'heart'	dgialo 'yellow'
qui 'who'	grasso 'fat'	mangiar 'to eat'	bianco 'white'
toutto 'all'	ové 'egg'	massar 'to kill'	noté 'night'
doué 'two'	piouma 'feather'	stella 'star'	caldo 'hot'
loungo 'long'	orékia 'ear'	piové 'it rains'	frédo 'cold'
picolo 'small'	ockio 'eye'	pietra 'stone'	nouovo 'new'
pechi 'fish'	nadzo 'nose'	sabia 'sand'	bonou 'good'
cané 'dog'	denti 'tooth'	terra 'earth'	nomé 'name'

(B) There are 8 words derivable from Spanish. LF *mirar* 'to see' is assumed to derive from Sp. *mirar* rather than It. *mirare* based on its meaning, especially in view of the common shift from 'to look at' to 'to see' in the Spanish verb (cf. Klee and Lynch 2009: 90 for American Spanish).

oumbré 'man'	négro 'black'
sangré 'blood'	mirar 'to see'
agoua 'water'	sabir 'to know'
sol 'sun'	ablar 'to say'

(C) There are twenty-three words derivable from either Italian or Spanish. LF *bévir* could derive from Sp. *beber* or be analogically formed on the basis of It. *bevuto* (Beretta 1992 mentions *bevere* for *bere* 'to drink' in L2 Italian).

qué 'what'	mano 'hand'	morir 'to die'	dar 'to give'
ouno 'one'	séno 'breast'	volar 'to fly'	louna 'moon'
grandé 'big'	intendir 'to hear'	caminar 'to walk'	montagnia 'mountain'
persona 'person'	sentir 'to hear'	vénir 'to come'	verdé 'green'
grano 'seed'	bévir 'to drink'	stendir 'to lie'	séco 'dry'
carne 'flesh'	dormir 'to sleep'	donar 'to give'	

(D) There are 7 Hispano-Italian doublets.

no ~ non 'not'
mouchéra / moukera ~ dona 'woman, wife'
cabessa ~ testa 'head'
camino ~ strada 'road'
mouchous ~ molto 'many'
inchito ~ pieno 'full'
sentar ~ sédir 'to sit'

(E) The remaining group is composed of 5 words.

forar 'to remove, take away, pull out, disorder, stand up; to pierce, make a hole'
natar 'to swim'
radiz 'root'
cinis 'ash'
roundo 'round'

The verb *forar* was analyzed in previous literature as a LF neologism; it is assumed to derive from Ven. *fora* 'out, outside' (It. *fuori*) while also incorporating the semantics of It. *forare* 'to pierce, make a hole in' in some of its meanings (Schuchardt 1909: 446; Cifoletti 1989: 66–67; 2004: 74). Cifoletti suggests that *fora* was extracted from nautical commands borrowed into Turkish and vernacular Arabic in which this adverb was misanalyzed as an imperative, setting into motion analogical processes; cf. such expressions as *fora!* 'lay out!; set the sail!,' *fora roba!* 'clear for action!,' *fora tenda!* 'strike the awnings!,' and *fora vele!* 'set the sails!' cited in Kahane et al. (1958: 222–224).[2] The remaining forms are probable inter-Romance hybrids: *radiz* 'root' (cf. Sp. *raíz*, It. *radice*), *natar* 'to swim' (cf. Sp. *nadar*, It. *nuotare*), *roundo* 'round' (possibly from Fr. *rond* with the Sp. It. masculine singular ending *-o* and vowel raising), and *cinis* 'ash' (cf. Sp. *ceniza* and its cognates in Meyer-Lübke 1911: 153; Sard. *čínus* in Wagner 1997: 107).[3]

In summary, from the total of 102 words, 59 (about 58 percent) are compatible in form with Italian, 15 (about 15 percent) with Spanish, 23 (about

[2] Baglioni (2010: 90) describes *forar* as a "neologismo dell'italiano nordafricano e levantino" [neologism of North African and Levantine Italian] and discusses additional proposed etymologies (pp. 438–439).

[3] *Cinis* has alternatively been analyzed as a Latinism (Schuchardt 1909: 457; Cifoletti 2004: 58; Operstein 2017c: 112).

23 percent) with both languages, and the remaining 5 (about 5 percent) consist of four probable hybrids and one innovation. Incorporated in these figures are seven Hispano-Italian doublets whose members are separately attributable to either Italian or Spanish, the doublet *sementza* ~ *grano* 'seed' whose first member is Italian while the second may be derived from either or both languages, and the doublet *dar* ~ *donar* 'to give' in which both members can derive from either or both languages.

5.2.2 200 Swadesh Wordlist

(A) There are ninety-eight words derivable from Italian. The words *largo* 'wide' and *bagniar* 'to wet' are assumed to derive from It. *bagnare* and *largo* rather than Sp. *bañar* and *largo* based on their meanings in LF.

toutto 'all'
e 'and'
cosa 'what'
cativo 'bad'
scorsa 'bark'
perké 'why'
ventro 'belly'
soffiar 'to blow'
osso 'bone'
bruchar 'to burn'
nébia 'cloud'
frédo 'cold'
dgiorno 'day'
sporco 'dirty'
cané 'dog'
orékia 'ear'
polvé 'dust'
terra 'earth'
mangiar 'to eat'
ové 'egg'
ockio 'eye'
cascar 'fall, flow'
lontano 'far'
grasso 'fat'
piouma 'feather'
fouogo 'fire'
pechi 'fish'
chinqoué 'five'
fioré 'flower'
piedi 'foot'
bonou 'good'
erba 'grass'
couoré 'heart'
pésanti 'heavy'
comé 'how'
caschar 'to hunt'
mi 'I'
sé 'if'
massar 'to kill'
ridir 'to laugh'
folia 'leaf'
sinistra 'left'
gamba 'leg'
loungo 'long'
nomé 'name'
stréto 'narrow'
vichino 'near'
collo 'neck'
nouovo 'new'
note 'night'
nadzo 'nose'
vekio 'old'
altro 'other'
dgiocar 'to play'
piové 'it rains'
rosso 'red'
dgiousto 'right'
corda 'rope'
salé 'salt'
sabia 'sand'
maré 'sea'
sementza 'seed'
pellé 'skin'
picolo 'small'
foumo 'smoke'
lischio 'smooth'
serpenté 'snake'
qoualqué 'some'
fendere 'to split'
pressar 'squeeze'
stella 'star'
bastone 'stick'
pietra 'stone'
dritto 'straight'
grosso 'thick'
qouesto 'this'
ti 'you'
tré 'three'
legar 'to tie'
lingoua 'tongue'
denti 'tooth'
albéro 'tree'
dgirar 'to turn'
dgitar 'to throw'
doué 'two'
caldo 'warm'
noi 'we'
bagniar 'to wet'
ove 'where'
bianco 'white'
qui 'who'
largo 'wide'
vento 'wind'
bosco 'woods'
vermé 'worm'
voi 'ye'
ano 'year'
dgialo 'yellow'

(B) There are fifteen words derivable from Spanish.

oumbré 'man'
mouchachou 'child'
sangré 'blood'
agoua 'water'
riou 'river'
cortar 'to cut'
sabir 'to know'
froutar 'to rub, scrub'
limpiar 'to rub, scrub, wash'
mirar 'to see'

sol 'sun'
négro 'black'
aki 'here'
ablar 'to say'
inchir 'to swell'

(C) There are forty-six words derivable from either Italian or Spanish.

bestia 'animal'
grande 'big'
respirar 'breathe'
vénir 'to come'
contar 'to count'
morir 'to die'
bévir 'to drink'
mamma 'mother'
montagnia 'mountain'
ouno 'one'
persona 'person'
séco 'dry'
padré 'father'
poco 'few'
combatir 'to fight'
volar 'to fly'
quatro 'four'
frouto 'fruit'
tirar 'to pull'
cantar 'to sing'
ciélo 'sky'
dormir 'to sleep'
sentir 'to smell'
donar 'to give'
dar 'to give'
verdé 'green'
mano 'hand'
intendir 'to hear'
sentir 'to hear'
tokkar 'to hit'
pensar 'to think'
tornar 'to turn'
caminar 'to walk'
secar 'to wipe'
roumpir 'to split'
ténir 'to hold'
in 'in'
lago 'lake'
stendir 'to lie'
vivir 'to live'
louna 'moon'
madré 'mother'
vomitar 'to vomit'
qué 'what'
qouando 'when'
con 'with'

(D) There are 5 Hispano-Italian doublets.

no ~ non 'not'
mouchous ~ molto 'many'
mouchéra / moukera ~ dona 'wife, woman'
camino ~ strada 'road'
sentar ~ sédir 'to sit'

(E) The remaining group is composed of twelve items.

forar 'to remove, take away, pull out, disorder, stand up; pierce, make a hole'
natar 'to swim'
cousir 'to sew'
poussar 'to push'
gantar 'to hold'
ténir paoura 'to fear'
radiz 'root'
cinis 'ash'
poudrido 'rotten'
là 'there'
ellou 'he'
elli 'they'

The above list contains an innovation (*forar*), five probable inter-Romance hybrids (*radiz* 'root,' *cinis* 'ash,' *natar* 'to swim,' *poudrido* 'rotten' [Sp. *podrido*, It. *putrido*], *ténir paoura* 'to fear' [Sp. *tener miedo*, It. *avere paura*]), two Gallo-Romance contributions (*poussar* 'to push' < Fr. *pousser*, *gantar* 'to hold' < Oc. *gantar*), and four words whose etymology is unclear: *là* 'there' may derive from Italian, French, or both; *cousir* 'to sew' may derive from Cat. *cosir*, Oc. *cóser*, Ven. *cuser*, and/or Sic. *cùsiri* (Castellanos 2007: 17; Baglioni 2017: 192); while the sources of *ellou* 'he' and *elli* 'they' are uncertain, as is clear from the large number of conjectures regarding the singular form: thus, Schuchardt (1909: 456) derives it from Sp. *él* or It. *egli*, Aslanov (2014: 130) from Ptg. *ele*, Cifoletti (1989: 59) from old or dialectal Venetian, and Baglioni (2017: 192) from Venetian or Spanish.[4]

In summary, from the total of 181 words, 103 (about 57 percent) are compatible in form with Italian, 20 (about 11 percent) with Spanish, 46 (about 25 percent) with both languages, and the remaining 12 (about 7 percent) consist of Gallo-Romance contributions, inter-Romance hybrids, an innovation, and words with uncertain etymology. Incorporated in these figures are five Hispano-Italian doublets whose members are separately attributable to either Italian or Spanish, the doublet *fendir* ~ *roumpir* 'to split' whose first member is Italian while the second may derive from either or both languages, and the doublet *ténir* ~ *gantar* 'to hold' whose first member may derive from Italian, Spanish, or both, and the second derives from Occitan (Castellanos 2007: 17).

5.3 Lexical Layers

5.3.1 Romance Component

In quantitative terms, the main Romance lexical components in the *Dictionnaire*'s LF are Italian, Spanish, and French, in that order (Cornelissen 1992: 221n1). Among the three components, the French is of a more recent introduction than the other two. Apart from historical facts ("the chronology of colonial penetration"; Heath 1989: 153), this conclusion is prompted by language-internal evidence, including the fact that the French words are adapted to preestablished phonological and morphological patterns of LF. Examples of phonological adaptation of the Gallicisms, such as replacement of [y] with [u] or [i], were given in Chapter 4 (see also Cifoletti 1980: 17–21; 2004: 47–50). Examples of morphological adaptation are shown below in (1). In these, the French nouns are adapted to LF with the gender markers *-o* / *-a*, the French infinitives acquire the LF imperfective endings *-ar* / *-ir*, and the French past participles the LF perfective endings *-ato* / *-ito* / *-uto*. Each of these grammatical markers is of Spanish, Italian, or a combined Hispano-Italian origin (see also Schuchardt 1909: 456; Cifoletti

[4] Derek C. Carr (p.c.) suggests Sp. *ello* 'it' as a possible source of *ellou*, with *elli* as a pseudo-Italian plural thereof.

1989: 87–88; Baglioni 2017: 195–196). Nissabouri (1997) discusses similar modification of French loanwords in Moroccan Arabic, whose effect is to align their shape with that of earlier loans from Spanish.

(1) biéra 'beer' (< Fr. bière)
verro 'glass' (< Fr. verre)
bagueta 'little stick' (< Fr. baguette)
rifouso 'refusal' (< Fr. refus)
avalar, avalato 'to swallow' (< Fr. avaler, avalé)
cedar, cédouto 'to give up' (< Fr. céder, cédé)
composir, composito 'to arrange' (< Fr. composer, composé)

Some of the Gallicisms additionally betray their recent date of introduction and marginal place in the LF lexicon by their semantic content and limited distribution. No words of French origin except, possibly, *roundo*, are present in the 100-item basic vocabulary list, and only one (*poussar*) is in the 200-item list. The small number of French-derived words in LF's basic vocabulary, together with their total absence from certain areas of the *Dictionnaire* and their semantic sophistication, has prompted the following analysis:

[N]on si trova nessun francesismo sicuro nelle sei pagine di Dialogues, nel Prèface, e tutte le volte che, nella parte lessicale, un termine è spiegato con una perifrasi ... dunque i vocaboli di sicura origine francese compaiono soltanto come glosse isolate, al di fuori di ogni contesto. Inoltre, mentre le parole di uso più comune, come è naturale, compaiono in diversi punti del *Dictionnaire*, pochissimi francesismi sono attestati due volte ... e nessun francesismo compare più di due volte. Se si guarda poi ai significati che sono resi da questi vocaboli di origine francese, si trovano dei concetti che non devono essere stati di uso quotidiano, specialmente per una lingua di scambio, di livello non elevato, e senza tradizioni culturali: di fronte a termini come *sacrificateur*, *sagacita*, *sepulcrale*, *subsistentza*, *superstitzioné*, *surviventé*, è lecito domandarsi se avrebbe avuto la possibilità di essere compreso un eventuale colono o militare francese che li avesse usati. (Cifoletti 1980: 18)

[No undisputed Gallicism is found in the six pages of Dialogues, the Preface, or each time when, in the lexical part, a word is explained with a periphrasis, so that words of undisputed French origin appear only as isolated glosses outside any context. Also, while the more commonly used words naturally appear in various parts of the *Dictionnaire*, very few Gallicisms are attested twice, and none appears more than twice. If we look at the meanings rendered by these words of French origin, we find concepts that must not have been in daily use, especially for a lowly exchange language without cultural traditions: faced with words like *sacrificateur*, *sagacita*, *sepulcrale*, *subsistentza*, *superstitzioné*, *surviventé* one might wonder whether there ever existed any French settler or soldier who would have used them.]

The abstract or elevated semantic content of many of the Gallicisms suggests that they may have been introduced into LF "from above." French enjoyed, at the time, the status of "the European language of diplomacy, aristocratic society, science, learning and literature" (Argent et al. 2014: 1). It was the usual language of communication in the diplomatic milieu of Algiers: "French is in general use in the society of the foreign agents residing here" (Shaler 1826: 13). Since it was from this milieu that the *Dictionnaire* had sprung into being, it is possible that some of the French words owe their presence in the *Dictionnaire*'s LF to the way this contact language was used by this social stratum. It is also likely that the more abstract or elevated of the Gallicisms were reserved for the acrolectal varieties of LF; the existence of such varieties will be addressed in Chapter 9.

The presence in the LF lexicon of significant Spanish and Italian components has given rise to competing historical interpretations. Schuchardt's remarks below appear to indicate that he regards this as an indication of LF's polygenesis, with the Spanish-based variety developing later than, and independently from, the Italian-based one:

> Just as Lingua Franca in the Eastern and Middle Mediterranean evolved out of Italian, so in the Western Mediterranean it evolved from Spanish, though at a later period. . . . The Lingua Franca with Spanish and Italian coloration blends them together with one another in different gradations so that perhaps only the western and eastern extremities are monochromatic. Reciprocal influence arose quite naturally, almost unavoidably; the initial structures of both had only the grammar, or, better, lack of grammar, in common, but there was also a vast majority of words in common – if we eliminate minor discrepancies in pronunciation. The geographical mid-point of this essentially uniform Lingua Franca is formed by Algiers. (Schuchardt 1979: 34–35)

The proposals by Castellanos (2007) and Aslanov (2014) assume that LF had developed in the Western Mediterranean, with the Iberian component predating the Italian. The two proposals differ in their details, which include the assumed linguistic basis of the original LF. Thus, Castellanos (2007: 2) hypothesizes that LF came into being sometime between the tenth and fifteenth centuries, after the commercial expansion of Romance-speaking Franks in the Western Mediterranean had brought them into contact with North African Arabs and Berbers. In subsequent centuries, it spread outward and was Italianized in territories east of Algiers. Castellanos hypothesizes that the lexicon of the original LF was "bàsicament occitano-català i toscano-ligur (pisano-genovès)" [basically Occitan-Catalan and Tuscan-Ligurian (Pisan-Genoese)] (p. 4) and identifies a number of specific Occitan-Catalan contributions, both lexical and structural (such as the noun suffixes *-on*, *-un*, *-dor* and the infinitive endings *-ar*, *-ir*; pp. 5–6). He suggests that Spanish could initially have influenced LF indirectly, by reinforcing certain Occitan-Catalan solutions such as the aforementioned endings *-ar*, *-ir* and suffixes *-on*, *-dor*, and sees the most significant direct Spanish influence on LF as taking place after the fifteenth or sixteenth century in Algiers and the territories west of it (p. 5n8). Aslanov (2014), taking as his starting point the observation that LF shares "many striking isoglosses with Portuguese" (p. 123), argues for the probable Portuguese nucleus in LF. This hypothesis is based on two structural developments that LF shares with Portuguese, extension of the copular uses of the locative copula *(e)star* and periphrastic pronominal possession. Aslanov argues for the existence of "a Portuguese-based Lingua Franca, originally used in Algarve or on the Portuguese-conquered Moroccan shores" (p. 131) and its subsequent spread to the whole of Maghreb.

In spite of their divergent hypotheses about the earliest lexical/structural layer of LF, Aslanov and Castellanos are in essential agreement as regards the view of LF as a product of contact among Romance speakers,[5] built on an Iberian foundation. Aslanov (2014) sees the purpose of LF as aiding "communication between speakers of different Romance languages who had been brought into contact as a result of trade, war or captivity" (p. 123), and its formation as an "attempt to find a lowest common denominator for Italo-Romance and Ibero-Romance languages" (p. 132) (see also Aslanov 2010: 110). As part of this argument, he attributes elimination of nominal plural in LF to the irreconcilable structural difference between Ibero-Romance and Italo-Romance plural markers *-s* and *-i*. In a related publication, he connects the facilitating role of LF in inter-Romance communication with the lack of a generalized knowledge of the mutually intelligible, supra-dialectal standard forms of the respective Romance languages:

> [G]li spagnoli o gli italiani di oggi non necessitano di nessuna lingua franca, neanche dell'inglese, la lingua franca moderna, per capirsi l'uno con l'altro. Però qualche secolo fa, quando la conoscenza della lingua standard ... non era diffusa in tutta la popolazione ... la lingua franca offriva una soluzione comoda laddove italofoni e locutori di lingue iberoromanze si incontravano. (Aslanov 2016: 40)
>
> [The Spaniards or Italians of today need no lingua franca – not even English, the modern lingua franca, – in order to understand one another. But a few centuries ago, when the knowledge of the standard languages was not widespread among the population, Lingua Franca offered a convenient solution where Italian speakers and speakers of Ibero-Romance languages met.]

Castellanos (2007), for his part, speaks of "[l]a neutralització interromànica ... sobre la base dels rudiments de llatí medieval que eren utilitzats en el conjunt de la Romània, per a fer-se entendre els parlants de les diferents llengües filles del llatí, en llurs contactes mutus" [inter-Romanic neutralization on the basis of the

[5] A conjecture along these lines was also advanced by Collier (1977: 283): "The language appears to have arisen when groups of different Romance-language speakers were captives of a dominant Arabic-speaking group."

Table 5.2. *Total and core vocabulary in the* Dictionnaire*'s Lingua Franca*

Lexical source	100-word Swadesh list	200-word Swadesh list	*Dictionnaire* as a whole
Italian	58%	57%	58%
Spanish	15%	11%	6%
Italian or Spanish	23%	25%	over 31%
Other Romance languages, hybrids, or innovations	5%	7%	
Non-Romance languages	0%	0%	under 5%

rudiments of Medieval Latin which were used in Romance-speaking territories by speakers of different Romance languages for making themselves understood in their mutual contacts] (p. 3). He discerns evidence of inter-Romance neutralization, e.g., in the absence in LF of Gallo-Romance front rounded vowels (p. 4). Reliance on their shared knowledge of Latin makes the creators of LF give preference to "full" nominal forms (those that are closer to their Latin sources) over truncated ones; for example, *bono* 'good' and *vino* 'wine' are preferred over their Catalan cognates *bo* and *vi* (p. 3).

The etymological composition of the vocabulary of the *Dictionnaire*'s LF contributes potentially useful information to clarifying the diachronic relationship between the Spanish and Italian components of the LF of Algiers. Table 5.2 shows that, while the percentage of Italian words remains stable across all sections of the vocabulary, that of Spanish words grows the closer one moves to the lexical core, from 6 percent in the total vocabulary to 11 percent in the 200 Swadesh wordlist and to 15 percent in the 100 list. This synchronic snapshot is compatible with a diachronic scenario in which a Spanish-based contact vernacular is being relexified by Italian, with the periphery of the lexicon succumbing to relexification earlier than the core. This interpretation derives support from similar reasoning adopted by some researchers of Papiamentu: although the Portuguese lexical component of Papiamentu is heavily outweighed by the Spanish one, its presence in the language's core vocabulary, in a proportion whose estimates range from 5 percent to 25 percent (Jacobs 2012: 17), has prompted a diachronic interpretation in which a Portuguese-based contact vernacular is being lexically expanded by Spanish (Green 1988: 464; see also Grant 2008; Jacobs 2012).

A concrete illustration of the ongoing relexification process is provided by Hispano-Italian doublets (see 2 below and Appendix B).

(2) a. Selected Hispano-Italian doublets in Anonymous (1830a)

Italian	Spanish	
figlio	mouchachou	'son'[6]
padron	maestro	'owner'
parola	palabra	'word'
pianto	lagrima	'tear'
timone	timoun	'helm, rudder'
piou	mas	'more'
débole	flaco	'weak'
vouoto	basio	'empty'
parlar	ablar	'to speak'
star	estar	'to be'
avir	ténir	'to have'
vouotar	basiar	'to empty'
scaldar	escaldar	'to heat'
domandar	quérir	'to ask'

b. Hispano-Italian doublets in Haedo (1612)

Italian	Spanish	
testa	cabeza	'head'
cane	perro	'dog'
parlar	dezir	'to say, speak'
pecato	pecado	'sin'
bono	bueno	'good'
non	no	'no, not'
acosi	assi	'so'

Other synchronic evidence of relexification is supplied by etymologically hybrid complex words and multiword lexemes in which elements from both lexifiers are found side by side (illustrated in 3).

(3) Selected Hispano-Italian hybrids in Anonymous (1830a)

tapétos	'rug'	(It. tappeto, Sp. -s)
hinchito	'full'	(Sp. henchir, It. -ito)
escondouto	'to hide' (perfective)	(Sp. esconder, It. -uto)
agoua di salé	'brine'	(Sp. agua; It. di, sale)
moukera del filio	'daughter-in-law'	(Sp. mujer, It. figlio)

[6] The *Dictionnaire* gives both *figlio* and *mouchachou* as translations for French *fils* 'son' but only *mouchachou* for French *enfant* 'child,' which is the reason *figlio* was not included among the Swadesh list items. Similarly for the doublet *parlar* ~ *ablar*: while the *Dictionnaire* lists both verbs as translations for Fr. *parler* 'to speak,' only *ablar* is given as the translation for Fr. *dire* 'to say.'

mouchou bello	'magnificent'	(Sp. mucho, It. bello)
mouchou gratzia	'I am much obliged to you'	(Sp. mucho, It. grazie)
mirar bonou	'to reflect'	(Sp. mirar, It. buono)

A diachronic confirmation of the relexification process derives from a comparison between the LF lexicons of Haedo (1612) and Anonymous (1830a), which shows a reversal of the relative proportion of Spanish- and Italian-derived words: 41 percent Spanish to 17 percent Italian words in Haedo (1612) versus 6 percent Spanish to 58 percent Italian words in Anonymous (1830a).

The deep entrenchment of the Spanish lexical items in the LF of Algiers is confirmed by their phonological shape and high usage frequency, as well as etymological doublets in which both items derive from different stages or different varieties of Spanish. The first of these characteristics is pointed out by Cifoletti (1989: 88), who observes that Spanish-derived words in LF "presentano modificazioni fonetiche tipiche dell'arabo" [present phonetic modifications typical of Arabic]. This characteristic, not shared (or not to the same extent) by words from other Romance sources, points to a longer presence of the Spanish words in the LF of Algiers. The factors that may account for this include the longer history of Spanish presence in Algeria and the settlement there of significant numbers of Iberian Muslims whose Arabic incorporated a large number of Spanish loans (Lapesa 1981; Heath 1989; Corriente 1997; Guella 2011; Sayahi 2014; Vicente 2020).

The potentially high usage frequency of the Spanish words follows from their containing such high-frequency items as kinship and body-part terms; modal verbs; basic verbs of motion, possession, perception, cognition, and verbal communication; adjectives for basic properties; and "words of very general usage" (Schuchardt 1979: 41), among them *dios* 'God,' *amigo* 'friend,' and *nada* 'nothing' (see 4 below).

(4) Selected Spanish-derived LF words outside the Swadesh wordlists

mouchacha	'girl, daughter'
amigo	'friend'
ladron	'thief, rascal'
scriban	'secretary'
bouriqua	'donkey'
cabra	'goat'
tartouga	'turtle'
bakalaou	'cod'
ratoun	'rat'
bentana	'window'
sartan	'frying pan'
serradoura	'lock'
pagnio	'cloth'

plata	'silver'
paga	'salary'
douros	'piaster'
dios	'God'
adios	'goodbye'
domingo	'Sunday'
escadra	'squadron'
scopéta	'rifle, gun'
locou	'crazy'
nada	'nothing'
escapar	'to escape'
escondir	'to hide'
componir	'to tidy up'
poudir	'to be able'

The high frequency of Spanish-derived lexemes is also apparent when comparing the usage frequency of the members of various doublets and triplets. For example, in the doublet *avir* ~ *ténir* 'to have,' Spanish-derived *ténir* is found in several analytic verb lexemes and more than ten example sentences, while Italian-derived *avir* is not utilized in examples or multiword lexemes. The semantic equivalence of *avir* and *ténir* is established in the *Dictionnaire*'s preface, where it is stated that "[l]e verbe avir ou tenir (avoir), ne s'emploie pas comme auxiliaire, mais seulement comme verbe possessif" [the verb avir or tenir (to have) is not used as an auxiliary but only as a possessive verb]. In the triplet *quérir* ~ *volir* ~ *désirar* 'to want,' Spanish-derived *quérir* is found in about ten example sentences and two analytic lexemes, while neither Italian-derived *volir* nor French-derived *désirar* is found in multiword lexemes, *volir* is used in one example sentence, and *désirar* in none. In the doublet *ablar* ~ *parlar* 'to speak,' only Spanish-derived *ablar* is used in examples and multiword lexemes. In the doublet *palabra* ~ *parola* 'word,' only Spanish-derived *palabra* is used in the dialogues. In the doublet *mouchou* ~ *molto* 'very,' Spanish-derived *mouchou* is used more often and in more contexts than Italian-derived *molto*.

The last characteristic arises from the fact that the Spanish lexical component is not uniform phonologically but reflects, for certain words, either different periods of entry or a mixture of conservative and innovating input dialects (or, indeed, both). Thus, the *Dictionnaire*'s spelling <cabessa> for Spanish <cabeça> 'head' points to a source dialect in which <ç> had a fricative ([s]) pronunciation. In Pananti (1817), this word is recorded as <cavezza>, which points to an affricate ([ts]) realization of the sibilant (vol. 1, p. 133). Since the affricate realization precedes the fricative one historically, these variants may have entered LF at different times;

alternatively, preservation of the affricate in <cavezza> may point to a conservative input dialect, such as Judeo-Spanish. Another instance of the same type are variant shapes of Spanish *mujer* 'woman,' given in the *Dictionnaire* as <mouchéra> and <moukera>. Provided <ch> is not an unusual orthographic choice for [k] or an attempt to spell [x] or [χ], the variant <mouchéra> reflects the earlier or a more conservative palatal realization of the medial consonant while <moukera> reflects its pronunciation following its retraction to a velar or uvular fricative. Similarly, <baschiar> 'to go down' may derive from older or dialectal realization of Sp. *bajar*, though derivation from Cat. *baixar* and/or Sic. *(ab)basciari* (Baglioni 2017: 192) is equally possible (see related observations in Schuchardt 1909: 459; Cifoletti 1989: 65; 2004: 71; and Chapter 4).

5.3.2 Non-Romance Component

The non-Romance component of the *Dictionnaire*'s LF lexicon, which amounts to about 5 percent of the total (Cornelissen 1992: 221), is unevenly divided between the Indo-European and the "exotic" portions (Russo 2001: 226). The former comprises a Grecism (*aspra* 'money, coin'), an Anglicism (*flinta*), and a handful of Latinisms (*viator* 'traveler,' *brakio* 'arm,' *imago* 'image')[7] (Schuchardt 1909: 457; Cifoletti 1989: 66; 2004: 58). The latter consists of Turkish and Arabic words, some of which entered LF via its Romance lexifiers rather than directly, and stands out by its meager contingent of nonnouns, of which there are only three: two adjectives (*maboul* 'crazy' and *meskin* 'poor, wretched, unfortunate') and one adverb (*dgiaba* 'for free') (see Schuchardt 1909: 447; Table 5.3). Unlike Romance-origin lexemes, which run the whole gamut of semantic and functional categories, from the core to the margins of the lexicon, from the concrete to the abstract, and from content to function words, non-Romance lexemes, with the exception of *brakio* 'arm,' are confined to lexical periphery and consist entirely of content items (see also Baglioni 2017: 188, 197ff.).

[7] In Baglioni (2017: 195n13), *imago* is analyzed as a Gallicism furnished with Sp. It. *-o*. Cifoletti's (2004: 58) list of the Latinisms also includes *oundé*, *papas*, and the aforementioned *cinis* 'ash.' *Oundé*, which appears in the dialogue phrase *oundé ti vénir?* 'Where are you coming from?,' may also derive from Old Spanish *onde* 'whence,' with mid vowel raising (cf. *oumbré* 'man' < Sp. *hombre*) (see Penny 2002: 132). Clewlow (1990: 59–60) notes the presence of *onde* in his recordings of Judeo-Spanish as spoken by Sephardim from Rhodes, and Grant (2008) remarks on its presence in Antillean Spanish. *Papas* is given in the *Dictionnaire* as the translation of Fr. *langouste* 'lobster,' while Haedo (1612) uses *Papaz* with the meaning 'Christian priest'; the semantic shift underlying this usage is discussed by Schuchardt (1909: 453) (see also Cohen 1912: 461–462; Souag 2005: 168). Russo (2001: 252) and Cifoletti (2004: 62) treat *papas* as an Arabism, and it is included in the list of "exotica" below.

Table 5.3. *Turco-Arabic lexical stratum in Lingua Franca*

Semantic field	Lingua Franca word	Gloss
Social and political relations	douar bacha dey sultan drogman ousif piskéri sbendout arab nemsa roumi	'town, village, hamlet' 'dey, pasha' 'dey' 'sultan' 'interpreter' 'black; slave' 'porter' 'robber' 'Arab' 'Austrian' 'Greek'
Agriculture and vegetation	rouss limoun arangi[a] festouk castali tout aneb esbinac carchouf salata	'rice' 'lemon' 'orange' 'pistachio' 'chestnut' 'mulberry' 'jujube' 'spinach' 'artichoke' 'lettuce'
Food and drink	carafa giara tassa barmil scherrub ~ cherub sorbet zoukaro pilaf safran	'jug' 'pitcher; jar' 'cup; glass; bowl; bucket' 'barrel; cask' 'drink; liqueur' 'syrup; liqueur' 'sugar' 'pilaf' 'saffron'
Warfare and hunting	nouba arsenal yatagan tobgi yoldach amiraute ~ amirante captan corsan	'garrison' 'arsenal' 'dagger; sabre' 'gunner' 'janissary; soldier' 'admiral; vice-admiral' 'captain' 'corsair'
The house	baraca banno skifa harem casana sofa	'barrack; hut' 'bath; sweating room' 'entrance hall' 'harem' 'closet' 'sofa'

Table 5.3. *(cont.)*

Semantic field	Lingua Franca word	Gloss
	materasso taoula	'mattress' 'table, board'
Possession	meskin fondouk magazino dgiaba bakchich cantar taba	'poor; wretched; unfortunate' 'market' 'store' 'for free' 'gift' 'quintal' 'seal'
Motion	sérigia ~ serigia eskima ~ esquima caravana galéra sandal catramé scala	'saddle; packsaddle' 'bridle' 'caravan' 'galley' 'fishing boat' 'tar' 'stairs; wharf'
Clothing and grooming	bernus dgiléko tourbanti marêïa fouta saboun	'coat' 'vest' 'turban' 'mirror' 'napkin, towel' 'soap'
Religion and belief	seubt chetan marabout mouzoulmin	'Sabbath' 'satan; devil' 'marabout; saint' 'Muslim, Mahometan'
Animals	raï taour papas	'shepherd' 'bull' 'lobster'
Law	cadi assassino	'cadi; judge' 'murderer; murder'
Physical world	roubié schiroco	'spring' 'south'
The body	abouba gandoufa	'plague' 'plague'
Cognition	maboul	'crazy'

[a] See Cohen (1912: 344–345) and Borg (1996: 142) regarding this word in Algerian Arabic and in Maltese, respectively.

Table 5.3 contains the total of eighty words. These compose the majority of the *Dictionnaire*'s LF words identified as "orientalismi" in Russo (2001: 228–252) – sixty-one in total – and nineteen items from a similar list in Cifoletti (2004: 58–63), including *arab*, *bakchich*, *banno*, *baraca*, *barmil*, *cantar*, *captan*, *castali*, *chetan*, *corsan*, *gandoufa*, *nemsa*, *piskéri*, *roubié*, *saboun*, *salata*, *sbendut*, *taoula*, and *taour*. The following items were excluded: *cavala* 'mare' and *bey* 'governor' from Russo (2001); and *brodou* 'broth,' *calceta* 'stocking,' *francis* 'French,' and *sala* 'room, hall, study, apartment' from Cifoletti (2004). The word *bey* appears in the vocabulary entry Fr. *gouverneur* > LF *gobernator (arabe bey)* 'governor / gobernator (Arabic bey),' and is not clearly meant as a LF word, while the remaining items could have entered LF from Romance languages without assuming the agency of Arabic (see also Baglioni 2017: 197–202).

The semantic field labels under which the items are organized in Table 5.3 are those used in the Loanword Typology project (Haspelmath and Tadmor 2009a). One of the stated goals of that project was to uncover cross-linguistic generalizations regarding the borrowability of words from different semantic domains (Haspelmath and Tadmor 2009b: 7, 22–34). In line with the project's empirical findings, partially summarized in table 6 of Tadmor (2009: 64), the Turkish and Arabic words in LF behave like loanwords in being concentrated in lexical-semantic domains cross-linguistically most permeable to intercultural influences. These comprise the functioning and organization of society (the fields labeled in Table 5.3 as social and political relations, warfare and hunting, motion, possession, law, and religion and belief) and living conditions (the fields labeled in Table 5.3 as food and drink, agriculture and vegetation, animals, the house, and clothing and grooming). In further alignment with the findings of the Loanword Typology project (Tadmor 2009: 64), certain semantic domains are not represented in LF's Turco-Arabic lexical stratum – kinship, basic actions and technology, spatial relations, quantity, time, sense perception, emotions and values, speech and language, and function words –, while the domains of the physical world, the body, and cognition are represented by the total of five lexical items. These consist of the words for south (*schiroco*, synonymous with its Romance doublet *metzo giorno*), spring (*roubié*, synonymous with its Romance doublet *prima vera*), crazy (*maboul*, synonymous with its Romance doublet *locou*), and plague (*abouba* and *gandoufa*). Baglioni (2017: 198) notes the absence of words for abstract concepts in the Arabic stratum.

The small percentage of the Turkish and Arabic words in the LF lexicon, the marked phonological shape of some of them, and their concentration in semantic domains cross-linguistically most prone to borrowing, give them the appearance of loans inserted into a Romance recipient language, involving recipient-language agentivity (Van Coetsem's 1988; Winford 2005: 376–377). This appearance is strengthened by the preponderance in this lexical stratum of nouns and the total absence of verbs and function words; both characteristics agree with the cross-linguistic borrowability hierarchies which posit that nouns are borrowed more easily than other parts of speech, and content words more easily than function words (Muysken 1981; Van Hout and Muysken 1994: 41–42; Haspelmath 2008: 48–50; Tadmor 2009: 61–63).

5.4 Lexicon Structure

5.4.1 Lexical Sources

Cross-linguistic studies of pidgins show that, taken as a class, pidgins share a number of attributes with respect to their lexicons. A succinct summary of the pertinent issues is provided in Parkvall and Bakker (2013: 33–35, 47); additional sources of typological information about pidgin lexicons include Bakker (1994: 36–37), Holm (2000: 107–108, 134–135), Juvonen (2016), and Parkvall (2016, 2019).

The first pertinent point is that the bulk of the lexicon of a pidgin derives either from a single source language or, less often, from two source languages in approximately equal proportions. It is assumed that the latter scenario obtains when neither of the two groups in contact is socially dominant (Bakker 1994: 36–37; 2008: 137; Parkvall and Bakker 2013: 33; Parkvall 2019: 269–272).

In the *Dictionnaire*, over 95 percent of the LF vocabulary derives from Romance languages, the leading lexical source being Italian (58 percent), followed by Spanish (6 percent) and French (4 percent); while an additional 27 percent of the Romance lexemes defy individual attribution. The next most important documentary source on LF, Haedo (1612), contains the lexicon of about 100 word types comprising about 41 percent Spanish words, 17 percent Italian words, and an additional 39 percent of Romance words that are not separately attributable (Cornelissen 1992; see Appendix C.2). The provenance of the LF lexicon is thus unlike that of a typical pidgin in that, rather than being derived predominantly from a single lexical source language, or from two languages in equal measure, it is drawn from several Romance languages in contact in proportions that vary diachronically and geographically.[8] Moving from the total to the core vocabulary, the *Dictionnaire*'s LF again fails to fit the generalization that most pidgins derive 90 percent or more of their core lexicon from a single source (Parkvall and Bakker 2013: 47; see Table 5.2). The provenance of its

[8] Regarding geographical variation in LF, see Chapter 1. The following succinct description from Desfontaines (1838: 19–20), who notes that "à Tunis elle [elle = LF] a beaucoup de rapport avec l'italian; à Bône et dans les environs, elle diffère peu de provençal; enfin, à Alger et du côté de Maroc, c'est un mélange d'italian et d'espagnol" [in Tunis, it has much in common with Italian; in Bona and its vicinity, it differs little from Provençal; lastly, in Algiers and Morocco, it is a mixture of Italian and Spanish], is particularly useful.

lexicon thus distances the *Dictionnaire*'s LF from typical pidgins and assimilates it to another type in the typology of contact outcomes: a koine. As remarked by Siegel (2001: 182–183), in koineization "there is no one 'lexifier'; several of the varieties in contact share in providing the lexical and morphological content."

5.4.2 Lexicon Size

The number of distinct lexemes in a pidgin is "usually below 2000, and in many cases below 1000 or even 500" (Parkvall and Bakker 2013: 33; see also Holm 2000: 107–108; Parkvall 2019: 264). Against this background, the lexicon of the *Dictionnaire*'s LF, which comprises about 2,035 lexemes (Baglioni 2017: 187), is atypically large. As shown below, it is also atypical, from the perspective of pidgins, in its lexical richness, including in having a substantial number of synonyms, some of which clearly have specialized senses and usages; and in its detailed preservation of suppletive, semantic, and idiomatic patterns of its Romance lexifiers.

5.4.3 Lexical Richness

One of the characteristic properties of pidgin discourse is its particularly low type-token ratio (TTR) (Parkvall and Bakker 2013: 34–35). The TTR is calculated by dividing "the number of unique words (types) in a text ... by the total number of words (tokens)" (Robinson 2008: 142). The TTR of the *Dictionnaire*'s LF may be compared with both that of its main Romance lexifiers and that of English thanks to the availability of the learner's dialogues from Vergani (1823) (see Chapter 3) in all of these languages. A full-scale study of the lexical diversity of this parallel mini-corpus is undertaken in Operstein (2020); Table 5.4 provides an illustration in the form of the *Dictionnaire*'s first dialogue in five languages (Anonymous 1830a: 93; Vergani 1823: 199; Rementería y Fica 1826: 192–193; Guichet 1855: 182–183). Since the French prompts in the *Dictionnaire* were slightly modified in relation to the original prompts in Vergani (1823), two of the Italian, Spanish, and English sentences have been modified accordingly (see Table 5.5 and Tables 3.3 and 3.13 in Chapter 3). In addition, the Spanish version has been supplied with the sentence *No es verdad* [This is not true].

The TTRs in the first dialogue, expressed as percentages[9] rounded to the nearest whole number, are shown in Table 5.6. Also included is the TTR of the combined LF samples from Haedo (1612) (see Appendix C). The figures in Table 5.6 show that the TTR of LF in the first dialogue (39 percent) and in

[9] See, e.g., Baker (2006: 52) and Crystal (2008: 276) on the use of percentages to express the TTR.

Table 5.4. *Dialogue No. 1 in five languages*

French	Lingua Franca	Italian	Spanish	English
Cela est vrai.	qouesto star véro.	È vero.	Es verdad.	It is true.
Cela n'est pas vrai.	qouesto non star véro.	Non è vero.	No es verdad.	That is not true.
Cela n'est que trop vrai.	qouesto star tropo véro.	Quest' è pur troppo vero.	Esta es la pura verdad.	That is but too true.
J'en doute.	mi doubitar di questo.	Ne dubito.	Lo dudo.	I doubt it.
Il n'y a point de doute.	non tenir doubio.	Non v'è dubbio alcuno.	No hay duda alguna.	There is no doubt.
Que voulez-vous parier?	cosà volir scométir?	Che volete scommettere?	Qué quiere V. apostar?	What will you bet?
J[a] gagerais quelque chose.	mi scométir qualqué cosa.	Scommetterei qualche cosa.	Apostaría cualquier[a] cosa.	I would bet something.
Je gagerais ce que vous voudrez.	mi scométir cosa ti quérir.	Scommetterò quel che volete.	Apostaré lo que V. quiera.	I will bet what you please.
Croyez-moi, je puis vous l'assurer.	ti crédir per mi, mi poudir asicourar per ti.	Credetemi; ve lo posso assicurare.	Créame V. puedo asegurárselo.	Believe me, I can assure you of it.
C'est ainsi.	star acoussi.	È così.	Es así.	It is so.
Je crois que oui.	mi pensar si.	Credo di sì.	Creo que sí.	I believe so.
Je crois que non.	mi pensar no.	Credo di no.	Creo que no.	I believe not.
Je dis que oui.	mi ablar si.	Dico di sì.	Digo que sí.	I say yes.

Table 5.4. *(cont.)*

French	Lingua Franca	Italian	Spanish	English
Je dis que non.	mi ablar no.	Dico di no.	Digo que no.	I say no.
Sur ma parole.	per la palabra di mi.	Sulla mia parola.	Sobre mi palabra.	Upon my word.
Je dis la vérité.	mi ablar dgiousto.	Dico la verità.	Digo la verdad.	I speak the truth.
Je vous crois.	mi crédir per ti.	Vi credo.	Os creo.	I believe you.
Je n'en crois pas une parole.	mi non crédir ouna palabra.	Non ne credo una parola.	Yo no creo una palabra.	I do not believe a word of it.
Je ne saurais croire.	mi non poudir crédir.	Non posso crederlo.	No puedo creerlo.	I cannot believe it.
Cela est faux.	qouesto star falso.	Quest' è falso.	Es falso.	That is false.

Table 5.5. *Changes to the Italian, Spanish, and English sentences*

Language	Original sentence	Modified sentence
French	*Qui en doute?* *Je dis toujours la vérité.*	*J'en doute.* *Je dis la vérité.*
Italian	*Chi ne dubita?* *Dico sempre la verità.*	*Ne dubito.* *Dico la verità.*
Spanish	*Quién lo duda?* *Digo siempre la verdad.*	*Lo dudo.* *Digo la verdad.*
English	*Who doubts it?* *I always speak the truth.*	*I doubt it.* *I speak the truth.*

Haedo's (1612) LF samples (43 percent) are comparable with those of LF's lexifiers and English. The TTR figures of typical pidgins, on the other hand, are much lower; for example, Ayafor and Green (2017: 47) give the figure of 3 percent for Cameroon Pidgin English. This suggests that the lexical richness

Table 5.6. *Type–token ratios in Dialogue No. 1 and Haedo (1612)*

Language	Types	Tokens	TTR	Source of the language sample
Lingua Franca	30	77	39%	Anonymous (1830a: 93)
Lingua Franca	101	233	43%	Haedo (1612); Cifoletti (1989: 163–164)
French	39	88	44%	Anonymous (1830a: 93)
English	36	81	44%	Guichet (1855: 182–183)
Spanish	32	71	45%	Rementería y Fica (1826: 192–193)
Italian	35	65	54%	Vergani (1823: 199)

of the LF of Algiers, as recorded in the key documentary sources, aligns it with its Romance lexifiers rather than with typical pidgins.

5.4.4 *Lexical Doublets*

The richness of the *Dictionnaire*'s LF vocabulary is further apparent in the abundance of lexical choices. Some of these come in the form of monolexemic and multiword equivalents for the same concepts (see 6a below). A more numerous category are referential synonyms (lexical doublets) (Hellinger 1985: 58; Cornelissen 1992: 222; Cifoletti 2004: 55–56; Selbach 2009: 226; Baglioni 2017: 193). Most doublets derive from LF's main lexifiers, Italian and Spanish; these were illustrated earlier in this chapter. Doublets involving a different combination of the source languages, as well as triplets, are exemplified in (6b) and (6c) below (see also Appendix B).

(6)
a. salar — mettir salé — 'to put salt in'
zoukar — mettir zoukaro — 'to put sugar in'
agioudar — dar agioudo — 'to help'
permettir — dar licentzia — 'to allow'
favorisar — counchar favour — 'to favor'
ringratziar — ablar gratzia — 'to thank'
piové — cascar agoua — 'it rains'

b. canoniéré (< It.) — tobgi (< Tu.) — 'gunner'
tavola (< It.) — taoula (< Ar.) — 'table, board'
prima vera (< Sp. It.) — roubié (< Ar.) — 'spring'
locou (< Sp.) — maboul (< Ar.) — 'crazy'
dar (< Sp. It.) — donar (< Fr. Cat.) — 'to give'
componir (< Sp.) — rangiar (< Fr.) — 'to tidy up'

c. bekiéré (< It.) verro (< Fr.) tassa (< Ar. Sp. Fr.) 'glass, cup'
far (< It.) fazir (< Sp. Ptg.) counchar (< Sic. It.)[10] 'to make, do'
volir (< It.) quérir (< Sp. Ptg.) désirar (< Fr.) 'to want'

The *Dictionnaire* provides ample evidence for semantic differentiation and collocational specialization in at least some of the doublets. One example is the specialization of *germana* in the meaning of 'sister' and of *sorella* in that of 'sister-in-law' (< Cat. *germana* 'sister,' It. *sorella* 'sister'). Spanish *escala* is selected for translating Fr. *échelle* 'ladder,' and Italian *scala* for Fr. *quai* 'quay' and *escalier* 'stairs.' Arabic *seubt* translates Fr. *sabbat* 'Sabbath,' and Italian *sabato* renders Fr. *samedi* 'Saturday.' Spanish-, Catalan-, or Sicilian-derived *baschiar* translates Fr. *descendre* 'to go down,' and Italian-derived *bassar* renders Fr. *baisser* 'to lower.' Arabic-, Spanish-, or French-derived *tassa* translates Fr. *écuelle* 'bowl,' *gobelet* 'cup,' *seau* 'bucket,' and *verre* 'glass,' while the meanings of Italian-derived *bekiéré* and French-derived *verro* are confined to those of 'cup' and 'glass,' respectively. Although Fr. *entendu* (sic) 'to hear' is translated with both French-derived *intendir* and Italian-derived *sentire*, only the latter verb is actually used in the dialogues.

The LF translation of Fr. *femme* 'woman, wife,' given as "mouchéra, (épouse), dona, (dame)," suggests that the primary sense of *mouchéra* (< Sp. *mujer*) is 'wife' and that of *dona* (< It. *donna*), 'woman.' This inference is strengthened by the translation of Fr. *belle-fille* 'daughter-in-law,' which is *moukera del filio* ('the son's wife'). LF *cabessa* (< Sp. *cabeza* 'head'), listed as one of the translations for both Fr. *tête* 'head' (*testa*, *cabessa*) and Fr. *esprit* 'spirit, mind' (*spirito*, *cabessa*), differs from its doublet *testa* (< It. *testa* 'head') in being used in idiomatic expressions. In the *Dictionnaire*, this noun is found in the idiom *ténir cabessa*, while a near-contemporary source, Pananti (1817), employs it twice in the idiom *star buona cavezza* (see 7a-b). *Testa*, also used twice in Pananti's passage, refers both times to the physical head in the collocation *testa tagliara* 'to cut the head off' (see 7c).

(7) a. *questo umbré ténir cabessa*
this man have.IMPF head
'cette homme à de l'esprit'[11]
'this man is clever' (lit. 'this man has head')
(Anonymous 1830a: 32)

b. *ti star buona cavezza*
2s be.IMPF good head
'you are clever' (lit. 'you are good head')
(Pananti 1817: 133)

[10] Cifoletti (2004: 58) derives *counchar* from Sic. *cunzari*; but see Baglioni (2017: 193).

[11] Here and elsewhere, the French translations in sentence-long examples represent the French prompts from the *Dictionnaire* and preserve the original orthography and capitalization.

c. *ma poi testa tagliara, perchè saper cose*
but then head cut.IMPF because know.IMPF things
'but then he cut their heads off because they knew things'
(Pananti 1817: 133)

Collocational specialization is also evident in some of the verbal synonyms. For example, *dar* rather than *donar* ('to give') is used for creating multiword verbal lexemes, as in *dar scorta* 'to escort,' *dar agioudo* 'to help,' *dar licentzia* 'to allow.' In the doublet *avir* ~ *ténir* ('to have'), only the second verb is used in analytic verb lexemes, as in *ténir paoura* 'to be scared,' *ténir febra* 'to have fever,' *ténir fantétzia* 'to be stubborn.' In the triplet *far* ~ *fazir* ~ *counchar* ('to do, make'), the verbs appear to be interchangeable in some but not all of their uses. For example, while 'it is necessary to do' is rendered as *bisogna far, fazir counchar*, and 'to hurry' as *far presto*, *fazir presto*, or *counchar presto*, the meteorological expressions translating Fr. *il fait chaud* 'it is hot,' *il fait froid* 'it is cold,' and *il fait du vent* 'it is windy' are constructed with the verb *fazir*, suggesting that these phrases were conventionalized in LF.

The existence of lexical choices for a substantial number of concepts is at variance with the conception of LF as lexically poor, and with classifying LF as a pidgin, since synonymy is typically not an expected feature of pidgins (Velupillai 2015: 31). The richness of LF's lexicon is further apparent in the organization of selected semantic domains, examined next.

5.4.5 Lexical Typology

LF displays substantial complexity in its detailed continuity with its lexifiers in the area of lexical typology, "characteristic ways in which language . . . packages semantic material into words" (Lehrer 1992: 249; cited after Koptjevskaja-Tamm et al. 2016: 434). Selected examples of how LF distributes semantic material across its lexical units are given in Table 5.7. They reveal that, in common with Italian and Spanish, and in most instances also French, LF combines the meanings of 'time' and 'weather' in one lexeme, that it lexically distinguishes between 'arm' and 'hand,' 'leg' and 'foot,' 'face' and 'cheek,' and between verbs of centripetal and centrifugal motion ('to come' versus 'to go'), and that it uses different words to convey the different senses of 'old,' 'to ask,' and 'to know' (Ricca 1993; Brown 2001; Koch 2001; Peeters et al. 2006: 90–94; Enrique-Arias 2010: 108; Stefenelli 2011: 566; Stolova 2015; Koptjevskaja-Tamm et al. 2016: 443).

The meaning of *vekio* ('aged') is emphasized by the derivative *vekiétza* 'old age' and that of *antico* ('ancient') by the collocation *tempo antico*, which translates Fr. *anciennement* 'formerly.' The division of the semantic domain of oldness into separate adjectives is also emphasized by the existence of separate

Table 5.7. *Selected semantic domains in Lingua Franca*

Lingua Franca	Italian	Spanish	French	Gloss
brakio	braccio	brazo	bras	‘arm’
mano	mano	mano	main	‘hand’
gamba	gamba	pierna	jambe	‘leg’
piedi	piede	pie	pie	‘foot’
fachia	faccia	cara	visage	‘face’
gouanchia	guancia	mejilla	joue	‘cheek’
venir	venire	venir	venir	‘to come’
andar	andare	ir	aller	‘to go’
tempo	tempo	tiempo	temps	‘time; weather’
domandar	domandare	preguntar	demander	‘to ask’
quérir	chiedere	pedir		
sabir	sapere	saber	savoir	‘to know’
conoschir	conoscere	conocer	connaître	
vekio	vecchio	viejo	vieux	‘old’
antico	antico	antiguo	ancien	

antonyms for each of the senses of ‘old,’ *dgiovine* ~ *picolo* (‘young’) and *nouovo* (‘new’). The generic-knowledge verb is found in the collocation *non sabir* ‘to not know’; while the senses of *conoschir*, ‘to meet’ and ‘to be acquainted with,’ are exemplified in (8a, 8b). The exchanges in (8c)–(8f) contrast the senses of the deictic verbs of motion *andar* and *vénir*, and the examples in (8g) and (8h) contrast the different senses of *tempo*.

(8) a. *ti conoschir per ellou?*
2s know.IMPF DOM 3s.M
‘Le connaissez vous?’
‘Do you know him?’
(Anonymous 1830a: 96)

b. *mi ténir piacher conoschir per ellou.*
1s have.IMPF pleasure meet.IMPF DOM 3s.M
‘Je serais bien aise de faire sa connaissance.’
‘I would be pleased to meet him.’
(Anonymous 1830a: 96)

c. *oundé ti vénir?*
whence 2s come.IMPF
'D'où venez-vous?'
'Where have you come from?'
(Anonymous 1830a: 95)

d. *mi vénir della* casa *di mi.*
1s come.IMPF of.ART house of 1s
'Je viens de chez moi.'
'I have come from my home.'
(Anonymous 1830a: 95)

e. *ové ti andar?*
where 2s fo.IMPF
'Où allez-vous?'
'Where are you going?'
(Anonymous 1830a: 95)

f. *mi andar in casa del Signor.*
1s go.IMPF in house of.the gentleman
'Je vais chez Monsieur M.'
'I am going to Mr. M.'s.'
(Anonymous 1830a: 95)

g. *molto tempo ti non mirato Signor M.?*
much time 2s NEG see.PF Mr. M.
'Y a-t-il long-tems que vous n'avez vu Monsieur M.?'
'Has it been long since you've seen Mr. M.?'
(Anonymous 1830a: 94)

h. *Comé star il tempo?*
how be.IMPF the weather
'Quel temps fait-il?'
'How is the weather?'
(Anonymous 1830a: 97)

LF's lexical continuity with its Romance lexifiers is further apparent in its well-developed vocabularies of color and kinship, and its possession and psychological verbs. LF's color terminology, as recorded in the *Dictionnaire*, comprises seven of the basic color terms (MacLaury 2001: 1228) – *bianco* 'white,' *négro* 'black,' *rosso* 'red,' *dgialo* 'yellow,' *verdé* 'green,' *blou* 'blue,' and *griso* 'gray' – as well as *kiaro* 'clear,' *oscouro* 'dark,' *biondo* ~ *rousso* 'blond,' *dorato* (for Fr. *doré* 'gilded, golden'), and the general word for 'color' (*color*). Its kinship terminology consists of *mamma* ~ *madre* 'mother,' *padre* 'father,' *figlio* ~ *mouchachou* 'son,' *mouchacha* 'daughter,' *fratello* ~ *cognato* 'brother,' *germana* 'sister,' *zio* 'uncle,' *zia* 'aunt,' *nipoté* 'nephew,' *nipota* 'niece,' *mouchéra* 'wife,' *moukera del filio* 'daughter-in-law,' *madre* 'mother-in-law,' *sorella* 'sister-in-law,' and the general term for 'kinsperson' (*sangré*). Predicative possession is expressed by means of a transitive construction in which the possessor and possessed noun phrases are coded as arguments of the verb 'to have,' a device inherited from LF's Romance lexifiers (illustrated in 9a) (Isačenko 1974; Stassen 2001: 955). LF also behaves syntactically like its Romance lexifiers in its ability to code the experiencer arguments of psychological verbs as both syntactic subjects (in 9b) and objects (in 9c) (Koch 2001: 1171–1172).

(9) a.

mi	*tenir*	*thé*	*mouchou*	*bonou …*
1s	have.IMPF	tea	very	good

'J'ai du thé délicieux …'
'I have some excellent tea'
(Anonymous 1830a: 97)

b.

mi	*quérir*	*mouchou*	*per*	*ti.*
1s	want.IMPF	very	DOM	2s

'je vous estime'
'I respect you'
(Anonymous 1830a: 32)

c.

qouando	*piacher*	*per*	*ti.*
when	please.IMPF	DOM	2s

'Quand il vous plaira.'
'Whenever you like.'
(Anonymous 1830a: 96)

Some of the above lexical and semantic distinctions are far from being universal (Koch 2001; Brown 2001, 2013), and some present considerable difficulties in the SLA context (see, e.g., Taylor 1985 on the difficulty of the Spanish lexical pair *saber/conocer* for English speaker learners). Their presence in a contact language can only be explained if the distinctions were essential and natural for its creators, and if the linguistic forms expressing these distinctions were common in the feature pool (the mixture of linguistic variants)[12] that fed its formation. The fact that many of the linguistic forms in question are transparently cognate in the participating languages would have ensured their survival in LF through mutual reinforcement (cf. Mufwene 2008: 119). As noted by Siegel (1997: 132), "the most common forms may have the best chance of survival, while the most idiosyncratic have the worst chance." The lexical typology of LF thus offers additional support for the hypothesis that inter-Romance koineization played an essential role in its formation and continued use.[13]

[12] See Mufwene (2001) regarding the feature pool concept, and Chapter 9 for further discussion.

[13] Of related interest is Parkvall's (2010) investigation of the Eurocentricity of Esperanto. The non-exhaustive list of features that align Esperanto typologically with the Indo-European languages of Europe includes a large color vocabulary, the lexical distinction between *blue*

5.4.6 Suppletion Patterns

LF displays further lexical complexity in continuing a number of the suppletion patterns of its Romance lexifiers. These include both the structural patterns themselves and the forms through which the suppletive relationships are realized (see Table 5.8). The grammatical domains underlying the suppletive relationships are summarized in (10) (see Mel'čuk 2006: 405–467); the corresponding regular formations are addressed in Chapter 6.

(10) Suppletion domains in Lingua Franca

a. Verb ~ deverbal noun:
   non ablar ~ silentzio, dormir ~ suono, tokkar ~ colpo
b. Noun ~ denominal adjective:
   oumbré ~ oumano
c. Inchoative ~ causative:
   morir ~ massar
d. Cardinal number ~ ordinal numeral:
   ouno ~ primo / primiéré, doué ~ ségoundo
e. Cardinal number ~ name of ten:
   doué ~ venti
f. Adjective ~ comparative degree:
   bonou ~ melior
g. Adverb ~ comparative degree:
   béné ~ mélio
h. Male ~ female:
   taour ~ vaka

5.4.7 Idiomatic Structure

The lexicon of the *Dictionnaire*'s LF contains a number of multiword expressions traceable to similar or identical conventionalized multiword expressions, or prefabs, in one or more of LF's Romance lexifiers. I am borrowing the term *prefab* from Erman and Warren (2000: 31), who define it as "a combination of at least two words favored by native speakers in preference to an alternative combination which could have been equivalent had there been no conventionalization." The rationale for considering prefabs together with LF's lexicon is that close affinity between prefabs and lexical units has long been recognized in the literature. For example, Pawley and Syder (1983: 191–192) speak of

and *green* and between *he* and *she*, the use of relative pronouns, the lack of morphological reduplication, and certain semantic features, such as combining the meanings of 'wear' and 'carry' in the same verb.

Table 5.8. *Selected suppletion patterns in Lingua Franca*

Lingua Franca	Italian	Spanish	French	Gloss
morir ~ massar	morire ~ uccidere	morir ~ matar	mourir ~ tuer	'die' ~ 'kill'
taour ~ vaka	toro ~ vacca	toro ~ vaca	taureau ~ vache	'bull' ~ 'cow'
non ablar ~ silentzio	tacere ~ silenzio	callar ~ silencio	se taire ~ silence	'to be silent' ~ 'silence'
dormir ~ souono	dormire ~ sonno	dormir ~ sueño	dormir ~ sommeil	'to sleep' ~ 'sleep'
tokkar ~ colpo	(colpire ~ colpo)	pegar / (golpear) ~ golpe	frapper ~ coup	'to hit, strike' ~ 'a blow'
oumbré ~ oumano	uomo ~ umano	hombre ~ humano	homme ~ humain	'man' ~ 'human'
bonou ~ melior	buono ~ migliore	bueno ~ mejor	bon ~ meilleur	'good' ~ 'better'
béné ~ mélio	bene ~ meglio	bien ~ mejor	bien ~ mieux	'well' ~ 'better'
ouno ~ primo, primiéré	uno ~ primo	uno ~ primero	un ~ premier	'one' ~ 'first'
doué ~ ségoundo	due ~ secondo	dos ~ segundo	deux ~ (deuxième)	'two' ~ 'second'
doué ~ venti	due ~ venti	dos ~ veinte	deux ~ vingt	'two' ~ 'twenty'

clause-length or longer *lexicalized sentence stems*, stable form-meaning combinations whose "fixed elements form a standard label for a culturally recognized concept, a term in the language," and hypothesize that "by far the largest part of the English speaker's lexicon consists of complex lexical items including several hundred thousand lexicalized sentence stems" (p. 215; see also Erwin and Warren 2000: 36; Bannard 2006).

A selection of Romance-origin prefabs in LF is given in Table 5.9. Many provide verbal shortcuts for recurrent social interactions: conventional formulae for the social rituals of greeting, leave-taking, and asking and replying about someone's health; meteorological expressions; expressions relating to

Table 5.9. *Selected multiword expressions in Lingua Franca*

Lingua Franca	Italian	Spanish	French	Gloss
ténir febra	avere la febbre	tener fiebre	avoir la fièvre	'to have fever'
ténir paoura	avere paura	tener miedo	avoir peur	'to be scared'
fasir paoura	far paura	dar miedo[a]	faire peur	'to scare'
fazir caldo	fa caldo	hace calor	il fait chaud	'it is hot'
fazir frédo	fa freddo	hace frío	il fait froid	'it is cold'
fazir vento	tira vento	hace viento	il fait du vent	'it is windy'
cosa bisognio counchar?	cosa bisogna fare?	qué hay que hacer?	que faut-il faire?	'what needs to be done?'
bon dgiorno Signor	buon giorno signore	buenos días señor	bonjour monsieur	'good morning sir'
bona séra	buona sera	buenas tardes	bonsoir	'good evening'
come ti star?	come stai?	cómo estás?	comment vas-tu?	'how are you?'
mi star bonou	sto bene	estoy bien	je suis bien	'I am well'
mi star béné acoussi	sto bene così	estoy bien así	je suis bien comme ça	'I am fine like this'
adios amigo	addio amico	adiós amigo	adieu mon ami	'good-bye friend'
qué ora star?	che ora è?	qué hora es?	quelle heure est-il?	'what time is it?'
cosa ténir?	che (cosa) ha?	qué tiene?	qu'a-t-il?	'what's the matter?'
non andar bonou	non va bene	no va bien	elle ne va pas bien	'it doesn't work'
andar avanti	va avanti	se adelanta	elle avance	'it is fast'
andar indiétro	va indietro	se atrasa	elle retarde	'it is slow'
per la palabra di mi	sulla mia parola	sobre mi palabra	sur ma parole	'upon my word'
star buona genti	è un buon'uomo	es buena gente	c'est un bon homme	'he's good people'
pold esser[b]	può essere	puede ser	peut-être	'perhaps'

Table 5.9. *(cont.)*

Lingua Franca	Italian	Spanish	French	Gloss
counchar favour[c]	fare un favore	hacer un favor	faire une faveur	'to do a favor'
pastar pano	impastare il pane	amasar el pan	pétrir le pain	'to knead bread'
contar di nouovo	contare di nuovo	contar de nuevo	compter de nouveau	'to count again'
con ségréto	in segreto	en secreto	en secret	'secretly'
in vita	in vita	con vida	en vie	'alive'

[a] Majorcan Spanish *hacer miedo* (Enrique-Arias 2010: 111). [b]See Cifoletti (2004: 57) and Baglioni (2017: 192) on the source of this expression. [c]Misprinted in the *Dictionnaire* as <councharfavour>.

telling the time; and a few other recurrent verbal and prepositional prefabs (cf. a useful taxonomy of multiword expressions in Parra Escartín et al. 2018).

Some of the prefabs may be traceable to a subset of LF's lexifiers, or even a single lexifier: compare the example in (11a) with the expression *fare colazione* 'to have breakfast (lunch)' in Italian, and the exampes in (11b) and (11c) with the expressions *dire juste* 'to say it as it is' (Hummel 2017: 31) and *je vais bien* 'I am well' in French.

(11) a. *ti* *fato* *colatzioné?*
2s do.PF breakfast
'Avez-vous déjeuné?'
'Have you had breakfast?'
(Anonymous 1830a: 96)

b. *mi* *ablar* *dgiousto.*
1s speak.IMPF just
'Je dis la vérité.'
'I speak the truth.'
(Anonymous 1830a: 93)

c. *mi* *andar* *bonou …*
1s hear.IMPF good
'je me porte bien'
'I am well.'
(Anonymous 1830a: 61)

The number and variety of Romance-origin prefabs in LF shows that its lexical continuity with the lexifiers extends far beyond the etymology of individual lexemes and encompasses that of idioms, which necessarily also includes the discourse and cultural practices in which the idioms are embedded. The idiomatic structure of LF is essentially Romance, a conclusion that has a bearing on its taxonomic status and the reasons for its morphosyntactic continuity with the lexifiers (see Owens 1996 regarding the role of idiomatic structure in genetic classification and Owens 2018: 210–212 on the impact of the diachronic stability of discourse patterns on morphosyntactic stability).

5.5 Chapter Summary

The lexical composition, lexical richness, lexical typology, suppletive patterns, and idiomatic structure of the *Dictionnaire*'s LF all show its detailed and interlocking continuity with its Romance lexifiers, while distancing it from pidgins.

The Romance lexicon of the *Dictionnaire*'s LF consists of three diachronic layers, each dominated by a particular lexifier: Spanish, Italian, or French. The most recent layer is French, and it is still lean at the evolutionary stage captured by the *Dictionnaire*. The French lexical items linger in the periphery of the lexicon, and are adapted to the Hispano-Italian phonological and morphological structures of LF. The French layer will continue to expand over the course of the nineteenth century, as will be reflected in the LF textual samples to appear after 1830 (Faidherbe 1884; Cifoletti 1989: 32–33; 1994a; 1994b). The Italian layer is numerically the most substantial of the three and occupies the intermediate diachronic position. The Spanish layer is the oldest; it includes some of the most basic and/or frequent vocabulary and displays the highest degree of adaptation to the vocalism of Berber and Arabic. A substantial number of Spanish-derived words are duplicated by referentially similar Italian-derived lexemes, which suggests that, at the time of the *Dictionnaire*'s compilation, the process of relexification of Spanish lexical items with Italian ones was in progress. The comparative antiquity of the Spanish lexical layer, and the ongoing relexification, are also revealed by a comparison of the LF vocabularies of Haedo (1612) and Anonymous (1830a), which shows a significant drop in the percentage of Spanish words over the intervening two and a half centuries, from about 41 percent in 1580 to about 6 percent in 1830 (Cornelissen 1992). Perhaps not surprisingly, given the common historical processes at work, the three Romance lexical layers in the LF of Algeria correspond to the three diachronic layers of Romance loans in Algerian Arabic, with the Spanish layer at the bottom, the French layer on top, and the Italian layer in between (Cohen 1912: 452–453, Guella 2011: 83–85; Heath 1989: 152–156; Lanly 1962; Souag 2005).

A considerable number of LF words cannot be traced to a specific Romance source language. The difficulty of tracing LF words to specific sources has been repeatedly noted by researchers of LF, including Cornelissen (1992: 220–221), Cifoletti (2004: 56), Baglioni (2017: 189), and Russo (2001: 220–226), who explains: "È impresa morto ardua differenziare l'apporto delle singole lingue romanze nel *Dictionnaire*; in parte perché addattamenti fonetici e morfologici ne hanno modificato l'aspetto" [Identifying the contributions of individual Romance languages in the *Dictionnaire* is a very difficult task, partly because phonetic and morphological adaptations have modified their appearance]. The issue of multiple etymologies is far from being unique to the study of LF, however, as it is routinely confronted by researchers of language contact and contact languages. Thus, Cohen (1912: 445) notes that some Romance loans in Algerian Arabic can be derived from both Spanish and Italian, and Heath (1989: 152–156) comments on a similar issue with respect to Romance loans in MCA. It has been suggested that up to 50 percent of the vocabulary of Tok Pisin is traceable to more than one language (Zuckermann 2003: 55, citing Mühlhäusler 1986: 2). Even more comparable to the LF situation is the case of Portuguese- and Spanish-lexified Papiamentu: according to the estimate cited in Green (1988: 463), only 35 percent of the words in the 100 Swadesh list of Papiamentu are separately attributable to Spanish or Portuguese, while 40 percent may derive from either language. Over half of the overall Romance lexical component of Papiamentu is "not differentially attributable," while "the remainder can be ascribed to Spanish and Portuguese in the approximate ratio 3:1" (Green 1988: 464; see also Jacobs 2012: 17n16).

For a number of LF lexemes, a single etymological source cannot account for the totality of their semantic, phonological, morphological, and/or syntactic properties. Thus, LF *forar*, discussed in Section 5.2.1, translates Fr. *percer* 'to pierce' and a range of verbs which have in common the meaning of removing or taking something away (*arracher* 'to pull,' *débrider* 'to unbridle,' *écarter* 'to remove,' *emporter* 'to take away,' *enlever* 'to remove,' *ôter* 'to take away'). As discussed by Cifoletti (2004: 74), this LF neologism conflates the semantics of Venetian *fora* 'out, outside' with that of Italian *forare* 'to pierce, make a hole in,' which is phonetically similar. The *Dictionnaire* uses LF *mirar* to translate French *voir* 'to see,' *apercevoir* 'to notice,' and *viser* 'to aim.' While the first two meanings are derivable from Spanish *mirar* 'to look at,' with the common semantic shift from 'to look at' > 'to see,' the third is traceable to phonetically similar Italian *mirare* 'to aim.' LF *fondouk* 'market' has the phonetic shape of Arabic /funduq/ while being semantically closer to Italian *fondacco* (Cifoletti 2004: 61–62). The process underlying these developments has been described in language-contact literature under various labels, including lexical conflation and lexical hybridization (Zuckermann 2003: 53–56).

Phonological hybrids are also present and include the forms in (12). Morphological hybrids include the many forms in which French stems are combined with Hispano-Italian suffixes or word markers, such as *intendouto* 'heard' (< Fr. *entendre*, It. *-uto*) and *bagueta* 'little stick' (< Fr. *baguette*, Sp. It. *-a*), as well as the numerals *diechisetté* 'seventeen,' *diechiotto* 'eighteen,' and *diechinové* 'nineteen,' in which Italian-derived numbers are assembled into a French morphological pattern (< It. *dieci* 'ten,' *sette* 'seven,' *otto* 'eight,' *nove* 'nine'; cf. Fr. *dix-sept* 'seventeen,' *dix-huit* 'eighteen,' *dix-neuf* 'nineteen') (see Baglioni 2010: 268 and Chapter 6).

(12)	fromagio	'cheese'	(< Fr. fromage, It. formaggio)[14]
	rimportar	'to gain'	(< It. riportare, Fr. remporter)
	sedjiournar	'to stay'	(< It. soggiornare, Fr. séjourner)
	dovinar	'to guess'	(< It. indovinare, Fr. deviner)
	risponsa	'answer'	(< Fr. réponse, It. risposta, possibly also Eng. response)
	riposta	'solution'	(< It. risposta, Fr. réponse, possibly also Eng. riposte)

With respect to lexical items with hybrid syntactic properties, Coates (1971: 28) observes that LF *mouchou* 'very; much,' though derived phonetically from Spanish *mucho*, behaves syntactically like Italian *molto* 'very.' This observation stems from the use of *mouchou* before adjectives (including adjectives used adverbially, as in *star mouchou bonou* 'he is very well'), where Spanish calls for the use of *muy* 'very' (Butt and Benjamin 2004: 110). Another instance is the verb *goustar* 'to taste; to like, approve,' which appears to combine the phonetic shape of Spanish *gustar* and/or Italian *gustare* with the transitivity of French *goûter* in the sense of 'to like' (see 13b) (Whitley 1995; Koch 2001: 1171–1172).

(13) a.

mi	*tenir*	*thé*	*mouchou*	*bonou;*
1s	have.IMPF	tea.M	very	good.M

mi	*quérir*	*ti*	*goustar*	*per*	*ellou.*
1s	want.IMPF	2s	taste.IMPF	DOM	3s.M

'J'ai du thé délicieux; je veux que vous en goutiez.'
'I've got some delicious tea, I want you to try it.'
(Anonymous 1830a: 97)

b.

ti	*goustar*	*qouesta*	*cosa?*
2s	like.IMPF	this	thing

'Approuvez-vous cette chose?'
'Do you like this thing?'
(Anonymous 1830a: 13)

[14] Similar forms are cited by Hull (1985: 252) for French-influenced Egyptian Italian, including *fromaggio* 'cheese' and *rincontrare* 'to meet' (It. *incontrare*, Fr. *rencontrer*).

In addition to over 95 percent of its vocabulary, LF also shares with its Romance lexifiers the fact of possessing Latinisms, both lexical (*imago* 'image,' *brakio* 'arm,' *viator* 'traveler') and structural: for example, some of the compounding patterns, such as the structure of teen numerals; some of the suppletion patterns, such as *bonou* 'good' ~ *melior* 'better'; and some of the finely grained semantic distinctions, such as *sabir* (generic knowledge) ~ *conoschir* (specific knowledge), are ultimately traceable to patterns inherited from Latin (*bonus* ~ *melior*, *scire* ~ *cognoscere*).

The leading non-Romance lexical component of LF is Arabic. At about 3 percent of the total vocabulary size, it does not exceed the Arabic components of Romance languages which have been in direct contact with Arabic historically (Schuchardt 1909; Aslanov 2014). There is no discernible structural influence of Arabic on LF outside the domain of phonology, where it is strongest in words of Spanish origin (Cifoletti 1989, 2004). The Arabic and Turkish words in LF are similar in essential ways to loanwords in noncontact languages: e.g., consonant-final nouns from these sources tend not to acquire a final vowel in LF, Turkish and Arabic words tend not to participate in LF's morphological processes,[15] are not subjected to internal analysis in the way words from Romance sources are,[16] are not found in the core vocabulary, consist predominantly of nouns, contain no verbs or function words, and pertain to semantic domains most prone to intercultural influences. The perceived foreignness of the Turkish and Arabic words is emphasized by the use of orthographic conventions that differ from the ones normally employed for the same consonants in words of Romance origin (see Chapter 4).

The comparatively minor Arabic contribution to LF is addressed by Aslanov (2014, 2016), who views it as evidence of LF's functioning more as a means of

[15] The only exception is the adjective *maboul* 'crazy,' recorded together with the feminine form *maboula*. The source of the feminine gender marker *-a* in this word is unclear, as it is shared by Arabic, Italian, and Spanish (Cifoletti 2004: 41).

[16] The Turkish-origin suffix *-gi* in *tobgi* 'gunner' (< Tu. *topçu*) appears to be unanalyzed in LF, though it is productive in Algerian Arabic (Cohen 1912: 456, 462–463; Benkato 2020: 202; cf. *saahgi* 'watchmaker,' *bouabidgi* 'cobbler,' *kandakchi* 'gunsmith' in the *Dictionnaire*'s Arabic vocabulary), other Arabic languages (cf. *dukkanži* 'one who owns a shop,' *ʔahwaži* 'coffee-maker, one who owns a coffee-house' in Butros 1973: 93), and Romance languages which have been in contact with Turkish (cf. Romanian *barcă* 'boat' →*barcagiu* 'ferryman,' *lapte* 'milk' →*laptagiu* 'milkman' in Şăineanu 1900: 52–53; Pascu 1916: 410–412; Rainer 2016c: 519; and Judeo-Spanish *pleito* 'quarrel' →*pleytedjí* 'quarrelsome person' in Bunis 2016: 413). The Arabic-origin suffix *-i*, found in the *Dictionnaire*'s gentilic/ethnic designations *roumi* 'Greek' and *piskéri* 'porter' ('Biskran'), also appears to be unanalyzed in LF. It is found in Turkish (Urban 2015: 39) and in Romance languages which have been in contact with Turkish or Arabic (cf. Spanish *magrebí* 'Maghrebi,' *marroquí* 'Moroccan,' *alfonsí* 'Alfonsine' in Walsh 1971; Schweickard 1993; Romanian *limoniu* 'lemon-yellow,' *samaniu* 'straw-yellow' in Şăineanu 1900: 53–54).

communication among Europeans from different nations than between the latter and Arabs:

> L'assenza relativa dell'arabo nella lingua franca . . . potrebbe corroborare l'idea secondo la quale la lingua franca svilupattasi in Algeria, Tunisia e Tripolitana in prima età moderna serviva più all'intercomprensione fra cristiani provenienti da vari orizzonti linguistici . . . che alla comunicazione fra arabi e cristiani. (Aslanov 2016: 31)

> [The comparative absence of Arabic in Lingua Franca could corroborate the idea that the Lingua Franca that developed in Algeria, Tunisia and Tripolitania in the early modern period served more for mutual understanding among Christians from different linguistic horizons than for communication between Arabs and Christians.]

Baglioni (2017) reaches a similar conclusion:

> [F]rom a lexical point of view, the Algerian LF, as documented by the *Dictionnaire* and all other sources, is a clearly (Italo-)Romance-based variety, whose Arabic component is much less relevant than that of Spanish, Portuguese and Sicilian. The main contact processes that can be reconstructed must have been between the Romance languages . . . (Baglioni 2017: 203)

As discussed in this chapter, the specifically Romance features of the LF lexicon extend to levels of organization that transcend the etymology of the lexemes and encompass lexical typology (ways of packaging semantic material into words), idiomatic structure (multiword expressions and underlying discourse practices), and suppletion patterns (including both the domains of suppletion and its exponence). These numerous, specific, and interlocking correspondences point to a substantial degree of continuity between LF and its Romance lexifiers, confirming the crucial role of inter-Romance koineization in its formation and transmission.

6 The Word Formation

This chapter examines the word formation patterns of the *Dictionnaire*'s LF. Its purpose is twofold: to provide a descriptive analysis of the patterns, and to situate them in relation to the word formation patterns of LF's Romance lexifiers and those of pidgins. To this end, the chapter first surveys the word formation mechanisms of the main Romance lexifiers of LF and pidgins (in Sections 6.1 and 6.2, respectively). Section 6.3 describes the predominant word formation pattern attested in the *Dictionnaire* and provides a preliminary discussion of LF noun and verb morphology. Sections 6.4–6.8 look, respectively, at suffixation, prefixation, suppletion, compounding, and multiword lexical expressions. Section 6.9 examines how the different word formation mechanisms interact in a single functional domain, that of valency/transitivity alternations. Section 6.10 summarizes the findings and relates them to the question of LF's taxonomic status.

6.1 Lexifiers

In the Romance lexifiers of LF, the most productive and varied word formation mechanism is affixation, particularly suffixation.[1] In both Italian and Spanish,

[1] This synopsis is based on the following publications: Rohlfs (1969), Iacobini (2004, 2015), Voghera (2004), Butt and Benjamín (2004), Patota (2006), Real Academia Española (2010), Kabatek and Pusch (2011), Masini (2011), Bauer (2011), Varela (2012), Buchi and Chauveau (2015), Forza and Scalise (2016), and Rainer (2016a, 2016b, 2016c). These sources do not necessarily agree in their analysis, terminology, or classification of Romance word formation patterns. For example, the place of syntagmatic compounds in the taxonomy of lexeme-building devices is unsettled, derivation of deverbal action nouns by means of the word marker *-o/-a/-e/-Ø* is categorized non-uniformly, and different functional analyses of the theme vowel lead to non-uniform treatment of conversion and parasynthesis (Voghera 2004; Buenafuentes de la Mata 2007; Alonso Ramos 2009; Rifón Sánchez 2011: 234n2; Varela 2012: 209; Rainer 2016a: 2636; 2016b: 2717; 2016c: 517, 519–521). The synopsis offered here represents one possible approach to analyzing Romance word formation. Patterns that are not relevant to word formation in LF, such as blending, clipping, abbreviations, neoclassical compounds, and nominal compounds formed by juxtaposing two nouns (some of these gained currency only in the twentieth century), are excluded from discussion.

the final unstressed vowel of the noun (the word marker),[2] if present, is suppressed during suffixation (see 1a); the same is generally true of the adjective inflection marker (see 1b). The theme vowel of the verb, located between the lexical root and inflection markers, is treated in some analyses as a derivational suffix in its own right (Varela 2012: 214; see 1c).

(1) a. It. *finestr-a* 'window' → *finestr-ino* 'car window'
Sp. *cor-o* 'choir' → *cor-al* 'choral'

b. It. *bell-o* 'beautiful' → *bell-ezza* 'beauty'
Sp. *clar-o* 'clear' → *clar-idad* 'clarity'

c. It. *martell-o* 'hammer' → *martell-a-re* 'to hammer'
Sp. *sal* 'salt' → *sal-a-r* 'to salt'

The examples in (1) above show that suffixes can change the lexical category of the base. Prefixes, by contrast, do not have this ability; cf. It. *caricare* 'to load' → *s-caricare* 'to unload,' Sp. *leal* 'loyal' →*des-leal* 'disloyal.' Prefixes and suffixes may be added to a base simultaneously; in Romance linguistics, this type of derivation is known as parasynthesis (Iacobini 2004: 165; Varela 2012: 214; Rainer 2016c: 517). The theme vowels *-a-* and *-i-* in the parasynthetic verbs in (2) are assumed to act as derivational suffixes (Varela 2012: 214).

(2) It. *burr-o* 'butter' → *im-burr-a-re* 'to butter'
It. *pian-o* 'level' → *s-pian-a-re* 'to level'
It. *dolc-e* 'sweet' → *ad-dolc-i-re* 'to sweeten'
Sp. *cuchill-o* 'knife' → *a-cuchill-a-r* 'to stab'
Sp. *dulc-e* 'sweet' → *en-dulz-a-r* 'to sweeten'
Sp. *roj-o* 'red' → *en-roj-ec-er* 'to go red'

Nonaffixal derivation is possible but is less productive than affixation. It comprises – apart from a number of processes which are not relevant in the context of this chapter, such as clipping, blending, and abbreviation – conversion (see 3a) and the process in (3b) variably classified as conversion or back-formation.

(3) a. It. *parlare* 'to speak' → *il parlare* 'dialect'
It. *povero* 'poor' → *i poveri* 'the poor'
Sp. *bueno* 'good' → *el bueno* 'the good guy'
lo bueno 'the good thing'
b. It. *arrivare* 'to arrive' → *arrivo* 'arrival'
It. *sostare* 'to stop' → *sosta* 'stop'
Sp. *retener* 'to retain' → *retén* 'stop, checkpoint'
Sp. *costar* 'to cost' → *costo*, *coste*, *costa(s)* 'cost(s)'

[2] See Harris (1991: 28; 1992: 66, 1996) and Acquaviva (2009) regarding word markers in Spanish and Italian.

Compounding is, similarly, less productive than affixation. In both Italian and Spanish, the lexical categories of the bases are mostly nouns, adjectives, and verbs, less often adverbs or prepositions; while the resulting compounds are almost exclusively nouns or adjectives. Examples illustrating the most relevant compound types are shown below in (4); verb-noun compounds form a particularly productive pattern in the Romance lexifiers of LF.

(4) a. Italian

cavatappi 'corkscrew'	(*cavare* 'pull out,' *tappi* 'corks')	(V-N)
terracotta 'terracotta'	(*terra* 'earth,' *cotta* 'baked')	(N-A)
mezzaluna 'half-moon'	(*mezzo* 'half,' *luna* 'moon')	(A-N)
sottobosco 'undergrowth'	(*sotto* 'under,' *bosco* 'wood')	(P-N)
malfatto 'badly done'	(*male* 'badly,' *fatto* 'done')	(Adv-Pple)

b. Spanish

sacacorchos 'corkscrew'	(*sacar* 'pull out,' *corchos* 'corks')	(V-N)
hierbabuena 'mint'	(*hierba* 'grass,' *bueno* 'good')	(N-A)
mediodía 'noon'	(*medio* 'half,' *día* 'day')	(A-N)
sobremesa 'tablecloth'	(*sobre* 'on,' *mesa* 'table')	(P-N)
maleducado 'ill-mannered'	(*mal* 'badly,' *educado* 'educated')	(Adv-Pple)

The Romance lexifiers of LF also possess a number of lexeme-building mechanisms which are located halfway between composition (morphology) and phraseology (syntax). For our purposes, the most relevant of these are nominal syntagmatic compounds and multiword verbal lexemes. Syntagmatic compounds are "new names for concepts [formed] on the basis of lexical patterns with internal syntactic structure" (Rainer 2016a: 2714). Examples of the most common types of syntagmatic compounds in Italian and Spanish – noun-adjective, adjective-noun, and noun-preposition-(article)-noun – are given in (5).

(5) a. Italian

anima gemella 'soulmate'	(*anima* 'soul,' *gemella* 'twin')
terza età 'the elderly'	(*terza* 'third,' *età* 'age')
coda di cavallo 'ponytail'	(*coda* 'tail,' *di* 'of,' *cavallo* 'horse')
cavallo da corsa 'racehorse'	(*cavallo* 'horse,' *da* 'for,' *corsa* 'racing')
luce del giorno 'daylight'	(*luce* 'light,' *del* 'of the,' *giorno* 'day')

b. Spanish

comida rápida 'fast food'	(*comida* 'food,' *rápida* 'fast')
medio hermano 'half-brother'	(*medio* 'half,' *hermano* 'brother')
perro de caza 'hunting dog'	(*perro* 'dog,' *de* 'of,' *caza* 'hunting')
asesino en serie 'serial killer'	(*asesino* 'killer,' *en* 'in,' *serie* 'series')
orden del día 'agenda'	(*orden* 'order,' *del* 'of the,' *día* 'day')

Multiword verbal lexemes include particle verbs, constructions in which a verb is followed by a locative particle (see 6a); and light verb constructions, in which a verb is followed by a noun, adjective, adverb, or prepositional phrase complement (see 6b). Particle verbs have different degrees of productivity in different Romance languages; thus, Italian is ahead of Spanish in the number and variety of its particle verbs. The verbs that tend to occur more often in particle verb constructions in Italian, and to combine with more particles, are "generic motion verbs, deictic verbs, and verbs of putting or removal" (Iacobini 2015: 634). These include *andare* 'to go,' *venire* 'to come,' *mettere* 'to put,' and *tirare* 'to pull.' Light verb constructions tend to be built around semantically bleached support verbs like *have*, *do/make*, *give*, *take*, and *put*. Dubský (1963: 43, 48) notes alternation and competition between some of the support verbs in Old Spanish (see also Enrique-Arias 2010: 111). Both particle verb and light verb constructions may have noncompositional, idiomatic meanings, as seen in Italian *fare fuori* 'to kill' (lit. 'to do out') and Spanish *tomar el pelo* 'to pull somebody's leg' (lit. 'to take the hair') (Polák 1949; Dubský 1963; Alonso Ramos 1998; Salvi 2001; Iacobini and Masini 2007; Calvo Rigual 2008; Iacobini 2009, 2015; Guglielmo 2010; Rainer 2016b, 2016c).

(6)

a. Particle (phrasal) verbs

It. *andare fuori* 'to go out'	(*andare* 'to go,' *fuori* 'out')
It. *portare via* 'to take away'	(*portare* 'to carry,' *via* 'away')
It. *venire giù* 'to come down, descend'	(*venire* 'to come,' *giù* 'down')
It. *mettere sotto* 'to put under, to run over'	(*mettere* 'to put,' *sotto* 'under')
Sp. *volver atrás* 'to go back'	(*volver* 'to turn,' *atrás* 'behind')
Sp. *dejar fuera* 'to leave out'	(*dejar* 'to leave,' *fuera* 'out')

b. Light (support) verb constructions

It. *fare presto* 'to hurry up'	(*fare* 'to do,' *presto* 'soon')
It. *fare una telefonata* 'to make a phone call'	(*fare* 'to make,' *una* 'a,' *telefonata* 'call')
It. *dare fuoco* 'to set fire'	(*dare* 'to give,' *fuoco* 'fire')
It. *avere fame* 'to be hungry'	(*avere* 'to have,' *fame* 'hunger')
Sp. *acabar mal* 'to come to a bad end'	(*acabar* 'to end,' *mal* 'badly')
Sp. *echar un vistazo* 'to take a look'	(*echar* 'to throw,' *un* 'a,' *vistazo* 'look')
Sp. *hacer alusión* 'to allude to'	(*hacer* 'to make,' *alusión* 'allusion')
Sp. *dar fin* 'to end'	(*dar* 'to give,' *fin* 'end')

Another, much less productive, pattern that is intermediate between lexicon and syntax is reduplication, as seen in It. *piccolo piccolo* 'very small,' *pian piano* 'very slowly,' *fuggi fuggi* 'stampede'; and Sp. *mujer mujer* 'real woman,' *tonto tonto* 'very stupid,' *muy muy grande* 'very big.'

Table 6.1. *Vocabulary enrichment mechanisms in pidgins*

Mechanism	Description
Polysemy	Limited vocabulary leads to "a staggering amount of polysemy" in content and functional items. Many pidgins have a single multipurpose adposition.
Multifunctionality	The same invariable word is used in different part-of-speech categories.
Multiword lexical expressions	(Nominal) compounds, circumlocutions, analytic verbal lexemes composed of the verb DO/MAKE and a noun complement.

6.2 Pidgins

The main vocabulary enrichment strategies of pidgins are polysemy ("one word having many meanings"), multifunctionality ("one word having many syntactic uses"), and creation of multiword lexical expressions: circumlocutions ("lexical items consisting of phrases rather than single words"), (nominal) compounds, and analytic verbal lexemes with the verb DO/MAKE (Parkvall and Bakker 2013: 33–35; the descriptions in parentheses are from Holm 2000: 108). Pidgins typically lack "derivation, reduplication, infixation, suprafixation, allomorphy, any synthetic structures" (Parkvall and Bakker 2013: 46). Table 6.1 summarizes the vocabulary-enriching techniques of pidgins, based on the discussion in Parkvall and Bakker (2013: 33–35, 36–37, 46) and Parkvall (2019: 264–265).

Plag (2009b) makes similar predictions regarding word formation patterns in creoles. In this and several related publications, he pursues the hypothesis that "creoles originate as conventionalized interlanguages of an early developmental stage" (p. 339):

> If creoles are conventionalized interlanguages, we would expect to find word-formation systems with the following properties:
>
> – frequent use of circumlocutions
> – very little affixation in comparison to the lexifier
> – in cases of affixation, overgeneralizations and innovative use of inherited affixes
> – very productive compounding, with transfer effects concerning headedness
> – productive multifunctionality (Plag 2009b: 346–347)

The word formation systems of creoles thus overlap to a considerable extent with those of pidgins, particularly as regards the nonproductivity of affixation and productive use of multifunctionality, compounding, and circumlocutions.[3] The similarities are broadly attributable to universals of naturalistic SLA, particularly where there is a significant genetic and/or typological distance between the source and target languages (see Cysouw 2013; Schepens et al. 2013).

6.3 Predominant Pattern

The best-represented word formation mechanism in the *Dictionnaire*'s LF is derivation. A number of derivational patterns are discernible, the most common of which is illustrated in (7). The examples below take no account of the direction of the derivation, which is addressed in the discussion that follows. The *Dictionnaire* records over a hundred verb-noun pairs of the type(s) shown in (7), which is significantly more than any other word formation pattern.

(7)

a.

Noun with the word marker *-o*		Verb	
balo	'dance'	balar	'to dance'
trotto	'trot'	trottar	'to trot'
soffio	'breath'	soffiar	'to breathe'
viagio	'journey'	viagiar	'to travel'

b.

Noun with the word marker *-a*		Verb	
peska	'fishing'	peskar	'to fish'
caschia	'hunting'	caschar	'to hunt'
paga	'pay'	pagar	'to pay'
fouga	'flight'	fougir	'to flee'

c.

Noun with the word marker *-e*		Verb	
salé	'salt'	salar	'to salt'
fioré	'flower'	fiorïr	'to blossom'

d.

Noun with the word marker Ø		Verb	
saboun	'soap'	sabounar	'to soap'
favor	'protection'	favorir	'to protect'

In the nouns in (7), the shared base is furnished with the word marker *-o*, *-a*, *-e*, or zero (Ø). The majority of the nouns have the word markers *-o* (over 50) or *-a* (over 30), which reflects their overall preponderance in the *Dictionnaire*'s LF. Their perception as an important part of the noun category is indicated by the adaptation to LF of a number of Romance-origin nouns ending in *-e* or a consonant (see 8).

[3] See Plag (2009b: 339ff.) and Booij (2007: 81–85) regarding the fluidity of the boundary between compounds and circumlocutions.

(8)

moukera ~ mouchéra	'woman'	(< Sp. mujer)
biéra	'beer'	(< Fr. bière)
bagueta	'little stick'	(< Fr. baguette)
verro	'glass'	(< Fr. verre)
pano[4]	'bread'	(< It. pane)
généro	'sort, kind'	(< It. genere)
ventro	'stomach'	(< It. Fr. ventre)

In the verbs in (7), the shared base is furnished with a theme vowel and an inflectional ending, as in *fin-é* 'end' → *fin-i-r* / *fin-i-to* 'to end.' The LF verb has only two inflectional endings, *-r* (deriving from the Romance infinitive) and *-to* (deriving from the Italian past participle). The *-r* form is the unmarked form of the verb; it is used in nonpast, imperfective, and imperative contexts and in verbal complements, and is glossed IMPF (imperfective) in the examples below. The *-to* form is found only in perfective or past contexts; it is glossed in the examples as PF (perfective). The imperfective form distinguishes two theme vowels, *-a-* and *-i-*, and the perfective form distinguishes three, *-a-*, *-i-*, and *-u-*. In both verb forms, *-a-* is the predominant theme vowel; it generally derives from the Spanish / Italian theme vowel *-a-* or French theme vowel *-e-* (see 9a). The theme vowel *-i-* conflates the Spanish / Italian theme vowels *-i-* and *-e-*; more rarely, it reflects the first conjugation vowel of the lexifiers (see 9b). In the perfective, the theme vowel *-u-* is less frequent than either *-a-* or *-i-* (see 9c).

(9)

a. LF imperfective with the theme vowel *-a-*

comminchiar	'to begin'	(< It. comminciare)
escapar	'to escape'	(< Sp. escapar)
cédar	'to give up'	(< Fr. céder)

b. LF imperfective with the theme vowel *-i-*

ridir	'to laugh'	(< It. ridere)
fiorïr	'to blossom'	(< It. fiorire)
fazir	'to do, make'	(< Sp. Ptg. fazer)
inchir	'to fill'	(< Sp. henchir)
composir	'to arrange'	(< Fr. composer)

c. LF perfective

comminchiato	'to begin'	(< It. comminciato)
fiorito	'to blossom'	(< It. fiorito)
conoschiuto	'to know'	(< It. conosciuto)
escapato	'to escape'	(< Sp. escapar, It. -ato)
fazito	'to do, make'	(< Sp. Ptg. fazer, It. -ito)
inchito	'to fill'	(< Sp. henchir, It. -ito)

[4] Also *pané*.

escondouto	'to hide'	(< Sp. esconder, It. -uto)
avalato	'to swallow'	(< Fr. avaler, It. -ato)
composito	'to arrange'	(< Fr. composer, It. -ito)
cédouto	'to give up'	(< Fr. céder, It. -uto)

In some of the verb-noun pairs in (7), the probable direction of the derivation is from the noun to the verb (as in *salé* 'salt' → *salar* 'to salt'), while in others it is from the verb to the noun (as in *caschiar* 'to hunt' → *caschia* 'hunting'). From the viewpoint of the typology of derivational processes, this represents two separate patterns. As noted in Section 6.1, derivation of denominal verbs of the type Sp. *sal* 'salt' → *salar* 'to salt' may be qualified as suffixal ("it is commonly assumed that the thematic vowel of the verb acts as a derivational suffix"; Varela 2012: 214). The opposite process – derivation of deverbal nouns by removing part of the verbal lexeme, as in It. *sostare* 'to stop' → *sosta* 'stop' – is considered nonaffixal derivation, including when accompanied by the addition to the noun of a word marker (Rifón Sánchez 2011; Varela 2012; Rainer 2016c: 520). This analysis may be extended to LF. Also in line with the situation in the lexifiers is the variety of semantic relations that obtain in the verb-noun pairs. Disregarding the direction of the derivation, we find such pairings as verb-agent noun, verb-instrument noun, verb-location noun, verb-result/object noun, and verb-event/action noun (see Lavale Ortiz 2011: 110–111; Rainer 2016c: 518; and the examples in 10).

(10)	*assassinar*	'to murder'	*assassino*	'murderer'
	gouidar	'to guide'	*gouida*	'guide'
	ségar	'to saw'	*séga*	'saw'
	sabounar	'to lather'	*saboun*	'soap'
	caschar	'to hunt'	*caschia*	'hunting'
	peskar	'to fish'	*peska*	'fishing'
	cousinar	'to cook'	*cousina*	'kitchen'
	caminar	'to walk'	*camino*	'road'
	gouadagniar	'to earn'	*gouadagnio*	'earnings'
	scométir	'to bet'	*scometza*	'bet'

6.4 Suffixation

The *Dictionnaire*'s LF has inherited from its lexifiers a fair amount of derivational affixation (see representative word families in 11). The majority of the inherited derivational patterns involve suffixation, and the majority of the suffixes derive nouns. Both characteristics are continuous with the lexifier patterns: "In Romance, nouns boast the most articulate array of suffixes" (Rainer 2016c: 518; see also Iacobini and Thornton 1994: 282). There is some evidence that LF not only preserved the inherited derivational devices but also actively used them to construct new words. Thus, Cifoletti (2004: 56, 74) hypothesizes that *forar* 'to remove, discard, pull out,' *balador* 'dancer,' *fougidor* 'deserter, runaway, renegade,' *biancador* 'launderer,' and *cazéria* 'barracks' may have been created in LF language-internally.[5]

(11)	senso	'sense'	séga	'saw'
	sensato	'sensible'	ségar	'to saw'
	sensationé	'sensation'	segador	'sawyer'
	sensibilé	'sensitive'	ségadoura	'sawing'
	sensibilita	'sensitivity'		

6.4.1 Deverbal Nouns

Several inherited patterns involve derivation of nouns from verbs. About nineteen nouns are nominalizations of the past participle; the majority of these end in *-a*. This number includes the forms exemplified in (12b), in which the derivational relationship is obscured by inherited allomorphy.

(12)	a.	volar	'to fly'	volata	'flight'
		fritar	'to fry'	fritata	'omelet'
		vendir	'to sell'	vendita	'sale'
		vestir	'to dress'	vestito	'garment'
		dgémir	'to moan'	dgémito	'moan'
	b.	piangir	'to cry'	pianto	'tear, sob'
		soridir	'to smile'	soriso	'smile'
		succedir	'to succeed'	succeso	'success'
		promettir	'to promise'	promessa	'promise'
		scométir	'to bet'	scometza	'bet'

The most frequent suffix deriving action nouns is *-tzion* ~ *-tion*; some eighteen verb-noun pairs of this type are attested in the *Dictionnaire*.

(13)	séparar	'to separate'	séparatzion	'separation'
	permettir	'to allow'	permitzion	'permission'
	pounir	'to punish'	pounitzion	'punishment'

About ten deverbal nouns are derived by means of *-ntza*.

(14)	miscolar	'to mix'	miscolantza	'mixture'
	ignorar	'to ignore'	ignoranza	'ignorance'
	sfidar	'to mistrust'	sfidentza	'mistrust'
	obédir	'to obey'	obédientza	'obedience'

[5] The etymology of *forar* is discussed in Chapter 5. See Dakhlia (2008: 345) for an alternative etymology of *cazéria*; Derek C. Carr (p.c.) suggests Sp. *casería* as another potential source for this word.

About eight deverbal nouns are formed by means of *-mento* (see 15). In the case of *campamento*, the corresponding verb is not recorded, though there is a related noun (*campo*).

(15)

ornar	'to decorate'	ornamento	'ornament'
armar	'to arm'	armamento	'arms'
movir	'to move'	movimento	'movement'
combatir	'to fight'	combatimento	'battle'
(campo	'camp, field')	campamento	'camp'

About seven nouns are formed with the suffix *-oura* ~ *-doura* ~ *-toura*. Included in this number is *verdoura* 'gardening, greenery' (< *verde* 'green').

(16)

serrar	'to shut'	serradoura	'lock'
aprir	'to open'	appertoura	'opening'

Most agent nouns are derived by means of the suffix *-dor* ~ *-tor*. The *Dictionnaire* contains about sixteen relevant verb-noun pairs; *-dor* is the more frequent allomorph. The last noun in (17) below is based on the lexifier past participle and contains a different allomorph of the stem.

(17)

peskar	'to fish'	peskador	'fisherman'
caschar	'to hunt'	caschador	'hunter'
cantar	'to sing'	cantador	'singer'
bévir	'to drink'	bévidor	'drinker'
vincir	'to conquer'	vincitor	'victor'
mentir	'to lie'	mentitor	'liar'
succedir	'to succeed'	successor	'successor'

The suffix *-or* derives both agent and nonagent nouns; there are about five relevant verb-noun pairs (see 18) and a larger number of nouns in *-or* whose corresponding verb is not recorded.

(18)

scoultar	'to sculpt'	scoultor	'sculptor'
saltar	'to jump'	saltor	'jumper'
amar	'to love'	amor	'love'
sudar	'to sweat'	sudor	'sweat'

In several cases, the verb corresponding to the agent noun is not recorded; instead, the noun is derivationally related to another noun or an adjective (see 19). As mentioned previously, Cifoletti (2004) views *biancador* 'launderer' as a probable language-internal innovation of LF.

(19)

lavoro	'work'	lavorador	'worker'
bianco	'white'	biancador	'launderer'
sédouctzion	'seduction'	sedouctor	'seducer'

Other deverbal agent noun suffixes are infrequent (see 20).

(20)

corrir	'to run'	corriéré	'messenger'
gouardar	'to guard, supervise'	gouardian	'guard, warden'
commandar	'to order'	comandanté	'commander'

6.4.2 *Deadjectival Nouns*

Quality nouns can be derived from adjectives by means of *-etza* ~ *-essa*. There are about sixteen such adjective-noun pairs; the variant *-essa* occurs once. The inflectional ending of the adjective is removed before the addition of the noun-forming suffix.

(21)

largo	'wide'	largetza	'width'
riko	'rich'	rikétza	'wealth'
locou	'mad'	loketza	'madness'
grandé	'large'	grandetza	'size'
alto	'high'	altessa	'height'

Another pattern of quality noun derivation involves adding to the adjective the suffix *-ita (-ità)* ~ *-ta*. The *Dictionnaire* records about nineteen nouns with this suffix, including the last two in (22) whose base adjectives are not recorded.

(22)

oscouro	'dark'	oscourita	'darkness'
cativo	'bad, nasty'	cativià	'nastiness'
vero	'true'	verita	'truth'
sensibilé	'sensitive'	sensibilita	'sensitivity'
libéro	'free'	liberta	'freedom'
(pounir	'punish')	impounità	'impunity'
(probar	'prove')	probità	'integrity'

A handful of deadjectival nouns are formed by means of other suffixes.

(23)

proudenté	'prudent'	proudentza	'prudence'
impatienté	'impatient'	impatientza	'impatience'
fourbo	'crafty'	forbéria	'craftiness'

6.4.3 *Denominal Nouns*

The suffix *-iére* ~ *-iero* ~ *-ier* derives agent and instrument nouns from other nouns. There are about seventeen nouns with this suffix, including two whose corresponding base nouns are not recorded (see 24). In *mariniére* 'rower' ~ *mariniéro* 'sailor,' different allomorphs of the suffix are attached to the same base. This continues the state of affairs in the lexifier: as noted by Serianni (1989: 117–118), some Italian masculine nouns in *-iere* have a variant in *-iero* due to variable adaptation of this borrowed suffix, which is consonant-final in the donor language (< Fr. *-ier*).

(24)

canon	'cannon'	canoniéré	'gunner'
timone	'rudder'	timoniéré	'helmsman'
tintoura	'dye'	tintouriéré	'dry cleaner'
prigeon	'prison'	prigioniéré	'prisoner'
candella	'candle'	candéliéré	'torch'
zoukro	'sugar'	zoukriéro	'sugar bowl'
scola	'school'	scolier	'schoolboy'
(armar	'to arm')	armouriéro	'gunsmith'
(serrar	'to lock')	serruriero	'locksmith'

Other examples of denominal noun derivation may be seen in (25).

(25)

cavalo	'horse'	cavaléria	'cavalry'
séda	'silk'	sédaria	'silk factory'
orlogio	'clock'	orlogiaïo	'clockmaker'
galina	'hen'	galinaïo	'henhouse'
vela	'sail'	vélamé	'veil'
moska	'fly'	mousquita	'cranefly'
louna	'moon'	lounetta	'glasses'
forno	'oven'	fornello	'stove'

6.4.4 *Derived Verbs*

Approximately sixteen verbs are derived from adjectives without any derivational affix other than the theme vowel, predominantly *-a-*. The adjective agreement marker is removed prior to adding the theme vowel. The derived verbs appear mostly to have causative semantics (Rainer 2016c: 519).

(26)

sporco	'dirty'	sporcar	'to make dirty'
limpio	'clean'	limpiar	'to clean'
libéro	'free'	libérar	'to free'
contento	'glad'	contentar	'to satisfy'

About eleven verbs are derived from nouns and adjectives by means of suffixes. The suffixes with the most occurrences are *-ific-* and *-iz-* or their variants.

(27)

dgiousto	'just'	dgioustificar	'to justify'
forti	'strong'	fortificar	'to strengthen'
favor	'favor'	favorisar	'to favor'
netto	'clean'	néttegiar	'to clean'

Over a dozen verbs are formed by simultaneous addition of a prefix and a suffix to a noun or adjective base (parasynthesis).

(28)

nouovo	'new'	rinovar	'to renew'
frédo	'cold'	rifrédar	'to cool'

caldo	'hot'	scaldar	'to heat'
sicouro	'safe'	assicourar	'to assure'
kiaro	'clear, transparent'	diskiarar	'to declare'
flamma	'flame'	infiamar	'to set fire to'
caténa	'chain'	incadénar	'to chain up'
rico	'rich'	enrikir	'to make rich'

6.4.5 Derived Adjectives, Adverbs, and Numerals

Approximately fourteen adjectives are derived by means of *-to* ~ *-ato*. Included in this group are denominal adjectives and adjectivized past participles (these latter form the majority). The last adjective in (29) exhibits inherited allomorphy.

(29)	senso	'sense'	sensato	'sensible'
	fortouna	'happiness, fortune'	fortounato	'happy'
	ornar	'to adorn'	ornato	'ornate'
	ousar	'to use'	ousato	'used'
	inchir	'to fill'	inchito	'full'
	morir	'to die'	morto	'dead'
	perdir	'to lose'	perso	'lost'

Several adverbs are derived from the feminine form of the base adjective by means of the suffix *-mente*.

(30)	simplo	'simple'	simplamente	'simply'
	altro	'other'	altramente	'differently

LF also uses the masculine form of adjectives in adverbial function (see 31). This use continues similar use in its Romance lexifiers, cf. *parlare forte* 'to speak loudly,' *vedere chiaro* 'to see clearly,' *mirare giusto* 'to aim straight' in Italian; *hablar alto* 'to speak loudly,' *respirar hondo* 'to breathe deeply' in Spanish; *parler haut* 'to speak loudly,' *dire juste* 'to say it as it is' in French (Serianni 1989: 494; Butt and Benjamin 2004: 438; Hummel 2017: 20–31).

(31) a. *mi ablar dgiousto.*
1s speak.IMPF just
'Je dis la vérité.'
'I speak the truth.'
(Anonymous 1830a: 93)

b. *mi sentir bonou.*
1s hear.IMPF good
'J'entends bien.'
'I hear (you) well.'
(Anonymous 1830a: 93)

The majority of the numerals in the *Dictionnaire* preserve the derivational and suppletive patterns of the lexifiers. An exception are the analytically formed *diechisetté* 'seventeen,' *diechiotto* 'eighteen,' and *diechinové* 'nineteen' (lit. 'ten-seven,' 'ten-eight,' 'ten-nine'), the corresponding numerals in Italian being *diciassette*, *diciotto*, and *diciannove*. In his discussion of similar forms in Tunisian chancery Italian, *deci sette* 'seventeen' and *dieci nove* 'nineteen,' Baglioni (2010: 268) points to the probable influence of French *dix-sept* 'seventeen' (lit. 'ten-seven') and *dix-neuf* 'nineteen' (lit. 'ten-nine') on the structure of these numerals.

(32)

1–10	11–19	20–90	Ordinals
oun '1'	oundichi '11'		primo, primiéré '1st'
doué '2'	dodichi '12'	venti '20'	ségoundo '2nd'
tré '3'	trédichi '13'	trenta '30'	tertzo '3rd'
qouatro '4'	qouatordichi '14'	qouaranta '40'	
chinqoué '5'	qouindichi '15'		
seï '6'	sedichi '16'	sessanta '60'	
sété '7'	diechisetté '17'	settanta '70'	settimo '7th'
otto '8'	diechiotto '18'		
nové '9'	diechinové '19'	novanta '90'	
diéchi '10'			

6.4.6 *Other Suffixal Patterns*

The *Dictionnaire* contains evidence of additional patterns of suffixation, each represented by a small number of tokens. A selection of these additional patterns is given in (33).

(33)

a.

Verb		Noun	
fabricar	'to manufacture'	fabricanté	'manufacturer'
gouarantir	'to guarantee'	gouarantia	'guarantee'
desiderar	'to wish'	desiderio	'desire'
prégar	'to request'	préguiéra	'request'
passar	'to pass'	passagio	'passage'
servir	'to serve'	servitou	'servitude'
gouardar	'to guard'	gouardia	'guard'

b.

Noun		Adjective	
vergognia	'shame'	vergognioso	'shameful'
senso	'sense'	sensibile	'sensitive'
lodé	'praise'	lodévolé	'commendable'
Algiéri	'Algiers'	Algérino	'Algerian'

c.

Adjective		Noun	
dgiousto	'just'	dgioustitia	'justice'
dgiovine	'young'	dgioventù	'youth'
malato	'ill'	malattia	'illness'

d.

Verb		Adjective	
pesar	'to weigh'	pesanti	'heavy'
ridir	'to laugh'	ridicoulé	'ridiculous'
lodar	'to praise'	lodevolé	'commendable'

e.

Noun		Noun	
terra	'earth, ground'	terreno	'territory'
fronté	'front'	frontiéra	'border'

6.5 Prefixation

Prefixation is less important than suffixation in LF word formation. This state of affairs agrees with that of LF's lexifiers.

The three negative prefixes – *in-* ~ *im-*, *dis-*, and *s-* – are employed in the derivation of antonyms.

(34)

certo	'certain'	incerto	'uncertain'
outilé	'useful'	inoutilé	'useless'
possibilé	'possible'	impossibilé	'impossible'
patzientza	'patience'	impatientza	'impatience'
piacher	'to please'	dispiacher	'to displease'
armar	'to arm'	disarmar	'to disarm'
cargar	'to load'	scaricar	'to unload'
ricordar	'to remember'	scordar	'to forget'

The (etymologically spatial) prefix *in-* ~ *im-* is seen in the verbs in (35).

(35)

piégar	'to fold'	impiégar	'to employ'
prestar	'to lend'	imprestar	'to borrow'
—		implorar	'to implore'

The verbs and nouns in (36) contain various allomorphs of the prefix *re-* ~ *ri-*; the *ri-* allomorph predominates.

(36) a.

scaldar	'to heat'	riscaldar	'to reheat'
mettir	'to put'	rimettir	'to put back'
conoschir	'to know'	riconoschir	'to recognize'
dgitar	'to throw'	ridgitar	'to reject'
frédo	'cold'	rifrédar	'to cool'
nouovo	'new'	rinovar	'to renew'

b.

fortza	'strength'	rinfortzo	'reinforcements'
gratzia	'thanks'	ringratziar	'to thank'

c.

venir	'to come'	revenir	'to return'
tirar	'to pull'	rétirar	'to withdraw'

d. intrar	'to enter'	rintrar	'to come back'
contar	'to count'	racontar	'to tell'

Other etymological prefixes have few occurrences and do not appear to form discernible morphological or semantic patterns, at least from the viewpoint of the recorded LF data (see 37).

(37)

salidor	'assailant'	assalidor	'besieger'
dormir	'to sleep'	adormir	'to put to sleep'
parté	'part'	aparté	'separately'
ridir	'to laugh'	soridir	'to smile'
segouir	'to follow'	prosegouir	'to chase'

Some of the derivationally related pairs in the *Dictionnaire*'s LF appear to calque the formal and semantic patterns of French (see 38).

(38)

Lingua Franca	French	
rispondir ~ risponsa	répondre ~ réponse	'to answer' ~ 'answer'
assicourar ~ rassicourar	assurer ~ rassurer	'to assure' ~ 'to reassure'
testa ~ intestato	tête ~ entêté	'head' ~ 'stubborn'

6.6 Suppletion

In common with its Romance lexifiers, LF displays derivational suppletion, instances in which the semantic relationship between the members of a derivational set is the same as in the other sets whereas the formal relationship is not (cf. definitions of suppletion in Mel'čuk 1976: 52; 1994: 358). An example of derivational suppletion in Italian is given in (30): here, the adjectival counterpart to *formaggio* 'cheese' does not have the same formal relationship to it as the other adjectives to their nouns (Serianni 1989: 192–194).

(39)

Noun	Adjective
legno 'wood'	legnoso
ferro 'iron'	ferroso
fumo 'smoke'	fumoso
formaggio 'cheese'	caseario

Following the dominant approach in the literature on suppletion, the relationship of suppletion is understood here as being free from etymological considerations: the forms in a suppletive relationship may be etymologically distinct (as in *formaggio* ~ *caseario*) or they may come from the same etymological source (as in It. *madre* 'mother' ~ *materno* 'maternal,' both ultimately from Lat. *mater*) (see Mel'čuk 1994: 355ff.; 2006: 416ff.; Veselinova 2006: 14 for pertinent discussion). The criterion of shared phonological material between the forms in a suppletive relationship gives rise to the distinction between strong suppletion, as in *formaggio* ~ *caseario*, and weak suppletion, as in *madre* ~ *materno* (Dressler 1985).

The suppletion patterns in the *Dictionnaire*'s LF have one of three sources: inheritance from lexifiers, suppletion due to different etymological sources of the allomorphs, and suppletion due to language-internal change. Inherited suppletion patterns are illustrated in (40), where the last row in each set illustrates the corresponding derivational relationship (even if the pattern in question is not productive in the data at our disposal; see also Table 5.8 in Chapter 5). The sets (40a), and (40c) through (40g), represent strong suppletion; while the remaining sets are examples of weak suppletion. The suppletive pattern in (40f) was inherited from the lexifiers, however, the verb 'to be silent' has been analytically recreated in LF (this common situation is addressed in Mel'čuk 2006: 424).

(40)
a. Masculine — Feminine
taour 'bull' — vaka 'cow'
[cavalo 'horse' — cavala 'mare']

b. Noun — Adjective
oumbré 'man' — oumano 'human'
[vergognia 'shame' — vergognioso 'shameful']

c. Number — Teen
doué 'two' — venti 'twenty'
[tré 'three' — trenta 'thirty']

d. Number — Ordinal
oun 'one' — primo, primiéré 'first'
doué 'two' — ségoundo 'second'
[sété 'seven' — settimo 'seventh']

e. Verb — Causative
morir 'to die' — massar 'to kill'
[dormir 'to sleep' — adormir 'to put to sleep']

f. Verb — Noun
non ablar 'to be silent' — silentzio 'silence'
[sentir 'to feel' — sentimento 'feeling']

g. Verb — Noun
dormir 'to sleep' — souono 'sleep'
tokkar 'to hit, strike' — colpo 'a blow'
[vendir 'to sell' — vendita 'sale']

h. Verb — Noun
prendir 'to take' — préza 'taking'
[vendir 'to sell' — vendita 'sale']

i.	<u>Verb</u>	<u>Adjective</u>
	perdir 'to lose'	perso 'lost'
	[adormir 'to put to sleep'	adormito 'asleep']

Suppletive sets due to different etymological sources of the allomorphs are exemplified in (41). The different provenance of the allomorphs is revealed by their phonological shape: for example, the members of the first two sets, *flamma* ~ *infiamar* and *riclamar* ~ *kiamar*, display different treatment of Lat. *fl* and *cl*, [fl] and [kl] versus [fj] and [kj], respectively (Repetti and Tuttle 1987).

(41)	flamma 'flame'	infiamar 'to set fire to'
	riclamar 'to ask for'	kiamar 'to call'
	caténa 'chain'	incadénar 'to chain up'
	scaricar 'to unload'	cargar 'to load'
	viator 'traveler'	viagiar 'to travel'
	prigeon 'prison'	imprisonar 'to imprison'
	brakio 'arm'	embrachiar 'to embrace'
	tradir 'to betray'	trahisoun 'betrayal'
	tradir 'to betray'	traïdor 'traitor'
	scrivir 'to write'	scriban 'secretary'

The sets in (42) differ in the height of a vowel. This difference may be due to different etymological sources of the words, which would make these sets a subgroup of those in (41). Alternatively, it may be due to the raising of mid vowels in LF (see Schuchardt 1909; Cifoletti 1989, 2004; Castellanos 2007; and Chapter 3).

(42)	<u>Mid vowel allomorph</u>		<u>High vowel allomorph</u>	
	s**é**courità	'safety'	s**i**couro	'safe'
	f**o**rbéria	'guile'	f**ou**rbo	'cunning'
	f**o**rno	'oven'	f**ou**rniéré	'baker'
	m**o**ska	'fly'	m**ou**squita	'cranefly'
	sedji**o**rno	'stay'	sedji**ou**rnar	'to stay'

6.7 Compounding

The *Dictionnaire*'s LF has few compounds without a linking morpheme between the constituents. These consist of nominal, adjectival, and numeral compounds inherited from the lexifiers (see 32 above and 43a below) and several forms which may represent LF neologisms (see 43b). Based on their formal model in the lexifiers – represented by such compounds as *cavatappi* in Italian, *sacacorchos* in Spanish, and *tirebouchons* in French ('corkscrew'), all of which literally mean 'pull out corks' – the LF compounds *fora-tapa* 'corkscrew' and *fora-bala* 'bullet-forceps' are best analyzed as verb-noun compounds.[6] The alternative – to analyze *fora-* as the adverb *fora* 'out, outside' – is less attractive.

(43) a.

passeporto	'safe-conduct'	(V-N)
gouarda sol	'umbrella'	
metzo giorno	'midday, afternoon, south'	(A-N)
prima vera	'spring'	
campo santo	'cemetery'	(N-A)
sottoterréno	'underground'	(P-N)
benvenouto	'welcome'	(Adv-Pple)

b.

fora-tapa	'corkscrew'	(V-N)
fora-balla	'bullet-forceps'	
diechisetté	'seventeen'	(Num-Num)
diechiotto	'eighteen'	
diechinové	'nineteen'	

6.8 Multiword Lexemes

The types of multiword lexical expressions in the *Dictionnaire*'s LF represent a subset of those of its Romance lexifiers. Among these we find nominal syntagmatic compounds (in Section 6.8.1), particle verbs (in Section 6.8.2), and light verb constructions (in Section 6.8.3). Other types of multiword lexemes are examined in Section 6.8.4.

6.8.1 Syntagmatic Compounds

There are two types of syntagmatic compounds in the *Dictionnaire*'s LF. The more numerous type consists of joining two nouns by means of the preposition *di* 'of, from' (see 44). This type continues the noun-preposition-(article)-noun syntagmatic compound type of the lexifiers (see Section 6.1), and some of the compounds have exact equivalents in the lexifiers: compare the forms in (44) with *grasso di porco* 'lard,' *albero di arance* 'orange tree,' *palla di cannone* 'cannonball,' *saluto di cannone* 'gun salute,' *carretta da cannone* 'gun carriage,' *fazzoletto da collo* 'neckerchief' in Italian; *bala de cañón* 'cannonball,' *agua de limón* 'lemonade' in Spanish; *volée de canon* 'cannon shot,' *salut de canon* 'gun salute,' *balle de canon* 'cannonball' in French. Also as in the lexifiers, a number of semantic relationships may obtain between the head and

[6] Another compound built to the same pattern is mentioned by Shaw (1757: 144): "[T]he common *apricot* occasions a variety of fevers and dysenteries, and is therefore known in the *Frank* language by the name of *Matza Franca*, or the *killer of Christians*" (the italics are in the original; cf. *massar* 'to kill,' *franco* 'Frank' in the *Dictionnaire*).

complement nouns, including those of possession (*moukera del filio* 'daughter-in-law'), material (*piato di terra* 'earthenware plate'), origin (*grasso di porco* 'lard'), and purpose (*cortello di barba* 'razor').

(44)

French	Lingua Franca	Literal gloss	Gloss
boulet	balla di canone	'ball of cannon'	'cannonball'
volée de canon	volata di canone	'shot of cannon'	'cannon shot'
salve de canon	saluto di canone	'salute of cannon'	'gun salute'
affût	carreta di canone	'carriage of cannon'	'gun carriage'
limonade	agoua di limoun	'water of lemon'	'lemonade'
saumure	agoua di salé	'water of salt'	'brine'
sain-doux	grasso di porco	'fat of pig'	'lard'
rasoir	cortello di barba	'knife of beard'	'razor'
fichu	fatzoletto di collo	'handkerchief of neck'	'neckerchief'
palmier	albéro di datoli	'tree of date'	'palm tree'
oranger	olbero d'arangi	'tree of orange'	'orange tree'
faïence (plat de)	piato di terra	'plate of earth'	'earthenware plate'
belle-fille	moukera del filio	'wife of the son'	'daughter-in-law'

The second type are syntagmatic compounds consisting of an adjective and a noun (see 45). These continue the A-N and N-A compound types of the lexifiers (see Section 6.1).

(45)

French	Lingua Franca	Literal gloss	Gloss
sentier	picolo camino	'little road'	'path'
caisson	picola cassa	'little box'	'case'
baguette	picolo bastone	'little stick'	'rod'
hachoir	cortello grosso	'large knife'	'cleaver'

The preposed adjective *picolo* in the above lexemes appears to be functionally equivalent to a diminutive suffix. This is a feature of LF's lexifiers, cf. the equivalence between *un discorsetto amichevole* and *un piccolo discorso amichevole* 'a little friendly speech' in Italian noted by Serianni (1989) and between and *un barecito* and *un pequeño bar* 'a little bar' in Spanish (Butt and Benjamin 2004).[7] In French, periphrastic diminutive with *petit* 'little' has replaced the diminutive suffix *-et(te)* (Bauer 2011: 540). In some of the earlier examples, repeated in (46a) for convenience, it was seen that what are

7 "[G]li aggettivi intensificatori anteposti esprimono spesso un contenuto semantico simile a quello dei suffissi accrescitivi e diminutivi" [Preposed intensifying adjectives often express similar semantic content to that of augmentative and diminutive suffixes] (Serianni 1989: 204). In the Spanish examples, suffixed diminutives differ from their analytic counterparts in their degree of (in)formality (Butt and Benjamin 2004: 550).

etymologically diminutive suffixes can be used in LF for word formation. This feature is also a part of the lexifier structure, cf. the Spanish examples in (46b) (Butt and Benjamin 2004: 553).

(46) a. Lingua Franca

forno	'oven'	fornello	'stove'
moska	'fly'	mousquita	'cranefly'
louna	'moon'	lounetta	'glasses'

b. Spanish

palo	'stick'	palillo	'toothpick'
cama	'bed'	camilla	'stretcher'
guerra	'war'	guerrilla	'guerrilla warfare'

6.8.2 *Particle Verbs*

The *Dictionnaire*'s LF contains a small number of particle verbs, constructions in which a verb is followed by a locative particle. The verbs found in these constructions are a subset of the "generic motion verbs, deictic verbs, and verbs of putting or removal" (Iacobini 2015: 634) used for the same purpose in the lexifiers (see Section 6.1). The LF constructions continue those found in Italian (see 47).

(47)

andar fora	'to go away'	(It. *andare fuori*)
portar fora	'to take away'	(It. *portare fuori*)
star fora	'to be out'	(It. *stare fuori*)
sarar dentro	'to lock up'	(It. *serrare dentro*)
mettir dentro	'to put inside'	(It. *mettere dentro*)
andar avanti	'to be fast'	(It. *andare avanti*)
andar indiétro	'to be slow'	(It. *andare indietro*)

6.8.3 *Light Verb Constructions*

LF's light verb constructions combine verbs with noun, adjective, adverb, or prepositional phrase complements. The verbs that tend to participate in this type of lexeme formation are semantically bleached, or delexicalized (Sinclair 1991: 113), and include *ténir* 'to have,' *far* ~ *fazir* ~ *counchar* 'to do, make,' *dar* 'to give,' *mettir* 'to put,' *forar* 'to remove, take away, pull out,' and *ablar* 'to say, speak,' though others, like *andar* 'to go' and *venir* 'to come,' are also used. A representative sample of periphrastic verb lexemes in LF is given in (48); additional examples may be seen in Cifoletti (1989: 151–154). A number of the lexemes have exact equivalents or at least close models in one or more of the lexifiers: cf. *mettere la briglia* 'to bridle,' *contare di nuovo* 'to recount,' *fare provviste* 'to supply' in Italian; *mettre la bride* 'to bridle,' *compter de nouveau* 'to recount' in French; *contar de nuevo* 'to recount' in Spanish (see also Table 5.9 in Chapter 5 and 50 below).

(48)

French	Lingua Franca	Literal gloss	Gloss
raser	forar barba	'to remove beard'	'to shave'
saigner	forar sangré	'to take out blood'	'to bleed'
sarcler	forar erba	'to pull out grass'	'to weed'
traire	forar late	'to draw milk'	'to milk'
sceller	mettir taba	'to put seal'	'to seal'
ferrer	mettir ferro	'to put iron'	'to shoe'
brider	méttir l'eskima	'to put the bridle'	'to bridle'
enterrer	mettir in terra	'to put in ground'	'to bury'
éclairer	far loumé	'to make light'	'to light'
nuire	far malé	'to do badly'	'to harm'
approvisionner	far provista	'to do supply'	'to supply'
il fait froid	fazir frédo	'to make cold'	'to be cold'
secourir	dar agioudo	'to give help'	'to help'
escorter	dar scorta	'to give escort'	'to escort'
souffrir	ténir dolor	'to have pain'	'to suffer'
effrayé	ténir paoura	'to have fear'	'to be afraid'
accourir	venir presto	'to come soon'	'to come running'
(se) hâter	andar ~ fazir presto	'to go ~ make soon'	'to hasten'
reflechir	mirar bonou	'to look well'	'to think'
répeter, redire	ablar ancora	'to say again'	'to repeat'
récompter	contar di nouovo	'to count again'	'to recount'

Some of the multiword verbal lexemes recorded in the *Dictionnaire* are also recorded in Haedo (1612); these include *anda presto* 'hurry up,' *porta fora* 'take away,' and *tener febre* 'to have a fever.' Haedo's other lexemes of this type, such as *dole cabeza* 'to have a headache,' *cerrar boca* 'to keep one's mouth shut,' *abrusar vivo* 'to burn alive,' and *hazer malato* 'to pretend to be ill,' have exact models in one or more of the lexifiers (cf. Sp. *duele la cabeza* 'to have a headache,' *cerrar la boca* 'to keep one's mouth shut'; It. *bruciare vivo* 'to burn alive,' *fare il malato* 'to pretend to be ill').

In some cases, the *Dictionnaire* lists the multiword and monolexemic alternatives for the same concept side by side (see 49).

(49)

French	Lingua Franca	Gloss
brave	bonou, ténir coragio ('to have courage')	'brave'
intrépide	intrépido, tenir coragio ('to have courage')	'intrepid'
saler	salar, mettir salé ('to put salt')	'to salt'
sucrer	zoukar, mettir zoukaro ('to put sugar')	'to sugar'
ranger	rangiar, componir, mettir in logo ('to put in place')	'to arrange'
soigner	servar, tenir coura ('to have care')	'to look after'
permettre	permettir, dar licentzia ('to give permission')	'to allow'

aider, secourir	agioudar, dar agioudo ('to give help')	'to help'
favoriser	favorisar, counchar favour ('to do favor')	'to favor'
remercier	ringratziar, ablar gratzia ('to say thanks')	'to thank'
baguette	bagueta, picolo bastone ('little stick')	'rod'

The analytic strategy of verbal lexeme formation illustrated in (48) and (49) has had a long and productive history in Romance languages, and has ample parallels in the lexifiers of LF. Examples of similarly structured or identical verbal periphrases in Italian and Spanish may be seen in (50) (Serianni 1989: 183, 379; Patota 2006: 70).

(50)

Italian	Spanish	Literal gloss	Gloss
avere sete	*tener sed*	'to have thirst'	'to be thirsty'
avere paura	*tener miedo*	'to have fear'	'to be afraid'
fare freddo	*hacer frío*	'to make cold'	'to be cold'
andare a cavallo	*andar a caballo*	'to go on horseback'	'to ride'

Also as in LF, many of the periphrastic verbal lexemes in the lexifiers are paraphrasable with monolexemic equivalents (see the examples in 51) (Polák 1949: 66; Dubský 1963: 46; Berruto 1983a: 64; Serianni 1989: 379; Renzi 2001: 427; Iacobini and Masini 2007: 161; Real Academia Española 2010).

(51)

Multiword lexeme	Monolexeme	Gloss
Sp. *dar un paseo* ('to give a walk')	*pasear*	'to walk'
Sp. *andar a caballo* ('to go on horseback')	*cabalgar*	'to ride'
Sp. *hacer mención* ('to make mention')	*mencionar*	'to mention'
It. *fare una passeggiata* ('to do a walk')	*passeggiare*	'to walk'
It. *andare a cavallo* ('to go on horseback')	*cavalcare*	'to ride'
It. *dare fuoco* ('to give fire')	*incendiare*	'to set fire to'
It. *fare soldi* ('to make money')	*guadagnare*	'to earn'
It. *andare fuori* ('to go out')	*uscire*	'to go out'
It. *andare giù* ('to go down')	*scendere*	'to go down'
Fr. *avoir recours* ('to have recourse')	*recourir*	'to use'
Fr. *prendre la fuite* ('to take flight')	*fuir*	'to flee'

6.8.4 *Other Multiword Lexemes*

French adjectives in the *Dictionnaire* are occasionally translated into LF by means of light verb constructions.

(52)

French	Lingua Franca	Literal gloss	Gloss
brave	ténir coragio[8]	'to have courage'	'brave'
sinueux	tenir dgiro	'to have turn'	'winding'

[8] The noun *coragio* is not listed as an independent entry.

timide	tenir vergonia	'to have shame'	'shy'
effrayé	ténir paoura	'to have fear'	'scared'
nuisible	fasir malé	'to do badly'	'harmful'

The following exemplify the use of relative clauses in noun and adjective formation.

(53)

French	Lingua Franca	Literal gloss	Gloss
suffisant	qué bastar	'which suffices'	'sufficient'
soigneux	qué tenir coura	'which has care'	'tidy'
bienfaiteur	quello que fasir béné	'he who does well'	'benefactor'

Several verbs and adjectives are formed by modifying the base lexeme with *non ~ no* 'no, not,' *mouchou ~ molto* 'much, very,' *tropo* 'too much,' or *oun poco* 'a little.'

(54)

French prompt	Lingua Franca	Literal gloss	Gloss
taire	non ablar	'to not speak'	'to be silent'
déplaire	non piacher	'to not please'	'to displease'
opposer (s')	non quérir	'to not want'	'to oppose'
mécontent	non contento	'not happy'	'unhappy'
injuste	non jiousto	'not just'	'unjust'
surpayer	pagar tropo	'to pay too much'	'to overpay'
estimer	quérir mouchou	'to love much'	'to esteem'
magnifique	mouchou bello	'very beautiful'	'magnificent'
opulent	molto riko	'very rich'	'opulent'
délicieux	molto bouno	'very good'	'delicious'
tiède	oun poco caldo	'a little hot'	'warm'

Several French adverbs and an adjective are translated into LF with prepositional phrases (see 55). The use of prepositional phrases in these functions is a feature that LF shares with its Romance lexifiers, cf. *con pazienza* 'with patience' ('patiently'), *con gioia* 'with joy' ('gladly'), *per fortuna* 'by luck' ('luckily'), *in vita* 'alive' in Italian; *con frequencia* 'with frequency' ('frequently'), *con locura* 'with madness' ('passionately'), *con vida* 'alive' in Spanish; *en secret* 'secretly,' *en vie* 'alive,' *par hasard* 'by chance' in French (Butt and Benjamin 2004: 437–438; Patota 2006: 70).

(55)

French	Lingua Franca	Literal gloss	Gloss
secrètement	con ségréto	'with secret'	'secretly'
soigneusement	con coura	'with care'	'carefully'
simultanément	in l'estesso tempo	'at the same time'	'simultaneously'
vis-à-vis	in fachia	'in face'	'face to face'
vivant	in vita	'in life'	'alive'
par hasard	per fortouna	'by luck'	'luckily'

Table 6.2. *Lexical encoding of valency alternations in Lingua Franca*

Lingua Franca	Italian	Spanish	French	Gloss
morir ~ massar	morire ~ uccidere	morir ~ matar	mourir ~ tuer	'die' ~ 'kill'
cascar ~ dgitar	cadere ~ gettare	caer ~ tirar	tomber ~ jeter	'fall' ~ 'throw'
sentar / restar ~ laschiar	restare ~ lasciare	quedar ~ dejar	rester ~ laisser	'stay' ~ 'leave'
richévir ~ dar / donar	ricevere ~ dare	recibir ~ dar	récevoir ~ donner	'receive' ~ 'give'
intrar ~ métir	entrare ~ mettere	entrar ~ meter	entrer ~ mettre	'go in' ~ 'put (in)'
dormir ~ adormir	dormire ~ addormentare	dormir ~ adormir	dormir ~ endormir	'sleep' ~ 'put to sleep'
imparar ~ impirir	imparare ~ insegnare	aprender ~ enseñar	apprendre ~ instruir	'learn' ~ 'teach'

6.9 Valency Alternations

The interplay between the different word formation techniques presented in the preceding sections may be illustrated by focusing on a single functional domain, such as valency (transitivity) alternations. LF expresses such alternations through a combination of lexical, morphological, and analytic means, showing continuity with the expression of this functional domain in the lexifiers (Lavale Ortiz 2007; Cennamo 2015).

Examples of valency alternations expressed lexically are given in Table 6.2 (see a discussion of such opposite-valence verb pairs in Lavale Ortiz 2007: 9–11). The forms in the column labeled "French" are the French prompts from the *Dictionnaire* corresponding to the LF translations in the first column. The pair *dormir* ~ *adormir*, though derivationally related, may be viewed as an instance of lexical alternation due to the nonproductivity of this pattern in our LF data. The pair *imparar* ~ *impirir* may be due to a simple typo, in which case it belongs to the pattern of labile verbs, to be discussed immediately below.

LF can also express different valency (transitivity) with the same labile (ambitransitive) verb (Haspelmath 1993: 92). This inference follows from the *Dictionnaire*'s entries in which the French prompt can have both an inchoative and a causative (or an intransitive and a transitive) reading (see 56a), and from entries in which the same LF verb translates two French verbs differing in valency and/or transitivity, or both active and pronominal forms of the same verb (see 56b). The verb lability (ambitransitivity) in LF is continuous with the same phenomenon in its Romance lexifiers, as is clear from the French prompts in (56a) and the probable Romance sources of the LF verbs in question, which include Spanish *sanar* 'to heal' (tr. ~ intr.) for LF *sanir*, Spanish *vestir* and/or Italian *vestire* 'to dress' (tr. ~ intr.) for LF *vestir*, Italian *bruciare* 'to burn' (tr. ~ intr.) for LF *bruchar*, Italian *cominciare* (tr. ~ intr.) for LF *comminchiar*, Italian *principiare* (tr. ~ intr.) for LF *principiar*, and Italian *finire* (tr. ~ intr.) for LF *finir*.

(56)		French		Lingua Franca
	a.	guérir	'to cure' ~ 'to get better'	sanir
		brûler	'to burn' (tr. ~ intr.)	bruchar
		refroidir	'to cool down' (tr. ~ intr.)	rifrédar
		commencer	'to begin' (tr. ~ intr.)	comminchiar, principiar
		finir	'to end' (tr. ~ intr.)	finir, spachiar
	b.	vêtir	'to dress' (tr.)	vestir
		habiller (s')	'to dress' (intr.)	
		rompre	'to break' (tr.)	rompir
		rompre (se)	'to break' (intr.)	
		réveiller	'to wake up' (tr.)	suzar
		réveller (se)	'to wake up' (intr.)	
		relever	'to raise'	rilévar, alsar
		relever (se)	'to rise'	

Morphological expression of valency is seen in denominal and deadjectival causative verbs. Some of the verbs are derived via suffixation, and others parasynthetically. Causative denominal and deadjectival verbs are plentiful in LF's Romance lexifiers; examples include *impastare* 'to knead' (< *pasta* 'dough'), *impaurire* 'to frighten' (< *paura* 'fear'), *chiarire* 'to clarify' (< *chiaro* 'clear'), *arrichire* 'to make rich' (< *ricco* 'rich') in Italian; and *avergonzar* 'to embarrass' (< *vergüenza* 'embarrassment'), *apenar* 'to shame' (< *pena* 'shame'), *secar* 'to dry' (< *seco* 'dry'), *enfriar* 'to cool' (< *frío* 'cold') in Spanish.

The number of denominal causatives in the *Dictionnaire* is small (see 57a). For some, the *Dictionnaire* supplies an analytic alternative in the form of a light verb followed by an abstract noun complement which supplies the core meaning of the verbal lexeme (see 57b).

(57)	a.	loumé	'light'[9]	alloumar	'to light (up)'
		coragio	'courage'[10]	incoragiar	'to encourage'

[9] Attested in the entry *far loumé* 'to light (up)' (Fr. *éclairer*).

[10] Attested in the entries *ténir coragio* (Fr. *brave* 'brave') and *tenir coragio* (Fr. *intrépide* 'intrepid').

flamma	'flame'	infiamar	'to set fire to'
pasta	'dough'	pastar	'to knead'
favour	'favor'	favorisar	'to favor'

b. alloumar ~ far loumé 'to light (up)'
favorisar ~ counchar favour[11] 'to favor'

The sentences in (58) further illustrate LF's ability to create analytic causatives on the basis of abstract nouns.

(58) a. *ti* *fato* *vergognia* *per* *mi.*
2s do.PF shame DOM 1s
'Vous m'avez fait un affront.'
'You have humiliated me.'
(Anonymous 1830a: 11)

b. *qouesto* *fazir* *pena* *per* *mi.*
this do.IMPF shame DOM 1s
'cela me fait scrupule'
'this embarrasses me'
(Anonymous 1830a: 74)

Most deadjectival verbs in LF appear to have causative semantics (see 59a). The forms in (59b) suggest that the *Dictionnaire*'s LF also has the ability to form inchoative and causative verbs from adjectives with the help of the support verbs *tornar* 'to turn' and *vernir*.[12]

(59) a.	sporco	'dirty'	sporcar	'to make dirty'
	dopio	'double'	dopiar	'to double'
	forti	'strong'	fortificar	'to strengthen'
	netto	'clean'	néttegiar	'to clean'
	caldo	'hot'	scaldar	'to heat'
	rico	'rich'	enrikir	'to make rich'
b.	rosso	'red'	tornar rosso	'to blush'
	bello	'beautiful'	tornar bello ~ vernir bello	'to grow lovelier'
	dritto	'straight'	tornar dritto	'to make straight'

There are further instances of analytic expression of valency (transitivity) that involve using the light verbs *far* ~ *fazir* 'to do, make,' *laschiar* 'to let,' *tornar* 'to turn,' and *ténir* 'to have.' In the examples in (60), opposite-valence verb pairs are built by using the verbs *fasir/ténir* and *far/tornar* in combination

[11] Spelled in the *Dictionnaire* as one word.
[12] The verb *vernir* is attested only in this entry; Cifoletti (1989: 148) wonders if this is an error for *venir* 'to come.' Cf. the use of *venir* 'to come' for *devenir* 'to become' in North African French (Lanly 1955: 205).

with noun complements. The use of these verbs for expressing valency (transitivity) alternations in LF is continuous with similar uses in the lexifiers. For example, in Italian *fare* 'to make' in combination with abstract nouns can function as a causative to *avere* 'to have' with the same nouns, as seen in the pair *fare paura* 'to scare' / *avere paura* 'to be scared' (Salvi 2001: 92–94).

(60)	fasir paoura	'to scare'	ténir paoura	'to be scared'
	far vergognia	'to humiliate'[13]	tenir vergonia	'bashful'[14]
	far amigo	'to reconcile'	tornar amigo	'to get reconciled'[15]

The examples in (61) illustrate the causative use of LF *fazir* 'to do, make' and *laschiar* 'to let' in combination with lexical verbs. Both constructions are continuous with the corresponding causative constructions of the lexifiers consisting of a finite light verb – typically 'to do, make' (Fr. *faire*, It. *fare*, Sp. *hacer*) for strong (Spanish) or various (French, Italian) degrees of causation and 'to let' (Fr. *laisser*, It. *lasciare*, Sp. *dejar*) for weak causation – followed by the infinitive of a lexical verb (Simone and Cerbasi 2001; Lavale Ortiz 2007; Cennamo 2015). Comparable examples from Italian are provided in (61c) and (61d). The causative verb 'to do, make,' and the corresponding causative construction, are further grammaticalized in French and Italian than they are in Spanish (Simone and Cerbasi 2001: 468; Soares da Silva 2012).

(61) a. *fazir scaldar agoua; mi quérir counchar thé.*
make.IMPF heat.IMPF water 1s want.IMPF make.IMPF tea
'Faites chauffer de l'eau; je veux faire du thé.'
'Have some water heated; I want to make tea.'
(Anonymous 1830a: 97)

b. *ti laschiar counchar per mi.*
1s let.IMPF do.IMPF DOM 1s
'Laissez-moi faire.'
'Let me do it.'
(Anonymous 1830a: 95)

c. *Faccio cantare una canzone.*
make.PRES.1s sing.INF a song
'I have a song sung.'
(Maiden and Robustelli 2013: 274)

d. *La mamma lascia preparare le valigie a Carla.*
the mom let.PRES.3s prepare.INF the suitcases to Carla
'Mom lets Carla pack the suitcases.'
(Patota 2006: 143)

13 See the example (58a) above. 14 Translates Fr. *timide*.

15 This is my interpretation of the entries Fr. *réconcilier* : LF *far amigo* and Fr. *réconcilier (se)* : *far tornar amigo*.

The preceding exposition has shown that LF employs a combination of lexical, morphological, and analytic means for expressing valency (transitivity) alternations, displaying both typological and specific continuity with its Romance lexifiers with respect to the means of expression in this functional domain.

6.10 Chapter Summary

This chapter has shown that the word and lexeme formation strategies of LF, as recorded in the *Dictionnaire*, are either inherited from or parallel with the corresponding strategies of LF's Romance lexifiers. A specific point of agreement is the use of affixation, particularly suffixation, as the best-developed word formation technique. LF further agrees with its lexifiers in having a richer repertoire of noun-forming suffixes as compared to suffixes that derive other word classes. The difference between LF and its lexifiers in the domain of derivational affixation consists in the number and variety of the patterns, with only a fraction of the lexifier patterns represented in LF. A related difference is the level of productivity of the inherited patterns; in particular, the pattern with the largest number of tokens in LF (Section 6.3) is not the most productive one in its lexifiers. Rainer (2016c: 520) notes, however, that derivation of deverbal action nouns of this type "witnessed a spectacular rise in medieval Romance" and "was only contained as a consequence of the massive relatinization of the category of action nouns." The prevalence of this derivational pattern in LF may therefore be the consequence of its comparative independence from its lexifiers, particularly as regards their registers most prone to relatinization. Metzeltin (2007) makes a similar point with respect to the evolution of Romanian, which he considers more "natural" than that of Western Romance languages because it was less constrained by prescriptive tendencies and the presence of the Latin model.

Other specific points of agreement between the word and lexeme formation of LF and its Romance lexifiers include moderate use of compounding as compared to affixation, and preference for syntagmatic over lexical nominal compounds. Some of LF's syntagmatic compounds, like *grasso di porco* 'lard' and *agoua di limoun* 'lemonade,' were likely inherited from one or more of its lexifiers. Also in common with its Romance lexifiers, LF exhibits a certain degree of suppletion in its derivational morphology. The sources of the suppletive patterns – inheritance from the lexifiers, different etymological provenance of the suppletive allomorphs, and language-internal developments – are the same as in other languages that exhibit suppletion. Multifunctionality, or the use of one and the same word in different part-of-speech categories, is not only limited in scope but also continues similar patterns in the lexifiers (see 62). Reduplication is uncharacteristic of LF, with only two examples supplied by the *Dictionnaire*: *poco poco* 'shortly, soon' (translating French *incessament*, *tantôt*, and *bientôt*), and *siémé siémé* 'together' (translating French *ensemble*). The nonproductivity of reduplication in LF continues the state of affairs in Latin and Romance languages, where this device is used sparingly (cf. *fortis, fortis* 'very strong' in Latin; *due occhi neri, neri* 'two very black eyes' in Italian) (Korletjanu 1974: 177–180, 223).

(62)

Lingua Franca	Lexifier
piacher 'to please' (v.), 'pleasure' (n.)	It. *piacere* (verb, noun)
parlar 'to speak' (v.), 'language' (n.)	It. *parlare* (verb, noun)
poudir 'to be able' (v.), *poder* 'power' (n.)	Sp. *poder* (verb, noun)
vekio 'old' (adj.), 'old man; veteran' (n.)	It. *vecchio* (adjective, noun)
dolce 'sweet' (adj.), 'sweet(s)' (n.)	It. *dolce* (adjective, noun)
doppo 'afterward' (adv.), 'after' (prep.)	It. *dopo* (adverb, preposition)
vichino 'close' (adj.), 'near' (adv.), 'neighbor'(n.)	It. *vicino* (adjective, adverb, noun)
ségoundo 'second' (adj.), 'according to' (prep.)	It. *secondo* (adjective, preposition)
sopra 'above' (adv.), 'on' (prep.)	It. *sopra* (adverb, preposition)
il sopra 'surface' (n.)	It. *il sopra* (noun)

LF further agrees with its lexifiers in its preference for analytic techniques of new lexeme formation. This preference has deep roots in the Romance domain, as already Archaic and Vulgar Latin constructed new verbal lexemes analytically, e.g., with the verbs *dare* 'to give,' *capere* 'to take,' *facere* 'to do, make,' and *habere* 'to have,' as in *verba facere* 'to speak,' *finem facere* 'to end,' *habere desiderium* 'to wish' (Polák 1949; Dubský 1963; Korletjanu 1974; Baños 2012). Similar multiword verbal lexemes abound in modern Romance languages, particularly their colloquial registers and L2 varieties, which tend to be less constrained by prescriptive norms. Berruto (1983a: 64–65) notes a plethora of verbal periphrases with "all-purpose verbs" (*verbi tuttofare*) in *italiano popolare*,[16] among them *fare un'emigrazione* 'to make an emigration' for *emigrare* 'to emigrate,' *far soldi* 'to make money' for *guadagnare* 'to earn,' *dar botte* 'to give blows' for *picchiare* 'to beat up.' In its multiword verbal lexemes, LF makes use of such support verbs as *far* ~ *fazir* ~ *counchar* 'to do, make,' *dar* 'to give,' *métir* 'to put,' and *ténir* 'to have,' in many cases continuing the specific periphrases of one or more of its lexifiers, cf. *fazir frédo* 'it's cold,' *ténir paoura* 'to be afraid' (*hacer frío*, *tener miedo* in Spanish; *far freddo*, *avere paura* in Italian). The support verbs used for creating multiword

16 "L'italiano popolare . . . corrisponde grosso modo alla lingua italiana usata dai ceti sfavoriti, con scarsa disponibilità e fruizione di beni materiali e culturali e con basso livello di scolarità ed istruzione" [*Italiano popolare* roughly corresponds to Italian used by disadvantaged classes with poor availability and use of material and cultural resources and a low level of schooling and education] (Berruto 1983b: 486).

lexemes in LF descend from high-frequency lexifier verbs that are basic in their corresponding semantic fields and are commonly used in complex predicates of various kinds (Viberg 2001: 1304; Baños 2012: 38n2). Analytic verbal lexemes of the type seen in LF are common in Western European languages (Polák 1949). Jespersen (1942: 117) notes "the general tendency of Mod[ern] E[nglish] to place an insignificant verb, to which the marks of person and tense are attached, before the really important idea," offering as examples verbal lexemes constructed with some of the same verbs that are used for this purpose in LF: *have* (*have a chat*), *take* (*take a drive*), *make* (*make a plunge*), *give* (*give a push*). Various Romance languages have also expanded the use of particle verbs, such as *andare fuori* 'to go out' and *buttare via* 'to throw away' in Italian, which were marginal in Latin (Iacobini and Masini 2007: 161; Rainer 2016c: 516). By exhibiting similar particle verbs, such as *andar fora* 'to go away' and *andar indiétro* 'to be slow,' LF fits into the general Romance diachronic drift toward a more analytic morphosyntax.

The way of forming new adjectives in LF by preposing adverbs such as 'very' is conceptually not unlike the analytic way of forming the degrees of comparison of adjectives that had replaced the earlier synthetic constructions of Latin, e.g., *magis altus* ~ *plus altus* 'more high' (*más alto* in Spanish, *più alto* in Italian) for *altior* 'higher.' The formation of antonyms by preposing a free negative morpheme, and other types of analytic paraphrases, also abound in native-speaker speech and writing directed at second language learners of Romance languages. Moretti's (1988) analysis of readings adapted for foreign and second language learners of Italian, for instance, shows such paraphrases as *non simpatico* 'not nice' for *antipatico* 'disagreeable,' *quasi nascosto* 'almost hidden' for *seminascosto* 'half-hidden,' *braccia magre* 'skinny arms' for *braccine* 'arms (diminutive),' *dare indietro* 'to give back' for *restituire* 'to return,' and *fare la corte* 'to court' for *corteggiare*.

In conclusion, the word and lexeme formation strategies of the *Dictionnaire*'s LF are characterized by features and phenomena that are both typologically and specifically Romance.[17] LF's word and lexeme formation continue those of its Romance lexifiers with a considerable degree of detail, exhibiting the prevalence of suffixation, less productive use of prefixation, a moderate amount of derivational suppletion, moderate use of lexical compounds, preference for nominal syntagmatic compounds, little use of reduplication, and overall preference for analytic lexeme formation techniques. LF's reliance on the vocabulary enrichment strategies characteristic of pidgins, on the other hand, – multifunctionality, circumlocutions, and polysemy – is less in evidence. The few lexical items that exhibit multifunctionality in LF,

[17] See Anderson (1985) on using word formation as a parameter in typological classification.

such as *parlar* 'to speak; language,' do so in the lexifiers as well (cf. It. *parlare*, Fr. *parler* 'to speak; dialect'). The circumlocutions that are present in the data, such as the rendering of adverbs and adjectives by means of prepositional phrases (*in vita* 'in life' for Fr. *vivant* 'alive') or translation of adjectives with relative clauses (*qué bastar* 'which suffices' for Fr. *suffisant* 'sufficient'), invariably rely on syntactic patterns inherited from the lexifiers. These patterns remain available in the lexifiers for paraphrasing in a variety of contexts, including in writing directed at second- and foreign-language learners and for creating dictionary definitions. For example, Richelet (1811) defines Fr. *suffisant* 'sufficient' as *qui suffit* 'which suffices,' and *vivant* 'alive' as *qui est en vie* 'who is in life' (see Section 3.6.5 of Chapter 3). The *Dictionnaire* contains no extravagant circumlocutions along the lines of a "big fellow box spose whiteman fight him he cry too much" (claimed as the lexical expression for piano in Tok Pisin; see Mühlhäusler 1979: 227).

The "staggering amount of polysemy" that characterizes the lexicon of typical pidgins is not a feature of the *Dictionnaire*'s LF. On the contrary, we find a number of lexical choices in the form of doublets (*généro* ~ *sorté* ~ *maniéra* 'sort, kind'), a combination of mono- and multiword lexemes (*piové* ~ *cascar agoua* 'it rains'), or both (*réfletir* ~ *pensar* ~ *mirar bonou* 'to reflect'). There is evidence that at least some of the doublets were semantically differentiated or collocationally specialized (see Chapter 5). The patterns of polysemy in the *Dictionnaire* are selective in the sense of being found in what appear to be some of the more common and/or better established words, and in some cases reflect the polysemy patterns of the lexifiers. For example, the verbs meaning *do/make*, *give*, and *put* are polysemous (or semantically bleached), and used in a variety of support functions, in both LF and the lexifiers. Similarly, while the more common words in (63a) are polysemous, their less common (near-)synonyms in (63b) are listed or used in the *Dictionnaire* with one meaning each.

(63) a. More common

amigo	'friend; ally; favorite'
mangiaria	'breakfast; meal; ragout; provisions'
lanchia	'boat; barque; canoe; launch; small craft'
sentar	'to live; stay; dwell; remain; sojourn; be located; sit down'

b. Less common

favorito	'favorite'
colatzioné	'breakfast'
batello	'boat'
restar	'to remain'
sedjournar	'to sojourn'

Furthermore, as mentioned at the beginning of this chapter (Section 6.2), polysemy at the grammatical pole of the lexicon translates into many pidgins' having a single multifunctional adposition. Contrary to this expectation, LF is well endowed with prepositions, having no less than nine simple prepositions (*a* 'to,' *di* 'of, from,' *in* 'in,' *con* 'with,' *per* 'for, by,' *sopra* 'on,' *sotto* 'under,' *doppo* 'after,' *da* 'at'), three complex prepositions (*fora di* 'out of,' *contra di* 'against,' *per metzo* 'through'), and four articulated prepositions (*al* 'to the' (m.), *alla* 'to the' (f.), *del* 'of the' (m.), *della* 'of the' (f.)). These features reveal LF's continuity with Romance languages in the area of word and lexeme formation, and argue against grouping LF with pidgins.

7 The Inflection

This chapter continues an examination of the structural features of the *Dictionnaire*'s LF by focusing on its inflectional categories and the means by which they are expressed. It begins with a brief survey of inflection in pidgins (Section 7.1) and the Romance lexifiers of LF (Section 7.2). The purpose of the survey is to map out the anticipated structural and typological limits for the inflectional categories of LF and their morphosyntactic expression. Section 7.3 looks at the inflection classes and inflectional categories of LF nominals and their exponence. Section 7.4 does the same for LF verbs. Section 7.5 looks at the expression of pronominal possessors and pronominal objects in the *Dictionnaire*'s LF. Whenever necessary, the *Dictionnaire*'s data is contrasted with Haedo's (1612). Section 7.6 summarizes the conclusions.

7.1 Pidgins

This section examines inflection in pidgins. The description below is based on the cross-linguistic surveys of pidgin languages by Bakker (2003), Roberts and Bresnan (2008), Parkvall and Bakker (2013), and Parkvall (2016, 2019).

Bakker (2003: 11) and Roberts and Bresnan (2008: 270) identify three sources of inflections in pidgins: inheritance from the lexifier(s), borrowing from other languages in contact, and innovation, either via grammaticalization of content items or by copying of patterns from other languages in contact. Of these, retention of lexifier inflections constitutes the most substantial category and follows a cline, from full to partial retention, to partial or full lexicalization, and to complete loss (Roberts and Bresnan 2008: 270, 277–278). In his typological survey of inflection in about thirty pidgins, Bakker (2003: 23) has found that the inheritability of verbal and nominal inflectional categories follows the hierarchies in (1).

(1)	number > case > gender	(nouns)
	TMA > valence > number > person > gender	(verbs)

Roberts and Bresnan (2008: 274–277), following Booij (1994, 1996), separate inflection into inherent (syntax-independent, close to derivation) and contextual (syntax-dependent) types. In Romance languages, inherent inflection includes such categories as TAM marking on verbs and gender and number marking on nouns, while contextual inflection includes subject agreement markers on verbs and gender and number agreement markers on adjectives (see Bauer 2004; Matasović 2018). The typological survey of inflection in twenty-nine pidgins undertaken in Roberts and Bresnan (2008) has revealed that the inheritability of inflections correlates with their division into the inherent and contextual types in that the former are about twice as likely as the latter to be inherited by pidgins (p. 278; see also Parkvall 2019: 265). The findings of Roberts and Bresnan (2008) provide additional evidence for the asymmetrical treatment of the two inflection types in contact situations, including cross-linguistic borrowability of inflectional morphology (Gardani et al. 2015), inheritability of inflections in creoles (Plag 2008a), and principled selectivity in the maintenance and loss of inflections in language attrition and other contact scenarios (Booij 1994: 32–34).

Parkvall and Bakker (2013) provide the following useful list of "[f]eatures typically absent from pidgins," which includes a number of inflectional features:

- In the area of morphology: inflection, derivation, reduplication, infixation, suprafixation, allomorphy, any synthetic structures;
- In the nominal realm: gender marking, case marking, number marking, definite and indefinite articles, large sets of demonstratives, adjectival agreement;
- In the verbal realm: person agreement, tense-mood-aspect marking, valence, voice and gender marking;
- In the area of functional categories: definite and indefinite articles, possessive pronouns, moderate or large sets of prepositions, more than one or a few question words, demonstratives, clause connectors. (Parkvall and Bakker 2013: 46)

Parkvall (2016) examines the behavior of three representative pidgins, Chinook Jargon, Français-Tirailleur, and Yokohamese, with respect to the ten features summarized in Table 7.1 (this is table 4 in the original publication with an added header row). Though the summary is based on three specific pidgins, Parkvall observes that "the following typical configuration . . . also, by and large, applies to pidgins in general."

As a final observation, Bakker (2003: 13–14) and Parkvall and Bakker (2013: 36) note that some pidgins systematically distinguish between selected parts of speech. One of their examples is the verb in Tay Boi (Vietnamese Pidgin French), which ends in *-er* regardless of the infinitive ending in the lexifier (see also Parkvall 2019: 266). This observation, and this example, will be revisited in Section 7.7.

Table 7.1. *Summary of the features considered in the three pidgins*

Category	Features
PERSONAL PRONOUNS	Usually three persons and two numbers, but little else
TENSE/MOOD/ASPECT	No grammaticalized markers at all
ADPOSITIONS	Often zero, sometimes extremely frequent use of one single item
ARTICLES	Usually absent
DEMONSTRATIVES	Usually no distance contrasts
GENDER / NOUN CLASSES / CLASSIFIERS	Neither grammatical nor biological gender (or comparable systems)
COPULA	Not inherited from the lexifier. For the most part absent, but sometimes grammaticalized from other material
NEGATION	Free and invariable particle, often preverbal
NOMINAL NUMBER	Not obligatorily marked
WORD ORDER	Few or no exceptions to whatever order is dominant

Source: Parkvall (2016)

7.2 Lexifiers

Italian and Spanish, the main lexifiers of the *Dictionnaire*'s LF, belong to the Romance structural type. The latter is usually characterized by simultaneous reference to the shared synchronic traits of Romance languages and the diachronic developments which define their shared evolution out of the Latin structural type (e.g., Kabatek and Pusch 2011). Viewed from the perspective of their structural distance from Latin, Italian and Spanish are located at the more conservative, less innovating pole of the Romance structural-typological continuum (Simone 2010; Carlier et al. 2012). The description of Romance inflection below follows the approach of taking into account both synchronic traits and diachronic developments, and places particular emphasis on the interplay between the inherited synthetic and innovating analytic components of inflection (Schwegler 1990; Haspelmath and Michaelis 2017).

7.2.1 Synchronic Features

The synchronic Romance inflectional categories may be illustrated with examples from Italian. The following description is based on the typological outline of Italian morphology in Berretta (1992: 130–131), with the additional sources to be referred to as needed. The description is necessarily selective in its coverage, being limited to areas of interest to this chapter and focusing on modern standard varieties of Italian and, where applicable, Spanish; the purpose here is not to downplay the historical, geographical, dialectal, social, or other kinds of variation in the Romance lexifiers of LF but to use the modern standard varieties as reference points for introducing the Romance inflectional categories ("the *kinds* of categories which are expressed in the grammar") and their exponence ("the *means* by which a given grammatical category is expressed") (Maiden 1995: 236).

Italian nouns morphologically mark the categories of number and gender (Berretta 1992; Maiden 1997). These are expressed via portmanteau endings on nouns and agreement between the head noun and other elements of the noun phrase (articles, demonstratives, quantifiers, possessives, adjectives), and between the subject and the verb. The example in (2) illustrates the portmanteau marker of number and gender *-e* in the noun *amiche* '(female) friends,' and the agreement between the noun and the definite article, possessive, and adjective in the noun phrase *le tue simpatiche amiche* 'your nice (female) friends,' and between the subject *amiche* and both elements of the verb phrase *sono partite* 'have left.'

(2)	*L-e*	*tu-e*	*simpatich-e*	*amich-e*	*sono*	*part-it-e.*
	the-F.PL	2S.POSS-F.PL	nice-F.PL	friend-F.PL	be.PRES.IND.3PL.SBJ	leave-PAST.PPLE-F.PL

'Your nice (female) friends have left.'
(Berretta 1992: 131)

In Spanish, the expression of plurality and gender marking in nouns and adjectives is more transparent than in Italian; compare the forms in (3).

(3)	Spanish	Italian	
	hij-o buen-o	figli-o buon-o	'good son'
	hij-o-s buen-o-s	figl-i buon-i	'good sons'
	hij-a buen-a	figli-a buon-a	'good daughter'
	hij-a-s buen-a-s	figli-e buon-e	'good daughters'

In both Italian and Spanish, nouns are divided into several inflection classes. This division is rooted in diachrony, and is addressed in Section 7.2.2.

Italian and Spanish retain the category of case only in personal pronouns, e.g., Italian *io* 'I' ~ *me*, *mi* 'me'; Spanish *yo* 'I' ~ *me*, *mí* 'me.' The object pronouns distinguish between stressed (tonic) and unstressed (clitic) forms. In the sentences below, the examples in (4a) and (4b) show the stressed pronoun and their respective equivalents in (4a') and (4b') the corresponding clitic pronoun.

(4)	a. *Carla*	*guarda*	*me.*
	Carla	look.PRES.IND.3S.SBJ	1S.DO

'Carla is looking at me.'
(Patota 2006: 191)

a.' *Carla mi guarda.*
Carla 1S.DO look.PRES.IND.3S.SBJ
'Carla is looking at me.'
(Patota 2006: 191)

b. *Carla parla a me.*
Carla speak.PRES.IND.3S.SBJ PREP 1S.IO
'Carla is speaking to me.'
(Patota 2006: 191)

b.' *Carla mi parla.*
Carla 1S.IO speak.PRES.IND.3S.SBJ
'Carla is speaking to me.'
(Patota 2006: 191)

Clitic pronouns may function as possessors (see 5a). Such constructions may be equivalent to constructions with dedicated possessives (see 5b).

(5) a. *Ti sarò sempre amica.*
2S.IO be.FUT.1S.SBJ always friend
'I'll always be your friend.'
(Cordin 2001: 621)

b. *Sarò sempre tua amica.*
be.FUT.1S.SBJ always 2S.POSS.F.S friend
'I'll always be your friend.'
(Cordin 2001: 621)

In both Italian and Spanish, the verb morphologically marks the categories of TAM and person/number of the subject (see 2, 4, and 5 above). Parts of the verb paradigm contain a semantically empty theme vowel, located between the lexical root and inflectional markers (Savoia 1997), which forms the basis for dividing the verbs into inflection classes. This aspect of the verbal morphology is rooted in diachrony, and is discussed in Section 7.2.2.

Some of the Italian inflectional markers, such as the markers of the past participle and imperfect tense, are transparent, while others display a high degree of fusion. This latter aspect was observed in the portmanteau number/gender marker *-e* in (2), and may be further seen in the expression of TAM, person, and number marking on the verbs in (2), (4), and (5). There is also a high degree of allomorphy in both lexical and inflectional morphemes; compare, for example, Italian *ved-o* and Spanish *ve-o* 'I see' with It. Sp. *vis-to* 'seen' (Berretta 1992: 131). In Italian, additional complexity is introduced into the verb morphology by the clitic pronouns. As seen in (6), the past participle *visto* agrees in number and gender with the object when expressed by a clitic pronoun but not when expressed by a noun.

(6) a. *L-e* *ho* *vis-t-e.*
PRO.DO-F.PL have.PRES.IND.1S.SBJ see-PAST.PPLE-F.PL
'I have seen them' (the female friends).
(Berretta 1992: 131)

b. *Ho* *vis-t-o* *l-e* *amich-e.*
have.PRES.IND.1S.SBJ see-PAST.PPLE-M.S the-F.PL friend-F.PL
'I have seen the (female) friends.'
(Berretta 1992: 131)

The above interplay between the synthetic and analytic components is shared by the inflectional systems of all modern Romance languages and is part of their common inheritance and evolution from Latin. Some of the principal diachronic processes that have led to the formation of the Romance inflectional systems are surveyed in Section 7.2.2.

7.2.2 Diachronic Features

7.2.2.1 Drift toward Analyticity The evolution from Latin to Romance languages is characterized by a drift from a more synthetic toward a more analytic morphosyntax. The drift consists in replacing synthetic inflectional forms with periphrastic functional equivalents (inflectional periphrases; Bonami 2015). In the verb, it involves using verbal periphrases in which a nonfinite lexical verb is combined with an inflected auxiliary expressing such categories as tense, mood, voice, and person: compare *amor* 'I am loved' in Latin (synthetic passive voice) with *sono amato* 'id.' in Italian and *soy amado* 'id.' in Spanish (analytic passive voice). In the adjective, it involves periphrastic comparative and superlative constructions: compare *fortior* 'stronger'/*fortissimus* 'strongest' in Latin with *più forte* 'stronger'/*il più forte* 'strongest' in Italian and *más fuerte* 'stronger'/*el más fuerte* 'strongest' in Spanish. In nouns and personal pronouns, the drift is manifested as the reduction or loss of morphological case distinctions and growing reliance on word order and prepositions to express grammatical relations. Thus, the synthetic expression of possession by means of the genitive case of the possessor noun was replaced in spoken Latin with the prepositional periphrasis consisting of *de* 'of' followed by the ablative case of the possessor, as in *caballus de Petro* 'horse of Peter' for *Petris equus* 'Peter's horse' (Korletjanu 1974: 166–168). Descendants of this construction live on in Romance languages, including Italian (*il cavallo di Pietro*) and Spanish (*el caballo de Pedro*). In a later but related development, polysemy of the third-person possessive adjective – in Spanish, *su* can mean 'his,' 'her,' 'their' (m.), 'their' (f.), 'your' (sg.), or 'your' (pl.) – has led to the use of prepositional periphrases with *de* 'of' to supplement and/or replace the dedicated possessives, as in *su casa de él* 'his house of him' > *la casa de él* 'the house of him,' 'his house' (Penny 2002: 142–143;

Orozco 2012: 206–207; 2018: 62–64). In Italian, *la sua casa* 'his/her house' is ambiguous with respect to the gender of the possessor, whereas *la casa di lui* 'the house of him,' 'his house' and *la casa di lei* 'the house of her,' 'her house' are explicit in this respect (Rohlfs 1968: 122; Cordin 2001: 620). The Latin dative case was replaced with the periphrasis consisting of *ad* 'to' followed by the accusative case of the nominal, as in *litteras ad te mitto* 'I am sending letters to you' for *litteras tibi mitto* 'I am sending you letters' in Cicero's correspondence (Grandgent 1927: 128; Korletjanu 1974: 162, 166–168). This example also illustrates the fact that the analytic constructions were initially used side by side with, or as stylistic variants of, the corresponding synthetic forms. Other diachronic changes leading to greater analyticity of the Romance morphosyntax include the development of clitic pronouns, articles, and complementizers (Schwegler 1990; Vincent 1997c).

7.2.2.2 Reduction of Noun Inflection Classes Latin nouns were divided into five inflection classes (declensions). The first three declensions were large and robust, whereas the fourth and the fifth were small, and nouns from these two declensions began to migrate to one of the first three already in Latin. The examples in (7) (from Korletjanu 1974: 163–165; Lloyd 1987: 156; Penny 2002: 126–127) show that the Romance forms continue the modified rather than the original declensions. As a result of this migration, both main Romance lexifiers of LF have only three noun inflection classes; as Grandgent (1927: 125) puts it, "[o]f the five Latin declensions, the three big ones absorbed the two little ones." Formally, first-declension nouns in both Italian and Spanish end in *-a* (as in It. *figlia* ~ Sp. *hija* 'daughter') and second-declension nouns in *-o* (as in It. *figlio* ~ Sp. *hijo* 'son'). Third-declension nouns end in *-e* in Italian (*mente* 'mind,' *luce* 'light') and either *-e* or a consonant in Spanish (*mente* 'mind,' *luz* 'light') (Maiden 1995: 97–98; Penny 2002: 126–127).[1]

(7)

Latin				Italian	Spanish	
socrus	(IV)	>	(I)	suocera	suegra	'mother-in-law'
nurus	(IV)	>	(I)	nuora	nuera	'daughter-in-law'
rabies	(V)	>	(I)	rabbia	rabia	'rage'
fides	(V)	>	(III)	fede	fe	'faith'

7.2.2.3 Hypercharacterization of Gender In both Italian and Spanish, there is a strong correlation between the noun word marker[2] *-a* and the feminine

[1] For details of these develoments, see, e.g., D'Achille and Thornton (2003) for Italian and Harris (1992) for Spanish.

[2] See Harris (1991) regarding this term.

gender, and between the noun word marker *-o* and the masculine gender. Penny (2002: 124) observes that in Old Spanish the correlation was even stronger, with only two nouns – the feminine *mano* 'hand' and the masculine *día* 'day' – contravening it. As a consequence of this correlation, third-declension nouns in both languages tend to migrate to the first or second declensions based on their gender; in the specialist literature, this process is sometimes labeled "hypercharacterization of gender" (Lloyd 1987: 156–157; Penny 2002: 125). Examples of this process in the evolution of Spanish include *infanta* 'princess' and *cuchara* 'spoon' (from earlier *infante* and *cuchar*) (Malkiel 1967a: 239; 1967b: 1241; Penny 2002: 125). This Romance tendency has roots in Vulgar Latin, where forms like *nepta* for Classical Latin *neptis* 'niece' achieved "a sharper characterization of gender, a neater 'fit' between form and meaning" (Malkiel 1983: 597).

Hypercharacterization of gender is also attested in Romance adjectives. Those that descend from Latin adjectives of the type *bonus* (m.)/*bona* (f.)/ *bonum* (n.) 'good' distinguish gender in their endings (*buono* ~ *buona* in Italian, *bueno* ~ *buena* in Spanish), whereas those that descend from the type *grandis* (m. f.)/*grande* (n.) 'big' are gender-neutral (It. Sp. *grande*). Shifting of *grandis*-type adjectives to the *bonus* type was also a feature of Vulgar Latin, with the forms *pauper mulier non paupera mulier* and *tristis non tristus* recorded in the Appendix Probi (Penny 2002: 128). As seen in (8a) below, the outcomes of this process are language-specific (Grandgent 1927: 127; Malkiel 1967a: 239; 1967b: 1241; Patota 2006: 75). Hypercharacterization of gender is attested in Judeo-Spanish and Judeo-Italian (see the forms in 8b and 8c from Penny 2004: 189 and Rubin 2016: 321, respectively).

(8) a.

Latin	Italian	Spanish	
paupere	povero, -a	pobre	'poor'
alacre	allegro, -a	alegre	'cheerful'
triste	tristo, -a ~ triste	triste	'sad'
acre	agro, -a	agro, -a[3]	'bitter, sharp'

b.

Spanish	Judeo-Spanish	
libre	libro, -a	'free'
firme	firme, -a	'firm'
grande	grande, -a	'big'

c.

Italian	Judeo-Italian	
pane	pano	'bread'
notte	not(t)a	'night'
grande	gran(n)o	'big'

[3] Later changed to *agrio, -a* (Malkiel 1967b: 1233ff.).

Table 7.2. *Verb classes in Latin*

Inflection class	Inflection class marker	Example	Gloss
I conjugation	*ā*	*voc-ā-re*	'to call'
II conjugation	*ē*	*val-ē-re*	'to be strong'
III conjugation	*ĕ*	*vinc-ĕ-re*	'to conquer'
IV conjugation	*ī*	*ven-ī-re*	'to come'

Table 7.3. *Verb classes in Italian and Spanish*

Form	Language	I conjugation	II conjugation	III conjugation
INFINITIVE	ITALIAN	cant-a-re	vend-e-re	dorm-i-re
	SPANISH	cant-a-r	vend-e-r	dorm-i-r
PAST PARTICIPLE	ITALIAN	cant-a-to	vend-u-to	dorm-i-to
	SPANISH	cant-a-do	vend-i-do	dorm-i-do

7.2.2.4 Reduction of Verb Inflection Classes Latin verbs are divided into inflectional classes (conjugations) based on the theme vowel in the present active infinitive (see Table 7.2).

Among the four Latin conjugations, only the first (*-āre*) and the fourth (*-īre*) "were genuinely productive" (Penny 2002: 171). In the evolution from Latin to Romance, the number of the verb classes was consequently reduced (see Table 7.3). The forms illustrated in Table 7.3 – the infinitive and the past participle – "are the main loci of retention of conjugational distinctions" (Maiden 2011: 208).

The processes leading to the reduction of the verb classes included merger of the second (*-ēre*) and third (*-ĕre*) conjugations, migration of second- and third-conjugation verbs to the first or fourth conjugations, and growth of the latter through absorption of verbs from other sources, including verbs from the other classes, derived, and borrowed verbs (Grandgent 1927; Korletjanu 1974; Napoli and Vogel 1990; Penny 2002; Maiden 2011, 2016). Some of these processes were under way already in Latin, as seen in *fugere et non fugire* recorded in the Appendix Probi (Korletjanu 1974: 194). In Italian, only the verbs in *-are* and the *-isc-* subclass of the verbs in *-ire* are synchronically productive (Iacobini and Thornton 1994: 280; Schwarze 1999: 3). In Spanish, only the *-ar* conjugation is synchronically productive, in the sense that new verbs are accommodated to the morphology of this conjugation (Stovicek 2010: 31).

7.2.2.5 Copularization of Latin *stare* Another relevant process is grammaticalization of Lat. *stare* 'to stand' and its intrusion into the functional territory of Lat. *esse* ~ VL **essere* 'to be.' This development has reached different degrees of completion in different Romance languages. In Italian, *stare* has evolved some copular and auxiliary functions; for example, it is used for forming the continuous tense, as in *sto correndo* 'I am running.' In Spanish and Portuguese, *estar* has reached the most advanced degree of copularization (Pountain 1982; Hengeveld 1992). It has been found that copularization of *estar* is accelerated in certain types of contact settings (see Silva-Corvalán 1986; Lipski 1993: 224 for Spanish).

7.3 Nominals

7.3.1 Nouns

In the *Dictionnaire*'s LF, nouns may end in [a], [o], [e], [i], [u], or a consonant. Nouns ending in [a] and [o] form the majority, or about 67 percent, of the total of just over a thousand nouns.[4] Of these, a little over 400 nouns (about 40 percent of the total) end in [a], and slightly over 270 (about 27 percent of the total) end in [o]. Etymologically, these groups consist of nouns that end in [a] or [o] in the source languages (see 9a, 9b) and a small number of predominantly Romance nouns that end in [e] or a consonant in the source languages (see 9c, 9d). Cifoletti (1989: 46; 2004: 38) observes that consonant-final words of non-European, mainly Arabic, origin remain consonant-final in LF, except when they become vowel-final due to the loss of word-final pharyngeals (see 9e, 9f).

(9)	a.	Nouns in -o		Nouns in -o
		amigo	'friend'	(< Sp. amigo)[5]
		domingo	'Sunday'	(< Sp. domingo)
		pagnio	'cloth'	(< Sp. paño)

[4] All calculations were done manually and are to be taken as indicating only the order of size of each word class.

[5] The language labels in the brackets indicate that the shape of the LF word is compatible with that of the Romance word listed there. As discussed in Chapter 5, the source language for many of the LF words is uncertain, and more than one Romance source for some of the words is likely (Schuchardt 1909; Cornelissen 1992; Russo 2001; Castellanos 2007; Baglioni 2017). Heath (1989: 152) notes a similar issue in connection with Romance loans in MCA: "In some cases [...] we may not know which Romance form was the immediate prototype (and [...] it is quite possible that the MCA form has a multiple Romance source)."

	martello	‘hammer’	(< It. martello)
	dginokio	‘knee’	(< It. ginocchio)

b.	Nouns in -a		Nouns in -a
	bouriqua	‘donkey’	(< Sp. borrica)
	camischia	‘shirt’	(< It. camiscia)
	germana	‘sister’	(< Cat. germana)
	mantéga	‘butter’	(< Cat. mantega)
	agouilla	‘needle’	(< Cat. agulla, Ptg. agulha)

c.	Nouns in -o		Nouns in -e or -C
	verro	‘glass’	(< Fr. verre)
	ventro	‘belly	(< Fr. It. ventre)
	tigro	‘tiger’	(< Fr. It. Sp. tigre)

d.	Nouns in -a		Nouns in -e or -C
	fébra	‘fever’	(< It. febbre, Cat. febre)
	scoura	‘axe’	(< It. scoure)
	biera	‘beer’	(< Fr. bière)
	amanda	‘almond’	(< Fr. amande)
	flinta	‘platinum’	(< Eng. flint)
	mouchéra ~ moukera	‘woman’	(< Sp. mujer)

e.	Nouns in -C		Nouns in -C
	rouss	‘rice’	(< Ar. /ru:z/)
	tout	‘mulberry’	(< Ar. /tu:t/)

f.	Nouns in -V		Nouns in [ʕ]
	taba	‘seal’	(< Ar. /ṭa:baʕ/)
	roubié	‘spring’	(< Ar. /rbi:ʕ/)

Several nouns that end in [o] in the source language display a final [u] in LF (see 10a). The shift from [o] to [u] in LF has been explained as assimilation to the vowel systems of the Berber and/or Arabic substrate or adstrate in LF (see Schuchardt 1909; Cifoletti 2004; Castellanos 2007; Chapter 3); variation in the height of the final vowel is seen in the pronoun *ello* ~ *ellou* ‘he.’ The group of [u]-final nouns also includes nouns that end in [u] in the source language (see 10b).

(10)	a.	riou	‘stream’	(< Sp. río, Cat. riu)
		mouchachou	‘boy’	(< Sp. muchacho)
		bakalaou	‘cod’	(< Sp. bacalao)
		brodou	‘broth’	(< It. brodo)
	b.	vertou	‘virtue’	(< It. virtù)
		servitou	‘slavery’	(< It. servitù)
		dgioventù	‘youth’	(< It. gioventù)

Nouns ending in [e] form slightly over 11 percent of the total number of nouns. This group is composed of nouns that end in [e] in the source languages, in either singular or plural (see 11). The word for 'bread' shows variation between the *e*- and *o*-final forms, *pané* ~ *pano* (< It. *pane*); the *-e* ~ *-o* variants are also seen in *mariniére* 'rower' ~ *mariniéro* 'sailor.'

(11)	a.	bové	'ox'	(< It. bove)
		nipoté	'nephew'	(< It. nipote)
		couoré	'heart'	(< It. cuore)
		païsé	'country'	(< It. paese)
		paché	'peace'	(< It. pace)
		sangré	'blood'	(< Sp. sangre)
	b.	scarpé	'shoe'	(< It. scarpa, pl. scarpe)
		cortiné	'curtain'	(< It. cortina, pl. cortine)
		coquiaré	'spoon'	(< Sic. cucchiara)[6]
		ové	'egg'	(< It. uovo)[7]

A small number of nouns (under 3 percent) end in [i]. This group includes nouns ending in *-i* in the singular in the source language (see 12a) and those that end in *-e* in the singular and *-i* in the plural in the source language (see 12b). While the change from *-e* > *-i* may be in part phonetic, motivated by the same tendency toward mid-vowel raising as the change from *-o* > *-u*, the fact that these nouns refer to objects that are paired (feet), come in large sets (teeth), or are typically seen in large quantities (fish, partridges, people), suggests that they are more likely to derive from the lexifier plural forms. This inference is also suggested by the sense differentiation between *dolche* 'sweetness; sweet, supple' (< It. *dolce*) and *dolci* 'preserves' (< It. *dolci*) and the adaptation of the plurals in (12c).

(12)	a.	martédi	'Tuesday'	(< It. martedì)
		mercolédi	'Wednesday'	(< It. mercoledì)
		tobgi	'gunner'	(< Ar. tobgi < Tu. topçu)[8]
		piskéri	'porter'	(< Ar. biskri)[9]
	b.	piedi	'foot'	(It. piede, pl. piedi)
		denti	'tooth'	(It. dente, pl. denti)

6 Rohlfs (1954: 78); Baglioni (2017: 192).

7 Rohlfs (1968: 36–38); Baglioni (2017: 191).

8 Due to the absence of vowel harmony in *tobgi*, Cifoletti (1980: 35) entertains the possibility that this is "una formazione autonoma dell'arabo" [an autonomous formation of Arabic] rather than a direct loan from Turkish; this issue is further addressed in Cifoletti (2004: 59n7).

9 An ethnonym based on the city name Biskra (Cifoletti 1980: 35; 2004: 144n4). "Some immigrant groups ... specialised in niche occupations which they dominated (without having a legally recognised monopoly): Jijelis were bakers, Mzabis bath-house managers, Biskris porters and couriers" (McDougall 2017: 36).

	genti	'man, people'	(It. gente, pl. genti)
	pechi	'fish'	(It. pesce, pl. pesci)
	pernichi	'partridge'	(It. pernice, pl. pernici)
c.	gouanti	'glove'	(It. guanto, pl. guanti)
	detti	'finger'	(It. dito, pl. diti)
	piselli	'pea'	(It. pisello, pl. piselli)
	fagioli	'bean'	(It. fagiolo, pl. fagioli)
	datoli	'date'	(Gr. δάκτυλος)[10]
	mobili	'furniture'	(It. mobile, pl. mobili)
	forbichi	'scissors'	(It. forbice, pl. forbici)

Consonant-final nouns constitute about 18 percent of the total number of nouns. Nearly half of these are Romance nouns ending in the suffixes *-tzion* ~ *-ion*, such as *permitzion* 'permission,' and *-tor* ~ *-dor* ~ *-or*, such as *peskador* 'fisherman.' Other word-final consonants in nouns of Romance provenance include /l/ (*sol* 'sun'), /s/ (*dios* 'God'), /t/ (*scorbut* 'scurvy'), /d/ (*nord* 'north'), /k/ (*esbinac* 'spinach'), /j/ (*convoï* 'convoy'), /m/ (*harem* 'harem') (*esbinac* and *harem* are ultimately from Arabic). Two of the final /s/s derive from the Spanish plural marker: *douros* 'piaster' (< Sp. *duro*, pl. *duros*) and *tapétos* 'carpet,' an apparent cross between Italian *tappeto* and Spanish *tapetes*. Words of Arabic and Turkish origin enrich the inventory of word-final consonants with /b/ (*cherub* 'drink'), /f/ (*carchouf* 'artichoke'), and /ʃ/ (*bakchich* 'gift').

In summary, from among the nouns recorded in the *Dictionnaire*, those ending in [a] constitute about 40 percent, those ending in [o] about 27 percent, and those ending in [e] or a consonant about 29 percent of the total. Slightly under 4 percent of the nouns end in [i] or [u]. Over 80 percent of nouns end in a vowel, and of these, over 80 percent end in [a] and [o]. The [i]- and [u]-final nouns continue in part the minority noun classes of the Romance lexifiers and in part result from the effects of language contact, such as mid-vowel raising and adaptation of source nouns in their plural form.

A look at the LF nouns documented in Haedo (1612) reveals a compatible picture in that there is also a clear preference for vowel-final nouns, with 94 percent of the nouns ending in a vowel and well over 80 percent of these ending in [a] and [o] (see Table 7.4, based on Cifoletti's 1989: 163–164 glossary of the LF lexical items appearing in that work). Unlike the *Dictionnaire*'s, Haedo's LF does not have nouns ending in [u] or [i].[11]

[10] On *datoli* 'date,' see Baglioni (2010: 432–433). In connection with the forms in (12c), the French loans /ligạ/ 'glove' (< Fr. *les gants* 'the gloves') and /libạ/ 'stocking' (< Fr. *les bas* 'the stockings') in MCA are of interest (Heath 1989: 127).

[11] Compare Haedo's Romanicized ending of *niçarane* 'Christian' with Cervantes's *nizaraní* (Walsh 1971: 168).

Table 7.4. *Noun classes in Haedo's Lingua Franca*

Nouns ending in [a] (16 out of 33)	Nouns ending in [o] (11 out of 33)	Nouns ending in [e] (4 out of 33)	Nouns ending in a C (2 out of 33)
bastonada	barbero	cane	Papaz
boca	Christiano	Fe	patron
cabeza	diablo	febre	
campaña	Dio	niçarane	
carta	forato		
casa	Iudio		
cosa	mundo		
fantasia	pecato ~ pecado		
hora	perro		
manera	tempo		
parola	vellaco		
terra			
testa			
tortuga			
ventura			
volta			

In both main lexifiers of LF, the *-o* and *-a* noun classes are numerically predominant and synchronically productive (Harris 1992: 68; Thornton 1996: 90; D'Achille and Thornton 2003: 227; Acquaviva 2009: 51). For Spanish, Harris (1991: 33) indicates that the *-o* and *-a* nouns (the "inner core") outnumber the *-e* and consonant-final nouns (the "outer core") by about two to one. In a related publication, Harris (1992: 68) argues that Spanish nouns, adjectives, and adverbs ending in *-o* and *-a* are "prototypical Spanish substantives": they are "the least marked in morphological terms" and "numerically preponderant by a large margin." For Italian, D'Achille and Thornton's (2003: 213) calculation indicates that from among 4557 noncompound nouns in the basic vocabulary of Italian, about 38 percent end in *-o*, about 36 percent in *-a*, and about 21 percent in *-e* (see also Iacobini and Thornton 1994: 279). Even taking into account the incomplete nature of our documentation of LF, the LF noun classes in Haedo (1612)

Table 7.5. *Noun classes in Lingua Franca*

Nouns in …	Anonymous (1830a)	Haedo (1612)	Italian basic vocabulary
-a	40%	48%	36%
-o	27%	33%	38%
-e and/or *-C*	29%	18%	21%
Other	4%	–	5%

and the *Dictionnaire* still show remarkable continuity with the noun declension classes of its major lexifiers (see Table 7.5).

7.3.2 Adjectives

The LF adjectives listed in the *Dictionnaire*, about 190 in total, fall into three groups. The largest (about 73 percent) is composed of adjectives ending in *-o* in the masculine and *-a* in the feminine (see the examples in 13). One adjective, *locou*, *-a* 'crazy' (< Sp. *loco*, *-a*), ends in [u] in the masculine form due to mid-vowel raising; variation in the height of the final vowel is exhibited by *bono* ~ *bonou* 'good.'

(13)	dgialo	'yellow'	(< It. giallo)
	nouovo	'new'	(< It. nuovo)
	flaco	'thin'	(< Sp. flaco)
	locou	'crazy'	(< Sp. loco)

Though the feminine counterpart is provided for only a minority of the *-o*/*-a* adjectives, the fact that the adjectives in *-o* have a feminine counterpart is explicitly stated in the *Dictionnaire*'s preface, with *bono* / *bona* 'good' given as an example ("[l]es adjectifs en *o* ont seuls un féminin" [only the adjectives in *o* have a feminine]; "[m]ais les adjectifs en *e* n'ont pas de féminin" [but the adjectives in *e* have no feminine]), and is also evident in the syntactic agreement features to be examined in Section 7.3.3 and in Chapter 8. The *Dictionnaire*'s LF vocabulary normally uses only the masculine form of the adjective as the citation form (see 14a), though in some cases the feminine form is supplied as well (see 14b).

(14)	a.	French	Lingua Franca	
		haut	alto	'high'
		juste	dgiousto	'just'
		riche	rico	'rich'
		sale	sporco	'dirty'

b.

French	Lingua Franca	
bas, basse	basso, bassa	'low'
sec, sèche	séco, séca	'dry'
beau, belle	bello -la	'beautiful
rond -de	roundo, da	'round'

The next largest group of adjectives (about 20.5 percent) end in *-e*; as in the lexifiers, these are gender-neutral. Included in this group are two adjectives that end in *-e* in the lexifier but *-i* in LF, due either to mid-vowel raising or to having been adopted in the plural form (see 15b). Variation in the final vowel is seen in *grandé* ~ *grandi* 'big, vast.'

(15) a. verdé 'green' (< It. Sp. verde)
dolche 'sweet' (< It. dolce)

b. forti 'strong' (< It. forte, pl. forti)
pésanti 'heavy' (< It. pesante, pl. pesanti)

Consonant-final adjectives (under 5 percent) include the Arabic-derived *maboul* 'crazy,' which stands out in having a feminine counterpart, *maboula*. Given that the feminine gender marker *-a* is shared by Arabic, Spanish, and Italian (Cifoletti 2004: 41), its specific source in *maboula* is unknown. The adjective *blou* 'blue' (< It. *blù*; invariable) is in a group by itself (see 16).

(16)

natural	'natural'	(< Sp. natural)
soupérior	'upper'	(< Sp. superior)
meskin	'poor; wretched; unfortunate'	(< Ar. [miski:n])
blou	'blue'	(< It. blù)

Some of the adjectives display hypercharacterization of gender:

(17)

savento	'learned'	(< Fr. savant)
simplo	'simple'	(< Sp. Fr. simple)
tristo	'sad'	(< Sp. It. Fr. triste; also It. tristo)

In summary, LF shows the same two morphological classes of adjectives as its lexifiers: the substantially larger *-o/-a* class and the smaller *-e*/consonant-final class; within the latter, the adjectives in *-e* are more numerous than those ending in a consonant. The proportions are similar in LF's Romance lexifiers; for example, Harris (1991: 34) observes that in Spanish most adjectives are "prototypical inner core words with *-o* in the masculine and *-a* in the feminine." For the basic vocabulary of Italian, Iacobini and Thornton (1994: 279) provide the figures of 65.3 percent adjectives in *-o / -a* versus 31.7 percent in *-e*. With the exception of *maboul / maboula* 'crazy,' the only LF adjectives to inflect for gender are the *-o / -a* group. In this feature, LF likewise agrees with its lexifiers: for example, the subtype of adjectives like *español / española* 'Spanish,' with no gender marker in the masculine and *-a* in the feminine, is, similarly, small in Spanish (Harris 1991: 34–35). The handful of adjectives recorded in Haedo's (1612) LF examples fall into the same categories as in the *Dictionnaire*, with the majority belonging to the *o- / a-* class (*bono* 'good,' *vivo* 'alive,' *malato* 'sick'). Thus, it may be concluded that LF shows detailed continuity with its Romance lexifiers with respect to the morphological classes of the nominals and in terms of prototypicality of the classes ending in *-o* and *-a* (nouns) and *-o* / *-a* (adjectives) (Harris 1991, 1992).

7.3.3 Gender

In the *Dictionnaire*'s nouns, the gender distinction can be expressed lexically or morphologically. A lexically expressed gender distinction is seen in nouns referring to humans and animals (in 18).

(18)	padré	'father'	madré	'mother'
	fratello ~ cognato	'brother'	germana	'sister'
	oumbré	'man'	mouchéra ~ dona	'woman'
	taour	'bull'	vaka	'cow'

Morphologically expressed gender distinctions are shown in (19). These examples illustrate the correlation between the noun ending *-a* and the feminine gender, and the noun ending *-o (-ou)* and the masculine gender. The use of an etymologically diminutive suffix to express the feminine gender in *galina* 'hen' continues a similar pattern in the lexifier (Serianni 1989: 124–126).

(19)	mouchachou	'son'	mouchacha	'daughter'
	nipoté	'nephew'	nipota	'niece'
	zio	'uncle'	zia	'aunt'
	cavalo	'horse'	cavala	'mare'
	gallo	'rooster'	galina	'hen'

Some names of animals are listed in the *Dictionnaire* in only one, presumably gender-neutral, form; these are *cabra* 'goat,' *bouriqua* 'donkey,' *okia* 'goose,' *camello* 'camel,' *lépéro* 'hare,' *moulo* 'mule,' *porco* 'pig,' and *vitello* 'calf.' The examples in (20) show that, just as in the lexifiers, the word markers *-o* / *-a* may also reflect non-gender-related lexical distinctions, both with and without semantic contiguity between the words so distinguished.[12]

(20)	lampo	'lightning'	lampa	'lamp'
	porto	'harbor'	porta	'door'

[12] Examples from the lexifiers include *panno* 'cloth' / *panna* 'cream' in Italian and *naranjo* 'orange tree' / *naranja* 'orange' in Spanish (Serianni 1989: 112; Harris 1991: 36n13).

pianto	'tear'	pianta	'plant'
païo	'pair'	païa	'straw'

Morphological expression of the gender distinction is also found in the third person personal pronoun, articles, adjectives, and demonstratives (see 21).

(21)

Masculine		Feminine	
ello ~ ellou	'he'	ella	'she'
il	'the'	la	'the'
oun	'a'	ouna	'a'
qouesto	'this'	qouesta	'this'
qouello	'that'	qouella	'that'
séco	'dry'	séca	'dry'

In the verb, the gender distinction is recorded in the perfective form that derives from the Italian past participle; in the *Dictionnaire*'s preface, this verb form is described etymologically as "le participe passé en *ito* ou *ato*, fém. *ita*, *ata*" [the past participle in *ito* or *ato*, feminine *ita*, *ata*]. The LF vocabulary supplies the feminine form for selected verbs (see 22), however, due to the absence of female participants in the textual examples (see Chapter 3), the use of the feminine form is not illustrated.

(22)

French	Lingua Franca	
assassiner, assassiné -ée	assassinar -ato -ata	'to murder'
baiser, baisé -ée	bachiar, bachiato -a	'to kiss'

Several kinds of evidence point to the unmarked status of the masculine gender (etymologically masculine singular) in the *Dictionnaire*'s LF. They include the use of the masculine forms of the demonstratives as neutral demonstrative pronouns (in 23a), the masculine forms of adjectives in adverbial function (in 23b), and the masculine forms of nouns when employed generically (in 23c). The unmarked status of the masculine gender in LF continues its unmarked status in the lexifiers (see Prado 1982; Harris 1991 for Spanish; Sabatini 1993; Maiden 1995; Thornton 2003 for Italian). The basicness of the masculine singular is also apparent in the SLA of Italian, as revealed by its early acquisition and use as the default form (Crotta 1988: 252; Valentini 1990: 342–344; Berretta 1992: 140).

(23) a. *qouest-o star vér-o.*
this-M be.IMPF true-M
'Cela est vrai.'
'This is true.'
(Anonymous 1830a: 93)

b. *mi ablar dgioust-o.*
1s speak.IMPF just-M
'Je dis la vérité.'

'I speak the truth.'
(Anonymous 1830a: 93)

c.

qué	*poudir*	*counchar*	*il*	*Françis*	*contra*	*di*	*Algieri?*
what	be.able.IMPF	do.IMPF	the.M	French	against	of	Algiers

'Que peuvent faire les Français contre Alger?'
'What can the French do against Algiers?'
(Anonymous 1830a: 98)

Outside lexicon and morphology, gender is signaled via syntactic agreement between the head noun and other elements of the noun phrase (articles, demonstratives, quantifiers, adjectives), and between the subject and predicative adjectives. For example, (24a) and (24b) below show the attributive adjective *bonou* / *bouona* 'good' agreeing in gender with the nouns *thé* and *genti*, and the examples in (24c) and (24d) show the definite article *il* / *la* and predicative adjectives *bello* and *pronta* agreeing in gender with the nouns *tempo* and *mangiaria*, respectively. The sentence in (24a), additionally, shows that the third person singular personal pronoun *ellou* agrees in gender with the antecedent noun *thé*.

(24) a.

mi	*tenir*	*thé*	*mouchou*	*bon-ou;*
1s	have.IMPF	tea.M	very	good-M

mi	*quérir*	*ti*	*goustar*	*per*	*ell-ou.*
1s	want.IMPF	2s	taste.IMPF	DOM	3S-M

'J'ai du thé délicieux; je veux que vous en goutiez.'
'I've got some delicious tea, I want you to try it.'
(Anonymous 1830a: 97)

b.

star	*bouon-a*	*genti.*
be.IMPF	good-F	man.F

'C'est un brave homme.'
'He is good people.'
(Anonymous 1830a: 94)

c.

il	*tempo*	*star*	*bell-o.*
the.M	weather.M	be.IMPF	beautiful-M

'Il fait beau temps.'
'The weather is nice.'
(Anonymous 1830a: 97)

d.

ti	*venir*	*dgiousto,*	*la*	*mangiaria*	*star*	*pront-a.*
2s	come.IMPF	just	the.F	breakfast.F	be.IMPF	ready-F

'Vous venez à propos, le déjeuné est prêt.'
'You have come just in time, the breakfast is ready.'
(Anonymous 1830a: 96)

The LF textual samples in Haedo (1612), likewise, point to a productive use of grammatical gender. This is seen, e.g., in the gender agreement between *cosa* and *questa* in (25a), *forato* and *aquel* in (25b), *volta* and *altra* in (25c), and *Papaz* and *Christiano* in (25d); and in such other phrases as *dessa manera* 'in this way' and *de otra manera* 'in another way' (otherwise). The adjective *bono / bona* 'good' agrees in gender with *barbero* in *barbero bono* 'good doctor' and *bastonada* in *bona bastonada* 'good beating.' Against this background of consistently applied gender agreement, the partial lack of it in *la Papaz Christiano* (in 25d) stands out. Haedo's examples also illustrate the unmarked status of the masculine gender in LF, as seen in the use of the masculine forms of the demonstratives as neutral demonstrative pronouns in (25d) and (25e) and the adverbial use of the masculine form of the adjective in (25f), and also in *correr bono* 'run well.'

(25) a. *...ancora no estar tempo de parlar quest-a cosa*
yet NEG be.IMPF time of speak.IMPF this-F thing.F
'it is not yet time to speak of this thing'
(Haedo 1612, in Cifoletti 1989: 159)

b. *...pillar y meter en aquel forato...*
take.IMPF and put.IMPF in that.M hole.M
'take (it) and put (it) in that hole'
(Haedo 1612, in Cifoletti 1989: 160)

c. *Mira no trovar mi altr-a volta...*
see.IMPF NEG find.IMPF 1S other-F time.F
'See that I do not find (it) again'
(Haedo 1612, in Cifoletti 1989: 161)

d. *...que la Papaz Christian-o fazer aquest-o*
that the.F priest.M Christian-M do.IMPF this-M
'that the Christian priest do this'
(Haedo 1612, in Cifoletti 1989: 160)

e. *mirar Iafer, que est-o estar gran pecado...*
see.IMPF Iafer that this-M be.IMPF big sin
'look Iafer, for this is a great sin'
(Haedo 1612, in Cifoletti 1989: 160)

f. *Assi, assi, hora estar buen-o...*
like.this like.this now be.IMPF good-M
'Like this, like this, now (he) is well'
(Haedo 1612, in Cifoletti 1989: 158)

In summary, the LF of Algiers has inherited from its lexifiers both the category of gender and the morphosyntactic means by which it is expressed, word endings and syntactic agreement between the head noun and other elements of the noun phrase, and between the subject and predicate adjectives. In common with its lexifiers, LF appears to treat the masculine (etymologically masculine singular) gender as the unmarked default form. In light of Bakker (2003) and Roberts and Bresnan (2008), if LF is categorized as a pidgin, the preservation in it of nominal gender, and of syntactic agreement with respect to gender – an instance of contextual inflection – are both unexpected.

7.3.4 Number

The evidence regarding the status of the category of number in LF is less conclusive. The *Dictionnaire*'s preface informs the readers that "[l]es noms n'ont pas de pluriel" [nouns have no plural] and gives *l'amigo* as the LF equivalent of French *les amis* 'the friends.' This statement is borne out by the examples below, which illustrate the absence of plural marking after a numeral (in 26a) and when the plural reference is present in the corresponding French prompt (26b–26d). The example in (26d), additionally, shows the absence of number agreement between the (etymologically) singular noun and plural demonstrative.

(26) a. *mi pensar non star tré ora.*
1s think.IMPF NEG be.IMPF three hour
'Je pense qu'il n'est pas trois heures.'
'I think it's not yet three o'clock.'
(Anonymous 1830a: 97)

b. *qué poudir counchar il Françis contra di Algieri?*
what be.able.IMPF do.IMPF the French against of Algiers
'Que peuvent faire les Français contre Alger?'
'What can the French do against Algiers?'
(Anonymous 1830a: 98)

c. *sé quérir paché l'Yoldach fazir gribouila.*
if want.IMPF peace the'janissary make.IMPF fuss
'S'il veut la paix les Turcs feront tapage.'
'If (he) wants peace, the janissaries will make a fuss.'
(Anonymous 1830a: 98)

d. *Quest-i Signor star amigo di mi.*
this-M.PL gentleman.M.S be.IMPF friend.M.S of 1S
'Ces Messieurs sont mes amis.'
'These gentlemen are my friends.'
(Anonymous 1830a: n.p.)

The plural reference of the singular forms in (26b) and (26c) – *il Françis* 'the French' (< Sp. *francés*) and *l'Yoldach* 'janissaries' (< Tu. *yoldaş*) – has a formal parallel in Arabic and the Romance lexifiers of LF. Heath (1989) indicates that borrowed ethnonyms in MCA, including /fṛanṣiṣ/ 'French,' /ingliz/ 'English,' /ṣblyun/ 'Spaniards,' /aḷṃan/ 'Germans,' /šinwa/ 'Chinese (people),' /mṛṛuk/ 'Moroccans,' and /marikan/ 'American' (< Sp. *francés*, *inglés*, *español*, *alemán*; *Fr. espagnol*, *allemand*, *chinois*, *Maroc*; Eng. *American*) have invariable form for all genders and numbers, noting that

MCA borrowings that involve names of nationalities contrast a zero plural or collective form with a suffixed singular form, as in /ṣblyun/ 'Spanish people' / /ṣblyun-i/ '(a) Spaniard' (p. 135). Cifoletti (1980: 35) derives many of the LF ethnonyms, including *francis*, from Arabic rather than directly from Romance sources. In the Romance lexifiers of LF, the formal parallel takes the form of the use of singular count nouns with generic plural meaning (see 27).

(27) a. *il romano è amante della buona tavola*
the Roman be.PRES.3S lover of.the good table
'Romans are lovers of good food'
(Serianni 1989: 208)

b. *el español, cuando está de vacaciones,*
the Spaniard when be.PRES.3S of Vacations

come mucho marisco
eat.PRES.3S much shellfish
'Spaniards, when they're on holiday, eat a lot of shellfish'
(Butt and Benjamin 2004: 30)

On the other hand, Cifoletti (1989: 49–50; 2004: 42) draws attention to the existence of number distinction in LF personal pronouns and one or two nouns, and the number agreement between the plural noun and article in *lé merkantzié* (see 28).

(28)

French	Lingua Franca	
je / nous	mi / noi	'I' / 'we'
tu / vous	ti / voi	'you' (sg.) / 'you' (pl.)
il, elle / ils	ellou, ella / elli	'he,' 'she' / 'they'
oreille	orékia -é	'ear,' 'ears'
quelquefois	qoualqué volta	'sometimes'
autrefois	altré volté	lit. 'other times'
marchandise	mercantzia	'merchandise' (sg.)
(mes) marchandises	lé merkantzié (di mi)	'(my) merchandise' (pl.)

The glossing of etymologically plural nouns like *douros* 'piaster' (< Sp. *duro*, pl. *duros*) and *scarpé* 'shoe' (< It. *scarpa*, pl. *scarpe*) as singulars argues for the nonproductivity of the category of number in the *Dictionnaire*'s LF. The form *mouchous*, used in translating French *plusieurs* 'many; people,' may contain an ananalyzed plural marker; the same form is found in *mouchous bello* 'very beautiful' (translating French *admirable* 'admirable'). Still, it may be argued that the apparent hybrids like *tapétos* 'carpet' (< It. *tappeto*, Sp. -*s*) and *coustié* 'chop' (< Sp. *costilla*, It. -*e*), in which an Ibero-Romance noun is combined with an Italo-Romance plural marker or vice versa, indicate that this category was not entirely unpoductive. In summary, in contrast with the clear evidence regarding the productivity of the category of gender, the data contained in the *Dictionnaire* is inconclusive as to whether the category of nominal number was productive in LF. The LF fragments in Haedo (1612) contain no plural nominals and provide no independent evidence with respect to this issue.

7.4 Verbs

7.4.1 Inflection

Verb inflection in the *Dictionnaire*'s LF has both synthetic and analytic components. The only inflectional distinction morphologically marked on the LF verb, other than the gender in the perfective form (see Section 7.3.3), is aspect. Two aspectual forms are distinguished, the *r*-form (imperfective) and the *to*-form (perfective). The former derives from the Romance infinitive and functions as the unmarked form of the verb; it is found in a greater number of examples, is used in imperfective and imperative contexts, and is the form of the verb when used as a complement of another verb. The latter derives from the Italian past participle, is recorded in fewer examples, and is used with reference to discrete events in the past or perfective events (see Cifoletti 1989: 54; 2004: 43). The refunctionalization of the lexifier infinitive and past participle forms in LF may be appreciated from the examples in (29).

(29) a. *mi* *doubitar* *di* *qouesto.*
1s doubt.IMPF of this
'J'en doute.'
'I doubt this.'
(Anonymous 1830a: 93) (*r*-form; present)

b. *qué* *servir* *touto* *qouesto*?
what serve.IMPF all this
'A quoi servira tout cela?'
'What will all this accomplish?'
(Anonymous 1830a: 95) (*r*-form; future)

c. *qui* *star* *qouesto* *signor* *qué* *poco* *poco* *ablar* *per* *ti.*
who be.IMPF this gentleman that little little speak.IMPF DOM 2s
'Qui est-ce Monsieur qui vous parlait tantôt.'
'Who is the gentleman that spoke with you just now?'
(Anonymous 1830a: 96) (*r*-form; imperfective past)

d. *sarar* *la* *porta.*
close.IMPF the door
'Fermez la porte.'
'Close the door.'
(Anonymous 1830a: 95) (*r*-form; imperative)

Table 7.6. *Relationship between tense and aspect in Spanish*

	Perfective aspect	Imperfective aspect
PRESENT TENSE	–	*Present*
PAST TENSE	*Preterit*	*Imperfect*

e. *mi non poudir crédir.*
1s NEG be.able.IMPF believe.IMPF
'Je ne saurais croire.'
'I can't believe (it).'
(Anonymous 1830a: 93) (*r*-form; verb complement)

f. *mi mirato in casa di ti.*
1s see.PF in house of 2s
'Je l'ai vu chez vous.'
'I saw (him) at your house.'
(Anonymous 1830a: 96) (*to*-form; punctual past)

g. *mi venouto aposto per far mangiaria con ti.*
1s come.PF specially for do.IMPF breakfast with 2s
'Je suis venu exprès pour déjeuner avec vous.'
'I have come specially to have breakfast with you.'
(Anonymous 1830a: 97) (*to*-form; perfective event)

The aspectual nature of the opposition between the *r*- and *to*-forms is indirectly supported by the typological analysis of tense and aspect systems in Dahl (1985). In application to Romance languages, this approach conceptualizes the relationship between tense and aspect as one of subordination of the former to the latter, with present and past tense distinguished only in the imperfective aspect, and the perfective aspect restricted to past time reference. This analysis is applied to Spanish in Table 7.6, based on Bybee (1995: 444–445), with the Spanish inflectional categories given in italics. Bybee's (1995) argument for the analysis encapsulated in Table 7.6 includes a semantic component ("the present is inherently imperfective") and a formal one (the imperfect and present forms have the same stem whereas the preterit has a different stem) (pp. 445–446). The two-form verb system of the *Dictionnaire*'s LF shows conceptual similarity with this organization, with the *to*-form confined to contexts describing discrete events in the past and perfective events and the *r*-form occupying the remaining space. The potentially contributing effect of the Arabic verb system, in which the perfective is used for punctual or perfective events in the past and imperfective for present, future, or imperfective past events (Heath 1989: 21), cannot be ruled out (Fronzaroli 1955: 239–241).

The *Dictionnaire* records several inflected forms of Romance verbs: the impersonal *basta* (< Sp. It. *basta* 'it is enough'), *bisogna* (< It. *bisogna* 'it is necessary'), *piové* (< It. *piove* 'it rains'); and *pold* in the expression *pold esser* (< Ven. *pold esser* 'maybe'; Baglioni 2017: 192) (see 30a, 30c, 31). The French prompts for three of these are nonverbal (*assez* 'enough' for *basta*, *pluie* 'rain' for *piové*, *peut-être* 'maybe' for *pold esser*), while French *falloir* 'to be needed' is translated into LF with both *bisogna* (< It. *bisogna* 'it is necessary') and *bisognio* (< It. *bisogno* 'need') (see 30c). These facts suggest that in the *Dictionnaire*'s LF the inflected forms may be functioning as unanalyzed expressions, especially in light of the verbal forms provided in response to the corresponding verbal prompts in French (compare 30a with 30b).

(30) a.

French nonverb	Lingua Franca	
assez	basta	'enough'
pluie	piové	'rain'
peut-être	pold esser	'maybe'

b.

French verb	Lingua Franca	
suffire	bastar	'to be enough'
pleuvoir, il pleut	piovir	'to rain, it rains'
pouvoir	poudir	'to be able'

c.

French	Lingua Franca	
besoin	bisognio	'need'
falloir	bisogno, bisogna	'to be needed'[13]

(31) *non counchar per mi, il café basta.*
NEG make.IMPF for 1S the coffee is.enough
'N'en faites pour moi, le café me suffit.'
'Don't make (tea) for me, coffee is enough.'
(Anonymous 1830a: 97)

The examples of LF in Haedo (1612) support the inference that the opposition between the *r*- and *to*-forms was aspectual in nature, while at the same time supplying evidence of variation in the realization of each member of the opposition. An examination of the glossary of Haedo's (1612) LF compiled by Cifoletti (1989: 163–164) shows that, in addition to the Romance infinitive, the imperfective member of the opposition is realized by the second person singular imperative and the third person singular present indicative forms of the Romance verb (see Table 7.7). A count of the relevant tokens shows that the inflected forms constitute a minority; in percentage terms, about 84 percent (fifty-three out of sixty-three verb tokens) are expressed by the Romance

[13] The source of *bisogna* is further discussed in Section 7.4.4.

Table 7.7. *Romance verb forms realizing the Lingua Franca imperfective in Haedo (1612)*

Infinitive				2s imperative and 3s present indicative	
Type	Token	Type	Token	Type	Token
abrusar	1	morir	2	anda	1
andar	4	parlar	5	dole	1
cerrar	1	pillar	4	ha	1
correr	1	poder	1	guarda	2
curar	2	portar	1	mira	2
dezir	2	responder	1	piglia	1
donar	1	saber	2	porta	1
estar	10	sentar	1	ven	1
fazer	1	tener	3		
forar	2	trabajar	2		
hazer	1	trovar	1		
meter	1	venir	1		
mirar	2				

infinitive, about 10 percent (six out of sixty-three) by the imperative, and about 6 percent (four out of sixty-three) by the third person singular present. Even taking into account this variation, the predominant form realizing the imperfective member of the opposition is the refunctionalized Romance infinitive. This becomes especially clear when the contexts in which the inflected forms occur, and the relative number of tokens for verbs appearing in both inflected and uninflected forms, are brought to bear on the issue. For example, both occurrences of the inflected form *guarda* are in the frozen expletive *guarda diablo*; the only occurence of *dole* is in the prefab *dole cabeza* 'have a headache'; 5 of the 6 imperative forms are found in the same textual fragment, with *anda*, *piglia*, and *porta* occuring in quick succession (*Anda presto*[14] *piglia, porta fora* 'Hurry up, pick it up, take it away'); the imperatives *anda* and *piglia* occur only once each whereas the corresponding infinitives *andar* and *pillar* each occur four times. The majority of the inflected forms in Haedo's LF (6 out of 8) are used only once each, and no form is used more

[14] The light verb construction *andar presto* 'to hurry' is also recorded in the *Dictionnaire*.

than twice. The verbs with the largest number of tokens, *estar* (10) and *parlar* (5), appear only in the Romance infinitive form.

The Romance verb forms reflected in Haedo's LF – the infinitive, the third person singular present indicative, and the second person imperative – make a recurrent appearance, either individually or in combination, as the default (unmarked) forms in contact situations involving Romance languages. Thus, Heath (1989: 105) observes that Spanish verbs tend to be borrowed into MCA in the infinitive form, and there is also "a small number of documented borrowings ending in weak /a/ vs. /i/; most of these appear to be based directly on the Sp[anish] familiar S[in]g[ular] imperative and involve verbs commonly used in commands (the examples are mostly nautical in nature)." The shape of Romance verbal loans adapted to the weak-final verb class in Maltese indicates that the most likely Romance verb forms to have served as their basis are the third person singular present indicative and/or second person singular imperative (Mifsud 1995: 115). The infinitive is the unmarked form of the verb in both Italian and Spanish foreigner talk (Lipski n.d.). In spontaneously acquired L2 Italian, the unmarked verb form tends to be the third person singular present indicative, a fact explained by its being the least marked verb form formally and the minimal common denominator of the paradigm, cf. *parla* 's/he speaks,' *parla-re* 'to speak,' *parla-to* 'spoken,' *parla-ndo* 'speaking' (Berretta 1992: 142; see also Chapter 9). Given this typological support, the presence of a mixture of uninflected and inflected Romance verb forms in Haedo's LF is likely to reflect actual variation in this area.

7.4.2 Auxiliaries

In the Romance lexifiers of LF, auxiliary verbs are combined with nonfinite forms of lexical verbs to express tense and voice (auxiliaries proper) as well as modality (modal auxiliaries) (Serianni 1989: 391ff.). The auxiliaries proper comprise the verbs *to be* and *to have*. The *be*-verbs of the lexifiers (Spanish *ser*, Italian *essere*) are not retained in the *Dictionnaire*'s or Haedo's LF. The *have*-verbs are retained, but only as verbs of possession.[15] This fact is specifically recorded in the *Dictionnaire*'s preface, where it is stated that "[l]e verbe *avir* ou *tenir* (avoir), ne s'emploie pas comme auxiliaire, mais seulement comme verbe possessif" [the verb *avir* or *tenir* (have) is not used as an auxiliary but only as a verb of possession] (illustrated in 32a and 32b with *ténir*; *avir* does not appear in textual examples). As shown in (32c)–(32e), *ténir* is also used as an impersonal existential verb.

[15] In Italian and French, descendants of Latin *habere* 'to hold, possess' (Fr. *avoir*, It. *avere*) are used in both auxiliary and possessive functions. In Spanish, *haber* serves only as an auxiliary, while the possessive function has been taken over by the descendant of Latin *tenere* 'to hold' (Sp. *tener*). In Portuguese, both functions are fulfilled by *ter* (Lat. *tenere*) (Pulgram 1978: 5–6).

(32) a. *mi tenir questo dgiardino*
1s have.IMPF this garden
'je possède cette campagne'
'I own this garden'
(Anonymous 1830a: 61)

b. *questo umbré ténir cabessa*
this man have.IMPF head
'cet homme à de l'esprit'
'this man is witty'
(Anonymous 1830a: 32)

c. *ténir poco tempo.*
have.IMPF little time
'Il y a peu de temps.'
'There is little time.'
(Anonymous 1830a: 96)

d. *genti hablar tenir gouerra.*
people say.IMPF have.IMPF war
'On dit que nous avons a guerre.'
'They say there is war.'
(Anonymous 1830a: 96)

e. *non tenir doubio.*
NEG have.IMPF doubt
'Il n'y a point de doute.'
'There is no doubt.'
(Anonymous 1830a: 93)

The LF fragments in Haedo (1612) suggest that the degree to which the *have*-auxiliary was lost varied. In the example in (33), the only one of its kind in Haedo (1612), the perfective form *portato* (spelled *por tato*) is used in the same fragment once with and once without an auxiliary. The auxiliary-full perfective may be a carryover from the writer's native language: as observed by Fronzaroli (1955: 238), "non si deve dimenticare che chi conosceva le lingue romanze avrà contaminato la lingua franca di forme più vicine a quelle" [it should not be forgotten that those who knew Romance languages would have contaminated Lingua Franca with forms closer to those]. The example in (33) also illustrates the use of *tener* 'to have' as an existential verb.

(33) *... porque tener aqui tortuga? Qui por tato de campaña?*
why have.IMPF here turtle who bring.PF from field

gran vellaco estar, qui ha por tato.
big scoundrel be.IMPF who has bring.PF
'why is there a turtle here? Who has brought it? He who has brought it is a big scoundrel.'
(Haedo 1612; in Cifoletti 1989: 161)

The modal auxiliaries in the *Dictionnaire*'s LF consist of the verbs in (34a) (illustrated in 34b–34d). Italian-derived *volir* 'to want' is used only in the one example; there are no examples with *dévir* 'to have to do.'

(34) a.

poudir	'to be able'	(< Sp. poder)
dévir	'to have to do'	(< Sp. deber, It. dovere)
quérir	'to want'	(< Sp. querer)
volir	'to want'	(< It. volere)

b. *qué poudir counchar il Françis contra di Algieri?*
what be.able.IMPF do.IMPF the.M French against of Algiers
'Que peuvent faire les Français contre Alger?'
'What can the French do against Algiers?'
(Anonymous 1830a: 98)

c. *Bonou? qué ti quérir mangiar.*
well what 2s want.IMPF eat.IMPF
'Bien, que voulez-vous prendre?'
'Well, what would you like to eat?'
(Anonymous 1830a: 97)

d. *cosà volir scométir?*
what be.able.IMPF do.IMPF
'Que voulez-vous parier?'
'What would you like to bet?'
(Anonymous 1830a: 93)

Haedo (1612) records the modal use of *poder* and *saber* 'to be able to' (cf. Serianni 1989: 395) (see 35).

(35) a. *Si cane dezir ... no poder trabajar ...*
if dog say.IMPF NEG be.able.IMPF work.IMPF
'If the dog says he can't work'
(Haedo 1612; in Cifoletti 1989: 158–159)

b. *...mirar como mi estar barbero bono, y saber curar...*
look.IMPF how 1s be.IMPF doctor good and know.IMPF cure.IMPF
'look what a good doctor I am and how I can cure'
(Haedo 1612; in Cifoletti 1989: 158)

7.4.3 Copula

LF does not inherit from its lexifiers the descendants of the Latin copula *esse(re)* 'to be' and instead fully grammaticalizes those of Latin *stare* 'to stand' (LF *(e)star* < Sp. Ptg. *estar*, It. *stare*). In both the *Dictonnaire* and

Haedo (1612), *(e)star* functions only as a copula (see 36); the *Dictionnaire*'s description of it as an auxiliary may be due to a misunderstanding (this point is addressed in Cifoletti 2004: 43).

(36) a. *qouesto non star vero.*
this NEG be.IMPF true
'Cela n'est pas vrai.'
'This is not true.'
(Anonymous 1830a: 93)

b. *commé star il fratello di ti?*
how be.IMPF the brother of 2S
'Comment se porte votre frère?'
'How is your brother?'
(Anonymous 1830a: 94)

c. *...mirar como mi estar barbero bono...*
see.IMPF how 1S be.IMPF doctor good
'look what a good doctor I am'
(Haedo 1612; in Cifoletti 1989: 158)

d. *... no parlar que estar malato.*
NEG say.IMPF that be.IMPF sick
'don't say that you are sick'
(Haedo 1612; in Cifoletti 1989: 159)

Haedo (1612) also documents the copular use of *sentar* (< Sp. Ptg. *sentar(se)* 'to sit (down)') (shown in 37a). In the *Dictionnaire*, this verb is used only as a lexical verb with such meanings as 'to live,' 'to stay,' and 'to sit (down)' (illustrated in 37b and 37c). The copular use of *sentar* in Haedo's LF is paralleled by its use as a copula, subsequntly discontinued, in contemporaneous literary imitations of Afro-Portuguese (Lipski 2014: 368).

(37) a. *... Dio grande sentar ...*
God big be.IMPF
'God is great'
(Haedo 1612; in Cifoletti 1989: 159)

b. *ové sentar?*
where sit.IMPF
'Où demeure-t-il?'
'Where does (he) live?'
(Anonymous 1830a: 96)

c. *ti sentar.*
2S sit.down.IMPF
'Asseyez-vous.'
'Sit down.'
(Anonymous 1830a: 95)

7.4.4 Grammaticalization

The analytic component of verbal inflection in LF includes the grammaticalized use of It. *bisogno* 'need, necessity' as a future marker (see 38a). This form's other use is to express obligation, in which function it alternates with *bisogna* (see 38b, 38c).

(38) a. *bisogno andar domani.*
FUT go.IMPF tomorrow
'Nous irons demain.'
'We'll go tomorrow.'
(Anonymous 1830a: 96)

b. *cosa bisognio counchar?*
what need do.IMPF
'Que faut-il faire?'
'What needs to be done?'
(Anonymous 1830a: 94)

c. *bisogna far*
need do.IMPF
'il faut faire'
'it needs to be done'
(Anonymous 1830a: 34)

In light of the variant forms of the noun *bisogno* ~ *bisogna* in the lexifier (Baglioni 2010: 142), it is unclear whether the source of *bisogna* in LF is the noun, the impersonal verb *bisogna* (< It. *bisogna* 'it is necessary'), or both. The *Dictionnaire* gives both *bisogno* and *bisogna* as translations for French *falloir* 'to need, to have to.'

Typologically oriented studies, such as Bybee and Pagliuca (1987) and Bybee (1995), identify three main diachronic sources of future markers: verbs of desire, verbs of movement, and verbs and phrases expressing "obligation, necessity, or predestination." The co-opting of Italian *bisogno* 'need, necessity' for the expression of futurity in LF conforms to this cross-linguistic trend while also having specific parallels in the Romance domain, beginning with the Romance synthetic future, which arose from a Latin construction expressing necessity or obligation (Bourciez 1967: 117–118; Korletjanu 1974: 193–194; Bybee 1995: 451).

7.4.5 Conjugations

The *Dictionnaire*'s LF distinguishes two verb classes (conjugations) in the *r*-form, *-ar* and *-ir*. The bulk of the *-ar* verbs derive from first-conjugation verbs in the lexifiers (see 39a) and the bulk of the *-ir* verbs reflect second- and third-conjugation lexifier verbs (see 39b). In a handful of cases, LF *-ir* verbs derive from first-conjugation lexifier verbs, or the verb belongs to more than one conjugation in LF (see 39c, 39d) (Schuchardt 1909: 456).

(39)	a.	ablar	'to say'	(< Sp. hablar)
		mirar	'to see'	(< Sp. mirar)
		dgiocar	'to play'	(< It. giocare)
		dgitar	'to throw'	(< It. gettare)
		alloumar	'to light'	(< Fr. allumer)
		avalar	'to swallow'	(< Fr. avaler)
	b.	rompir	'to break'	(< Sp. romper)
		escondir	'to hide'	(< Sp. esconder)
		inchir	'to fill'	(< Sp. henchir)
		crédir	'to believe'	(< It. credere)
		volir	'to want'	(< It. volere)
		capir	'to understand'	(< It. capire)
	c.	sanir	'to heal'	(< Sp. sanar)
		composir	'to arrange'	(< Fr. composer)
	d.	sédar ~ sédir	'to sit (down)'	(< It. sedere)
		imparar ~ impari	'to learn' ~ 'to teach'[16]	(< It. imparare)

The number of *-ar* verbs exceeds that of *-ir* verbs by about three to one, with about 320 (74 percent) of the former and about 110 (26 percent) of the latter. These percentages are close to Iacobini and Thornton's (1994: 279) figures for the basic vocabulary of Italian, which show 68.1 percent of verbs in *-are*. Two of the LF verbs are attested in both conjugations (see 39d above). The *Dictionnaire* does not list the *to*-form for each and every verb, however, where supplied, it is overwhelmingly *-ato* for the *-ar* verbs and mostly *-ito* for the *-ir* verbs (see 40a, 40b). The *-uto* form is attested in the verbs shown in (40c, 40d); only two of these belong to the *-ar* conjugation. Some of the forms in *-uto* appear to have been assembled in LF language-internally: compare *escondir / escondouto* 'to hide' in LF with *esconder / escondido* in Spanish.

(40)	a.	***-ar / -ato***	
		ablar, -ato	'to say'
		andar, -ato	'to go'
		amousar, -ato	'to entertain'
		sarar, -ato	'to close'
	b.	***-ir / -ito***	
		adormir, -ito	'to put to sleep'

16 Derek C. Carr (p.c.) suggests the possibility of contamination with Sp. *impartir* 'to give, impart.'

composir, -ito	'to arrange'
cousir, -ito	'to sew'
fazir, -ito	'to do, make'

c. ***-ar / -uto***

cédar, -outo	'to give up'
sédar, -outo	'to sit (down)'

d. ***-ir / -uto***

avir, -outo	'to have'
bévir, -outo	'to drink'
conoschir, -uto	'to know'
crédir, -outo	'to believe'
deffendir, -outo	'to defend'
dévir, -outo	'to owe'
dispendir, -outo	'to spend'
escondir, -outo	'to hide'
fendir, -outo	'to split'
intendir, -outo	'to hear'
vénir, -outo	'to come'

The *-ir* verbs in (41) show different stem allomorphs in the *to*-form (or its lexicalized adjectival form).

(41)

***r*-form**	***to*-form**	
fingir	finto	'to feign'
pingir	pinto	'to paint'
vincir	vinto	'to defeat'
morir	morto	'to die'
rompir	roto	'to break'
scrivir	scrito	'to write'
perdir	perso	'to lose'

In Haedo's LF, the *r*-form distinguishes three rather than two conjugations (see 42). Only two *to*-forms are recorded in that source: *portato* and *(e)scripto*.

(42)

-ar	***-er***	***-ir***
abrusar	correr	dezir
andar	fazer ~ hazer	morir
cerrar	meter	venir
curar	poder	
donar	responder	
estar	saber	
forar	tener	
mirar	(dole)	
parlar	(ha)	
pillar		
portar		
sentar		

trabajar
trovar
(guarda)

The merger of the *-er* verbs with *-ir* verbs in the *Dictionnaire*'s LF has been attributed to phonological causes, namely, raising of mid vowels due to assimilation to the vocalism of North African Arabic and Berber (Schuchardt 1909; Castellanos 2007). This analysis is indirectly supported by the treatment of Spanish verbs in MCA, as reported by Heath (1989: 105): these are mostly borrowed in the infinitive form and end in /-aṛ/ and /-iṛ/ ~ /-ir/ in the receiving language. Cifoletti advances a complementary hypothesis:

Credo perciò che la generalizzazione della desinenza *-ir* sia da attribuire più che altro al bisogno di semplificare e normalizzare, anche se possono avervi giocato un ruolo le difficoltà di pronuncia di alcuni arabofoni. (Cifoletti 1989: 40)

[That is why I believe that the generalization of the ending *-ir* is attributable mostly to the need to simplify and standardize, even if the pronunciation difficulties of some Arabic speakers may have played a part in it as well.]

As discussed in Chapter 4, Cifoletti's hypothesis is supported by the consideration that the [e] > [i] shift before a word-final [r] is specific to verbs and is not extended to nouns. For example, Sp. *poder* 'to be able' is reflected in LF as *poudir* and Sp. *poder* 'power' as *poder*; Sp. *deber* / It. *dovere* 'to owe' is reflected as *dévir* and It. *dovere* 'duty' as as *dovéré*. A small number of second-conjugation lexifier verbs are recorded with both endings (*piachir* ~ *piacher* 'to please' < It. *piacere*; *mettir* ~ *metter* 'to put' < Sp. *meter*, It. *mettere*), suggesting variation in actual usage.

In conclusion, the *Dictionnaire*'s verb classes show continuity with the verb classes (conjugations) of the lexifiers in that (1) the *-ar* class is the more productive inflection class (this is also true of Haedo's LF, with the recorded fragments containing fifteen *-ar* versus twelve *-er* / *-ir* verbs), (2) the neutralization of the conjugational distinctions affects non–first conjugation (non-*ar*) verbs, and (3) verbs of the *-ar* class show no stem allomorphy, with all such allomorphy confined to verbs of the *-ir* class (see a discussion of these developmental trends in Maiden 2011).

7.5 Pronouns

As discussed in Section 7.2.1, in the Romance lexifiers of LF personal pronouns distinguish the category of case, the oblique pronouns additionally distinguish between tonic and clitic forms, and there are also dedicated pronominal possessives. In the *Dictionnaire*'s LF, the system of personal pronouns is drastically simplified (see 43).

(43)

mi andar	'I go'	noi andar	'we go'
ti andar	'you (sg.) go'	voi andar	'you (pl.) go'
ellou andar	'he goes'	elli andar	'they go'
ella andar	'she goes'		

The above formal reduction has brought about the development of analytic means for signaling pronominal objects and possessors. As noted in Section 7.2.2.1, the Romance lexifiers of LF use the preposition descending from Latin *de* to express possession when the possessor is a noun or selected personal pronouns. The *Dictionnaire*'s LF agrees with its lexifiers in using a descendant of this preposition to signal nominal possessors, and increments this evolutionary trend by completely grammaticalizing this possessive construction: while in the lexifiers the analytic possessive construction with pronominal possessors is either stylistically marked (Cordin 2001) or distributionally restricted (Orozco 2012), in LF it is used even with singular pronouns of the first and second person (see 44).

(44) a. *mi andar in casa del Signor.*
1s go.IMPF in house of.the gentleman
'Je vais chez Monsieur M.'
'I am going to the gentleman's house.'
(Anonymous 1830a: 95)

b. *per la palabra di mi.*
by the word of 1s
'Sur ma parole.'
'Upon my word.'
(Anonymous 1830a: 93)

c. *commé star il fratello di ti?*
how be.IMPF the brother of 2s
'Comment se porte votre frère?'
'How is your brother?'
(Anonymous 1830a: 94)

The single possessive form recorded in Haedo (1612), shown in (45), indicates that there is likely to have been variation in the expression of pronominal possession. As in the case of variation in the expression of the aspectual opposition, with the more lexifier-like forms (imperatives, third person singulars, auxiliary-ful perfects) coexisting with the more basilectal forms (infinitives, auxiliary-less perfects), variation in the expression of pronominal possession, with more lexifier-like forms like *tuya* thrown into the mixture, is consistent with the hypothesis of LF being located on a pidgin-koine continuum (see Chapter 9).[17]

[17] The variety of variant structures increases if the LF textual samples from different areas and periods are treated as a single corpus. In the area of pronominal possession, for example, this

(45) ... *si venir ventura andar a casa tuy-a*
if come.IMPF luck go.IMPF to house.F your-F
'if luck comes your way, you'll go home'
(Haedo 1612; in Cifoletti 1989: 159)

The analytic expression of pronominal possessors is paralleled in the *Dictionnaire*'s LF by the analytic marking of direct and indirect pronominal objects (see 46a, 46b). The LF DOM marker has as its source the Italian-derived preposition *per* 'by, for,' which continues to maintain its spatial and benefactive functions in other contexts. The examples in (46c), (46d), and (46e) show that the *Dictionnaire*'s LF does not use *per* to mark direct or indirect nominal objects.

(46) a. *dispiacher mouchou per mi.*
displease.IMPF very DOM 1S
'J'en suis bien fâché.'
'I am very sorry.'
(Anonymous 1830a: 94)

b. *ti crédir per mi, mi poudir assicourar per ti.*
2S believe.IMPF DOM 1S 1S be.able.IMPF assure.IMPF DOM 2S
'Croyez-moi je puis vous l'assurer.'
'Believe me, I can assure you.'
(Anonymous 1830a: 93)

c. *molto tempo ti non mirato Signor M.?*
much time 2S NEG see.PF mister M.
'Y a-t-il long-tems que vous n'avez vu Monsieur M.?'
'Has it been long since you've seen Mr. M.?'
(Anonymous 1830a: 94)

d. *aprir la bentana.*
open.IMPF the window
'Ouvrez la fenètre.'
'Open the window.'
(Anonymous 1830a: 95)

e. *ti dar una cadiéra al Signor.*
2S give.IMPF a chair to.the gentleman
'Donnez une chaise à Monsieur.'
'Give the gentleman a chair.'
(Anonymous 1830a: 94)

The use of *per* to mark pronominal objects is also found in the LF fragments in Gigio Artemio Giancarli's play *La Zingana* (1545) and the plays of Carlo

variation would include postposed possessives of the Southern Italo-Romance type: compare *casama* 'my house' (in *Contrasto della Zerbitana*) with *casa tuya* 'your house' (in Haedo 1612) and *la casa di mi* 'my house' (in the *Dictionnaire*) (Minervini 1996a: 250).

Goldoni, though its use in these sources is less regular and differs in details from that of the *Dictionnaire* (Zago 1986: 125; Operstein 1998, 2007: 242–244). In connection with this use, Schuchardt (1909: 460) notes the marking of objects by means of *pour* 'for' in the Judeo-French of Algiers.

Both Italian and Spanish display differential object marking, albeit at different stages of grammaticalization. LF thus agrees with its main lexifiers in the fact of the existence of this phenomenon while differing from them in the choice of the preposition grammaticalized as the DOM marker and the type of objects selected for such marking (see Chapter 9).

7.6 Chapter Summary

Viewed from the perspective of pidgins, the inflectional categories of LF and/or their exponence present a number of unexpected features. These are summarized in (47).

(47) a. Pronouns and nominals
- Gender distinction in the third person pronoun
- Gender distinction in nominals
- Gender agreement in the noun phrase
- Gender agreement in the clause
- Lack of a productive number marking on nouns

b. Verbs
- Gender marking in the perfective
- Morphologically marked aspect distinction
- Allomorphy in selected verb forms
- Grammaticalized future marker
- Causative construction with the verbs *do/make* and *let*

c. Functional categories
- Inherited definite and indefinite articles
- Inherited distance contrast in demonstratives
- A substantial number of prepositions
- A substantial number of question words
- A substantial number of clause connectors

The features in (47a) and (47b) are unexpected in light of Parkvall and Bakker's (2013) and/or Parkvall's (2016, 2019) indications that gender distinction in nouns and personal pronouns, TAM marking, grammaticalized TAM markers, synthetic structures in general, adjectival agreement, expression of valence, and allomorphy are typically absent from pidgins. The presence of adjectival agreement in LF is additionally unexpected in light of Roberts and Bresnan's (2008) prediction that gender agreement, being an instance of contextual inflection, is an unlikely candidate for retention in a pidgin. Simultaneous presence of gender marking and absence of a productive number marking on nouns are unexpected in light of Bakker's (2003) finding that pidgins are more likely to inherit number than gender marking from their lexifiers. With respect to the functional categories listed in (47c), the *Dictionnaire*'s LF has inherited from its Romance lexifiers definite and indefinite articles (*il/la* 'the,' *oun/ouna* 'a'); distal and proximate demonstratives (*qouello/qouella* 'that,' *qouesto/qouesta* 'this'); nine simple, three complex, and four articulated prepositions (*a* 'to,' *di* 'of, from,' *in* 'in,' *con* 'with,' *per* 'for, by,' *sopra* 'on,' *sotto* 'under,' *doppo* 'after,' *da* 'at'; *fora di* 'out of,' *contra di* 'against,' *per metzo* 'through'; *al* 'to the (m.),' *alla* 'to the (f.),' *del* 'of the (m.),' *della* 'of the (f.)'); several clause connectors (*qué* 'that, which,' *il/la qouale* 'which,' *sé* 'if,' *qouando* 'when'); and a variety of question words (*qui* 'who,' *cosa* 'what,' *qué* 'what, which,' *ové* 'where, whither,' *oundé* 'whence,' *commé* 'how,' *perqué* 'why,' *qouando* 'when,' *qouanto* 'how much, how many').

The structural retentions listed in (47) are supplemented by retentions that relate more specifically to the Romance morphological background of LF, including preservation of the Romance inflectional classes in nouns, adjectives, and verbs. The noun and adjective classes of LF continue those of its lexifiers with a high degree of faithfulness, while also exhibiting the related phenomenon of hypercharacterization of gender. Also as in the lexifiers, the expression of gender in LF is accomplished both morphologically via word endings and syntactically via agreement. LF further matches its lexifiers in the apparently unmarked status of the masculine gender. The number of verb classes in the *Dictionnaire*'s LF is reduced by comparison with its lexifiers, however, the reduction proceeds in the same direction as in the lexifiers, with the diachronically unstable conjugation with the thematic vowel *-e-* merging with the more productive *-i-* conjugation, and with the *-a-* conjugation being numerically the stronger of the resulting two conjugations.

In the introduction, a mention was made of Bakker's (2003) and Parkvall and Bakker's (2013) observation that some pidgins explicitly mark certain parts of speech. Formally, this is achieved by adding a certain morpheme to each member of the respective word class, "even though they are never applied completely consistently" (Bakker 2003: 13). One of the examples is the verb in Tay Boi, which ends in *-er* regardless of the infinitival ending in its lexifier French. It would seem that the reduction of verb classes in LF, with only two such classes distinguished in the unmarked verb form, *-ar* and *-ir*, may be viewed as an instance of this phenomenon. Bakker's (2003: 13) observation that such formal marking of word classes is rare in the world languages but is found in some artificial languages like Esperanto resonates with Schuchardt's impression:

Table 7.8. *Word classes in Lingua Franca compared with Italian*

Part of speech	Lingua Franca	Italian basic vocabulary	Italian L1 acquisition
NOUNS	58%	61%	67%
VERBS	25%	20%	20%
ADJECTIVES	11%	15%	12%

In its primary features Lingua Franca is thus reminiscent of "planned" languages in general; and in the composite nature of its lexicon and a certain formal agreement between its components of varied origin, it is reminiscent of the sort of language that Neo-Latin or Novi Latin reveals itself to be. (Schuchardt 1979: 32)

LF shows the same division into word classes as its lexifiers, in which respect it also differs from pidgins, which tend to have fewer parts of speech (Parkvall and Bakker 2013: 39). LF distinguishes all of the parts of speech recognized by the Italian and Spanish grammatical traditions: articles, nouns, adjectives, pronouns, verbs, adverbs, prepositions, conjunctions, and interjections (Serianni 1989: 83–84; Real Academia Española 2010: 10–11). A rough manual calculation shows that the relative sizes of the major word classes in the *Dictionnaire*'s LF are comparable with those of the corresponding word classes in Italian. In Table 7.8, the column labeled "Italian Basic Vocabulary" represents the percentages of each major word class in the about 7,000 word basic vocabulary of Italian (De Mauro 1991); the figures are cited after Iacobini and Thornton (1994: 278). The column labeled "Italian L1 Acquisition" represents the percentage of words in each major word class in a vocabulary of 527 words produced by children between the ages of eight and thirty months acquiring Italian as their first language (cited after Lo Duca et al. 2009: 13). All nonround percentages have been rounded off to the nearest whole number.

The inflectional innovations of LF are plausibly conditioned by the loss of lexifier functional categories and/or their means of expression. Thus, refunctionalization of nonfinite Romance verb forms into members of an aspectual opposition and grammaticalization of It. *bisogno* 'need' into a future marker may be connected with the nonretention in LF of Romance verbal inflection and nonmodal auxiliaries. Complete grammaticalization of the Romance locative copula *(e)star* may be correlated with the nonretention in LF of the Romance copula derived from Latin *esse(re)*. Complete grammaticalization of the analytic possessive construction with *di* 'of' is connected with the loss in LF of Romance possessives and pronominal clitics. The development of an

Table 7.9. *Inflectional innovations in Lingua Franca*

Loss	Innovation
Copula descending from Latin *esse(re)*	Copularization of *(e)star*
- Verbal inflection - Nonmodal auxiliaries	- Refunctionalization of the lexifier infinitive and past participle into members of an aspectual opposition - Grammaticalization of *bisogno* into a future marker
- Possessives - Pronominal clitics	Grammaticalization of the analytic possessive construction with *di*
- Pronominal case - Pronominal clitics	- Analytic marking of pronominal objects - Grammaticalization of *per* into a DOM marker

analytic means of signaling personal pronominal objects and grammaticalization of *per* as the DOM marker may be connected with the nonretention in LF of the pronominal case distinctions and clitic pronouns of the lexifiers. These losses of lexifier inflectional material and the corresponding innovations of LF are summarized in Table 7.9.

In summary, the structural features of LF include a high degree of retention of lexifier inflectional categories and the morphosyntactic means by which they are expressed, resulting in typological continuity between LF and its lexifiers in the area of inflection. The continuity is seen not only in the retentions but also in the direction of LF's innovations, including reduction in the number of verb classes, copularization of *(e)star*, and the development of DOM, which proceed in the same direction as the corresponding developments in the lexifiers. The high-contact environment that engendered LF and supported its continued existence appears to have served as a catalyst for some of the processes that were under way in one or more of the lexifiers.

Many of the LF structural features and innovations have parallels not only in the diachronic evolution of Romance languages but also in their various contact and L2 varieties. For example, hypercharacterization of gender has been reported in Judeo-Italian (*pano* for *pane* 'bread,' *gran(n)o* for *grande* 'big'), *italiano popolare* (*moglia* for *moglie* 'woman,' *paieso* for *paese* 'country'), Italian interlanguages (*padro* for *padre* 'father,' *meso* for *mese* 'month,' *lavatricia* for *lavatrice* 'washing machine'), and English borrowings in American Italian (*Broccolino, giobba, fensa* for *Brooklyn, job, fence*) (Berruto 1983a: 57; 2012: 215; Valentini 1990: 342; Berretta 1992: 138; Schmid 1992: 293; Rubin 2016: 321). Omission of *essere* and a less constrained adverbial use of adjectives have been noted for *italiano popolare*

(Berruto 1983a: 57, 60). Hybrid formations similar to LF *tapétos* 'carpet' (It. *tappeto*, Sp. *-s*) have been described for *cocoliche*, the mixed language of Italian immigrants in Argentina (cf. *fuciles* 'guns' < It. *fucile*, Sp. *-s*); and Italian interlanguages of Spanish speakers in Switzerland (cf. *amicos* 'friends,' *parolas* 'words' < It. *amico*, *parola*, Sp. *-s*; *coseche* 'harvests' < Sp. *cosecha*, It. *-e*) (Schmid 1993: 407, 411; Berruto 2012: 217). These parallels, and many others besides, emphasize the role of inter-Romance koineization in the origin of LF.

8 The Syntax

The preceding two chapters have identified a substantial degree of continuity between the *Dictionnaire*'s LF and its Romance lexifiers in the domains of inflection and word formation. The present chapter continues this endeavor by focusing on LF's syntax. Section 8.1 looks at the structure of the noun phrase, and Sections 8.2–8.6 examine, respectively, those of the copular, verbal, interrogative, and imperative clauses, and of complex sentences. The syntactic structures of LF are compared with the corresponding structures in one or both of its main lexifiers to demonstrate probable antecedents or parallels for the constructions and word order features seen in LF. In the concluding section, the structural features and developmental trends of the LF syntax are situated in relation to those of its Romance lexifiers.

8.1 Noun Phrase

8.1.1 Agreement

In the *Dictionnaire*'s LF, grammatical gender is realized in part via syntactic agreement between the head noun and modifying elements of the noun phrase, and between the subject noun and predicative adjectives. The examples below, repeated here for convenience from Chapter 7, illustrate gender agreement between the masculine noun *thé* 'tea' and the attributive adjective *bonou* (in 1a), and between the feminine noun *mangiaria* 'breakfast,' the definite article *la*, and the predicative adjective *pronta* (in 1b). Syntactic gender agreement is also recorded by Haedo (1612), which evidences the diachronic stability of this feature in the LF of Algiers (see also Cifoletti 2004).

(1) a. *mi tenir thé mouchou bon-ou;*
1s have.IMPF tea.M very good-M

mi quérir ti goustar per ell-ou.
1s want.IMPF 2s taste.IMPF DOM 3s-M
'J'ai du thé délicieux; je veux que vous en goutiez.'

'I've got some delicious tea, I want you to try it.'
(Anonymous 1830a: 97)

b.

ti	*venir*	*dgiousto,*	*la*	*mangiaria*	*star*	*pront-a.*
2s	come.IMPF	just	the.F	breakfast.F	be.IMPF	ready-F

'Vous venez à propos, le déjeuné est prêt.'
'You have come just in time, the breakfast is ready.'
(Anonymous 1830a: 96)

The *Dictionnaire*'s LF has no productive category of nominal number. Syntactic agreement with respect to number is found in the isolated example in (2a). In the sentence in (2b), from the *Dictionnaire*'s preface, the plural reference of the noun is inferred from the accompanying demonstrative. This arrangement is conceptually similar to the analytic expression of number in Italian indeclinable nouns; compare *il re* 'the king' with *i re* 'the kings' (Patota 2006: 56). Apart from the examples in (2), there is no evidence of the use of syntactic means to signal nominal number in the *Dictionnaire*'s LF.

(2) a.

l-é	*merkantzi-é*	*di*	*mi*
the-F.PL	merchandise-F.PL	of	1s

'mes marchandises'
'my merchandise'
(Anonymous 1830a: 50)

b.

Quest-i	*Signor*	*star*	*amigo*	*di*	*mi.*
this-M.PL	gentleman.M.S	be.IMPF	friend.M.S	of	1s

'Ces Messieurs sont mes amis.'
'These gentlemen are my friends.'
(Anonymous 1830a: n.p.)

8.1.2 Articles

8.1.2.1 Forms As in its Romance lexifiers, the definite and indefinite articles in LF are preposed. The forms of the articles, with the spelling variation omitted, are shown in (3).

(3)

Masculine		Feminine	
oun amigo	'a friend'	ouna palabra	'a word'
il tempo	'the weather'	la palabra	'the word'
l'amigo	'the friend'	l'eskima	'the bridle'

The *Dictionnaire*, additionally, records several forms in which the article is fused with the preceding preposition into a single word (cf. Patota 2006: 64). Only two prepositions, *a* 'to, at' and *di* 'of,' are attested in articulated forms, which consist of the masculine *al*, *del* and feminine *alla*, *della* (see 4).

The preposition *in* 'in' is not merged with the following article in *in l'estesso tempo* 'at the same time' (cf. *nello stesso tempo* in Italian).

(4) a. *mi andar in casa del Signor.*
1s go.IMPF in house of.the mister
'Je vais chez Monsieur M.'
'I am going to the house of Mr. (M.).'
(Anonymous 1830a: 95)

b. *mirar qué ora star al orlogio di ti.*
see.IMPF what hour be.IMPF at.the watch of 2s
'Voyez quelle heure il est à votre montre.'
'See what time is it on your watch.'
(Anonymous 1830a: 97)

Based on the phrase- and sentence-long examples recorded in the *Dictionnaire*, the *Dictionnaire*'s LF uses determined and determinerless nouns in ways that are similar to its Romance lexifiers. For convenience of presentation, each noun type is discussed below separately.

8.1.2.2 Count Nouns Common count nouns tend to have the definite article in both subject and object positions. This feature is inherited from LF's Romance lexifiers, in which it reflects the obligatorification of the definite article in these positions: "In Romance, articles before common count nouns occurring as arguments of a verb (usually considered the 'core' domain) became obligatory quite early" (Wall and Octavio de Toledo 2016: 350). The examples in (5) illustrate this feature with respect to the subject noun phrase *il Bacha* 'the Pasha' (in 5a, 5b) and the object noun phrases *la porta* 'the door' and *la bentana* 'the window' (in 5c, 5d). The determined count nouns in (5c) and (5d) contrast with the determinerless mass noun in (5e) (to be discussed in Section 8.1.2.4).

(5) a. *dounqué bisogno il Bacha quérir paché.*
so need the pasha want.IMPF peace
'Le Pacha sera donc obligé de demander la paix.'
'So the Pasha will be forced to ask for peace.'
(Anonymous 1830a: 98)

b. *perqué il Bacha tenir fantétzia.*
because the pasha have.IMPF pride
'Parce que le Pacha est entèté.'
'Because the Pasha is stubborn.'
(Anonymous 1830a: 98)

c. *sarar la porta.*
close.IMPF the door
'Fermez la porte.'

'Close the door.'
(Anonymous 1830a: 95)

d. *aprir la bentana.*
open.IMPF the window
'Ouvrez la fenètre.'
'Open the window.'
(Anonymous 1830a: 95)

e. *portar café.*
bring.IMPF coffee
'Apportez le café.'
'Bring coffee.'
(Anonymous 1830a: 95)

The use of the definite article before common count nouns in LF parallels their use in contemporary Spanish (in 6a) and Italian (in 6b).[1]

(6) a. *El rey habló con los ministros.*
the king speak.PRET.3s with the ministers
'The King spoke with the ministers.'
(Butt and Benjamin 2004: 27)

b. *Il gatto sta dormendo nel mio letto.*
the cat be.PRES.3s sleeping in.the my bed
'The cat is sleeping in my bed.'
(Kupisch 2012: 739)

8.1.2.3 Generic Nouns Generic nouns tend to be determined when used as subjects and determinerless when used as verb or prepositional objects. This contrast obtains between the subject *la mangiaria* 'the breakfast' in (7a) and the object *mangiaria* in (7a'), and between the subject *il Françis* 'the French' in (7b) and the prepositional object *Francis* in (7b'). Given the absence of a productive nominal plural, the generic nouns are formally (etymologically) singular in LF.

(7) a. *ti venir dgiousto, la mangiaria star pront-a.*
2s come.IMPF just the.F breakfast.F be.IMPF ready-F
'Vous venez à propos, le déjeuné est prêt.'
'You have come just in time, the breakfast is ready.'
(Anonymous 1830a: 96)

a.' *mi venouto aposto per far mangiaria con ti.*
1s come.PF specially for do.PF breakfast with 2s

[1] Most comparative examples are drawn from the normative varieties of the lexifiers, abstracting away from exceptions and variation. Given the diversity of diachronic, diatopic, and diastratic inputs to LF, the examples, and the varieties from which they are drawn, are chosen as convenient reference points for the constructions illustrated.

'Je suis venu exprès pour déjeuner avec vous.'
'I have come especially to have breakfast with you.'
(Anonymous 1830a: 97)

b. *qué poudir couchar il Françis contra di Algieri?*
what be.able.IMPF do.IMPF the.M French against of Algiers
'Que peuvent faire les Français contre Alger?'
'What can the French do against Algiers?'
(Anonymous 1830a: 98)

b.' *con Francis.*
with French
'Avec les Français.'
'With the French.'
(Anonymous 1830a: 98)

Similar distinctions in article use with generic nouns may be found in Spanish and Italian. Compare, for instance, the determined subject *los belgas* 'Belgians' (in 8a) with the bare prepositional object *ingleses* 'English people' (in 8b) in Spanish (MacKenzie 2003: 8; Butt and Benjamin 2004: 29ff.; Real Academia Española 2010: 289–290, 294ff.). The sentences in (8c)–(8e) illustrate generic plural subjects, and verb and prepositional objects, in Italian (Benincà 1980; Giorgi 2001: 326; Kupisch 2012: 739–740; Maiden and Robustelli 2013: 76ff.).

(8) a. *Los belgas beben mucha cerveza.*
the Belgians drink.PRES.3PL much beer
'Belgians drink a lot of beer.'
(Butt and Benjamin 2004: 29)

b. *Le gusta salir con ingleses.*
3S.OBL please.PRES.3S go.out.INF with English.PL
'S/he likes going out with English people.'
(Butt and Benjamin 2004: 32)

c. *I gatti dormono molto.*
the cats sleep.PRES.3PL much
'Cats sleep a lot.'[2]
(Kupisch 2012: 739)

d. *Ho sentito rumori.*
have.PRES.1S hear.PPLE rumors
'I've heard rumors.'
(Patota 2006: 64)

e. *Sono venuto con amici.*
be.PRES.1S come.PPLE with friends

[2] Non-generic reading ('The cats sleep a lot') is also possible (Kupisch 2012: 739).

'I've come with friends.'
(Patota 2006: 65)

The LF example in (9a) has a determinerless generic subject *genti* 'people, person.' The examples in (9b) and (9c) illustrate similar usage in Spanish and Italian, respectively, with postverbal subjects, and the examples in (9d)–(9f) illustrate similar usage with preverbal subjects in Italian, Spanish, and Brazilian Portuguese (see Lapesa 1987; Munn and Schmitt 1999; Benincà et al. 2001: 186; Renzi 2001: 388–390; MacKenzie 2003: 7–8; Butt and Benjamin 2004: 31; Maiden and Robustelli 2013: 78).

(9) a. *genti hablar tenir gouerra.*
people say.IMPF have.IMPF war
'On dit que nous avons la guerre.'
'They say there is war.'
(Anonymous 1830a: 98)

b. *Caían bombas por todas partes.*
fall.IMPF.3PL bombs on all sides
'Bombs were falling everywhere.'
(Butt and Benjamin 2004: 31)

c. *Arrivava gente da tutte le parti.*
arrive.IMPF.3PL people from all the sides
'People came in from everywhere.'
(Patota 2006: 65)

d. *Studenti e colleghi hanno telefonato.*
students and colleagues have.PRES.3PL telephone.PPLE
'Students and colleagues have called.'
(Kupisch 2012: 740)

e. *agentes de la autoridad lo detuvieron*
agents of the authority him arrest.PRET.3PL
'law enforcement agents arrested him'
(Lapesa 1987: 66)

f. *Criança(s) faz(em) muito barulho.*
child(ren) make.PRES.3S(PL) much noise
'Children make a lot of noise.'
(Schmitt 1996: 259)

In the following pair of sentences, the mass noun *agoua* 'water' is used without a determiner in both subject and object positions. The semantic overlap between mass nouns and plural count nouns is discussed, e.g., in Benincà (1980: 53), Benincà et al. (2001: 185), Benincà (2012), and MacKenzie (2003: 8).

(10) a. *agoua cascar*
water flow.IMPF
'L'eau coule.'
'Water flows.'
(Anonymous 1830a: 23)

b. *cascar agoua.*
flow.IMPF water
'Il pleut.'
'It's raining.'
(Anonymous 1830a: 98)

8.1.2.4 Count Nouns with Generic Meaning The example (7b) in Section 8.1.2.3 illustrated the use of a determined count noun, *il Françis* 'the Frenchman,' with generic meaning. Further examples of this usage include *l'Algérino* 'the Algerian' in (11a), *l'Yoldach* 'the janissary' in (11b), and *il Françis* 'the Frenchman' in (11c) and (11d).

(11) a. *mi pensar l'Algérino non combatir.*
1s think.IMPF the'Algerian NEG fight.IMPF
'Je pense que les Algériens ne se batront pas.'
'I think Algerians will not fight.'
(Anonymous 1830a: 98)

b. *sé quérir paché l'Yoldach fazir gribouila.*
if want.IMPF peace the'janissary make.IMPF fuss
'S'il veut la paix les Turcs feront tapage.'
'If he wants peace, Turks will make a fuss.'
(Anonymous 1830a: 98)

c. *per mare nada, ma per terra il Françis star mouchou forti.*
by sea nothing but by land the French be.IMPF very strong
'Par mer rien, mais par terre ils sont redoutables.'
'By sea nothing, but the French are very strong on the ground.'
(Anonymous 1830a: 98)

d. *sé il Françis sbarkar, Algiéri star perso.*
if the French disembark.IMPF Algiers be.IMPF lost
'Si les Français débarquent Alger est perdu.'
'If the French disembark, Algiers is lost.'
(Anonymous 1830a: 98)

While the above usage may be the simple consequence of the nonproductivity of nominal number in LF, the use of singular count nouns with generic meaning has parallels in LF's Romance lexifiers (Serianni 1989: 208; Butt and Benjamín 2004: 30) (see the examples in 12).

(12) a. *El inglés es un excelente marino*
the English be.PRES.3S an excellent worker
'The English are excellent seamen'
(Real Academia Española 2010: 290)

b. *il tedesco è un gran lavoratore*
the German be.PRES.3S a great worker
'the Germans are great workers'
(Serianni 1989: 208)

8.1.2.5 Mass Nouns The definite article is omitted with partitive mass nouns in verb object position. This includes nouns referring to substances, such as *agoua* 'water' and *thé* 'tea' in (13a), and the abstract noun *paché* 'peace' in (13b) and (13c).

(13) a. *fazir scaldar agoua; mi quérir counchar thé.*
make.IMPF heat.IMPF water 1S want.IMPF make.IMPF tea
'Faites chauffer de l'eau; je veux faire du thé.'
'Heat up water, I want to make tea.'
(Anonymous 1830a: 97)

b. *dounqué bisogno il Bacha quérir paché.*
so need the pasha ask.for.IMPF peace
'Le Pacha sera donc obligé de demander la paix.'
'So the Pasha will be forced to ask for peace.'
(Anonymous 1830a: 98)

c. *perqué non counchar paché*
why NEG want.IMPF peace
'Pour quoi ne fait-on pas la paix?'
'Why not make peace?'
(Anonymous 1830a: 98)

Similar omission of the definite article before partitive mass nouns is found in Spanish (see 14a, 14b) and Italian (see 14c, 14d) (Rohlfs 1968: 118; Renzi 2001: 392–394; Butt and Benjamin 2004: 30–32; Patota 2006: 65; Maiden and Robustelli 2013: 76ff.).

(14) a. *Quiero cerveza.*
want.PRES.1S beer
'I want (some) beer.'
(Butt and Benjamin 2004: 30)

b. *Quieremos paz.*
want.PRES.1PL peace
'We want peace.'
(Butt and Benjamin 2004: 32)

c. *Qui vendono birra.*
here sell.PRES.3PL beer
'They sell beer here.'
(Maiden and Robustelli 2013: 77)

d. *Abbiamo speranza.*
have.PRES.1PL hope
'We have hope.'
(Patota 2006: 65)

The examples in (15) show that the mass noun *café* 'coffee' is determined in the subject position and determinerless in the verb object position, which appears to indicate that at least some mass nouns behave similarly to generic nouns in LF (see Section 8.1.2.3). Butt and Benjamin (2004: 30) point to their overlap in Spanish by observing that "the difference between generic and partitive mass nouns . . . is not always obvious, as in the sentence *como carne* 'I eat meat,' where *carne* apparently refers to meat in general." It has been suggested that plural count nouns and mass nouns may have similar semantic and syntactic properties (Benincà 1980: 53; Benincà et al. 2001: 185; MacKenzie 2003: 8; Benincà 2012). In the absence of a productive nominal plural, mass nouns and generic count nouns are morphologically not distinguished in LF.

(15) a. *non counchar per mi, il café basta.*
NEG make.IMPF for 1s the coffee enough
'N'en faites pas pour moi, le café me suffit.'
'Do not make (tea) for me, coffee will do.'
(Anonymous 1830a: 97)

b. *ti quérir café?*
2s want.IMPF coffee
'Voulez-vous du café?'
'Would you like coffee?'
(Anonymous 1830a: 97)

c. *portar café.*
bring.IMPF coffee
'Apportez le café.'
'Bring coffee.'
(Anonymous 1830a: 97)

8.1.2.6 Nouns Modified by a Qualifier A noun that takes no article when used by itself may do so when modified by a qualifier, which in our data is nearly always a possessive phrase with *di* 'of.' The sentences below present examples of determined and determinerless nouns functioning as objects of the prepositions *per* 'by, for,' *di* 'of, from,' and *a* 'to, at.'

(16) a. *per mare nada, ma per terra il Françis star mouchou forti.*
by sea nothing but by land the French be.IMPF very strong
'Par mer rien, mais par terre ils sont redoutables.'
'By sea nothing, but the French are very strong on the ground.'
(Anonymous 1830a: 98)

b. *per la palabra di mi.*
by the word of 1s
'Sur ma parole.'
'Upon my word.'
(Anonymous 1830a: 93)

c. *qouando ti mirar per ellou*
when 2s see.IMPF DOM 3S.M
saloutar mouchou per la parte di mi.
greet.IMPF much by the part of 1s
'Quand vous le verrez faites lui mes compliments.'
'When you see him, pay him my respects.'
(Anonymous 1830a: 94)

d. *andar fora di casa.*
go.IMPF out of house
'Sortez de la maison.'
'Go out of the house.'
(Anonymous 1830a: 95)

e. *mi vénir della casa di mi.*
1s come.IMPF from.the house of 1s
'Je viens de chez moi.'
'I've come from home.'
(Anonymous 1830a: 95)

f. *mirar qué ora star al orlogio di ti.*
see.IMPF what hour be.IMPF at.the watch of 2s
'Voyez quelle heure il est à votre montre.'
'See what time is it on your watch.'
(Anonymous 1830a: 97)

The preposition *in* 'in' behaves differently in that the addition of a qualifier to its object noun does not cause the noun to become determined (see the noun *casa* 'house' in 17a–17c). The example in (17d) shows that this feature may not be confined to the noun *casa*, which is determinerless in certain common verb-object and preposition-object collocations in both main lexifiers of LF (Serianni 1989: 184; Renzi 1997: 168; 2001: 426; MacKenzie 2003: 3, 10–12; Patota 2006: 70; Maiden and Robustelli 2013: 74).

(17) a. *star in casa?*
see.IMPF in house
'Est-il à la maison?'

'Is he at home?'
(Anonymous 1830a: 94)

b. *mi mirato in casa di ti.*
1s see.PF in house of 2s
'Je l'ai vu chez vous.'
'I saw (him) at your house.'
(Anonymous 1830a: 96)

c. *mi andar in casa del Signor.*
1s go.IMPF in house of.the gentleman
'Je vais chez Monsieur M.'
'I am going to the house of Mr. (M.).'
(Anonymous 1830a: 95)

d. *in strada grandi.*
in big street
'Dans la grand' rue.'
'In the big street.'
(Anonymous 1830a: 96)

The addition of a modifying phrase or adjective to a noun does not automatically make it specific. For example, *genti* 'people, person' in (18a) remains generic and determinerless despite the addition of a modifying adjective, and *amigo* 'friend' in (18b) remains generic and determinerless despite the addition of a possessive phrase. Both resulting noun phrases are in predicative position and semantically classificatory rather than identificatory (Lapesa 1987: 60; MacKenzie 2003: 10).

(18) a. *star buona genti.*
be.IMPF good person
'C'est un brave homme.'
'He is good people.'
(Anonymous 1830a: 94)

b. *Questi Signor star amigo di mi.*
these gentleman be.IMPF friend of 1s
'Ces Messieurs sont mes amis.'
'These gentlemen are my friends.'
(Anonymous 1830a: n.p.)

A similar distinction in the use of the definite article, depending on whether the noun is used by itself or with a qualifier, is observed, e.g., in Spanish: compare *religión* 'religion' in (19a) with *la religión* 'the religion' in (19b). In (19c), the noun *religión* remains generic and determinerless despite the addition of a qualifying adjective. The predicative noun phrase *hombre serio* 'serious man' in (19d) is also generic (classificatory) and determinerless (Butt and Benjamin 2004: 31, 43).

(19) a. *Estamos hablando de religión.*
be.PRES.1PL talk.GRD of religion
'We're talking about religion.'
(Butt and Benjamin 2004: 31)

b. *Estamos hablando de la religión de los antiguos persas.*
be.PRES.1PL talk.GRD of the religion of the ancient Persians
'We're talking about the religion of the ancient Persians.'
(Butt and Benjamin 2004: 31)

c. *Estamos hablando de religión antigua.*
be.PRES.1PL talk.GRD of religion ancient
'We're talking about ancient religion.'
(Butt and Benjamin 2004: 31)

d. *el doctor Urdino es hombre serio*
the doctor Urdino be.PRES.3S man serious
'Doctor Urdino is a serious man'
(Butt and Benjamin 2004: 43)

8.1.2.7 Verb–Object Units The *Dictionnaire*'s LF contains a number of analytic verbal lexemes composed of a transitive verb and a determinerless direct object noun. The majority of these are built with the support verbs *far/fazir/counchar* 'to do, make,' *mettir* 'to put,' *ténir* 'to have,' *forar* 'to take away, remove,' and *dar* 'to give,' though other verbs are used as well; the nouns in these units may be count or mass (see the examples in 20). At least some of these constructions are inherited from LF's Romance lexifiers (see Cifoletti 1989: 151–154 and Chapter 5 of this book).

(20) a. *questo umbré ténir cabessa*
this man have.IMPF house
'cet homme à de l'esprit'
'this man is witty'
(Anonymous 1830a: 32)

b. *ténir fébra.*
have.IMPF fever
'Il a la fièvre.'
'He's got fever.'
(Anonymous 1830a: 94)

c. *non tenir doubio.*
NEG have.IMPF doubt
'Il n'y a point de doute.'
'There is no doubt.'
(Anonymous 1830a: 93)

d. *ti fato colatzioné?*
2S do.PF breakfast

'Avez-vous déjeuné?
'Have you had breakfast?'
(Anonymous 1830a: 96)

e. *qouesto fasir paoura.*
this make.IMPF fear
'cela est effrayant'
'this is scary'
(Anonymous 1830a: 29)

f. *fazir vento.*
make.IMPF wind
'Il fait du vent.'
'It's windy.'
(Anonymous 1830a: 98)

g.

French	Lingua Franca	Literal gloss	Gloss
saler	mettir salé	'to put salt'	'to salt'
sceller	mettir taba	'to put seal'	'to seal'
embraser	mettir fugo	'to put fire'	'to set fire'
raser	forar barba	'to remove beard'	'to shave'
traire	forar laté	'to draw milk'	'to milk'
escorter	dar scorta	'to give escort'	'to escort'
secourir	dar agiudo	'to give help'	'to help'
est entêté	tenir fantétzia	'to have *fantasia*'[3]	'to be stubborn'

Both Italian and Spanish use bare nouns in common, idiomatic verb-object collocations, such as *tener coche* 'to have a car,' *buscar casa* 'to look for a house' in Spanish and *avere paura* 'to be afraid,' *cercare lavoro* 'to look for work' in Italian (Serianni 1989: 183; Renzi 2001: 427; MacKenzie 2003: 11–12; Butt and Benjamin 2004: 40, 43; Patota 2006: 70; Maiden and Robustelli 2013: 70). MacKenzie (2003) observes that, unlike in *tener un coche* 'to have a car,' the determinerless object in *tener coche* forms an indivisible unit with the verb, with the resulting meaning being something like 'to be a car owner.' A similar close linkage between the verb and its object obtains in comparable units in Italian, which are often paraphrasable with a single verb (Renzi 2001: 427–429; Maiden and Robustelli 2013: 76ff.; see also Chapters 5 and 6 of this book).

The examples in (21a) show that not all verb-object collocations in the *Dictionnaire*'s LF contain a bare noun. It is possible that the constructions in (21a) were intended as paraphrases and, as a result, do not occupy the same slot on the lexicon-syntax continuum as the units in (20). This view appears supported by the comparable paraphrases in Richelet (1811), which may have influenced the *Dictionnaire*'s compilers (see 21b and Chapter 3).

[3] On the meanings of *fantasia* see Faidherbe (1884: 108) ("un mot qui résume tout: *fantasia*" [a word that sums up everything: *fantasia*], Broughton (1840: 279–280), and Cifoletti (1979).

(21) a.

French	Lingua Franca	Literal gloss	Gloss
brider	méttir l'eskima	'to put the bridle'	'to bridle'
débrider	forar l'esquima	'to remove the bridle'	'to unbridle'
éteindre	massar il fouogo	'to kill the fire'	'to extinguish'
assiéger	far il sedio	'to make the siege'	'to besiege'
seller	mettir la sérigia	'to put the saddle'	'to saddle'
défoncer[4]	forar il foundo	'to remove the bottom'	'to knock out the bottom'

b.

French word	Paraphrase in Richelet (1811)
brider	mettre une bride 'to put a bridle'
débrider	oter la bride 'to remove the bridle'
éteindre	etouffer le feu 'to smother the fire'
assiéger	mettre le siége devant une place . . . 'to put the siege in front of a place'
seller	mettre la selle sur le dos d'un cheval . . . 'to put a saddle on the back of a horse'
défoncer	oter le fond d'un tonneau 'to remove the bottom of a barrel'

8.1.2.8 Noun–*di*–Noun Units When *di* 'of' is used as the linking element of a syntagmatic nominal compound, the following noun, with one exception, does not take a determiner (see 22a). When *di* 'of' is used as the marker of possession, on the other hand, the possessor noun is furnished with the definite article (see 22b, 22c). Like the verb-object units with a determined noun discussed in the preceding section, the exceptional unit in which the second noun is determined – *moukera del filio* – may be more syntactic than lexical in nature.

(22) a.

French	Lingua Franca	Literal gloss	Gloss
fichu	fatzoletto di collo	'handkerchief of neck	'neckerchief'
rasoir	cortello di barba	'knife of beard'	'razor'
meuble	roba di casa	'stuff of house'	'furniture'
sain-doux	grasso di porco	'fat of pig'	'lard'
saumure	agoua di salé	'water of salt'	'brine'
palmier	albéro di datoli	'tree of date'	'date palm'
belle-fille	moukera del filio	'wife of the son'	'daughter-in-law'

b. *d' ordine del Bacha*
of order of.the house
'par arrêt du Pacha'

[4] Spelled <déforcer>.

'by the order of the Pasha'
(Anonymous 1830a: 14)

c. *mi andar in casa del Signor.*
1s go.IMPF in house of.the gentleman
'Je vais chez Monsieur M.'
'I am going to Mr. M.'s house.'
(Anonymous 1830a: 95)

A similar contrast in Spanish is illustrated in (23) with examples taken from Butt and Benjamin (2004: 32) and MacKenzie (2003: 9).

(23) a. *la carne de vaca* *la ropa de niño*
the meat of cow the clothes of child
'beef' 'children's clothes'

b. *la carne de la vaca* *la ropa del niño*
the meat of the cow the clothes of the child
'the meat of the cow' 'clothes belonging to the boy'

8.1.2.9 Personal Titles The only personal title recorded in the *Dictionnaire* is *Signor*; it is determinerless when used as a vocative and determined otherwise.

(24) a. *bon dgiorno Signor.*
good day mister
'Bon jour, Monsier.'
'Good day, sir.'
(Anonymous 1830a: 93)

b. *ti dar una cadiéra al Signor.*
2s give.IMPF a chair to.the gentleman
'Donnez une chaise à Monsieur.'
'Give the gentleman a chair.'
(Anonymous 1830a: 94)

The above difference is observed in both Spanish and Italian (Serianni 1989: 172, 185; Butt and Benjamin 2004: 37).

(25) a. *el señor Moreira*
'Mr. Moreira'
(Butt and Benjamin 2004: 37)

a.' *pase usted, señor Sender*
'come in Mr. Sender'
(Butt and Benjamin 2004: 37)

b. *Il signor Bruschino*
'Mr. Bruschino'
(Serianni 1989: 172)

b.' *dottor Lombardo, senta una cosa*!
'listen, doctor Lombardo!'
(Serianni 1989: 185)

8.1.2.10 Indication of Time The LF construction in (26a) appears to be a calque of the corresponding construction in French. The construction used in Italian and Spanish is given in (26b).

(26) a. *poco poco star qouatr'ora.*
little little be.IMPF four'hour
'Il est bientôt quatre heures.'
'It's almost four o'clock.'
(Anonymous 1830a: 97)

b. *Sono le quattro.*
Son las cuatro.
be.PRES.3PL the.F.PL four
'It's four o'clock.'

8.1.3 Other Determiners

In addition to the definite article, the determiners in the *Dictionnaire*'s LF include the indefinite article, cardinal and ordinal numerals, quantifiers, and demonstrative, interrogative, and indefinite adjectives. As in the lexifiers, these are prenominal (Serianni 1989; Renzi 1997).

The use of the indefinite article *oun / ouna* in LF parallels its use in the lexifiers (see 27a–27c). The part of speech status of *francis* and similar ethnic designations in (27d) – as adjectives or substantivized adjectives – is unclear.

(27) a. *mi andar mirar oun amigo.*
1s go.IMPF see.IMPF a friend
'Je vais voir un ami.'
'I am going to see a friend.'
(Anonymous 1830a: 95)

b. *ti dar una cadiéra al Signor.*
2s give.IMPF a chair to.the mister
'Donnez une chaise à Monsieur.'
'Give the gentleman a chair.'
(Anonymous 1830a: 94)

c. *mi non crédir ouna palabra.*
1s NEG believe.IMPF a word
'Je n'en crois pas une parole.'
'I don't believe a word.'
(Anonymous 1830a: 93)

d. *star francis ...*
be.IMPF French
'Il est français ...'
'He is French / a Frenchman'
(Anonymous 1830a: 96)

The sentences in (28) illustrate the prenominal position of the demonstrative adjective *qouesto / qouesta* and the gender agreement between it and the noun.

(28) a. *quest-o umbré ténir cabessa*
this-M man.M have.IMPF house
'cet homme à de l'esprit'
'this man is witty'
(Anonymous 1830a: 32)

b. *ti goustar qouest-a cosa*?
2S like.IMPF this-F thing.F
'Approuvez-vous cette chose?'
'Do you like this thing?'
(Anonymous 1830a: 13)

The sentences in (29) illustrate the prenominal position of the interrogative adjective *qué* (in 29a), indefinite adjective *qoualké* (in 29b), quantifiers *molto*, *mouchou*, *poco* (in 29c-29e), and numerals (in 29f, 29g).

(29) a. *Gouerra, con qué natzion*?
war with which nation
'La guerre, avec quelle nation?'
'A war, with which nation?'
(Anonymous 1830a: 98)

b. *mi poudir servir per ti per qoualké cosa*?
1S be.able.IMPF serve.IMPF DOM 2S for some thing
'Puis-je vous servir en quelque chose?'
'Can I do anything for you?'
(Anonymous 1830a: 94)

c. *molto tempo ti non mirato Signor M.*?
much time 2S NEG see.PF mister M.
'Y a-t-il long-tems que vous n'vez vu Monsieur M.?'
'Has it been long since you've seen Mr. M.?'
(Anonymous 1830a: 94)

d. *mouchou tempou di conoschir per ellou?*
much time of know.IMPF DOM 3S.M
'Y a-t-il long-temps que vous le connaissez?'
'Have you known him long?'
(Anonymous 1830a: 96)

e. *ténir poco tempo.*
have.IMPF little time

'Il y a peu de temps.'
'Not long.'
(Anonymous 1830a: 96)

f. *mi pensar non star tré ora.*
1s think.IMPF NEG be.IMPF three hour
'Je pense qu'il n'est pas trois heures.'
'I think it's not yet three o'clock.'
(Anonymous 1830a: 97)

g. *primo piano*
first floor
'I,er étage'
'first floor'
(Anonymous 1830a: 32)

8.1.4 Adjectives

The *Dictionnaire* records few examples of noun phrases with attributive adjectives. In these, the adjectives can follow the noun, as in *cortello grosso* 'cleaver' ('large knife') and the examples in (30a, 30b), or they can precede it (in 30c, 30d). The position of a degree word in relation to the adjective is illustrated in (30b). The examples in (30d) are translations of the French prompts supplied in parentheses.

(30) a. *in strada grandi.*
in big street
'Dans la grand' rue.'
'On the big (main) street.'
(Anonymous 1830a: 96)

b. *mi tenir thé mouchou bonou …*
1s have.IMPF tea.M very good
'J'ai du thé délicieux …'
'I've got some very good tea …'
(Anonymous 1830a: 97)

c. *star buona genti.*
be.IMPF good person
'C'est un brave homme.'
'He is good people.'
(Anonymous 1830a: 94)

d. *picola cassa* 'box' (Fr. *caisson*)
picolo camino 'path' (Fr. *sentier*)
picolo bastone 'little stick' (Fr. *baguette*)

The position of the attributive adjective in Romance languages can be both pre- and postnominal, and be subject to many factors, including syntactic, semantic, pragmatic, lexical, and phonological (Nespor 2001; Butt and Benjamin 2004: 60–66; Patota 2006: 78–80; Bernardini 2011). The postnominal position generally elicits the literal meaning of an adjective and is considered unmarked; a postposed adjective is semantically autonomous with respect to the noun and supplies objective descriptive information about it. The prenominal position is marked, implies close semantic linkage between the adjective and noun, refers to an inherent and known property of the noun, and may be utilized for nonliteral, subjective, or metaphorical uses. In the literature, the order adjective-noun has been likened to a nominal compound and noun-adjective to modification by a relative clause (Maiden 1995: 114–115; Vincent 2007: 58–60; Cornilescu and Dinu 2013: 456); the order of adjectival modification has also been analyzed in terms of the syntheticity/analyticity dichotomy, with preposed modification representing the synthetic option and postposed the analytic one (Picone 1996: 18–19). Vincent (2007: 59) writes, with reference to the phrase *un vecchio amico* 'an old friend' – as opposed to *un amico vecchio* – in Italian: "Because noun and adjective unite to form a complex concept in this way, they are equivalent to what might in another language be a single word such as *buddy* or a compound like *soulmate.*" In Italian, preposed adjectives can be modified by *più* 'more' and *meno* 'less' but not, for example, by *molto* 'very' (Giorgi 2001: 317). Spoken and written modalities of Italian differ in their use of the prenominal position: while in the former it is mostly used in fixed expressions, in the latter it constitutes a stylistic choice (Scarano 2000, as summarized by Bernardini 2011). For some attributive adjectives, differences in placement may result in significant semantic differences: compare, for example, *certe idee* 'certain ideas' with *idee certe* 'ideas which are certain' in Italian (Maiden 1995: 114), *un buen amigo* 'good as a friend' with *un amigo bueno* 'a good friend and a good person' in Spanish (Butt and Benjamin 2004: 65), or *un homme honnête* 'a man who is honest and trustworthy' with *un honnête homme*, a phrase which combines the senses of "both a man of probity and a cultivated man," in French (Smith 2006: 169).

The small number of relevant examples in the *Dictionnaire* does not allow an in-depth study of attributive adjective placement in LF, however, they are sufficient to evidence continuity with the syntax of attributive adjectives in the lexifiers. For example, *buono* 'good' has the meaning of subjective evaluation in *buona genti* 'good people' (30c) while in *thé mouchou bonou* 'very good tea' (30b) it "predicates some property of the noun which is not inherent in the noun's meaning" (Maiden 1995: 114). The postposed position of *bonou* in the second example is also apparently due to its being modified by *mouchou* 'very.' The prenominal position of *picolo* 'small, little' in the examples in (30d) reflects the formation of new lexemes to express new concepts. The function of *picolo* in these items may be compared with that of a diminutive suffix (Serianni 1989: 204). In summary, the syntax of attributive adjectives in LF, with some evidence of functional differentiation between the pre- and postnominal placement of adjectives, is clearly continuous with the state of affairs in LF's Romance lexifiers.

8.1.5 *Possession*

The *Dictionnaire*'s LF expresses attributive possession by means of the preposition *di* 'of' placed between the possessee and the possessor. The latter may be a noun, as in (31a), or a personal pronoun, as in (31b).

(31) a. *mi andar in casa del Signor.*
1s go.IMPF in house of.the gentleman
'Je vais chez Monsieur M.'
'I am going to the house of Mr. (M.).'
(Anonymous 1830a: 95)

b. *commé star il fratello di ti?*
how be.IMPF the brother of 2s
'Comment se porte votre frère?'
'How is your brother?'
(Anonymous 1830a: 94)

The above possessive construction represents the end point in the grammaticalization of a periphrastic possessive that the lexifiers initially used with nominal possessors (cf. *la casa de Juan* 'Juan's house' in Spanish, *la casa di Gianni* 'Gianni's house' in Italian). With pronominal possessors, the lexifiers have both a dedicated set of possessive adjectives and the ability to use the periphrastic construction for disambiguation, contrast, or emphasis (Cordin 2001: 620–621; Maiden and Robustelli 2013: 158ff.). For example, the gender of the possessor in Italian *la sua casa* 'his/her house' may be disambiguated by using the periphrastic *la casa di lui* 'his house' or *la casa di lei* 'her house' while in Spanish *su casa*, which is ambiguous with respect to the gender, person, and number of the possessor, may be disambiguated by the use of the periphrases *la casa de él* 'his house,' *la casa de ella* 'her house,' *la casa de ellos* 'their (m.) house,' *la casa de ellas* 'their (f.) house,' *la casa de Usted* 'your (sg.) house,' or *la casa de Ustedes* 'your (pl.) house' (Orozco 2012: 219). In LF, elimination of the category of possessives has paved the way for complete grammaticalization of the periphrastic possessive construction which, in the lexifiers, continues to be stylistically marked and/or distributionally constrained.

8.2 Copular Clauses

Copular clauses are formed with the copula *(e)star*, which derives from the locative copulas in its lexifiers, Spanish *estar* and Italian *stare*.

The examples in (32a)–(32e) illustrate LF copular clauses with nominal, adjectival, prepositional (possessor and locational), and adverbial predicates, respectively. The examples in (32b) and (32f) show that the predicative adjective agrees with the subject in gender. The sentences in (32d), (32e), and (32g) show that the subject of a copular clause may be left unexpressed. The examples in (32f) and (32g) show that the negative morpheme precedes the copula.

(32) a. *Questi Signor star amigo di mi.*
these gentleman be.IMPF friend of 1s
'Ces Messieurs sont mes amis.'
'These gentlemen are my friends.'
(Anonymous 1830a: n.p.)

b. *il tempo star bello.*
the weather be.IMPF beautiful
'Il fait beau temps.'
'The weather is fine.'
(Anonymous 1830a: 97)

c. *qouesto libro star di mi.*
this book be.IMPF of 1s
'ce livre est à moi'
'this book is mine'
(Anonymous 1830a: 49)

d. *star in casa?*
be.IMPF in house
'Est-il à la maison?'
'Is he at home?'
(Anonymous 1830a: 94a)

e. *no, star forà.*
NEG be.IMPF outside
'Non, il est sorti.'
'No, he is out.'
(Anonymous 1830a: 94a)

f. *qouesto non star vero.*
this NEG be.IMPF true
'Cela n'est pas vrai.'
'This is not true.'
(Anonymous 1830a: 93)

g. *non star bouonou.*
NEG be.IMPF well
'Il n'est pas bien.'
'He is not well.'
(Anonymous 1830a: 94)

The functioning of *(e)star* as the only copula in LF is related to nonretention in it of the Romance copula deriving from Latin *esse(re)* 'to be.' The complete copularization of *(e)star* in LF represents the end point in the grammaticalization of Latin *stare* 'to stand,' its ultimate etymological source. One of the syntactic effects of this development is nondistinction in LF between nominal and locational predicates.

The entry *porter (se)* in the *Dictionnaire*'s LF vocabulary, reproduced in (33a) and (33b), indicates that *(e)star* is interchangeable with *andar* 'to go' in the prefab *star bonou* ~ *andar bonou* 'to be well'; compare, in particular, (33b) with (33c). Interchangeability of these verbs in this prefab continues similar interchangeability within the same and across different Romance languages, cf. *je suis bien* ~ *je vais bien* 'I am fine' in French, *cómo andas*? for *cómo estás*? 'how are you doing?' in Spanish (Butt and Benjamin 2004: 244, 425; Maiden 1995: 157–158).

(33) a.

Porter (Se), je me porte bien, comment vuos portez-vous, etc.	star *ou* andar, mi andar bonou, comme ti star?

b.

mi	*andar*	*bonou,*	*comme*	*ti*	*star*?
1s	go.IMPF	well	how	2s	be.IMPF

'je me porte bien, comment vuos (sic) portez-vous'
'I am fine, and how are you?'
(Anonymous 1830a: 61)

c.

non	*star*	*bouonou.*
NEG	be.IMPF	well

'Il n'est pas bien.'
'He is not well.'
(Anonymous 1830a: 94)

8.3 Verbal Clauses

The basic constituent order in the example sentences and dialogues supplied in the *Dictionnaire* is SVO (see 34a, 34b). The subject (in 34c) and the direct object (in 34d) may be left unexpressed. Adverbs and prepositional phrases follow the verb (34d–34f); the negative morpheme precedes it (in 34g, 34h). A sentence may begin with a subordinating conjunction (in 34i). The examples in (34a), (34c), and (34i) illustrate LF's predicative possessive construction with *ténir* 'to have,' and (34h) shows the use of *ténir* as an impersonal existential verb. The example in (34g) shows double negation, and the one in (34e) illustrates the adverbial use of a masculine (etymologically masculine singular) adjective.

(34) a.

questo	*umbré*	*ténir*	*cabessa*
this	man	have.IMPF	head

'cet homme à de l'esprit'

'this man is witty'
(Anonymous 1830a: 32)

b. *ti conoschir per ellou?*
2s know.IMPF DOM 3s.M
'Le connaissez vous?'
'Do you know him?'
(Anonymous 1830a: 96)

c. *ténir fébra.*
have.IMPF fever
'Il a la fièvre.'
'He has a fever'
(Anonymous 1830a: 94)

d. *mi mirato iéri.*
1s see.PF yesterday
'Je l'ai vu hier.'
'I saw him yesterday.'
(Anonymous 1830a: 94)

e. *mi ablar dgiousto.*
1s speak.IMPF just
'Je dis la vérité.'
'I speak the truth.'
(Anonymous 1830a: 93)

f. *mi vénir della casa di mi.*
1s come.IMPF from.the house of 1s
'Je viens de chez moi.'
'I've come from home.'
(Anonymous 1830a: 95)

g. *mi non sentito nada.*
1s NEG hear.PF nothing
'Je n'ai rien entendu.'
'I haven't heard anything.'
(Anonymous 1830a: 98)

h. *non tenir doubio.*
NEG have.IMPF doubt
'Il n'y a point de doute.'
'There is no doubt.'
(Anonymous 1830a: 93)

i. *perqué il Bacha tenir fantétzia.*
because the pasha have.IMPF pride
'Parce que le Pacha est entèté.'
'Because the Pasha is stubborn.'
(Anonymous 1830a: 98)

The direct object of *dar* 'to give' precedes the indirect object (in 35a). The direct object precedes the prepositional phrase (in 35a, 35b). This is also the unmarked order in LF's Romance lexifiers (Benincà et al. 2001: 135; Ledgeway 2011: 408; Dryer and Gensler 2013).

(35) a. *ti dar una cadiéra al Signor.*
2s give.IMPF a chair to.the gentleman
'Donnez une chaise à Monsieur.'
'Give the gentleman a chair.'
(Anonymous 1830a: 94)

b. *mi poudir servir per ti per qoualké cosa?*
1s be.able.IMPF serve.IMPF DOM 2s for some thing
'Puis-je vous servir en quelque chose?'
'Can I do anything for you?'
(Anonymous 1830a: 94)

Several modal, causative, perception, and motion verbs, including *poudir* 'to be able,' *quérir* 'to want,' *volir* 'to want,' *andar* 'to go,' *sentir* 'to hear,' *fazir* 'to do, make,' and *laschiar* 'to let,' can form complex predicates with other verbs, which invariably appear in the imperfective form (see the examples in 36).

(36) a. *mi andar spasségiar.*
1s go.IMPF walk.IMPF
'Je vais me promener.'
'I am going for a walk.'
(Anonymous 1830a: 95)

b. *cosà volir scométir?*
thing want.IMPF bet.IMPF
'Que voulez-vous parier?'
'What would you like to bet?'
(Anonymous 1830a: 93)

c. *mi sentito ablar di ellou.*
1s hear.IMPF speak.IMPF of 3S.M
'J'ai entendu parler de lui.'
'I've heard about him.'
(Anonymous 1830a: 96)

d. *mi non poudir crédir.*
1s NEG be.able.IMPF believe.IMPF
'Je ne saurais croire.'
'I can't believe it.'
(Anonymous 1830a: 93)

e. *fazir scaldar agoua; mi quérir counchar thé.*
make.IMPF heat.IMPF water 1s want.IMPF make.IMPF tea

'Faites chauffer de l'eau; je veux faire du thé.'
'Heat up water; I want to make tea.'
(Anonymous 1830a: 97)

f. *ti laschiar counchar per mi.*
1s let.IMPF do.IMPF DOM 1s
'Laissez-moi faire.'
'Let me do it.'
(Anonymous 1830a: 97)

The complex predicates in LF are continuous with the corresponding constructions in its Romance lexifiers, including infinitival constructions with modal, causative, and perception verbs and periphrastic futures with the verb *to go*, as in *va faire* 'is going to do' in French (Harris 1988: 229; Maiden 1995: 160–163; Vincent 1997a: 173). LF's analytic causatives with *fazir* 'to do' and *laschiar* 'to let' are continuous with the corresponding periphrastic causatives in the lexifiers (see the Italian examples in 37 and Chapter 6 of this book).

(37) a. *La mamma fa preparare il pranzo a Carla.*
the mom make.PRES.3s prepare.INF the dinner to Carla
'Mom makes Carla prepare dinner.'
(Patota 2006: 143)

b. *La mamma lascia preparare le valigie a Carla.*
the mom let.PRES.3s prepare.INF the suitcases to Carla
'Mom lets Carla pack the suitcases.'
(Patota 2006: 143)

The future / irrealis marker *bisogno*, grammaticalized in this function from Italian *bisogno* 'need,' is placed before the subject or, in the absence of an overt subject, before the verb (see 38).

(38) a. *bisogno mi andar.*
FUT 1s go.IMPF
'J'irai' ~ 'Que j'aille'
'I will go' ~ 'That I go'
(Anonymous 1830a: n.p.)

b. *bisogno andar domani.*
FUT go.IMPF tomorrow
'Nous irons demain.'
'We'll go tomorrow.'
(Anonymous 1830a: 96)

c. *bisogno andar mirar per ellou siémé siémé.*
FUT go.IMPF see.IMPF DOM 3S.M together
'Nous irons le voir ensemble.'
'We'll go see him together.'
(Anonymous 1830a: 96)

Several verbs in the *Dictionnaire*'s LF, including *fazir* 'to do, make,' *ténir* 'to have,' *(e)star* 'to be,' *piacher* 'to please,' and *dispiacher* 'to displease,' are or may be used impersonally (see 39). The sentences in (39f) and (39g) stand out in that the impersonal use of *cascar* 'to flow' is expressed via the word order.

(39) a. *non tenir doubio.*
NEG have.IMPF doubt
'Il n'y a point de doute.'
'There is no doubt.'
(Anonymous 1830a: 93)

b. *non star tardi.*
NEG be.IMPF late
'Il n'est pas tard.'
'It's not late.'
(Anonymous 1830a: 97)

c. *qouando piacher per ti.*
when please.IMPF DOM 2S
'Quand il vous plaira.'
'Whenever it pleases you.'
(Anonymous 1830a: 96)

d. *dispiacher mouchou per mi.*
displease.IMPF very DOM 2S
'J'en suis bien fâché.'
'I am very sorry.'
(Anonymous 1830a: 94)

e. *fazir vento.*
make.IMPF hot
'Il fait du vent.'
'It's windy.'
(Anonymous 1830a: 98)

f. *cascar agoua.*
flow.IMPF water
'Il pleut.'
'It rains.'
(Anonymous 1830a: 98)

g. *agoua cascar*
water flow.IMPF
'L'eau coule'
'The water flows'
(Anonymous 1830a: 23)

The *Dictionnaire*'s LF has grammaticalized the preposition *per* 'for, by' into a marker of pronominal objects. Unlike its lexifiers, LF personal pronouns do not distinguish between subject and oblique forms, which may explain the need for a syntactic marking of grammatical relations. Cifoletti (2004: 47) observes that *per* marks both direct and indirect objects with the first and second person pronouns, and only direct objects with the third person pronouns.

(40) a. *ti conoschir per ellou?*
2s know.IMPF DOM 3S.M
'Le connaissez vous?'
'Do you know him?'
(Anonymous 1830a: 96)

b. *ti fato vergognia per mi.*
2s do.PF shame DOM 1s
'Vous m'avez fait un affront.'
'You have humiliated me.'
(Anonymous 1830a: 11)

c. *qouando piacher per ti.*
when please.IMPF DOM 2s
'Quand il vous plaira.'
'Whenever it pleases you.'
(Anonymous 1830a: 96)

Both main lexifiers of LF display the phenomenon of differential object marking (DOM). The difference with LF consists in the preposition grammaticalized as the DOM marker, the arguments selected for the marking, and the degree of grammaticalization and generalization of the phenomenon. The examples below illustrate DOM in Spanish (in 41a), Italian (in 41b), and *cocoliche* (in 41c) (Serianni 1989: 95; Berretta 1989, 1990, 1991; Maiden 1995: 264; Butt and Benjamin 2004: 333–339; Berruto 2012: 154, 217).

(41) a. *No conozco a Feliciano.*
NEG know.PRES.1S DOM Feliciano
'I don't know Feliciano.'
(Butt and Benjamin 2004: 334)

b. *A Giorgio, questi argomenti non l'hanno convinto.*
DOM Giorgio these arguments NEG 3S.M'have.PRES.3PL convince.PPLE
'These arguments haven't convinced Giorgio.'
(Berretta 1991: 214)

c. *vedo a mio fratello.*
see.PRES.1S DOM my brother
'I see my brother'
(Berruto 2012: 217)

The development of DOM in LF may be correlated with the functional expansion of *per* in the context of naturalistic acquisition of Italian as a second language (Bernini 1987; see Operstein 2007 and Chapter 9). Alternatively, or in addition, DOM could have been replicated from languages with which LF was in contact, a number of which possess this feature: Heine and Kuteva (2003) argue that language-internal and contact-induced grammaticalization often act together to effect a structural change. Language-internal grammaticalization and copying have both been identified as potential sources of inflectional material in contact languages (Bruyn 2008; Roberts and Bresnan 2008). With specific reference to DOM, replication from other languages in contact has been proposed, e.g., by Döhla (2016), who argues that the development of DOM in Andalusian Arabic and Maltese was induced by their contact, respectively, with Iberian Romance vernaculars and Old Sicilian.

The *Dictionnaire*'s data capture DOM at an incipient evolutionary stage in that it is confined to the marking of objects expressed by personal pronouns, which occupy the highest slots in the animacy and definiteness hierarchies (Rohlfs 1971; Berretta 1991; Döhla 2016). As seen in (42), direct nominal objects show no DOM marking.

(42) a. *molto tempo ti non mirato Signor M.?*
much time 2S NEG see.PF mister M.
'Y a-t-il long-tems que vous n'vez vu Monsieur M.?'
'Has it been long since you've seen Mr. M.?'
(Anonymous 1830a: 94)

b. *aprir la bentana.*
open.IMPF the window
'Ouvrez la fenètre.'
'Open the window.'
(Anonymous 1830a: 95)

Related to the phenomenon of DOM is the issue of the distinction (or lack thereof) between direct and indirect objects in LF. Both Spanish and Italian display the tendency toward formal syncretism between direct and indirect object pronouns, which is more pronounced in some varieties than in others (cf. the phenomena of *leísmo* and *loísmo* in Spanish) (Kabatek and Pusch 2011: 85; Vázquez and Miglio 2016: 70–71). For indirect nominal objects, Romance languages generally use the preposition *a* 'to,' however, both Spanish and Italian also use this preposition for introducing some direct nominal objects as part of the DOM phenomenon (Vincent 1997b: 209), compare *hablo a la niña* 'I speak to the girl' with *veo a la niña* 'I see the girl' in Spanish. LF marks both direct and indirect pronominal objects by *per*, but distinguishes direct from indirect nominal objects by using the preposition *a* 'to' with the latter, compare *ti non mirato Signor M.* 'you didn't see Mr. M.'

with *ti dar una cadiéra al Signor* 'give a chair to the gentleman.' Based on these facts, LF is typologically similar to its lexifiers both in the tendency toward nondistinction between direct and indirect objects and in carrying out this tendency only partially (with pronominal but not with nominal objects).

In several examples, the preposition *di* 'of, from' marks the complements of verbs, adverbs, and/or prepositions (see 43). This use is continuous with similar uses of this multifunctional preposition in the lexifiers (see, e.g., Vincent 1997b: 209–210 for Italian).[5]

(43) a. *mi doubitar di qouesto.*
1s doubt.IMPF of this
'J'en doute.'
'I doubt this.'
(Anonymous 1830a: 93)

b. *mi non impachiar di qouesto.*
1s NEG care.IMPF of this
'Je ne me soucie pas de cela.'
'I don't care about this.'
(Anonymous 1830a: 93)

c. *andar fora di casa.*
go.IMPF out of house
'Sortez de la maison.'
'Go out of the house.'
(Anonymous 1830a: 95)

d. *qué poudir counchar il Françis contra di Algieri?*
what be.able.IMPF do.IMPF the.M French against of Algiers
'Que peuvent faire les Français contre Alger?'
'What can the French do against Algiers?'
(Anonymous 1830a: 98)

8.4 Interrogative Clauses

Polar questions in the *Dictionnaire*'s LF are structurally indistinguishable from declarative clauses and are signaled by intonation:

Rien dans la forme du langage ne marque l'interrogation, qui ne se fait sentir que par l'inflexion interrogative de la voix. (Anonymous 1830a: n.p.)

[Nothing in the form of the language marks questions, which are conveyed only by the interrogative inflection of the voice.]

[5] Of related interest are innovative uses of the preposition *di* in L2 Italian, including its extension to environments in which the target language employs other prepositions or no preposition at all, as well as its definite-article-like and DOM-marker-like uses (Bernini 1986, 1987; Berretta and Crotta 1991; Moretti 2000).

The use of intonation for signaling polar questions, without any syntactic marking, has parallels in both main lexifiers of LF (see, e.g., Rossano 2010: 2759 and Maiden and Robustelli 2013: 147 for Italian and Butt and Benjamin 2004: 540 for Spanish). The *Dictionnaire*'s dialogues supply examples of polar questions both with and without overt subjects.

(44) a. *ti quérir café?*
2s want.IMPF coffee
'Voulez-vous du café?'
'Would you like coffee?'
(Anonymous 1830a: 97)

b. *ti conoschir per ellou?*
2s know.IMPF DOM 3s.M
'Le connaissez vous?'
'Do you know him?'
(Anonymous 1830a: 96)

c. *sentir per mi?*
hear.IMPF DOM 1s
'M'entendez-vous?'
'Do you hear me?'
(Anonymous 1830a: 96)

d. *capir?*
understand.IMPF
'Comprenez-vous?'
'Do you understand?'
(Anonymous 1830a: 96)

In content questions, the question word or interrogative phrase is placed at the beginning of the clause. The question words in the *Dictionnaire* include *qui* 'who,' *qué* 'what, which,' *cosa* 'what,' *commé* 'how,' *perqué* 'why,' *ové* 'where,' *oundé* 'whence,' and *qouanto* 'how many, how much.' If the subject is expressed by a personal pronoun, the order of the subject and verb is not inverted; otherwise, it is inverted (compare 45a with 45b and 45c). The subject of a content question may be left unexpressed (see 45d–45f).

(45) a. *Commé ti star?*
how 2s be.IMPF
'Comment vous portez-vous?'
'How are you?'
(Anonymous 1830a: 93)

b. *commé star il fratello di ti?*
how be.IMPF the brother of 2s
'Comment se porte votre frère?'
'How is your brother?'
(Anonymous 1830a: 94)

c. *Comé star il tempo*?
how be.IMPF the weather
'Quel temps fait-il?'
'How is the weather?'
(Anonymous 1830a: 97)

d. *qué pensar?*
what think.IMPF
'Qu'en pensez-vous?'
'What do you think?'
(Anonymous 1830a: 94)

e. *di qué païsé star*?
from what country be.IMPF
'De quel pays est-il?'
'What country is he from?'
(Anonymous 1830a: 96)

f. *cosà volir scométir*?
what want.IMPF bet.IMPF
'Que voulez-vous parier?'
'What would you like to bet?'
(Anonymous 1830a: 93)

The examples in (46) provide further illustration of the word order difference in content questions related to the nature of the subject.

(46) a. *cosa ti quérir counchar*?
what 2s want.IMPF do.IMPF
'Que voudriez-vous faire?'
'What would you like to do?'
(Anonymous 1830a: 94)

b. *qué poudir counchar il Françis contra di Algieri?*
what be.able.IMPF do.IMPF the.M French against of Algiers
'Que peuvent faire les Français contre Alger?'
'What can the French do against Algiers?'
(Anonymous 1830a: 98)

c. *cosa ti ablar*?
what 2s say.IMPF
'Que dites-vous?'
'What are you saying?'
(Anonymous 1830a: 96

d. *qué servir touto qouesto*?
what serve.IMPF all this
'A quoi servira tout cela?'
'What will all this serve?'
(Anonymous 1830a: 95)

Both Spanish and Italian require inversion of the subject and verb in most content questions (Butt and Benjamin 2004: 539–540; Rossano 2010: 2764; Maiden and Robustelli 2013: 147–148; see the Italian examples in 47).

(47) a. *Cosa sottolinei tu?*
what underline.PRES.2s 2s
'What do you underline?'
(Rossano 2010: 2764)

b. *Quanto costa un casco?*
how.much cost.PRES.2s a helmet
'How much does a helmet cost?'
(Rossano 2010: 2764)

Optional noninversion of subjects in content questions has been noted, e.g., for Caribbean Spanish, where it has been connected with the increase in the frequency of overt pronominal subjects and analyzed as part of an overall drift toward a rigid SVO order (Brown and Rivas 2011). An example is *qué tú piensas*? for the normative *qué piensas tú*? 'what do you think?.' Though the details of noninversion in Caribbean Spanish do not match those of LF in every respect – for example, Brown and Rivas note that it is attested not only with pronominal but also with certain types of nominal subjects – the Spanish facts provide a plausible explanatory model for the noninversion of pronominal subjects in LF, namely, the tendency toward a fixed SVO word order. The fixed preverbal position of pronominal subjects in LF may also be connected with their use as functional equivalents of person inflection, which finds a parallel in the Romance domain in the obligatorification of preverbal subject pronouns in French and some other Romance varieties (Benincà 1997: 123; Kabatek and Pusch 2011: 83–84).

The LF example in (48a) illustrates the use of the preverbal position for topicalization, with the subject moved before the question word. The Italian example in (48b), along with the French prompt in 48(a), show that LF shares this topicalization strategy with its Romance lexifiers.

(48) a. *E il padré di ti commé star?*
and the father of 2s how be.IMPF
'Et Monsieur votre père comment est il?'
'And your father how is he?'
(Anonymous 1830a: 94)

b. *Ma tu che ruolo avrai?*
but 2s what role have.FUT.2s
'But you which role will you have?'
(Rossano 2010: 2765)

8.5 Imperative Clauses

The imperatives in the *Dictionnaire*'s LF dialogues are structurally indistinguishable from declaratives and polar questions. They invariably employ the imperfective form of the verb, with or without the subject pronoun; examples of the latter type appear to be more common. Both types of imperatives have functional equivalents in LF's Romance lexifiers, where both uninflected infinitives and verb forms inflected for person may be used as imperatives (Lipski n.d.).

(49) a. *intrar.*
come.in.IMPF
'Entrez.'
'Come in.'
(Anonymous 1830a: 95)

b. *spétar oun poco.*
wait.IMPF a little
'Attendez un peu.'
'Wait a while.'
(Anonymous 1830a: 95)

c. *ti sentar.*
2s sit.down.IMPF
'Asseyez-vous.'
'Sit down.'
(Anonymous 1830a: 95)

d. *ti métir oun poco piou zoukro.*
2s put.IMPF a little more sugar
'Mettez-y un peu plus de sucre.'
'Add a little more sugar.'
(Anonymous 1830a: 97)

8.6 Complex Sentences

The *Dictionnaire*'s dialogues contain examples of sentences consisting of more than one clause. The coordinate clauses are joined asyndetically (see 50).

(50) a. *ti venir dgiousto, la mangiaria star pronta.*
2s come.IMPF just the breakfast be.IMPF ready
'Vous venez à propos, le déjeuné est prêt.'
'You've come just in time, the breakfast is ready.'
(Anonymous 1830a: 96)

b. *mi tenir thé mouchou bonou;*
1s have.IMPF tea very good

mi quérir ti goustar per ellou.
1s want.IMPF 2s taste.IMPF DOM 3s

'J'ai du thé délicieux; je veux que vous en goutiez.'
'I've got some delicious tea, I want you to try it.'
(Anonymous 1830a: 97)

And the same is true of the complement clauses in (51).

(51) a. *ti quérir mi andar con ti?*
2s want.IMPF 1s go.IMPF with 2s
'Voulez-vous que j'aille avec vous?'
'Do you want me to come with you?'
(Anonymous 1830a: 95)

b. *mi pensar l'Algérino non combatir.*
1s think.IMPF the'Algerian NEG fight.IMPF
'Je pense que les Algériens ne se batront pas.'
'I think Algerians will not fight.'
(Anonymous 1830a: 98)

c. *mi pensar star meïo.*
1s think.IMPF be.IMPF better
'Il me semble qu'il vaudrait mieux.'
'I think this would be better.'
(Anonymous 1830a: 95)

d. *genti hablar tenir gouerra.*
people say.IMPF have.IMPF war
'On dit que nous avons la guerre.'
'They say there is war.'
(Anonymous 1830a: 98)

e. *mi star contento mirar per ti.*
1s be.IMPF happy see.IMPF DOM 2s
'Je suis bien aise de vous voir.'
'I am happy to see you.'
(Anonymous 1830a: 93)

f. *mi ténir piacher conoschir per ellou.*
1s have.IMPF pleasure know.IMPF DOM 3S.M
'Je serais bien aise de faire sa connaissance.'
'I would be happy to meet him.'
(Anonymous 1830a: 96)

Several sentences contain clause-combining morphemes. These include *per* 'for' in the same-subject purpose clause in (52a), *qué* 'that' in the relative clause in (52b), *sé* 'if' in the conditional clause (in 52c), and *quando* 'when' in the temporal clause in (52d).

(52) a. *mi venouto aposto per far mangiaria con ti.*
1s come.PF specially for do.PF breakfast with 2s
'Je suis venu exprès pour déjeuner avec vous.'

'I have come specially to have breakfast with you.'
(Anonymous 1830a: 97)

b. *qui star qouesto signor qué poco poco ablar per ti.*
who be.IMPF this gentleman that little little speak.IMPF DOM 2S
'Qui est-ce Monsieur qui vous parlait tantôt.'
'Who is the gentleman that spoke with you just now?'
(Anonymous 1830a: 96)

c. *sé quérir paché l'Yoldach fazir gribouila.*
if want.IMPF peace the'janissary make.IMPF fuss
'S'il veut la paix les Turcs feront tapage.'
'If he wants peace, the Turks will make a fuss.'
(Anonymous 1830a: 98)

d. *qouando ti mirar per ellou*
when 2S see.IMPF DOM 3S.M

saloutar mouchou per la parte di mi.
greet.IMPF much by the part of 1S
'Quand vous le verrez faites lui mes compliments.'
'When you see him, pay him my respects.'
(Anonymous 1830a: 94)

Even though the number and variety of complex sentences in the *Dictonnaire*'s dialogues are limited, each of the recorded sentence types and clause-combining morphemes is inherited from LF's Romance lexifiers. The complementizer-like use of *di* 'of' in (53) also has parallels in Romance languages (Maiden 1995: 207; Vincent 1997a: 171–172; Camus Bergareche 2013).

(53) *mouchou tempou di conoschir per ellou?*
much time of know.IMPF DOM 3S.M
'Y a-t-il long temps que vous le connaissez?'
'Have you known him long?'
(Anonymous 1830a: 96)

8.7 Chapter Summary

The preceding descriptive and comparative study indicates that the syntactic structures of the *Dictionnaire*'s LF combine features inherited from its Romance lexifiers and innovations. Constructions shared with the lexifiers include the word order features summarized in Table 8.1, which is based on Greenberg (1963), Sőrés (1995), and Dryer and Haspelmath (2013). As seen in the table, the *Dictionnaire*'s LF has inherited from its lexifiers the orders determiner-noun, numeral-noun, preposition-noun, DOM marker-pronoun, possessed-possessor, noun-relative clause, degree word-adjective, negative morpheme-verb, modal auxiliary-verb, verb-adverb, the relative order of the direct and indirect objects of the verb 'to give,' the basic subject-verb-object

Table 8.1. *Word order features of the* Dictionnaire*'s Lingua Franca*

Word order	Italian	Spanish	Lingua Franca	Gloss
ARTICLE-NOUN	*un amico*	*un amigo*	*oun amigo*	'a friend'
DEMONSTRATIVE-NOUN	*questo signore*	*este señor*	*qouesto signor*	'this gentleman'
NUMERAL-NOUN	*tre ore*	*tres horas*	*tré ora*	'three hours'
PREPOSITION-NOUN	*in casa*	*en casa*	*in casa*	'at home'
DOM-PERSONAL PRONOUN	*a lui*	*a él*	*per ellou*	'him'
POSSESSED-POSSESSOR [NOUN]	*la casa del signore*	*la casa del señor*	*casa del Signor*	'the house of the gentleman'
POSSESSED-POSSESSOR [PRONOUN]	*la casa di lui*	*la casa de él*	*casa di mi*	'his house' (It. Sp.) 'my house' (LF)
ADJECTIVE-NOUN	*buona gente*	*buena gente*	*bouona genti*	'good people'
NOUN-ADJECTIVE	*strada grande*	*calle grande*	*strada grandi*	'big street'
NOUN-RELATIVE CLAUSE	*quel Signore che parlava con voi poco fa*	*aquel señor que hablaba con V. poco ha*	*qouesto signor qué poco poco ablar per ti*	'the gentleman that spoke with you just now'
DEGREE WORD-ADJECTIVE	*molto forte*	*muy fuerte*	*mouchou forti*	'very strong'
VERB-ADVERB	*andare fuori*	*ir afuera*	*andar fora*	'to go out (side)'
NEGATOR-VERB	*non sta bene*	*no está bien*	*non star bouonou*	'is not well'
AUXILIARY-VERB	*(ve lo) posso assicurare*	*puedo asegurar (selo)*	*mi poudir assicourar (per ti)*	'I can assure (you)'

Table 8.1. *(cont.)*

Word order	Italian	Spanish	Lingua Franca	Gloss
SUBJECT-VERB-NOMINAL OBJECT	*il popolo vuole pace*	*el pueblo quiere paz*	*l'Yoldach fazir gribouila*	'people want peace' (It. Sp.), 'Turks will make a fuss' (LF)
VERB-DIRECT OBJECT-INDIRECT OBJECT	*date una sedia al Signore*	*dad una silla al señor*	*ti dar una cadiéra al Signor*	'give a chair to the gentleman'

order with nominal objects, and both the noun-adjective and adjective-noun orders. Also inherited are periphrastic causatives with the verbs *make* and *let*, predicative possession with the verb *have*, double negation, the adverbial use of adjectives, obligatory fronting of the interrogative phrase in content questions, subject-verb inversion in content questions with subjects not expressed by personal pronouns, the use of fronting for topicalization, the ability to begin a clause with a subordinating conjunction, and functional differentiation between the preposed and postposed order of attributive adjectives (Maiden 1995: 263, 267). Also inherited are the gender agreement in the noun phrase and between the subject and predicative adjective, the unmarked status of the masculine gender, principled ways of using bare and determined nouns, the ability to make functional use of variations in the constituent order, and substantial sets of prepositions, question words, and clause-combining morphemes (Serianni 1989: 121; Maiden 1995: 107). LF is also similar to its lexifiers in its tendencies toward partial nondistinction between direct and indirect objects, copular use of motion verbs, and the use of prepositions as complementizers and object markers. These inherited syntactic properties firmly align LF typologically with its Romance lexifiers, while at the same time distancing it from pidgins, which have few prepositions, clause connectors, and question words and typically lack adjectival agreement, inherited articles, and functional use of word order differences (Parkvall and Bakker 2013: 46).

Syntactic innovations seen in LF are motivated by contact-induced reduction in lexifier structural categories and/or their exponence (Maiden 1995: 236). The structural losses include noninheritance of the lexifier clitic pronouns, case distinctions in personal pronouns, possessive adjectives, morphological person marking on the verb, and a copula deriving from Latin *esse(re)*. In some cases, these losses led to compensatory expansion of functionally related lexifier constructions; in others, they resulted in complete elimination of the affected construction types. In particular:

1. Nonretention in LF of a copula deriving from Latin *esse(re)* has brought about complete grammaticalization of the locative copula *(e)star*, ultimately from Latin *stare* 'to stand,' whose syntactic effects include identical encoding of nominal and locational predicates. In the lexifiers, the descendants of Lat. *stare* (Sp. *estar*, It. *stare*) are only partially grammaticalized and used alongside those of *esse(re)*.
2. Nonretention in LF of the Romance possessive adjectives has brought about complete grammaticalization of the periphrastic pronominal possessive construction with *di* 'of.' Compared to the lexifiers, this construction has lost its marked character and expanded its functional range: periphrastic pronominal possessives are stylistically marked in Italian (Cordin 2001: 620) and are constrained in Spanish by linguistic and social factors including the person of the possessor, the nature of the possessed noun, the syntactic position of the possessive phrase, and the speaker's education (Orozco 2012). The full grammaticalization in LF of *(e)star* and the periphrastic possessive construction confirms the accelerating effect of intense language contact on morphosyntactic changes whose inception predates the contact (Lanly 1962; Vintilă-Rădulescu 1968; Silva-Corvalán 1986; Chaudenson 2001; Orozco 2012: 232–233; 2018: 33, 57).
3. Nonretention in LF of the Romance clitic pronouns has brought about the fixing of the basic SVO order. The basic SOV order of the lexifiers, which is obligatory when the object is expressed by a clitic pronoun, was eliminated in LF; compare, for example, the SVO order of a sentence like *mi crédir per ti* 'I believe you' in LF with the SOV order of its equivalents in Spanish (*yo te creo*) and Italian (*io ti credo*). The tendency toward the fixing of the SVO order is further apparent in the absence of subject-verb inversion in content questions when the subject is expressed by a personal pronoun (a similar developmental trend exists in Caribbean Spanish; see Brown and Rivas 2011).
4. Elimination of morphological person marking on the verb is partially compensated in LF by the use of overt pronominal subjects, though in the variety reflected in the *Dictionnaire* their use is not obligatory. The use of free personal pronouns to mark subjects in LF is paralleled by the obligatorification of subject pronouns in Romance languages (Kabatek and Pusch 2011: 83–84; Orozco 2018: 122) and their overuse in contact varieties thereof (cf. Lanly 1955: 207, 210; 1962: 216 for North African French).

5. Elimination of case distinctions in personal pronouns is compensated in LF by the development of DOM, which is also a feature of several Romance languages, including their contact varieties (cf. Moretti 2000 for L2 Italian). The differences between LF and its lexifiers with respect to DOM are of the same degree and kind as between different Romance languages (Kabatek and Pusch 2011: 84–85).

In conclusion, the syntactic constructions of the *Dictionnaire*'s LF are clearly continuous with those of its Romance lexifiers. The inherited syntactic constructions are considerably less varied as LF lacks such categories as passive, reflexives, possessives, nonmodal auxiliaries, and number agreement. Similar structural reduction is noted in other contact varieties of Romance languages; for example, Hull (1985: 249–250) notes the loss of certain tenses and the use of *che* as the only relativizer in Egyptian Italian, and Lanly (1955, 1962) makes similar observations with respect to North African French (see congruent observations in Chaudenson 2001: 162). The syntactic innovations of LF result from functional expansion of the directly related lexifier constructions and have close parallels in the Romance domain. The syntactic continuity between LF and its lexifiers fully bears out Whinnom's (1965: 524) assessment that "the syntax of Sabir, however simplified, is beyond question Romance: the word-order is a Romance word-order."

9 The Lingua Franca

The preceding chapters have shown that, in spite of the commonly accepted classification of LF as a pidgin, a close scrutiny of the variety recorded in the *Dictionnaire* reveals a number of non-pidgin-like characteristics. The present chapter considers the place of the *Dictionnaire*'s LF in the taxonomy of outcomes of language contact. Revisiting the key structural features of this variety of LF, it shows that, while some of the features are consistent with a pidginization account of its origin, others receive a more convincing explanation within the framework of koineization. Following a background discussion of the issue in Section 9.1, Section 9.2 focuses on the structural characteristics of LF which may be attributed to pidginization processes, and Section 9.3 on those which are attributable to koineization. Section 9.4 concludes the chapter, and the book, by discussing the view of LF as a structural continuum ranging from basilectal lects, more typical of speakers with non-Romance linguistic backgrounds, to acrolectal ones, more typical of speakers of Romance languages.

9.1 Introduction

The place of LF in the taxonomy of linguistic systems is an issue of long standing. It was first brought to public attention in an open discussion in the London literary magazine *Athenaeum* (Clarke and Bonaparte 1877). The exchange was prompted by the publication of the essay *On the Existence of Mixed Languages*, written in response to "an advertisement offering a prize for an Essay on the subject of Mixture in Languages" (Clough 1876: n.p.; see Lang 1992: 64; Operstein 2007: 235; Appendix D). One of the discussants, Hyde Clarke, denied LF the status of a separate language ("there is no such separate language as Lingua Franca"), while the other, Prince Louis-Lucien Bonaparte, offered a different take:

> The Indo-Portuguese of Ceylon, the Negro-Dutch of the Danish-American islands, the different French-creolese dialects, etc., stand in the same dialectal relation to the literary languages of Portugal, Holland, and France, as the LF does to the standard Italian. (Clarke and Bonaparte 1877: 640)

An earlier view essentially along the same lines as Bonaparte's is expressed in Anonymous (1852):

D'après quelques érudits, la langue franque et son congénère le *sabir* ne seraient qu'un dialecte roman, ce que ferait remonter leur origine à la langue des Cicéron, des Virgile, des Jules César. (cited in Cifoletti 1989: 195)

[According to some scholars, Lingua Franca and its congener *sabir* are nothing more than a Romance dialect, which would take their origin back to the language of Ciceros, Virgils, Julius Caesars.]

In contemporary linguistic literature, LF is usually classified as a pidgin (e.g., Foltys 1984–1985: 1–2; Bakker 1994: 27; Smith 1994: 355; Holm 2000: 15; Thomason 2001: 162; Couto 2002: 169; Velupillai 2015: 151).[1] On the basis of a structural comparison between LF and known cross-linguistic properties of pidgins, Couto (2002: 169) concludes: "Enfim, por qualquer critério que o abordemos, a LF confirma a unanimidade reinante no meio crioulístico de que ela é um pidgin" [In short, no matter what criterion we apply, LF confirms the unanimity prevailing in the creolist milieu that it is a pidgin]. In the face of this apparent unanimity, the following reservations are instructive:

Although Lingua Franca is traditionally categorized as a pidgin language, there is some reason to qualify this classification. As was already observed by Schuchardt (1909), some of its linguistic features, such as the generalized use of the infinitive, suggest that Lingua Franca may perhaps be more accurately viewed as a form of Foreigner Talk. Other linguists (e.g., Minervini 1996)[2] have claimed that it should rather be seen as a second-language variety of Italian. And since Italian and Spanish, the languages that formed the basis for Lingua Franca, were closely related dialects rather than separate languages five centuries ago, it might perhaps more appropriately be categorized as a koiné, i.e. the product of dialect convergence. (Arends 2005: 625)

Pidgins are conceptualized as a distinct type in the typology of contact languages (Thomason 1997, 2001; Bakker and Matras 2013; Parkvall 2019), though, as summarized by Parkvall and Bakker (2013: 19–25), attempts at defining this language type satisfactorily generally have not been successful. In their own typological study of pidgins, the first of its kind in its extent and scope, Parkvall and Bakker distill a small set of linguistic and social criteria which they consider "essential parts of pidginhood" (p. 21) and which they employ to set pidgins apart from other linguistic systems, including creoles, L2 varieties, and natively spoken languages. The structural criterion in this set merely states that a pidgin "is highly reduced lexically and grammatically

[1] Also Mufwene (1997: 56) (see related discussion in Tuten 2003: 76–79).
[2] Minervini (1996a).

compared to its input languages" (p. 22). This criterion forms part of the provisional definition of pidgins that Parkvall and Bakker adopt:

A pidgin is a language which (a) functions as a ***lingua franca****, and which (b) is lexically and structurally* ***extremely limited*** *in its communicative possibilities.* (Parkvall and Bakker 2013: 25, italics original)

The views outlined in the above-quoted passage from Arends (2005) derive in part from the ambiguous structural features of LF. As shown in Chapters 5–8 of this book, alongside features and developments that the *Dictionnaire*'s LF shares with pidgins – such as the loss or reduction of lexifier function words and inflectional categories, and replacement of synthetic structures with analytic ones – it also displays a number of unexpected developments and retentions of lexifier material. Thus, in the nominal system it retains gender marking on adjectives and personal pronouns, gender agreement in the noun phrase, articles, and proximal and distal demonstratives. In the verb system, it distinguishes aspect via suffixes on the verb and has the ability to express valence alternations by means of analytic causatives and inchoatives. In the area of functional categories, it has definite and indefinite articles and an array of clause connectors, question words, and prepositions. In the area of lexicon, it displays a substantial vocabulary rich in synonyms and well-developed derivational morphology. In the area of syntax, it makes functional use of word-order differences by inverting the order of nominal subjects and verbs in content questions, using the preverbal position for topicalization, and differentiating between the pre- and postnominal placement of adjectives.

Yet another property which makes the *Dictionnaire*'s LF atypical, from the perspective of pidgins, is its mutual intelligibility with at least some of its Romance lexifiers, for, as noted by Parkvall and Bakker (2013: 23), "[p]idgins tend to be mutually incomprehensible with their respective input languages" (see also Thomason 1997: 83). LF's instant intelligibility to Romance speakers is clear from Haedo's (1612) description: "los christianos," he says, "se acomodan al momento a aquel hablar" [Christians adapt themselves at once to this dialect] (cited in Cifoletti 1989: 158; see also Operstein 2007). The criterion of mutual intelligibility with the lexifiers not only distances LF from pidgins but also brings it closer to koines, the outcome of contact between genetically related, typologically similar, and mutually intelligible linguistic systems (Siegel 1985: 365).

LF additionally differs from pidgins in the provenance of its lexicon. While pidgin languages derive the bulk of their lexicons either from a single lexifier or from two lexifiers in roughly equal numbers,[3] the vocabulary of LF derives

[3] "Most pidgins derive almost all of their vocabulary from one language .... There are also pidgins with a mixed lexicon deriving from two languages ... ." (Bakker 2008: 137). "The pidgin lexicon in most documented cases derives primarily from one single language, with only

from several Romance languages, in proportions that vary historically and geographically. For example, one of the differences between the LF of Goldoni and the *Dictionnaire*'s is the abundance of Venetianisms in the former variety (Zago 1986); post-1830 sources document an increase in the number of Gallicisms and Arabisms in the LF of Algiers (Cifoletti 1994a, 1994b). Haedo (1612) provides a vivid illustration of the dynamics of relexification by remarking on sudden infusion of Portuguese words into the LF of Algiers "despues que de Tetuan, y Fez truxeron a Argel grandissimo numero de portugueses, que se perdieron en la batalla del Rey de Portugal, don Sebastian" [after they brought to Algiers from Tetuan and Fez a very large number of Portugese who were lost in the battle of the King of Portugal Don Sebastian] (cited in Cifoletti 1989: 158). The etymological composition of its lexicon, like mutual intelligibility with its lexifiers, makes LF similar to koines: as emphasized by Siegel (2001: 182–183), in koineization "there is no one 'lexifier'; several of the varieties in contact share in providing the lexical and morphological content."

The structural characteristics of the *Dictionnaire*'s LF may be understood by reference to the sociohistorical context in which it became stabilized: the multilingual slaving cultures and societies of the Maghreb between the sixteenth and nineteenth centuries (Cifoletti 2000, 2004). In this linguistic ecology, LF was used both for in-group communication among individuals with Romance language backgrounds – captives from Romance-speaking lands – and out-group communication between them and the local population, including their Arabic-, Turkish-, and Berber-speaking masters, as well as with fellow captives from non-Romance-speaking nations. The formation and continued transmission of LF thus necessarily involved two radically different types of contact: contact among genetically related, typologically congruent, and to various degrees mutually intelligible Romance languages, and contact between Romance and non-Romance languages. The two types of contact would have taken place concurrently and in the same sociolinguistic space, producing an outcome that is structurally nonuniform. While contact of the first type is expected to produce an outcome that is typologically congruent with the participating linguistic systems and is best understood within the framework of koineization, contact of the second type is expected to result in a more drastic restructuring of the lexifiers' structures and receives a better account within the framework of pidginization.

minor contributions from the other speech varieties involved .... However, there are also some pidgins where the lexicon is derived from two languages in roughly equal numbers, probably in special social circumstances" (Parkvall and Bakker 2013: 33).

The mechanisms of language change underlying pidginization and koineization, though fundamentally similar (cf. Mufwene 1997, 2001; Siegel 1997, 2001), differ in some of their aspects:

> Koineization is similar to pidginization in that both processes arise from contact between speakers of different linguistic varieties and may result in a new variety, which usually shows features of the varieties in contact and is reduced and simplified in comparison. However, the two processes are fundamentally different in other ways. The varieties in contact which lead to koineization are more typologically similar than those which lead to pidginization. Furthermore, koineization is a slow, gradual process which requires continued contact and integration among the speakers of the different varieties, whereas pidginization is a rapid process not requiring such integration. (Siegel 1985: 376)

The structural dimension highlighted in the above passage concerns the degree of typological congruence among the languages in contact, and the social one revolves around the degree of social and cultural integration among the speakers. As each dimension admits of a continuum of variation, the contact variety to emerge from a given contact situation may also be conceptualized as located on a continuum between a typical pidgin and a typical koine. When the contact situation involves both related and unrelated languages, and both culturally homogeneous and heterogeneous groups, as is the case here, the linguistic outcome of the contact is expected to combine the structural characteristics of a pidgin and a koine.

This chapter attempts to separate the structural components of LF which may be attributed to pidginization from those attributable to koineization. Methodologically, this involves two types of comparisons. The first consists in comparing selected key structural features of LF with the corresponding features of naturalistically acquired and foreigner talk versions of its lexifiers. This approach rests on the large body of research which connects pidginization with processes underlying naturalistic second language acquisition (SLA) and the formation of foreigner talk (FT), a speech register used by native speakers for communication with "outsiders who are felt to have very limited command of the language or no knowledge of it at all" (Ferguson 1971: 143). FT may be one of a range of simplified registers handled by a speech community; Ferguson (1971: 143) observes that such registers are embedded in the community's culture and are "culturally transmitted like any other part of the language and may be quite systematic and resistant to change." Clements (2003: 247) argues "that the difference between natural L2 varieties and pidgins is one of degree and not of type" and reports on research on Hiri Motu which suggests that this pidgin had its beginnings in Motu FT (p. 250; see Lal and Fortune 2000: 72, Thomason 2001: 83). Thomason and Kaufman (1988) provide additional examples of deliberate native-speaker simplification in FT and emphasize its role as a "social distancer" (p. 175) aimed at impeding access to the full language. Lanly (1962: 37–39) attributes certain structural characteristics of North African French to deliberate simplification by native speakers.

Ferguson and DeBose (1977) argue that pidgins are the outcome of interaction and mutual accommodation between SLA and FT versions of the lexifier. More recently, Plag (2008a, 2008b, 2009a, 2009b) has fleshed out the hypothesis that creoles are conventionalized interlanguages (learners' varieties) of an early stage by systematically comparing cross-linguistic findings on L2 acquisition of selected structural features with the corresponding features of creoles. In light of this theoretical background (see also Chaudenson 2001: 154–161; Siegel 2008a), it is legitimate to look for evidence of pidginization in an explicit comparison between the key structural features of LF and the corresponding features of FT and L2 varieties of its Romance lexifiers.

Unlike pidginization, which may disrupt the typological continuity between the lexifier and the contact variety based on it, koineization produces an outcome that is typologically continuous with the participating linguistic systems (Siegel 1985: 371; 2001: 183). In light of this distinction, it is legitimate to look for evidence of koineization in a typological comparison between LF and its Romance lexifiers. As noted in Chapter 7, the Romance linguistic type is commonly defined by taking into account both the synchronic structural features of Romance languages and their shared structural-typological evolution from Latin. This approach will be followed in the discussion below.

9.2 Pidginization

In this section, selected key structural features of the *Dictionnaire*'s LF are compared with the corresponding features in naturalistically acquired and foreigner talk varieties of its lexifiers. The features in question are the use of the Romance infinitive as the unmarked verb form, the use of the Romance past participle as the other verb form, and elimination of lexifier functional elements and morphosyntactic categories. Since the LF variety captured in the *Dictionnaire* is heavily Italianized, the focus of the remarks below is on Italian FT and naturalistically acquired L2 Italian, particularly learners' varieties arising from untutored (unguided, naturalistic, spontaneous) acquisition of Italian in the context of immigration. As emphasized by Vedovelli (1983), immigrants acquiring the language of the host country informally form a coherent sociolinguistic and socioeconomic group:

Tali parlanti sono adulti, si trovano in situazione di immigrazione, hanno appreso la lingua italiana al di fuori delle strutture formative, sotto la spinta dei bisogni sociali legati al loro ruolo di manodopera: essi hanno appreso l'italiano 'spontaneamente.' (Vedovelli 1983: 354)

[Such speakers are adults, are found in the situation of immigration, have learned Italian outside formal structures, under the pressure of social needs tied to their role as laborers; they have learned Italian 'spontaneously.']

Bernini (1986: 179) stresses that, in untutored SLA, communication and acquisition take place simultaneously and in a context of cultural distance between the learners and the locals, with the learners' inferior social status inherent in communications of the type workman/foreman, tenant/landlord, immigrant/policeman. The inferior status of the foreign workers in countries in which there are large numbers of them is also emphasized by Berretta (1988b: 376), who speaks of "uno stereotipo dello straniero 'inferiore'" [an 'inferior' foreigner stereotype] prompting the use of FT. These extra-linguistic considerations make a comparison between LF and Italian interlanguages spontaneously acquired in the context of immigration particularly appropriate.[4]

9.2.1 *Imperfective*

9.2.1.1 Data In the *Dictionnaire*'s preface, the verb system of LF is described as consisting of two verb forms, one deriving from the Romance infinitive and the other from the Romance past participle:

Les verbes ne se conjuguent pas, ils n'ont que deux temps: l'infinitif qui est toujours terminé en *ir* ou *ar*, et le participe passé en *ito* ou *ato*, fém. *ita*, *ata*. Ex.: *fazir* faire, *fazito* fait; *andar* aller, *andato* allé. (Anonymous 1830a: n.p.)

[The verbs are not conjugated, they have only two tenses: the infinitive that always ends in *ir* or *ar* and the past participle in *ito* or *ato*, feminine *ita*, *ata*. Examples: *fazir* 'do,' *fazito* 'done'; *andar* 'go,' *andato* 'gone.']

The LF verb form deriving from the infinitive functions as the unmarked member of the above opposition: in the examples, it is found in imperfective contexts (see 1a, 1b), is used as the imperative (in 1c), and is the form of the verb when functioning as the complement of another verb (in 1d). As discussed in Chapter 7, in Haedo's (1612) LF the imperfective member of the two-form verb opposition is additionally realized by the second person singular imperative and third person singular present indicative forms.

(1) a. *mi pensar l'Algérino non combatir.*
1s think.IMPF the'Algerian NEG fight.IMPF
'Je pense que les Algériens ne se batront pas.'

[4] See Chaudenson (2001: 154ff.) and Mufwene (2010: 378) regarding the usefulness of the studies on naturalistic SLA for understanding creolization.

'I think Algerians won't fight.'
(Anonymous 1830a: 98)

b. *perqué non counchar paché*
why NEG want.IMPF peace
'Pour quoi ne fait-on pas la paix?'
'Why not make peace?'
(Anonymous 1830a: 98)

c. *portar café.*
bring.IMPF coffee
'Apportez le café.'
'Bring coffee.'
(Anonymous 1830a: 97)

d. *mi non poudir crédir.*
1s NEG be.able.IMPF believe.IMPF
'Je ne saurais croire.'
'I can't believe it.'
(Anonymous 1830a: 93)

9.2.1.2 Discussion Italian FT and naturalistically acquired L2 Italian both tend to use a single verb form as the unmarked form of the verb. The specific form fulfilling this function varies.

In Italian FT, the unmarked verb form is the infinitive (see the examples in 2). The reasons proposed for this choice include the use of the infinitive as the basic, citation form of the verb, both in Italian and in Romance languages in general; its use in commands; its overall frequency; and its perception by native speakers as a simple verb form well adapted for use with nonnatives (Berretta 1992: 141–143; Berruto 1993; Lipski 2002: 130; Bernini 2010b; Maiden 2011: 209). Another factor is the conservative and conventionalized nature of the FT register, emphasized by Ferguson (1971). Spinazzola (1984) found the FT in Goldoni's play *Una delle ultime sere del carnovale* similar to the contemporary FT elicited through a questionnaire, confirming the diachronic stability of this register in Italian. Lipski (n.d.) shows that the use of the infinitive as the basic verb form is common to the FT registers of several Romance languages, and is an instance of deliberate simplification by native speakers. In Spanish-speaking communities, this feature has been culturally transmitted as an integral part of the FT register for at least the last 500 years. Lipski's (n.d.) own study of elicited Spanish FT reveals that the incidence of infinitives in this register is positively correlated with cultural literacy in Spanish.

(2) a. *Io lavorare Bergamo. Tu?*
1s work.INF Bergamo 2s
'I work in Bergamo. And you?'
(Bernini 1986: 179)

b. *quale* *hotel* *cercare?*
which hotel look.for.INF
'Which hotel are you looking for?'
(Berretta 1992: 142)

c. *forse* *tu* *volere* *ostello* *per* *la* *gioventù*
perhaps 2s want.INF hostel for the youth
'Maybe you want a youth hostel?'
(Berretta 1992: 142)

In Italian interlanguages acquired spontaneously in Italy, the unmarked form of the verb tends to be the third person singular present indicative. In regular verbs of the first and second conjugation, this is formally the least marked form, being the minimal common denominator of the paradigm, cf. *parla* 'speaks,' *parla-re* 'to speak,' *parla-to* 'spoken,' *parla-ndo* 'speaking' (Berretta 1992: 142). Lipski (n.d.) points to the default status of the 3sg in L2 varieties of Romance languages, referencing its high text frequency and "relatively depleted verb morphology." The basicness of the third person singular in language contact and acquisition settings, and its pivotal role in verbal restructuring, are emphasized by Chaudenson (2001: 174). Another verb form attested as the default form in L2 varieties is the second person singular present indicative. This choice of form has been explained by its high frequency in spoken discourse, particularly as an impersonal second person singular (Bernini 1989: 198–199).

In Italian interlanguages of learners who receive little native-speaker input, have little ability to elaborate this input, and/or are exposed to large amounts of FT, the unmarked verb form is the infinitive (Berretta 1992: 140–141, 143; see the examples in 3). Berretta (1992) reports certain preference for the infinitive as the unmarked verb form in speakers whose L1 is Chinese, an isolating language, and mentions two other speakers with different L1s who oscillate between the present and the infinitive as basic forms. The infinitive also emerges as the basic verb form in L2 Italian which developed in the 1980s and 1990s among immigrants of various origins in German-speaking areas of Switzerland, functioning as a kind of lingua franca of the immigrant workforce (see Section 9.4.3). The use of the infinitive in that variety correlates with acquisition of Italian with little native-speaker input and strong exposure to FT (Berretta 1992: 141, 143; Dal Negro 1994; Berruto 2012: 60, 220).

(3) a. *volere* *una* *bicchiera?*
want.INF a glass
'Do you want a glass?'
(Berruto 1991: 345; the speaker's L1 is Serbo-Croatian)

b. *tu* *dove* *studiare?*
2s where study.INF

'Where do you study?'
(Berretta 1992: 141; the speaker's L1 is German)

c. *sabato* *domeniga* *stare* *casa*
Saturday Sunday be.INF home
'Saturday and Sunday I will be at home.'
(Banfi 1986: 233; the speaker's L1 is Arabic)

d. *io pensare quella bambina cercare per balone*
1s think.INF that girl look.for.INF for ball
'I think that girl is looking for a ball.'
(Berruto 1991: 347; the speaker's L1 is Greek)

e. *per me meglio quando io tutto scrivere*
for 1S.OBL better when 1s all write.INF
'it would be better for me to write everything down'
(Berretta 1988b: 220; the speaker's L1 is German)

In summary, the use of the Romance infinitive as the unmarked verb form in the *Dictionnaire*'s LF may be traced back to conventionalized, conservative, culturally transmitted FT registers of its Romance lexifiers. The congruence among the lexifiers with respect to the presence of this feature in their respective FT registers may have played a role as well (see Mufwene 2001, 2008; Ansaldo 2009; Clements 2012, 2014 on the impact of frequency, congruence, and perceptual salience on the retention of lexifier material in contact varieties). As discussed in Chapter 7, the Romance infinitive was refunctionalized in LF into the imperfective member of an aspect-based opposition. The, much less frequent, use of the second person singular imperative and third person singular indicative as alternative exponents of this aspectual form in the LF of Haedo (1612) is explainable by the presence of L2 varieties in the feature pool leading to the formation of LF (see Section 9.4.1).

9.2.2 *Perfective*

9.2.2.1 Data The second verb form in LF derives from the Italian past participle; though the LF vocabulary lists both the feminine and the masculine forms, only the latter is attested in textual examples (see Chapters 3 and 7). As illustrated in (4), it is used for perfective events or discrete events in the past (see also Cifoletti 2004: 43).

(4) a. *ti fato colatzioné?*
2s do.PF breakfast
'Avez-vous déjeuné?
'Have you had breakfast?'
(Anonymous 1830a: 96)

b. *mi non sentito nada.*
1s NEG hear.PF nothing
'Je n'ai rien entendu.'
'I haven't heard anything.'
(Anonymous 1830a: 98)

c. *mi mirato iéri.*
1s see.PF yesterday
'Je l'ai vu hier.'
'I saw him yesterday.'
(Anonymous 1830a: 94)

9.2.2.2 Discussion In naturalistic acquisition of Italian as a second language, TAM marking is acquired ahead of person marking. Within TAM, the first distinction to be expressed morphologically is aspectual, while the time of action is initially expressed by temporal adverbs and discourse strategies. Person morphology emerges later, and its absence is initially compensated for by explicit subject pronouns, which are not obligatory in native Italian (Berretta 1992: 132). Acquisition of the verb system proceeds through a consistent sequence of stages irrespective of the learners' first languages (cf. Klein and Perdue 1997). Of relevance here are the first two stages, described as follows in Berretta (1992: 132–135) (see also Crotta 1988; Giacalone Ramat and Banfi 1990; Berretta and Crotta 1991).

Premorphological stage. This stage is characterized by a mixture of different verb forms acquired in response to their frequency in the input. The forms are acquired as morphologically unanalyzed lexical units.

Aspectual opposition stage. At this stage, there emerges an opposition between the imperfective, expressed by the present indicative; and the perfective, expressed by the past participle. The present is the unmarked form in this opposition, appearing in the present, future, and past imperfective contexts; the past participle appears in past perfective and, more rarely, future perfective contexts. Early acquisition of the past participle in *-to* is explained by its morphological transparency, leading to analogical formations like *rispondato* for *risposto* (Italian *rispondere* 'to answer'). The resulting opposition of the type *parla / parlato* is analyzable as primarily aspectual and only secondarily temporal. It characterizes not only early interlanguages but also those that have become fossilized, suggesting that it captures the minimum necessary for communication. Infinitives also appear at this stage, mostly as dependent forms, more rarely in competition with the present indicative as the basic verb form.

Examples of auxiliary-less past participles in naturalistically acquired Italian interlanguages are given in (5).

(5) a. *Monika telefonato di Germania*
Monika telephone.PPLE of Germany
'Monika called from Germany'
(Bernini 1987: 143; the speaker's L1 is German)

b. *combaniato uno di bartire Egitto*
accompany.PPLE one of leave.INF Egypt
'I accompanied one who was leaving for Egypt'
(Bernini 1987: 142; the speaker's L1 is Arabic)

c. *Bambini dato botte a serpente. Mangiato banane tante.*
children give.PPLE blows to snake eat.PPLE bananas many

Anche Maliko mangiato banane tante. Anche io botte a serpente.
also Maliko eat.PPLE bananas many also 1S blows to snake
Dopo serpente morto.
then snake die.PPLE
'The children beat the snake. They ate many bananas. Maliko ate many bananas, too. I beat the snake, too. Then the snake died.'
(Berretta 1988a: 380; the speaker's L1 is Swahili)

d. *noi conosciuto loro on the boat*
1PL meet.PPLE 3PL on the boat
'We met them on the boat'
(Crotta 1988: 245; the speaker's L1 is Cantonese)

e. *quando venire n'italia loro autato*
when come.INF in.Italy 3PL help.PPLE
'When I arrived in Italy, they helped me'
(Banfi 1986: 233; the speaker's L1 is Arabic)

The use of auxiliary-less past participles as perfective verb forms has also been noted in naturalistically acquired L2 Spanish (see the examples in 6). Clements (2009: 151) hypothesizes that the L1 Mandarin speaker in his study "has identified the Spanish past participial suffix *-do* as another perfective marker."

(6) a. *Mi tio machado Estados Unido.*
my uncle leave.PPLE United States
'My uncle came to the Unted States.'
(Clements 2009: 151)

b. *Tu sabe Yuen Taiwan venido?*
2S knows Yuen Taiwan come.PPLE
'You know Yuen, who came from Taiwan?'
(Clements 2009: 151)

c. *Yuen más detlás viene. Yo más temprano llegado.*
Yuen more behind comes 1S more early arrive.PPLE

'Yuen came afterward. I came before her.'
(Clements 2009: 151)

The use of past participles unaccompanied by auxiliaries is found in some versions of Italian FT (illustrated in 7). Omission of the auxiliaries is part of the more general tendency to omit function words in extreme versions of FT.

(7) *Io pittore. Io nato Bergamo, pero io lavorare per Milano.*
1s painter 1s be.born.PPLE Bergamo but 1s work.INF for Milan

Milano grande città. Monografia, fatta Milano. [. . .] *Mio padre,*
Milan great city monograph make.PPLE Milan my father

mio papà, pittore, era Engadina. Dipingere acquarelli.
my dad painter was Engadin paint.INF watercolors

Voi conoscere Engadina? [. . .]
2PL know.INF Engadin
'I am a painter. I was born in Bergamo but I am working in Milan. Milan is a great city. The monograph, it was made in Milan. My father, my dad, a painter, was from Engadin. He painted watercolors. Do you know Engadin?'
(Berretta 1988a: 376)

In Simplified Italian of Ethiopia (SIE), the verb system consists of the infinitive and past participle (see 8). The latter is used "as a simple past tense," the former in the other contexts. On the part of the nonnative speakers of Italian examined by Habte-Mariam (1976), the only published source on this variety, SIE appears to represent a continuum of naturalistically acquired L2 varieties fossilized in the early stages.

(8) a. *bɛnire domani*
come.INF tomorrow
'Come tomorrow.'
(Habte-Mariam 1976: 178)

b. *kwando tu bɛnuto, ɨyo ja finito*
when 2s come.PPLE 1s already finish.PPLE
'When you came, I had already finished.'
(Habte-Mariam 1976: 178)

In summary, the aspect-based two-form verb system of the *Dictionnaire*'s LF is found in naturalistically acquired early-stage and fossilized Italian interlanguages. The use of past participles without auxiliaries in these varieties is reinforced by two tendencies, the lag in the acquisition of the auxiliaries by L2 learners and their suppression by native speakers in drastically reduced versions of FT. As discussed in Chapter 7, the Romance past participle was grammaticalized in LF as the perfective member of the aspectual opposition.

9.2.3 *Morphosyntactic Reduction*

The *Dictionnaire*'s LF lacks a number of structural categories and functional elements of its Romance lexifiers. These include nominal number, person inflection on verbs, case distinction in personal pronouns, pronominal clitics and possessives, nonmodal auxiliaries, and the copula deriving from Lat. *esse(re).* These losses may be attributed to reduction of functional elements and categories in extreme FT and rudimentary SLA varieties of the lexifiers.

Cross-linguistic studies show that the kinds of free functional elements that tend to be omitted in FT and SLA varieties include copulas, auxiliaries, articles, prepositions, and pronominal clitics (Ferguson 1971: 147; Ferguson and DeBose 1977: 104; Berretta 1988b: 219; 1992: 138–139; Berruto 1993; Bernini 2010b). In naturalistically acquired L2 Italian, the probability of some of these elements' being omitted is correlated with their phonetic and semantic salience; for example, *è* 's/he is,' *ho* 'I have,' and *ha* 's/he has' are more likely to be omitted than *sono* 'I am; they are,' *siamo* 'we are,' or *abbiamo* 'we have'; and the prepositions *per* 'for, by' and *con* 'with' are less likely to be omitted than the purely grammatical *a* before infinitives and genitive *di* (Berretta 1992: 138–139). Examples of omission of functional elements in L2 Italian are given in (9); the omitted elements are italicized in the native equivalents.

(9) a. *quando* *guerra* *finito*
when war end.PPLE
'quando *la* guerra *è* finita'
'when the war ended'
(Berretta 1988b: 219; the speaker's L1 is German)

b. *non* *cabito*
NEG understand.PPLE
'non *ho* capito'
'I did not understand'
(Bernini 1986: 180; the speaker's L1 is Arabic)

c. *va* *lavorare*
goes work.INF
'va *a* lavorare'
's/he is going to work'
(Berretta 1988b: 219; the speaker's L1 is German)

Processes that characterize naturalistic L2 acquisition of Italian are summarized by Vedovelli (1989: 88; 1991a: 427; 1991b: 128):

- Use of free morphemes, resulting in a lack of agreement, invariable forms, replacement of synthetic forms with analytic ones;
- Reduction of noun and verb morphology, including TAM, number, and person marking;

- Overgeneralization of the present indicative or infinitive forms and the past participle;
- Elimination of the copula, frequent absence of the main verb, omission or incorrect use of function words (articles, prepositions, auxiliaries);
- A reduced system of personal pronouns, possessive adjectives, and demonstratives;
- Use of repetition to express plurality, large quantities, or progressive actions;
- A high degree of variability in grammatical agreement;
- Analogical formation of verb forms;
- Transfer features.

Some of the most salient features of Italian FT are summarized by Valentini (1994: 398–399):

- Omission of function words and free functional morphemes (articles, prepositions, clitic pronouns, auxiliaries, copulas);
- Use of the infinitive instead of inflected verb forms;
- Presence of nonobligatory subject pronouns;[5]
- Generalization of the negative morpheme *no / niente*;
- Preference for short sentences and parataxis;
- Massive presence of questions;
- Preference for the more frequent lexemes, hypernyms, and concrete terms;
- Frequent repetitions and reformulations with paraphrases or synonyms.

Berretta (1986: 329) further notes that clitic pronouns tend to be replaced in Italian FT with stressed pronominal forms, while omission of verbal morphology finds a functional substitute in the use of explicit subjects, expressed via stressed pronouns or lexical items (Berretta 1988: 383–384). The presence of these features in FT is variable, with the most drastically restructured varieties observed in situations of strong asymmetry in the social status of the interlocutors (Valentini 1994: 399). This characteristic of the FT register is also stressed by Fergusen and DeBose (1977):

> [. . .] FT registers may vary in degree of 'foreignness,' i.e., the incidence of FT features may vary from slight to very full depending chiefly on the speaker's assessment of the addressee's status and level of competence in the language. More typical of FT variation, however, is the 'vertical' dimension of 'talking up' versus 'talking down'. (p. 105)

[5] The comparable feature in French is emphasized by Lanly (1955, 1962) and Chaudenson (2001: 176) in connection with its evolution in colonial settings.

Table 9.1. *Typological discontinuities between Lingua Franca and its Romance lexifiers*

Romance lexifiers	Lingua Franca
Nonmodal auxiliaries	No nonmodal auxiliaries
Copula derived from **esse(re)*	No copula derived from **esse(re)*
Possessives	No possessives
Clitic pronouns	No clitic pronouns
Person inflection on verbs	No person inflection on verbs
Number inflection on nouns	No number inflection on nouns
Case distinction in personal pronouns	No case distinction in personal pronouns
Infinitive	Imperfective
Past participle	Perfective

Other factors causing structural variation in FT include the individual speaker's ability to perceive and reduce complexity in their native language and the frequency of their contacts with nonnatives (Bernini 2010b). The latter factor leads Valentini (1994: 407) to conjecture that the conventionalized FT register of the type envisaged by Ferguson and DeBose (1977) has to be specially acquired by native speakers through frequent contact with nonnatives.

9.2.4 Summary

The loss of the lexifiers' functional elements and structural categories in LF may be seen as a result of mutual accommodation between the FT and SLA varieties of the lexifiers, particularly the more drastically restructured FT and the more rudimentary SLA ones. One outcome of this process is a disruption of the typological continuity between the lexifiers and the contact variety based on them; such disruption may be interpreted as evidence of pidginization (Siegel 1985, 2001).

Some of the more salient morphosyntactic differences between LF and its Romance lexifiers, attributable to such processes, are summarized in Table 9.1. The first four comprise losses of free functional elements of the lexifiers,[6] the

[6] Clitic pronouns are acquired in parallel with verbal morphology and are said to be located halfway between free morphemes and verbal inflection (see Berretta 1986: 329; 1988a).

next three concern elimination of functional categories expressed via bound morphology, and the remaining two capture functional differences between categories that are formally identical, nonfinite verb forms in the lexifiers versus members of an aspectual opposition in LF.

It is possible that the absence in LF of the functional elements of the lexifiers was not categorical. As noted in Chapter 7, the LF passages in Haedo (1612) include a small number of inflected Romance verb forms, such as the imperative *mira* 'look' and the third person singular present *dole* 'hurts'; and both *ha portato* and the auxiliary-less *portato* for 'has brought.' The *Dictionnaire* marks singular and plural on a couple of nouns (cf. *orékia, -é* 'ear(s)') and lists a few inflected verb forms like *piové* 'it rains.' These facts point to the existence of different degrees of restructuring of the lexifier grammar in LF, which in turn suggests the existence of more pidgin-like and more koine-like idiolects.

9.3 Koineization

This section revisits selected structural features and diachronic developments of LF showing continuity with the corresponding features and evolutionary trends of its Romance lexifiers. The features to be reviewed are the etymological composition of the LF lexicon, word formation, verb classes, copula, personal pronouns, pronominal possession, and differential object marking.

9.3.1 Vocabulary

As discussed in Chapter 5, the lexicon of the *Dictionnaire*'s LF is overwhelmingly Romance. Its most numerous lexical components are Italian, Spanish, and French; lexical contributions from non-Romance languages are minor or nonexistent, with no Berber words, a handful of Turkish, Greek, and Latin words, and an Arabic component not exceeding those of Sicilian, Spanish, or Portuguese (Aslanov 2014). Cornelissen (1992) estimates that the LF vocabulary contains 58% Italo-Romance words, 27% words existing in more than one Romance language, and 6% Spanish, 4% French, 3% Arabic, and 2% Turkish, Portuguese, and Catalan words. Neither of the Swadesh wordlists in LF contains words from non-Romance sources. The Romance lexical mixture is emphasized by doublets deriving from different Romance languages, like *quérir* ~ *volir* 'to want' (< Sp. *querer*, It. *volere*); and hybrids whose features derive from different Romance sources (e.g., LF *forar* combines the semantics of Ven. *fora* 'out, outside' and It. *forare* 'to pierce, to make a hole in').

LF's lexical continuity with Romance languages extends to its word and lexeme formation techniques, which rely more on inherited mechanisms than the strategies characteristic of pidgins (multifunctionality, circumlocutions, polysemy) (Holm 2000; Parkvall and Bakker 2013). Multifunctionality (using "semantically and syntactically underspecified forms in different syntactic environments"; Plag 2009b: 356) is uncharacteristic of the *Dictionnaire*'s LF: in the few recorded cases, such as *parlar* 'to speak' ~ 'language' and *vekio* 'old' ~ 'old man,' LF's patterns merely continue those of the lexifiers (*parlare* 'to speak' ~ 'dialect,' *vecchio* 'old' ~ 'old man' in Italian). Since multifunctionality is attested in early stages of L2 acquisition of Romance languages, and in fossilized interlanguages, of speakers with typologically distant L1s (cf. Moretti 1990 for Italian and Clements 2003 for Spanish), its underutilization in LF may be correlated with the large number of Romance speakers among its creators and users. Polysemy is remarked upon in sources that postdate the *Dictionnaire* (e.g., Anonymous 1852), however, in the *Dictionnaire*'s LF, which boasts a substantial vocabulary and a number of synonymous word pairs, it is not excessive and distributed across the lexemes in a principled way. LF lacks an all-purpose preposition, a trait specifically mentioned by Arends (1997) as distinguishing LF from pidgins. LF matches its Romance lexifiers in its lexical typology, suppletion patterns, and in having periphrastic equivalents for a number of its verbs (Polák 1949; Dubský 1963). The sections below briefly recapitulate the strategies of complex word and multiword lexeme formation in the *Dictionnaire*'s LF, which also match those of its Romance lexifiers.

9.3.1.1 Affixation As noted in Chapter 5, the single most important word formation device in Romance languages is affixation, particularly suffixation (Rainer 2016a). LF preserves a fair amount of Romance derivational affixation (see 10) and also uses Romance derivational patterns to create new words: Cifoletti (2004: 56, 74) mentions *balador* 'dancer,' *fougidor* 'deserter,' *biancador* 'launderer,' *cazéria* 'barracks,' and *forar* 'to remove, discard, pull out' as possible LF innovations (see also Schuchardt 1909: 446).

(10) a.

VERB		ACTION NOUN	
peskar	'to fish'	peska	'fishing'
caschar	'to hunt'	caschia	'hunting'
pagar	'to pay'	paga	'pay'
fougir	'to flee'	fouga	'flight'

b.

VERB		ACTION NOUN	
séparar	'to separate'	séparatzion	'separation'
occoupar	'to occupy'	occoupatzion	'occupation'
permettir	'to allow'	permitzion	'permission'
pounir	'to punish'	pounitzion	'punishment'

c.

VERB		AGENT NOUN	
peskar	'to fish'	peskador	'fisherman'
caschar	'to hunt'	caschador	'hunter'
cantar	'to sing'	cantador	'singer'
bévir	'drink'	bévidor	'drinker'

d.

NOUN		AGENT NOUN	
canon	'cannon'	canoniéré	'gunner'
timone	'rudder'	timoniéré	'helmsman'
tésoro	'treasure'	tésoriéré	'treasurer'
tintoura	'dye'	tintouriéré	'dry cleaner'

e.

ADJECTIVE		CAUSATIVE VERB	
sporco	'dirty'	sporcar	'to make dirty'
limpio	'clean'	limpiar	'to clean'
vouoto	'empty'	vouotar	'to empty'
inqouiéto	'anxious'	inqouiétar	'to worry'

f.

ADJECTIVE		QUALITY NOUN	
largo	'wide'	largetza	'width'
sporco	'dirty'	sporquetza	'filth'
locou	'crazy'	loketza	'craziness'
grandé	'large'	grandetza	'greatness'

g.

ADJECTIVE		QUALITY NOUN	
cativo	'bad'	cativitä	'nastiness'
sincéro	'sincere'	sincérita	'sincerity'
oscouro	'dark'	oscourita	'darkness'
sensibilé	'sensitive'	sensibilita	'sensitivity'

h.

VERB		ANTONYM	
piacher	'to please'	dispiacher	'to displease'
armar	'to arm'	disarmar	'to disarm'
onorar	'to honor'	disonorar	'to dishonor'

i.

ADJECTIVE		ANTONYM	
certo	'certain'	incerto	'uncertain'
outilé	'useful'	inoutilé	'useless'
possibilé	'possible'	impossibilé	'impossible'

9.3.1.2 Compounding LF makes limited use of compounding without a linking morpheme. It includes a handful of compounds inherited from the lexifiers (illustrated in 11a) and two probable neologisms built to a common lexifier pattern (in 11b).

(11) a. campo santo 'cemetery'
sottoterréno 'underground'

b. fora-tapa 'corkscrew'
fora-balla 'bullet-forceps'

The *Dictionnaire* also contains syntagmatic nominal compounds of the type noun-*di*-noun (the majority type), noun-adjective, and adjective-noun (see 12). These continue common Romance patterns, cf. *luna di miele* 'honeymoon,' *terzo mondo* 'third world' in Italian; *ojo de buey* 'porthole,' *perro caliente* 'hot dog' in Spanish.

(12)

French	Lingua Franca	Literal gloss	Gloss
saumure	agoua di salé	'water of salt'	'brine'
sain-doux	grasso di porco	'fat of pig'	'lard'
boulet	balla di canone	'ball of cannon'	'cannonball'
rasoir	cortello di barba	'knife of beard'	'razor'
hachoir	cortello grosso	'large knife'	'cleaver'
sentier	picolo camino	'little road'	'path'

9.3.1.3 Multiword Lexemes Examples of multiword verbal LF lexemes are given in (13). These are created by combining verbs with object nouns, adverbs, adjectives, or prepositional phrases; the majority are built by using as support verbs semantically bleached verbs like *far ~ fazir* 'to do, make,' *dar* 'to give,' *mettir* 'to put,' and *forar* 'to remove, discard, pull out.'

(13)

French	Lingua Franca	Literal gloss	Gloss
éclairer	far loumé	'to make light'	'to light'
sceller	mettir taba	'to put seal'	'to seal'
enterrer	mettir in terra	'to put in ground'	'to bury'
raser	forar barba	'to remove beard'	'to shave'
saigner	forar sangré	'to let blood'	'to bleed'
surpayer	pagar tropo	'to pay too much'	'to overpay'

Some multiword lexemes are formed by modifying the base verb or adjective with *non* 'no, not,' *molto ~ mouchou(s)* 'very,' or *oun poco* 'a little.'

(14)

French	Lingua Franca	Literal gloss	Gloss
taire	non ablar	'not to speak'	'to be silent'
injuste	non jiousto	'not just'	'unjust'
opulent	molto riko	'very rich'	'opulent'
magnifique	mouchou bello	'very beautiful'	'magnificent'
tiède	oun poco caldo	'a little hot'	'warm'

Each of the above techniques of multiword lexeme formation continues patterns found in the lexifiers, some of which, in turn, continue tendencies present already in Latin (Korletjanu 1974). In a number of cases, as in *fazir frédo* 'it's cold,' LF continues specific multiword lexemes of the lexifiers (cf. *hacer frío* in Spanish, *far freddo* in Italian).

Table 9.2. *Verb classes in Lingua Franca*

	-ato	*-ito*	*-outo*
-ar	*escapar* *escapato*	—	*sédar* *sédouto*
-ir	—	*fazir* *fazito*	*vénir* *vénouto*

In summary, the word and lexeme formation patterns in the *Dictiononaire*'s LF continue those of its Romance lexifiers: affixation and a range of multiword lexeme types, particularly noun-*di*-noun compounds and verbal lexemes with semantically bleached support verbs. Patterns that are less productive in the lexifiers, such as prefixation, compounding, and repetition, are correspondingly less productive in LF. In its word and lexeme formation, the *Dictionnaire*'s LF emerges as typically Romance.

9.3.2 Verb Classes

9.3.2.1 Data The *Dictionnaire*'s preface states that the LF verb form deriving from the Romance infinitive ends in *-ar* or *-ir*, and the one deriving from the Romance past participle ends in *-ato* or *-ito* (see Section 9.2.1.1). This description captures the bulk of the forms recorded in the body of the *Dictionnaire*, though it misses the patterns in *-ir* ~ *-outo*, *-ar* ~ *-outo*, and the verbs whose past participles are irregular (see Table 9.2 and the examples in 15 below).

Romance infinitives of the first conjugation (those ending in *-ar* in Spanish, *-are* in Italian, and *-er* in French) are generally adapted to the LF imperfective in *-ar*, and those of the remaining conjugations to the LF imperfective in *-ir* (see Table 9.3).

The adaptation patterns of Romance infinitives which deviate from the majority patterns in Table 9.3 are illustrated in (15) (see also Schuchardt 1909: 456–457).

(15)	sanir	'to cure, recover'	(< Sp. sanar, It. sanare)
	composir	'to arrange'	(< Fr. composer)
	sédir ~ sédar	'to sit down'	(< It. sedere)
	imparir	'to teach'	(< It. imparare)
	imparar	'to learn'	

The *Dictionnaire* does not provide the perfective form for each and every LF verb; where provided, the patterns of adaptation are generally as shown

Table 9.3. *Adaptation of Romance infinitives in Lingua Franca*

Lingua Franca		Spanish	Italian	French
-ar	*ablar*	*hablar*		
	mirar	*mirar*		
	cascar		*cascare*	
	mangiar		*mangiare*	
	avalar			*avaler*
	désirar			*desirer*
-ir	*escondir*	*esconder*		
	inchir	*henchir*		
	conoschir		*conoscere*	
	fougir		*fuggire*	
	intendir			*entendre*
	sortir			*sortir*

in Table 9.4, with the French forms in *-é*, *-i*, and *-u* adapted to the LF forms in *-ato*, *-ito*, and *-outo*, respectively; and the Spanish form in *-ado* adapted as *-ato*, and the one in *-ido* as *-ito* or *-outo*. Irregular past participles are generally inherited intact (though not in the case of *fazir* 'to do'; see 16).

(16)

Lingua Franca	Source forms	
perdir / perso	It. perdere / perso	'to lose'
fingir / finto	It. fingere / finto	'to feign'
rompir / roto	Sp. romper / roto	'to break'
fazir / fazito	Ptg. fazer / feito	'to do'

The next section addresses the question of how the LF distinction between two verb classes in the imperfective (*-ar*, *-ir*) and three in the perfective (*-ato*, *-ito*, *-outo*) may be contextualized in relation to the verb class systems of its lexifiers.

9.3.2.2 Discussion Classical Latin verbs are divided into inflectional classes (conjugations) based on the theme vowel in the present active infinitive (see Table 9.5).

Of the four Latin conjugations, the first (*-āre*) and the fourth (*-īre*) were the most numerous and the most clearly differentiated morphologically. This state

Table 9.4. *Adaptation of Romance past participles in Lingua Franca*

Lingua Franca		Spanish	Italian	French
-ato	*ablato*	*hablado*		
	cascato		*cascato*	
	avalato			*avalé*
-ito	*inchito*	*henchido*		
	fougito		*fuggito*	
	enrikito		*(arrichito)*	*enrichi*
-uto	*escondouto*	*escondido*		
	conoschiuto		*conosciuto*	
	intendouto			*entendu*

Table 9.5. *Verb classes in Latin*

Inflection class	Inflection class marker	Example	Gloss
I conjugation	ā	am-ā-re	'to love'
II conjugation	ē	flor-ē-re	'to blossom'
III conjugation	ĕ	fug-ĕ-re	'to flee'
IV conjugation	ī	aud-ī-re	'to hear'

of affairs continues in Romance languages, where the first and the fourth conjugations are the most productive and numerically predominant. The degree of productivity of the fourth conjugation varies from language to language: thus, French has about 4,000 first conjugation (*-er*) verbs and about 300 fourth conjugation (*-ir*) verbs (Korletjanu 1974: 196). In Romanian, 392 out of 803 basic high-frequency verbs belong to the first (*-a*) conjugation and 263 to the fourth (*-i*) conjugation; borrowed verbs are incorporated into one of these conjugations (Chitoran 2002: 53; Costanzo 2011: 81). The first conjugation had swelled already in Vulgar Latin thanks to in-migration of verbs from the other classes, novel formations such as *cantare* for *canere* 'to sing,' and incorporation of Greek borrowings (Korletjanu 1974: 194–196). The first conjugation continues to grow in individual Romance languages, while at the same time developing a "propensity for resistance to allomorphy" (Maiden 2011: 212):

[T]hroughout the history of virtually all Romance languages the first conjugation contains the overwhelming majority of lexical verbs, and is the predominant one used for derived forms, the production of neologisms, and borrowing (as was already the case in Latin; see Sihler 1995: 528). (Maiden 2011: 212)

The second (*-ēre*) and third (*-ĕre*) conjugations had merged in Vulgar Latin and remain unproductive in Romance languages (Korletjanu 1974: 195–196). These verb classes have also suffered some attrition due to migration of the verbs to the more productive first or fourth conjugations: for example, third-conjugation verbs in *-io* (e.g., *fugio, fugĕre* 'to flee') and some second-conjugation verbs in *-ēo* (e.g., *floreo, florēre* 'to flourish') have migrated to the fourth conjugation (cf. *huir* 'to flee' in Spanish, *fiorire* 'to flourish' in Italian). The process of attrition continued throughout the individual histories of the Romance languages, resulting in differences in the class membership of individual verbs; compare, for example *hervir* 'to boil' and *poseer* 'to own' in Spanish with *ferver* and *possuir* in Portuguese (< Latin *fervēre, possidēre*) (Stovicek 2010: 3). The strong status of the first and fourth conjugations, as compared to the second and third, is also evident in the patterns of neutralization of inflection class distinctions:

By far the commonest type of partial conjugational neutralization involves loss of distinction between non-first conjugation verbs, resulting in a binary opposition between first conjugation and non-first conjugation. There are also a few cases in which the fourth conjugation remains distinct, and the others are neutralized. I am unaware of any neutralization affecting first and fourth, and leaving second and third conjugations distinct. (Maiden 2011: 207)

The general development of inflectional verb classes in the evolution from Latin to Romance is characterized by the following trends (based on Korletjanu 1974; Maiden 2011, 2016):

- Reduction in the number of verb classes;
- Growth of the first (*-āre*) and fourth (*-īre*) conjugations;
- Merger of the second (*-ēre*) and third (*-ĕre*) conjugations;
- Migration of second- and third-conjugation verbs to the first or fourth conjugation;
- The first conjugation is kept distinct, with neutralizations affecting the other conjugations;
- "[I]n most Romance languages the sole, or predominant, productive class is the first conjugation" (Maiden 2016: 509);
- "Across Romance, at least three conjugational distinctions are preserved in the infinitive" (Maiden 2016: 509);

Table 9.6. *Verb classes in Italian and Spanish*

Language	Form	First conjugation	Second conjugation	Third conjugation
Italian	Infinitive	*lev-a-re*	*vend-e-re*	*dorm-i-re*
	Past participle	*lev-a-to*	*vend-u-to*	*dorm-i-to*
Spanish	Infinitive	*llev-a-r*	*vend-e-r*	*dorm-i-r*
	Past participle	*llev-a-do*	*vend-i-do*	*dorm-i-do*

- "[T]he infinitive and the past participle are the main loci of retention of conjugational distinctions" (Maiden 2011: 208).

Italian and Spanish each distinguish three verb conjugations in the infinitive (Napoli and Vogel 1990; Butt and Benjamin 2004; Patota 2006). Outside the infinitive, the neutralization of conjugational distinctions appears to be more advanced in Spanish than in Italian: for example, Italian has a three-way distinction in the past participle, while Spanish has merged the past participles of non–first conjugation verbs (Maiden 2011: 205; 2016: 510) (see Table 9.6).[7]

In Italian, only the *-are* verbs and a subclass of the *-ire* verbs (those with the augment *-isc-*) are synchronically productive (Schwarze 1999: 3). The *-are* verbs show no stem allomorphy, while the *-ire* verbs have it only in the present indicative and subjunctive. The most stem allomorphy is displayed by the *-ere* conjugation (Da Tos 2012: 98–101; Maiden 2016: 510–511).

In Spanish, the *-ar* conjugation has retained all of its members and acquired new ones through borrowing from non-Romance languages, in-migration of verbs from the other classes, and accommodation of derived (denominal, deadjectival) verbs; this conjugation is "the main recipient of verbs from other sources" (Penny 2002: 172). The *-ir* conjugation has retained all surviving *-īre* verbs and acquired new members through borrowing from Germanic, learned borrowings from Latin, and migrated *-er* verbs. The *-er* conjugation has acquired few new verbs and has lost a number of its members to the *-ir* class; in medieval texts, some originally *-er* verbs appear in both *-er* and *-ir* forms (Penny 2002: 172–173). In present-day Spanish, only the *-ar* conjugation is synchronically productive in the sense that new verbs are accommodated to the morphology of this conjugation (Stovicek 2010: 31).

7 The *-ere* conjugation in Italian consists of *vedére*-type and *léggere*-type verbs (Maiden 2011: 202; 2016: 509).

Seen against the background of the above diachronic trends, the structural developments of the *Dictionnaire*'s LF proceed in the same direction as, and increment,[8] the corresponding developments in the lexifiers. By reducing the number of verb classes in the imperfective, LF increments the Romance diachronic trend to reduce the number of conjugations in the infinitive. The way in which this reduction is achieved – via merger of non–first conjugation verbs – mirrors the corresponding developments in the lexifiers. The way the merger proceeds in LF – through elimination of the *-er* class in favor of the *-ir* class – is also in agreement with the Romance diachronic trend to strengthen the *-ir(e)* conjugation at the expense of the *-er(e)* one. The phonological basis of the *-er* / *-ir* merger in LF, hypothesized by some researchers, also fits in with the Romance developments where the merger of the *-er(e)* and the *-ir(e)* verbs has a basis in phonological neutralizations (Penny 2002: 173; Maiden 2016: 510). Finally, although the *-ir* class contains both the *-ir* and the *-er* verbs of the lexifiers, *-ar* is still the much larger verb class. The preponderance of *-ar* verbs in LF is also in line with the Romance diachronic trend to swell the *-a-* class at the expense of the other classes and by using it as the main repository for borrowings and neologisms. The productivity of the *-ar* class is confirmed by the neologism *forar*, which is adapted to the *-ar* conjugation.

The two-class system of the LF imperfective, in which the *-ar* class contains descendants of the Latin first conjugation and the *-ir* class those of the Latin second, third, and fourth conjugations, finds parallels in some Romance languages, such as Sicilian (Costanzo 2011: 81) and Calabrese (Gardani 2016: 235). A more distant parallel is the merger between non–first conjugation past participles in Spanish and Portuguese (Harris-Northall 1996; see Table 9.7). After the Italian lexical layer (re-)introduced into LF the participle with the theme vowel *-u-*, there arose an unusual, from the Romance perspective, situation in which the number of conjugation classes in the past participle (*-ato*, *-ito*, *-outo*) is greater than in the infinitive (*-ar*, *-ir*). As observed by

[8] The notion of incrementation is taken from Labov (2007: 346), where it describes the process "in which successive cohorts and generations of children advance the change beyond the level of their caretakers and role models, and in the same direction over many generations." Here, it is used in the sense of advancing a change beyond its original scope. The following observations, made in connection with innovative developments in L2 Italian, are pertinent in projecting a similar notion onto a contact environment: "Gli apprendenti hanno sviluppato potentiali già contenuti nel sistema ma non attivati dai parlanti nativi . . . . Così, le varietà di apprendimento ed i fenomeni storici dei parlanti nativi vanno considerati due manifestazioni differenti di costrizioni in parte simili" [The learners have developed potentials already present in the system but not activated by native speakers. Thus, learners' varieties and the historical phenomena of native speakers should be considered two different manifestations of partially similar constraints] (Moretti 2000: 467). The issue of acceleration of ongoing changes in situations of intense language contact is addressed, e.g., by Vintilă-Rădulescu (1968), Silva-Corvalán (1986), Chaudenson (2001), and Orozco (2018).

Table 9.7. *Verb class mergers in Spanish, Portuguese, and Lingua Franca*

Language	Form	First conjugation	Second conjugation	Third conjugation
Medieval Spanish/ Portuguese	Infinitive	*-ar*	*-er*	*-ir*
	Past participle	*-ado*	*-udo*	*-ido*
Modern Spanish/ Portuguese	Infinitive	*-ar*	*-er*	*-ir*
	Past participle	*-ado*	*-ido*	
Lingua Franca	Imperfective	*-ar*	*-ir*	
	Perfective	*-ato*	*-uto*	*-ito*

Table 9.8. *Evolution of verb classes from Latin to Romance to Lingua Franca*

Latin > Romance	Romance > Lingua Franca
The number of verb classes in the infinitive is reduced from 4 to 3	The number of verb classes in the imperfective is reduced from 3 to 2
The *-e-* class is reduced or eliminated	The *-e-* class is eliminated
The *-i-* class is expanded	The *-i-* class is expanded
The *-a-* class predominates	The *-a-* class predominates

Maiden (2011: 204), "in no part of the Romance verb paradigm is the number of conjugational distinctions ever greater than in the infinitive."

The above developmental trends, summarized in Table 9.8, show continuity with the corresponding developments in LF's Romance lexifiers.

9.3.3 Copula *(e)star*

9.3.3.1 Data The *Dictionnaire* provides the following information about the verb *(e)star*:

Il n'y a qu'un seul verbe auxiliaire, *star* être, qui s'emploie également pour nos deux auxiliaires *être* et *avoir*. (Anonymous 1830a: n.p.)

[There is only one auxiliary verb, *star* 'to be,' which is employed for our two auxiliaries *be* and *have*.]

Though *star* is described above as an auxiliary, it is, in fact, used as an auxiliary only in the example *mi star andato* 'j'aurais été' ('I would go'), which is given in the preface immediately above this description. Cifoletti (2004: 43) notes that this example does not correspond to anything otherwise known about LF, and Foltys (1987: 67) offers a similar assessment. In the LF vocabulary and dialogues, *star* functions only as a copula (see 17).

(17) a. *il tempo star bello.*
the weather be.IMPF beautiful
'Il fait beau temps.'
'The weather is fine.'
(Anonymous 1830a: 97)

b. *qouesto libro star di mi.*
this book be.IMPF of 1s
'ce livre est à moi'
'this book is mine'
(Anonymous 1830a: 49)

c. *no, star forà.*
NEG be.IMPF outside
'Non, il est sorti.'
'No, he is out.'
(Anonymous 1830a: 94a)

9.3.3.2 Discussion Italian and Spanish each have two copulas, one derived from Latin *esse* / VL **essere* 'to be' and/or *sedere* 'to sit,' and the other from Latin *stare* 'to stand.' In Spanish, only *ser* (< *sedere*) occurs with nominal complements and only *estar* (< *stare*) with locative adverbial complements. With past participle and adjective complements, the choice of a copula results in semantic differences (exemplified in 18) (see Pountain 1982: 139–141).

(18) a. *Juan está enfermo.*
Juan *estar* ill
'Juan is ill.'
(Pountain 1982: 140)

b. *Juan es enfermo.*
Juan *ser* ill
'Juan is an invalid.'
(Pountain 1982: 140)

The diachronic evolution underpinning the above synchronic situation involved gradual semantic bleaching of *stare* and its encroachment on the functional domains of **esse(re)*, a development shared with other Romance languages. From the pan-Romance perspective, the degree of copularization of *stare* is at its most advanced in Spanish and Portuguese, with the contrast between the two copulas developed most consistently in Spanish (Pountain 1982: 139, 144). Catalan is behind its Iberian neighbors in the degree of grammaticalization of *stare*; Pountain (1982: 157) speaks of a "later 'drift' of Catalan towards a Castilian-like situation." In Italian and Romanian, *stare* has developed some additional lexical meanings as well as some copular and auxiliary functions; for example, Italian, like Spanish, uses this verb to form the continuous tense, as in It. *sto lavorando* / Sp. *estoy trabajando* 'I am working' (Butt and Benjamin 2004: 237). In French, only selected forms of *stare* survive in fixed expressions and as suppletive forms of the **esse(re)* paradigm (Pountain 1982: 146–147).

The evolution of *stare* into the only copula in LF may be seen as the end point of an evolutionary drift that has its roots in Latin and has attained different stages in different Romance languages. The drift in question consists of progressive copularization of *stare* and concomitant curtailment of the functional domains of **esse(re)*. In Spanish and Portuguese, the descendants of *stare* are only partially grammaticalized and are in complementary distribution and/or competition with those of **esse(re)*. In the contact situation that produced LF, the ongoing displacement of **esse(re)* by *stare* was accelerated, resulting in complete loss of the former and full copularization of the latter. Aslanov (2014: 129) offers a similar assessment: "The generalization of *star* at the expenses of *ser* (Italian *essere*) is a way to systematize to the extreme a structural drift that appears only occasionally in Portuguese". The potentially accelerating effect of language contact on this change is emphasized by Silva-Corvalán (1986):

> The innovation examined here undoubtedly represents part of an evolutionary trend in Spanish and other Romance languages. Given such a situation, the result of language contact will be acceleration of the change. It may be argued that one further condition is necessary for this rapid diffusion, namely reduced access or lack of access to formal varieties of the language, as well as to those institutions which maintain conservative and prescriptive language norms. (Silva-Corvalán 1986: 603–604)

The lack of exposure to normative language as a factor favoring restructuring is emphasized by Chaudenson (2001: 163–165). Both factors – intense language contact and lack of normative pressure – can be assumed as motivating factors in the expansion of *(e)star* to all copular functions in LF. The complete grammaticalization of *(e)star* in LF also suggests that the starting point for this evolution is more likely to have been provided by the linguistic systems in which this verb was already at least partially grammaticalized, such as Spanish and/or Portuguese, than by those in which it was primarily used as a lexical verb. (According to Geeslin and Guijarro-Fuentes 2008, contact with Catalan inhibits the expansion of *estar* in Spanish.) Additional support for the probable Spanish and/or Portuguese origin of LF *(e)star* derives from studies of SLA and FT: *estar* was used as the default copula in imitations of Moorish speech on the sixteenth-century Spanish stage (Lipski 2002: 121–122); *stare* is one of the two copulas in SIE (the other being *ce* < It. *c'e* 'there is')

Table 9.9. *Personal pronouns in the* Dictionnaire*'s Lingua Franca*

	Singular	Plural
1st person	*mi*	*noi*
2nd person	*ti*	*voi*
3rd person	*ellou* (m.) *ella* (f.)	*elli*

(Habte-Mariam 1976; Pulgram 1978); *essere* tends to be omitted about half of the time in Italian FT (Berruto 1993: 2281); *ser* is usually deleted while *estar* is usually kept, at least in its locative function, in Spanish FT (Thompson 1991).

9.3.4 Personal Pronouns

9.3.4.1 Data The LF system of personal pronouns, as presented in the *Dictionnaire*'s preface and examples, consists of the forms shown in Table 9.9. Other personal pronoun forms of the lexifiers (clitics, possessors, other case forms) do not survive in LF.[9] Their elimination has obliterated formal distinctions between subject pronouns, object pronouns, and pronominal possessors, prompting the development of new or foregrounding of existing analytic means to signal these differences. Reduction in the number of pronominal forms in LF is thus inseparable from the development of periphrastic pronominal possession and differential object marking. The latter will be examined in Section 9.4.5; the former is illustrated in (19) and discussed immediately below.

(19) a. *commé star il fratello di ti?*
how be.IMPF the brother of 2s
'Comment se porte votre frère?'
'How is your brother?'
(Anonymous 1830a: 94)

b. *qouesto libro star di mi*
this book be.IMPF of 2s
'ce livre est mien'
'this book is mine'
(Anonymous 1830a: 49)

c. *mi andar in casa del Signor.*
1s go.IMPF in house of.the gentleman

[9] The only exception is *loro, di loro* given as translations for Fr. *leur* 'their.'

'Je vais chez Monsieur M.'
'I am going to the gentleman's house.'
(Anonymous 1830a: 95)

9.3.4.2 Discussion The development from the Latin to the Romance linguistic type involved a drift toward a more analytic morphosyntax. In personal pronouns, this drift is manifested in the loss of morphological case distinctions and reliance on word order and prepositions to express grammatical relations (see Chapter 7).

Based on parallel developments in European-lexified creoles, some researchers derive the LF pronouns *mi* 'I' and *ti* 'you (sg.)' from the oblique forms of the corresponding lexifier pronouns. Cifoletti (1989: 59–60) derives them from the subject pronouns in Venetian, pointing to the distinction between the subject and oblique forms *ɨyo / me* (1sg) and *tu / te* (2sg) in SIE and preference for the subject forms of personal pronouns in Italian FT. Northern Italo-Romance does not distinguish between subject and oblique stressed pronouns in the first and second person singular (Vanelli 1997: 107). Under either theory of origin, the formal reduction of the system of personal pronouns in LF may be seen as a continuation of the Romance diachronic trend to reduce the number of case forms of personal pronouns. This formal reduction brings about complete grammaticalization in LF of the Romance periphrastic possessive construction.

In both Italian and Spanish, descendants of the Latin preposition *dē* are used for expressing possession when the possessor is a noun, cf.:

(20) a. *Hai visto la nuova macchina di Andrea?*
have.PRES.IND.2s seen the new car of Andrea
'Have you seen Andrea's new car?'
(Patota 2006: 62)

b. *La casa de Juan es bonita.*
the house of Juan be.PRES.IND.3s beautiful
'Juan's house is beautiful'
(Orozco 2010a: 191)

In both languages, the use of this periphrastic construction is also extended to personal pronoun possessors. In Italian, the construction with *di* is used with third person pronouns to disambiguate their gender reference (Rohlfs 1968: 122; Cinque 1996: 73) (see 21).

(21) a. *nella camera di lui*
in.the room of 3S.M
'in his room'
(Rohlfs 1968: 122)

b. *nella camera di lei*
in.the room of 3S.F
'in her room'
(Rohlfs 1968: 122)

In Spanish, the possesive construction with *de* can occur with any personal pronoun except for the first and second (informal) person singular (Orozco 2010a: 192–193) (see 22).

(22)

la casa mía	'my house'
la casa tuya	'your (sg.) house'
la casa de Usted	'your (sg.) house'
la casa de él	'his house'
la casa de ella	'her house'
la casa de nosotros	'our (m.) house'
la casa de nosotras	'our (f.) house'
la casa de Ustedes	'your (pl.) house'
la casa de ellos	'their (m.) house'
la casa de ellas	'their (f.) house'

In both languages, the periphrastic possesive construction with pronominal possessors is stylistically marked and/or distributionally restricted (Cordin 2001; Orozco 2012). The *Dictionnaire*'s LF has expanded its scope by extending it to all contexts and all persons. This develoment may have been reinforced by the presence of periphrastic possessives in Maghrebi Arabic (Aslanov 2014: 125; see also Obediente 1997: 161n2). Presence in the substrate languages of structures congruent with the corresponding structures in the lexifier ensures their selection into the contact variety (cf. Mufwene 2001: 23; 2008: 119; 2010: 375). In this case, the structures in question may be not only typologically congruent but also related: in Heath's (2015) view, the relevant possessive morphemes in Maghrebi Arabic, *di* ~ *d-* ~ *dyal*, derive from its contact with Late Latin and its periphrastic possessive construction with *dē*.

In summary, the complete grammaticalization of the periphrastic possessive construction in the *Dictionnaire*'s LF is inseparable from the formal simplification of its system of personal pronouns. Both developments show continuity with and incrementation of the corresponding diachronic trends in the lexifiers. The complete replacement of a synthetic with an analytic means of expressing pronominal possession in LF is in line with the synthetic-to-analytic diachronic drifts in the histories of Romance languages whose pace tends to pick up in certain types of contact situations (Schwegler 1990; Orozco 2010b: 215–216; 2018: 32, 68).

9.3.5 *Differential Object Marking*

9.3.5.1 Data In the *Dictionnaire*'s LF, direct and indirect objects expressed by personal pronouns are preceded by *per* (see 23a–23c). Direct objects expressed by nouns do not receive such marking (see 23d, 23e).

(23) a. *mi crédir per ti.*
1s believe.IMPF DOM 2s
'Je vous crois.'
'I believe you.'
(Anonymous 1830a: 93)

b. *respondir per mi.*
answer.IMPF DOM 1s
'Répondez-moi.'
'Answer me.'
(Anonymous 1830a: 96)

c. *ti conoschir per ellou?*
2s know.IMPF DOM 3s.M
'Le connaissez vous?'
'Do you know him?'
(Anonymous 1830a: 96)

d. *molto tempo ti non mirato Signor M.?*
much time 2s NEG see.PF mister M.
'Y a-t-il long-tems que vous n'vez vu Monsieur M.?'
'Has it been long since you've seen Mr. M.?'
(Anonymous 1830a: 94)

e. *ti dar una cadiéra al Signor.*
2s give.IMPF a chair to.the gentleman
'Donnez une chaise à Monsieur.'
'Give a chair to the gentleman.'
(Anonymous 1830a: 94)

LF *per* derives from It. *per* 'for, to, by, through.' The *Dictionnaire* lists it as a spatial preposition (Fr. *par* 'by') and as a dative/benefactive/purposive one (Fr. *pour* 'for'). These uses of *per* are found side by side with its use as a DOM marker (see 24).

(24) a. *per mare nada, ma per terra il Françis star mouchou forti.*
by sea nothing but by land the French be.IMPF very strong
'Par mer rien, mais par terre ils sont redoutables.'
'By sea nothing, but on the ground the French are formidable.'
(Anonymous 1830a: 98)

b. *mi venouto aposto per far mangiaria con ti.*
1s come.PF specially for do.PF breakfast with 2s
'Je suis venu exprès pour déjeuner avec vous.'

'I have come specially to have breakfast with you.'
(Anonymous 1830a: 97)

c. *non* *counchar* *per* *mi,* *il* *café* *basta.*
NEG make.IMPF for 1S the coffee enough
'N'en faites pas pour moi, le café me suffit.'
'Do not make (tea) for me, coffee will do.'
(Anonymous 1830a: 97)

9.3.5.2 Discussion As a group, Romance languages display formal marking of a subset of direct objects. The objects so marked stand out in terms of such features as animacy, definiteness, specificity, or topicality. The DOM marker typically develops out of the Latin preposition *ad* 'to, toward' or *per* 'by, through,' which accounts for the label "prepositional accusative" (*accusatif prépositionnel, acusativo preposicional, accusativo preposizionale*) applied to this phenomenon in Romance linguistics (Rohlfs 1971; Bossong 1991; Moretti 2000; Fiorentino 2010). The phenomenon may be illustrated with the Spanish examples in (25). In (25a), the direct object is marked by *a* because it "denotes a known or identified human being." In (25b), the direct object is not so marked because it "is not individually particularized" (Butt and Benjamin 2004: 333–334).[10]

(25) a. *No* *conozco* *a* *Feliciano*
NEG know.PRES.1S DOM Feliciano
'I don't know Feliciano'
(Butt and Benjamin 2004: 334)

b. *No* *conozco* *un* *solo* *farmacéutico* *en* *todo* *Bruselas*
NEG know.PRES.1S a single pharmacist in all Brussels
'I don't know a single pharmacist in the whole of Brussels'
(Butt and Benjamin 2004: 334)

DOM is attested in all branches of the Romance language family and has been studied to varying degrees of detail in Spanish, Portuguese, Catalan, Romanian, Italian, Sardinian, Sicilian, Corsican, Engadin, Gascon, and French (e.g., Rohlfs 1971; Berretta 1990, 1991; Moretti 2000; Iemmolo 2010; Berruto 2012; Fagard and Mardale 2014; Neuburger and Stark 2014; Schwenter 2014). The individual Romance languages differ in the degree of grammaticalization and other details of the phenomenon. The most systematic use of DOM is attested in Spanish and Romanian, while French, for instance, displays it as an optional pragmatic device to express topicalization, contrast, or emphasis (Berretta 1990; Iemmolo 2010; Fagard and Mardale 2014). Rohlfs (1971: 328–333) hypothesizes that the object-marking prepositions were initially employed as a stylistic device for placing the object in relief, suggesting that

[10] A direct object marked by a DOM marker may be doubled by a pronominal clitic coreferential with it. Differential marking of indirect objects is discussed, e.g., by Bilous (2011) and Pineda (2012).

DOM in Romance languages may have originated with objects expressed by personal pronouns.

In a comparative study of DOM in Romance and Semitic, Bossong (1991: 157) finds that in both language families the accusative case marker tends to be formally identical with, and derive from, the dative case marker. In systems with differential marking of direct objects, the objects so marked are not prototypical due to their animacy or definiteness (see also Berretta 1990: 179; Iemmolo 2010). Bossong hypothesizes that this lack of alignment between the semantic and syntactic properties of the marked objects explains the choice of the dative marker as the source of the DOM marker:

> In typical DOM languages, only those direct objects tend to be marked which share a more or less great amount of semantic features with prototypical subjects while those direct objects showing prototypical object properties tend to be left unmarked. [...] Positive object marking inside a DOM system marks subject-like objects. In this perspective, the formal identity of ACC and DAT markers in so many languages can easily be explained: prototypical datives have the same semantic properties as prototypical subjects. (Bossong 1991: 162)

LF agrees with the above Romance phenomena with respect to the objects selected for DOM (personal pronouns, which are prototypical subjects) and the source of the DOM marker (a spatial preposition). The evolution of *per* into a marker of pronominal objects in LF may be conceptualized as shown in (26).

(26) spatial preposition > purposive/benefactive/dative preposition > DOM marker

The grammaticalization of *per* into a DOM marker in LF finds typological parallels in the grammaticalization of Lat. *per* into a DOM marker in Romanian (*pe*) and in functional expansion of Italian *per* in naturalistically acquired L2 Italian. Bernini (1987: 139–141) notes that in early-stage Italian interlanguages *per* surfaces not only with the meanings of goal/purpose/benefactive but also with that of dative, which he interprets as an extension of the former usage (see 27).

(27) a. *io mandato lettera ber lui*
1s send.PPLE letter to 3s.M
'I sent a letter to him'
(Bernini 1987: 140)

b. *lui mandato lettera ber me*
3s.M send.PPLE letter to 1s
'He sent a letter to me'
(Bernini 1987: 140)

c. *io scritto ber Farid*
1s write.PPLE to Farid

Table 9.10. *Extension of* per *in Lingua Franca and related varieties*

Linguistic system	Nouns	Personal pronouns	Indirect object	Direct object
Italian interlanguages	+	+	+	–
Simplified Italian of Ethiopia	–	+	+	–
Dictionnaire's Lingua Franca	–	+	+	+

'I wrote to Farid'
(Bernini 1987: 140)

In SIE, *bɛr* (< *per*) marks indirect pronominal objects (see 28).

(28) a. *non dire bɛr luy*
NEG tell.INF to 1S.M
'Don't tell him'
(Habte-Mariam 1976: 178)

b. *noy dato soldi bɛr loro*
1PL give.PPLE money to 3PL
'We gave them money'
(Habte-Mariam 1976: 178)

As summarized in Table 9.10, the expansion of *per* in Italian interlanguages and in the *Dictionnaire*'s LF includes both shared and nonshared uses. The use of *per* to mark direct pronominal objects appears to point to its greater degree of grammaticalization in LF.

In summary, the development of DOM in LF parallels its development in Romance languages, includiing such details as the choice of the object-marking preposition and the type of objects singled out for differential marking. Simultaneous functioning of *per* as a preposition with spatial and nonspatial meanings and as a DOM marker is parallel to the functioning of *a* in Spanish and *pe* in Romanian. As in the case of the periphrastic possessive construction, the existence of DOM in other languages present in the contact environment, including Romance and Semitic languages, may have contributed to this development (see, e.g., Döhla 2016 on the proposal that Andalusian Arabic and Maltese developed DOM as a result of contact with Romance languages).[11] The presence of DOM-like phenomena in the early

[11] Also of potential interest is the use of both *per* and *a* as DOM markers in Judeo-Italian translations from Hebrew calquing the syntax of the source language, cf. *temero lu pupelo*

Table 9.11. *Typological continuity between Lingua Franca and its Romance lexifiers*

Romance languages	Lingua Franca
Lexical units formed through affixation	Lexical units formed through affixation
Lexical units formed through compounding	Lexical units formed through compounding
Lexical units formed though multiword lexemes	Lexical units formed through multiword lexemes
Stare partially copularized	*Stare* fully copularized
Stare encroaches on the domains of **esse(re)*	*Stare* replaces **esse(re)*
Case distinctions in personal pronouns reduced	Case distinctions in personal pronouns lost
Periphrastic pronominal possessives supplement possessive adjectives	Periphrastic pronominal possessives replace possessive adjectives
Development of DOM	Development of DOM
Verb classes in the infinitive reduced (4 > 3)	Verb classes in the imperfective reduced (3 > 2)
Verb class in *-e-* is reduced	Verb class in *-e-* is lost
Verb class in *-a-* predominates	Verb class in *-a-* predominates

stages of naturalistic acquisition of Italian hints at the probable role of contact in the development of DOM in Romance languages as well.

9.3.6 Summary

The features examined in this section are summarized in Table 9.11. They point to a high degree of typological continuity between LF and its Romance lexifiers, which may be interpreted as evidence of koineization in its genesis and transmission (Siegel 1985, 2001). The role of SLA and FT phenomena is evident in some of the developments in Table 9.11. For example, grammaticalization of *stare* in LF proceeds in tandem with the loss of the copula derived from **esse(re)*, found in both FT and SLA; the development of DOM-like phenomena is attested in naturalistic acquisition of Italian as L2; and the reduction of verb classes in the LF *r*-form has been attributed to the effects of SLA (Cifoletti 1989: 40; see Chapter 4).

per Dumedet 'and the people feared the Lord,' *amarai a-Domedet* 'you will love the Lord' (Rubin 2016: 322–323).

9.4 The Lingua Franca

9.4.1 *Formative Processes*

Mufwene (1997, 2001) and Siegel (1997, 2001) have shown that the formation of different types of contact languages, including koines and pidgins, involves similar underlying mechanisms. These comprise mixing (creation of a pool of linguistic features originating in different varieties), leveling (loss of minority variants), simplification (elimination of marked variants and irregular patterns), formation of hybrid forms, reallocation of the leftover variants to new stylistic or sociolinguistic functions, and focusing (stabilization) (see also Trudgill 2004, 2011; Kerswill and Trudgill 2005; Mufwene 2008, 2009; Siegel 2008b; Ansaldo 2009; Kerswill 2010; Operstein 2015: 4–5). The *Dictionnaire*'s LF supplies linguistic evidence for each of these processes.

The mixing process is seen in the presence in LF of different lexical strata, and is especially conspicuous in lexical doublets, such as the ones in (29).

(29)

Italian	Spanish	
testa	cabessa	'head'
parola	palabra	'word'
débole	flaco	'weak'
vouoto	basio	'empty'
piou	mas	'more'
star	estar	'to be'

An instance of leveling may be seen in the nonoccurrence in the *Dictionnaire* of inflected Romance verbs beyond items like *piové* 'it rains' and *basta* 'enough,' apparently lexicalized. As discussed in Chapter 7, selected inflected forms of the verb are present in Haedo's LF as minority variants realizing the LF impefective. Similarly, while Haedo (1612) offers such variants as Italian-derived *Dio* for 'God' and the synthetic possessive *tuya* 'your (sg.),' the *Dictionnaire* records only Spanish-derived *dios* for the former and analytic *di ti* for the latter.

Simplification of lexifier grammars includes elimination of morphosyntactic categories, such as number in nouns and adjectives, case in personal pronouns, and person inflection on verbs. Examples of regularization of irregular patterns include hypercharacterization of gender and elimination of verb allomorphy, cf. It. *bere / bevuto* 'to drink' > LF *bévir / bevuto*, Ptg. *fazer / feito* (Sp. *fazer / fecho*) > LF *fazer / fazito*.

The *Dictionnaire*'s data is particularly rich in hybrid forms. For example, the perfectives in (30a) combine Spanish or French verb stems with Italian endings, the nouns in (30b) combine French stems with Hispano-Italian word markers, the multiword lexemes in (30c) combine Spanish and Italian lexical items, the examples in (30d) are Franco-Italian phonological hybrids, and the ones in (30e) are semantic hybrids: *forar* 'to remove, take away, pull out, disorder, stand up; to pierce, make a hole' combines the meanings of Ven. *fora* 'out, outside' and It. *forare* 'to pierce, make a hole in' (Cifoletti 2004: 74); *mirar* 'to see, notice; aim' appears to combine those of Sp. *mirar* 'to look at' (> 'to see') and It. *mirare* 'to aim.' The item *mouchou bello* in (30c), additionally, illustrates Coates's (1971: 28) observation that *mouchou* "derives morphemically from Spanish, but syntactically from Italian."

(30)	a.	ablato	'speak'	<	Sp. habl-	It. -ato
		escondouto	'hide'	<	Sp. escond-	It. -uto
		amousato	'amuse'	<	Fr. amus-	It. -ato
		composito	'arrange'	<	Fr. compos-	It. -ito
	b.	verro	'glass'	<	Fr. verre	Sp. It. -o
		bagueta	'stick'	<	Fr. baguette	Sp. It. -a
	c.	moukera del filio	'daughter-in-law'	<	Sp. mujer	It. figlio
		mouchou bello	'magnificent'	<	Sp. mucho	It. bello
	d.	risponsa	'response'	<	Fr. réponse	It. risposta
		riposta	'solution'	<	It. risposta	Fr. réponse
	e.	forar	'to remove; to pierce'	<	Ven. fora	It. forare
		mirar	'to see; to aim'	<	Sp. mirar	It. mirare

Possible examples of reallocation may be found in the semantic or collocational specialization of lexical doublets. Thus, *germana* (< Cat. *germana* 'sister') and its doublet *sorella* (< It. *sorella* 'sister') differ in that the former is specialized in the meaning of 'sister' and the latter in that of 'sister-in-law'; *cabessa* (< Sp. *cabeza* 'head') appears to differ from its doublet *testa* (< It. *testa* 'head') in its ability to be used figuratively, cf. the idiom *ténir cabessa* 'to have a head' ('to be witty'). Similarly, only the first verb in the doublets *dar / donar* 'to give' and *ténir / avir* 'to have' is used for creating multiword verbal lexemes.

Stabilization of LF appears to have taken place between the late sixteenth and early nineteenth centuries (Cifoletti 2000, 2004). The LF variety recorded in the *Dictionnaire* is certainly structurally coherent.

9.4.2 Feature Pool

Siegel (1997) hypothesizes that the mixture of linguistic variants (the "feature pool")[12] present in the contact environment leading to the

[12] See Mufwene (2001) regarding the concept of a feature pool.

formation of "stable pidgin and creole languages" is composed of the following categories of input:

From superstrate speakers:

- various regional and social dialects of the superstrate
- various versions of foreigner talk
- second language varieties of nonnative speakers (e.g., of other European languages)
- existing pidgins with the same lexifier language
- existing creoles with the same lexifier language
- second language versions of existing stable pidgins or creoles ('Tok Masta')

From substrate speakers:

- second language versions of various superstrate models with some transfer from
  first languages
  indigenous lingua francas
  foreigner talk versions of these languages
- previously heard pidginized forms of the superstrate
- existing stable pidgins
- existing creoles
- second language versions of existing stable pidgins or creoles (Siegel 1997: 132)

Applied to the contact situation that preceded the stabilization of Maghrebi LF between the sixteenth and nineteenth centuries, the feature pool was conceivably composed of variants drawn from the following linguistic subsystems:

1. various regional and social dialects of Italo- and Ibero-Romance vernaculars;
2. various foreigner talk versions of Italo- and Ibero-Romance vernaculars;
3. various second language versions of Italo- and Ibero-Romance vernaculars;
4. existing contact and pidginized varieties of Italo- and/or Ibero-Romance vernaculars;
5. existing varieties of LF.

The native varieties in (1) and (2) above would have been produced by Romance-speaking converts to Islam and their descendants, Iberian Muslims and Sephardic Jews and their descendants, Romance-speaking captives, slaves, soldiers and administrators manning the Spanish presidios in North Africa, and Romance-speaking foreign agents and their families (Vincent 2004; Epalza and Slama-Gafsi 2010). The nonnative varieties in (3) would have been produced by non-Romance-speaking Europeans, Muslims who had spent some time in captivity in Romance-speaking territories, and those of the Iberian Muslims and Jews who had resided in other Romance-speaking lands prior to settling in the Maghreb. The L2 and/or pidginized varieties that may have been present in the mixture also include those presented in contemporary letters and theater as *habla de negro* (Spanish of sub-Saharan Africans), *lengua de moros* (Spanish of Iberian Muslims), *língua de preto* (Portuguese of sub-Saharan Africans), *greghesco* (Italian of Greeks), *schiavonesco* (Italian of Slavs), and in musical compositions known as *moresche* (songs in L2 Italian of African slaves) and *todesche* (songs in L2 Italian of German lancers).[13] Additionally, non-Maghrebi varieties of LF could have been brought to the Maghreb: for example, the LF-speaking characters in Goldoni's plays include Turkish and Greek merchants and an Armenian peddler (Zago 1986). That this complex ethnolinguistic mosaic actually existed in Algiers is known from Haedo's description:

> Dejemos aparte que hay muy muchos turcos y moros que han estado captivos en España, Italia y Francia, y, por otra parte, una multitud infinita de renegados de aquellas y otras provincias, y otra gran copia de judíos que han estado acá, que hablan español, italiano y francés muy lindamente. Y aún todos los hijos de renegados y renegadas, que en la teta deprendieron el hablar natural cristianesco de sus padres y madres, le hablan tan bien como si en España o Italia fueran nacidos. (Haedo 1612, cited in Epalza and Slama-Gafsi 2010: 103)

> [Let us leave aside that there are many Turks and Moors who had been captives in Spain, Italy and France and, on the other hand, an infinite multitude of renegades from these and other provinces, and another great plenty of Jews who had been here, who speak Spanish, Italian and French very beautifully. And then there are all the children of renegades who learned at their mother's breast the natural Christian speech of their fathers and mothers and speak it as well as if they had been born in Spain or Italy.]

The linguistic subsystems in (1) through (5) above form a structural continuum which comprises idiolects that are close to the lexifiers (collectively, the acrolect) and those that are distant from it (collectively, the basilect). The acrolectal pole of the continuum is composed of native-speaker varieties, mildly restructured FT varieties, and advanced L2 varieties of the lexifiers; and the basilectal pole is composed of rudimentary and fossilized L2 varieties, severely restructured FT varieties, and pidginized varieties of the lexifiers. The formative processes at the acrolectal end would have been of a kind that produces a koine and those at the basilectal end of a kind that produces a pidgin.

[13] Teyssier (1959); Weber de Kurlat (1963); Amelung (1964); Coates (1970); Cortelazzo (1970–1971, 1972, 1980, 1983); Coutelle (1971, 1977); Lazzerini (1977); Cardamone (1981); Folena (1983); Kahane and Kahane (1985); Bierbach (1988); Lipski (2005); Santos Morillo (2010); Operstein (2012); Salvatore (2012).

The structural features contributed to the LF continuum by its basilectal end reflect the FT and SLA strategies that take place between typologically distant, mutually incomprehensible languages spoken by culturally distant speakers. They comprise innovations which disrupt the typological continuity between LF and its Romance lexifiers and include a two-form verb system based on nonfinite verb forms of the lexifiers, loss of free functional elements of the lexifiers (nonmodal auxiliaries, the copula derived from **esse(re)*, clitic pronouns, possessives), and wholesale elimination of a range of functional categories, including nominal number, case distinctions in personal pronouns, and TAM and person inflection on verbs. The structural features contributed to the LF continuum by its acrolectal end reflect the FT and SLA strategies that take place among typologically similar, mutually intelligible varieties spoken by culturally homogeneous speakers. They reflect continuity between LF and its Romance lexifiers and comprise two types of features: retentions of Romance structural patterns, including nominal gender, gender agreement, word-order features, definite and indefinite articles, word-formation mechanisms, and idioms; and innovations in the form of hybrid forms and developments which advance or run parallel to the corresponding developments in the lexifiers, including full grammaticalization of the copula *(e)star* and periphrastic possessive construction, development of differential object marking, reduction of verb classes in the infinitive, and elimination of case distinctions in personal pronouns. The two types of innovations which set LF apart from its lexifiers are conceptually similar to the two types of innovations identified by Chaudenson (2001) in French-lexified creoles in relation to French:

> As one might expect, creoles show two principal types of innovation in relation to French. The first consists of the continuation of forms or processes which were, and occasionally still are, present in certain French varieties. In this respect North American French varieties are, on many points, the most advanced state of French .... The second type of innovation consists of forms or processes external to F^0 as a variation model. It is evidently in this area that the slaves' languages can be claimed to have influenced their appropriations of the target language. However, this type of innovation could also encompass more general phenomena due either to restructuring tied to exolingual communication or to general (indeed universal) strategies of language learning. (These influences are of course not mutually exclusive.) (Chaudenson 2001: 182–183)

An even closer typological parallel to the historical LF situation is provided by the use of Italian as a language of interethnic communication in German-speaking areas of Switzerland in the 1980s and 1990s, to be examined next.

9.4.3 Fremdarbeiteritalienisch

The use of Italian as an interethnic lingua franca in German-speaking areas of Switzerland was first noted in publications dating from the 1970s, and first described in Berruto et al. (1990) (also Berruto 1991: 334–335). Berruto (2012: 220) delimits the temporal extent of the basilectal pole of the Italian-based lingua franca (Fremdarbeiteritalienisch 'guest worker Italian') by the 1980s and 1990s (see also Moretti 1993b: 405–407; Bernini 2010a).

The historical events leading up to the establishment of Italian as an interethnic lingua franca in Switzerland are summarized in Schmid (1994: 17–21). Of immediate relevance is mass migration into Switzerland after the Second World War, bringing the total number of foreign workers to 721,000 in 1964. Of these, 66 percent were Italians, while the next two most numerous groups, Germans and Spaniards, constituted 11 percent taken together. The majority of the Italian immigrants came from the South (60 percent) and a minority from the North (26 percent). After the economic crisis of 1974, the influx of foreign workers picked up in the 1980s, including from countries like Turkey and Yugoslavia, resulting in a resident foreign population of 1,140,474, or 16.9 percent of the total, in 1991; 33 percent of the resident foreigners were Italians and 10.1 percent, Spaniards.

Schmid (1994: 19–23) notes that, in Switzerland, the presence of foreign workers is viewed as a passing, economically driven phenomenon, with a certain rotation of the workforce aimed as impeding its stabilization in the country (e.g., he points to the existence of different types of stay permits). The foreign workers likewise view their residence in the country as temporary and driven by economic necessity, plan to return to their countries of origin, have little contact with the local population outside the work sphere, and are not socially integrated in the host society. Their motivation to acquire German is instrumental rather than integrative. The combination of the social segregation of the foreign population and the feeling of the nonpermanence of their stay in the country creates favorable conditions for the emergence of an auxiliary language:

> L'etnicizzazione della forza lavoro all'interno di una struttura gerarchica costituische infatti un tratto caratterizzante della società svizzera e, dal punto di vista sociolinguistico, una condizione necessaria per l'adozione di una lingua veicolare esocomunitaria tra la popolazione immigrata. (Schmid 1994: 20)

> [Ethnicization of the workforce inside a hierarchical structure, in fact, constitutes a characteristic trait of the Swiss society and, from the sociolinguistic point of view, a necessary condition for the adoption of an out-group vehicular language among the immigrant population.]

According to the research carried out at the time, the acquisition of Italian by foreign workers proceeded naturalistically. The target language input included native varieties ranging from "TV Italian" to various regional forms of Italian and to foreigner talk, and also included a range of nonnative varieties. For speakers with non-Romance L1s, an important type of input were Italian interlanguages of speakers with other Romance L1s, particularly Spanish and Catalan (Berruto 1991: 337; Moretti 1993a; Schmid 1994: 32).[14]

The foreign workers studied by Berruto (1991) were of diverse provenance and spoke different L1s, including various Italo-Romance varieties, Spanish, Catalan, Portuguese, Greek, Serbian, Croatian, Albanian, Turkish, Amharic, and Arabic. Their occupations revolved around manual work, including construction, the textile industry, and the service industry, e.g., cleaning and restaurants. Their linguistic repertoire was composed of the L1, used with their fellow-countrymen, and two L2s, Swiss German and FAI, which could be acquired simultaneously and could both be used in the work environment. Unlike Swiss German, FAI was also used outside work as a kind of "we-code," "lingua di classe" [class language], or "lingua dei lavoratori" [workers' language], guaranteeing the foreign workers a minimum of social integration in the host country (Berruto 1991: 335–336). The status of Italian as the language of the working class is emphasized by other researchers as well:

> L'atteggiamento di questo parlante riflette una forte identificazione con l'italiano come "lingua degli operai," opposta al tedesco che come codice dominante è connotato dai valori e dalle norme della società locale. Pare che questa funzione di *we-code* giochi un ruolo non insignificante nella diffusione dell'italiano, creando una sorta di "solidarietà lingüística" tra gli immigrati. (Schmid 1994: 29)
>
> [The attitude of this speaker reflects strong identification with Italian as a "workers' language," opposed to German which, as a dominant code, is endowed with the values and norms of the local society. It seems that this function as a *we-code* plays a not insignificant role in the spread of Italian, creating a kind of "linguistic solidarity" among the immigrants.]

The domains of use of lingua franca Italian included workplaces with predominantly foreign workforce (building, catering, textile industry, the service sector), the public domain (shops, doctors, lawyers, social workers), and social interaction (between neighbors, at sports events) (Schmid 1994: 27–34).

In attempting to explain why Italian was chosen as the contact language among the immigrants, Berruto (1991: 342) observes that Swiss German is marked as the we-code of the Swiss, the dominant social stratum, and that FAI therefore fills a communicative void. Other proposed reasons include the presence of Italian in the Swiss linguistic space (9.8 percent of the Swiss residents had Italian as their native language in 1980; see Berruto 1991: 336n11), and a large proportion of Italian speakers among the immigrants (38 percent in Berruto's study), combined with a large proportion of speakers of closely related languages (11 percent of speakers of Spanish and

[14] In this connection, cf. the issue of basilectization of lexifiers in linguistic ecologies "where nonnative speakers have served as models for new learners" (Mufwene 2010: 373).

Portuguese). These factors are similar to the sociolinguistic situation in Algiers, where the largest proportion of the captives and slaves were speakers of Romance languages.

The Italian-based lingua franca is similar to LF in several respects, including in functioning as a means of interethnic communication, in being a target of acquisition among foreign workers with different Romance and non-Romance L1s, and in not being based on the language of the host country's dominant social group. It is also similar to LF structurally, including with respect to its ambiguous taxonomic status: in the literature, this linguistic variety has been variously categorized as a koine, a pidgin, a partial pidgin, and a continuum of interlanguages (Berretta 1986: 333n5; Berretta 1988a: 381; Berruto 1991: 333, 342). Table 9.12 shows that the conditions under which the lingua franca Italian appears to have functioned and been transmitted in Switzerland, summarized here after Berruto (1991: 340–341), are comparable in a number of respects to those of Maghrebi LF.

The linguistic output of the foreign workers is described as a continuum of varieties with different degrees of approximation to the target depending on such factors as the speakers' opportunities and motivation to learn Italian, as well as their L1's genetic and typological distance from Italian. The continuum comprised both rudimentary interlanguages fossilized at early stages and advanced, morphologically rich interlanguages principally spoken by speakers with Romance L1s. Interlanguages of the first type were sufficiently homogeneous to be referred to by a single label; Berruto (1991) refers to them collectively as Fremdarbeiteritalienisch (FAI). As seen in the examples in (31), FAI shares a number of specific structural features with LF, including the use of the infinitive as the unmarked form of the verb and of the past participle as the perfective or past tense form.

(31) a. *sono turchi, sono portolesi, italiani, spagnoli, greci,*
are Turks are Portuguese Italians Spaniards Greeks

tutti insieme parlare italiano [. . .]
all together speak.INF Italian

quando fare pausa mezzogiorno tutti parlare italiano
when make.INF rest noon all speak.INF
'There are Turks, there are Portuguese, Italians, Spaniards, Greeks, all speak Italian together. When there is a break at noon, all speak Italian together.'
(Berruto 1991: 338; the speaker's L1 is Greek)

b. *io pensare quella bambina cercare per balone*
1s think.INF that girl look.for.INF for ball
'I think that girl is looking for a ball.'
(Berruto 1991: 347; the speaker's L1 is Greek)

c. *quando io arrivato, io parlare solo francese*
when 1s arrive.PPLE 1s speak.INF only French

Table 9.12. *Lingua Franca versus lingua franca Italian*

Lingua franca Italian	Lingua Franca
Used in a multilingual environment without a shared language	Used in a multilingual environment without a shared language
There is a linguistic and in part also cultural distance between the relevant ethnic groups	There is a linguistic and in part also cultural distance between the relevant ethnic groups
Used in part among nonnative speakers	Used among nonnative speakers
Acquired in part from nonnative speakers	Acquired from nonnative speakers
Develops in, and is typically tied to, the work environment	Develops in, and is typically tied to, the work environment
Used as an auxiliary language and fulfills restricted communicative needs	Used as an auxiliary language and fulfills restricted communicative needs
Used as a means of communication among immigrants of different origins, with Italians, and in part also with the local population	Used as a means of communication among speakers of different origins, with Romance language speakers, and the local population
The basis of lingua franca Italian is not the dominant indigenous language (German)	The lexifier of Lingua Franca is not the dominant indigenous language (Arabic)
The language learned by the immigrants is not socially superior but one without social distance	The lexifier of Lingua Franca is not socially superior but one without social distance
The foreigners are often in contact and mix freely with native speakers of Italian	Lingua Franca users were often in contact with native speakers of the lexifiers
The linguistic input is richer than in typical situations of pidgin formation	The linguistic input included both natively and nonnatively spoken lexifiers
There is a social consensus about lingua franca Italian as a "workers' language"	There is a social consensus about Lingua Franca as a language in its own right

Source: After Berruto (1991)

'When I came, I spoke only French.'
(Berruto 1991: 346; the speaker's L1s are Kikongo and Lingala)

d. *e* *lui* *come* *mangiato* *banana* *buttato* *por* *terra*
and 3S.M as eat.PPLE banana throw.PPLE on ground
'And as soon as he ate the banana he threw it on the ground.'
(Berruto 1991: 345; the speaker's L1 is Albanian)

Schmid (1993: 405–407; 1994: 32) conceptualizes the linguistic reality of the Italian-based lingua franca as a structural continuum dependent on the

Table 9.13. *Continuum of variation in Italian-based lingua franca, based on Schmid (1994)*

L2 Italian of non-Romance speakers	L2 Italian of Romance speakers	*Italiano popolare*
basilect	mesolect	acrolect

Table 9.14. *Continuum of variation in Italian-based lingua franca, based on Schmid (1992, 1994)*

L2 Italian of non-Romance speakers	L2 Italian of Romance speakers
basilect	acrolect

speakers' L1s. The acrolectal end of the continuum is composed of L1 and L2 Italian of speakers of other Italo-Romance languages (*italiano popolare*) whereas the basilectal end consists of L2 Italian of speakers of non-Romance languages, such as Turkish and Greek. The mesolectal range comprises L2 Italian of speakers of other Romance languages, such as Spanish and Portuguese (see Table 9.13).[15]

In an earlier publication, Schmid (1992) found that the types of restructuring found in *italiano popolare* are also observed in the L2 Italian of Spanish speakers. This leads to the possibility of merging the mesolectal and acrolectal varieties of the Italian-based lingua franca into one category (shown in Table 9.14).

A similar approach may be adopted with respect to the linguistic continuum represented by LF. It is likely that the greatest structural difference in the production of LF obtained between Romance and non-Romance language speakers, with variations within each type of output being smaller than between the two types. These opposing poles of the LF structural range are captured in Table 9.15 with the labels "basilect" and "acrolect." The structural differences between the two poles were likely to have been accompanied by lexical ones: it is conceivable that the basilectal varieties contained a greater proportion of non-Romance words and the acrolectal ones incorporated

[15] Schmid's approach is validated by quantitative studies on the linguistic distance effect in SLA. For example, Schepens, van der Slik and van Hout (2013) show that the difficulty of learning Dutch as a L2 is generally predictable from the linguistic distance between the target language and the learner's L1.

Table 9.15. *Continuum of variation in Lingua Franca*

Lingua Franca of non-Romance speakers	Lingua Franca of Romance speakers
basilect	acrolect

borrowings from prestige Romance languages Italian and French. It also bears mentioning that the non-Romance speaker group included not only Turkish, Berber, and Arabic speakers but also speakers of various non-Romance European languages, for, as observed by Planas (2004),

[L]es captifs provenant de l'Europe du Nord n'ont sans doute pas bénéficié des mêmes facilités de communication que les captifs originaires des territoires méditerranéens, car leurs langues natales, trop éloignées des langues latines méditerranéennes, ne leur permettaient pas d'accéder à une compréhension globale de la *lingua franca* ou de langues latines majoritairement parlées dans les régences. (p. 248)

[The captives from Northern Europe no doubt did not enjoy the same ease of communication as those from Mediterranean lands because their native tongues, too remote from Mediterranean Romance languages, did not allow for a comprehensive understanding of Lingua Franca or Romance languages widely spoken in the regencies.][16]

The likely existence of basilectal LF was facilitated by the presence in the area's languages of a robust and steadily growing Romance lexical component on which the local population could draw in its dealings with Franks. Instructive typological parallels to this situation are provided by the massive amounts of English loanwords in Japanese and French loanwords in English:

The existence of a large number of loanwords derived from English provides a Japanese person, regardless of English proficiency, with a resource for communicating with English speakers who do not know Japanese. . . . [T]here is no doubt that a large corpus of English-derived words within one's own language has the potential to aid communication with English speakers, in a similar way that a native speaker of English can often comprehend words in the romance [sic] languages such as French, due to their similarities to Latin or French-derived words in English. (Kay 1995: 74–75)

The likely existence of acrolectal LF is supported by the contemporaneous use of Italian as a language of diplomacy, seafaring, and commerce. From the sixteenth through the eighteenth centuries, Italian was the default language of

[16] The statement by a German-speaking eyewitness that LF "demjenigen, der Spanisch oder Italienisch versteht, es möglich macht, sich mit den Algierern so ziemlich zu verständigen" [enables him who understands Spanish or Italian to pretty much communicate with Algerians] (Herman H. 1837: 95) confirms this insight.

communication between the Ottoman Empire and Europe; in Egypt and Tunisia, it served as a language of communication between Europeans of different nationalities well into the nineteenth century (Sammarco 1937: 147–150; Triulzi 1971: 158; Cifoletti 1983: 1263–1264; Baglioni 2010: 17; 2015: 47). To illustrate the default status of Italian in diplomatic correspondence, Cremona (2002: 26) describes how, toward the end of the sixteenth century, diplomatic communication between the Sultan and Queen Elizabeth I of England would involve writing the original missive in Turkish, translating it into Italian, drafting the reply in English, and finally dispatching it in Italian. Two thirds of the documents generated by the French consulate in Tunis during the seventeenth century were written in Italian (p. 27). These were often written by nonnatives; Baglioni (2010) and Minervini (2011) emphasize the probable role of Sephardic Jews from Livorno (Leghorn) in the elaboration of this written variety of Italian. In Tunis, it was this influential community that "gradually came to impose on the other Europeans their language" (Loth 1905: 318, cited in Triulzi 1971: 158). In Algiers, the Leghorn Jews often served as intermediaries between the European consuls and Turkish authorities (Singer 1907: 386). Owing to the Iberian origin of this community, the lexicon of Judeo-Livornese incorporated a significant number of Iberian (Spanish, Judeo-Spanish, and/or Portuguese) words (Orfano 2016; Rubin 2016: 332–333).

The mixed linguistic character of chancery Italian (ChI) is emphasized by Cremona (2002):

> We have no time to say much about the linguistic features of the Italian of the French and English consular documents from Tunis and Tripoli. It is enough here to state that it was generally a Tuscan-based Italian, of the chancery type, but one handled by non-Italians for the most part, and so containing substantial numbers of Gallicisms and other -isms, and generally including many Italian dialectal features. (p. 28)

Baglioni's (2010) study of 132 documents produced between 1590 and 1703 at the French and British consulates and the Ottoman Chancery in Tunis indicates that this written variety not merely co-existed with LF in the same linguistic space but also shared with it a number of specific lexical and structural features. Thus, shared lexical choices include *donar(e)* 'to give,' *pigliar(e)* 'to take,' *desirar* 'to want,' *sentar(e)* 'to stay, remain,' *forar(e)* 'to throw away, take away,' *limpiar(e)* 'to clean,' *mantega* 'butter,' *datoli* 'date(s),' LF *sangré* / ChI *sengre* 'blood,' LF *platzà* / ChI *plassa* 'place,' LF *scopéta* / ChI *scopetta* 'rifle' (see also Cremona 1996: 89, 95). Shared structural features include analytically formed *deci sette* and *dieci nove* for Italian *diciassette* 'seventeen' and *diciannove* 'nineteen', respectively; copular use of ChI *stare* / LF *(e)star*; sigmatic plurals (e.g., *bancos* 'benches' in ChI, *douros* 'piaster' in LF); Italianized French past participles (e.g., ChI *composato*, LF *composito* < Fr. *composé* 'composed'); and hypercharacterization of gender (e.g., LF *intéresso* 'interest' < It. *interesse*, *moukera* 'woman' < Sp. *mujer*; ChI *paezo* 'country' < It. *paese*, *molla* 'woman' < It. *moglie*). Shared phonological features include underdifferentiation of geminates, raising of mid vowels (e.g., LF *païsé* 'country,' *favour* 'favor' ~ ChI *paise*, *favoure* < It. *paese*, *favore*), prosthetic [e] before initial sC-clusters (e.g., LF and ChI *escambio* 'exchange' < It. *scambio*), prenasal lowering of [e] (e.g., ChI *tranta* 'thirty' < It. *trenta*, LF *sartan* 'frying pan' < Sp. *sartén*) and raising of [a] (e.g., LF and ChI *encora* 'again' < It. *ancora*). These numerous and specific correspondences suggest that ChI and LF may have formed different poles of the same linguistic reality.

The division of LF into basilectal and acrolectal varieties is supported by post-1830 sources. An article published anonymously in 1852 distinguishes between what it refers to as *petit sabir* and *grand sabir*:

> Depuis la conquête algérienne, par suite des richesses nouvelles que cette langue à acquises, on a été amené à lui reconnaître deux variétés: le *petit sabir*, c'est-à-dire le *sabir* primitif, dans toute sa simplicité originelle; le *grand sabir*, c'est-à-dire le *sabir* revu, corrigé et considérablement augmenté. Quand nous disons corrigé, nous nous trompons du tout au tout, car, autant le *petit sabir* brille par sa reserve, autant le *grand sabir* se fait remarquer par sa licence. (Anonymous 1852; quoted after Cifoletti 1989: 195)

> [After the Algerian conquest, as a result of the new riches that this language has acquired, we have been led to recognize two varieties of it: *petit sabir*, that is to say the original *sabir*, in all its original simplicity; and *grand sabir*, that is to say a revised, improved, and considerably expanded *sabir*. When we say improved we are completely off the mark, for, just as *petit sabir* shines by its restraint, so is *grand sabir* notable by its license.]

Though the above source attributes the origin of the distinction between *petit sabir* and *grand sabir* to the postconquest period, Cifoletti (2004: 50) observes that the existence of two ways of speaking LF, one more reduced (*una modalità più ristretta*) and the other more expansive (*una modalità più ampia*), must have predated the French conquest of Algeria.

A comparable testimony is contained in a letter from Alfred Morel-Fatio to Hugo Schuchardt, dated 9 February 1882. In it, Morel-Fatio speaks in terms of "two Linguas Francas":

> Ici, autant que je puis le constater, il y a deux langues franques: La première est parlée au port entre les marins des divers pays romans qui se comprennent à l'aide du gemeinromanisch; la seconde est celle qu'emploie les Arabes et Kabiles pour se faire comprendre de la population chrétienne. (Morel-Fatio 1882a; see also Nolan 2020: 73)

> [Here, as far as I can tell, there are two Linguas Francas: the first is spoken at the port among sailors from various Romance countries who understand one another with the help of gemeinromanisch [common Romance]; the second is the one used by Arabs and Kabyles for making themselves understood by the Christian population.]

In conclusion, it is likely that there existed a continuum of ways of speaking LF in Algiers, and elsewhere in North Africa, that ranged from basilectal to acrolectal. The basilect/acrolect distinction in LF may have mirrored a similar distinction in the use of its Romance lexifiers; e.g., the use of Italian in the same linguistic ecologies varied according to whether it was used for extra-group communication ("per le relazioni tra indigeni ed Europei" [for relations between natives and Europeans]) or for intra-group one ("come lingua di scambio fra Europei di origini differenti" [as an exchange language among Europeans of different origins]) (Cifoletti 1983: 1263).[17] The formative processes at the basilectal end, constrained both by a linguistic distance between the participating systems and a cultural and socio-psychological one between the individuals, would have been characterized by a more drastic restructuring of the lexifiers. The formative processes at the acrolectal end, eased by a linguistic homogeneity of the participating systems and a cultural one of the speakers, would have involved a milder degree of restructuring. This difference in the restructuring processes is emphasized by Clements (2003: 247), who observes that "[i]n a pidginization situation with typologically very distinct languages, one would expect the mutual linguistic accommodation to be less successful and the dependence on universal tendencies to be greater." Simultaneous presence of different degrees of restructuring in the formation of LF may be held responsible for its combining the characteristics of a pidgin and a koine. It is likely that the attention of contemporary observers was drawn toward the basilectal end of the continuum because of its greater distinctiveness, just as, in recent times, it was the basilectal end of the Italian-based lingua franca continuum that was sufficiently distinctive to merit a special label.

[17] I use the terms intra-group and extra-group to parallel Parodi and Luján's (2014a, 2014b, 2017) and Luján's (2017) use of these terms to characterize the evolution of Latin American Spanish, conceptualized as resulting from two types of contact: intra-group contact among speakers of different Peninsular Spanish dialects, and extra-group contact between them and speakers of American indigenous languages.

Appendix A Swadesh Wordlists

(a) The LF entries are given in the *Dictionnaire*'s orthography. The spelling variants, if any, are provided only where relevant.

(b) With the exception of one or two lexical items which appear only in the dialogues, such as *combatir* 'to fight,' most of the words below are from the LF vocabulary. A few were extracted from related entries: for example, though the vocabulary lacks the entry for 'other,' the LF word for this meaning surfaces in translations of French *successivement* (*ouno dopo l'altro* 'one after another') and *autrefois* (*altré volte* 'other times').

(c) In the tables below, the column labeled "English" provides the Swadesh list meanings in English, cited here after Campbell (2013: 449–451) and McMahon and McMahon (2005: 38–39); see also useful compilations in Rea (1973: 361–366) and Brann (1994: 155–158).

(d) The column labeled "French" contains the French equivalents (or near-equivalents) of the Swadesh list meanings in the *Dictionnaire*. Only the masculine form is listed for the adjectives, and only the infinitive form for the verbs.

(e) The column labeled "Lingua Franca" gives the LF translations of the corresponding French entries. Where applicable, only the masculine form is listed for the adjectives, only the singular form for the nouns, and only the imperfective form for the verbs.

(f) The columns labeled "Spanish" and "Italian" occasionally provide the sources or cognates of the LF words rather than the current translations of the corresponding Swadesh list meanings. For example, the entries for the first and second person singular pronouns contain the oblique rather than the subject forms, the entries for 'rain' are given as Sp. *llueve*/It. *piove* 'it rains' rather than *lluvia*/*pioggia* 'rain' to match the LF form *piové*, and Sp. *tocar*/It. *toccare* 'to touch' are listed as corresponding to the LF translation for Fr. *frapper* 'to hit' (*tokkar*). In the case of more than one possible equivalent, only the cognate of the LF form is given, even if this is not the current term for the Swadesh list meaning. For example, the Spanish equivalents of LF 'knee,' 'long,' and 'dog' are given as *hinojo*, *luengo*, and *can* rather than *rodilla*, *largo*, and *perro*, respectively, and *ammazzare* rather than *uccidere* is listed as the Italian equivalent of LF 'to kill' (*massar*). In the case of semantically related words, only the cognate or source of the LF word is listed, even if this is not the exact Swadesh list equivalent in the respective language. For example, the Spanish equivalents of 'to say' and 'to see' are given as *hablar* 'to speak' and *mirar* 'to look at' rather than *decir* and *ver* to match the corresponding words in LF (*ablar*, *mirar*). If the source of the "Italian" form is an Italo-Romance language other than Italian, the Italian cognate is listed instead. For example, *me* 'I,' *te* 'you,' *fuori* 'outside,' and *ammazzare* 'to kill' are used as stand-ins for their Venetian cognates, which are assumed to be the actual sources of the LF words.

A.1 100 Wordlist

	Lingua Franca	French	Spanish	Italian	English
1	mi	moi	mí	me	I
2	ti	tu	ti	te	you
3	noi	nous	nosotros	noi	we
4	qouesto	ce, cela	este	questo	this
5	qouello	ceci, celui	aquel	quello	that
6	qui	qui	quién	chi	who
7	qué	quoi, que	qué	che	what
7a	cosa	que		cosa	
8	non	non		non	not
8a	no		no		
9	toutto	tout	todo	tutto	all
10	mouchous	plusieurs	muchos		many
10a	molto (genti)	multitude		molti	
11	ouno	un	uno	uno	one
12	doué	deux	dos	due	two
13	grandé	grand	grande	grande	big
14	loungo	long	luengo	lungo	long
15	picolo	petit	pequeño	piccolo	small
16	moukera	femme	mujer		woman

(cont.)

	Lingua Franca	French	Spanish	Italian	English
16a	dona			donna	
17	oumbré	homme	hombre	uomo	man
18	persona	personne	persona	persona	person
19	pechi	poisson	pez	pesce	fish
20	–	–			bird
21	cané	chien	can	cane	dog
22	–	–			louse
23	albéro	arbre	árbol	albero	tree
24	grano	grain	grano	grano	seed
24a	sementza	semence	simiente	semenza	
25	folia	feuille	hoja	foglia	leaf
26	radiz	racine	raíz	radice	root
27	scorsa	écorce	corteza	scorza	bark
28	pellé	peau	piel	pelle	skin
29	carné	viande	carne	carne	flesh
30	sangré	sang	sangre	sangue	blood
31	osso	os	hueso	osso	bone
32	grasso	graisse	grasa	grasso	fat
33	ové	oeuf	huevo	uovo	egg
34	–	–			horn
35	–	–			tail
36	piouma	plume	pluma	piuma	feather
37	–	–			hair
38	testa	tête		testa	head
38a	cabessa		cabeza		
39	orékia	oreille	oreja	orecchia	ear
40	ockio	oeil	ojo	occhio	eye
41	nadzo	nez	nariz	naso	nose
42	–	–			mouth

(cont.)

	Lingua Franca	French	Spanish	Italian	English
43	denti	dent	diente	dente	tooth
44	lingoua	langue	lengua	lingua	tongue
45	–	–			claw
46	piedi	pied	pie	piede	foot
47	dginokio	genou	hinojo	ginocchio	knee
48	mano	main	mano	mano	hand
40	ventro	ventre	vientre	ventre	belly
50	collo	col	cuello	collo	neck
51	séno	sein	seno	seno	breast
52	couoré	coeur	corazón	cuore	heart
53	–	–			liver
54	bévir	boire	beber	bere	drink
55	mangiar	manger	comer	mangiare	eat
56	–	–			bite
57	mirar	voir	mirar	vedere (mirare)	see
58	intendir	entendu (sic)	entender	intendere	hear
58a	sentir		sentir	sentire	
59	sabir	savoir	saber	sapere	know
60	dormir	dormir	dormir	dormire	sleep
61	morir	mourir	morir	morire	die
62	massar	tuer	matar	ammazzare	kill
63	natar	nager	nadar	nuotare	swim
64	volar	voler	volar	volare	fly
65	caminar	marcher	caminar	camminare	walk
66	vénir	venir	venir	venire	come
67	(stendir)	(étendre)	(extender)	(stendere)	lie
68	sédir	s'asseoir		sedersi	sit
68a	sentar		sentarse		
69	forar	lever (se)	(fuera)	(fuori)	stand

(cont.)

	Lingua Franca	French	Spanish	Italian	English
70	donar	donner	donar	donare	give
70a	dar		dar	dare	
71	ablar	dire	ablar	dire	say
72	sol	soleil	sol	sole	sun
73	louna	lune	luna	luna	moon
74	stella	étoile	estrella	stella	star
75	agoua	eau	agua	acqua	water
76	piové	pluie	llueve	piove	rain
77	pietra	pierre	piedra	pietra	stone
78	sabia	sable	arena	sabbia	sand
79	terra	terre	tierra	terra	earth
80	nébia	nuage	niebla	nebbia	cloud
81	foumo	fumée	humo	fumo	smoke
82	fouogo	feu	fuego	fuoco	fire
83	cinis	cendre	ceniza	cenere	ash
84	bruchar	brûler	quemar	bruciare	burn
85	camino	route	camino		road
85a	strada			strada	
86	montagnia	montagne	montaña	montagna	mountain
87	rosso	rouge	rojo	rosso	red
88	verdé	vert	verde	verde	green
89	dgialo	jaune	amarillo	giallo	yellow
90	bianco	blanc	blanco	bianco	white
91	négro	noir	negro	nero	black
92	noté	nuit	noche	notte	night
93	caldo	chaud	cálido	caldo	hot
94	frédo	froid	frío	freddo	cold
95	pieno	plein	lleno	pieno	full
95a	inchito		henchido		

(cont.)

	Lingua Franca	French	Spanish	Italian	English
96	nouovo	nouveau	nuevo	nuovo	new
97	bonou	bon	bueno	buono	good
98	roundo	rond	redondo	rotondo	round
99	séco	sec	seco	secco	dry
100	nomé	non (sic)	nombre	nome	name

A.2 200 Wordlist

	Lingua Franca	French	Spanish	Italian	English
1	toutto	tout	todo	tutto	all
2	e	et	y	e	and
3	bestia	bête	bestia	bestia	animal
4	cinis	cendre	ceniza	cenere	ash
5	a, in	à, en	a, en	a, in	at
6	–	–			back
7	cativo	mauvais	malo	cattivo	bad
8	scorsa	écorce	corteza	scorza	bark
9	perké	parce que	porque	perche	because
10	ventro	ventre	vientre	ventre	belly
11	grandé	grand	grande	grande	big
12	–	–			bird
13	–	–			bite
14	négro	noir	negro	nero	black
15	sangré	sang	sangre	sangue	blood
16	soffiar	souffler	soplar	soffiare	blow
17	osso	os	hueso	osso	bone
18	respirar	respirer	respirar	respirare	breathe
19	bruchar	brûler	quemar	bruciare	burn

(cont.)

	Lingua Franca	French	Spanish	Italian	English
20	mouchachou	enfant	muchacho	bambino	child
21	nébia	nuage	nieble	nebbia	cloud
22	frédo	froid	frío	freddo	cold
23	vénir	venir	venir	venire	come
24	contar	compter	contar	contare	count
25	cortar	couper	cortar	tagliare	cut
26	dgiorno	jour	día	giorno	day
27	morir	mourir	morir	morire	die
28	–	–			dig
29	sporco	sale	sucio	sporco	dirty
30	cané	chien	can	cane	dog
31	bévir	boire	beber	bere	drink
32	séco	sec	seco	secco	dry
33	–	–			dull
34	polvé	poussière	polvo	polve	dust
35	orékia	oreille	oreja	orecchia	ear
36	terra	terre	tierra	terra	earth
37	mangiar	manger	comer	mangiare	eat
38	ové	oeuf	huevo	uovo	egg
39	ockio	oeil	ojo	occhio	eye
40	cascar	tomber	caer	cascare	fall
41	lontano	loin	lejos	lontano	far
42	grasso	graisse	grasa	grasso	fat
43	padré	père	padre	padre	father
44	ténir paoura	effrayé	tener miedo	avere paura	fear
45	piouma	plume	pluma	piuma	feather
46	poco	peu	poco	poco	few
47	combatir	se battre	combatir	combattere	fight
48	fouogo	feu	fuego	fuoco	fire

(cont.)

	Lingua Franca	French	Spanish	Italian	English
49	pechi	poisson	pez	pesce	fish
50	chinqoué	cinq	cinco	cinque	five
51	–	–			float
52	cascar				flow[1]
53	fioré	fleur	flor	fiore	flower
54	volar	voler	volar	volare	fly
55	–	–			fog[2]
56	piedi	pied	pie	piede	foot
57	quatro	quatre	cuatro	quattro	four
58	–	–			freeze
59	frouto	fruit	fruto	frutto	fruit
60	donar	donner	donar	donare	give
60a	dar		dar	dare	
61	bonou	bon	bueno	buono	good
62	gerba ~ erba	herbe	hierba	erba	grass
63	verdé	vert	verde	verde	green
64	–	–			guts
65	–	–			hair
66	mano	main	mano	mano	hand
67	ellou ~ ello	lui, il	él	lui, egli	he
68	testa	tête	testa	testa	head
68a	cabessa		cabeza		
69	intendir	entendu (sic)	entender	intendere	hear
69a	sentir		sentir	sentire	
70	couoré	coeur	corazón	cuore	heart
71	pésanti	lourd	pesado	pesante	heavy
72	aki	ici	aquí	qui	here

[1] See the entry "fall." [2] See the entry "cloud."

(cont.)

	Lingua Franca	French	Spanish	Italian	English
73	tokkar	frapper	tocar	toccare	hit
74	ténir	tenir	tener	tenere	hold
74a	gantar				
75	come	comment	como	come	how
76	caschar	chasser	cazar	cacciare	hunt
77	–	–			husband
78	mi	moi	mí	me	I
79	–	–			ice
80	sé	si	si	se	if
81	in	dans, chez, à	en	in	in
82	massar	tuer	matar	ammazzare	kill
83	sabir	savoir	saber	sapere	know
84	lago	lac	lago	lago	lake
85	ridir	rire	reír	ridere	laugh
86	folia	feuille	hoja	foglia	leaf
87	sinistra	gauche	izquierda	sinistra	left
88	gamba	jambe	pierna	gamba	leg
89	(stendir)	(étendre)	(extender)	(stendere)	lie
90	vivir	vivre	vivir	vivere	live
91	–	–			liver
92	loungo	long	luengo	lungo	long
93	–	–			louse
94	oumbré	homme	hombre	uomo	man
95	mouchous	plusieurs	muchos		many
95a	molto (genti)			molti	
96	louna	lune	luna	luna	moon
97	madré	mère	madre	madre	mother
97a	mamma		mamá	mamma	
98	montagnia	montagne	montaña	montagna	mountain

(cont.)

	Lingua Franca	French	Spanish	Italian	English
99	–	–			mouth
100	nomé	non (sic)	nombre	nome	name
101	stréto	étroit	estrecho	stretto	narrow
102	vichino	proche	cerca	vicino	near
103	collo	col	cuello	collo	neck
104	nouovo	nouveau	nuevo	nuovo	new
105	noté	nuit	noche	notte	night
106	nadzo	nez	nariz	naso	nose
107	non	non		non	not
107a	no		no		
108	vekio	vieux	viejo	vecchio	old
109	ouno	un	uno	uno	one
110	altro	successivement	otro	altro	other
111	persona	personne	persona	persona	person
112	dgiocar	jouer	jugar	giocare	play
113	tirar	tirer	tirar	tirare	pull
113a	forar		(fuera)	(fuori)	
114	poussar	pousser	empujar	spingere	push
115	piové	pluie	llueve	piove	rain
116	rosso	rouge	rojo	rosso	red
117	dgiousto	juste	justo	giusto	right
118					right[3]
119	riou	ruisseau	río	fiume	river
120	camino	route	camino		road
120a	strada			strada	
121	radiz	racine	raíz	radice	root
122	corda	corde	cuerda	corda	rope

[3] See the entry "straight."

(cont.)

	Lingua Franca	French	Spanish	Italian	English
123	poudrido	pourri	podrido	putrido	rotten
124	froutar	frotter	frotar	strofinare	rub
124a	limpiar		limpiar		
125	salé	sel	sal	sale	salt
126	sabia	sable	arena	sabbia	sand
127	ablar	dire	hablar	dire	say
128	–	–			scratch
129	maré	mer	mar	mare	sea
130	mirar	voir	mirar	vedere	see
130	grano	grain	grano	grano	seed
130a	sementza	semence	simiente	semenza	
132	cousir	coudre	coser	cucire	sew
133	–	–			sharp
134	–	–			short
135	cantar	chanter	cantar	cantare	sing
136	sédir	s'asseoir		sedersi	sit
136a	sentar		sentarse		
137	pellé	peau	piel	pelle	skin
138	ciélo	ciel	cielo	cielo	sky
139	dormir	dormir	dormir	dormire	sleep
140	picolo	petit	pequeño	piccolo	small
141	sentir	sentir	sentir	sentire	smell
142	foumo	fumée	humo	fumo	smoke
143	lischio	uni	liso	liscio	smooth
144	serpenté	serpent	serpiente	serpente	snake
145	–	–			snow
146	qoualqué	quelque	algunos	qualche	some
147	–	–			spit
148	fendir	fendre		fendere	split
148a	roumpir		romper	rompere	

(cont.)

	LINGUA FRANCA	FRENCH	SPANISH	ITALIAN	ENGLISH
149	pressar	presser	presionar	pressare	squeeze
150	toccar con yatagan	sabrer			stab[4]
151	forar	lever (se)	(fuera)	(fuori)	stand
152	stella	étoile	estrella	stella	star
153	bastone	bâton	bastón	bastone	stick
154	pietra	pierre	piedra	pietra	stone
155	dritto	droit	derecho	dritto	straight
156	–	–			suck
157	sol	soleil	sol	sole	sun
158	inchir	emplir	henchir	riempire	swell[5]
159	natar	nager	nadar	nuotare	swim
160	–	–			tail
161	qouello	ceci, celui	aquel	quello	that
162	là	là	ahi	la	there
163	elli	ils	ellos	loro	they
164	grosso	épais	grueso	grosso	thick
165	–	–			thin
166	pensar	penser	pensar	pensare	think
167	qouesto	ce, cela	este	questo	this
168	ti	tu	ti	te	you
169	tré	trois	tres	tre	three
170	dgitar	jeter	tirar, echar	gettare	throw
171	légar	amarrer	ligar	legare	tie
172	lingoua	langue	lengua	lingua	tongue
173	denti	dent	diente	dente	tooth
174	albéro	arbre	árbol	albero	tree

[4] See the entry "hit."

[5] The *Dictionnaire*'s entry for Fr. *gonfler* 'to swell' is probably a typo (Cifoletti 1989: 110). The above table uses the nearest entry.

(cont.)

	Lingua Franca	French	Spanish	Italian	English
175	tornar	tourner	tornar	tornare	turn
175a	dgirar		girar	girare	
176	doué	deux	dos	due	two
177	vomitar	vomir	vomitar	vomitare	vomit
178	caminar	marcher	caminar	camminare	walk
179	caldo	chaud	cálido	caldo	warm
180	limpiar	laver	limpiar	lavare	wash
181	agoua	eau	agua	acqua	water
182	noi	nous	nosotros	noi	we
183	bagniar	mouiller	bañar	bagnare	wet
184	qué	quoi, que	qué	che	what
184a	cosa	que		cosa	
185	qouando	quand	cuando	quando	when
186	ove	où	donde	dove	where
187	bianco	blanc	blanco	bianco	white
188	qui	qui	quién	chi	who
189	largo	large	largo	largo	wide
190	moukera	femme	mujer	moglie	wife
191	vento	vent	viento	vento	wind
192	–	–			wing
193	secar	essuyer	secar	seccare	wipe
194	con	avec	con	con	with
195	dona	femme	mujer	donna	woman
196	bosco	forêt	bosque	bosco	woods
197	vermé	ver	gusano	verme	worm
198	voi	vous	vosotros	voi	ye
199	ano	an, année	año	anno	year
200	dgialo	jaune	amarillo	giallo	yellow

Appendix B Doublets

(1) The tables below contain the following types of forms:
  (a) Lexical doublets (referential synonyms). These may derive from different languages (as in *pieno* ~ *inchito* 'full' < It. *pieno*, Sp. *henchido*) or from the same language (e.g., *appertoura* ~ *bouko* 'hole, opening' < It. *apertura*, *buco*).
  (b) Etymological doublets (cognates). These may derive from different languages (e.g., *mouchou* ~ *molto* 'very' < Sp. *mucho* ~ It. *molto* < Lat. *mŭltus* 'much'); from the same language (e.g., *poudir* 'to be able' ~ *poder* 'power' < Sp. *poder*); or from different dialects (e.g., *moukera* ~ *mouchéra* 'woman, wife' < Sp. *mujer*, J.-Sp. *muʒer* < Lat. *mŭliere* 'woman, wife') (Meyer-Lübke 1911: 423).

(2) With the sole exception of *roba di casa* 'furniture,' multiword lexemes are not included. This means that of the three lexemes listed as translations for French *réflechir* 'to reflect' – *réfletir*, *pensar*, *mirar bonou* – only the first two are included.

(3) The column labeled "French" contains the French prompts from the *Dictionnaire*'s LF vocabulary. The column labeled "Compatible forms" contains compatible forms in the lexifiers; only one such form is listed for each LF word. For example, LF *dar* 'to give,' *roumpir* 'to split,' *pensar* 'to reflect,' *donar* 'to give,' and *rinovar* 'to renew' may derive from Sp. *dar*, *romper*, *pensar*, Cat. *donar*, and It. *rinnovare* – the forms given in the table – or they may derive, respectively, from It. *dare*, *rompere*, *pensare*, Fr. *donner*, and Sp. *renovar*. Sp. *rabiar* and Fr. *ranger* rather than It. *arrabiare* and *arrangiare* are listed as probable sources for LF *rabiar* and *rangiar* (see Cifoletti 2004: 39–41).

(4) The source of *mangiaria* 'breakfast' is unclear (Schuchardt 1909: 447). The origin of *forar* is discussed in Chapter 5, that of *gribouilla* in Cifoletti (2004: 74–75), and that of *cazéria* in Venture de Paradis (1898: 84), Cifoletti (2004: 74), and Dakhlia (2008: 345). The provenance of LF *spachiar* 'to finish' is addressed in Borg (1996: 143). On the convoluted

history of *drogman* ~ *trucheman* 'interpreter,' see Minervini (1996b: 57–58) and the references cited in that publication.

(5) Unless otherwise noted, the source words in Arabic, Turkish, and Sicilian are cited after Russo (2001), Cifoletti (2004), and/or Baglioni (2017). The source words in Venetian are cited after Boerio (1867); Catalan and Occitan words are cited after Castellanos (2007).

(6) The issue of multiple-source etymologies is addressed in Chapter 5. For further discussion of lexical synonymy in LF see, e.g., Cornelissen (1992: 221–222) and Cifoletti (1989: 32, 63; 2004: 55–56).

B.1 Doublets

Lexeme 1	Lexeme 2	French	English	Compatible forms
agioudar	favorisar	'seconder'	'to help'	Cat. ajudar, Fr. favoriser
basiar	vouotar	'vider'	'to empty'	Sp. vaciar, It. vuotare
baschiar	bassar	'descendre'; 'baisser'	'to lower'; 'to go down'	Cat. baixar, It. abbassare
brachiar	alloumar	'allumer'	'to light'	Sic. (s)braçiari,[1] Fr. allumer
comminchiar	principiar	'commencer'	'to begin'	It. cominciare, principiare
domandar	quérir	'demander'	'to ask'	It. domandare, Sp. querer
escaldar	scaldar	'échauffer, chauffer'	'to heat, warm'	Sp. escaldar, It. scaldare
estar	star	'être'	'to be'	Sp. estar, It. stare
fendir	roumpir	'fendre'	'to split'	It. fendere, Sp. romper
finir	spachiar	'finir'	'to end'	It. finire, Ven. spichiàr[2]
gouarantir	servar	'garantir'	'to guarantee'	It. garantire, servare

[1] Baglioni (2017: 192). [2] Borg (1996: 143) derives *spachiar* from Sic. *spicciari*.

(cont.)

Lexeme 1	Lexeme 2	French	English	Compatible forms
goustar	tastar	'goûter'	'to taste'	Sp. gustar, It. tastare
incendiar	bruchiar	'incendier'	'to burn'	It. incendiare, bruciare
intendir	sentir	'entendu'	'to hear'	Fr. entendre, It. sentire
irritar	rabiar	'irriter, s'irriter'	'to anger, get angry'	Sp. irritar, rabiar
méfidar	sfidar	'méfier (se)'	'to be wary of'	Fr. se méfier, It. sfidarsi
occadzionar	cagionar	'occasionner'	'to cause'	Fr. occasionner, It. cagionare
parlar	ablar	'parler'	'to speak'	It. parlare, Sp. hablar
poder	poudir	'pouvoir' (n.); 'pouvoir' (v.)	'to be able'; 'power'	Sp. poder
prendir	chiapar	'prendre'	'to take'	It. prendere, Ven. chiapàr
préparar	componir	'preparer'	'to prepare'	Sp. preparar, componer
raccommodar	rangiar	'raccommoder'	'to repair'	It. raccomodare, Fr. ranger
rangiar	componir	'ranger'	'to tidy up'	Fr. ranger, Sp. componer
reflétir	pensar	'refléchir'	'to reflect'	It. riflettere, Sp. pensar
rilévar	alsar	'relever (se)'	'to raise / rise'	It. rilevare, Sp. alzar
rinovélar	rinovar	'renouveler'	'to renew'	It. rinnovellare, rinnovare
rimandar	mandar	'renvoyer'	'to send back'	It. rimandare, Sp. mandar
rimarkar	mirar	'remarquer'	'to notice'	It. rimarcare, Sp. mirar
gouadagniar	rimportar	'remporter'	'to gain'	It. guadagnare, riportare

(cont.)

Lexeme 1	Lexeme 2	French	English	Compatible forms
sagiar	provar	'essayer'	'to try'	It. saggiare, provare
sédar	sédir	'(s')asseoir'	'to sit (down)'	It. sedere
sedjiournar	sentar	'séjourner'	'to stay'	Fr. séjourner, Sp. sentar
sentar	sédir	's'asseoir'	'to sit down'	Sp. sentar, It. sedere
sentar	restar	'rester'	'to stay'	Sp. sentar, It. restare
simoular	fingir	'simuler'	'to feign'	It. simulare, fingere
sitouar	logar	'situer'	'to place'	Sp. situar, Ven. logàr
soupliar	prégar	'supplier'	'to beg'	Fr. supplier, It. pregare
ténir	avir	'avoir'	'to have'	Sp. tener, It. avere
tirar	forar	'tirer'	'to pull'	It. tirare, Ven. fora
tornar	dgirar	'tourner'	'to turn'	It. tornare, girare
vigilar	gouardar	'veiller'	'to watch over'	It. vigilare, guardare
amigo	favorito	'favori'	'favorite'	Sp. amigo, It. favorito
appertoura	bouko	'ouverture'	'hole'	It. apertura, buco
batello	lanchia	'bateau'	'boat'	It. battello, Sp. lancha
caméra	sala	'chambre'	'room'	It. camera, sala
camino	strada	'chemin, route'	'road'	Sp. camino, It. strada
canoné	canon	'canon'	'cannon'	It. cannone, Fr. canon
canoniéré	tobgi	'canonier'	'gunner'	It. cannoniere, Tu. topçu

(cont.)

Lexeme 1	Lexeme 2	French	English	Compatible forms
capello	baréta	'chapeau'	'hat'	It. cappello, Ven. barèta
caserna	cazéria	'caserne'	'barracks'	Cat. caserna[3]
colatzioné	mangiaria	'dejeuner'	'breakfast'	It. colazione, mangiare
dolor	malé	'souffrance'	'suffering'	Sp. dolor, It. male
drogman	trucheman	'interprète'	'interpreter'	Fr. trucheman[4]
escala	scala	'echelle'; 'escalier, quai'	'ladder'; 'stairs, quay'	Sp. escala, It. scala
figoura	fachia	'figure'	'face'	It. figura, faccia
figoura	imago	'image'	'picture'	It. figura, Lat. imago[5]
falta	colpa	'faute'	'mistake'	Sp. falta, It. colpa
figlio	mouchachou	'fils'	'son'	It. figlio, Sp. muchacho
finetza	forbéria	'ruse'	'cunning'	It. finezza, furberia
fortza	forsa	'force,' 'effort'	'effort,' 'strength'	It. forza, Ptg. força
fortification	fortificatzion	'fortification'; 'retranchement'	'fortification; retrenchment'	Fr. fortification, It. fortificazione
fossa	tomba	'fosse'	'grave'	It. fossa, tomba
fratello	cognato	'frère'	'brother'	It. fratello, cognato
gandoufa	abouba	'peste'	'plague'	Ar. ɣandu:f, ħbu:b

3 See Venture de Paradis (1898: 84), Cifoletti (2004: 74), and Dakhlia (2008: 345) regarding the source(s) of *cazéria*.
4 See Minervini (1996b: 57–58) regarding the etymology of *drogman* ~ *trucheman*.
5 Also Fr. *image* (Baglioni 2017: 195n13).

(cont.)

Lexeme 1	Lexeme 2	French	English	Compatible forms
germana	sorella	'soeur'; 'belle-soeur'	'sister'; 'sister-in-law'	Cat. germana, It. sorella
grano	sementza	'blé, grain'; 'semence'	'wheat, grain'; 'seed'	Sp. grano, It. semenza
gréco	roumi	'grec'	'Greek'	It. greco, Ar. ru:mi
gribouilla	baroufa	'dispute'	'quarrel'	Ferr. gribullar,[6] It. baruffa[7]
lagrima	pianto	'larme'	'tear'	Sp. lagrima, It. pianto
lettera	carta	'lettre'	'letter'	It. lettera, Sp. carta
madré	mamma	'mère'	'mother'	Sp. madre, It. mamma
maestro	padron	'propriétaire'	'owner'	Sp. maestro, It. padrone
mariniére	mariniéro	'rameur'; 'marin, matelot'	'rower'; 'seaman, sailor'	It. mariniere, mariniero
méfidentza	sfidentza	'méfiance'	'distrust'	Fr. méfiance, It. sfidanza
metzo giorno	schiroco	'sud'	'south'	It. mezzogiorno[8]
mobili	roba di casa	'meuble'	'furniture'	It. mobili, roba
opinion	pensier	'opinion'	'opinion'	Sp. opinión, It. pensiero/e
parola	palabra	'parole'	'word'	It. parola, Sp. palabra

[6] The etymology given in the table is based on Nigra (1901: 290): "ferr. *sgrisular* e *grimullar* (= *gribullar*) 'fermentare, principiare a bollire,' e dicesi del bollire dell'olio, del burro e simili, e del fermentare e frizzare del vino" [Ferr. *sgrisular* and *grimullar* (= *gribullar*) 'to ferment, to begin to boil,' and is said of the boiling of oil, of butter and the like, and of the fermentation and effervescence of wine."

[7] The phrase *faisait baroufa* is mentioned by Lanly (1955: 208) for North African French.

[8] See Russo (2001: 231–232) regarding the etymology of *schiroco*.

(cont.)

Lexeme 1	Lexeme 2	French	English	Compatible forms
patria	païzé	'patrie'	'motherland'	It. patria, paese
permitzion	licentzia	'permission'	'permission'	Fr. permission, It. licenza
perrouquère	barbiéré	'perruquier'	'barber'	It. perruchiere, barbiere
polvé	polvéré	'poussière'; 'poudre (à tirer)'	'dust'; '(gun) powder'	It. polve, polvere
pounta	spina	'pointe'	'point, thorn'	It. punta, spina
protection	favor	'protection'	'protection'	Sp. favor, Fr. protection
rango	logo	'rang'	'rank'	Sp. rango, It. luogo
régalo	bakchich	'présent, récompense'; 'étrenne'	'gift, reward'; 'tip'	Sp. regalo, Tu. bahşiş
ricerka	riquiesta	'recherche'	'search'	It. ricerca, richiesta
roubié	prima vera	'printemps'	'spring' (season)	Ar. rbi:ʕ, Sp. primavera
sabato	seubt	'samedi'; 'sabbat'	'Saturday'; 'Sabbath'	It. sabato, Ar. sabt
santo	marabout	'saint'	'saint'	Sp. santo, Fr. marabout
scherrub	sorbet	'liqueur'	'liqueur'	Ar. šara:b,[9] Fr. sorbet
sitouation	logo	'sitouation'	'position'	Fr. situation, It. luogo
skiavo	ousif	'esclave, serf'; 'nègre, esclave'	'slave'; 'Black, slave'	It. schiavo, Ar. wṣi:f
sociéta	compania	'société	'society'	It. socièta, compagnia

[9] See Cifoletti (2004: 61) regarding the specific source form(s).

(cont.)

Lexeme 1	Lexeme 2	French	English	Compatible forms
soupa	tzoupa	'potage'; 'soupe'	'soup'	Fr. soupe, It. zuppa
tavola	taoula	'planche'	'table, board'	It. tavola, Ar. ṭåwla
testa	cabessa	'tête'	'head'	It. testa, Sp. cabeza
tetto	terrassa	'toit'	'roof'	It. tetto, Fr. terrasse
timoun	timone	'timon'; 'gouvernail'	'helm'; 'rudder'	Sp. timón, It. timone
vapor	foumo	'vapeur'	'steam'	Sp. vapor, It. fumo
vigilia	gouardia	'veille'	'night watch'	It. vigilia, guardia
zoukaro	zoukro	'sucre'	'sugar'	It. zucchero, Fr. sucre
basio	vouoto	'vide'	'empty'	Sp. vacío, It. vuoto
biondo	rousso	'blond'	'fair' (color)	It. biondo, Ptg. ruço
débole	flaco	'faible'	'weak'	It. debole, Sp. flaco
dgiovine	picolo	'jeune'	'young'	It. giovane, piccolo
fermo	solido	'solidement'	'firmly'	It. fermo, solido
fino	fourbo	'rusé'	'crafty'	It. fine, furbo
spacioso	largo	'spacieux'	'spacious'	It. spazioso, largo
lingoua	parlar	'langage'	'language'	It. lingua, parlare
maboul	locou	'fou'	'crazy'	Ar. maḥbu:l, Sp. loco
pieno	inchito	'plein, rempli'	'full, filled'	It. pieno, Sp. henchido
molto	mouchou	'très'	'very'	It. molto, Sp. mucho

(cont.)

Lexeme 1	Lexeme 2	French	English	Compatible forms
no	non	'non'	'not'	Sp. no, It. non
piou	mas	'plus'	'more'	It. più, Sp. más

B.2 Triplets

Lexeme 1	Lexeme 2	Lexeme 3	French	English	Compatible forms
bekiéré	verro	tassa	'gobelet; glass'	'cup; glass'	It. bicchiere, Fr. verre, Ar. ṭa:sa ~ ṭassa[10]
généro	sorté	maniera	'sorte, espèce'	'sort, kind'	It. genere, sorte, maniera
mouchéra	moukera	dona	'femme'	'wife; woman'	Sp. mujer, J.-Sp. muʒer, It. donna
fazir	far	counchar	'faire'	'to do, make'	Sp. Ptg. fazer, It. fare, Sic. cunzari
froutar	limpiar	néttegiar	'frotter; nettoyer'	'to rub, clean'	Fr. frotter, Sp. limpiar, Fr. nettoyer
rimettir	donar	dar	'remettre'	'to give'	Fr. remettre, Cat. donar, Sp. dar
roular	rodar	involtar	'rouler, empaqueter'	'to roll, pack'	Fr. rouler, Sp. rodar, It. involtare
ténir	firmar	gantar	'retenir; ténir'	'to hold, keep'	Sp. tener, It. fermare, Oc. gantar
ritornar	tornar	révénir	'revenir,' '(s'en) retourner'	'to return'	It. ritornare, tornare, Fr. revenir

[10] See Russo (2001: 238–239). A Romance source is equally possible (Sp. *taza*, Cat. *tassa*, Fr. *tasse*).

B.3 Quadruplet

Lexeme 1	Lexeme 2	Lexeme 3	Lexeme 4	French	English	Compatible forms
quérir	volir	désirar	desidérar	'désirer, vouloir, souhaiter'	'to want, wish'	Fr. desirer, Sp. querer, It. volere, desiderare

Appendix C Type–Token Ratios

C.1 Dialogue No. 1

Lingua Franca: 30 types : 77 tokens = 0.39 (39%)

Type	Token	Type	Token	Type	Token	Type	Token
mi	14	véro	3	no	2	falso	1
star	5	ablar	3	volir	1	qoualqué	1
qouesto	5	scométir	3	quérir	1	acoussi	1
non	4	poudir	2	assicourar	1	tropo	1
ti	4	pensar	2	doubitar	1	ouna	1
crédir	4	palabra	2	doubio	1	la	1
per	4	di	2	dgiousto	1	tenir	1
cosa	3	si	2				

French: 39 types : 88 tokens = 0.443 (44%)

Type	Token	Type	Token	Type	Token	Type	Token
je, j,' moi	13	gagerais	2	doute (v.)	1	faux	1
que (conj.)	6	parole	2	doute (n.)	1	point	1
croire, crois, croyez	6	non	2	parier	1	trop	1
ne, n'	5	en (pron.)	2	assurer	1	ainsi	1
est	5	ce, c'	2	a (avoir)	1	y	1
vous	4	il, l' (pron.)	2	puis	1	que	1
cela	4	oui	2	saurais	1	ma	1
vrai	3	pas	2	quelque	1	de	1
dis	3	la	1	chose	1	sur	1
voulez, voudrez	2	une	1	verité	1		

Spanish: 32 types : 71 tokens = 0.451 (45%)

Type	Token	Type	Token	Type	Token	Type	Token
creo, créa, creer	6	V., se, os	5	me	1	alguna	1
no	6	quiere, quiera	2	se (dat.)	1	cualquiera	1
que (conj.)	6	palabra	2	esta	1	asegurar	1
es	5	puedo	2	mi	1	dudo	1
verdad	4	la (art.)	2	una	1	hay	1
lo	4	sí	2	yo	1	duda	1
digo	3	así	1	pura	1	cosa	1
apostar, apostaría, apostaré	3	sobre	1	falso	1	qué	1

Italian: 35 types : 65 tokens = 0.538 (54%)

Type	Token	Type	Token	Type	Token	Type	Token
è	6	sì	2	che	1	così	1
credo, credete, creder	5	ne	2	mi (dat.)	1	alcuno	1
di	4	parola	2	assicurare	1	qualche	1
non	4	volete	2	dubito	1	quel	1
vero	3	posso	2	cosa	1	la (art.)	1
dico	3	lo (pron.)	2	verità	1	sulla	1
scommettere, scommetterei, scommetterò	3	ve, vi (pron.)	2	dubbio	1	mia	1
quest'	2	v' (adv.)	1	falso	1	una	1
no	2	che (conj.)	1	purtroppo	1		

English: 36 types : 81 tokens = 0.444 (44%)

Type	Token	Type	Token	Type	Token	Type	Token
I, me	13	say	2	can	1	yes	1
believe	6	will	2	cannot	1	too	1
it	6	word	2	do	1	please	1
is	6	what	2	doubt (v.)	1	something	1
you	4	no	2	doubt (n.)	1	would	1
bet	3	of	2	truth	1	my	1
true	3	so	2	false	1	upon	1
that (dem.)	3	assure	1	there	1	the	1
not	3	speak	1	but	1	a	1

C.2 Haedo (1612)

101 types : 233 tokens = 0.433 (43%) (based on Cifoletti 1989: 163–164)

Type	Token	Type	Token	Type	Token
no, non	12	Fe	2	bastonada	1
estar	11	mundo	2	boca	1
si	9	cosi	2	cabeza	1
gran, grande	8	curar	2	cosa	1
y	7	responder	2	carta	1
Dio	6	saber	2	manera	1
que	6	trabajar	2	parola	1
como	5	fazer, hazer	2	patron	1
cane	5	morir	2	forato	1
parlar	5	dezir, dezirme	2	febre	1
pillar, piglia	5	venir, ven	2	tempo	1
andar, anda	5	guarda	2	terra	1
mirar, mira	4	escripto, scripto	2	tortuga	1
portar, porta, portato	4	qui	2	veccio	1
pecado, pecato	4	la	2	vellaco	1
mi	4	questo, questa	2	ventura	1
a	4	chito	1	volta	1
de	4	mucho	1	correr	1
bona, bono, bueno	4	muy	1	cerrar	1
tener	3	priu (i.e. più)	1	donar	1
fantasia	3	assi	1	abrusar	1
cornudo	3	acosi	1	forar	1
malato	3	aquel	1	meter	1
aca	3	esto	1	poder	1
en	3	aquesto	1	sentar	1
anchora	2	dessa	1	trovar	1
testa	2	aqui	1	dole	1
campaña	2	tuya	1	ha	1

(cont.)

Type	Token	Type	Token	Type	Token
casa	2	altra	1	con	1
hora, ora	2	presto	1	fora	1
perro	2	vivo	1	in	1
Papaz	2	Iudio	1	por	1
Christiano	2	niçarane	1	porque	1
diablo	2	barbero	1		

Appendix D Clarke–Bonaparte (1877) Exchange

Hyde Clarke
(No. 2583, 28 April 1877, p. 545)

In the prize essay 'On the Existence of Mixed Languages,' by J. Cresswell Clough,[1] one of the first sections is on the Lingua Franca of South Europe, at p. 11; and there are other references.

The author gives a definite statement, on the authority of Malte Brun, that "the Lingua Franca of the Mediterranean is a mixture of Catalan, Limousin, Sicilian, and Arabic, with other roots, especially Turkish. It originated in the slave establishments of the Moors and Turks."

Mr. Clough has various observations on the subject. I have written to him for a specimen of the language; but he courteously informs me he has not one at hand, and that he has never seen one. He thinks Lingua Franca may be obsolescent.

Of course, there is a general belief in Lingua Franca, and it is spoken of in many books of travel.

Some time ago, before Mr. Clough's book was written, I sent a request to *Notes and Queries* for specimens of Lingua Franca, but met with no response. As it is now used in support of a theory as to mixed languages and the true nature of English, I beg the favour of your giving publicity to my inquiry in the columns of the *Athenaeum*.

Hyde Clarke
(No. 2585, 12 May 1877, pp. 607–608)

The answer to my question has come. If information is anywhere to be found, as to any language, it is in that rich, philological library of the Prince Bonaparte, which is rendered more valuable by the liberality and courtesy with which its stores are placed at the service of scholars.

[1] Clough (1876).

Prince Bonaparte showed me all he has – a small 'Dictionnaire de la Langue Franque, ou Petit Mauresque, à l'usage des Français en Afrique,' published some years ago at Marseilles, and a page from the *Journal de l'Algérie*, giving a dialogue between a lady and a hammal. Prince Bonaparte knew two French officials who thought they had heard or seen Lingua Franca, and that is much about the same thing. The dictionary is a word-book of Italian, with an occasional form approaching Spanish, and, of course, some local words used in Algeria.

The opinion of Prince Bonaparte, who has bestowed so much attention on the dialects of Europe, is that the so-called Lingua Franca is Italian, and that in no place or case is it rightly to be called a dialect. This was the opinion to which I had already come, and the sight of the dictionary confirmed me; and it amounts to this, that there is no such separate language as Lingua Franca, which has been so long and so often referred to in books of Eastern travel.

The explanation of the name of this alleged language appears simple. In the late centuries of the Byzantine empire and early centuries of the Mussulman conquests, the Genoese and the Venetians carried on the commerce of Europe, as the remains and traditions of their factories are to be found in every port, and sometimes in inland towns. Thus this Italian, not the Lingua Toscana in bocca Romana, being the language of commerce with the lands of the Franks, was by the Greeks considered the language of the Franks. Italian it would not be called, because it was the language of the Genoese of the city, or it might be of the Venetians. When the Mussulmans became rulers, this Italian was still the Frank language, for they did not look on the Greeks as Franks. The dispersion of the Spanish Jews and of the Moors of Spain supplied a greater number of practitioners, who founded a cognate language.

When the trade came into the hands of the French, Dutch, and English merchant, he found his Greek and Jewish brokers speaking with him, not his own language of course, but what was called Lingua Franca; and the traveller visiting the factory, heard of this Lingua, found it cited in the bazaar, and professed by his dragoman. What is both Spanish and Italian passed muster with the Jews, but what was not was replaced by Spanish. Thus, as in some parts of Barbary, where there were more Jews and Moors than Italians, the Spanish words were more frequent. It will be noticed that the dictionary has an alternative suggestive title of Petite Mauresque. In Turkey I consider that Italian is being dethroned by French; but, on the other hand, among the Jews Spanish is being modified by Italian.

Louis-Lucien Bonaparte
(No. 2586, 19 May 1877, p. 640)

I THOROUGHLY agree with Mr. Hyde Clarke in considering the so-called Lingua Franca as Italian, but, at the same time, I think that the qualification of

Italian dialect cannot be denied to it. In fact, if Mr. Hyde Clarke admits, on the one hand, as I do, that the Lingua Franca is Italian, and on the other hand, recognizes that this kind of Italian is not the "Lingua Toscana in bocca Romana" (a popular denomination for the standard Italian, to which I would prefer that of "Lingua Toscana in bocca Toscana"), it seems to me that the difference between the Lingua Franca and the literary Italian ought to be indicated by the qualification of dialect applied to the first. Here is a short specimen of both: –

Lingua Franca, with Italian Orthography.	*Italian, Literal Translation.*
Bon giorno, Signor; comme ti star?	Buon giorno, Signore; come stai?
Mi star bono, e ti?	Io sto bene, e tu?
Mi star contento mirar per ti.	I son contento di vederti.
Grazia.	Grazie.
Mi pudir servir per ti per qualche cosa?	Poss' io servirti in qualche cosa?
Muciu grazia.	Molte grazie.
Ti dar una cadiera al Signor.	Dà una seggiola al Signore.
Non bisogna.	Non abbisogna.
Mi star bene acousì.	Io sto bene così.
Comme star il fratello di ti?	Come sta il tuo fratello?
Star muchiu bonu.	Sta molto bene.

The almost entire absence of grammatical forms, and the introduction of Spanish and other non-Italian words, secure to the Lingua Franca, according to my opinion, the rank of an independent Italian dialect quite distinct from the Genoese, the Venetian, &c. The Indo-Portuguese of Ceylon, the Negro-Dutch of the Danish-American islands, the different French-Creolese dialects, &c., stand in the same dialectal relation to the literary languages of Portugal, Holland, and France, as the Lingua Franca does to the standard Italian.

Hyde Clarke
(No. 2587, 28 May 1877, pp. 671–672)

It is a matter of regret to me to have misunderstood the Prince Bonaparte on one head, for I thought he denied to Lingua Franca the quality of a dialect, and regarded it only as a "parler."

However, I must demur to the title of dialect, because I doubt the existence of Lingua Franca, and only admit, with the Prince, Italian as the language, and this notwithstanding the compilation of a dictionary of Lingua Franca or *Mauresque*, as I should doubt a dictionary of the French or *Mauresque*, spoken in Algeria.

If Lingua Franca has an independent existence, then there will be something else besides a dialect, for there will be a number of sub-dialects for each port, according as the low Italian is badly spoken in Algiers, Tunis, or Smyrna, and other sub-dialects for each port, according to the population of each, Jewish, Arab, or Greek.

The claim for Lingua Franca is the same as if it were asserted there is a language or even dialect called Broken English, which is spoken differently by Frenchmen, Hollanders, Germans, Danes, Spaniards, Italians, Greeks, &c., for Lingua Franca is not in the same condition as Indo-Portuguese or Negro-Dutch.

As Prince Bonaparte has well laid down, Italian is a language spoken by Italians or others in the Levant, and I add that it is spoken to them differently, according as it comes from the mouth of a Greek, a Moor, and more particularly of a Spanish Jew. If a Spanish Jew in Algiers speaking Italian uses, as he would in speaking French, Spanish words, *mucho* for *molto*, *bono* for *bene*, or *gracia* for *grazie*, that constitutes a "parler," and not a dialect. This does not prove that a Greek would use *mucho* for *molto*. English and French are much altered by Levantines and Greeks, and particularly when a local term, as Han or Khan, Konak, Bazar, Janissary, is introduced, but no one maintains that English or French is Lingua Franca. French is, perhaps, as largely used as Italian as a common language in Mediterranean countries, and with a strong flavor of Provençal, as the Italian has of Genoese, Neapolitan, or Venetian. French, too, is used a [sic] barbarously by some ill-trained practitioners, but it would hardly be safe for philologists to establish a French Lingua Franca.

Louis-Lucien Bonaparte
(No. 2588, 2 June 1877, p. 703)

Mr. Hyde Clarke will not admit that the Lingua Franca is an Italian dialect, and that it stands in the same dialectal relation to the Italian as the Indo-Portuguese and the Negro-Dutch to the languages of Portugal and Holland. Evidence, however, is against him. In fact, what characterizes the Portuguese and Dutch dialects of Ceylon and the Danish-American islands is, above, all, the loss of the grammatical forms and the introduction of a certain number of words not used in Portugal or Holland. The same happens with the Lingua Franca, and it would be illogical to deny the quality of dialect to the last without denying it also to the former. Moreover, the Lingua Franca is spoken in several uniform sub-dialects and varieties, according to certain localities, such being the case with all dialects.

In the Lingua Franca of Algiers *muciu*, and not *molto*, is the word for "much," and *muciu* would be used by Jews or Greeks, or any one else acquainted with the variety of Lingua Franca of that town.

I cannot admit that words peculiar to the Genoese, Neapolitan, or Venetian dialects are to be found in any important number in the Lingua Franca.

There is not along the shores of the Mediterranean such a thing as a French or an English Lingua Franca corresponding to the Italian Lingua Franca, as it would be impossible to establish for the French or English badly spoken in Mediterranean countries, or altered by Levantines and Greeks, the following grammatical rules which apply so well to the real Lingua Franca: – 1. The nouns have no plural: *amigo* "friend, friends." 2. The verbs have no conjugation, but only a periphrastic future and a participle ending in *ato* or *ito: mi*, *ti*, *ellu*, *noi*, *voi*, *elli*, *andar* mean not only "I go, thou goest, he goes, we go, you go, they go," but also "I went," &c.; *mi*, *ti*, *&c*., *bisogno andar*, stands for "I shall go, though wilt go, &c." 3. *Star* means both "to be" and "to have," when they are used as auxiliary verbs. 4. *Avir* or *tenir* means "to have," but only with the meaning of "to possess." 5. The direct regimen of the personal pronouns is preceded by the preposition *per: mi mirar per ellu*, "I see him."

The Lingua Franca is decidedly an Italian dialect differing from the standard Italian, particularly in its grammar, more than any real Italian dialect of Italy, and to such an extent that some Italians (wrongly, according to my opinion) refuse it even the qualification of Italian.

The linguistical difference between a dialect and a "parler" seems to me specious in the present case, and I conclude my remarks, the last I shall make on this rather dry subject, by stating that the Italian dialect called Lingua Franca ought not to be confounded with the regular Italian, more or less correctly spoken, as an acquired language, by a great number of natives of the Mediterranean countries.[2]

[2] A reviewer notes that the views expressed by Clarke and Bonaparte are both alive today, referencing Lafi (2004) as an example. I am grateful to the anonymous reviewer for this point and this reference.

References

Acquaviva, Paolo. 2009. The structure of the Italian declension system. In *Selected Proceedings of the 6th Décembrettes*, Fabio Montermini, Gilles Boyé & Jesse Tseng (eds.), 50–62. Somervile, MA: Cascadilla Proceedings Project.

Adams, Charles Francis (ed.). 1875. *Memoirs of John Quincy Adams Comprising Portions of His Diary from 1795 to 1848*. Vol. 7. Philadelphia, PA: J. B. Lippincott.

(ed.). 1876. *Memoirs of John Quincy Adams Comprising Portions of His Diary from 1795 to 1848*. Vol. 8. Philadelphia, PA: J. B. Lippincott.

Ahmed, Haoues. 2009. Code-switching and borrowing in Algeria. *Revue Sciences Humaines* 32: 97–107.

Ageron, Charles-Robert. 1991. *Modern Algeria: A History from 1830 to the Present*. Michael Brett (ed. & trans.). Trenton, NJ: Africa World Press.

Allwood, Jens. 1998. Some frequency based differences between spoken and written Swedish. In *Papers from the XVIth Scandinavian Conference of Linguistics*, 18–29. Turku University: Department of Linguistics.

Alonso Ramos, Margarita. 1998. *Étude sémantico-syntaxique des constructions à verbe support*. PhD dissertation, University of Montreal.

2009. Delimitando la intersección entre composición y fraseología. *Lingüística Española Actual* 31: 243–275.

Amelung, Peter. 1964. *Das Bild des Deutschen in der Literatur der italienischen Renaissance (1400–1559)*. Munich: Max Hueber.

Anderson, Stephen R. 1985. Typological distinctions in word formation. In *Language Typology and Syntactic Description*, vol. 3, *Grammatical Categories and the Lexicon*, Timothy Shopen (ed.), 3–56. Cambridge: Cambridge University Press.

Anonymous. 1830a. *Dictionnaire de la langue franque ou petit mauresque, suivi de quelques dialogues familièrs et d'un vocabulaire de mots arabes les plus usuels; à l'usage des Français en Afrique*. Marseilles: Typographie de Feissat ainé et Demonchy.

1830b. *Alger. Topographie, population, forces militaires de terre et de mer, acclimatement et resources que le pays peut offrir à l'armée d'expédition, precedé d'un résume historique; suivi d'un précis sur le service des troupes pendant un siège et orné d'un plan très exact de la ville et de ses environs. Par un Français qui a résidé à Alger*. Marseilles: Typographie de Feissat ainé et Demonchy.

1852. La lanque sabir. *L'Algérien*, May 11.

Ansaldo, Umberto. 2009. *Contact Languages: Ecology and Evolution in Asia*. Cambridge: Cambridge University Press.

Arce, Ángeles. 1988. Principales gramáticas y diccionarios bilingües en la España del XIX. In *En el siglo XIX italiano*, 7–15. Salamanca: Ediciones de la Universidad.

Arends, Jacques. 1997. The Lingua Franca hypothesis: A review of the evidence. Paper read at the meeting of the Society for Pidgin and Creole Linguistics, London, June.

1998. A bibliography of Lingua Franca. *The Carrier Pidgin* 26: 4–5, 33–35.

2005. Lingua Franca. In *Encyclopedia of Linguistics*, Philipp Strazny (ed.), vol. 1, 625–626. New York: Fitzroy Dearborn.

Argent, Gesine, Vladislav Rjéoutski & Derek Offord. 2014. European francophonie and a framework for its study. In *European Francophonie: The Social, Political and Cultural History of an International Prestige Language*, Vladislav Rjéoutski, Gesine Argent & Derek Offord (eds.), 1–31. Oxford: Peter Lang.

Aslanov, Cyril. 2002. Quand les langues romanes se confondent… La Romania vue d'ailleurs. *Langage et société* 99: 9–52.

2006. *Le français au Levant, jadis et naguère: à la recherche d'une langue perdue.* Paris: Honoré Champion.

2010. Débat sur l'ouvrage de Jocelyne Dakhlia, *Lingua franca: histoire d'une langue métisse en Méditerranée. Langage et Société* 134: 103–113.

2014. Lingua Franca in the Western Mediterranean: Between myth and reality. In *Congruence in Contact-induced Language Change: Language Families, Typological Resemblance, and Perceived Similarity*, Juliane Besters-Dilger, Cynthia Dermarkar, Stefan Pfänder & Achim Rabus (eds.), 122–136. Berlin: De Gruyter.

2016. La lingua franca fra ieri e oggi. In *Intercomprensione: lingue, processi e percorsi*, Elisabetta Bonvino & Marie-Christine Jamet (eds.), 29–41. Venice: Edizioni Ca' Foscari.

Ayafor, Miriam & Melanie Green. 2017. *Cameroon Pidgin English: A Comprehensive Grammar*. Amsterdam: John Benjamins.

Baglioni, Daniele. 2010. *L'italiano delle cancellerie tunisine (1590–1703): edizione e commento linguistico delle "Carte Cremona."* Rome: Scienze e Lettere.

2011. Lettere dall'impero ottomano alla corte di Toscana (1577–1640). *Un contributo alla conoscenza dell'italiano scritto nel Levante. Lingua e Stile* 46: 3–70.

2015. Italian loanwords in Maltese and the vocabulary of "Levant Italian." In *Perspectives on Maltese Linguistics*, Albert Borg, Sandro Caruana & Alexandra Vella (eds.), 45–58. Berlin: Akademie.

2016. L'italiano fuori d'Italia: dal Medioevo all'Unità. In *Manuale di linguistica italiana*, Sergio Lubello (ed.), 125–145. Berlin & Boston: Walter de Gruyter.

2017. The vocabulary of the Algerian Lingua Franca. *Lexicographica* 33: 185–205.

2018. Attestazioni precinquecentesche della lingua franca? Pochi dati, molti problemi. In *Migrazioni della lingua: nuovi studi sull'italiano fuori d'Italia. Atti del Convegno internazionale dell'Università per Stranieri di Perugia, 3–4 maggio 2018*, Francesca Malagnini (ed.), 69–91. Florence: Franco Cesati.

Baker, Paul. 2006. *Using Corpora in Discourse Analysis*. London: Continuum.

Bakker, Peter. 1994. Pidgins. In *Pidgins and Creoles: An Introduction*, Jacques Arends, Pieter Muysken & Norval Smith (eds.), 25–39. Amsterdam: John Benjamins.

2003. Pidgin inflectional morphology and its implications for creole morphology. In *Yearbook of Morphology 2002*, Geert Booij & Jaap van Marle (eds.), 3–33. Dordrecht: Kluwer.

2008. Pidgins versus creoles and pidgincreoles. In *The Handbook of Pidgin and Creole Studies*, Silvia Kouwenberg & John Victor Singler (eds.), 130–157. Boston: Wiley-Blackwell.

Bakker, Peter & Yaron Matras (eds.), *Contact Languages: A Comprehensive Guide*, Berlin: De Gruyter Mouton.

Banfi, Emanuele. 1986. L'italiano degli altri. *Italiano e Oltre* 5: 231–234.

Bannard, Colin. 2006. *Acquiring phrasal lexicons from corpora*. PhD dissertation, University of Edinburgh.

Baños, José Miguel. 2012. Verbos soporte e incorporación sintáctica en latín: el ejemplo de *ludos facere*. *Revista de Estudios Latinos* 12: 37–57.

Bauer, Brigitte L. M. 2011. Word formation. In *The Cambridge History of the Romance Languages*, Martin Maiden, John C. Smith & Adam Ledgeway (eds.), vol. 1, 532–563. Cambridge: Cambridge University Press.

Bauer, Laurie. 2004. The function of word-formation and the inflection-derivation distinction. In *Words in Their Places: A Festschrift for J. Lachlan Mackenzie*, Henk Aertsen, Mike Hannay & Rod Lyall (eds.), 283–292. Amsterdam: Vrije Universiteit.

Benincà, Paola. 1980. Nomi senza articolo. *Rivista di Grammatica Generativa* 5: 51–62.

1997. Sentence word order. In *The Dialects of Italy*, Martin Maiden & Mair Parry (eds.), 123–130. London: Routledge.

2012. Determiners and relative clauses. *Iberia* 4: 92–109.

Benincà, Paola, Giampaolo Salvi & Lorenza Frison. 2001. L'ordine degli elementi della frase e le costruzioni marcate. In *Grande grammatica italiana di consultazione*, Lorenzo Renzi, Giampaolo Salvi & Anna Cardinaletti (eds.), 129–239. Bologna: il Mulino.

Benkato, Adam. 2020. Maghrebi Arabic. In *Arabic and Contact-Induced Change*, Christopher Lucas & Stefano Manfredi (eds.), 197–212. Berlin: Language Science Press.

Bernardini, Pietra. 2011. Qualificativi, aggettivi. In *Enciclopedia dell'italiano*. www.treccani.it/enciclopedia/aggettivi-qualificativi_(Enciclopedia-dell'Italiano)/.

Bernini, Giuliano. 1986. L'italiano senza maestro. *Italiano e Oltre* 1: 179–183.

1987. Le preposizioni nell'italiano lingua seconda. *Quaderni del Dipartimento di Linguistica e Letterature Comparate* 3: 129–152.

1989. Strategie di costruzione dei paradigmi verbali in lingua seconda. *Quaderni del Dipartimento di Linguistica e Letterature Comparate* 5: 195–208.

2010a. Italiano come pidgin. In *Enciclopedia dell'italiano*. www.treccani.it/enciclopedia/italiano-come-pidgin_(Enciclopedia-dell'Italiano)/.

2010b. Foreigner talk. In *Enciclopedia dell'italiano*. www.treccani.it/enciclopedia/foreigner-talk_(Enciclopedia-dell'Italiano)/.

Berretta, Monica. 1986. Per uno studio dell'apprendimento dell'italiano in contesto naturale: il caso dei pronomi personali atoni. In *L'apprendimento spontaneo di una seconda lingua*, Anna Giacalone Ramat (ed.), 329–353. Bologna: Il Mulino.

1988a. "Che sia ben chiaro ciò di cui parli": riprese anaforiche tra chiarificazione e semplificazione. *Annali della Facoltà di Lettere dell'Universita di Cagliari* n.s. 8: 367–389.

1988b. Interferenza ed elaborazione autonoma nell'apprendimento dell'italiano come lingua seconda. *Quaderni del Dipartimento di Linguistica e Letterature Comparate* 4: 213–231.

1989. Sulla presenza dell'accusativo preposizionale in italiano settentrionale: note tipologiche. *Vox Romanica* 48: 13–37.

1990. Sull'accusativo preposizionale in italiano. In *Parallela 4. Morfologia / Morphologie*, Monica Berretta, Piera Molinelli & Ada Valentini (eds.), 179–189. Tübingen: Gunter Narr.

1991. Note sulla sintassi dell'accusativo preposizionale in italiano. *Linguistica* 31: 211–232.

1992. Marcatezza in morfologia e apprendimento di lingue seconde. *Quaderni del Dipartimento di Linguistica e Letterature Comparate* 8: 129–156.

Berretta, Monica & Giuseppina Crotta. 1991. Italiano L2 in un soggetto plurilingue (cantonese-maltese-inglese): sviluppo di morfologia. *Studi Italiani di Linguistica Teorica ed Applicata* 20: 285–331.

Berruto, Gaetano. 1983a. L'italiano popolare e la semplificazione linguistica. *Vox Romanica* 42: 38–79.

1983b. Una nota su italiano regionale e italiano popolare. In *Scritti linguistici in onore di Giovan Battista Pellegrini*, Paola Benincà, Manlio Cortelazzo, Aldo Luigi Prosdocimi, Laura Vanelli & Alberto Zamboni (eds.), 481–488. Pisa: Pacini.

1991. *Fremdarbeiteritalienisch*: fenomeni di pidginizzazione dell'italiano nella Svizzera tedesca. *Rivista di Linguistica* 3: 333–367.

1993. Italiano in Europa oggi: *foreigner talk* nella Svizzera tedesca. In *Omaggio a Gianfranco Folena*, 2275–2290. Padova: Programma.

2012. *Sociolinguistica dell'italiano contemporaneo*. 2nd ed. Rome: Carocci.

Berruto, Gaetano, Bruno Moretti & Stephan Schmid. 1990. Interlingue italiane nella Svizzera tedesca. Osservazioni generali e note sul sistema dell'articolo. In *Storia dell'italiano e forme dell'italianizzazione*, Emanuele Banfi & Patrizia Cordin (eds.), 203–228. Rome: Bulzoni.

Bierbach, Christine. 1988. Tedesco, francese, spagnolo e tutti quanti: la perception de la différence linguistique et l'articulation de stéréotypes nationales dans des texts italiens autour de 1600. In *Actes du XVIII Congrès Internacional de Linguistique et de Philologie Romanes*, Dieter Kremer (ed.), vol. 5, 129–143. Tübingen: Max Niemeyer.

Bilous, Rostyslav. 2011. *Transitivité et marquage d'objet différentiel*. PhD dissertation, University of Toronto.

Birmingham, John C., Jr. 1976. Papiamentu: The long-lost Lingua Franca? *The American Hispanist* 2: 8–10.

Blum, Shoshana & E. A. Levenston. 1978. Universals of lexical simplification. *Language Learning* 28: 399–415.

Boerio, Giuseppe. 1867. *Dizionario del dialetto veneziano*. 3rd ed. Venice: Giovanni Cecchini.

Bonami, Olivier. 2015. Periphrasis as collocation. *Morphology* 25: 63–110.

Booij, Geert. 1994. Against split morphology. In *Yearbook of Morphology 1993*, Geert Booij & Jaap van Marle (eds.), 27–49. Dordrecht: Kluwer.

1996. Inherent versus contextual inflection and the split morphology hypothesis. In *Yearbook of Morphology 1995*, Geert Booij & Jaap van Marle (eds.), 1–16. Dordrecht: Kluwer.

2007. *The Grammar of Words: An Introduction to Linguistic Morphology*. 2nd ed. Oxford: Oxford University Press.

Borg, Alexander. 1996. On some Mediterranean influences on the lexicon of Maltese. In *Romania Arabica: Festschrift für Reinhold Kontzi zum 70*. Geburtstag, Jens Lüdtke (ed.), 129–150. Tübingen: Gunter Narr.

Bossong, Georg. 1991. Differential object marking in Romance and beyond. In *New Analyses in Romance Linguistics*, Dieter Wanner & Douglas A. Kibbee (eds.), 143–170. Amsterdam: John Benjamins.

Bourciez, Édouard. 1967. *Éléments de linguistique romane*. 5th ed. Paris: Librairie C. Klincksieck.

Brann, Conrad Max Benedict. 1994. Réflexions sur la langue franque (lingua franca): origine et actualité. *La Linguistique* 30: 149–159.

Bray, Laurent. 1986. Richelet's *dictionnaire françois* (1680) as a source of *La porte des siences* (1682) and Le Roux's *Dictionnaire comique* (1718). In *The History of Lexicography*, R. R. K. Hartmann (ed.), 13–22. Amsterdam: John Benjamins.

1990. La lexicographie française des origines à Littré. In *Wörterbücher. Ein internationales Handbuch zur Lexikographie*, Franz Josef Hausmann, Oskar Reichmann, Herbert Ernst Wiegand & Ladislav Zgusta (eds.), vol. 2, 1788–1818. Berlin: Walter de Gruyter.

Bresnier, Louis-Jacques. 1855. *Cours pratique et théorique de la langue arabe renfermant les principes détaillés de la lecture, de la grammaire et du style ainsi que les éléments de la prosodie, accompagné d'un traité du langage arabe usuel et de ses divers dialectes en Algérie*. Algiers: Bastide.

Breu, Walter. 1991. Abweichungen vom phonetischen Prinzip bei der Integration von Lehnwörtern. In *Slavistische Linguistik 1990: Referate des XVI. Konstanzer Slavistischen Arbeitstreffens Bochum/Löllingshausen 19.-21.9.1990*, Klaus Hartenstein & Helmut Jachnow (eds.), 36–70. Munich: Otto Sagner.

Broughton, Mrs. 1840. *Six Years Residence in Algiers*. 2nd ed. London: Saunders and Otley.

Brown, Cecil H. 2001. Lexical typology from an anthropological point of view. In *Language Typology and Language Universals*, Martin Haspelmath, Ekkehard König, Wulf Oesterreicher & Wolfgang Raible (eds.), vol. 2, 1178–1190. Berlin: Walter de Gruyter.

2013. Hand and arm. In *The World Atlas of Language Structures Online*, Matthew S. Dryer & Martin Haspelmath (eds.). Leipzig: Max Planck Institute for Evolutionary Anthropology. http://wals.info/chapter/129.

Brown, Esther L. & Javier Rivas. 2011. Subject-verb word-order in Spanish interrogatives: A quantitative analysis of Puerto Rican Spanish. *Spanish in Context* 8: 23–49.

Brower, Benjamin Claude. 2009. *A Desert Named Peace: The Violence of France's Empire in the Algerian Sahara, 1844–1902*. New York: Columbia University Press.

Bruyn, Adrienne. 2008. Grammaticalization in pidgins and creoles. In *The Handbook of Pidgin and Creole Studies*, Silvia Kouwenberg & John Victor Singler (eds.), 385–410. Chichester: Wiley-Blackwell.

Bryson, Thomas A. 1979. *An American Consular Officer in the Middle East in the Jacksonian Era: A Biography of William Brown Hodgson, 1801–1871*. Atlanta, GA: Resurgens.

Buchi, Éva & Jean-Paul Chauveau. 2015. From Latin to Romance. In *Word-Formation: An International Handbook of the Languages of Europe*, Peter O. Müller, Ingeborg Ohnheiser, Susan Olsen & Franz Rainer (eds.), vol. 3, 1931–1957. Berlin: Walter de Gruyter.

Buenafuentes de la Mata, Cristina. 2007. *Procesos de gramaticalización y lexicalización en la formación de compuestos en español*. PhD dissertation, Autonomous University of Barcelona.

Bunis, David M. 2016. Judezmo (Ladino). In *Handbook of Jewish Languages*, Lily Kahn & Aaron D. Rubin (eds.), 365–450. Leiden: Brill.

Butros, Albert. 1973. Turkish, Italian, and French loanwords in the colloquial Arabic of Palestine and Jordan. *Studies in Linguistics* 23: 87–104.

Butt, John & Carmen Benjamin. 2004. *A New Reference Grammar of Modern Spanish*. 4th ed. New York: McGraw-Hill.

Bybee, Joan L. 1995. Spanish tense and aspect from a typological perspective. In *Studies in Language Learning and Spanish Linguistics in Honor of Tracy Terrell*, Peggy Hashemipour, Ricardo Maldonado & Margaret van Naerssen (eds.), 442–457. San Francisco, CA: McGraw-Hill.

Bybee, Joan L. & William Pagliuca. 1987. The evolution of future meaning. In *Papers from the VIIth International Conference on Historical Linguistics*, Anna Giacalone Ramat, Onorio Carruba & Giuliano Bernini (eds.), 109–122. Amsterdam: John Benjamins.

Calvo Rigual, Cesáreo. 2008. I verbi sintagmatici italiani: appunti contrastivi con lo spagnolo e il catalano. In *Estudios y análisis de fraseología contrastiva: lexicografía y traducción*, Carmen González Royo & Pedro Mogorrón (eds.), 47–66. Alicante: Universidad de Alicante.

Camamis, George. 1977. *Estudios sobre el cautiverio en el Siglo de Oro*. Madrid: Gredos.

Campbell, Lyle. 2013. *Historical Linguistics: An Introduction*. 3rd ed. Cambridge, MA: MIT Press.

Campos-Astorkiza, Rebeka. 2012. The phonemes of Spanish. In *Handbook of Hispanic Linguistics*, José Ignacio Hualde, Antxon Olarrea & Erin O'Rourke (eds.), 89–110. Boston, MA: Wiley-Blackwell.

Camus Bergareche, Bruno. 1993a. Lingua franca y lengua de moros. *Revista de Filología Española* 73: 417–426.

1993b. El estudio de la lingua franca: cuestiones pendientes. *Revue de Linguistique Romane* 57: 433–454.

2013. On *deísmo*. Another case of variation in Spanish complementation. *Catalan Journal of Linguistics* 12: 13–39.

Cardamone, Donna G. 1981. *The canzone villanesca alla napolitana and Related Forms, 1537–1570*. Vol. 1. Ann Arbor, MI: UMI Research Press.

Carlier, Anne, Walter De Mulder & Béatrice Lamiroy. 2012. Introduction: The pace of grammaticalization in a typological perspective. *Folia Linguistica* 46: 287–301.

Cassidy, Frederic G. 1966. Multiple etymologies in Jamaican Creole. *American Speech* 41: 211–215.

Castellanos, Carles. 2006. *La lingua franca. Consideracions crítiques. Traducció del document Proves documentals de la Lingua Franca de*

Christian Foltys amb pròleg i notes de Carles Castellanos. Girona: Documenta Universitaria.

2007. La lingua franca, una revolució lingüística mediterrània amb empremta catalana. Paper presented at XII Internacional Colloquium of the North American Catalan Society, Halifax, Canada, May 11–13. www.uab.cat/Document/439/403/castellanos_linguafranca2007.pdf.

Cennamo, Michela. 2015. Valency patterns in Italian. In *Valency Classes in the World's Languages*, Andrej Malchukov & Bernard Comrie (eds.), vol. 1, 417–481. Berlin: De Gruyter Mouton.

Chatelain, René Julien. 1828. *Mémoire sur les moyens a employer pour punir Alger, et detruire la piraterie des puissances barbaresques; précédé d'un précis historique sur le caractère, les moeurs et la manière de combattre des musulmans habitant la côte d'Afrique, et d'un coup d'oeil sur les expéditions françaises tentées contre eux a diverses époques*. Paris: Anselin.

Chaudenson, Robert. 2001. *Creolization of Language and Culture*. London: Routledge.

Chitoran, Ioana. 2002. *The Phonology of Romanian: A Constraint-Based Approach*. Berlin: Mouton de Gruyter.

Cifoletti, Guido. 1975. Prestiti italiani nel dialetto del Cairo. *Incontri Linguistici* 2: 135–147.

1978. *Lingua franca* e *sabir*: Considerazioni storiche et terminologiche. *Incontri Linguistici* 4: 205–212.

1979. La parola *fantasia* nelle lingue del Mediterraneo. *Incontri Linguistici* 5: 139–145.

1980. *Il vocabolario della lingua franca*. Padova: CLESP.

1983. La lingua italiana in Egitto. In *Scritti linguistici in onore di Giovan Battista Pellegrini*, Paola Benincà, Manlio Cortelazzo, Aldo Luigi Prosdocimi, Laura Vanelli & Alberto Zamboni (eds.), 1259–1264. Pisa: Pacini.

1989. *La lingua franca mediterranea*. Padova: Unipress.

1991. L'influsso arabo sulla Lingua Franca. In *Atti della quinta giornata comparatistica*, Antonio Loprieno (ed.), 34–39. Perugia: Dipartimento di Linguistica e Filologia Romanza.

1994a. A proposito di lingua franca. *Incontri Linguistici* 17: 155–170.

1994b. Aggiornamenti sulla lingua franca mediterranea. In *Languages of the Mediterranean: Substrata – The Islands – Malta*, J. M. Brincat (ed.), 143–149. Malta: Institute of Linguistics, University of Malta.

2000. La lingua franca a Venezia nel settecento. In *Documenti letterari del plurilinguismo*, Vincenzo Orioles (ed.), 9–18. Rome: Il Calamo.

2002. Coincidenze lessicali tra la lingua franca e l'arabo tunisino. *Incontri Linguistici* 25: 125–150.

2004. *La lingua franca barbaresca*. Rome: Il Calamo.

2007. Lingue franche mediterranee. *Plurilinguismo* 14: 105–112.

Cinque, Guglielmo. 1996. Genitivo e genitivi pronominali nel DP italiano. In *Italiano e dialetti nel tempo: saggi di gramática per Giulio C. Lepschy*, Baola Benincà, Guglielmo Cinque, Tullio de Mauro & Nigel Vincent (eds.), 67–84. Rome: Bulzoni.

Clarke, Hyde & Louis-Lucien Bonaparte. 1877. Correspondence on Lingua Franca. *The Athenaeum: Journal of Literature, Science, the Fine Arts, Music and the Drama* 545, 607–608, 640, 671–672, 703.

Clements, J. Clancy. 2003. The tense-aspect system in pidgins and naturalistically learned L2. *Studies in Second Language Acquisition* 25: 245–281.

2009. *The Linguistic Legacy of Spanish and Portuguese: Colonial Expansion and Language Change*. Cambridge: Cambridge University Press.

2012. The Spanish-based creoles. In *Handbook of Hispanic Linguistics*, José Ignacio Hualde, Antxón Olarréa & Erin O'Rouke (eds.), 27–46. Oxford: Blackwell.

2014. Form selection in contact languages: Evidence from some Portuguese- and Spanish-lexified contact varieties. In *Portuguese-Spanish Interfaces: Diachrony, Synchrony, and Contact*, Patricia Amaral & Ana Maria Carvalho (eds.), 377–401. Amsterdam: John Benjamins.

Clewlow, David Frederick. 1990. *Judeo-Spanish: An Example from Rhodes*. MA thesis, University of British Columbia.

Clissold, Stephen. 1977. *The Barbary Slaves*. Totowa, NJ: Rowman and Littlefield.

Clough, James Cresswell. 1876. *The Existence of Mixed Languages*. London: Longmans, Green.

Coates, William A. 1970. The German Pidgin-Italian of the 16th-century *lanzichenecchi*. In *Papers from the Fourth Annual Kansas Linguistics Conference*, Herbert Harris (ed.), 66–74. Lawrence: University of Kansas.

1971. The Lingua Franca. In *Papers from the Fifth Kansas Linguistics Conference*, Frances Ingemann (ed.), 25–34. Lawrence: University of Kansas.

Cohen, Marcel. 1912. *Le parler arabe des juifs d'Alger*. Paris: H. Champion.

Collier, Barbara. 1977. On the origins of Lingua Franca. *Journal of Creole Studies* 1: 281–298.

Collison, Robert L. 1982. *A History of Foreign-Language Dictionaries*. London: André Deutsch.

Cordin, Patrizia. 2001. I possessivi: pronomi e aggettivi. In *Grande grammatica italiana di consultazione*, Lorenzo Renzi, Giampaolo Salvi & Anna Cardinaletti (eds.), 619–630. Bologna: il Mulino.

Cornelissen, Ralf. 1992. Zur Lingua Franca des Mittelmeers. In *Beiträge zur sprachlichen, literarischen und kulturellen Vielfalt in der Philologien*, Gabriele Birken-Silverman & Gerda Rössler (eds.), 217–228. Stuttgart: Franz Steiner.

Cornilescu, Alexandra & Anca Dinu. 2013. Adjectives and specificity. *Revue Roumaine de Linguistique* 58: 455–480.

Corriente, Federico. 1997. *A Dictionary of Andalusi Arabic*. Leiden: Brill.

Cortelazzo, Manlio. 1965. Che cosa s'intendesse per "lingua franca." *Lingua Nostra* 26: 108–110.

1970–1971. Il linguaggio schiavonesco nel Cinquecento veneziano. *Atti dell'Istituto Veneto di Scienze, Lettere ed Arti* 130: 113–160.

1972. Nuovi contributi alla conoscenza del grechesco. *Italia Dialettale* 35: 50–64.

1977. Il contributo del veneziano e del greco alla lingua franca. In *Venezia: centro di mediazione tra Oriente e Occidente (secoli XV-XVI). Aspetti e problemi*, Hans-Georg Beck, Manoussos Manoussacas & Agostino Pertusi (eds.), vol. 2, 523–535. Florence: Leo S. Olschki.

1980. Esperienze ed esperimenti plurilinguistici. In *Storia della cultura veneta*, vol. 3/II, *Dal Primo Quattrocento al Concilio di Trento*, Girolamo Arnaldi & Manlio Pastore (eds.), 183–213. Vicenza: Neri Pozza.

1983. Ancora un testo *schiavonesco*: la *Comedia de Ravanello*. *Atti e Memorie della Società Istriana di Archeologia e Storia Patria* 31 n.s.: 269–274.

Costanzo, Angelo Roth. 2011. *Romance conjugational classes: Learning from the peripheries*. PhD dissertation, Ohio State University.

Coutelle, Louis. 1971. *Le greghesco: réexamin des éléments néo-grecs dex textes comiques vénitiens du XVIe siècle*. Thessalonica: ELLENIKA.

1977. Grec, greghesco, lingua franca. In *Venezia: centro di mediazione tra Oriente e Occidente (secoli XV-XVI). Aspetti e problemi*, Hans-Georg Beck, Manoussos Manoussacas & Agostino Pertusi (eds.), vol. 2, 537–544. Florence: Leo S. Olschki.

Couto, Hildo Honório do. 2002. *A língua franca mediterrânea: histórico, textos e interpretação*. Brasilia: Plano.

Cremona, Joseph. 1996. L'italiano in Tunisi. La lingua di alcuni testi del tardo'500 e del'600. In *Italiano e dialetti nel tempo: saggi di grammatica per Giulio C. Lepschy*, Paola Benincà, Guglielmo Cinque, Tullio de Mauro & Nigel Vincent (eds.), 85–97. Rome: Bulzoni.

2002. Italian-based Lingua Francas around the Mediterranean. In *Multilingualism in Italy: Past and Present*, Anna Laura Lepschy & Arturo Tosi (eds.), 24–30. Oxford: Legenda.

Cresti, Federico. 2005. La population d'Alger et son évolution durant l'époque ottomane: un état des connaissances controversé. *Arabica* 52: 457–495.

Crotta, Giuseppina. 1988. Italiano L2 in un soggetto plurilingue: il sistema verbale. *Quaderni del Dipartimento di Linguistica e Letterature Comparate* 4: 241–257.

Crowley, Terry. 2008. Pidgin and creole morphology. In *The Handbook of Pidgin and Creole Studies*, Silvia Kouwenberg & John Victor Singler (eds.), 74–97. Wiley-Blackwell.

Crystal, David. 2008. *A Dictionary of Linguistics and Phonetics*. 6th ed. Oxford: Blackwell.

Cysouw, Michael. 2013. Predicting language-learning difficulty. In *Approaches to Measuring Linguistic Differences*, Lars Borin & Anju Saxena (eds.), 57–81. Berlin & Boston: De Gruyter Mouton.

Cysouw, Michael & Bernhard Wälchli. 2007. Parallel texts: Using translational equivalents in linguistic typology. *Sprachtypologie und Universalienforschung* 60: 95–99.

D'Achille, Paolo & Anna M. Thornton. 2003. La flessione del nome dall'italiano antico all'italiano contemporaneo. In *Italia linguistica anno Mille – Italia linguistica anno Duemila. Atti del XXXIV congresso internationale di studi della Società di Linguistica Italiana*, Nicoletta Maraschio & Teresa Poggi Salani (eds.), 211–230. Rome: Bulzoni.

Da Tos, Martina. 2012. *The intramorphological meanings of thematic vowels in Italian verbs*. PhD dissertation, University of Padova.

Dahl, Östen. (1985). *Tense and Aspect Systems*. Oxford: Basil Blackwell.

Dakhlia, Jocelyne. 2008. *Lingua Franca: histoire d'une langue métisse en Méditerranée*. Arles: Actes Sud.

Dal Negro, Silvia. 1994. Il sistema verbale di apprendenti di Italiano L2 nella Svizzera tedesca. *Rivista Italiana di Dialettologia* 18: 51–77.

Dan, Pierre. 1649. *Histoire de Barbarie et des corsaires, des royaumes, et des villes d'Alger, de Tunis, de Salé, & de Tripoly*. Paris: Pierre Rocolet.

Davis, Robert C. 2003. *Christian Slaves, Muslim Masters: White Slavery in the Mediterranean, the Barbary Coast, and Italy, 1500–1800*. Hampshire: Palgrave Macmillan.

De Mauro, T. 1991. *Il vocabulario di base della lingua italiana*. In *Guida all'uso delle parole*, 149–183. Rome: Editori Riuniti.

Desfontaines, Louiche René. 1838. *Fragmens d'un voyage dans les régences de Tunis et d'Alger fait de 1783 à 1786*. In *Peyssonnel et Desfontaines. Voyages dans les régences de Tunis et d'Alger*, M. Dureau de la Malle (ed.), Vol. 2. Paris: Librairie de Gide.

Devic, L. Marcel. 1876. *Dictionnaire étymologique des mots français d'origine orientale (arabe, persan, turc, hébreu, malais)*. Paris: Imprimerie Nationale.

Dictionnaire de l'Académie Françoise. 1762. 4th ed. 2 vols. Paris: Chez la Veuve de Bernard Brunet.

Döhla, Hans-Jörg. 2016. The origin of differential object marking in Maltese. In *Shifts and Patterns in Maltese*, Gilbert Puech & Benjamin Saade (eds.), 149–172. Berlin: De Gruyter Mouton.

Dressler, Wolfgang U. 1985. Suppletion in word formation. In *Historical Semantics – Historical Word-Formation*, Jacek Fisiak (ed.), 97–112. Berlin: Mouton de Gruyter.

Dryer, Matthew S. & Orin D. Gensler. 2013. Order of object, oblique and verb. In *The World Atlas of Language Structures Online*, Matthew S Dryer & Martin Haspelmath (eds.). Leipzig: Max Planck Institute for Evolutionary Anthropology. http://wals.info/chapter/1.

Dryer, Matthew S. & Martin Haspelmath (eds.). 2013. *The World Atlas of Language Structures Online*. Leipzig: Max Planck Institute for Evolutionary Anthropology. http://wals.info.

Dubský, Josef. 1963. Las formas descompuestas en el español antiguo. *Revista de Filología Española* 46: 31–48.

Enrique-Arias, Andrés. 2010. On language contact as an inhibitor of language change: The Spanish of Catalan bilinguals in Majorca. In Anne Breitbarth, Christopher Lucas, Sheila Watts and David Willis (eds.), *Continuity and Change in Grammar*, 97–118. Amsterdam: John Benjamins.

Epalza, Míkel de & Abdel-Hakim Slama-Gafsi. 2010. *El español hablado en Túnez por los moriscos o andalusíes y sus descendientes (siglos XVII-XVIII). Material léxico y onomástico documentado, siglos XVII-XXI*. Valencia: Universitat de València.

Erman, Britt & Beatrice Warren. 2000. The idiom principle and the open choice principle. *Text* 20: 29–62.

Fagard, Benjamin & Alexandru Mardale. 2014. Non, mais tu l'as vu à lui? Analyse(s) du marquage différentiel de l'objet en français. *Verbum* 26: 145–170. https://halshs.archives-ouvertes.fr/halshs-01121653/document.

Faidherbe, Louis Léon César. 1884. L'Alliance française pour la propagation de la langue française dans les colonies et des pays étrangers. *Revue Scientifique, Jan.* 26: 104–109.

Ferguson, Charles A. 1971. Absence of copula and the notion of simplicity: A study of normal speech, baby talk, foreigner talk, and pidgins. In *Pidginization and*

Creolization of Languages, Dell Hymes (ed.), 141–150. Cambridge: Cambridge University Press.

Ferguson, Charles A. & Charles E. DeBose. 1977. Simplified registers, broken language, and pidginization. In *Pidgin and Creole Linguistics*, Albert Valdman (ed.), 99–125. Bloomington: Indiana University Press.

Field, James A. 1969. *America and the Mediterranean World 1776–1882*. Princeton, NJ: Princeton University Press.

Finnie, David H. 1967. *Pioneers East: The Early American Experience in the Middle East*. Cambridge, MA: Harvard University Press.

Fiorentino, Giuliana. 2010. Accusativo preposizionale. In *Enciclopedia dell'italiano*. www.treccani.it/enciclopedia/accusativo-preposizionale_(Enciclopedia-dell'Italiano)/.

Folena, Gianfranco. 1983. Le lingue della commedia e la commedia delle lingue. In *Scritti linguistici in onore di Giovan Battista Pellegrini*, Paola Benincà, Manlio Cortelazzo, Aldo Luigi Prosdocimi, Laura Vanelli & Alberto Zamboni (eds.), 1485–1513. Pisa: Pacini.

Foltys, Christian. 1984–1985. Die Belege der Lingua Franca. *Neue Romania* 1: 1–37, 2: 133–134.

1987. Das *Dictionnaire de la langue franque* von 1830 und die Frage der sprachlichen Expansion in der Lingua Franca. *Neue Romania* 5: 60–84.

Forza, Francesca & Sergio Scalise. 2016. Compounding. In *The Oxford Guide to the Romance Languages*, Adam Ledgeway & Martin Maiden (eds.), 523–537. Oxford: Oxford University Press.

Fronzaroli, Pelio. 1955. Nota sulla formazione della lingua franca. *Atti e Memorie dell' Academia Toscana di Scienze e Lettere La Colombaria* 20 (n.s. 6): 211–252.

Frost, Arthur C. 1965. Sidi-Ferruch: History repeats itself. *Foreign Service Journal* 42: 8–10, 52.

Gardani, Francesco. 2016. Allogenous exaptation. In *Exaptation and Language Change*, Muriel Norde & Freek Van De Velde (eds.), 227–260. Amsterdam: John Benjamins.

Gardani, Francesco, Peter Arkadiev & Nino Amiridze. 2015. Borrowed morphology: An overview. In *Borrowed Morphology*, Francesco Gardani, Peter Arkadiev & Nino Amiridze (eds.), 1–23. Berlin: De Gruyter Mouton.

Geeslin, Kimberly L. & Pedro Guijarro-Fuentes. 2008. Variation in contemporary Spanish: linguistic predictors of *estar* in four cases of language contact. *Bilingualism: Language and Cognition* 11: 365–380.

Genty de Bussy, Pierre. 1839. *De l'établissement des Français dans la régence d'Alger, et des moyens d'en assurer la prospérité*. 2nd ed. Paris: Firmin Didot.

Giacalone Ramat, Anna & Emanuele Banfi. 1990. The acquisition of temporality: A second language perspective. *Folia Linguistica* 24: 405–428.

Giorgi, Alessandra. 2001. La struttura interna dei sintagmi nominali. In *Grande grammatica italiana di consultazione*, Lorenzo Renzi, Giampaolo Salvi & Anna Cardinaletti (eds.), 287–328. Bologna: il Mulino.

Grandgent, Charles H. 1927. *From Latin to Italian: An Historical Outline of the Phonology and Morphology of the Italian Language*. Cambridge, MA: Harvard University Press.

Grant, Anthony P. 2008. The Portuguese elements in Papiamentu. In *Linguistic Studies on Papiamentu*, Nicholas Faraclas, Ronnie Severing & Christa Weijer (eds.), 47–72. Curaçao: Fundashon pa Planifikashon di Idioma.

Green, John N. 1988. Romance creoles. In *The Romance Languages*, Martin Harris & Nigel Vincent (eds.), 420–473. New York: Oxford University Press.

Greenberg, Joseph H. 1963. Some universals of grammar with particular reference to the order of meaningful elements. In *Universals of Language*, Joseph H. Greenberg (ed.), 58–90. London: MIT Press.

Grion, Giusto. 1890–1892. Farmacopea e lingua franca del dugento. *Archivio Glottologico Italiano* 12: 181–186.

Guella, Noureddine. 2011. Emprunts lexicaux dans des dialectes arabes algériens. *Synergies Monde Arabe* 8: 81–88.

Guglielmo, Daniela. 2010. Parlare coi "verbi sintagmatici." In *La comunicazione parlata 3. Atti del congresso internazionale (Napoli, 23–25 febbraio 2009)*, Massimo Pettorino, Antonella Giannini & Francesca M. Dovetto (eds.), vol. 1, 3–21. Università degli Studi di Napoli L'Orientale. http://opar.unior.it/336/1/La_comunicazione_parlata_3_-_vol._I.pdf.

Guichet, J. 1855. *An Italian and English Grammar, from the Italian and French Grammar of Vergani and Piranesi, Exemplified in Twenty Lessons, with Exercises, Dialogues, and Entertaining Historical Anecdotes.* London: Charles H. Law.

The Encyclopaedia Britannica, or Dictionary of Arts, Sciences, and General Literature. 1856. 8th ed. Vol. 10. Edinburgh: Adam and Charles Black.

Habte-Mariam, Marcos. 1976. Italian. In *Language in Ethiopia*, M. L. Bender, J. D. Bowen, R. L. Cooper & C. A. Ferguson (eds.), 170–180. London: Oxford University Press.

Haedo, Fray Diego de. 1612. *Topographia e historia general de Argel.* Valladolid.

Hardgreaves, Mary W. M. & James F. Hopkins (eds.). 1981. *The Papers of Henry Clay*, vol. 6, *Secretary of State 1827.* Lexington, KY: University Press of Kentucky.

Harris, James W. 1991. The exponence of gender in Spanish. *Linguistic Inquiry* 22: 27–62.

1992. The form classes of Spanish substantives. In *Yearbook of Morphology 1991*, Geert Booij & Jaap van Marle (eds.), 65–88. Dordrecht: Kluwer.

1996. The syntax and morphology of class marker suppression in Spanish. In *Grammatical Theory and Romance Languages*, Karen Zagona (ed.), 99–122. Amsterdam: John Benjamins.

Harris, Martin. 1988. French. In *The Romance Languages*, Martin Harris & Nigel Vincent (eds.), 209–245. New York: Oxford University Press.

Harris-Northall, Ray. 1996. The Old Spanish participle in *-udo*: Its origin, use, and loss. *Hispanic Review* 64: 31–56.

Harvey, L. P. 2005. *Muslims in Spain: 1500 to 1614*. Chicago, IL: University of Chicago Press.

Harvey, L. P., R. O. Jones & Keith Whinnom. 1967. Lingua Franca in a *villancico* by Encina. *Revue de Littérature Comparée* 41: 572–579.

Haspelmath, Martin. 1993. More on the typology of inchoative/causative verb alternations. In *Causatives and Transitivity*, Bernard Comrie & Maria Polinsky (eds.), 87–120. Amsterdam: John Benjamins.

2008. Loanword typology: Steps toward a systematic cross-linguistic study of lexical borrowability. In *Aspects of Language Contact: New Theoretical, Methodological and Empirical Findings with Special Focus on Romancisation Processes*, Thomas Stolz, Dik Bakker & Rosa Salas Palomo (eds.), 43–62. Berlin: Mouton de Gruyter.

Haspelmath, Martin & Uri Tadmor (eds.). 2009a. *Loanwords in the World's Languages: A Comparative Handbook.* The Hague: De Gruyter Mouton.

Haspelmath, Martin & Uri Tadmor. 2009b. The Loanword Typology project and the World Loanword Database. In *Loanwords in the World's Languages: A Comparative Handbook*, Martin Haspelmath & Uri Tadmor (eds.), 1–34. The Hague: De Gruyter Mouton.

Haspelmath, Martin & Susanne Maria Michaelis. 2017. Analytic and synthetic: Typological change in varieties of European languages. In *Language Variation – European Perspectives VI*, Isabelle Buchstaller & Beat Siebenhaar (eds.), 3–22. Amsterdam: John Benjamins.

Heath, Jeffrey. 1984. Language contact and language change. *Annual Review of Anthropology* 13: 367–384.

1989. *From Code-Switching to Borrowing: Foreign and Diglossic Mixing in Moroccan Arabic*. London: Kegan Paul International.

2015. D-possessives and the origins of Moroccan Arabic. *Diachronica* 32: 1–33.

Heine, Bernd. 1979. Some linguistic characteristics of African-based pidgins. In *Readings in Creole Studies*, Ian F. Hancock, Edgar Polomé, Morris Goodman & Bernd Heine (eds.), 89–98. Amsterdam: John Benjamins.

Heine, Bernd & Tania Kuteva. 2003. On contact-induced grammaticalization. *Studies in Language* 27: 529–572.

Hellinger, Marlis. 1985. *English-orientierte Pidgin- und Kreolsprachen: Entstehung, Geschichte und sprachlicher Wandel.* Darmstadt: Wissenschaftliche Buchgesellschaft.

Hengeveld, Kees. 1992. *Non-verbal Predication: Theory, Typology, Diachrony*. Berlin: Mouton De Gruyter.

Herman, H. 1837. *Memorien aus Algier oder Tagebuch eines deutschen Studenten in französischen Diensten*. Bern: C. Fischer und Comp.

Hess, Andrew C. 1978. *The Forgotten Frontier: A History of the Sixteenth-Century Ibero-African Frontier*. Chicago: University of Chicago Press.

Hodgson, William B. 1829. Grammatical sketch and specimens of the Berber language preceded by four letters on Berber etymologies, addressed to the President of the Society by William B. Hodgson, Esq. Read October 2nd, 1829. *Transactions of the American Philosophical Society* 4 (n.s.): 1–48.

1836. Lettre de M. William B. Hodgson, ancien consul américain a Alger, à M. d'Avezac, Sécretaire générale de la Commission centrale, Paris, le 29 septembre 1836. *Bulletin de la Société de la Géographie de Paris*, 2nd ser., 4, No. 31 (October 1836): 247–250.

1844. *Notes on Northern Africa, the Sahara and Soudan, in Relation to the Ethnography, Languages, History, Political and Social Condition, of the Nations of Those Countries*. New York: Wiley and Putnam.

1845. Remarks on the past history and present condition of Morocco, Algiers, and the Barbary Regencies. In *Proceedings of the New York Historical Society for the Year 1844*, 162–168. New York: Press of the Historical Society.

Holm, John. 2000. *An Introduction to Pidgins and Creoles*. Cambridge: Cambridge University Press.

Honeyfield, John. 1977. Simplification. *TESOL Quarterly* 11: 431–440.

Hopkins, James F. & Mary W. M. Hardgreaves (eds.). 1973. *The Papers of Henry Clay*, vol. 5, *Secretary of State 1826*. Lexington, KY: University Press of Kentucky.

Hull, Geoffrey. 1985. La parlata italiana dell'Egitto. *L'Italia Dialettale* 48: 243–254.

Hummel, Martin. 2017. Adjectives with adverbial function in Romance. In *Adjective Adverb Interfaces in Romance*, Martin Hummel & Salvador Valera (eds.), 13–46. Amsterdam: John Benjamins.

Iacobini, Claudio. 2004. Parasintesi. In *La formazione delle parole in italiano*, Maria Grossmann & Franz Rainer (eds.), 165–188. Tübingen: Max Niemeyer.

2009. Phrasal verbs between syntax and lexicon. *Italian Journal of Linguistics* 21(1): 97–117.

2015. Particle verbs in Romance. In *Word-Formation: An International Handbook of the Languages of Europe*, Peter O. Müller, Ingeborg Ohnheiser, Susan Olsen & Franz Rainer (eds.), vol. 1, 626–658. Berlin: Walter de Gruyter.

Iacobini, Claudio & Francesca Masini. 2007. Verb-particle constructions and prefixed verbs in Italian: Typology, diachrony and semantics. In *On-line Proceedings of the Fifth Mediterranean Morphology Meeting (MMM5), Fréjus 15–18 September 2005*, Geert Booij et al. (eds.), 157–184. University of Bologna. http://mmm.lingue.unibo.it/.

Iacobini, Claudio & Anna Maria Thornton. 1994. Italiano in quantità. *Italiano e Oltre* 9: 276–285.

Iemmolo, Giorgio. 2010. Topicality and DOM: Evidence from Romance and beyond. *Studies in Language* 34: 239–272.

Institut de France. 1835. *Dictionnaire de L'Académie Française*. 6th ed. 2 vols. Brussels: J. P. Meline.

Isačenko, Alexander V. 1974. On *have* and *be* languages: A typological sketch. In *Slavic Forum: Essays in Linguistics and Literature*, Michael S. Flier (ed.), 43–77. The Hague: Mouton.

Ives, Ernest L. 1936a. Colonel Tobias Lear. *American Foreign Service Journal* 13: 185–187, 220–226.

1936b. An adventurer turns diplomat. *American Foreign Service Journal* 13: 601–605, 628–633.

1937. Our first language student. *American Foreign Service Journal* 6: 333, 360–362.

Jacobs, Bart. 2012. *Origins of a Creole: The History of Papiamentu and Its African Ties*. Berlin: De Gruyter Mouton.

Jespersen, Otto. 1942. *Modern English Grammar on Historical Principles. Part VI: Morphology*. Copenhagen: Ejnar Munksgaard.

Johanson, Lars. 2012. Mood meets mood: Turkic versus Indo-European. In *Morphologies in Contact*, Martine Vanhove, Thomas Stolz, Aina Urdze & Hitomi Otsuka (eds.), 195–203. Berlin: Akademie.

Juvonen, Päivi. 2008. Complexity and simplicity in minimal lexica: The lexicon of Chinook Jargon. In *Language Complexity: Typology, Contact, Change*, Matti

Miestamo, Kaius Sinnemäki & Fred Karlsson (eds.), 321–340. Amsterdam: John Benjamins.

2016. Making do with minimal lexica. Light verb constructions with MAKE/DO in pidgin lexica. In *The Lexical Typology of Semantic Shifts*, Päivi Juvonen & Maria Koptjevskaja-Tamm (eds.), 223–248. Berlin: De Gruyter Mouton.

Kabatek, Johannes & Claus D. Pusch. 2011. The Romance languages. In *The Languages and Linguistics of Europe: A Comprehensive Guide*, Bernd Kortmann & Johan van der Auwera (eds.), 69–96. Berlin: De Gruyter Mouton.

Kahane, Henry & Renée Kahane. 1976. Lingua Franca: The story of a term. *Romance Philology* 30: 25–41.

1985. A case of glossism: Greghesco and Lingua Franca in Venetian literature. In *Mélanges de linguistique dédiés à la mémoire de Petar Skok (1881–1956)*, M. Deanovíc et al. (eds.), 223–228. Zagreb: Djela Jugoslavenske Akademije Znanosti i Umjetnosti.

Kahane, Henry, Renée Kahane & Andreas Tietze. 1958. *The Lingua Franca in the Levant: Turkish Nautical Terms of Italian and Greek Origin.* Urbana, IL: University of Illinois Press.

Kay, Gillian. 1995. English loanwords in Japanese. *World Englishes* 14: 67–76.

Kennedy, Charles Stuart. 2015. *The American Consul: A History of the United States Consular Service, 1776–1924.* Washington, DC: New Academia.

Kerswill, Paul. 2010. Contact and new varieties. In *The Handbook of Language Contact*, Raymond Hickey (ed.), 230–251. Oxford: Wiley-Blackwell.

Kerswill, Paul & Peter Trudgill. 2005. The birth of new dialects. In *Dialect Change: Convergence and Divergence in European Languages*, Peter Auer, Frans Hinskens & Paul Kerswill (eds.), 196–220. Cambridge: Cambridge University Press.

Khan, Geoffrey. 2016. Judeo-Arabic. In *Handbook of Jewish Languages*, Lily Kahn & Aaron D. Rubin (eds.), 22–63. Leiden: Brill.

Klee, Carol A. & Andrew Lynch. 2009. *El español en contacto con otras lenguas.* Washington, DC: Georgetown University Press.

Klein, Wolfgang & Clive Perdue. 1997. The Basic Variety (or: Couldn't natural languages be much simpler?) *Second Language Research* 13: 301–347.

Klimenkowa, Alla. 2017. *Sprachkontakt und lexikalische Innovation in der karibischen Kontakwtzone: die Beispiele bozal, cimarrón und criollo.* Hamburg: Helmut Buske.

Knapp, Samuel L. 1833. Memoir of William Shaler. *The New-York Mirror* 10: 345.

Koch, Peter. 2001. Lexical typology from a cognitive and linguistic point of view. In *Language Typology and Language Universals*, Martin Haspelmath, Ekkehard König, Wulf Oesterreicher & Wolfgang Raible (eds.), vol. 2, 1142–1178. Berlin: Walter de Gruyter.

Koptjevskaja-Tamm, Maria, Ekaterina Rakhilina & Martine Vanhove. 2016. The semantics of lexical typology. In *The Routledge Handbook of Semantics*, Nick Riemer (ed.), 434–454. London: Routledge.

Korletjanu, Nikolai Grigorievich. 1974. *Issledovanie narodnoj latyni i ee otnoshenij s romanskimi jazykami* [A study of Vulgar Latin and its relationship with Romance languages]. Moscow: Nauka.

Kupisch, Tanja. 2012. Specific and generic subjects in the Italian of German-Italian simultaneous bilinguals and L2 learners. *Bilingualism: Language and Cognition* 14: 736–756.

Labov, William. 2007. Transmission and diffusion. *Language* 83: 344–387.

Lafi, Nora. 2004. La langue des marchands de Tripoli au XIXe siècle: langue franque et langue arabe dans un port méditerranéen. In *Trames de langues: usages et métissages linguistiques dans l'histoire du Maghreb*, Jocelyne Dakhlia (ed.). 215–222. Paris: Maisonneuve & Larose.

Lal, Brij V. & Kate Fortune (eds.). 2000. *The Pacific Islands: An Encyclopedia*. Honolulu, HI: University of Hawai'i Press.

Lang, George. 1992. The literary settings of Lingua Franca (1300–1830). *Neophilologus* 76: 64–76.

2000. *Entwisted Tongues: Comparative Creole Literatures*. Amsterdam: Rodopi.

Lanly, André. 1955. Notes sur le français parlé en Afrique du Nord. *Le Français Moderne* 23: 197–211.

1962. *Le français d'Afrique du Nord: étude linguistique*. Paris: Presses Universitaires de France.

Lapesa, Rafael. 1981. *Historia de la lengua española*. 9th ed. Madrid: Gredos.

1987. El sustantivo sin actualizador en español. In *Estudios lingüísticos, literarios y estilísticos* 2, 57–68. Valencia: Universitat de València.

Lapiedra Gutiérrez, Eva. 1997. *Cómo los musulmanes llamaban a los cristianos hispánicos*. Alicante: Instituto de Cultura "Juan Gil Albert."

Larzul, Sylvette. 2010. Grammatisation et lexicographie de l'arabe algérien au XIXe siècle. *Synergies Monde Arabe* 7: 89–100.

Laugier de Tassy, Jacques Philippe. 1725. *Histoire du royaume d'Alger avec l'état présent de son gouvernement, de ses forces de terre & de mer, de ses revenus, police, justice politique & commerce*. Amsterdam: Henri du Sauzet.

Lavale Ortiz, Ruth María. 2007. Causatividad y verbos denominales. *Estudios de Lingüística* 21: 171–207.

2011. Sensory-emotional denominal causative verbs. In *Spanish Word Formation and Lexical Creation*, José Luis Cifuentes Honrubia & Susana Rodríguez Rosique (eds.), 107–143. Amsterdam: John Benjamins.

Lazzerini, Lucia. 1977. Il *greghesco* a Venezia tra realtà e *ludus*: saggio sulla commedia poliglotta del Cinquecento. *Studi di Filologia Italiana* 35: 29–95.

Ledgeway, Adam. 2011. Syntactic and morphosyntactic typology and change. In *The Cambridge History of the Romance Languages*, Martin Maiden, John C. Smith & Adam Ledgeway (eds.), vol. 1, 382–471. Cambridge: Cambridge University Press.

Lehrer, Adrienne. 1992. A theory of vocabulary structure: Retrospectives and prospectives. In *Thirty Years of Linguistic Evolution: Studies in Honour of René Dirven on the Occasion of his Sixtieth Birthday*, Martin Pütz (ed.), 243–256. Amsterdam: John Benjamins.

Lévy, Simon. 1997. Du quelques emprunts possibles au portuguais dans les parlers du Maroc. *Estudios de Dialectología Norteafricana y Andalusí* 2: 173–180.

Lipski, John M. 1993. Origin and development of "ta" in Afro-Hispanic creoles. In *Atlantic Meets Pacific: A Global View of Pidginization and Creolization*, Francis Byrne & John Holm (eds.), 217–231. Amsterdam: John Benjamins.

2002. "Partial Spanish": Strategies of pidginization and simplification (from Lingua Franca to "Gringo Lingo"). In *Romance Phonology and Variation: Selected*

Papers from the 30th Linguistic Symposium on Romance Languages, Gainesville, Florida, February 2000, Caroline R. Wiltshire & Joaquim Campts (eds.), 117–143. Amsterdam: John Benjamins.

2005. *A History of Afro-Hispanic Language: Five Centuries, Five Continents*. Cambridge: Cambridge University Press.

2014. A historical perspective of Afro-Portuguese and Afro-Spanish varieties in the Iberian Peninsula. In *Portuguese-Spanish Interfaces: Diachrony, Synchrony, and Contact*, Patricia Amaral & Ana Maria Carvalho (eds.), 359–376. Amsterdam: John Benjamins.

n.d. On the source of the infinitive in Romance-derived pidgins and creoles. Ms. https://pdfs.semanticscholar.org/0cde/f7f7daf6b5253b8fa7f756dcdf881f00f35f.pdf.

Lloyd, Paul M. 1987. *From Latin to Spanish: Historical Phonology and Morphology of the Spanish Language*. Philadelphia: Memoirs of the American Philosophical Society.

Lo Duca, Maria G., Martina Ferronato & Elena Mengardo. 2009. "Indicazioni per il curricolo" e obiettivi di apprendimento sulle categorie lessicali: il riconoscimento del nome. In *Lingua e grammatica: teorie e prospettive didattiche*, Paola Baratter & Sara Dallabrida (eds.), 11–27. Milan: FrancoAngeli.

Lombardero Caparrós, Alberto. 2015. *The historiography of English language teaching in Spain: A corpus of grammars and dictionaries (1769–1900)*. PhD dissertation, Universitat Rovira i Virgili.

Loth, Gaston. 1905. *Le peuplement Italien en Tunisie et en Algérie*. Paris: Librairie Armand Colin.

Loving, Matthew. 2012. Collecting to the core – French dictionaries. *Against the Grain* 25: 82–83.

Luján, Marta. 2017. Spanish in the Americas: A dialogic approach to language contact. In *Language Contact and Change in Mesoamerica and Beyond*, Karen Dakin, Claudia Parodi & Natalie Operstein (eds.), 385–417. Amsterdam: John Benjamins.

Mackall, Leonard L. 1931. William Brown Hodgson. *Georgia Historical Quarterly* 15: 324–345.

MacKenzie, Ian. 2003. Bare nouns in Spanish. *Bulletin of Spanish Studies* 80: 1–12.

MacLaury, Robert E. 2001. Color terms. In *Language Typology and Language Universals*, Martin Haspelmath, Ekkehard König, Wulf Oesterreicher & Wolfgang Raible (eds.), vol. 2, 1227–1251. Berlin: Walter de Gruyter.

Maiden, Martin. 1995. *A Linguistic History of Italian*. London: Longman.

1997. Inflectional morphology of the noun and adjective. In *The Dialects of Italy*, Martin Maiden & Mair Parry (eds.), 68–74. London: Routledge.

2011. Morphological persistence. In *The Cambridge History of the Romance Languages*, Martin Maiden, John C. Smith & Adam Ledgeway (eds.), vol. 1, 155–214. Cambridge: Cambridge University Press.

2016. Inflectional morphology. In *The Oxford Guide to the Romance Languages*, Adam Ledgeway & Martin Maiden (eds.), 497–512. Oxford: Oxford University Press.

Maiden, Martin & Cecilia Robustelli. 2013. *A Reference Grammar of Modern Italian*. 2nd ed. London: Routledge.

Malkiel, Yakov. 1967a. Linguistics as a genetic science. *Language* 43: 223–245.

1967b. Multiple versus simple causation in linguistic change. In *To Honor Roman Jakobson: Essays on the Occasion of His Seventieth Birthday II*, 1228–1246. The Hague: Mouton.

1983. Etymology: New thoughts about possibilities for its rejuvenation. In *Scritti linguistici in onore di Giovan Battista Pellegrini*, Paola Benincà, Manlio Cortelazzo, Aldo Luigi Prosdocimi, Laura Vanelli & Alberto Zamboni (eds.), 589–624. Pisa: Pacini.

Mallette, Karla. 2014. Lingua Franca. In *A Companion to Mediterranean History*, Peregrine Horden & Sharon Kinoshita (eds.), 330–344. Chichester: John Wiley.

Mann, Charles C. 1993. Polysemic functionality of prepositions in pidgins & creoles: The case of 'fọ̀' in Anglo-Nigerian Pidgin. In *Atlantic Meets Pacific: A Global View of Pidginization and Creolization*, Francis Byrne & John Holm (eds.), 57–67. Amsterdam: John Benjamins.

Marcel, Jean-Joseph. 1799. *Vocabulaire français-arabe, contenant les mots principaux et d'un usage plus journalier*. Cairo.

1830. *Vocabulaire français-arabe du dialecte vulgaire d'Alger, de Tunis et de Marok, à l'usage des militaires français*. 2nd ed. Paris.

Masini, Francesca. 2011. Polirematiche, parole. In *Enciclopedia dell'italiano*. www.treccani.it/enciclopedia/parole-polirematiche_(Enciclopedia-dell%27Italiano)/.

Matasović, Ranko. 2018. *An Areal Typology of Agreement Systems*. Cambridge: Cambridge University Press.

McDougall, James. 2017. *A History of Algeria*. Cambridge: Cambridge University Press.

McMahon, April & Robert McMahon. 2005. *Language Classification by Numbers*. Oxford: Oxford University Press.

Medina Molera, Antonio. 2005. *Quijote e Islam*. Barcelona: Carena.

Mel'čuk, Igor. 1976. On suppletion. *Linguistics* 170: 45–90.

1994. Suppletion: Toward a logical analysis of the concept. *Studies in Language* 18: 339–410.

2006. *Aspects of the Theory of Morphology*. Berlin: Mouton de Gruyter.

Menegaldo, Maria Grazia. n.d. Criteri per la stesura di testi a scrittura controllata e per la semplificazione dei testi scritti. Materiali per la didattica, Progetto ALIAS: Approccio alla Lingua Italiana per Allievi Stranieri. www.itals.it/criteri-la-stesura-di-testi-scrittura-controllata-e-la-semplificazione-dei-testi-scritti.

Meouak, Mohamed. 2004. Langues, société et histoire d'Alger au XVIIIe siècle d'après les données de Venture de Paradis (1739–1799). In *Trames de langues: usages et métissages linguistiques dans l'histoire du Maghreb*, Jocelyne Dakhlia (ed.), 303–329. Paris: Maisonneuve & Larose.

Mesthrie, Rajend. 2006. Anti-deletions in an L2 grammar: A study of Black South African English mesolect. *English World-Wide* 27: 111–145.

Metzeltin, Miguel. 2007. La deriva tipológica del rumano. *Estudis Romànics* 29: 43–59.

Meyer-Lübke, Wilhelm. 1911. *Romanisches etymologisches Wörterbuch*. Heidelberg: Carl Winter's Universitätsbuchhandlung.

Mifsud, Manwel. 1995. *Loan Verbs in Maltese: A Descriptive and Comparative Study*. Leiden: Brill.

Minervini, Laura. 1996a. La lingua franca mediterranea: plurilinguismo, mistilinguismo, pidginizzazione sulle coste del mediterraneo tra tardo medioevo e prima età moderna. *Medioevo Romanzo* 20: 231–301.

1996b. Les contacts entre indigènes et croisés dans l'Orient latin: le rôle des drogmans. In *Romania Arabica: Festschrift für Reinhold Kontzi zum 70. Geburtstag*, Jens Lüdtke (ed.), 57–62. Tübingen: Gunter Narr.

2002. La formación de la *koiné* judeoespañola en el siglo XVI. *Revue de Linguistique Romane* 66: 497–512.

2006. L'italiano nell'Impero Ottomano. In *Lo spazio linguistico italiano e le "lingue esotiche": rapporti e reciproci influssi. Atti del XXXIX Congresso internazionale di studi della Società di Linguistica Italiana (Milano, 22–24 settembre 2005)*, Emanuele Banfi & Gabriele Iannàccaro (eds.), 49–66. Rome: Bulzoni.

2010. Lingua franca, italiano come. In *Enciclopedia dell'italiano.* www.treccani.it/enciclopedia/lingua-franca-italiano-come_(Enciclopedia-dell'Italiano)/.

2011. Gli ebrei dei porti adriatici come mediatori linguistici e culturali. In *L'Adriatico: incontri e separazioni (XVIII-XIX secolo)*, Francesco Bruni & Chryssa Maltezou (eds.), 193–203. Venice: Istituto Veneto di Scienze, Lettere ed Arti.

2014. El léxico de origen italiano en el judeoespañol de Oriente. In *La lengua de los sefardíes: tres contribuciones a su historia*, Winfried Busse (ed.), 65–104. Tübingen: Stauffenburg.

Morel-Fatio, Alfred. 1882a. Letter to Hugo Schuchardt dated 9 February 1882. http://schuchardt.uni-graz.at/id/letter/1400.

1882b. Letter to Hugo Schuchardt dated 7 March 1882. http://schuchardt.uni-graz.at/id/letter/1401.

Moretti, Bruno. 1988. Un caso concreto di semplificazione lingüística: le "letture semplificàte." *Studi Italiani di Lingüística Teorica ed Applicata* 17: 219–255.

1990. L'impiego effettivo della formazione delle parole nel discorso in italiano di non nativi (nella Svizzera tedesca). In *Parallela 4. Morfologia/Morphologie*, Monica Berretta, Piera Molinelli & Ada Valentini (eds.), 293–303. Tübingen: Gunter Narr.

1993a. Dall'*input* alla lingua obiettivo: aspetti del *continuum* dell'italiano *lingua franca* nella Svizzera germanofona. In *Actes du XX Congrès International de Linguistique et Philologie Romanes*, Gerold Hilty (ed.), vol. 3, 557–570. Tübingen: Francke.

1993b. Learning strategies for closely related languages: on the Italian spoken by Spanish immigrants in Switzerland. In *Current Issues in European Second Language Acquisition Research*, Bernhard Kettermann & Wilfried Wieden (eds.), 405–418. Tübingen: Gunter Narr.

2000. Le varietà di apprendimento e il potenziale delle lingue: l'esempio della marcatura dell'oggetto tra accusativo preposizionale e partitivo. *Romanische Forschungen* 112: 453–469.

Morgan, William D. & Charles Stuart Kennedy. 1991. *The US Consul at Work.* New York: Greenwood Press.

Morsly, Dalila. 1996. Alger plurilingue. *Plurilinguismes* 12: 47–80.

Mufwene, Salikoko S. 1997. Jargons, pidgins, creoles, and koines: What are they? In *The Structure and Status of Pidgins and Creoles*, Arthur K. Spears & Donald Winford (eds.), 35–70. Amsterdam: John Benjamins.

2001. *The Ecology of Language Evolution.* Cambridge: Cambridge University Press.

2008. *Language Evolution: Contact, Competition and Change*. New York: Continuum.

2009. The indigenization of English in North America. In *World Englishes: Problems, Properties, Prospects*, Thomas Hoffman & Lucia Siebers (eds.), 351–368. Amsterdam: John Benjamins.

2010. SLA and the emergence of creoles. *Studies in Second Language Acquisition* 32: 359–400.

2014. Globalisation économique mondiale des XVIIe-XVIIIe siècles, émergence des créoles, et vitalité langagière. In *Langues créoles, mondialisation, éducation. Proceedings of the 13th Colloquium of the Comité International des Etudes Créoles, Mauritius 2012*, Arnaud Carpooran (ed.), 23–79. Vacoas: Editions le Printemps.

Mühlhäusler, Peter. 1979. *Growth and Structure of the Lexicon of New Guinea Pidgin*. Canberra: Australian National University.

1986. *Pidgin and Creole Linguistics*. 2nd ed. Oxford: Basil Blackwell.

Munn, Allan & Cristina Schmitt. 1999. Against the nominal mapping parameter: Bare nouns in Brazilian Portuguese. In *Proceedings of North East Linguistic Society 29*, Pius Tamanji, Masako Hirotani & Nancy Hall (eds.), 339–353. Amherst, MA: GLSA.

Muysken, Pieter. 1981. Halfway between Quechua and Spanish: The case for relexification. In *Historicity and Variation in Creole Studies*, Arnold Highfield & Albert Valdman (eds.), 55–78. Ann Arbor, MI: Karoma.

Napoli, Donna Jo & Irene Vogel. 1990. The conjugations of Italian. *Italica* 67: 479–502.

Nerval, Gérard de. 1911. *Correspondance (1830–1855)*. Jules Marsan (ed.). 3rd ed. Paris: Mercure de France.

Nespor, Marina. 2001. Il sintagma aggettivale. In *Grande grammatica italiana di consultazione*, Lorenzo Renzi, Giampaolo Salvi & Anna Cardinaletti (eds.), 439–455. Bologna: il Mulino.

Neuburger, Kathrin A. & Elisabeth Stark. 2014. Differential object marking in Corsican. Regularities and triggering factors. *Linguistics* 52: 365–389.

Nichols, Roy F. 1950. Diplomacy in Barbary. *Pennsylvania Magazine of History and Biography* 74: 113–141.

Nigra, C. 1901. Note etimologiche e lessicali. *Archivio Glottologico Italiano* 15: 275–302.

Nissabouri, Abdelfattah. 1997. Sur l'hispanisation des mots d'emprunt en arabe marocain. *Estudios de Dialectología Norteafricana y Andalusí* 2: 187–196.

Nolan, Joanna. 2020. *The Elusive Case of Lingua Franca: Fact and Fiction*. Cham: Palgrave Macmillan.

Norden, Frederic Louïs. 1755. *Voyage d'Egypte et de Nubie*. Vol. 1. Copenhagen.

Obediente y Sosa, Enrique. 1997. *Biografía de una lengua: desarrollo y expansión del español*. Merida-Venezuela: Universidad de los Andes, Consejo de Publicaciones CDCHT.

Oltra Massuet, Maria Isabel. 1999. *On the notion of theme vowel: A new approach to Catalan verbal morphology*. MA thesis, Massachusetts Institute of Technology.

Operstein, Natalie. 1998. Was Lingua Franca ever creolized? *Journal of Pidgin and Creole Languages* 13: 377–380.

2007. On the status and transmission of Lingua Franca. In *Darъ Slovesьny: Festschrift für Christoph Koch zum 65. Geburtstag*, Wolfgang Hock & Michael Meier-Brügger (eds.), 235–249. Munich: Otto Sagner.

2012. Golden Age *poesía de negros* and Orlando di Lasso's *moresche*: A possible connection. *Romance Notes* 52: 13–18.

2015. Contact-genetic linguistics: Toward a contact-based theory of language change. *Language Sciences* 48: 1–15.

2017a. The Spanish component in Lingua Franca. *Language Ecology* 1: 105–136.

2017b. The syntactic structures of Lingua Franca in the *Dictionnaire de la langue franque*. *Italian Journal of Linguistics* 29(2): 87–130.

2017c. The orthography of the *Dictionnaire de la langue franque*. *Mediterranean Language Review* 16: 1–33.

2018a. Inflection in Lingua Franca: From Haedo's *Topographia* to the *Dictionnaire de la langue franque*. *Morphology* 28: 145–185.

2018b. Toward a typological profile of Lingua Franca: A view from the lexicon and word formation. *Language Sciences* 66: 60–82.

2018c. The making of the *Dictionnaire de la langue franque*. *Zeitschrift für romanische Philologie* 134: 1114–1153.

2018d. Lingua Franca between pidginization and koineization. *Journal of Pidgin and Creole Languages* 33: 309–363.

2019. The French connection: William Brown Hodgson's mission in Algiers and the *Dictionnaire de la langue franque*. *Mediterranean Language Review* 26: 67–89.

2020. Lexical diversity and the issue of the basilect/acrolect continuum in Lingua Franca. In review.

Oren, Michael B. 2007. *Power, Faith, and Fantasy: America in the Middle East, 1776 to the Present*. New York: W. W. Norton.

Orfano, Alessandro. 2016. *"In tutte le parole mettevano 'r bagitto. E poi piano piano è finita."* Aspetti lessicali e morfologici della parlata giudeo-livornese attuale. In *Actes du XXVIIe Congrès international de linguistique et de philologie romanes (Nancy, 20–25 juillet 2013). Section 11: Linguistique de contact*. Nancy: ATILF (online).

Orozco, Rafael 2010a. *A sociolinguistic study of Colombian Spanish in Colombia and New York City*. PhD dissertation, New York University.

2010b. Variation in the expression of nominal possession in Costeño Spanish. *Spanish in Context* 7: 194–220.

2012. The expression of nominal possession in the Spanish of Colombians in New York City. In *Colombian Varieties of Spanish*, Richard J. File-Muriel & Rafael Orozco (eds.), 205–233. Madrid: Iberoamericana.

2018. *Spanish in Colombia and New York City: Language Contact Meets Dialectal Convergence*. Amsterdam: John Benjamins.

Owens, Jonathan. 1996. Idiomatic structure and the theory of genetic relationship. *Diachronica* 13: 283–318.

2001. Creole Arabic: An orphan of all orphans. *Anthropological Linguistics* 43: 348–378.

2018. Why linguistics needs an historically oriented Arabic linguistics. In *Arabic in Contact*, Stefano Manfredi & Mauro Tosco (eds.), 207–232. Amsterdam: John Benjamins.

Pananti, Filippo. 1817. *Avventure e osservazioni sopra le coste di Barberia*. 2 vols. Milan.

Parkvall, Mikael. 2010. How European is Esperanto? A typological study. *Language Problems and Language Planning* 34: 63–79.

2016. Pidgin languages. In *Oxford Research Encyclopedia, Linguistics*. http://linguistics.oxfordre.com/.

2019. Pidgins. In *The Oxford Handbook of Language Contact*, Anthony P. Grant (ed.), 261–281. New York: Oxford University Press.

Parkvall, Mikael & Peter Bakker. 2013. Pidgins. In *Contact Languages: A Comprehensive Guide*, Peter Bakker & Yaron Matras (eds.), 15–64. Berlin: De Gruyter Mouton.

Parodi, Claudia & Marta Luján. 2014a. El español de América a la luz de sus contactos con el mundo indígena y el europeo. *Lexis* 38: 377–399.

2014b. Hacia una caracterización adecuada del español americano/Towards an adequate characterization of Spanish in the Americas. *Cuadernos de la ALFAL* 6: 10–28.

Parra Escartín, Carla, Almudena Nevado Llopis & Eoghan Sánchez Martínez. 2018. Spanish multiword expressions: Looking for a taxonomy. In *Multiword Expressions: Insights from a Multi-lingual Perspective*, Manfred Sailer & Stella Markantonatou (eds.), 271–323. Berlin: Language Science Press.

Pascu, Giorge. 1916. *Sufixele românești*. Bucharest: Librăriile SOCEC & Co.

Patota, Giuseppe. 2006. *Grammatica di riferimento dell'italiano contemporaneo*. Novara: Garzanti Linguistica.

Pawley, Andrew & Frances Hodgetts Syder. 1983. Two puzzles for linguistic theory: nativelike selection and nativelike fluency. In *Language and Communication 7:1*, J. C. Richards & R. W. Schmidt (eds.), 191–226. London: Longman.

Peeters, Bert, Marie-Odile Junker, Catherine Travis, Patrick Farrell, Pedro Perini-Santos & Brigid Maher. 2006. NSM exponents and universal grammar in Romance: Evaluators and descriptors; mental predicates. In *Semantic Primes and Universal Grammar: Empirical Evidence from the Romance Languages*, Bert Peeters (ed.), 79–109. Amsterdam: John Benjamins.

Pellow, Thomas. 1739. *The History of the Long Captivity and Adventures of Thomas Pellow, in South Barbary*. 2nd ed. London.

Penny, Ralph. 2000. *Variation and Change in Spanish*. Cambridge: Cambridge University Press.

2002. *A History of the Spanish Language*. 2nd ed. Cambridge: Cambridge University Press.

Peters, Ann M. 1983. *The Units of Language Acquisition*. Cambridge: Cambridge University Press.

Picone, Michael D. 1996. *Anglicisms, Neologisms and Dynamic French*. Amsterdam: John Benjamins.

Piesse, Louis. 1862. *Itinéraire historique et descriptif de l'Algérie comprenant le Tell et le Sahara*. Paris: Librairie de L'Hachette et Cie.

Pineda, Anna. 2012. Double object constructions and dative/accusative alternations in Spanish and Catalan: A unified account. *Borealis* 2: 57–115.

Pinheiro Chagas, Manoel (ed.). 1884. *Diccionario popular historico, geographico, mythologico, biographico, artistico, bibliographico e litterario*. Vol. 13. Lisbon: Typographia da Viuva Sousa Neves.

Plag, Ingo. 2008a. Creoles as interlanguages: Inflectional morphology. *Journal of Pidgin and Creole Languages* 23: 109–130.

2008b. Creoles as interlanguages: Syntactic structures. *Journal of Pidgin and Creole Languages* 23: 307–328.

2009a. Creoles as interlanguages: Phonology. *Journal of Pidgin and Creole Languages* 24: 119–138.

2009b. Creoles as interlanguages: Word-formation. *Journal of Pidgin and Creole Languages* 24: 339–362.

Planas, Natividad. 2004. L'usage des langues en Méditerranée occidentale à l'époque moderne. In *Trames de langues: usages et métissages linguistiques dans l'histoire du Maghreb*, Jocelyne Dakhlia (ed.), 241–257. Paris: Maisonneuve & Larose.

Polák, Václav. 1949. La périphrase verbale des langues de l'Europe occidentale. *Lingua* 2: 64–73.

Pountain, Christopher. 1982. *ESSERE/STARE as a Romance phenomenon. In *Studies in the Romance Verb. Essays Offered to Joe Cremona on the Occasion of His 60th Birthday*, Nigel Vincent & Martin Harris (eds.), 139–160. London: Croom Helm.

Prado, Marcial. 1982. El género en español y la teoría de la marcadez. *Hispania* 65: 258–266.

Pulgram, Ernst. 1978. Latin-Romance *habere*: Double function and lexical split. *Zeitschrift für romanische Philologie* 81: 1–8.

Quemada, Bernard. 1967. *Les dictionnaires du français moderne 1539–1863. Étude sur leur histoire, leurs types et leur méthodes.* Paris: Didier.

Quérard, J.-M. 1839. *La France littéraire, ou dictionnaire bibliographique des savants, historiens et gens de lettres de la France, ainsi que des littérateurs étrangers qui ont écrit en français, plus particulièrement pendant les XVIIIe et XIXe siècles.* Vol. 10. Paris: Firmin Didot Frères, Libraires.

Rainer, Franz. 2016a. Spanish. In *Word Formation: An International Handbook of the Languages of Europe*, Peter O. Müller, Ingeborg Ohnheiser, Susan Olsen & Franz Rainer (eds.), vol. 4, 2620–2640. Berlin: De Gruyter Mouton.

2016b. Italian. In *Word Formation: An International Handbook of the Languages of Europe*, Peter O. Müller, Ingeborg Ohnheiser, Susan Olsen & Franz Rainer (eds.), vol. 4, 2712–2731. Berlin: De Gruyter Mouton.

2016c. Derivational morphology. In *The Oxford Guide to the Romance Languages*, Adam Ledgeway & Martin Maiden (eds.), 513–522. Oxford: Oxford University Press.

Rea, John A. 1973. The Romance data of the pilot studies for glottochronology. In *Current Trends in Linguistics*, vol. 11, *Diachronic, Areal and Typological Linguistics*, Thomas A. Sebeok (ed.), 355–368. The Hague: Mouton.

Real Academia Española. 2001. *Diccionario de la lengua española*. 22nd ed. Madrid: Espasa Calpe.

2010. *Nueva gramática de la lengua española. Manual.* Madrid: Espasa Libros.

Rementería y Fica, Mariano de. 1826. *Gramática italiana simplificada y reducida a 20 lecciones con sus respectivas prácticas, diálogos, y una coleccion de trozos históricos en italiano para uso de los principiantes. Compuesta por M. A. Vergani. Acomodada a la lengua española por D. Mariano de Rementería y Fica, profesor de humanidades.* Madrid: Imprenta de D. Miguel de Burgos.

Renzi, Lorenzo. 1997. The structure of the noun phrase. In *The Dialects of Italy*, Martin Maiden & Mair Parry (eds.), 162–170. London: Routledge.

2001. L'articolo. In *Grande grammatica italiana di consultazione*, Lorenzo Renzi, Giampaolo Salvi & Anna Cardinaletti (eds.), 371–437. Bologna: il Mulino.

Repetti, Lori & Edward F. Tuttle. 1987. The evolution of Latin *PL*, *BL*, *FL* and *CL*, *GL* in Western Romance. *Studi Mediolatini e Volgari* 33: 53–115.

Ricca, Davide. 1993. *I verbi deittici di movimento in Europa: una ricerca interlinguistica*. Florence: La Nuova Italia.

Richelet, César-Pierre. 1680. *Dictionnaire françois, contenant les mots et les choses, plusieurs nouvelles remarques sur la langue françoise*. Geneva: Jean Herman Widerhold.

1761. *Dictionnaire portatif de la langue françoise, extrait du grand dictionnaire de Pierre Richelet*. 2nd ed. Lyon: Pierre Bruyset-Ponthus.

1811. *Dictionnaire portatif de la langue françoise, extrait du grand dictionnaire de Pierre Richelet, corrigé et augmenté par de Wailly*. 3rd ed. 2 vols. Lyon: Amable Leroy.

Rifón Sánchez, Antonio. 2011. Nominalizations of transfer verbs: Blocking, constraints and competition between affixes. In *Spanish Word Formation and Lexical Creation*, José Luis Cifuentes Honrubia & Susana Rodríguez Rosique (eds.), 233–254. Amsterdam: John Benjamins.

Robert, Adolphe, Edgar Bourloton & Gaston Cougny (eds.). 1891. *Dictonnaire des parlementaires français*. Vol. 3. Paris: Bourloton.

Roberts, Sarah J. & Joan Bresnan. 2008. Retained inflectional morphology in pidgins: A typological study. *Linguistic Typology* 12: 269–302.

Robinson, Stuart. 2008. Why pidgin and creole linguistics needs the statistitian: Vocabulary size in a Tok Pisin corpus. *Journal of Pidgin and Creole Languages* 23: 141–146.

Roches, Léon. 1904. *Dix ans à travers l'Islam, 1834–1844*. New ed. Paris: Perrin et Cie.

Rohlfs, Gerhard. 1954. *Die lexikalische Differenzierung der romanischen Sprachen.* Munich: Verlag der Bayerischen Akademie der Wissenschaften.

1968. *Grammatica storica della lingua italiana i dei suoi dialetti. Morfologia.* Turin: Giulio Einaudi.

1969. *Grammatica storica della lingua italiana e dei suoi dialetti. Sintassi e formazione delle parole*. Turin: Giulio Einaudi.

1971. Autour de l'accusatif prépositionnel dans les langues romanes. *Revue de Linguistique Romane* 35: 312–334.

Ross, Christopher. 1991. *The United States Mission in Algeria: A Historical Sketch.* https://dz.usembassy.gov/wp-content/uploads/sites/236/2017/04/U.S.-Mission-to-Algeria-A_Historical_Sketch.pdf.

Rossano, Federico. 2010. Questioning and responding in Italian. *Journal of Pragmatics* 42: 2756–2771.

Rossi, Ettore. 1928. La lingua franca in Barberia. *Rivista delle Colonie Italiane* n.n.: 143–151.

Roux, P. 1800. *Journal Typographique et Bibliographique, Publié par P. Roux, Troisième année (1er Vendémiaire au 30 Fruct. an VIII – 22 Sept. 1799, au 21 21 Sept. 1800)*. Paris: Chez l'Éditeur.

Rubin, Aaron D. 2016. Judeo-Italian. In *Handbook of Jewish Languages*, Lily Kahn & Aaron D. Rubin (eds.), 297–364. Leiden: Brill.

Russo, Michela. 2001. Orientalismi in un anonimo *Dictionnaire* della lingua franca (1830). *Zeitschrift für romanische Philologie* 117: 222–254.

Sabatini, Alma. 1993. *Il sessismo nella lingua italiana*. Rome: Istituto Poligrafico e Zecca dello Stato.

Said, Edward W. 1978. *Orientalism*. New York: Pantheon Books.

Şăineanu, Lazăr. 1900. *Influenţa orientală asupra limbei şi culturei române*. Vol. 1. Bucharest: Editura Librăriei Socec.

Salvatore, Gianfranco. 2012. Parodie realistiche. Africanismi, fraternità e sentimenti identitari nelle canzoni moresche del Cinquecento. *Kronos* 14: 97–130.

Salvi, Giampaolo. 2001. La frase semplice. In *Grande grammatica italiana di consultazione*, Lorenzo Renzi, Giampaolo Salvi & Anna Cardinaletti (eds.), 37–127. Bologna: il Mulino.

Sammarco, Angelo. 1937. *Gli italiani in Egitto: il contributo italiano nella formazione dell'Egitto moderno*. Alexandria: Edizioni del Fascio.

Santoro, Salvatore. 1996. Lingua Franca in Goldoni's *Impresario delle Smirne*. *Journal of Pidgin and Creole Languages* 11: 89–93.

Santos Morillo, Antonio. 2010 *¿Quién te lo vezó a dezir? El habla de negro en la literatura del XVI, imitación de una realidad lingüística*. PhD dissertation, University of Seville.

Savoia, Leonardo. 1997. Inflectional morphology of the verb. In *The Dialects of Italy*, Martin Maiden & Mair Parry (eds.), 75–86. London: Routledge.

Sayahi, Lotfi. 2005. Phonological adaptation of Spanish loanwords in Northern Moroccan Arabic. *University of Pennsylvania Working Papers in Linguistics* 11: 253–263.

2011. Contacto y préstamo léxico: el elemento español en el árabe actual. *Revista Internacional de Lingüística Iberoamericana* 9: 85–99.

2014. *Diglossia and Language Contact: Language Variation and Change in North Africa*. Cambridge: Cambridge University Press.

Schepens, Job, Frans van der Slik & Roeland van Hout. 2013. The effect of linguistic distance across Indo-European mother tongues on learning Dutch as a second language. In *Approaches to Measuring Linguistic Differences*, Lars Borin & Anju Saxena (eds.), 199–229. Berlin: De Gruyter Mouton.

Scarano, Antonietta. 2000. Aggettivi qualificativi, italiano parlato e articolazione dell'informazione. Preprint LABLITA 5.

Schmid, Stephan. 1992. Le interlingue di ispanofoni nella Svizzera tedesca: un tipo di italiano popolare? In *Linee di tendenza dell'italiano contemporaneo*, Bruno Moretti, Dario Petrini & Sandro Bianconi (eds.), 285–301. Rome: Bulzoni.

1993. Learning strategies for closely related languages: On the Italian spoken by Spanish immigrants in Switzerland. In *Current Issues in European Second Language Acquisition Research*, Bernhard Kettemann & Wilfried Wieden (eds.), 405–418. Tübingen: Gunter Narr.

1994. *L'italiano degli spagnoli. Interlingue di immigrati nella Svizzera tedesca*. Milan: FrancoAngeli.

Schmitt, Christina Job. 1996. *Aspect and the syntax of noun phrases*. PhD dissertation, University of Maryland at College Park.

Schuchardt, Hugo. 1909. Die Lingua franca. *Zeitschrift für romanische Philologie* 33: 441–461.

1979. On Lingua Franca. In *The Ethnography of Variation: Selected Writings on Pidgins and Creoles*, T. L. Markey (ed & trans.), 26–47. Ann Arbor, MI: Karoma.

1980. The Lingua Franca. In *Pidgin and Creole Languages: Selected Essays by Hugo Schuchardt*, Glenn G. Gilbert (ed & trans.), 65–88. Cambridge: Cambridge University Press.

Schwarze, Christoph. 1999. Inflectional classes in lexical functional morphology: Latin -sk- and its evolution. In *Proceedings of the LFG 99 Conference*, Miriam Butt & Tracy Holloway King (eds.). Manchester: University of Manchester/CSLI Publications. http://web.stanford.edu/group/cslipublications/cslipublications/LFG/4/lfg99schwarze.pdf.

Schwegler, Armin. 1990. *Analyticity and Syntheticity: A Diachronic Perspective with Special Reference to Romance Languages*. Berlin: Mouton de Gruyter.

Schweickard, Wolfgang. 1993. Ethnika auf *-í* im Spanischen und entsprechende Bildungen in anderen Sprachen. In *Verbum Romanicum: Festschrift für Maria Iliescu*, Johannes Kramer & Guntram A. Plangg (eds.), 327–334. Hamburg: Helmut Buske.

Schwenter, Scott A. 2014. Two kinds of differential object marking in Portuguese and Spanish. In *Portuguese-Spanish Interfaces: Diachrony, Synchrony, and Contact*, Patricia Amaral & Ana Maria Carvalho (eds.), 237–260. Amsterdam: John Benjamins.

Seager, Robert, II (ed.). 1982. *The Papers of Henry Clay*, vol. 7, *Secretary of State: January 1, 1828–March 4, 1829.* Lexington: University Press of Kentucky.

Selbach, Rachel. 2009. Norms, grammar, or a bit of style: Lingua Franca and the issue of languageness. In *LACUS Forum 34: Speech and Beyond*, Patricia Sutcliffe, Lois Stanford & Arle Lommel (eds.), 221–232. Houston, TX: LACUS.

Serianni, Luca 1989. *Grammatica italiana. Italiano commune e lingua letteraria.* Turin: Utet Libreria.

Shaler, Nathaniel Southgate. 1909. *The Autobiography of Nathaniel Southgate Shaler, with a Supplementary Memoir by His Wife.* Boston: Houghton Mifflin.

Shaler, William. 1824. *Communication on the Language, Manners, and Customs of the Berbers or Brebers of Africa. In a Series of Letters from William Shaler, Esq. Consul of the United States at Algiers, to Peter S. Duponceau, Esq.* Philadelphia: Abraham Small.

1826. *Sketches of Algiers, Political, Historical, and Civil; Containing an Account of the Geography, Population, Government, Revenues, Commerce, Agriculture, Arts, Civil Institutions, Tribes, Manners, Languages, and Recent Political History of That Country.* Boston: Cummings, Hilliard.

1830. *Esquisse de l'État d'Alger, considéré sous les rapports politique, historique et civil: contenant un tableau statistique sur la géographie, la population, le gouvernement, lesrevenus, le commerce, l'agriculture, les arts, les manufactures, les tribus, les moeurs, les usages, le langage, les événemens politiques et récens de ce pays. Traduit de l'anglais et enrichi de notes par M. X. Bianchi. Avec un plan d'Alger, du port, des fortifications, et d'une partie de la radé; dressé d'après les documens officiels et rectifié sur les lieux mêmes.* Paris: Librairie Ladvocat.

Shaw, Thomas. 1757. *Travels or Observations Relating to Several Parts of Barbary and the Levant.* 2nd ed. London.

Shuval, Tal. 1998. *La ville d'Alger vers la fin du XIIIe siècle: population et cadre urbain.* Paris: CNRS Éditions.

2000. The Ottoman Algerian elite and its ideology. *International Journal of Middle East Studies* 32: 323–344.

Siegel, Jeff. 1985. Koines and koineization. *Language in Society* 14: 357–378.

1997. Mixing, leveling, and pidgin/creole development. In *The Structure and Status of Pidgins and Creoles*, Arthur K. Spears & Donald Winford (eds.), 111–149. Amsterdam: John Benjamins.

2001. Koine formation and creole genesis. In *Creolization and Contact*, Norval Smith & Tonjes Veenstra (eds.), 175–197. Amsterdam: John Benjamins.

2008a. Pidgins/creoles and second language acquisition. In *The Handbook of Pidgin and Creole Studies*, Silvia Kouwenberg & John Victor Singler (eds.), 189–218. Oxford: Blackwell.

2008b. *The Emergence of Pidgin and Creole Languages.* Oxford: Oxford University Press.

Sihler, Andrew. 1995. *A New Comparative Grammar of Greek and Latin.* Oxford: Oxford University Press.

Silva-Corvalán, Carmen. 1986. Bilingualism and language change: The extension of *estar* in Los Angeles Spanish. *Language* 62: 587–608.

Simone, Raffaele. 2010. Lingue romanze e italiano. In *Enciclopedia dell'italiano.* www.treccani.it/enciclopedia/lingue-romanze-e-italiano_(Enciclopedia-dell%27Italiano)/.

Simone, Raffaele & Donato Cerbasi. 2001. Types and diachronic evolution of Romance causative constructions. *Romanische Forschungen* 113: 441–473.

Sinclair, John. 1991. *Corpus, Concordance, Collocation.* Oxford: Oxford University Press.

Singer, Isidore (ed.). 1907. *The Jewish Encyclopedia.* Vol. 1. New York: Funk and Wagnalls.

Smith, May. 2006. *The Influence of French on Eighteenth-century Russian: Semantic and Phraseological Calques.* Bern: Peter Lang.

Smith, Norval. 1994. An annotated list of creoles, pidgins, and mixed languages. In *Pidgins and Creoles: An Introduction*, Jacques Arends, Pieter Muysken & Norval Smith (eds.), 331–374. Amsterdam: John Benjamins.

Soares da Silva, Augusto. 2012. Stages of grammaticalization of causative verbs and constructions in Portuguese, Spanish, French and Italian. *Folia Linguistica* 46: 513–552.

Sőrés, Anna. 1995. Rapports génetiques et typologiques dans l'étude synchronique des langues romanes. *Revue Romane* 30: 41–79.

Souag, Lameen. 2005. Notes on the Algerian Arabic dialect of Dellys. *Estudios de Dialectología Norteafricana y Andalusí* 9: 151–180.

Spinazzola, Margherita. 1984. Mo fème el servizio de parlar Italian: A comparative analysis of foreigner talks. *Quaderni di Filologia Germanica della Facoltà di Lettere e Filosofia dell'Universita di Bologna* 3: 261–266.

Spiro, Socrates. 1937. Nota sulle parole italiane nell'arabo moderno parlato d'Egitto. In *Gli italiani in Egitto: il contributo italiano nella formazione dell'Egitto moderno, Angelo Sammarco*, 191–200. Alexandria: Edizioni del Fascio.

Stassen, Leon. 2001. Predicative possession. In *Language Typology and Language Universals*, Martin Haspelmath, Ekkehard König, Wulf Oesterreicher & Wolfgang Raible (eds.), vol. 2, 954–960. Berlin: Walter de Gruyter.

Stefenelli, Arnulf. 2011. Lexical stability. In *The Cambridge History of the Romance Languages*, Martin Maiden, John C. Smith & Adam Ledgeway (eds.), vol. 1, 564–584. Cambridge: Cambridge University Press.

Stolova, Natalya. 2015. *Cognitive Linguistics and Lexical Change: Motion Verbs from Latin to Romance*. Amsterdam: John Benjamins.

Stovicek, Thomas William. 2010. *A developmental history of the Hispano-Romance verb conjugations*. PhD dissertation, Ohio State University.

Swiggers, Pierre. 1991–1993. Autour de la "Lingua Franca": une lettre de Marcel Cohen à Hugo Schuchardt à propos de la situation linguistique à Alger. *Orbis* 36: 281–290.

Tadmor, Uri. 2009. Loanwords in the world's languages: Findings and results. In *Loanwords in the World's Languages: A Comparative Handbook*, 55–75. Martin Haspelmath & Uri Tadmor (eds.), 1–34. The Hague: De Gruyter Mouton.

Tagliavini, Carlo. 1932. Divagazioni semantiche rumene e balcaniche. *Archivum Romanicum* 16: 333–383.

Taylor, Kathy. 1985. *Saber* and *Conocer*. *Hispania* 68: 649–655.

Teyssier, Paul. 1959. *La langue de Gil Vicente*. Paris: Klincksieck.

Theroux, Paul. 2003. *Dark Star Safari: Overland from Cairo to Capetown*. Boston, MA: Houghton Mifflin.

Thomason, Sarah G. 1997. A typology of contact languages. In *The Structure and Status of Pidgins and Creoles*, Arthur K. Spears & Donald Winford (eds.), 71–88. Amsterdam: John Benjamins.

2001. *Contact Languages*. Edinburgh: Edinburgh University Press.

Thomason, Sarah Grey & Terrence Kaufman. 1988. *Language Contact, Creolization, and Genetic Linguistics*. Berkeley, CA: University of California Press.

Thompson, Roger. 1991. Copula deletion in Spanish foreigner-talk: Using questionnaires as a research tool. *Journal of Pidgin and Creole Languages* 6: 89–106.

Thornton, Anna Maria. 1996. On some phenomena of prosodic morphology in Italian: Accorciamenti, hypocoristics and prosodic delimitation. *Probus* 8: 81–112.

2003. L'assegnazione del genere ai prestiti inglesi in italiano. In *Italiano e inglese a confronto*, Anna-Vera Sullam Calimani (ed.), 57–86. Florence: Franco Cesati.

Tirosh-Becker, Ofra. 2019. Linguistic analysis of an Algerian Judeo-Arabic text from the 19th century. *La Linguistique* 55: 193–212.

Triulzi, Alessandro. 1971. Italian-speaking communities in early nineteenth century Tunis. *Revue de l'Occident Musulman et de la Méditerrannée* 9: 153–184.

Trudgill, Peter. 2004. *New-Dialect Formation: The Inevitability of Colonial Englishes*. Edinburgh: Edinburgh University Press.

2011. *Sociolinguistic Typology: Social Determinants of Linguistic Complexity*. Oxford: Oxford University Press.

Trumper, John. 1997. Calabria and southern Basilicata. In *The Dialects of Italy*, Martin Maiden & Mair Parry (eds.), 355–364. London: Routledge.

Tuten, Donald N. 2003. *Koineization in Medieval Spanish*. Berlin: Mouton De Gruyter.

Urban, Mateusz. 2015. *The Treatment of Turkish Etymologies in English Lexicography: Lexemes Pertaining to Material Culture.* Krakow: Jagiellonian University Press.

Valentini, Ada. 1990. Genere e numero in italiano L2. In *Parallela 4. Morfologia/ Morphologie*, Monica Berretta, Piera Molinelli & Ada Valentini (eds.), 335–345. Tübingen: Gunter Narr.

1994. Un caso di comunicazione esolingue: il *foreigner talk. Quaderni del Dipartimento di Linguistica e Letterature Comparate* 10. 397–411.

Van Coetsem, Frans. 1988. *Loan Phonology and the Two Transfer Types in Language Contact.* Dordrecht: Foris.

Van Hout, Roeland & Pieter Muysken. 1994. Modeling lexical borrowability. *Language Variation and Change* 6: 39–62.

Vanelli, Laura. 1997. Personal pronouns and demonstratives. In *The Dialects of Italy*, Martin Maiden & Mair Parry (eds.), 106–115. London: Routledge.

Varela, Soledad. 2012. Derivation and compounding. In *Handbook of Spanish Linguistics*, José Ignacio Hualde, Antxon Olarrea & Erin O'Rourke (eds.), 207–226. Hoboken, NJ: Wiley-Blackwell.

Vázquez Rozas, Victoria & Viola G. Miglio. 2016. Constructions with subject vs. object experiencers in Spanish and Italian: a corpus-based approach. In Yoon, Jiyoung & Stefan Th. Gries (eds.), *Corpus-Based Approaches to Construction Grammar*, 65–102. Amsterdam: John Benjamins.

Vedovelli, Massimo. 1983. Testi e testimonianze di lavoratori stranieri in Italia. In *Italia linguistica: idée, storia, strutture*, Federico Alvano Leoni, Daniele Gambarara, Franco Lo Piparo & Raffaele Simone (eds.), 353–364. Bologna: Il Mulino.

1989. Gli immigrati stranieri in Italia: note sociolinguistiche. *Studi Emigrazione* 26: 68–94.

1991a. Apprendimento linguistico nel contesto dell'immigrazione. *Scuola Democratica* 3–4: 19–130.

1991b. L'immigrazione straniera in Italia: note tra sociolinguística e educazione linguistica. *Studi Italiani di Linguistica Teorica ed Applicata* 2: 411–435.

Velupillai, Viveka. 2015. *Pidgins, Creoles and Mixed Languages: An Introduction.* Amsterdam: John Benjamins.

Veneroni, Giovanni. 1700. *Le maître italien dans sa derniere perfection, nouvellement reveu, corrigé, et augmenté par l'Autheur. Contenant tout ce qui est necessaire pour apprendre facilement, & en peu de tems la langue italiene. Par le Sieur de Veneroni, Secretaire Interprete du Roi en la Langue Italiene.* 8th ed. Paris: Chez Michel David.

1800. *Maître italien ou grammaire françoise et italienne de Veneroni, Contenant tout ce qui est nécessaire pour apprendre facilement la Language Italianne. Nouvelle édition ... par C. M. Gattel, Professeur de Grammaire générale à l'école centrale du Département de l'Isère.* Avignon: Offray fils, Imprimeur-Libraire.

1823. *The Complete Italian Master Containing the Best and Easiest Rules for Attaining that Language. By Signor Veneroni, Italian Secretary to the French King.* London.

Venier, Federica. 2012. *La corrente di Humboldt. Una lettura di La lingua franca di Hugo Schuchardt.* Rome: Carocci.

Venture de Paradis, Jean-Michel. 1898. *Alger au XIXe siècle.* Algiers: Adolphe Jourdan.

Vergani, Angelo. 1823. *Grammaire italienne, simplifiée, et réduite a XX leçons; avec des Thèmes, des Dialogues et un petit Recueil de traits d'histoire en Italien, à l'usage des commençans; par Vergani. Nouvelle édition, corrigée et augmentée par M. Piranesi, Membre de l'Académie des Arcades de Rome.* Paris: Théofile Barrois Fils, Libraire.

Veselinova, Ljuba N. 2006. *Suppletion in Verb Paradigms: Bits and Pieces of the Puzzle.* Amsterdam: John Benjamins.

Vianello, Nereo. 1955. "Lingua franca" di Barberia e "lingua franca" di Dalmazia. *Lingua Nostra* 16: 67–69.

Viberg, Åke. 2001. Verbs of perception. In *Language Typology and Language Universals*, Martin Haspelmath, Ekkehard König, Wulf Oesterreicher & Wolfgang Raible (eds.), vol. 2, 1294–1309. Berlin: Walter de Gruyter.

Vicente, Ángeles. 2020. Andalusi Arabic. In *Arabic and Contact-Induced Change*, Christopher Lucas & Stefano Manfredi (eds.), 225–244. Berlin: Language Science Press.

Vincent, Bernard. 2004. La langue espagnole en Afrique du Nord: XVIe-XVIIIe siècles. In *Trames de langues: usages et métissages linguistiques dans l'histoire du Maghreb*, Jocelyne Dakhlia (ed.), 105–111. Paris: Maisonneuve & Larose.

Vincent, Nigel. 1997a. Complementation. In *The Dialects of Italy*, Martin Maiden & Mair Parry (eds.), 171–178. London: Routledge.

1997b. Prepositions. In *The Dialects of Italy*, Martin Maiden & Mair Parry (eds.), 208–213. London: Routledge.

1997c. Synthetic and analytic structures. In *The Dialects of Italy*, Martin Maiden & Mair Parry (eds.), 99–105. London: Routledge.

2007. Learned vs popular syntax: Adjective placement in early Italian vernaculars. In *Languages of Italy: Histories and Dictionaries*, Anna Laura Lepschy & Arturo Tosi (eds.), 55–75. Ravenna: Longo.

Vintilă-Rădulescu, Ioana. 1968. Français créole et français régional d'Afrique du nord. *Revue Roumaine de Linguistique* 13: 645–649.

Voghera, Miriam. 2004. Polirematiche. In *La formazione delle parole in italiano*, Maria Grossmann & Franz Rainer (eds.), 56–68. Tübingen: Max Niemeyer.

Wagner, Max Leopold. 1997. *La lingua sarda. Storia, spirito e forma.* Nuoro: Ilisso.

Wall, Albert & Álvaro Sebastián Octavio de Toledo y Huerta. 2016. Exploring and recycling: Topichood and the evolution of Ibero-Romance articles. In *Exaptation and Language Change*, Muriel Norde & Freek Van de Velde (eds.), 341–375. Amsterdam: John Benjamins.

Walsh, John K. 1971. The Hispano-Oriental derivational suffix *-í*. *Romance Philology* 25: 159–172.

Weber de Kurlat, Frida. 1963. Sobre el negro como tipo cómico en el teatro español del siglo XVI. *Romance Philology* 17: 380–391.

Weiss, Gillian. 2011. *Captives and Corsairs: France and Slavery in the Early Modern Mediterranean.* Stanford, CA: Stanford University Press.

Whinnom, Keith. 1965. The origin of the European-based creoles and pidgins. *Orbis* 14: 509–527.

1977a. Lingua Franca: Historical problems. In *Pidgin and Creole Linguistics*, Albert Valdman (ed.), 295–310. Bloomington, IN: Indiana University Press.

1977b. The context and origins of Lingua Franca. In *Langues en contact – Pidgins – Creoles – Languages in Contact*, Jürgen Meisel (ed.), 3–18. Tübingen: Gunter Narr.

Whitley, Stanley M. 1995. *Gustar* and other psych verbs: A problem in transitivity. *Hispania* 78: 573–585.

Winford, Donald. 1997. Introduction: On the structure and status of pidgins and creoles. In *The Structure and Status of Pidgins and Creoles*, Arthur K. Spears & Donald Winford (eds.), 1–31. Amsterdam: John Benjamins.

2005. Contact-induced changes: Classification and processes. *Diachronica* 22: 373–427.

Zago, Renata. 1986. Lingua franca nelle commedie di Goldoni. *Quaderni Utinensi* 7–8: 122–126.

Zuckermann, Ghil'ad. 2003. *Language Contact and Lexical Enrichment in Israeli Hebrew*. New York: Palgrave Macmillan.

Index

For EU product safety concerns, contact us at Calle de José Abascal, 56–1°, 28003 Madrid, Spain or eugpsr@cambridge.org.

www.ingramcontent.com/pod-product-compliance
Ingram Content Group UK Ltd.
Pitfield, Milton Keynes, MK11 3LW, UK
UKHW020403140625
459647UK00020B/2622
* 9 7 8 1 1 0 8 9 9 9 8 5 4 *